The Refugees Among Us

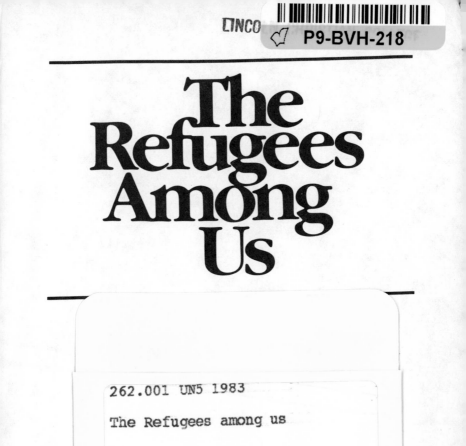

The Refugees Among Us

Unreached Peoples
'83

Edward R. Dayton
Samuel Wilson
Editors

Cover design by Steven Heassler.
Printed in U.S.A.

ISBN: 0-912552-38-7
LC: 82-061991

Contents

5

Introduction

*This is a book about refugees. More importantly, it is a book about the challenge and opportunities that the refugees of this world bring to the Church of Christ. It is a book that can change your life and the life of your church. In it, you will find stories that will thrill you and others that will tug at your heart. For this is a book about **people.** Its purpose is to link up the people of God with some hurting people of the world who need to know about Christ.*

This is an exciting day in the life of Christ's Church. In the midst of wars and rumors of wars, in the pressures of a growing humanism and secularism in both modern and modernizing societies, the Church is growing. The growth has many dimensions. The long-awaited **World Christian Encyclopedia** has surveyed all the countries of the world, and the editors have concluded that 32.8% of the people of planet Earth call themselves Christians. Even in countries where Christianity is outlawed, there are numbers of covert Christians.

But there are other dimensions of growth besides the numerical. Renewal movements are sweeping through many Protestant churches and many different

Roman Catholic and Orthodox churches. The Holy Spirit is powerfully at work filling and empowering the Body of Christ. Such a renewal is reaching out to millions upon millions of nominal Christians who have yet to understand the true meaning of the gospel.

But this journey inward on the part of the Church has in turn multiplied the number of men and women embarked upon the journey outward, the journey towards proclaiming the gospel of the kingdom to those who have never heard because they have had no chance to hear.

Since the inception of the **Unreached Peoples** series in 1979, new concepts of mission are being expressed in the everyday vocabulary of the Church. **Unreached peoples, hidden peoples, frontier missions** express new ways of looking at the world. The eminent Western missiologist Ralph Winter sees the Church on a third, and hopefully final, phase of the modern mission movement. In the first phase, missionaries from the West touched the shores of Africa, Asia and Latin America. In the second phase they moved inland in such organizations as the China Inland Mission, the Africa Inland Mission and the Sudan Interior Mission. In both these phases the primary dimension in describing the task was geography. In the third phase, Winter sees the Church moving deeper into the societies of the world, the **people groups** that make up the basic dimensions of humanity. For although the **World Christian Encyclopedia** indicates that in all 223 countries listed there are some Christians, over two billion people have never heard the gospel and will never be reached by a natural expansion of the Church within the countries in which they live. They are separated by barriers of language, culture, religion, class or racial segregation, or barriers created by the situations within which they find themselves. These are the **unreached** people groups of the world, and to them the **Unreached Peoples** series is dedicated. It is to those particular people groups called

8

refugees--for them, and about them--that this specific volume is dedicated.

The Unreached Peoples Series

The **Unreached Peoples** series began in 1979. This is the fifth volume in the series, which has been sponsored by the Strategy Working Group of the Lausanne Committee for World Evangelization (LCWE). The series finds its genesis in the work done for the International Congress on World Evangelization held at Lausanne, Switzerland, in 1974, where the LCWE had its beginning. The Missions Advanced Research and Communications Center (MARC), a ministry of World Vision International, was asked by the 1974 program committee to prepare a picture of the current status of world evangelization. As the MARC staff corresponded with Christian leaders around the world, it became apparent that the terms **evangelized** and **unevangelized** were inadequate to describe the task before us. We found two extremes. On the one hand, there were many places in the world where people described themselves as Christians, but their lack of attendance at worship and their other Christian practices and life-style indicated that they had little or no commitment to Christ. By some dimension they may be **evangelized,** but they need a fresh call to turn to God and to accept Christ as Savior and Lord. On the other hand, there were places where there was a Christian presence but no apparent response. Were these people evangelized? Out of these discussions emerged the concept of **unreached** rather than **unevangelized.**

Since its founding in 1966, MARC has centered its philosophy of world evangelization around the people group. The analysis that was done jointly by Donald McGavran and Edward R. Dayton at the School of World Mission at Fuller Seminary indicated that the country-by-country approach to missions was no longer viable. It had been a good beginning for the earlier era of modern missions: it pointed direction, and it outlined an area for research. But within the national boundaries were thousands of people groups. Often the national boundaries disguised or hid these people groups. Often even the Church within the country was unaware of their presence.

McGavran and Dayton worked through an analysis of needed world evangelization, based on McGavran's earlier insight which came from people movements Christward or movements on the part or whole of some ethnic group, clan, tribe or other segment of society. More than two-thirds of the young churches have sprung from such movements. As the analysis continued, it became obvious that the most useful unit of evangelizaion was neither the country nor the individual, but a vast variety of subgroups--people groups. It was also obvious that the Christian world was woefully ignorant about the number and complexity of the people groups. We had identified thousands of language groups and seen the power of such definition to attract and motivate cross-cultural missionaries, but the more subtle and specific people groups had seldom been defined, except by some social anthropologists and sociologists.

On the basis of this research the first unreached peoples directory was prepared for the International Congress in 1974. Based on reports from around the world, it listed 434 unreached people groups.

Subsequent to Lausanne, the LCWE was formed and constituted four working groups--Communications, Intercession, Theology and Education, and Strategy. The Strategy Working Group (SWG) requested World Vision International, the parent agency of MARC, to make the services of that research and strategy organization available to work with SWG. World Vision was pleased to accede to that request. The result has been a series of publications focusing on unreached peoples and on developing strategies to reach them. This book is one in that series.

Other Publications

In addition to the **Unreached Peoples** series, SWG and MARC have published a **World Christianity** series, the purpose of which is to give a country-by-country view of the status of Christianity. At this writing, the series includes volumes on the Middle East, Eastern Asia, Southern Asia, and Central America and the Caribbean. **Planning Strategies for Evangelism** is a workbook which has gone trhough six revisions as it has been field-tested. **That Everyone May Hear** is a small study book that attempts to spell out the theory behind a people group approach to world evangelization. The first edition was translated into Spanish, Chinese, Japanese and French. It is now in its third edition.

Consultation on World Evangelization

These and other materials were utilized by LCWE in preparation for the Consultation on World Evangelization (COWE) held in Thailand, June 16-26, 1980. The primary purpose of the Consultation was to evaluate the work of LCWE and to consider prayerfully whether LCWE should continue.

In preparation for COWE, 17 coordinators were appointed in the major categories of Muslims, Hindus, Buddhists, mystics and cultists, Marxists, traditional Chinese, secularists, traditional religionists, refugees, nominal Protestants, nominal Catholics, nominal Orthodox, large cities, the inner city, and the poor. These coordinators in turn appointed conveners all over the world to discuss the challenge of reaching specific people groups in these larger categories. Hundreds of study groups were convened, and their reports were synthesized into a major report by each coordinator. The COWE then discussed each of these areas in a series of mini-consultations as well as regional groups. A great deal of new information and new insight was gained which has now been published as the Lausanne Occasional Papers (see **Resources**).

The Present Volume

The editors wish to express their appreciation to Burt N. Singleton, manager of World Vision's Research and Information Division and the special consultant for this volume. Not only has he done extensive research on refugees, he has experienced firsthand involvement with them. He was Operations Officer on **Seasweep,** the rescue and assistance vessel World Vision placed in the South China Sea to aid refugees attempting to flee Indochina in small boats.

Since this volume is one of a series, we will begin by giving you a report on the status of reaching the unreached of the world. This will be followed by an article by Ed Dayton on the role of the local church in reaching unreached peoples.

In Part 2, we turn to the challenging story of those people groups called refugees. Ray Bakke outlines for us the history of refugees and the impact they have had on the task of world evangelization. Burt Singleton talks about finding and ministering to refugees. L. P. Verora tells us about refugees in transit and finding ministries to refugees through families.

Loc Le-Chau and Burt Singleton analyze for us how the Strategy Working Group unreached peoples approach can be applied to refugees. Gary Coombs will challenge you with what one local church has been able to do in reaching four different representative groups of refugees. Finally in Part 2, Sam Wilson draws conclusions on the lessons we have learned from all of this.

Part 3 of this volume follows other volumes in giving a number of expanded descriptions of refugee people groups. This section is preceded by a world overview of refugees, but then moves on to give you some specific examples of refugee groups and the potential for reaching them with the gosepl.

Part 4 continues the practice of presenting a registry of the unreached people groups of the world. Here you will find the groups listed alphabetically, by religion, by country, by language and by receptivity. Here also you will find ways of getting further information on particular groups of people to whom God may be leading you in a ministry of prayer, financial support or specific efforts to communicate the gospel to them.

Although it is our privilege to be listed as co-editors of this volume, it should immediately be recognized that such a work can never be the product of two people. In addition to our consultant, Burt Singleton, and the hundreds of men and women throughout the world who have given ungrudgingly of their time, we want to recognize each of those who have contributed both missiological articles and case studies. The huge task of managing the unreached peoples database has been in the hands of Paul Hawley, Research Associate at MARC. Research Associates John Pentecost and Martha Fiege of the Research and Information Division have been responsible for computerizing the database and answering innumerable research questions. Members of the MARC staff, especially Kimberly Finn, have also contributed significantly to the production of this volume.

Future Volumes

Unreached Peoples '84 is already in work. Its purpose is to give a status report on the involvement of mission agencies in attempts to reach unreached people groups. A questionnaire has gone to mission agencies, in both the West and the Two-Thirds World, asking for their analysis of what has been done to date and indicating their plans for the future.

Edward R. Dayton
Samuel Wilson

Monrovia, California

13

Lausanne Committee for World Evangelization as of 1982

One outcome of the International Congress on World Evangelization held in Lausanne, Switzerland, in the summer of 1974, was a mandate from the more than 2400 participants to form an ongoing committee. The "Spirit of Lausanne" was a powerful new thrust for completing the task of world evangelization. The Lausanne Committee for World Evangelization (LCWE) was born in a meeting in Mexico City, January 20-23, 1975. The Committee drew up a constitution, named 48 charter members, and elected Leighton Ford as president and Gottfried Osei-Mensah as executive secretary.

The Committee had its first major meeting at Willowbank, Bermuda, in January 1978. At that time it received a report from its Strategy Working Group on the concept of viewing the world as people groups. The Committee accepted the basic concept and determined that this should be the central focus of a planned Consultation on World Evangelization at Pattaya, Thailand, in 1980.

During June 16-26, 1980, the LCWE convened the Consultation on World Evangelization at Pattaya. Six hundred participants and 230 consultants, observers and guests were present. As a result of that Consultation, the decision was made to reaffirm the mandate of Lausanne and to continue the work of the movement.

The central offices of LCWE are located at Whitefield House, 186 Kennington Park Road, London SE11 4BT, England. Two Working Groups and two Advisory Groups carry out its basic ministries. The current listing of committee and group members follows:

Lausanne Committee

The Rev. Francisco Anabalon (Chile)
Mr. Ramez Atallah (Egypt)
Dr. Saphir Athyal (India)
Dr. Peter Beyerhaus (West Germany)
Mrs. Vonette Bright (U.S.A.)
Dr. Chun Chae Ok (Korea)
Dr. Wade T. Coggins (U.S.A.)
Dr. Robert Coleman (U.S.A.)
The Rt. Rev. A. Jack Dain (Australia)
The Rev. Rene Diadanso (Cameroon)
Dr. Mariano Di Gangi (Canada)
Dr. Nilson Fanini (Brazil)
Mr. Ajith Fernando (Sri Lanka)
Dr. Leighton Ford (U.S.A.)
The Rev. Andrew Furuyama (Japan)
Mrs. Emmy Gichinga (Kenya)
The Rev. Juan Gili (Spain)
The Rev. Geziel Nunes Gomes (U.S.A.)
Dr. Fritz Hoffman (East Germany)
Dr. C. B. Hogue (U.S.A.)
Dr. Donald E. Hoke (U.S.A.)
Dr. George Hunter (U.S.A.)
Dr. Abd-el-Masih Istafanous (Egypt)
The Rt. Rev. Festo Kivengere (Uganda)
Mr. A. T. Victor Koh (Singapore)
Mr. Gordon Landreth (England)
Dr. Samuel Libert (Argentina)
Dr. Branko Lovrec (Yugoslavia)

Dr. Dirinda Marini-Bodho (Zaire)
The Rev. Horst Marquardt (Germany)
Dr. James Massey (U.S.A.)
The Rev. John J. Matulessy (Indonesia)
Dr. Billy Melvin (U.S.A.)
Dr. W. Stanley Mooneyham (U.S.A.)
Dr. Agne Nordlander (Sweden)
Dr. Emilio Antonio Nunez (Guatemala)
Mr. Samuel Odunaike (Nigeria)
The Rev. Gottfried Osei-Mensah (England)
Dr. Cho-Choon Park (Korea)
Dr. Pablo E. Perez (Mexico)
The Rt. Rev. John Reid (Australia)
Mr. D. John Richard (India)
The Rev. Simon H. Sircar (Bangladesh)
The Rev. Alfredo Smith (Peru)
Dr. John Stott (England)
Mr. John Tooke (South Africa)
Dr. C. Peter Wagner (U.S.A.)
The Rev. Thomas Wang (Hong Kong)
Dr. I Ben Wati (India)
Dr. Warren Webster (U.S.A.)
Rev. Canon James Wong (Singapore)
Dr. Thomas Zimmerman (U.S.A.)
The Rev. Isaac Zokoue (France)

Honorary Life Member

Dr. Billy Graham (U.S.A.) Ex-Officio

Lausanne Committee Alternates:

Mr. Isaac Ababio (Ghana)
The Rev. Fouad Accad (Lebanon)
Dr. Robinson Cavalcanti (Brazil)
Mr. Eric Gay (Switzerland)
The Rev. Tom Houston (United Kingdom)
The Rev. Siman Ibrahim (Nigeria)
Dr. Jay Kesler (U.S.A.)
Dr. Frank S. Khair-Ullah (Pakistan)
Dr. Erwin Kolb (U.S.A.)

Mr. Fred Magbanua Jr. (Philippines)
Mrs. Iqbal K. Massey (Cyprus)
Mr. Caesar B. Molebatsi (South Africa)
The Rev. Archie B. Parrish (U.S.A.)
Mr. John Ray (Pakistan)
Dr. Bong Rin Ro (Taiwan)
Dr. George Samuel (India)
The Rev. Rolf Scheffbuch (Germany)
The Rev. Eliseau Simeao (Angola)
The Rev. David Stewart (New Zealand)
The Rev. Tite Tienou (U.S.A.)
Dr. Robert H. Wilson (U.S.A.)
Dr. Norvald Yri (Tanzania)

Theology Working Group

Dr. Saphir Athyal (India)
Dr. Wilson Chow (U.S.A.)
The Rev Peter Kuzmic (Yugoslavia)
Dr. Dirinda Marini-Bodho (Zaire)
Dr. Samuel Moffett (U.S.A.)
The Rt. Rev. John Reid (Australia)
Dr. Agne Nordlander (Sweden)

Strategy Working Group

Mr. Edward R. Dayton (U.S.A.)
Mr. Patrick Johnstone (England)
Mr. A. T. Victor Koh (Singapore)
Dr. Gail Law (Hong Kong)
Rev. Don M. McCurry (U.S.A.)
Miss Kirsti Mosvold (Norway)
Dr. George Samuel (India)
The Rev. Peter Savage (Mexico)
The Rev. Viggo Sogaard (Denmark)
Dr. Warren Webster (U.S.A.)

Intercession Advisory Group

Mrs. Vonette Bright (U.S.A.)
Mr. Chou Sun Ae (Korea)
Mr. Dennis Clark (United Kingdom)

Mrs. Millie Dienert (U.S.A.)
Mr. Fritz Hoffmann (Germany)
Mr. Armin Hoppler (Switzerland)
Mrs. M. Mapalieij-Mantik (Indonesia)
The Rev. N. Lawrence Olson (Brazil)
Mr. Jan-Aage Torp (Norway)

Communications Advisory Group

Dr. Sigurd Aske (Norway)
The Rev. Horst Marquardt (West Germany)
The Rev. Viggo Sogaard (Denmark)
Lausanne Staff

The Rt. Rev. A. Jack Dain (Australia)
Mr. Bill Jefferson (U.S.A.)
The Rev. Gottfried Osei-Mensah (England)
Miss Jane Rainey (England)

Lausanne Offices

The Rev. Gottfried Osei-Mensah, Executive Secretary
    LCWE
    Whitefield House
    186 Kennington Park Road
    London SE11 4BT, England

Mr. Bill Jefferson
    LCWE
    P. O. Box 3500
    Wheaton, Illinois 60187

MARC Office

Dr. Samuel Wilson, Director
    MARC
    919 West Huntington Drive
    Monrovia, California 91016

Part 1

The Unreached
and How to
Reach Them

Reaching the Unreached: A Status Report

Edward R. Dayton

*The historical development of the concept of **people groups** as the basis for a strategy of evangelization is traced here through the various steps of acceptance and application. The desire by mission organizations to define and reach specific people groups has necessitated understanding of cultural factors that may related to the acceptance of the gospel. Four important facets are currently being explored: a theological foundation for reaching the unreached, the concept of the people group, the concept of evangelism strategy, and the relationship between evangelism and social responsibility.*

The history of the Church ebbs and flows like the tides of the sea. Why it should be so, we cannot explain. We can only measure the tides of history and then hope future historians will find us more faithful. It was during one of the ebb tides of the Church that William Carey wrote his small tract **An Enquiry Into the Obligation of Christians to Use Means for the Conversion of the Heathen.** As is often the case, God used the known facts of the world to challenge men and women with the needs of the world. Carey's **Enquiry** is full of facts and figures about the world, as best he knew them. Carey estimated that only one-third of the countries of the world had been touched by the gospel. And yet in the midst of this apparent low point in the Church's concern for the regions beyond, the Spirit was at work in miraculous ways. In 1793, Carey and his two friends could barely raise expenses for their passage to India. Not very many people were interested in their desire to take the Good News to the people of Asia. No one came to see them off. Yet one year later, when a shipload of missionaries sailed down the Thames heading for the islands of the South Seas, thousands of British Christians lined the shores to wish them godspeed. The modern mission movement had begun. It continued unabated for over 100 years. There were few national boundaries that were not crossed by the missionaries of the gospel.

But once again, the forward movement of the Church altered after what appeared to be a high point in the mission movement at the World Missionary Conference at Edinburgh in 1910. It was soon replaced by a spirit of pessimism and doubt. The human destruction of a World War and the theological debates that raged in North America brought about a "rethinking of missions." The challenge of crossing cultural barriers to bring the Good News no longer appeared to attract the elite of Western universities as it had in earlier years. The large Western denominational mission organizations declined in size, while the so-called "faith missions" sent increasing number of Bible-school-trained men and women to fill the gap. By 1960, researchers noted that for the first time within the North American mission force, the numbers of missionaries associated with the Evangelical Foreign Missions Association (EFMA) and the Interdenominational Foreign Mission Association (IFMA) equaled the number of missionaries represented by the Division of Overseas Ministries of the U.S. National Council of Churches.

The rise of faith missions was accompanied by a decline in attempts by the Church to research the task that lay before it. During the early 1900s, the major data of William Carey had been replaced by extensive research on the status of the world and the movement of the Church to evangelize the world. In 1925, the last **World Missionary Atlas** was published. It was an extensive volume with maps of every country in the world locating churches and missionaries. After 1924, there occurred what some observers have termed "the Babylonian captivity of research."

Defining the Task

During the 1950s, a missionary to India with a Yale Ph.D. in education began to take note of surprisingly new movements toward Christ. Donald McGavran witnessed "people movements" in which large numbers of individuals apparently accepted Christ en masse. Stimulated by what was happening in India, McGavran looked for the cause of the phenomenon. In 1960 he founded the Institute of Church Growth at Northwest Christian College in Eugene, Oregon. McGavran challenged veteran missionaries, dissatisfied with the progres they were making, to look anew at the task before them. He pointed them to the tools of anthropology and research. A small cadre of men and women were attracted to Eugene. In 1965, McGavran and the Institute of Church Growth moved to Pasadena, California, and McGavran was installed as Dean of the Fuller Theological Seminary School of World Mission and the Institute of Church Growth. Western missionaries and church leaders from all over the world were attracted to the new School of World Mission. An experienced faculty of mission thinkers assembled around McGavran, and masters and doctoral theses on "church growth" flowed forth from the school. McGavran insisted that the Church was intended to grow. Intuitively, men and women with the same burden for reaching the world believed him and came to learn how they too could obtain "church growth eyes."

At the core of the church growth movement was the concept of setting goals, looking into the future, prayerfully trying to imagine what kind of a church one would like to see planted in a particular place, among a particular people.

In 1964, a 40-year-old engineering executive sensed the call of God in his life and with his family came to Fuller to study theology. In the first few months of his studies, Ed Dayton encountered Ted Engstrom, executive vice president of World Vision International, and what had started as a series of studies leading toward a local pastorate was turned to researching and understanding what God was doing in the world. Dayton was startled by the apparent lack of application of the tools of systems and sociology to the mission task of the Church. When McGavran came to Fuller in 1965, he encouraged Ed Dayton to apply his tools of systems thinking and long-range planning to the task of world mission.

In 1966, McGavran and Dayton were both invited to the Berlin Congress on World Evangelization, jointly sponsored by Billy Graham and the magazine **Christianity Today.** In order to provide a technological overview of the task of the Church, a new agency was born, the Missions Advanced Research and Communication Center (MARC). In 1967, while McGavran continued to direct the School of World Mission, Dayton moved MARC to World Vision, where it became a Division of World Vision International.

Redefining the Task

During their time together at Fuller, McGavran, anthropologist Alan Tippett, Dayton, and three other missionaries devoted a ten-week seminar to applying the tools of strategic planning to the task of world evangelization. In the midst of this seminar it became obvious that thinking about the world in terms of countries, castes or tribal groups was not sufficient. The idea of the **people group** was born.

Although the number of case histories and studies from the School of World Mission continued to multiply, McGavran was not satisifed. In 1966, he persuaded a major foundation to finance extensive research on the status of Christianity in Latin America. Under McGavran's direction, William Read, Harmon Johnson and Victor Monterroso completed the authoritative **Latin American Church Growth** (Eerdmans, 1969).

Meanwhile, MARC was discovering the same dearth of hard data. In 1967 MARC was commissioned by the Divison of Overseas Ministries to undertake the previous work of the Missionary Research Library and produce a **Directory of Foreign Missions from North America.** (In 1953, the MRL had identified 244 agencies from the United States and Canada; in subsequent years this number was to rise to over 700.)

But the data on the status of Christianity in the world had also fallen on hard times. The last edition of the **World Christian Handbook,** which had been published in 1968, was quoting the **Encyclopedia Britannica,** which in turn was quoting the **Handbook!** The editorship of the next **World Christian Handbook** had come into the hands of David Barrett, an Anglican researcher in Nairobi, Kenya. He invited Francois Houtart and Ed Dayton to join him in the task of producing a greatly expanded and comprehensive edition. While this work was being undertaken, MARC began to produce **Status of Christianity Profiles** on numbers of countries. When in 1972 the program committee of the planned International Congress on World Evangelization (ICOWE) was looking for a research source to put the status of Christianity before the Congress, MARC and the School of World Mission were the logical candidates. When the

Congress was convened in Lausanne in 1974, MARC had produced 53 **Status of Christianity Profiles** on countries and major states of the world and an **Unreached Peoples Directory** listing 424 specific unreached people groups.

At the Congress, Dr. Ralph Winter, then on the faculty of the School of World Mission, challenged the delegates with the fact that not only are over three-quarters of the world not Christian, but of these people over two billion are isolated from the gospel by cultural, social, religious and other barriers. These are the **unreached** peoples of the world. At that time, Winter's research indicated that local churches would never reach 80% of the non-Christians of the world without sending cross-cultural missionaries, and less that 5% of the total missionary force was directed toward them.

But the ICOWE at Lausanne not only defined the magnitude and nature of the task, it also produced a new statement on the task of world evangelization. The Lausanne Covenant (see **Resources**) became an umbrella under which Christian men and women, local churches, denominations and mission agencies from all over the world could join hands in the task of taking the Good News to every tribe, tongue, people and country.

Communicating the Task

The Lausanne Committee for World Evangelization (LCWE) was formed out of the ICOWE. Members of the Committee, as well as others who were motivated by the spirit of Lausanne, brought together men and women within their regions and countries to communicate to them the task of world evangelization. For example, where MARC had identified ten unreached people groups in the country of Kenya, a conference at Lenana, Kenya, in 1975 challenged its participants with the fact that there were 12 unreached people groups within Kenya. Similar conferences included (among others) one in Nigeria, one in Papua New Guinea and the Solomon Islands, the Chinese Congress on World

Evangelization in 1976, a Pan-African Conference, an All-India Conference, a Ghana Congress, and a Congress on Evangelism for Malaysia and Singapore.

In 1977, Ralph Winter left the Fuller School of World Mission to found the U.S. Center for World Mission. Winter had the dream and vision to bring together numbers of mission agencies in one location to focus on specific major blocks of unreached people groups. Winter popularized the concept of **hidden peoples.** He saw that not only were many people groups unreached, but they were not identified or even recognized by the Church which might be in close proximity to them. There was no church in their midst. Winter saw this as a new frontier to cross and popularized the phrase **Frontier Missions.** Student movements, such as the Student Missions Fellowship, the Summer Institutes of International Studies (SIIS) and the triennial North American mission conference sponsored by Inter-Varsity Christian Fellowship at Urbana, Illinois, had brought unreached peoples to the attention of thousands of collegians. Young people in Europe were not immune. What was intended to be a gathering of 1500 young people at Mission '76 in 1976 attracted 2800 young men and women. In 1980, their numbers swelled to 7000. As this volume goes to press, 10,000 are expected to attend Mission '83 in Geneva.

In June 1980, the LCWE convened the Consultation on World Evangelization (COWE) at Pattaya, Thailand. Meanwhile, the LCWE had sponsored a Consultation on the Homogeneous Unit Principle in Pasadena, California, in 1977; a consultation on Gospel and Culture at Willowbank, Bermuda, in 1978; and a North American Consultation on Muslim Evangelization at Glen Eyrie, Colorado, also in 1978. The research of MARC and the Strategy Working Group was published in **Planning Strategies for World Evangelization** and in a more simplified book, **That Everyone May Hear** (see **Resources).** The **Unreached Peoples** series began that same year.

Committing to the Task

As churches, missions and Christians were challenged to search for the hidden or unreached peoples around them, the Spirit moved in their midst, and responses came from all over the world. The emerging missions already at work in many of the Two-Thirds World countries renewed their efforts. In 1981 the Friends Missionary Prayer Band of India was sending 195 missionaries across cultural and language barriers throughout India. The Evangelical Church of West Africa was sending missionaries to reach Hausa-speaking people in Nigeria and beyond. In 1979, the World Evangelical Fellowship established its Missions Commission, whose first meeting focused on unreached peoples. Numbers of Western mission agencies appointed specific personnel to seek out and mobilize themselves toward reaching unreached people. In 1980, the Evangelical Foreign Missions Association asked its member mission agencies to analyze how many unreached people groups they were currently attempting to reach and laid before them the challenge of increasing that number by 1990. As a result, the EFMA missions committed themselves to reach, by that date, more than double the number of unreached groups they were already reaching. New commitments to research and action are typified by a yearly meeting to exchange data on unreached peoples in Sumatra, Indonesia, and by a recent survey of unreached peoples in Kenya carried out jointly by World Vision of Kenya and Daystar Communications.

Individual agencies like International Missions of the Foursquare Church have set specific targets for reaching a given number of previously unreached peoples.

In late 1980, encouraged by Ralph Winter, a good number of Western and emerging mission agencies came together in Edinburgh to commit themselves to the task of reaching unreached peoples. As one direct result, a European ad hoc group has convened twice to research the unreached of that continent.

Youth With A Mission (YWAM) challenged their leadership specifically to call their members to the long task of training for cross-cultural missions.

One of the three consultations of the **I Will Build My Church** conference planned for Wheaton in the summer of 1983 focuses on the frontier mission task of the church.

Sharpening the Focus

The growing movement briefly described above has filled the minds and captured the imaginations of the Church throughout the world. Millions of Christians have been led to pray in a new way. The number of young men and women committing their lives to the task of reaching unreached peoples continues to grow.

But any new movement goes through a continuous process of defining its terms and sharpening its focus. The renewed concern for the task of evangelization raises new questions about the mission of the Church. The Lausanne Covenant had stated that the primary commission of the Church was evangelization. Yet those at Lausanne repented of the failure of the Church to have a concern for the human needs of the world. The Lausanne Covenant called for the whole Church to carry out the complete task of mission. Some at Lausanne, however, felt that the Lausanne Covenant did not go far enough. As a result, in June 1982 a Consultation on the Relationship Between Evangelism and Social Responsibility in Grand Rapids, Michigan, was jointly convened by the World Evangelical Fellowship and the Lausanne Committee for World Evangelization, resulting in new understandings. Although the task of evangelization continued to be stressed as primary, it was more clearly recognized that announcing the Good News of the kingdom must include a concern for all dimensions of human life.

As local churches in the West saw the prayer concern for the unreached peoples of the world, they began to explore ways they could become more directly involved. Since the task of becoming a cross-cultural missionary requires extensive training and a special calling, how could local church members become involved beyond going themselves and praying? In response to this felt need, the U.S. Center for World Mission, MARC, LCWE and members of other mission agencies met to define the task in such a way that members of local churches, both in the West and in Two-Thirds World countries, could become directly involved. The result of their discussions led to defining the task of reaching unreached peoples in six steps (see the article "Reaching the Unreached: The Role of the Local Church").

In addition to defining six definite phases of attempts to reach unreached peoples, the meeting, convened by the North American Lausanne Committee, also recognized that some confusion has arisen over the number of unreached people groups of the world. To dramatize the task more clearly, Ralph Winter and the U.S. Center had initially calculated that there were some 25,000 ethnolinguistic groups in the world, 16,750 of which were labeled unreached people groups. Theoretically, if one adds up the population of all these groups, it equals the population of the world. However, the Lausanne definition of a people group (see **Definitions**) encompasses more than ethnolinguistic groups. It recognizes that there are other sociological groupings and that people may be members of more than one social group. Thus, as soon as a part of one ethnolinguistic group is broken away from its basic group, as in the case of ethnic Chinese refugees from Indochina, another people group is formed.

The same meeting also pointed out to the Lausanne

Strategy Working Group that the definition of an "unreached people group" as one being less than 20% practicing Christian was at times misleading. This definition, which had been based on sociological theory (see **Unreached Peoples '81**), in one sense was so broad that people had difficulty believing that there were any **reached** people groups. In responding to this criticism, the Lausanne Strategy Working Group at its March 1982 meeting agreed to a modification of a definition worked out at the Edinburgh '80 Congress (see **Definitions**).

Meanwhile, in the spring of 1982, the long-awaited **World Christian Encyclopedia** was released by Oxford University Press. This 1010-page volume presented a picture of the status of Christianity in the world unlike any that had ever preceded it. But in addition to merely defining the number of Christians in each country, senior editor David Barrett went further in coming up with measurements of the degree of "evangelization" of a population or country. This opened up the whole question of priority for reaching particular groups.

Barrett also divided the world into 8990 "major constituent peoples, sub-peoples and cultures" based upon seven stylized racial colors and thirteen geographic races. Again, this was an attempt to be all-inclusive in enumerating the people of the world.

Inherent in the concept of an unreached people group is the Strategy Working Group notion that each people group is unique and therefore demands a unique evangelistic strategy. The methodology for discovering God's best strategy for people groups had been presented in the book **That Everyone May Hear** and in the work preceding and during the Consultation on World Evangelization at Pattaya. However, numbers of people felt that the approach appeared too Western, led to the potential of founding a racist church, and focused too much on unreached people to the neglect of the one billion people who could be reached by evangelistic methods based on the expansion of local churches. In response to recommendations at Pattaya, the Lausanne Strategy Working Group and Theology Working Group met jointly to review the Lausanne strategy summed up in **That Everyone May Hear** and the audiovisual by the same name (see **Resources**). As a result of that meeting, the book was revised and is scheduled for release as a third edition in 1983. The audiovisual that had been used so extensively throughout the world to challenge thousands of Christians to renewed effort to unreached peoples was expanded, and four new audiovisuals were planned for 1983: theological foundations to reach unreached peoples as defined by the Lausanne Covenant; the concept of the people group; the concept of strategy; and the relationship between evangelism and social responsibility (see **Resources**).

The Lausanne Committee for World Evangelization is scheduled to meet in January 1983 to consider its work during the next ten years and to lay long-range plans for the future.

Edward R. Dayton is the founder of the Missions Advanced Research and Communication Center (MARC), a ministry of World Vision International. He is currently vice-president for the Mission and Evangelism Group in World Vision and has written extensively on management and mission strategy.

Reaching the Unreached: The Role of the Local Church

Edward R. Dayton

By definition, reaching an unreached people group requires well-trained and adequately prepared cross-cultural missionaries. There are times when a local church can constitute itself as a mission society and, on the basis of extensive prayer, thoughtful planning, and dedicated commitment, be used by God to reach an unreached people group that may be geographically close to them. However, most of the time, in most situations around the world, the local church's role is not so clear.

As the awesome and challenging fact of over two billion non-Christians living in unreached people groups has grasped the minds and hearts of local churches of the West, their response has been predictable: "What can **we** do? How can we become involved in reaching the unreached?"

At the same time, numbers of Western mission agencies have been challenging their members to move beyond people groups within which there is already an established and effective Church, to attempt to bring the gospel to those who have never heard. We need new support. New missionaries need to be recruited, trained and supported. God's people need to provide the resources to support them.

The dilemma of helping the local church to have a direct interest in an unreached people, particularly in another country, was a concern of a group of mission leaders who met in Chicago in 1982. They saw that the major task before them was to describe some way to join hands with each other and with local churches to reach a specific unreached people group. The resulting program has been adopted under various names and in different forms by different mission agencies and churches. However, at its core is a way of looking at the world's people groups in terms of **attempts to reach them.**

Although this program has nondenominational mission agencies as its primary focus, mission agencies as its primary focus, it can be easily adapted for denomination agencies and churches. While the data in the Registry of Unreached Peoples in this volume attempts to describe statistics about unreached people groups, this program sees unreached peoples in the perspective of those attempting to reach them. It goes without saying that since reaching the unreached is, in the final analysis, an action of God through His Church, supportive prayer is essential at all stages

Stages of Identification and Evangelization

The program sees the task in six stages: an unreached people group is (1) **Reported,** (2) **Verified,** (3) **Evaluated,** (4) **Selected,** (5) **Supported** and (6) **Engaged.** Notice that these stages are described in terms of the **evangelistic need** of the people group.

Let us examine these stages in greater detail:

Stage 1 - Reported. If someone has reported a group as possibly unreached, the data may be very sparse. However, by listing it in the Registry of Unreached Peoples and identifying it as a people group in **Stage 1,** the way is open for others to move into **Stage 2** and for focused prayer to begin. This initial identification can be extremely important. God often uses such scanty data to open the eyes of others who may be very close to this particular unreached people group.

Stage 2 - Verified. The group has been verified both as a people group and as an **unreached** people group. First, it is important that we understand that they are a **people group** (see **Definitions**). The whole strategy of reaching unreached peoples centers around the idea that if a strong indigenous church is planted among the people group, it can spread the gospel along natural social lines within the group. But we also need to know if it is an **unreached** people group. For example, as of this writing the churches of Kenya are doing an extensive survey of all the people groups of Kenya. They have identified numbers that are reached--those in which there is a strong indigenous church that appears to have the potential of evangelizing the entire group. They are verifying other groups as unreached people.

Stage 3 - Evaluated.. Adequate research has been completed to permit interested Christians outside this people group to make a decision to attempt to reach it. This research may be carried out by local Christians, by other national Christians who are not close to the group, or by expatriate missionaries. Two basic kinds of information are needed: (1) the characteristics of the people group--we need to know enough about the people in this group and their needs so that we can attempt to discover God's unique strategy for reaching them with the gospel--and (2) potential obstacles to reaching this group, such as political boundaries beyond which it is illegal to spread the Christian gospel or citizens of some nations are not allowed.

In other words, after a group has been **evaluated,** it

may appear either that for the moment the door to reaching them is not open, or that we have the information needed for the right cross-cultural agency, either new or old, to decide to attempt to reach them.

Stage 4 - Selected. Up to **Stage 3** all we have had is research, and hopefully a great deal of prayer. At **Stage 4** we move beyond research to action. Some church or mission agency sufficient for the task has made a commitment to reach this people group. At one extreme it may be a local church that has decided to create a mission society to attempt to reach a group that lies very close to them. At the other extreme, there may be a well-funded and long-established mission agency, either national or expatriate, that believes God is calling it to reach this particular people.

At this point the mission agency can announce its intention to attempt to reach this people group through the various media that are available to it, including the MARC Unreached Peoples Desk (see **Definitions**). The mission agency may actually seek out one or more individuals who would be interested in supporting their efforts to reach this particular people group. Or the mission agency may go ahead in faith and begin its work with whatever resources it has, counting on future support.

Stage 5 - Supported. There are adequate resources, usually from the local churches or the denominations, for the mission agency to move ahead. In other words, the mission agency has either approached the local church or the local church has approached the mission agency, and the local church has received information enough to believe that it should get involved in reaching this unreached people group. This may mean receiving special reports from the mission agency, directly or through the agency's regular literature. It may also mean a special emphasis within the local church to focus the interest and concern of the membership on this particular people group; for this the mission agency would be expected to provide the local church with the kind of information it needs.

Stage 6 - Engaged. Initial field work is begun with the intent of planting an evangelizing, culturally indigenous church. What is meant by "field work" is that a qualified missionary, someone with cross-cultural gifts, either is preparing to, or actually has made contact with the unreached people group. Here again, it is important that there be a stream of information back to the local church that is sufficient to provide the needed prayer and material support.

It is important to recognize that just because an unreached people group has now been **engaged** does not complete the process or obviate the need for more engagement. Indeed, one agency with two missionaries may have an engaged unreached people group, when eventually one hundred missionaries may be needed, including those from other agencies.

Who Is Involved in the Program?

There are a number of groups who can benefit from the program.

Local churches need to know what opportunities exist for their involvement in the various stages. They may simply wish to pray. They may want to get involved in supporting the efforts of missions or of research agencies in reporting, verifying and evaluating unreached people groups. They may want to submit to the Unreached Peoples Desk reports on specific people they believe constitute an unreached people group. At the next level, they may want to tell a mission agency that they are ready to support efforts to reach a particular people group, if the mission agency selects it for its work. Beyond this, they will want to become involved in supporting the work of the mission agency.

Again, it is important to recognize that these local

churches may be living a few miles away from an unreached people group, or they may be separated by oceans. Both situations need their concern.

Christian organizations motivating local churches to the task of world mission will need the kind of information supplied by this program. For example, in the United States, the **Association of Church Missions Committees (ACMC)** attempts to keep its members informed about how they can carry out their mission programs more effectively. Youth and campus organizations, such as **Inter-Varsity Christian Fellowship,** the **International Fellowship of Evangelical Students,** and **Campus Crusade for Christ International,** all of which have a concern for challenging young people with reaching the unreached, will also be helped.

Mission agencies need to know about, verify and study the feasibility of reaching unreached people groups, and then move on to selecting them, committing themselves to reaching them. They need to be able to announce their selection to others to provide the basis for cooperation or to avoid duplicate efforts. They then need to communicate, to the local churches and the Christian public, information that will permit local churches to support people groups by name and provide prayer, financial and personnel support.

Research agencies and mission schools that have expertise in gathering and storing information and doing supportive research on their own or with mission agencies need to be able to tell those mission agencies and local churches about such efforts.

Mission training schools engaged in training personnel who will be directly involved in reaching the unreached need to have the information to help those they are training make a decision for the future. **Seminaries,** which train pastors and other Christian workers whose ministry may involve mission interpretation, need to have an understanding of the worldwide task of reaching unreached peoples and progress toward meeting the challenge.

How the Program Works

A group is **reported** as an unreached people group, and this report reaches the ears of an agency, a local church or one of a number of research agencies, such as MARC or the U.S. Center for World Mission, who are involved in tracking the status of unreached people groups. The information is listed in missions periodicals or in this **Unreached Peoples** annual.

This report challenges a research agency, a local church or a mission agency to **verify** that this group is indeed unreached and that it is a people group. The Registry of Unreached Peoples is updated. Again research agencies, mission agencies or local churches may have their interest aroused.

A mission agency or research agency announces the name of a **verified** unreached people group that it would like to research further to **evaluate** the feasibility of reaching it. It may specifically ask for assistance from local churches in supporting this research, or it may use resources it already has.

One or more local churches respond to such an announcement by requesting information needed to **support** whatever activity will help move a given unreached people group toward the next stage of evangelization. The mission agency or research agency then supplies the local churches with sufficient information to enable them to support the effort with prayer, finances and sometimes personnel.

When the process of **evaluation** and **verification** is completed, the mission agency announces it has **selected** a particular people group and thus has committed itself to reach it. Ultimately, a local church may ask a mission agency or research agency whether it is willing to select a particular people group. The local church then responds by committing itself to support the effort with prayer, finances or possibly personnel. The mission agency then begins to **engage** the unreached people group and informs supporting churches of its progress.

During all this time, research agencies can publish the status of various unreached people groups in terms of the particular stage in which they fall, as noted above. Agencies, agency associations or church associations may choose to do the same.

If you would like further information about this program, write to the **Unreached Peoples Desk, MARC, 919 West Huntington Drive, Monrovia, CA 91016.**

Edward R. Dayton is the founder of the Missions Advanced Research and Communication Center (MARC), a ministry of World Vision International. He is currently vice-president for the Mission and Evangelism Group in World Vision and has written extensively on management and mission strategy.

Part 2

Reaching Refugees

Refugees and World Evangelization

Raymond J. Bakke

Refugees in biblical and historical perspective have been both ministered to and at the same time a source of ministry to others. God has used the mass movement of people to spread His Word to the four corners of the world. From the movement of the Jewish nation in the Old Testament to the dispersal of Christians throughout the known world in the first century A.D. to the early waves of American settlers, the entire history of Christianity demonstrates the principle that the Christian is indeed a refugee on the face of the earth. Today's opportunity for fellowship with refugee Christians and non-Christians alike places the Great Commission in a new perspective as the local church seeks to minister to the refugees in its midst. As in the past, today's refugee movements can and will contribute to the development of new forms of more effective ministry.

> "This is the century of homeless man."
> Elfan Rees, **We Strangers and Afraid**

From Pharaoh to Castro they come: millions of refugees, those involuntary migrants who are victims of politics, wars, and catastrophes. These are the "up-

45

rooted peoples," and their numbers have multiplied so rapidly all over the globe that scarcely one of the 223 nations of the world remains unaffected (Newland 1981). In fact, the validity of the contemporary missiological theme "Mission on Six Continents" is precisely shown at the interconnectedness of these massive movements of peoples which have destabilized entire regions of the world.

Broadly speaking, migration scholars identify at least four types of migratory movements:

1. Nomadism, or temporary and disruptive incursions into human settlements;

2. Invasions, or mass movements by conquering groups with the sudden displacement, resettlement, or assimilation of peoples;

3. Immigration, that "free" movement of peoples, often in very large numbers, the pattern of Australia and the United States in the 19th century; and

4. Forced migration, where the victims of international conflicts (or civil wars of international significance) force significant numbers of refugees.

World War II displaced some 40 million of people in Europe alone, but most of those (83%) stayed within their national boundaries. New in our time is the extent of international displacement. Unknown to many, for example, (probably because there have been no "boat people" to dramatize it) is the fact that about half the world's refugees at this time are Africans, moving from one country to another. The "extent and urgency of these situations are unprecedented," according to Ninan Koshy of the World Council of Churches. (The millions of African refugees became the agenda of a continent-wide church-sponsored gathering in Arusha, Tanzania, October 26-30, 1981, which was reported in **The Ecumenical Review,** Vol. 34, April 1982, p. 188.)

No one should minimize the human tragedy of today's refugees. Who has not met the battered exiles in their own neighborhoods or at least studied their tortured faces in magazines and heard their pathetic cries via television newscasts? Surely Christians need not trivialize or paternalize these uprooted peoples by supposing that their immediate needs (e.g., food, shelter, employment or medical care) are their deepest needs. Nor should observers lump them into stereotypical groups or categories apart from personal involvement with them. Experience and studies show a range from the uprooted ghetto refugees, driven into anomic social isolation, to underground refugees, invisible yet next door to us, to those who escape either by exiting or by assimilating into existing communities.

Perhaps the least appropriate of all reactions for host Christians is to "blame the victims" for what has happened to them (the "it serves them right" syndrome; cf. Ryan 1971). The contemporary fact of life is that refugees are treated as a problem when they leave their country and sometimes because they do not leave (e.g., Weiberg 1982). The psychological, social, economic, and religious motivations of the individual refugees are diverse and extraordinarily complex, though sociologists sometimes classify them in general terms such as "push" and "pull" factors (see Jansen 1969 for sociological definitions, and Chance and Butterworth 1981:33-50 for a clarification of their usefulness).

Nevertheless, many studies show that persons who have lost their roots are not normal persons, particularly in the first generation of their forced exile. While they may be classified as political, social, economic, cultural-intellectual or religious refugees, the range of extant psychological factors cuts across all these categories. Insecurities, anxieties, frustrations, fears, and bitterness may be masked by the more visible needs for food or clothing, but these psychological needs cannot be ignored by the refugees or the community for long without broad social consequences.

Perhaps you have assumed that the primary thrust of this essay would be the ministry of evangelism **to** refugees (the validity of which is without question here), rather than the role **of** refugees in world evangelization. However, to interpret these massive, oft-tragic human dramas from God's perspective in Scripture and history permits--indeed, requires--a perspective that God is **sending** the refugees into the world so that they may assist and further the historical tasks of world evangelization and church planting in ways we previously would have thought impossible.

If we were to ask the refugees we know whether placing their concrete experiences of suffering into a broad biblical or historical context would relativize and marginalize those unique experiences, they would say yes. It might even be experienced as our attempt to avoid responding to them personally. I have experienced selected hostility from American blacks who resent the inclusion of their history with that of other victims of forced migration, illustrating how pastoral care requires that we treat people uniquely in each existential situation. Yet, because Christianity as a historical faith has drawn, and continues to draw, theological meanings from the subsequent reflections on real experiences good or ill, we dare to do it.

Perspective is important. God has moved His peoples before (since Genesis 10 and 11), and He seems to be doing that again in large measure in our time. David Bosch (1980), in his helpful discussion of **Missio Dei,** rightly observes that evangelicals must learn to see the Great Commission as something God is doing rather than something we do independently of His action.

A Biblical Perspective

This people has already made its way into every city, and it is not easy to find any place in the habitable world which has not received this nation and in which it has not made its power felt (Strabo, cited in Josephus, Antiquities).

Forced to live in cities everywhere, the Jews of the Old Testament and intertestamental eras grappled with issues of faith and culture, developed new communication and catechetic styles, created new, diverse and historically significant liturgical patterns (the synagogue was invented in the diaspora), and translated the Scriptures into other languages. No one would deny that for the most part these changes were painfully experienced, but who among us would doubt their benefit, to an enriched and adaptive Judaism but more importantly to the rapid spread of first-century Christianity? (Michael Green, Blailock Neill, and numerous other writers like Harnak earlier have observed this. See also Banks 1980.)

Seen from this perspective, Abraham, then Israel itself, become paradigms for the modern refugee and the contemporary Church of Jesus Christ for a world in transit. The exodus of Israel from Egypt is well known. Less well known is the promise that he would drive out other nations before Israel then (Ex. 34:11) and continue to relocate other peoples throughout history (Acts 17:26). Who can doubt that the nearly simultaneous exodus of refugees from or to nearly all the nations of the earth has special kingdom significance?

If we reread Jeremiah's personal letter to the Jewish refugees forced into exile in Babylon after a terrible 900-mile march (Jer. 29:4ff), we may notice three rather specific instructions given the refugees themselves: first, they were to interpret these experiences as God's missionary call to them and not as a personal tragedy (vs. 4); second, they were to invest in their new environment and put down roots there vs. 5); third, they were to seek the welfare (shalom) of their host city, realizing that they would find their own personal welfare within the context of a healthy host community (vs. 7).

But can we assume, as we seem to be doing in this essay, that refugees are Christians? Not all are, by any measure. But many are. Some contemporary refugees come from new churches established by missionaries or nationals. Others have found Christ in the refugee camps because the gospel was faithfully and ingeniously proclaimed there. Others come from ancient Near Eastern churches overlaid with centuries of cultural tradition, having survived centuries of persecution in hostile environments. Obviously then, part of the responsibility of host churches is to make contact, then affirm and enable the refugee churches to do their evangelistic task in ways that use their unique gifts. One possible result will be the renewal of host churches in new partnerships with refugee churches directly for mission and evangelism in the same communities. Before, those groups were linked only symbolically by missionaries who alone experienced the big picture and mediated between the local and distant believers; now congregations will experience those wonderful dynamics directly.

There is much practical biblical instruction for Christians in host cultures and congregations engaged in refugee ministry:

1. Strangers and aliens should be welcomed into homes following Abraham's example found in Genesis 18:1-8. (This is enjoined in many other texts.)

2. Aliens should not be mistreated either by persons or policies because we, like Israel, should remember we have alien backgrounds or histories. In fact, we are to love strangers and sojourners as we love ourselves (Lev. 19:33, 34).

3. Material possessions should be shared with needy visitors. In a special way we are said to minister to

Christ and angels if we do this (Matt. 25; Rom. 12:13; Heb. 13:2).

4. We must insist that all aliens receive the full protection of just laws, for like Israel, we will be accountable for how aliens are treated (see Ex. 22:21-24). It is not enough, biblically speaking, to personally treat strangers well, if others in our communities or our laws treat foreigners unjustly. The biblical commands that require us to do justly also condemn our toleration of injustice, and the Hebrews understood this (cf. Watson 1959).

5. We must remember that "the earth is the Lord's" (Ps. 24:1) and the food supply (cattle of Ps. 50:10, 11). If He wants to redistribute His land and His wealth by shifting us around, that is fundamentally His privilege. Those of us who have much will always experience these changes as loss, but that is exclusively a human point of view.

Because the whole earth belongs to the Lord (not just my favorite parts), people may go to Moab or Egypt to escape famine or live as expatriates in distant lands like Babylon or Persia. In any case the God of the Bible is the God of the fatherless and the landless (Ps. 68:5-6).

Moreover, let us not forget that in his only New Testament letter sent exclusively to a single individual (Philemon), Paul, that intercontinental evangelist par excellence, suggests a theological rationale for refugee movements when he reflects on the theft and flight of Onesimus from Asia to Rome and back when he says: "Perhaps this is why he was parted from you for a while, that you might have him back for ever" (vs. 15). This kind of theological thinking resembles that of Mordecai who, as an alien in Persia and threatened by a pogrom against his people, could argue that Esther's ministry role as queen might have significant kingdom implications (Esther 4:14).

Clearly, the biblical materials from both Testaments embrace the ministry **of** as well as **to** the refugees.

A Historical Perspective

Yet, although they live in Greek and barbarian cities alike as each man's lot has been cast, and follow the customs of the country in clothing and food and the matters of daily living . . . they live in their own countries, but only as aliens. They have a share in everything as citizens, and endure everything as foreigners. Every fatherland is a foreignland, and yet for them every foreignland is a fatherland (letter to Diognetus 5:4, 5).

In his superb two-volume study **Strangers and Exiles: A History of Religious Refugees,** Fredrick Norwood summarizes:

The entire history of early Christianity demonstrates the principle that the Christian is indeed a refugee on the face of the earth. The theme that his destiny is not of this world, that he seeks a "Kingdom," that the end lies in the City of God beyond history, runs like a strong thread from Hebrews to Augustine (1969:112,113).

Beyond these first few centuries, readers are doubtless familiar with the mobile nature of medieval Christians, and perhaps familiar with the hospices and other institutions developed to care for the refugees of three continents during many centuries of church expansion amid cultural and political turbulence. Even then refugees helped spread the gospel. Chapters 5 and 6 of the Letter to Diognetus, dated around A.D. 140 **(Early Christian Fathers** 1953), contain remarkable explanations of early Christian morality and witness in the diaspora of the Roman Empire. (See also Schmid 1885, a truly remarkable source book.)

Perhaps the reader has also heard of the "Stranger Churches" for continental refugees in England during the Reformation of the 16th century, or has studied the tragic plight of French-speaking Huguenots after the Massacre of St. Bartholomew's Day in Paris and the simultaneous purge in other French cities, which killed at least 20,000 and spread both victims and the gospel as far as the New World colonies. Then again, who among us has not marveled at the energy and missionary vision developed among the Marian exiles and other Anglo refugees in Geneva, or by radical Mennonites who fled into Amsterdam and other cities along the Rhine and thus spread the gospel throughout the low countries of Europe? The contemporary observation of John Strype said it well: "These divers very learned and godly foreigners forward religion not a little" (Ecclesiastical Memorials II, 321). (I recommend two other studies that clarify the roles and significance of Reformation refugees in European cities: Bernd Moller, **Imperial Cities and the Reformation** (Forties), and Steven Ozment, **The Reformation in the Cities** (Yale).)

A Contemporary Perspective

> Give me your tired, your poor, your huddled masses yearning to breathe free . . . Send these homeless, tempest-tossed to me (Bartholdi, on the Statue of Liberty).

In the decade of the 1970s the numbers of immigrants into the U.S.A. equaled the 8.8 million of 1900-1910. Many are involuntary migrants, forced from their homelands to seek refuge here. The national experiences of both North and South America are matched by the experiences of Western Europe, which in turn might be called the "empire strikes back" syndrome, for virtually every colonial power has become host to the former colonials, much to the consternation of the nativists. Urban riots have ensued all over the globe, triggered in part by actions of--and reactions to--urban refugees.

The institutional church in formerly stable parish neighborhoods is only a little worse off amid these new migratory realities than the exclusively foreign missionary emphasis church for whom the mission was always "over there someplace." Neither congregation responds willingly or easily to the new realities.

Mortimer Arias (1982:69-81) is probably right when he reminds host churches especially in the U.S.A. that hospitality is a forgotten virtue and that Christians can now use the Johannine pattern of "come and see" evangelism with new appropriateness.

What then can we do?

1. Make contact with refugee groups by assisting refugee service organizations where they exist or founding them where they are needed and do not exist. I was reminded how significant this ministry is by a recent visit to the Chinese American Service League in Chicago where at least 9000 of the 40,000-plus Chinese immigrants have been assisted by credentialed and compassionate Christian social workers.

2. Provide space in church buildings and other support services for immigrant congregations.

3. Connect the believers of immigrant groups with believers at both ends of their migrant streams. Sometimes this means bringing the work of missionaries home or struggling to connect the resources lodged in the international mission board with the home mission people so that local multilingual leadership can be developed. Many host congregations need new lessons in cross-cultural understandings, i.e., fewer missionaries who come to take their money and leave without showing them what they need to know to be cross-culturally effective at home.

4. Both host and refugee believers need affirmation

for their special roles in God's worldwide evangelization task.

5. More than relief, which is necessary, refugees who find themselves either in pathological urban neighborhoods in their new countries (because the housing is cheaper), or as minorities in middle-class Anglo settings, will need sensitive support systems which provide a whole range of psychological and social services beyond the direct communication of the gospel.

6. By keeping informed and involved, we may influence the fundamental causes of the forced migration in the first place. We may, through a variety of networks and Christian international organizations, empower believers and others to regain control of their own countries and destinies.

7. We can certainly communicate the gospel clearly and patiently in the context of compassionate, caring relationships wherever we find the refugee.

These are but suggestions in principle. Many worthy models exist.

The U.S.A. achieved two remarkable successes in 1965 that bear on these discussions. First, a series of civil rights bills removed some internal barriers of structured racism. Second, and equally significant, immigration laws were implemented that removed race or national origin as principles of selectivity for refugees or others seeking entrance to the country.

A new, healthy globalism, however, has not resulted from the passage of these more just laws. Instead (and perhaps predictably) new sectionalisms, heightened nativism and shifts to racial and ideological consciousness have emerged in this country, even among some Christians.

Some Americans still believe the mythology of Israel Zangwill's play **The Melting Pot** (1909). Even our motto **E pluribus unum** (one from many) is taken to imply that the refugees and other immigrants must change to be as good as we are, or must earn their right to be here.

On the contrary, Christians recognize that many of the most culturally distant new refugees have values much closer to the biblical norms for behavior and family life than those of many resident culture-bound Christians. Who could possibly doubt the benefit of having Korean, Romanian, Arab, Kampuchean, Haitian or Filipino refugee Christians (to name but a few) who have fled oppression now living next door to us? Who can possibly fail to be strengthened by the testimonies of these new residents?

Obviously, there's another thing we can do: study the culture and history of the refugees. For that there are good sources in many languages. Some that have helped me to be much more sensitive and helpful to others include the following:

Harvard Encyclopedia of American Ethnic Groups (Harvard, 1981), Stephan Thernstrom ed., massive and superb studies with wide-ranging essays and helpful bibliographies. Thomas Bentz, **New Immigrants: Portraits in Passage** (Pilgrim, 1981), includes a listing of places where readers can get information for involvement (pp. 204-206). This perhaps ought to be read alongside the reprinted classic study by John Higham, **Strangers in the Land: Patterns of American Nativism, 1860-1925** (Atheneum, 1978 edition). Milton Gordon's **Assimilation in American Life** (Oxford University Press, 1964), Michael Novak's **The Rise of the Unmeltable Ethnics** (MacMillan, 1971), and Andrew Greely's little work **Why Can't They Be Like Us?** (Institute of Human Relations Press, 1969) are remarkably helpful in clarifying the limits of accommodation and assimilation among ethnic and/or refugee peoples. **Ethnic Chicago** by Jones and Holli (Eerdmans, 1981),

Oscar Handlin's **The Uprooted** (Atlantic Monthly Press, 1973), and **Puerto Rico and the Puerto Ricans** (especially the chapter on Puerto Ricans in the diaspora) by Lopez and Petras (Schenkman, 1974) vividly portray the pathos and alienation through psychological and sociological case histories in ways illustrative of other groups as well. Egon Mayer's **From Suburb to Shtetl: The Jews of Boro Park** (Temple, 1979) describes some of the adjustments a community of Jewish refugees made and how they adapted their religious and family patterns to survive and grow in their new setting.

The **Eastasia Edge** by Roy Hofheinz and Kent Calder (Basic Books, 1982) trumpets the message that "Asia is coming . . . indeed has come" and that we in the West shall never be the same again. **Migration Today: Current Issues and Christian Responsibility** is published annually and is available free from the World Council of Churches (150 route de Ferney, 1211 Geneva 20, Switzerland). The Winter-Spring 1981 issue of **Justice Ministries** is subtitled "The Church and Immigration" and has numerous helpful abstracts of books and articles dealing with refugees and resources. Published by the Institute for Church in Urban-Industrial Society (ICUIS), these materials are available at 5700 S. Woodlawn, Chicago, IL 60637.

Finally, a recent article in **The New York Times** (May 1982), reporting on the new tensions in New York's Chinatown, mentioned the remarkable fact that every province of mainland China is now represented by refugees in one very small section of Chinatown in one Western city. It sounds like a parable. Why is the Lord bringing so many international refugees from distant lands to live in our neighborhoods, if not so that they may be able to hear the gospel more clearly and respond to it more directly? Why indeed, unless they are to assume a new and significant role in world evangelization?

References Cited

Arias, Mortimer
  1982   "Centripetal Missions or Evangelization by Hospitality," **Missiology,** X:1, January.

Banks, Robert
  1980   **Paul's Idea of Community,** Eerdmans.

Bosch, David
  1980   **Witness to the World,** John Knox.

Chance and Butterworth
  1981   **Latin American Urbanization,** Cambridge.

Early Christian Fathers
  1953   Westminister.

Jansen, C.
  1969   "Some Sociological Aspects of Migration," in **Migration,** ed. J. A. Jackson, Cambridge.

Newland, Kathleen
  1981   **Refugees: The New International Politics of Displacement,** Washington, D.C.:   Worldwatch Institute.

Ryan, William
  1971   **Blaming the Victims,** Pantheon.

Schmid, C.
  1885   **The Social Results of Early Christianity,** trans. R. W. Dale, Wm. F. Skister, Ltd.

Watson, Thomas
  1959   **The Ten Commandments,** Banner of Truth Trust.

Weiberg, Gunner
  1982   "Why I Did Not Leave Nazi Germany in Time," **The Christian Century,** April 27, pp. 478-481.

Raymond Bakke *is a professor of ministry at North-ern Baptist Theological Seminary in Lombard, Illinois, and is co-founder of the Seminary Consortium for Urban Pastoral Education (SCUPE). He has over twenty years of urban ministry experience, including a ten-year inner-city pastorate. In 1980, Bakke served as the international coordinator for the mini-consultation on large cities at the Consultation on World Evangelization in Pattaya, Thailand.*

Finding and Ministering to Refugees

Burt N. Singleton

The general classification of "refugee" is too large to consider effectively as a single unreached people group. Even the country of origin does not sufficiently characterize the changing dynamic of the refugee situation. This article provides a framework against which to view the varying needs, fears and concurrent ministry opportunities which exist as refugees move to a place of final settlement.

Who Are Refugees?

The world is faced with a rising tide of suffering humanity, the debris of war, persecution and natural disaster we know as refugees. Estimates of today's refugee population vary between 14 and 18 million people. No one predicts a significant reduction in that number, and as political climates continue to destabilize, it is easy to identify several troubled regions of the world capable of producing additional thousands. Unfortunately, only a small percentage, estimated to be less than five percent, are refugees as a result of natural disasters. The remaining 95 percent are the result of human greed, betrayal of the popular will, lust for power, ethnic hatred and economic strains. No nation is entirely immune to the effects of today's millions of displaced people.

As we will see, the life cycle of refugees has various stages. Understanding these stages helps us to define them as different kinds of **people groups.** (See **Definitions.**) Each of these different **people groups** requires a particular evangelistic strategy to effectively reach them with the gospel. Frequently they can be reached by near-neighbor Christians. However, most of the time special mission organizations will be required. Unfortunately, the changing status of refugee groups has often left them ignored by Christians. This should not be so. It need not be so.

Refugees in History

The ebb and flow of this tide has been a phenomenon of history for both Jews and Christians. A place of refuge has been the goal of countless millions. Abraham was a refugee in Egypt due to a famine in Palestine (Gen. 12:10). Jacob and his family fled a later famine (Gen. 15:13). Joseph and Mary slipped quietly from Bethlehem to Egypt with their young child to escape the wrath of King Herod (Matt. 2:13-22). In more modern times, the Jews of Europe in the 1930s began an exodus in response to the wave of anti-Semitism. The root cause was largely misunderstood, and the world's economic condition was not conducive to resettlement of such large numbers. This largely unsuccessful refugee movement led to the Holocaust and the death of millions in the concentration camps and ovens of the Third Reich. Today, Soviet Jews subject to political harassment and imprisonment find great difficulty leaving Russia to find freedom in other countries.

Refugee status is also well-known to Christians. In the early 1950s, when Ho Chi Minh gained control of North Vietnam, almost 800,000 fled from the North to the South, most of them Catholics who feared persecution because of their faith. The murderous policies of Idi Amin in Uganda in the 1970s affected Christians as well as tribal peoples. Hundreds of thousands of Catholics and Protestants fled to the adjoining countries of Kenya, Zaire, Tanzania, Sudan and beyond.

In a sense, all Christians are refugees on earth. Peter reminds believers that "our citizenship is in heaven" (Phil. 3:20). In I Peter 2:11, believers are called "aliens" and "exiles." Even the Great Commission (Matt. 28:19, 20) suggests that God's people become refugees in order to carry His word to all the peoples of the earth. The unprecedented expansion of the Christian church in the first centuries came about as unnamed followers of Christ dispersed and, often fleeing for their lives, carried the Good News throughout the Roman Empire.

The Old Testament abounds in admonitions concerning the treatment of strangers. "The alien living with you must be treated as one of your native born. Love him as yourself . . . " (Lev. 19:34, cf. Ex. 12:49; Deut. 1:16; 27:19; Zech. 7:10; Mal. 3:5; Ezek. 47:22; Lev. 23:22; Deut. 24:19, 21; Deut. 26:12-13). The stranger was accorded the same ranking as the widow and orphan. Matthew equates the care of strangers to the care of Jesus Christ by the believer. No distinction is made in Scripture as to whether the alien/stranger has arrived simply as one on a journey or rather has fled war, political persecution, ethnic prejudice or starvation.

Today, however, the momentum of world politics and the complexity of national sovereignty have created a situation that confuses and divides the Church. Though we once classified refugees simply as "strangers," the cause of their flight having little or no bearing on their treatment, today we are faced with illegal aliens, applicants for asylum, economic refugees, political refugees, and thousands upon thousands who are hidden behind the clouds of political chicanery whose very existence is denied. The United Nations 1951 Convention, as amended by the 1967 Protocol, defines a refugee as a person who, "owing to well-founded fear of being persecuted for reasons of race, religion, nationality, membership of a particular social group or political opinion, is outside the country of his nationality and is unable or, owing to such fear, is unwilling to avail himself of the protection of that country." This definition excludes the many people displaced by natural or civil calamity within their own countries and those who cross national borders for reasons other than well-founded fear of persecution. In actual fact, however, people fleeing across national borders are classified according to the law of the country they enter.

The technical and sometimes tiresome question of who is and who is not a refugee has enormous significance for the displaced people themselves. The answer determines the degree of support and protection the individuals receive, as well as a long-term resolution of their plight.

The fundamental right refugee status gives people is the right not to be sent back against their will to the country from which they have fled. Governments of countries from which people flee have often disputed the validity of refugees' claims, calling them bandits, guerrilla fighters or simply illegal but voluntary migrants. The current regimes in Afghanistan and Vietnam have used these arguments as defense against charges of violating their own citizens' basic human rights.

Countries on the receiving end of refugee flows have also been known to dispute claims of refugee status. In 1979, when thousands of Kampucheans fled across the border into Thailand, they were not accorded refugee status. In fact, in June 1979, Thailand forced more than 40,000 Kampucheans back across the border. Haitians, who began arriving in the United States by boat during 1978, claimed political asylum, but were said by the United States Government to be economically motivated migrants.

The Haitian case exemplifies the ambiguous application of refugee status because it coincided with the acceptance in the United States of nearly 120,000 Cuban entrants, only a minority of whom could be considered to meet the conventional requirements for political asylum. The case was settled by a compromise that allowed both Cubans and Haitians to remain in the country, but denied them refugee status. Both groups were ambiguously classified as "entrants" and so received less federal assistance than refugees would have been given. They were also denied the international legal protection of the United Nations Convention and Protocol.

The distinction between political and economic refugees often is hazy, especially when the government of a particular country views those who attempt to leave it as potential troublemakers or even traitors. In the Soviet Union and in Cuba, for example, people who apply for exit visas often suffer harassment from the authorities. By the very act of attempting to emigrate, perhaps for economic reasons, people may make themselves politically suspect and therefore subject to persecution. By this peculiar circumstance, they may, in fact, become legitimate political refugees.

Separated from their home culture, refugees immediately become a different people group because of their circumstances and because of their needs. While they still retain the principal characteristics of their ethnic and national origin, the disruption of the normal social and economic order causes refugees to identify themselves as "separated people." As a large group of refugees seek asylum in various countries and resettle in still other countries, what began as a large people group becomes many smaller groups, each with its own unique characteristics.

Whatever the legal classification, to the Christian the refugees remain the biblical strangers in our midst. Their needs are **total.** Food, shelter and medical attention are only the most immediate concerns about the future, and the heartaches of the past constitute emotional trauma for the refugee. During periods of enforced idleness, the need for intellectual stimulation becomes increasingly manifest as physical problems diminish. Those who have helped refugees cope with their various needs have found many appropriate opportunities for evangelism. Thus, there are many ways and many opportunities to reach refugees with the gospel. To better understand this, we need to analyze the anatomy of the refugee's flight.

The Anatomy of Flight

A serious search for specific opportunities of refugee evangelism is assisted by an understanding of the total flight experience. Mass movements of refugees generally follow one or more of the patterns shown in Figure 1. Each individual situation, however, falls within a broad spectrum of extremes, not all of which can be described precisely. However, the common characteristic of all refugees is a sense of terrible loss and severe anxiety, both at a level incomprehensible to one who has never had the refugee experience. The trauma of flight produces strong residual psychological changes which may affect refugee behavior for years to come. Three residual characteristics have been identified as central to the trauma:

1. Feelings of guilt. These feelings may arise on account of the loss of loved ones because the refugee delayed flight or failed to protect them during attack or even because the refugee failed to produce basic necessities of food, medicine, clothing and so on for loved ones.

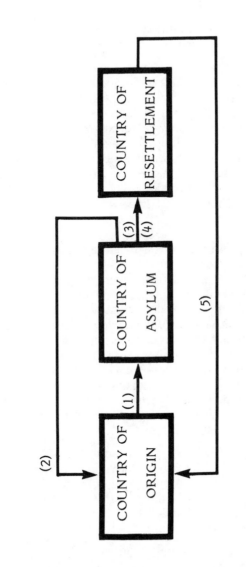

The Anatomy of Flight

Figure 1

2. A sense of invulnerability. This sometimes develops because the refugee has been through the worst and has survived.

3. Aggressiveness. This is frequently seen as an outgrowth of the first two. The displacement of guilt onto others, and a willingness to take risks because one is invulnerable, tend to make refugees more aggressive than they were before flight. This aggressiveness may be displayed in the form of increased violence, crime and suicide or, more productively, in an increased willingness to innovate, to take risks and to make the necessary effort to build a new life.

Within the Country of Origin

1. The perception of a threat. Some refugees sense the danger early, before a crisis makes orderly departure impossible. In this sense, anticipatory refugees resemble voluntary migrants who sometimes bring resources with them and make preparations for a new life in a new land. Most refugees, however, leave their homeland on a moment's notice, often in an atmosphere of panic or hysteria. Because the decision to leave is made within such a short time span, little thought is given to the consequences of flight. Recent interviews with a group of Indochinese refugees indicated that 85 percent began their flight within two hours to two days after making the decision to leave.

2. Deciding to flee. As a consequence of a panic decision to depart, the refugees may make inadequate preparations and an unwise choice of routes. Preparation for fleeing may also alert authorities to their intentions, introducing problems in an already tense situation.

3. The period of extreme danger and flight. During initial departure, some of the route may be through the country of origin or by boat where they are subject to extreme dangers of weather and, in some cases, pirates.

At this point, an interesting question is the role of the national church in the country of origin in assisting the departing refugee. For a mass exodus, the church may be overwhelmed with requests for assistance. Still, it would appear that this period represents an opportunity for viable Christian counsel and witness.

Country of Asylum

Referring to Figure 1, the first path represents the initial movement of the refugees to a country of asylum, out of their native country. They may travel through several other countries to reach the country of asylum, or it may be adjacent to their own country. They may be welcomed, tolerated or repelled. If allowed to remain in the country of asylum, they are generally gathered together with other refugees in some settlement. In whatever form the settlement may take, it becomes in the language of the country a "camp," if only to emphasize that it is, in the opinion of the host government, a temporary situation. Some "temporary" camps look much like villages, establishing self-government, schools, some industry and trade.

The camp experience becomes another form of trauma for the refugees. They are segregated from the host population, forced to share needed facilities, embarrassed by a lack of privacy of daily life within an overcrowded, limited and restricted area. These characteristics of camp existence give refugees a sense of dependency and a clear signal that they have a special and limited status and are definitely being controlled. It is generally in the camp that refugees must first face up to the loss of homeland, identity and former life. The possibility of a new life in a strange land awaits them. Anxiety, fear, frustration and emotional disturbances appear, and often refugees regress to a more infantile state. They become apathetic, helpless or aggressive, and in such a state lose a sense of structure and the ability to coordinate or to predict, as well as basic feelings of self-confidence.

During this status as refugees, they have not begun the process for attaining citizenship in the country of asylum. If they are judged and designated as bona fide refugees, United Nations and voluntary agencies will be permitted to provide assistance in meeting their needs. Depending primarily upon the host government's attitude toward the refugees, the national church in the country of asylum may or may not seize upon the ministry opportunity that is theirs. If the government and the church are willing, much refugee aid from Christian organizations can be handled through the local churches, giving them an opportunity to minister to neighbors, and at the same time, an understanding of the situation that caused these people to become refugees in the first place. Difficulties may arise if the refugees are of obviously higher economic status than those who seek to minister to them. The combination of debilitating factors experienced in the camp setting points to one of the greatest opportunities for evangelism in the entire refugee experience.

Country of Resettlement

Moving from the country of asylum, a choice among three dispositions is available for the refugees. First, the situation that caused them to flee their country may have changed, and they may return to their own country of their own free will. Depending upon the size of the refugee group, how long the group has been out of the country, their treatment received as refugees and the situation that exists in the country when they return, they may well form a separate people group, distinct from those who remained in the country. This has been noted in the Falkland Islands where those who fled the Argentine invasion were viewed with some disdain by those who remained. Even in their own country, sometimes refugee/survivors suffer a real sense of isolation from others who have not shared their traumatic experiences. The national church in the country of origin may now be faced with an evangelism strategy built upon unity, forgiveness and the rebuilding of lives in their own country.

Second, the host country may permit the refugees to resettle in that country. This is seldom the case, but it can occur when there are already large groups within the country of close ethnic similarity to the refugees, such as the Vietnamese of Chinese origin permitted to resettle in China. This change of status brings a new and unique set of problems, particularly if the government is motivated by political rather than humanitarian considerations. However, if the national church has built bridges to the refugee population during the time they were temporary guests, a follow-up resettlement activity is a natural extension. If such bridges have not been built, receptivity to the gospel on the part of the refugees may be somewhat less evident, **and** missionaries who have previously worked with this particular group of refugees in their country of origin may be better able to bridge the gap between the national church and the refugees.

A third movement possible from the refugee status in the country of asylum is to a third country for resettlement. Here the refugees have little hope or desire of returning to their native country and will undergo the cultural shock of starting life over, frequently with a new language, new climate and new occupation. Adjustment difficulties do not depend solely on the degree of cultural differences between the refugees and their hosts, although that is likely to be the most important factor.

Much also depends on the status of those who have fled. Are they young and active, professional or farmer, family or group or single men, well educated, whole village or small groups? How much have they suffered? Who has been lost or left behind? How long have they been persecuted, and how long were they in refugee camps?

What is the attitude of the receiving country? Does the host resent or welcome the refugees? Do the refugees have some claim on the receiving state? In resettlement in a third country, the national church has a major role to play. A simple attitude of friendliness and a desire to help may be the greatest single aspect of any workable evangelism strategy.

Readjustment and Resettlement

As a generalization, the pattern of refugee adjustment and resettlement in a new country over time has been analyzed in four stages:

1. The initial arrival period of the first few months. During this initial period, refugees will be confronted by the reality of what has been lost. From a high occupational and social status at home, they may have to plunge to the bottom of the social ladder, from professional to the service sector, from elite to an impoverished minority. They will be confronted by the loss of culture, identity and habits. Every action that used to be habitual or routine will require careful examination and consideration. Strains will appear at home because the husband cannot provide, the wife must work, the children fail to respect the old ways, and, because they acquire the culture more rapidly, the children patronize the parents. Nostalgia, depression, anxiety, guilt, anger and frustration are so severe that many refugees may even toy with the idea of going home.

2. The first and second years. This period may be characterized by the drive of refugees to recover what has been lost, to rebuild their lives. Some of the factors that cause initial downward mobility become less severe with time. Acculturation, language improvement, retraining programs and hard work and determination begin to take effect. During this period research indicates many refugees change jobs, go to school and move from their initial concentrated placement areas. They may also experience increased problems within the family, and their level of mental confusion is liable to shift and increase.

3. After four or five years. By this time, the refugees will have completed the major part of the adjustment. Less change occurs after this point. The dream of restoring one's old status conflicts with reality. By now, also, they have acquired the language and the culture, been retrained and worked hard. Still, their skills may be getting stale. Drive and determination may wane, discouragement may set in. The refugees may become resigned to the changes of their life and status. Many will be just surviving, acculturated enough to function, but far from assimilated or totally integrated.

4. After ten years. A refugee group will now have achieved a certain stability. The recovery of lost status will continue, but at a much slower pace. The total effect after the first decade is one of decline. Despite drive and determination, the total effect of exodus is to produce a lower status. Generally, the refugees have paid a high price for their flight.

Back to Country of Origin

A final movement is the eventual movement of resettled refugees from their foster country back to the country of origin. This group tends to arrive as individual families over a long period of time, but constitutes a cultural anomaly in their own country. Interviews indicate that this movement is the ultimate desire of a great many resettled refugees, usually based upon the condition of a major change in government. This movement certainly represents a unique opportunity for the national church in the country of origin. As they "catch up" on what has transpired in the country since their departure, locate lost friends and relatives and undergo reverse culture shock, there are many opportunities for the national church to help.

A last and perhaps most tragic group are those for whom none of the three basic movements from the country of asylum are available. These are the "residue" that remain in the camps for years. For some groups, flight from war and persecution is turned into lifelong, even generations of exile. The most prominent case is that of the Palestinians, most of whom were displaced over thirty years ago and are still awaiting a durable solution. Nearly two million have the status of refugees. But the Palestinians are not alone. Tens of thousands of Tibetans have remained stateless in India since 1959, and many still dream of returning to an independent Tibet. Some observers fear that the ethnic Somali refugees from Ethiopia who now reside in Somalia will become another long-term community of exiles. The bitter experience of prolonged statelessness certainly scars those who live through it. They represent perhaps the most tragic people group for which the church must design an evangelism strategy.

It is recognized that at any given time, refugees from a given country may be moving in all modes simultaneously. In each mode, however, although many of their ethnic and cultural characteristics would be held in common, the differences caused by where they have been and where they are now, from the strategist's point of view, are enough to consider them as separate people groups. As we seek to find and explore means by which refugees of the world can be brought to a saving knowledge of our Lord and Savior Jesus Christ, we see that at every turn opportunities exist to meet their special needs at their time of need. These opportunities may be available to and through the national churches in the countries in which these refugees happen to be or through specific mission organizations established to meet recognized opportunities. International and national aid notwithstanding, our ultimate responsibility as Christians is to meet the total needs of these peoples--physical, mental and spiritual.

Conclusion

We have seen that refugees form a special kind of people group, and that the characteristics of the group often divide and change over a relatively short period of time. Most refugee people groups are unreached. But at many stages of their journey, most are quite open to the Good News of rescue in Jesus Christ.

Burt N. Singleton, Jr. is the director of the Research and Information Division of World Vision International. During the height of the Vietnamese "Boat People" crisis, he served as the Operations Officer on board Seasweep, a service and supply ship operated on the South China Sea by World Vision to aid the refugees in their flight to freedom. In 1980, Singleton participated in the mini-consultation on refugees at the Consultation on World Evangelization in Pattaya, Thailand. In addition to his work through World Vision, he is a board member of the Navajo Gospel Mission.

Tensions in African Resettlement: The Cabindan Case

Arni Shareski
Jane Raffloer

The civil war in Angola, beginning in 1975, scattered more than a million refugees to neighboring countries. One group, a part of the Bakongo tribe living in the Cabinda region of Angola, were caught between two rival factions and fled to Zaire for refuge. Now virtually isolated from other Bakongans, their culture has experienced severe change through attempts to assimilate them into Zairean culture.

The Bakongo tribe had historically held traditional freehold in an area fronting on the Atlantic Ocean and stretching into the modern political boundaries of the Republic of the Congo, Zaire and Angola. A portion of the Bakongo tribe lived in a 2800-square-mile section of Angola called Cabinda. This province is cut off geographically from Angola by the land arm of Bas-Zaire which reaches from several hundred miles inland out to the Atlantic coast. This portion of Zaire forms a physical and political barrier that isolates Cabinda from Angola. The Bakongo people, who speak a language called Kikongo, number about 3,000,000.

The Bakongos are deeply steeped in animism, and in

Cabinda early Protestant missionaries met stubborn resistance. The first Christian and Missionary Alliance missionaries to arrive in 1884 attempted to enter Bakongo villages, but the inhabitants withheld permission to preach and asked the missionaries to leave. Roman Catholics established mission stations in the port town. Two more Protestant mission stations followed after several years and later became the responsibility of the Christian and Missionary Alliance. In the early 1970s responsibility again shifted to the Canadian Baptist Mission.

Although significant inroads were made among Bakongo people in Zaire, Cabindans proved more resistant. Only a small percentage of Cabindans had become Christian before political turmoil caused them to leave their province, and those segments of the population that were neither animist nor Christian might be considered Christo-pagan.

The official language in Zaire is French, but in Angola it was Portuguese. The Bakongo people in Zaire are able to read and write in Kikongo, their tribal language. However, in Cabinda, Bakongo people have emphasized Portuguese and use their tribal language only infrequently. As a consequence, few Cabindans read or write Kikongo but carry on most commerce and social interaction in Portuguese. It is probable that not more than 25% of Cabindans can read their own tribal language. Those able to read elementary Portuguese could number as many as 35% of the group.

Angola, a Portuguese colony since about 1600, was plunged into civil war in 1975 on the eve of receiving its independence. Though Portugal attempted to maintain its colonial presence by declaring Angola to be its province, little attention was paid by Angolans intent on receiving their independence like their neighbors. In 1975 a fierce, bloody rebellion broke out with Portugal, instigated primarily by three clandestine political parties operating in scattered areas of Angola. Even within the national political parties several factions struggled for power among the top leadership.

In Cabinda, the Front for the Liberation of the Enclave of Cabinda (FLEC), itself quite splintered into factions, fought one of the major Angolan political parties, the Popular Movement for the Liberation of Angola (MPLA), for control. FLEC, after its defeat by the MPLA, dispersed into smaller units and shifted to guerrilla warfare. Those who suffered the most at the hands of FLEC and MPLA were the Bakongo peoples living in Cabinda. At the height of the Angolan Civil War perhaps a million refugees fled into Zaire. Among these, the Cabindans escaped into Bas-Zaire to find relief from the bloodshed.

The Bakongo are no strangers to suffering. As early as 1961 a major uprising of the Bakongo people against the Portuguese in Angola resulted in at least 50,000 deaths. Innocent onlookers were killed without reason. Large groups of villagers, herded into church buildings, died when the buildings were set afire. When independence was finally gained from Portugal, the settlement brought no peace. Factions of the MPLA and FLEC continued their warring, and Cabindans continued to slip into the relative safety of Bas-Zaire.

Violence pervaded even the camps within Bas-Zaire as FLEC insurgents hiding within the camps skirmished along the borders.

Cabindan Refugees

In fleeing their homeland, Cabindans became a different kind of people group from their former identity as an ethno-linguistic group living within Angolan political boundaries. Those who escaped underwent significant social, emotional and psychological changes. They entered a strange region and left villages where their ancestors had dwelt for centuries. The violence

79

and fear of their war-torn homeland created a sense of groupness as they departed.

In Zaire, further factors shaped the distinctives which make them a people group. Although they were among their own tribal people, Cabindan knowledge of the Kikongo tribal language was minimal. Since they spoke little French or Kikongo they formed a Portuguese-speaking enclave within their own ethnolinguistic group. A traditional dependence on animism provided further distinctives. Local Zairean chiefs, at least Christo-pagans and in some cases Christians, objected strongly to Cabindan spirit worship, and insisted that refugees put away their fetishes and cease sacrificing to demons. These refugees became a different kind of people group because of a geographical shift, language differences, tribal and ethnic distinctives, traditional religious practices (now disallowed or resisted by their tribal neighbors), and a tendency toward suspicion by Zairean Bakongo people because of dangerous guerrilla elements believed harbored among their transplanted population.

In 1979, approximately 35,000 Cabindan refugees lived in Bas-Zaire, and 25,000 of these required assistance. United Nations camps could care for 15,000, but those living close to the border did not receive U.N. assistance. The International Rescue Committee and Catholic Relief Service, however, did operate close to the border.

Perhaps more than any other factor, instability characterizes life among the Cabindans. Shelling, caused by Zairean army units attempting to remove FLEC presence from refugee groups, continued. In turn, this instability caused the Zairean government to invoke earlier legislation that prevented refugees from living within 200 kilometers of the border. In April 1981, with this legal tool in hand, the government moved Cabindans living near the border deeper inland into one of the three United Nations camps located in the Lukula and Nsioni areas.

The Christian Response

The most immediate needs in evidence as the refugees initially entered Zaire were illness, weariness, fright and hunger. A number of refugees had been wounded during their escape to Zaire. Children fell victim to malnutrition sickness which distended the stomach, puffed the eyes shut and lowered immunity. Most refugees spent days and sometimes weeks hiding in tropical forests without shelter and under the continual onslaught of mosquitos.

Hospitals and medical facilities began operation in the mid-seventies along the border. In 1977, the Christian and Missionary Alliance organized a refugee camp and assisted refugees living in nearby Zairean villages. TEAR Fund established a dispensary near one of the camps, and other international agencies also provided assistance.

Over 1600 national pastors and church-related staff work in Bas-Zaire. The Christian and Missionary Alliance numbers around 100,000 believers, and the church has a strong evangelistic thrust. In six of the major refugee camps this church base carried out tent campaigns with over 1000 making commitments. A local pastor organized Bible instruction classes three nights a week for new converts, and a new church was built near a camp. Some food and milk was supplied, especially for the children, although funds were limited. Zairean Bakongo people have assisted their relatives from Cabinda with what little they have, though continuing droughts seriously threaten these resources. Educational facilities for children operate on a small scale, and a lending library ministry is under way. The lending libraries contain hundreds of Christian books in Portuguese, and the libraries will continue to be under the supervision of catechists from within the camps.

As of April 1982, the UNHCR indicated that all refugees living in Bas-Zaire, with the exception of some 20,000, are no longer receiving assistance. Those 20,000 should no longer requiring aid by the end of 1982.

Assessing the Future

The presence of large numbers of committed Zairean Christians within Bas-Zaire has formed a substantial base for ministry to these refugees. With Christian and Missionary Alliance assistance, an integrated ministry of caring for the full range of need among Cabindan refugees was initiated. Christian and Missionary Alliance missionaries rightly perceived Cabindan refugees as a unique people group and appropriately identified this group as a specific "mission field."

This people group, with its unique distinctives, is even now changing, and an understanding of what remains to be done to reach them must change as well. The immediate needs of disease, hunger and fatigue have been replaced by the longer-term effects of frequent moves and the attendant social confusion. Cabindan refugees now find themselves deeper inside Zaire. Speaking no French and very little Kikongo, they remain isolated, although their ability to support themselves has improved. Cabindan children are being educated in Zairean schools. As a consequence, they will learn their own tribal language and French, and further barriers will be raised between generations. This also must be understood as ministry plans are being made.

Currently, Zairean Christians, with some expatriate missionaries, are continuing to use tent evangelism and sustain schools and libraries already functioning. Gospel tracts and booklets are distributed, and some students from the Bible Institute at Kinkonzi are preaching in the camps during their vacation periods.

A critical key to understanding the future of an integrated ministry within Cabindan refugee enclaves is the identification of leadership within the camps, and an understanding of the nature and patterns of social interaction which are uniquely formed by the distinctives of this people group. It is debatable whether a Cabindan church should be founded within the camps or whether Kikongo-speaking churches nearby can assimilate believers. Yet it is very important that Portuguese-speaking Christian groups should flourish within the camps. Without this, an entire generation of Cabindans can be overlooked. Cabindans may not necessarily listen to their Bakongo relatives now that their initial physical needs have been met. But they may listen to Cabindan Christian leaders who have lived through the refugee experience and speak Portuguese. Strategies for Zairean Christians to reach this people group must incorporate these understandings.

Once food and illness have been dealt with at their most dramatic levels of need, important avenues of communication may be gained through literacy ministries. This work can be specifically addressed to the older Portuguese-speaking refugees to avoid unsettling generation gaps between Cabindan children learning Kikongo and French in their schools and the older Cabindans. The problem of animism requires further attention. The Zairean Christians may not have had recent experience with unbelievers engaged in animism and spirit worship. This may be a point at which expatriate missionary experience could serve Zairean pastors and church workers in Cabindan work. Some expatriates will still be needed to assist in liaison between United Nations officials and Cabindan refugees in the camps.

At the present time a strategy should also emphasize the continuing development of self-sufficiency among refugees, the bridging of barriers between Cabindans and their non-Portuguese-speaking neighbors, the spread of small Cabindan worship groups, teaching gatherings within the camps, and the training of Cabindan leadership. Attempts to implement this strategy among Cabindan refugees should consistently incorporate changing social models and patterns. Cabindans are completing the traumatic transition from a people with a homeland, to a refugee people group broken by fear and illness and scattered in border camps, to a people group regaining self-esteem yet very much disoriented in the confusion of the inland camps. Ultimately a vision must grow of Cabindans as a people group integrating with surrounding neighborhoods, increasing in literacy, gaining agricultural and commercial tools, retaining their tribal and social distinctives yet reaching out to evangelize other Cabindans and even those Zairean unbelievers living nearby. Only in the love, compassion and redemptive power of the gospel of Christ the refugee can be transformed into a place of viable Christian witness.

Jane Raffloer is a Christian and Missionary Alliance missionary currently on furlough. She has served for the last six years as the C.&.M.A. Field Director of Bas-Zaire. Her ministry included organizing women's retreats and conferences, as well as her involvement in ministering to refugees. She is a graduate of Nyack College in New York.

Arni Shareski, Assistant Vice President, Overseas Ministries of the Christian and Missionary Alliance, served as a missionary in Bas-Zaire from 1957 to 1967 before being appointed to his present responsibility. He is a graduate of the Canadian Bible College, Regina, Saskatchewan.

Refugees in Transit

L.P. Verora

In the interim period between the refugee camp and resettlement in the third country, refugees spend considerable time in processing centers. Two such centers in the Philippines are described, together with the opportunities for local congregations and other Christian organizations to minister to the refugees under these particular conditions. Somewhat more structured than the camp situation, the processing centers tend to group family and ethnic groups together, facilitating the presentation and propagation of the gospel. At the time when the refugee is faced with the prospect of imminent change, he is more open to change in the area of ministry.

The endless hours of waiting and wondering do not automatically cease when refugees are moved from the initial holding camps. Thousands are sent to processing centers where they have to wait until their documents are prepared. This study describes such an intermediate situation of refugees from Indochina who are in two such centers in the Philippines. It demonstrates the many opportunities available to local churches and

Christian organizations to work in such situations and points out the strong possibility of utilizing evangelical Christians among refugees to carry out a witness to their fellows. It also indicates that within many different groups of refugees there will be more closely defined people groups.

Philippine Processing Camps

There are a number of Asian countries involved in processing Indochinese refugees for resettlement. The refugee centers in the Philippines are among the largest. We will discuss two of these.

The Philippine Refugee Processing Center (PRPC) materialized at the United Nations International Conference on Indochinese Refugees held in Geneva, Switzerland, in July 1979. At this conference, the Philippine foreign minister offered temporary accommodation to 50,000 Indochinese refugees from the various first asylum countries in Southeast Asia. On November 12, 1979, the Philippine government and the UNHCR signed an agreement for the construction and operation of a Refugee Processing Center. Under the agreement, the Philippines would construct and operate the Center with funding provided by the United Nations. The Center would accommodate only pre-processed, pre-selected Indochinese refugees who had already been accepted by other countries for final resettlement.

The Philippine Refugee Processing Center is committed to providing a temporary but humane settlement for the Indochinese refugees. It serves as an appropriate sanctuary for their shelter and rehabilitation while they await final entry into the countries of resettlement.

Shelter

As the refugees complete the processing of their immigration papers (this usually takes from three months to three years), they are provided with community housing at the Center. The approach is to develop community life among the refugees and to assist them in adjusting to their would-be new environment. Thus, the planning framework and considerations are multidisciplinary in approach, incorporating community development as well as other physical, social, economic, political, ecological, occupational, religious and cultural inputs.

Bunkhouses are the main dwelling facilities constructed for the refugees. Each bunkhouse consists of ten units. Each unit in the bunkhouse is occupied by six to nine persons constituting a family. If a family has only a few members, relatives and friends are billeted with them. Billeting assignment is based on family, ethnic and friendship groupings. Thus, they quickly form "people groups." (See **Definitions**.) Basic necessities are provided to each family: kerosene stoves, eating and cooking utensils, mosquito nets, mats, blankets and food.

Bunkhouses are basically wood or sawali-framed structures with concrete floor slabs and cement asbestos roofings. Each unit is provided with electric lighting outlets and a sleeping loft accessible by means of a wooden ladder. All bunkhouses face an interior court, arranged in such a way that social interaction is encouraged and reinforced. Schoolhouses are in interior courts which also serve as the extension of the living areas of the basic family units. Toilet, shower, laundry and water facilities are strategically located between the rings of bunkhouses for accessibility to the residents.

There are also neighborhood facilities which include classroom buildings, meeting/assembly rooms, distribution shops and playgrounds. Cluster facilities--open market, administrative center, central home, guard post--are also found in the center. The administrative center, the largest of the cluster of facilities, consists of a central post, processing center, administrative building, staff dormitories, single-detached units, dining room/kitchen for the staff, guest house, garage with kerosene can storage, workshop and equipment shed, general warehouse, cold storage warehouse, commissary, guard post and fire brigade station.

Rehabilitation

The primary task of PRPC operations is the rehabilitation of the refugees. This implies their transformation from displaced individuals into persons well prepared for productive and meaningful life in the countries of their final destination. There is an understanding that change is the result of a process. It is during such a change that people are most open to new ideas and new understandings.

The rehabilitation or transformation of the refugees is based on their needs to overcome certain traumas caused by their previous experiences. More importantly, it is geared to adequately equipping them with the necessary behavior, attitudes, skills and technologies in preparation for their immigration. Among the skills that the refugees must develop substantially are language and vocational/occupational skills. They are also prepared for the culture and society of their countries of final resettlement.

Transformation Process

Physical, social, political, cultural, intellectual, religious and economic needs are considered in the transformation of the refugees. It is the intention of the PRPC to enable them to regain confidence and a sense of self-worth, to encourage them to become productive and participative individuals and to prepare them for a new life in their resettlement countries.

The refugees at PRPC are classified into various groupings:
- Age groups - infants, preschoolers, children,

youths, adults and those aged 46 and above
- Skilled and unskilled workers
- Formal leaders and their followers
- Speakers and non-speakers of English
- Religious groupings

On these various groupings are based the appropriate training programs, social and religious services and political structures for their rehabilitation. Again, note the similarity of the way the PRPC deals with refugees to the concept of "people group."

The rehabilitation of the refugees goes through three interrelated psycho-social processes: adaptation, capability building, and disengagement. Adaptation is geared towards the preparation of the refugees to be well-adjusted and to cope with and adjust to their physical and social environment. Capability building is the transformation of the refugees into productive and highly motivated temporary residents at the Center. Disengagement is the final transformation of the refugees into prospective immigrants, equipped for integration into the culture and society of their countries of resettlement.

Each of the rehabilitation processes consists of an integrated package of formal training programs and opportunities for community development. This is done at the Center through the Community Action and Social Services Group (CASSDEG). Various national and foreign volunteer agencies also sponsor other programs and services which are coordinated and monitored by CASSDEG.

Formal training programs are designed to enable the refugee to (1) develop and reinforce appropriate language skills, (2) acquire or reinforce vocational and occupational skills, (3) increase knowledge on the culture of the countries of resettlement and (4) develop or reinforce sociocultural skills.

Community development opportunities at the PRPC

consist of participation in community organization and involvement in sociocultural and religious activities.

CASSDEG-Initiated Programs

There are two major types of programs at the Center: CASSDEG and agency programs.

CASSDEG-initiated programs aim to provide the refugees with opportunities, services and facilities to enable them to participate actively in the creation of their own community. Community participation is encouraged to allow them to reestablish social ties and relationships, resume social tasks and obligations, and regain social competence.

CASSDEG-initiated programs include the following:

1. **Formal Refugee Orientation Program.** This is part of the processing for new arrivals aged 16 and above. The program gives opportunity to refugees to get acquainted with the Center--its facilities, services, programs, rules and regulations, sanctions and operations. At this early stage, they are motivated to build interest and participate in the Center's activities.

2. **Information Program.** This is aimed at maintaining smooth communication flow between the PRPC administration and the refugees. Announcements are made through the public address system of meetings and assemblies, and individual and group discussions with the leaders of the refugees. By and large, the program serves to motivate and encourage the refugees to involve themselves in the activities of the Center.

3. **Community Organization (CO).** Generally, the CO program seeks to enable the refugees to revive their sense of community and to mobilize them to participate actively in the Center's activities. Through the program, formal and recognized leaders of the refugees are identified. They are trained to maximize their roles for the benefit of their fellow refugees.

Also, community-based structures are organized at three levels: building brigades, block committees, and neighborhood councils.

4. **Work Credit System.** A mechanism is also initiated to monitor closely and evaluate the participation of the refugees in community programs and activities. For example, for every hour of work or training that a refugee goes through, he gets a certain number of credit points. Credit points are recorded in the passbook which is regularly evaluated by the CASSDEG and the Joint Volunteer Agency (agency in charge of resettlement). Each refugee is informed that he is obliged to meet a certain quota of points. Failure to meet them would mean a delay in the refugee's resettlement to a host country.

5. **Refugee Volunteer Service Program.** Volunteer refugees are being tapped as interpreters, artists and translators to assist the PRPC groups and participating agencies in implementing the various programs. Volunteer refugees, now comprising a major working group, also facilitate smooth operations of the Center. They participate in food distribution, maintenance of facilities, and sanitation activities.

Agency-Sponsored Programs

The agency-sponsored programs are designed to assist the refugees in developing and reinforcing their skills and in preparing them for productive life in their countries of resettlement.

1. **English as a Second Language (ESL) Course.** The course is designed to enable the refugees to acquire adequate and appropriate English language skills. It includes lessons in vocabulary, sentence patterns, grammar, usage and exercises in reading and writing.

The ESL course is undertaken by the International Catholic Migration Commission (ICMS). It is offered for four months to refugees aged 16 and above. Classes in German are also offered for those who will emigrate to West Germany.

2. Cross-Cultural Orientation. This orientation aims to prepare the refugees for eventual resettlement in the United States. Awareness sessions are conducted on Western culture and life-style, and American community life, traditions, beliefs, customs and body politic. Initial interim efforts in terms of lectures and film showings have been exerted by the World Relief Corporation, the Philippine Baptist Refugee Ministries and the Salvation Army.

3. Youth Guidance. Youth guidance aims to familiarize refugee children of school age (7-15 years old) with a structured learning environment. The program also intends to facilitate their adjustment to life within the PRPC and in the United States, their country of final resettlement.

The kind of education offered to school-age children is is in accordance with the American public school system. The curricula consist of English, mathematics, reading, writing, geography, Bible study and sports. Around 25 to 30 pupils attend each class for four months. World Relief Corporation conducts the classes.

4. Child Care. Services for the preschool children aged four to six years are provided through the child-care program. The program consists of a two-hour daily session on pre-prep instruction, creative play, feeding, and counseling for three months. It also provides for the physical, social, emotional and intellectual development of the preschool children. Caritas Manila is initiating the program.

5. Vocational Skills Training. The refugees are also provided with training in marketable skills to enable them to find employment or engage in productive activities in their countries of resettlement. Skills training include batik, basic typing, hair grooming, beauty culture, embroidery and basket weaving.

Vocational skills training takes eleven weeks on the average, two to three hours a day, Monday to Friday. The trainees are selected from among the new arrivals. The program is sponsored by the World Relief Corporation and the Salvation Army.

6. **Occupational Skills Training.** Separate from vocational skills training is occupational skills training. This program is designed to prepare the refugees to be economically productive and self-supporting upon resettlement.

The Philippine Baptist Refugee Ministries has launched an occupational skill training program among the physically capable male adults 18 to 65 years old. Courses offered are carpentry, plumbing and electronics.

Basic and advanced training is conducted in each of the courses. A total of 60 sessions in 12 weeks are held. Sessions include lectures, audiovisual presentations, demonstrations, discussions, problem solving, practice and examinations.

7. **Talent Development.** The objective of this program is to provide meaningful training to harness the musical and other talents of the refugees for recreation and entertainment. The program also provides a way for the constructive use of their leisure time.

The Salvation Army undertakes training in guitar playing, banduria playing, singing and dancing. Training is done one hour every weekday for four months. The program is offered to both male and female refugees, 12 to 25 years old, who show musical and choreographic inclination.

8. **Community-Based Health.** Supplementing the health service of the PRPC is the community-based health program. Additional medical staff from the

World Relief Corporation are fielded at the Center to conduct prenatal care, post-partum home visits, anti-malarial prophylaxis, classes for health aides and informal health education.

9. **Sports Program.** The World Relief Corporation also provides sports equipment to the neighborhoods as the need arises. Two basketball courts that double as volleyball courts have been constructed.

Support to Religious Activities

Participating agencies also coordinate religious services for the three existing religious groupings at the PRPC: Catholics, Protestants and Buddhists. Masses for the Catholics are celebrated on Saturdays and Mondays at the Catholic Chapel. These are coordinated by Caritas Manila. Sunday services and classes for the three Protestant churches (Lao, Kampuchean and Vietnamese) at the Center are also conducted under the auspices of the Philippine Baptist Mission, World Relief Corporation and Far East Broadcasting Company. Buddhist religious rites are held at the Center's Buddhist Temple. A second temple is being constructed at this writing.

Support is also given by the PRPC administration to sustain the implementation of agency programs and to ensure the coordination of institutional efforts. This includes (1) dissemination of information on available programs, (2) identification and organization of refugee trainers, (3) mobilization of participants, (4) follow-up of arrangements for requisition and maintenance of physical requirements, and (5) monitoring and evaluation of committed inputs.

Refugee-Initiated Economic Activities

Other than the CASSDEG-initiated and agency-sponsored programs are refugee-initiated economic activities. The refugees undertake, on their own, some economic activities to supplement their provisions and to put their time to productive use. Economic activities include (1) backyard gardening, (2) cafe and restaurant management, (3) retail store management, (4) basket weaving and (5) handicraft production.

PRPC Client Population

There are 16,603 refugees at the PRPC as of February 1982. Of this number, 9472 are Vietnamese, 6427 are Kampucheans and 704 are Laotians.

As early as January 1980, there had been 67,511 refugees processed: 32,287 Vietnamese, 22,527 Kampucheans, 12,757 Laotians. In the same period, there had been 51,944 refugees processed out: 23,184 Vietnamese, 16,532 Kampucheans, 12,238 Laotians.

The refugee population at the Center is increasing steadily due to new arrivals and new births. As of March 1982, there were, on the average, 2000 new arrivals monthly since January 1980 and around 1080 babies born to refugee parents within the PRPC. It is expected that the rate of refugee arrival at the Center will exceed the rate of departure.

Vietnamese Rehabilitation Center

Unlike the PRPC, the Vietnamese Rehabilitation Center caters exclusively to the transformation process of Vietnamese refugees. It is run like a camp under the Western Command of the Armed Forces of the Philippines.

The Vietnamese Rehabilitation Center (VRC) is located three kilometers from the city proper of Puerto Princesa, province of Palawan. Puerto Princesa is a second class city, but its outskirts and coastal areas are predominantly rural. Farming and fishing--with an admixture of trade, commerce, light industry and navigation--are still the main forms of occupation among its population.

Basically, the Vietnamese Rehabilitation Center has also the task of providing shelter and rehabilitation.

However, its services and programs are not as exhaustive and comprehensive as those at the PRPC.

Administratively, the VRC operates under the umbrella of the UNHCR-Interagency Volunteer Group. It is a co-institutional body of the Philippine Refugee Processing Center.

Programs

The VRC presently caters to the needs of 6122 Vietnamese refugees. Programs include health, language training, cultural orientation, skills, training, self-help projects, material assistance, counseling, sports and recreation.

Health. Health programs at the VRC consist of preventive health and sanitation, and medical and gynecological treatment.

Preventive health and sanitation covers family planning, prenatal care, day-care, home nursery, first aid, nursing class and information dissemination. Agencies involved are the United Nations High Commission for Refugees (UNHCR), the Sovereign Military Order of Malta (SMOM), the Philippine National Red Cross (PNRC), and the Rotary International.

Medical and gynecological treatment includes provisions of medicine, vaccination/immunization (DPT, polio), milk feeding for infants and individuals with special needs, provision of medical instrument/equipment, and dental treatment. Other than the UNHCR, SMOM and PNRC, the Rotary International, the Intergovernment Committee on Europe Migration (ICEM), the Western Command (Wescom) and the Japanese Embassy are also involved in this kind of treatment.

Language Training Cultural Orientation. There is also the language training cultural orientation program aimed at preparing the Vietnamese refugees for future resettlement. The program covers nursery classes (4-6 years old), elementary education/English classes, adult language training, cultural orientation, use of library facilities and visual aids (film showing/slides presentation). Agencies and institutions involved are Holy Trinity College (HTC), UNHCR, the Philippine Cultural Communication Service Corporation (PCCS), the Center for Assistance to Displaced Persons (CADP), the Church of Jesus Christ of Latter-day Saints (Mormons), the Filipino-Chinese Service Center for Vietnamese Refugees (FCSCVR), Wescom, PNRC and the Japanese Embassy.

Skills Training. Ongoing skills training at the VRC includes embroidery, dressmaking, tailoring, wooden shoemaking, radio repair, typing, general services and maintenance, painting, knitting and food service training. Agencies and institutions involved are CADP, the School for Philippine Craftsmen (SPC), Wescom, the National Council of Churches in the Philippines (NCCP), National Manpower and Youth Council (NMYC), UNHCR, the British Voluntary Service Overseas (BVSO), the Baptist World Alliance (BWA), the Norwegian Embassy and the United Nations Voluntary Fund for the Decade of Women (UNVFDW).

Self-Help Projects. Self-help projects help supplement the income and reinforce the skills of the refugees. They include cooperative canteen, vegetable gardening, bakery, noodle-making and restaurant/coffee shop. Agencies involved in these endeavors are the Catholic Relief Services (CRS), UNHCR, CADP and UNVFDW.

Material Assistance. Supplies such as traveling bags, blankets/bedding, clothing and cooking utensils are provided for the refugees. The CADP, UNHCR and CRS are deeply involved in this program.

Counseling. Counseling and allied services are provided to special groups of refugees. They are infants and preschoolers, unaccompanied minors, single parent families, young women, handicapped/disabled, elderly, financially needy, medical holds and long-staying individuals. Agencies involved in this kind of service are PNRC, HTC, UNHCR and CADP.

Sports, Recreation and Cultural Activities. The VRC refugees are also provided with sports, recreational and cultural activities: scouting, physical exercises, nonformal education, sports, musical programs, film showing and cultural entertainment. The UNHCR, Wescom and PNRC are the agencies most involved in them.

Religious Groupings. The refugees at VRC are either ancestor worshipers, Buddhists, Cao Daists, evangelicals or Catholics. Of the 6122 refugee population, eight percent (490) are ancestor worshipers; 43 percent (2632) are Buddhists; four percent (245) are Cao Daists; six percent (367) are evangelicals; 36 percent (2204) are Catholics; and three percent (184) belong to other religions. In other words, these refugees already have a surprisingly high number of Christians in their midst.

Some Christian education activities at the VRC include Bible studies and other spiritual gatherings. These, however, are minimal.

Analysis

In analyzing these two major camps in the Philippines, a number of things stand out as important to reaching these people for Christ.

The program segments people into family and community-based groupings, which facilitates group acceptance of new ideas and concepts. In other words, the camps tend to divide people into natural people groups for which specific evangelistic strategies could be designed.

There are a large number of Christians among these

refugees who are carrying on worship services in the three different languages and, with the encouragement of outside agencies, have a great potential for evangelizing others within the camps.

The government is already drawing on a large number of Christian organizations, who are thus carrying out a widespread program of "friendship evangelism" which can produce a fertile soil for the more natural spread of the gospel by the Christians in the camps.

In many ways, this is an outstanding case study of how an integrated strategy, aimed at strengthening the church that is already geographically close to a people group, can be utilized to spread the gospel.

Because of the natural reluctance of any government to encourage one religion over another, Christian agencies working within government camps cannot be actively involved in proselytizing. However, by coordinating the strategies of those agencies expertise in one area with those able to strengthen and encourage local churches and provide Christian education materials, the possibility of seeing large numbers of people come to Christ, even during their temporary sojourn in such camps as these, is very real.

L. P. Verora received his schooling from two Philippine universities in agricultural and development economics, public administration and management. He was formerly a documentation writer/program fellow in Development Communications at the International Institute of Rural Reconstruction (IIRR). Then he joined the public service as deputy director and eventually officer-in-charge of the multimillion-dollar Slum Improvement and Resettlement Program (SIRP), a joint undertaking of the World Bank, National Housing Authority and local government in the Philippines. Presently, the author is a staff specialist of World Vision Philippines.

Finding Ministry Through Families

James A. Edgren

The actual case histories presented here show that man's expectations are not always God's results. What began as an apparent failure in attempting to resettle one refugee family grew into a successful ministry to a community of refugees. In the process, the congregation learned to give with open hands, to be flexible and to be patient. Congregations who have experienced this type of ministry will see much that is quite familiar; others may learn from these experiences both the cautions and the rewards of such a ministry.

The Lord also will be a refuge for the oppressed, a refuge in times of trouble. And they that know thy name will put their trust in thee: for thou, Lord, hast not forsaken them that seek thee (Psalm 9:9-10).

The following cases involve people who were resettled in metropolitan Washington, D.C. The cases are discussed from the perspective of one congregation with a number of sponsoring families. The material is based upon personal interviews with the refugee families or individuals involved. Each case involves a different voluntary agency, differing religious and ethnic backgrounds and varied family makeup. The method of sponsorship also varied.

I. THE CASE OF L AND N AND THEIR FAMILY

Initial Contact--The Voluntary Agency

As a result of personal contacts, some familiarity with the work of World Relief Refugee Service (WRRS) and a deep-seated commitment to missions, the local congregation began to explore the possibility of sponsoring a refugee family. Because of this denomination's long association with ministry in Southeast Asia, it seemed appropriate to think in terms of sponsoring some of the "Boat People." Further, the presence in the church of a Vietnamese student, an earlier refugee, eased the fears of some that communication would be impossible. Consequently, in June of 1979, application was made to World Relief Refugee Service for a refugee family. This application was built on several families in the church who pledged to support the effort. WRRS communicated with the church leadership regarding the prospective sponsorship, pointing out both the rewards and disappointments that might possibly be experienced. Although staffed by former missionaries to Vietnam, and in some cases by Vietnamese nationals, WRRS was new to the sponsorship and resettlement ministry and was "feeling its way" as it began to place families in early 1979. WRRS informed the church that it could expect a family "in about six weeks."

The Church's Response and Commitment

A committee of interested volunteers was formed to deal with the various aspects of sponsorship, and the project was presented to the congregation at large. The pastor and several of the elders explained to the membership the level of financial, material and personal commitment that would be required, and the congregation voted to sponsor the family, commit financial resources, and back the committee members in the endeavor. Some members asked why a Christian family could not be sponsored, feeling that the church's first responsibility should be to the "brethren." WRRS had explained that there were very few Christian families for sponsorship and that non-Christian families would present opportunities for witness as well as assistance. With some of the initial questions satisfactorily answered, the committee began to plan for the sponsorship.

Preparing for the Family's Arrival

Armed with only a mimeographed instruction pamphlet and common sense, the committee set to work. The family, it was learned, was in one of the island camps of Malaysia awaiting resettlement and consisted of a young father (23) and mother (21) and two small children, ages two years and six months. Their religion was listed as Buddhist. A family of four did not present insurmountable problems to the committee, and they were soon able to interest six families in opening their homes to the refugee family.

A "family sharing" plan was devised whereby the refugees would be rotated from home to home for as long as it would take to get them established. The committee estimated that this would take perhaps three months, so each sponsoring family would host the refugees for two weeks at a time. This plan was preferred over the alternative of having the family stay with only one host for the entire period.

A refugee fund was established, and the church prepared to advance funds to each sponsor home as their turn came to host the refugee family. Each sponsoring family's out-of-pocket expenses were reimbursed. At the same time, an all-out collection effort was launched to obtain clothing, household items and furniture for the family. By the time the church received its two-week notice from WRRS, the committee was well along in its planning and had worked out arrangements to provide transportation, shopping, outfitting and other services for the family.

Arrival, Reception, First Impression

L and N and their two children arrived at Dulles International Airport on a very hot day in August, carrying their entire earthly belongings in one small duffel bag; each adult carried a child. They were tired and disheveled, having spent two full days in transit, and a bit bewildered by it all. A member of the congregation, along with the Vietnamese student, met them. Their faces brightened when they heard themselves addressed in Vietnamese, and some of their evident anxiety subsided. After brief introductions and words of welcome, they were taken to the home of the first host family and moved into a guest room to begin their new life in America.

Since they were totally exhausted, they spent their first two days mostly catching up on sleep. Their English was quite limited. L could use perhaps 25 words in English; N was limited to "hello" and "thank you." Although they were able to use Vietnamese-English dictionaries and undoubtedly could read more English (as we learned later), speaking was particularly difficult for them, so the Vietnamese student translated a lot over the phone in the first several days.

From the standpoint of the host families, the first impressions and first reactions were to fall in love with the "little" family--they were small in stature. For L and N it was all quite bewildering and overwhelming, but they adjusted rapidly.

The Family Sharing Plan

The family sharing plan proved to be quite workable, with each family able to devote the time and effort required for a two-week period. Several of the husbands in the sponsoring families scheduled their vacations to devote more time to the resettlement process. Other church families, who did not feel they could take a family into their homes, were supportive in providing extra foodstuffs and, on occasion, inviting the family over for dinner.

Meanwhile, the committee, several of whom were also hosting the family in their homes, coordinated the effort, receiving donated clothing and other materials. They distributed resources, disbursed money from the refugee fund, and spent countless hours driving the refugees to the various medical, dental and social service appointments.

It was decided that during the period of residence with each family, a maximum effort should be made to teach English to L and N. This project, while a good idea, only worked out in two of the sponsoring homes, primarily due to lack of time and training of the sponsors.

The decision was made at the outset not to put the family on welfare, but rather to attempt to find a job for L as soon as his English was sufficient. This decision was communicated to L and N with the help of a translator, and they seemed to accept it and understand the relative merits of this plan.

In subsequent discussion, it was discovered that the families who had hosted the refugees in their homes were the most intensely interested in further refugee ministry, while those who had not felt able to take in a family were somewhat less interested. All agreed that the experience had provided far more rewards than expected, and that the anticipated inconvenience was not nearly as great as they had feared. It had been, for each of the sponsoring families, a deep spiritual experience, not easily duplicated. The overall evaluation of the family sharing plan was that it not only had worked well but was probably the only plan that would have.

Escape Stories and Camp Experiences--Listening

As communication with L and N became easier, they began to tell of their escape from Vietnam, describing in great detail how they and several hundred others had left their homes clandestinely, meeting at designated locations, slipping out to the boats on the river and finally making their way out to the sea. L, who was a qualified marine diesel mechanic, had worked on the boats before and so was able to pay for his passage and that of his family with his maintenance and piloting skill. After many hardships and setbacks, a typhoon and the loss of a boat to the Communists, the little party (76 on this particular boat) managed to outmaneuver and outrun the government patrol boats and break out into the open sea. Here the bane of all Southeast Asian refugee flight awaited them, the Thai pirates. Due to the skill of the pilot and helmsman, they were able to outmanuever the pirates and escape the horrors perpetrated on other refugees by these modern-day marauders of the South China Sea.

After several days at sea, loaded with its human cargo, the boat made it into Malaysian waters and was finally able to put ashore. Payments to Malaysian authorities were necessary before the group was allowed to land, and eventually they made their way to one of the many refugee camps on the Malaysian islands.

The stories of life in the camps, told in similar detail by most of the refugees, are replete with tales of extortion, corruption, stealing of food and valuables, and the usual problems of a bureaucracy. Although specific details vary, and some camps were better run than others, the overall conditions were poor. Small "lean-to" shacks, hastily constructed shelters, were often all that the refugees had over their heads. Many of the islands had no drinking water, and fresh water had to be brought in daily by ship. Attempts by the United Nations High Commission for Refugees (UNHCR) and other agencies to alleviate conditions were often frustrated by an unwillingness on the part of local authorities to make changes.

For L and N, recalling these experiences was a painful process. They had taken pictures while in the camp, so we were able to share their experiences with them. Little Son Hair was born in the camps and was named accordingly (Son means "island" in Vietnamese). They had left family members behind. (L's father had been shot by the Communists while piloting his barge down a jungle river.) L received word while still residing with one of the families that his brother and family had drowned while escaping, but there were no eyewitnesses. Occasionally, letters from the camps or from Vietnam would reach the refugees, and this would lead to more reflection and some mild depression. Throughout this period, the importance of just listening was made clear to sponsors. One of the real values of the family sharing plan was that it gave the refugee family repeated opportunities to talk about the experiences of the escape and the camps. This was a valuable learning opportunity for the sponsoring community and a therapeutic experience for the refugees.

Christian Witness--Church and Home

From the very beginning, L and N attended the church. Since they had listed their religion as Buddhist, no attempt was made to coerce them to attend. They were just asked if they would like to come, and they indicated that they would. They also participated in family devotions in the various homes where they lived. Since two of their hosts were Army officers who had been in Vietnam, a great deal of conversation focused on the homeland. This was a cathartic experience, though somewhat painful, since for almost all the refugees, love of country is strong, and patriotic love of country was often the motivating factor in leaving. They could not stand to see their country destroyed by the regime.

L and N showed a great openness to Christian teachings and to the gospel. They were given Vietnamese-English New Testaments which they used in family devotions. The plan followed in one home was to read the verses in that day's Bible passage alternately in English and Vietnamese, with refugee and host each attempting to read in the other's language. Much laughter was shared in such endeavors.

As the weeks passed, the involvement of church families in the lives of the refugees became greater, as did their emotional investment in the success of the project. They became "our family" to the church people and a degree of possessiveness was observed. There was also much prayer that L and N would respond to the gospel and accept Christ as Savior and Lord. They were given Vietnamese literature, and the story of salvation was explained to them, using the "Four Spiritual Laws" in Vietnamese. However, since L's English (though better than N's) was not sufficient to express abstract spiritual concepts, the host families yearned for the opportunity to bear witness to this family in a way that they could clearly understand. Things were beginning to happen that would make this dream a reality.

Teaching English--The Career Center

The refugee committee of the church realized that the key to success with resettlement was the mastery of English. It became apparent that what they had thought of as the optimum plan (English classes in the home) was just not workable. Most of the hosts did not have the time to teach English in the home, although in subsequent experience this turned out to be the superior plan. Consequently, both L and N enrolled in the English classes at the Career Center in Arlington,

Virginia. Since most of the students at the Career Center were Vietnamese, a support group was immediately formed and contacts were made. Both L and N were delighted with this arrangement, for they were able to go to school most of the day and enjoy the company of other Vietnamese.

There were, however, several problems with the Career Center. First, the logistics of picking the refugees up every morning and afternoon required a major coordination effort. Various members of the congregation volunteered to provided transportation. In most cases, because of the hours, it was the host housewives who did the driving. This burden was not shared equally, and some of those providing transportation became discouraged. The Career Center was also a considerable distance from the church and homes of most members, yet it offered the many benefits of a cultural support group. Contacts made at the Career Center were to prove of great significance in the future.

Second, the English being taught at the center was not of the highest quality, since many of the teachers were persons for whom English was already a second language. The experience was often more social than educational.

Third, a good number of the refugees at the Career Center were on welfare, and they began to tell L and N of the "good life" in which one studied all day and socialized at night, and the government paid the bill. Although by American standards welfare checks are not large, to Vietnamese refugees fresh from the camps, without "green cards" (permanent resident status) they represent about as much as can be earned anyway. The system, as currently administered, offers little incentive to go out and get a job, when welfare payments are reduced by two-thirds of any salary earned. Although he offered no overt resistance to the suggestion of the committee that he get a job, the seeds were already planted in L's mind concerning the benefits of going on welfare.

Finally, the attendance of L and N at the Career Center meant babysitting services had to be provided daily on a rotating basis for their children. Since there were few who could provide this service during the day, most of the burden fell on four or five housewives.

All these problems together led to the decision to enroll L and N in a Fairfax County English program, since it was clear that they would eventually locate in Fairfax County. This was done, but only L went to classes. N stayed home with the children. In this program, L learned English much faster. There were only three other Vietnamese in the class, and the teacher was a native-born American. As his English improved, L was able to describe his skills and, receiving encouragement, began to look forward to the possibility of working.

The most important benefit derived from the Career Center and English class experience was finding the Vietnamese support group. Through these contacts, not only were the social relationships enhanced, but the host families were also introduced to a much larger group of Vietnamese from varying backgrounds. This larger group was to become increasingly significant to the ministry.

The First Job and Communication Problems

Through the Virginia Employment Commission, and a willingness on the part of the Coca Cola Company to take a risk on a refugee, L got a job as a diesel mechanic working on forklift trucks at a local Alexandria bottling plant. The small forklift diesel engines were a far cry from the marine diesel engines he was used to, but L adjusted quickly. His starting salary was $4.50 per hour, and he was soon able to obtain considerable overtime work at $6.75 per hour. Since he had no car, various members of the host families drove him to and from work.

It should be noted that without the understanding and concern of the Virginia Employment Commission staff (particularly one older gentleman) and the openness of the Director of Personnel at Coca Cola, it would have been almost impossible to place L in an American work setting. Getting the job, which paid as well as it did, was considered by the congregation to be an answer to prayer. It was also the result of a great deal of hard work.

Even though he was making good money (for a refugee in his first year) and liked his job, L continually talked of wanting to go to school. He had learned that going to school qualified one to receive welfare payments. The committee members counseled L about the importance of continuing to work, but a communication problem was developing. As autumn gave way to winter, L began to think of the possibility of working part time and going to school at night. His dissatisfaction with the job began to be evident, and it was clear that there were problems ahead.

The First Apartment

Once the job was secured, the committee was able to move quickly to obtain a suitable apartment. Research revealed that the waiting list for government-subsidized housing was so long that such an arrangment was out of the question. Also, it was learned that L's earnings disqualified him for certain social services, even though he had no assets. The committee had explained to L and N they would live with various families for about three months and then be settled in an apartment of their own. Further, it was explained, the church would pay the rent for the apartment for the first three months and contribute to their support for the next three months. After that, unless there were unforeseen difficulties, they would be on their own.

In obtaining an apartment, the church quickly learned that holding a job was not enough. The apartment managers had learned from experience that refugee families tend to move away, leaving them "holding the bag." Even the assurances of the church were not sufficient to secure a lease. The apartment manager understood only one thing: a financially solvent co-signer. A member of the congregation was able to co-sign the lease, and L and N and children moved in.

The church had rallied to provide furnishings for the new apartment. Rugs for the floors, curtains, beds and mattresses, sofa and chairs, dining room and kitchen tables, cooking utensils, dishes, a television set, a radio, a tape recorder for Vietnamese tapes, and numerous other items were supplied. The women of the church gave a "housewarming shower," and an open house was scheduled. Everyone was quite happy and thankful to the Lord for the provision of all these needs. Since L's place of employment was only about two miles away, and he still had no car, one young man donated his bicycle for use to and from work.

One of the best features of the apartment was its location in a complex that housed many other Vietnamese. It was not long before acquaintances and friendships developed. Several of the persons contacted at the Career Center lived in this complex, and soon a cultural support group was functional. For L, this meant evenings at cards and some gambling and drinking. For N, this meant loneliness and sitting home with two small children. They were now "established." From an American standpoint, this should have been cause for rejoicing; from a Vietnamese perspective this was fraught with many problems.

Cutting the Apron Strings

Although the church refugee committee consisted of

members who had been in Vietnam and had worked closely with Vietnamese, they underestimated the importance in Vietnamese culture of a total family group living under one roof. They judged that privacy and an apartment of their own would have high value for the L family. For N, the apartment symbolized loneliness and separation from loved ones and friends. She became increasingly withdrawn. She made little progress in learning English, and rarely went out, even to shop. Since they moved into the apartment in November, it was not long before the discomforts of a typical Washington winter began to be felt. This was a new experience for the L family. They had come straight from the tropics to Washington in August, and had not experienced really cold weather. Now the cold began to take its toll; as it got colder, they began to shiver in spirit as well as physically. They longed for a warmer climate.

Since the committee had taken the position that a "sink or swim" approach would work best in learning English and adjusting to American ways, the family was encouraged to make their own decisions and handle their own finances. A car was donated, L obtained a license, and independence was achieved. With this independence came estrangement. Rarely were they in church, unless they were called for or invited for dinner. Without intending to do so, the church was "cutting the strings," and this little family was drifting away.

Although financial support was still being given to them, by February L began to talk of quitting his job. He wanted to go to school. For him this was a recurring theme. He was encouraged to keep at it and reminded of his obligations, particularly to the church and to his co-signer; he responded to this counsel and agreed to stay on the job until April. His six-month lease would expire in April, and he would be free to move away, preferably to California. But he seemed to be experiencing great difficulty in communicating this to the church people, fearing he would lose face and commit a serious breach of social etiquette. He felt very strongly that he should honor his commitment, yet felt equally strongly that he should move to California.

Moving Away--Trauma

Without warning, L announced that N and the children would be flying to California within a week. In seeking to determine whether N was leaving on her own accord or was being sent, the leaders of the church committee interviewed both L and N. Nothing of substance could be learned. N was going to live with a "friend," and it would be "better there" for her. The church members most intimately involved with the family were stunned. What had gone wrong? How could someone who had been given all these advantages, after starting with only the clothes on their backs, pick up and just leave it all? Where had the church failed? Were there marital problems? What could be done to rectify the situation? Nothing. It was all over--quickly and painlessly. N and the children were gone.

Within hours after N's departure, two young, single Vietnamese males moved in with L. L gave notice to his employer and quit his job. He sold his car to a friend to raise money for N's ticket and sold his bicycle to another friend and the furnishings in the apartment to the boys who would occupy it after he left. All the goods so lovingly bestowed by the church people were disposed of in this way. The committee leadership met with L and pointed out that it would be a serious breach of ethics for him to move out without completing the term on his lease. To his credit, he agreed to stay until the lease expired. He asked the co-signer to assist his apartment mates in like manner, but the co-signer refused. Five days before the lease expired, but with final arrangements with the apartment management completed, L departed for California, leaving behind a number of saddened and confused church people.

The Legacy--Contacts for a Multiplied Ministry

At first reading, the foregoing case history might appear to be a disastrous way to start out. After all, is not refugee ministry supposed to be a rewarding experience, full of successes and results? After all that has been said up to this point about the joys of this ministry, is this what the prospective sponsor can expect? In some cases, yes. But that is not the point. There is an exciting "Part Two" to this case history that helps to bring the whole matter into focus. Later, we will analyze the cases presented; first, the other half of this story. It has do with what may be called **multiplied ministry.**

At about the time the church was considering sponsoring a refugee family, a Vietnamese couple with two children and one on the way had visited the church. They were interested in studying the Bible with someone who could answer their questions. Although both had Catholic backgrounds, they were interested in Protestant approaches to Christian living and wanted to see their own faith grounded in biblical understanding of what it meant to be a Christian. A relationship developed between them and several of the host families who had L and N in their homes. They were early refugees, had been in the United States for almost five years and spoke English rather well. They proved to be a great help in translating and providing cultural understanding and support.

Shortly after the move from the Arlington Career Center to the English program in Fairfax County, contact was made with a Vietnamese man by the name of Mr. G. Mr. G was studying English in the mornings and working at Mount Vernon Hospital evenings. He lived with his nephew and cousin in a small apartment in Alexandria. He was one of the first contacts made through L and N, and his story is next in this chapter.

While at the Career Center, L also made contact with another family that had been on the same boat in the escape. The head of this family, which consisted of husband and wife, two brothers and a sister, was a licensed ship's captain and had piloted the escape vessel. One of the host families was introduced to this family, and soon a relationship developed which led to repeated contacts and ministry.

As a result of earlier contacts, a Vietnamese picnic was arranged in the autumn at the home of one of the host families. About 30 Vietnamese attended, including some new faces that L brought with him. This contact with another family of three daughters led to further friendship and ministry which continued after the family moved out of the state.

The list of contacts is long. Through the apartment complex, an extended family of seven was contacted and given assistance, which led eventually to sponsorship of another family direct from the camps. The story of this family is another case in this chapter.

Thanks to the concern of L for the needs of fellow refugees, a family of 15, which had just lost the patriarch of the family in a freak accident, was contacted. In the middle of January, they were without blankets, shoes for the children, clothing or furniture. In spite of having just outfitted the N's apartment, the church nevertheless responded and miraculously met the most pressing and immediate needs. Out of this ministry came an extended and enduring relationship which proved to be a great opportunity.

The point of all this is that as a result of sponsoring **one** family, the church was able to make enduring contact with over **one hundred** Vietnamese and ethnic Chinese refugees. Although there was keen disappointment over the departure of L and N, the legacy they left behind was a legacy of relationships that had been forged as a result of their being there in the life of the church at that particular time. As a result of introductions made by L, several families in the church were able to expand their personal ministry beyond what they had ever dreamed. They found the rewards far outweighed the disappointments. There was a degree of personal grief over the departure of L and N and the children, but God gave an increase to assuage the grief.

II. THE CASE OF MR. G

Initial Contact

G had been sponsored through the U.S. Catholic Conference (USCC), but his sponsor had not been of much help to him, because he had little enough in the way of resources; G had to make it pretty much on his own. A devout Catholic, G had sought fellowship and support through the local Vietnamese Catholic Church which he attended whenever he could get there. Without transportation, he was walking several miles to work and several more to school, getting little sleep in the process. At this point, having been in the United States for about six months, he was introduced to us by L. Quickly, a warm friendship developed, and G became part of the expanding "family" of Vietnamese refugees in touch with the church.

Church and Family Assistance--Forging a Relationship

One of the church members spent two Saturdays searching for a car with G, finally finding one that was mechanically sound. Others invited him to dinners and picnics, and he became especially close to one family. As time went on, this family developed a deep and abiding relationship with G. He was a man of sensitivity and genuine concern. His own life had been overwhelmed in tragedy, but he was still a man for others. There were many lengthy talks on spiritual

117

matters, and G became a regular caller at this home. It was clear that G, a practicing Catholic, had a deep love for Jesus Christ and a submissive spirit regarding the hand of God in his life. He was encouraged in his Christian experience and often joined the family in prayers. Although never pressed to do so, he attended the church on occasion, but for the most part continued to be active in the Catholic Church. In the course of this developing relationship, he shared the story of his great loss with the family.

"Escape and Tragedy"

"Many Drown, Malaysia Lifts Ban. Malaysia decided on December 4, 1978, to lift its ban, admitting Vietnamese refugees stranded in boats off the Malaysia coast. At least 400 such refugees from four boats were permitted to land that day.

"The government reversed its policy after more than 300 Vietmanese drowned in several ships that capsized off the Malaysian and Thai coasts. In the worst incident, about 200 escapees from Vietnam died on November 22 when their fishing boat tipped over after it was towed away from the Malaysian shore by police at Kuala Trengganu, the capital of Trengganu state, where most refugees landed.

"The accident, which occurred about 150 yards offshore, was witnessed by a large crowd of villagers, many of whom were said to have expressed their hostility by throwing stones at the ship."

The foregoing account, taken from a yearly compilation of news stories on Indochinese refugees, was a horrible tragedy. A senseless and avoidable disaster, decried by the international press, but only another story of great suffering, to be dismissed with a sigh by most Americans. But for one sponsoring family, it was brought sharply into focus, for this was G's story.

When the boat capsized, G was separated from his wife and three of his children, who were in the lower part of the vessel. In the confusion, he was not able to find them, but was able to get hold of his youngest daughter and, against great odds, gain the safety of the shore. In the sinking of the ship, his wife and three children were drowned. The young daughter that he had rescued died shortly thereafter. He was suddenly a widower, bereft of his entire family, on a hostile shore, a homeless refugee. In recounting his story, G said that while he had understood the risks of escape, he had expected that perhaps the entire family would be wiped out and reunited in heaven. It had never occurred to him that he alone might survive. Heavy with his tragic loss, he assumed the responsibility of his nephew and cousin, and made his way via Boston to Washington, D.C., settling without the benefit of a sponsor in Alexandria. Having lost his own family, he was primarily concerned to help others, to adopt, as it were, another family through a ministry to them. This was to lead to one of the more exciting aspects of the **multiplied ministry** spoken of earlier.

Here was a man who understood suffering, who had sustained great loss but was not crushed by his loss. Rather, he emerged stronger, and those who were privileged to enjoy his friendship were inspired by his courage. God was making use of a refugee heart to reach other refugees, and the unfolding of that story is beautiful.

The Proposition--Challenge and Legacy

One Sunday, after L and N were established in their own apartment and most of their needs had been met, one of the host families was discussing what their next move ought to be in refugee sponsorship ministry. They had prayed about it and were trying to decide. Arriving home, they found G's car in their driveway and G sitting on their doorstep. Inviting him in, they discovered that he had been waiting there for several hours after returning from Mass.

It was not long before the purpose of this visit was revealed. He had received a letter from the wife of his former business partner in Vietnam. The wife had eight children and had escaped from Vietnam aboard the ship **Tung An.** After six months at sea, being denied entry at port after port, this vessel--loaded with some 2000 ethnic Chinese Vietnamese--had finally been allowed to land in the Philippine Islands. The family was in a refugee camp on the Bataan peninsula. Could G help them get to America? Overwhelmed by this request, G pointed out that he could not sponsor them since he was not a resident, being a recently arrived refugee himself. He had thought of going through USCC, the voluntary agency that had resettled him, but this family was not Catholic, and anyway, there was another reason: he wanted this family, who were nominal Buddhists (ancestor worshipers, really) to have a Christian sponsor. Then came the bombshell: Would this host family sponsor the refugee family of nine persons--a mother, six daughters and two sons? If not, he would understand and try to get a sponsor through USCC, despite the odds against it.

The host family was overwhelmed--not so much by the size of the refugee family but by the timing of G's visit. God was answering their prayers. They had been seeking guidance, and here came a proposition and an opportunity. They explained to G how timely his visit was. It was immediately clear to them that they should take this family. There was no hesitation. Space problems could be worked out. The children were consulted and agreed this was what they should do. They told G to write to the lady and tell her that effective that date, she had a sponsor.

Upon reflection, it became evident that God was

teaching this family something far greater than the nicety of charitable acts. He was demonstrating within their experience that an expanding **multiplied ministry** was possible for anyone; all that was required was a willing spirit. God had used the concern of a refugee, Mr. G, to challenge this family to expand its outreach. The family made no appeal to the church for support, although several church members pledged financial and material assistance when they heard about the project. Rather, the decision was made to sponsor directly, trusting that God would supply the needs. WRRS was contacted and asked to seek out this family and request assignment to WRRS, since a sponsor had come forward. Letters and telegrams were dispatched to the UNHCR for the Philippines, the United States Joint Voluntary Agencies (USJVA) and other agencies, requesting that the process be expedited. Packages of medicine and sundries, money orders for incidentals, and booklets full of English lessons were sent.

The home was made ready to receive the family. It was determined that the family could be adequately cared for by a little rearranging of the modest four-bedroom home into a multi-bed dormitory, sleeping a total of 14 persons. Clothing for each child was gathered from friends and unknown donors alike. The local thrift shop supplied other needed items at very small cost. Used furniture, additional mattresses and cots were made ready, and then the host family sat down to wait.

In the meantime, the letters went back and forth. From the refugees came continual requests to expedite the process. From the social welfare agencies, the USJVA and the UNHCR, came continual assurances that all was being done. From the voluntary agencies, the USCC and the WRRS, came the news that the family had been assigned to USCC before this sponsor had been identified, and a transfer would have to be made to WRRS, or no family.

At last came a telegram from the Philippines. It read simply, "Resettle July 24. Healthy. Waiting." All was in readiness. It was only a matter of time. Then the bottom dropped out.

Not only was the family not cleared to depart (several members did not pass the health test), but a cousin in California had come forward to sponsor the family. Because he was a relative, he had priority over the host family. No, he would not release the family, nor would USCC release them to WRRS. Telephone calls went back and forth, letters between the Philippines, California and northern Virginia. The refugee family wanted to come to Alexandria, not to California. No matter, said the bureaucracy, to California they would go. Immigration law is immigration law.

Needless to say, the host family was keenly disappointed. It had all seemed so clear. God had obviously spoken. The timing was no coincidence. All the emotional and material investment. Why? But God was at work in the midst of this discouragement as well. He was still teaching this family; now they were learning how to deal with dashed hopes. They were experiencing what refugees go through all the time. They were acquiring the rudiments of a refugee heart. Out of the ashes of their hopes sprang a new opportunity, directly related to the third case.

The contact with Mr. G had created a rich relationship and had also left a legacy: this time, a spirit of availability. Through G, this family had learned a valuable lesson, that God wanted them to be flexible, to be completely available. Perhaps a family of nine might have been too much; who knows? Perhaps it was only a testing to see if the family was ready to respond. In any event, instead of the nine, God did, in fact, send six to that family, but that is a part of the third story. The key to all this is that God did it His way.

Finding Ministry Through Families

III. THE CASE OF THE B FAMILY CLAN

Initial Contact--Concerned Families

Mr. and Mrs. B, along with their three girls and the three younger brothers of Mr. B, had been sponsored by Hebrew Immigrant Aid Society, Inc. (HIAS). They had arrived penniless in Washington, D.C., and had to borrow a quarter to make a phone call to a sponsor who was not there to meet them. Having been sponsored by a Vietnamese who provided little in the way of assistance, the B family was soon on its own in a small apartment in Falls Church. It was here, in early November, that they first made contact with L and N, and a friendship between the two families developed. One of the host families had planned a Vietnamese Thanksgiving dinner, and L and N, Mr. G and another family were invited. K and B, B's brothers and the children came with L and N. The dinner was the first indication of the close friendship that would grow between the B family and this host family. The B family had very little in the way of material goods. When their needs were made known to the congregation, one family committed their year-end bonus to outfit the family with winter clothing and took them shopping for groceries and staples as well. Other families began to provide some assistance as the needs of the L family were met. The B family came to church a number of times; Mrs. B, whose English was quite good, was able to understand the rudiments of the gospel message. The concern and compassion of just a few families in the church were the catalyst in forging a relationship that not only endured but produced new opportunities for ministry.

The B Family Story

Mrs. B's father had owned a successful business in Vietnam, and she and her brother had attended French language schools. In fact, French rather than Vietnamese was spoken in the home, and this helped Mrs. B to learn English quickly. When the Communists took over South Vietnam in 1975, the B family knew it was only a matter of time before Mrs. B's father would lose his business. Mr. B's family were also people of some means, owning an export-import business and a farm. The regime appropriated their property, and they had to move to the city. Once the decision had been made to attempt an escape, the family gathered money, jewelry, gold and other valuables from elders who could not or would not make the journey and used them to pay the bribes that were necessary to successfully escape from the country. The B family, Mr. B's three younger brothers and Mrs. B's parents were all able to escape, although on separate boats.

During the voyage, the B family's boat was stopped on the open sea and boarded by Thai pirates. All money, gold and valuables were stolen from them. One woman who refused to give up her hidden valuables was stripped naked and her clothes thrown into the sea. Mrs. B had sewn some money into her clothing, but when she saw what was done to this other woman, she gave up her money. A treasured gold wedding necklace was also taken from her. This treatment was typical of what many refugees suffered at the hands of Thai pirates. The refugees were rarely armed and therefore were helpless before the pirates, who often raped the women and were known to throw overboard those who resisted them. The B family was thankful to survive the ordeal even though they now were left with nothing. Mrs. B later told an American friend that she prayed that God would help them during this terrible time.

The B family spent about ten months in the camps in Malaysia. Mrs. B had a toddler and one baby in arms when she arrived and was pregnant with a third. Her third child was born during their stay. The family was in such straits that they had to clothe the new baby in newspaper until a kindly Chinese family provided some clothes. The mother told of not having sufficient milk for the children in the camps, and the entire family suffered from malnutrition. Mrs. B weighed about eighty pounds when she finally left Malaysia for America.

Relationship and Witness

Forging a relationship is a prerequisite to authentic ministry with another person, and this is no less true for refugees. As a result of the contact initiated through L and N, several of the church families became quite close to the B family. Many Sunday afternoons were spent by the adults in fellowship around the dinner table, while the children played together. English lessons were initiated in one of the homes after completion of a literacy course, and the format proved to be quite workable. Soon cousins and friends were attending these impromptu English classes.

During these visits, Mrs. B confided to one of her American friends her personal fears and discouragements, and this lady had many opportunities to share the love of Christ and the message of the gospel with her. Mrs. B was very open to the gospel and expressed interest in how it was applicable in living life under her circumstances. These women developed a close relationship, and God used it to minister encouragement and inspiration to both of them.

Sponsoring the H Family

About a year after the church had sponsored L and N, the American family that had been working with Mr. G to sponsor the refugee family of nine received word that this family would definitely not be coming to them. What should they do? They were physically, psychologically, emotionally and spiritually prepared to take this family into their home. Surely God must have some other plan. And indeed He did.

The B family had received word that Mr. B's sister, her husband and four children not only had escaped from Vietnam but after only six months in camp were on their way to the United States. The B family, with nine people already in a tiny two-bedroom apartment (they had picked up two cousins along the way), felt it their duty to sponsor their relatives and take in this family of six. Since Mr. B had been unable to obtain a job (he was going to school six hours a day), and Mrs. B had to care for and feed nine people on a welfare check, the thought of taking on six more mouths to feed was overwhelming. But the B family was prepared to do just that.

At this point, the host family, having seen their previous hopes dashed, offered to sponsor the new family. There was much rejoicing as this larger family unit was reunited after two years of separation. Mr. B's younger brother's wife had arrived earlier from Thailand, and so a part of the B family clan was together once again. Only the parents and several younger children remained in Vietnam.

For about three weeks, things went smoothly. Four hours of English lessons for the whole family were the order of each day. They children caught on quickly, and the parents made good progress as well. The family joined the host family for evening devotions and learned to read from the Bible. Although the H family was secularist (not even "nominal" Buddhist), they seemed to be quite open to the gospel and attended the church with the host family. A real closeness developed.

Then, as a result of some broken articles, a lack of discipline and cultural misunderstandings on both sides, the relationship was suddenly shattered in an emotional outburst. Tears flowed. Communication difficulties necessitated calling Mrs. B to translate in an attempt to iron out the problems. There was much hurt on both sides, as Mrs. H withdrew completely. The tensions that had developed over the inability to communicate feelings now came to the surface. The children of the host family became hostile as they saw their belongings abused and destroyed. The refugee family, it seemed, had arrived with nothing and understood neither the value of some things nor what the American culture demanded in the way of behavior. The inability to communicate left them bewildered and hostile. Not having had to struggle without any sponsor's help as did their relatives, the B family, they understood little of what was involved with sponsorship. The B family was humiliated because they realized what was involved and what it was costing the host (from an American perspective) to sponsor the H family.

Without a steady job, with virtually no English, and totally unprepared, the H family managed to find a well-to-do Vietnamese friend who found them a beautiful four-bedroom house in suburban Annandale, Virginia, co-signed a lease and guaranteed some work at an oriental market. Less than four weeks after their arrival, they moved into their new home.

Fortunately, much of the immediate hostility had been resolved, and so the host family provided them with beds, mattresses, tables and chairs, and helped them move, using private cars. The children were enrolled in the schools, and they began life on their own just one month after their arrival.

IV. OTHER OPPORTUNITIES FOR MINISTRY

The three case histories presented above illustrate some of the opportunities for ministry that arise when churches or individuals are flexible--available to the leading of God's Holy Spirit. The contacts with other Vietnamese and ethnic Chinese refugees continued to multiply as members of this congregation became more intimately involved with the various families. However, making a contact is not of much value unless it is followed up. This is where the opportunity for further ministry comes. To follow up these contacts and begin the work of forging lasting relationships, a spirit of hospitality and a sharing of time and material resources are essential. A number of events during this one-year period served these purposes and were the means of reaching many Vietnamese refugees with the gospel message while ministering to their physical needs as well. They are included here because they are intertwined with the three case histories we have discussed.

Significant Special Gatherings

Because of the importance of the extended family in Vietnamese culture, gatherings of family and clan members are events of major significance. American sponsors and host families have found that such gatherings provide a means for getting to know refugee families and establishing lasting relationships with them. In the case of this congregation, there were a number of such opportunities.

The Vietnamese-American picnic. Early in the fall, while the N family was still rotating among the various church families, one family held a picnic in their backyard to which they invited about 20 Americans and about 20 Vietnamese. However, the Vietnamese brought another ten or so. The Americans present tried their best to communicate with the Vietnamese, and those Vietnamese who could speak some English did yeoman service in translating. As a result of this gathering which served both Vietnamese and American dishes, new friendships were formed, and one family was assisted with moving and received much clothing and household goods. A young American couple volunteered to take the family to the museums the next day. Thanks to the help of several church ladies, the picnic was a success.

A Vietnamese-American Thanksgiving. Since the picnic had worked so well, one family was encouraged to share Thanksgiving dinner with the Vietnamese refugees. This event included 26 refugees from five families and provided an opportunity for the first time to communicate the spirit of Thanksgiving to God to the refugees in Vietnamese. The meal consisted of traditional American fare, with turkey and trimmings, as well as Vietnamese dishes. It was at this gathering that first contact with the B family was made.

A Vietnamese-American Christmas. In all of this, while the friendships that had been established were strengthened, members of the church were concerned that, except for literature in Vietnamese and Vietnamese-English Bibles that were given out, they had been unable to present with clarity the message of God's love in sending Jesus Christ to earth. The Christmas story would provide such an opportunity.

As a group of about 30 Vietnamese refugees and host family members gathered around the Christmas tree, the Christmas story was read, verse by verse, in Vietnamese and then in English. Then the children gathered on the floor, and the nativity set was used to act out the story as it was translated into Vietnamese by Mrs. B. Stockings were opened, gifts were distributed, and it was feast time again. On this occasion, the delicious Vietnamese egg rolls were part of the fare--a great experience for Americans and Vietnamese alike.

The Vietnamese supper. Somewhat later, the Reverend Tom Stebbins, a former Christian and Missionary Alliance missionary who was born in Vietnam and spoke the language fluently, was planning a speaking tour through the mid-Atlantic states. He was contacted and agreed to speak to a gathering of Vietnamese in April of 1980. The host family invited every Vietnamese refugee they knew to come to a special Vietnamese night at their home. Some of the Vietnamese ladies prepared egg and spring rolls and other Vietnamese delicacies. At last, the time had arrived when the Vietnamese would hear the message of the gospel clearly, in their own language, something the host families had been praying about for some time. This would be the "frosting on the cake."

When Tom and Donna Stebbins arrived (Donna was wearing the traditional Ao Dai, the Vietnamese national costume) and greeted the Vietnamese in unaccented dialect, they were warmly welcomed. Several new faces were on hand, invited by Mr. L and by the B family. As Tom Stebbins began to speak, he went around the room asking each of those present to tell his or her story. Midway through, he asked if they would sing the old Vietnamese national anthem. All promptly rose to their feet. Hearing that anthem sung was a moving experience for the Americans; it was no less moving for the Vietnamese. There were few dry eyes.

The stories were poignant. One young man had been imprisoned by the Communists for three months and 18 days in a cage so small that he could not stand erect or stretch out. He was 17 years old at the time of his escape. In another remarkable case, Tom Stebbins discovered that one young man present had become a Christian and had attended a Tin Lanh (Protestant) church in the very building, in fact, in the very room, that had once been Tom's office. Other amazing coincidences were recounted. The refugees knew of the Tin Lanh churches in Vietnam and were able to update Tom and Donna Stebbins on what had happened after the fall of Saigon.

Then came the opportunity for Tom to carefully explain in Vietnamese the basics of the Christian faith. All listened attentively. Afterward there were questions on various points. Mrs. B told one of the church ladies that now she felt she understood what Christianity was all about. It was an exciting and profitable evening.

These gatherings are mentioned because they often served as a catalyst in opening new avenues of service and witness. One young man who was present that night, Mr. T, came to stay with the host family for several days and was instrumental in opening contact with the Vietnamese Gospel Fellowship Church. The local congregation had known about this church but had not made any contact with the lay pastor. There was a reluctance to take any of the refugees there until it could be ascertained that the church would be a positive influence in their lives. Mr. T's involvement with that fellowship helped to bridge the gap, and one Sunday morning one of the church families attended the services, and still another avenue of ministry opened.

The Vietnamese Gospel Fellowship Church

Due to some early misunderstandings, the refugee committee of the sponsoring congregation did not avail themselves of the cultural support of the Vietnamese Gospel Fellowship Church. For one thing, the church was organized differently than the Vietnamese Tin Lanh churches with which the committee members were familiar. (The Vietnamese leadership felt they could have a wider impact if they did not identify with the Tin Lanh name, but the committee did not know this.) Since the fellowship was not affiliated with other Tin Lanh churches, the refugee committee did not know where the Vietnamese Gospel Fellowship stood doctrinally. Further, a mistranslation of some literature had led the committee to believe that the Fellowship was an eclectic group including Buddhists, Bahais, Cao Dais and other religionists. As a result, a valuable resource went untapped in the early stages of sponsorship. Not until after settlement of the H family was linkage established between the sponsoring congregation and the Vietnamese Gospel Fellowship.

The lay pastor of this fellowship and his wife, Mr. and Mrs. L, were instrumental in presenting the message of the gospel to the Vietnamese families brought to the church by American host families. The local

131

congregation invited the Vietnamese Gospel Church choir and Pastor L to present a service and were encouraged by their ministry. As a result of this new relationship, host families could now be assured that refugees being sponsored by them would hear the Word of God in their own language. The presence of the Vietnamese Gospel Fellowship in Arlington proved to be a great help for subsequent sponsorship.

Analyzing the Cases

In analyzing the three case histories which have been considered, an in-depth sociological study of the implications of each is not proposed. This sort of analysis had been done already by a number of secular writers. Dr. Gail Kelly analyzed several cases from the sociological perspective in her excellent study on settlement and adjustment of the First Wave refugees, **From Vietnam to America,** published in 1977. Dr. Tran Minh Tung studied adjustment from a mental health perspective, publishing his findings in 1980. Other analyses by Motero (1979), Kung (1969) Lui and Murata (1978) and Ruebbensaal (1978) highlight various adjustment problems from a sociological perspective and are worth perusing.

Rather, this analysis considers the common denominators and the spiritual impact of each experience. One seeks ways to minister more effectively and therefore must take seriously commonly observed patterns which affect that ministry. What are the lessons to be learned from these case histories? What should have been done differently? What can the sponsoring church learn about itself from these cases? What is their impact upon the life of the individual Christian? These are questions for which one should seek answers.

Experiences in Common

In each case, the refugee family went through a great deal of personal suffering and tragedy in the escape, during the voyage and in the camps. Although some had it easier than others, they all faced the prospect of abandoning all their earthly possessions. They either left without them, or had them forcibly taken from them by the pirates in the course of the voyage. They all shared in common this loss of material goods. Further, each of them experienced the loss of loved ones, either through death during the voyage (as in the case of Mr. G), or through uncorroborated reports after arrival (L's situation) or through leaving parents, children, or brothers and sisters behind, under a Communist regime, with only limited hope of ever seeing them again. Of the approximately 50 refugees interviewed, not one escaped without experiencing some loss of this type.

Another common experience was physical deprivation. Even those who had the most uneventful sea voyages went without food, or without water, sometimes for several days; in most cases they were cramped and crowded together in a fashion reminiscent of the colonial slavers. For others, the camps presented a problem, with inadequate water and sanitation and improper nutrition.

The refugees shared a common interest in going to school. The earlier the arrival, the more emphasis on going to school. Later arrivals, such as the H family, apparently had gotten the word that it was better to get a job, and so Mr. H obtained employment within a month of his arrival. (The job was, however, with a Vietnamese friend, not with an American firm.)

A Spirit of Openness

An openness to American cultural values. Although much has been written about the refugee's inability to adjust to American ways, the experience with the families studied was quite different. These families and individuals were all quite open to American ways and wanted to learn them as quickly as possible. Of all the author's Vietnamese contacts, only a small percentage evidenced serious depression or unhappiness with being in America. For most, this was a good place to live and raise their children. The difficulty in obtaining a job or jobs rarely was translated into any hostility.

The openness also extended to ways of doing things. All the refugees in this group were eager to learn. The Sunday afternoon English lessons were faithfully attended, even by those who had been in the United States for several years. The stubborn refusal to do things the way Americans do them, so often observed among some refugees and immigrants, was not often seen among these Boat People.

An openness to Christianity. The three cases chosen reflect three differing religious backgrounds. L and N were Buddhist, Mr. G was Roman Catholic, and the B family could best be characterized as secularist. Yet regardless of background, all were quite open to participate in family prayers, attend worship services and read the Bible with their hosts. As a result of some host families' practice of holding hands while saying grace before meals, subsequent visits in the homes of resettled refugee families also included this ritual before a meal.

Of course, the foregoing can be seen, not as openness to Christianity, but rather as a typical oriental trait of adjustment to folk ways so as not to offend one's host. But in these cases, the openness was genuine, accompanied by genuine questions and honest concerns. They wanted to know what it was all about. They could see that these sponsoring families gave of themselves, and many of the refugees wanted to know what made the difference in their lives.

An openness to new life-style. In each case, the families had been people of some means in Vietnam. These refugees were not illiterate peasants. They had to have either money, material resources or marketable skills in order to escape. Of the refugees interviewed through the various social contacts by the author, none were peasants. Most were either military personnel, businessmen, marketers, government workers, exporters, or small entrepreneurs. Most either owned property or had the means to do so. They were all well educated, including the women, and several were musically inclined.

With only one or two exceptions, most would start out in comparatively menial jobs, far below what they would have been doing in Vietnam. Yet there was virtually no complaining. They accepted starting again at the bottom of the ladder and the need to adapt themselves to their new life-style. In fact, many of them exemplify the "Horatio Alger" spirit prevalent in our national thinking a century ago. This is not to say that many are not discouraged. Much has been written in the secular press concerning the discouragement and depression of the Boat People. I am merely pointing out that in our experience we have not observed this to any great extent.

Lessons Learned

Perhaps the greatest learning has been on the part of the sponsoring congregation. But the problem is that we may have learned the wrong lessons; or if we learned the right lessons, we have drawn the wrong conclusions from them. But even this can be valuable. Out of all the lessons learned, we need mention only two, for these two are basic to the whole spiritual issue of ministry to refugees and encompass in one way or another most of the others.

Attitudes toward giving. When L and N left for California, having sold or bartered the various articles and furnishings that the church people had donated, there was not only a feeling of disappointment and discouragement, but there was also some repressed anger and hostility and a feeling that they had been used, that their gifts had been trampled underfoot. This is an understandable and quite normal reaction, but it is not biblical. Something was wrong with our reaction.

I suspect that the problem lay with our attitude toward giving. Very rarely are people (even Christians) able to give freely, that is, without some strings attached. Almost all giving has an object, and a concern for proper utilization of the gift toward that object. This is as it should be: good stewardship demands wise and careful giving. But, in the name of stewardship, many of us extract certain personal rewards in the act of giving which rob us of the true reward. Jesus said of the Pharisees, "Verily, they have their reward." Many Christians are like the Pharisees, extracting their reward through a vicarious enjoyment of the gift in its **proper** utilization, that is to say, in the manner **they** deem worthy of the gift. By taking this position, they have imposed a condition upon receiving the gift. "I will give you this rug **if** you will use it properly," or "This chair is yours, and for your use as long as it stays in this apartment." This kind of giving, while better than no giving at all, nevertheless falls short of the way God gives. He gives without strings.

It may well be that God was teaching this congregation through the experience of their own disappointment in what happened to the things they gave, that when something is given "as unto the Lord" it is given unconditionally, without strings. If the Lord chooses to "squander" the gift upon an unworthy recipient, that is His business. Here the story of the healing of the ten lepers comes to mind. Jesus healed them all, even though only one was thankful. From the world's standpoint, the gift was squandered on the other nine. But Christians cannot succumb to this type of reasoning. Christian giving must be "as unto the Lord," and not "as unto men."

136

The lesson to be learned in this case is that refugee ministry provides opportunity to give "as unto the Lord" to needy people, many of whom do not have the ability to avoid squandering the gift. Individual Christians who have learned this lesson have taken a giant step forward in being prepared to truly minister. When they can apply this concept to all their material goods, there is no limitation on what God can do through them. And that leads to the second major lesson learned.

Availability and patience. The willingness to give "as unto the Lord" leads to a state of availability and flexibility: availability to be used by God and flexibility as to where and how He will use you. The second lesson learned in working with the refugee families considered here was the **necessity to be flexible.** The best laid plans, the most carefully thought-out procedures often had to be scrapped. The difficulties in communication and the resultant misunderstandings led to such things as preparing a meal for ten and having no one show up. It was necessary to be prepared for late arrival on the part of refugee families--sometimes as much as an hour or more late.

One of the hardest things of all for the sponsoring congregation is when the sponsored family decides to pack up and move away, sometimes clear across the country--or, in a related case, to be prepared to take a family of nine and instead receive a totally different family of six. All these events point to one lesson to be learned--be flexible.

Finally, there is the matter of **patience.** It takes time to adjust to a totally different and confusing lifestyle. Things that Americans take for granted are totally unknown to many refugees. Sponsors need to exercise great patience in dealing with the refugees they take into their homes. These three attributes--**availability, flexibility and patience**--while obvious Christian virtues, need to be continually reemphasized in preparing to sponsor refugees.

Each of the voluntary agencies has prepared material on the practical aspects of sponsorship, and it is not for us to duplicate their efforts. It is important, rather, that we understand that the success or failure of refugee ministry often rests upon attitudes toward giving and being available. Hopefully, we have learned these lessons.

Multiplied Ministry

Earlier we made reference to **multiplied ministry** in connection with the contacts made by and through the originally sponsored family. These ministries--through multiplication of opportunity--illustrate how one congregation and one or two families within that congregation have seen their circle of ministry broadened by successive refugee family contact. I would suggest that this experience is not unusual, and it is what one can expect when refugee ministry is taken seriously.

References Cited

Kelly, Gail P.
>   1977   **From Vietnam to America: A Chronicle of the Vietnamese Immigration to the United States.** Boulder, CO: Westview Press.

King, E. F.
>   1973   "The Refugees in Flight: Kinetic Models and Forms of Displacement." **International Migration Review,** volume 7.

Lui, W. T., M. Lamanna, and A. Murata
>   1979   **Transition to Nowhere.** New York: Charter Spring Publishers, Inc.

Montero, Darrel
>   1979   **Vietnamese Americans: Patterns of Resettlement and Socioeconomic Adaptation in the United States.** Boulder, CO: Westview Press.

Ruebbensaal, Ann P.
    1978   "The Adjustment of Vietnamese Refugees to American Culture" (unpublished typescript). Washington, D.C.:   The American University.

Tung, Tran Minh
    1980   **Indochinese Patients.**   Washington, D.C.: Action for South East Asians, Inc.

Lieutenant Colonel James Edgren is a Chaplain in the United States Army and is stationed in Washington, D.C. He has a keen interest in missions and has been deeply involved both with national Christians and suffering people. Col. Edgren is pursuing a doctorate from Wesley Theological Seminary.

A Local Church Multiplies

Gary Coombs

What began as a ministry to refugees by a local church turned in reality into a church planting ministry. As a result of explaining and exemplifying their faith to others, a congregation became stronger with knowledge and experience in cross-cultural evangelism as well as holistic ministry. Ministry broadened to other people groups. The church is currently ministering to Cambodians, Vietnamese and Laotians as well as to Cubans. The guiding principle was to identify leaders within each refugee group, train such leadership and continue to work with them while staying in the background. Much of the ministry growth has been attributed to this strategy.

This is the story of one local American church's involvement with refugees from Indochina. It is a wonderful example of what one local church, motivated by the Holy Spirit, can do and how much can be learned by being cross-culturally sensitive to the task of reaching those from another culture.

Laurel Bible Chapel began its ministry to Indochina refugees by reaching out to Cambodians in 1975. Today, about 250 Cambodians come to the church on Sunday afternoons. The church is also involved with Vietnamese. They currently have a Bible class with translation into Vietnamese. The third group to which they minister are Laotians. One key Laotian who accepted Christ in 1980 has been instrumental in the development of ministries to over 150 Laotians in two different churches.

The three groups differ. The Vietnamese are more oriented toward Western ways. They tend to be a little more independent than Lao and Cambodians. Each group has its predominant Buddhist background. The Vietnamese have gotten away from Buddhism, likewise the Cambodians, except for some elements of Buddhism that are interwoven into their culture. The Lao hold more strongly to Buddhism, and there is greater community resistance to their turning to Christ. It is estimated that 90 percent of the Lao are Buddhist, but less than 50 percent of the Cambodians and Vietnamese would claim to be strongly Buddhist.

The Cambodians have been very receptive toward Christianity. Even those who claim to be Buddhist show little hostility. A large number of Cambodians have become Christians. The Vietnamese do not appear particularly hostile toward Christianity, but neither is there often a lot of interest. As with all the groups, it is easy for them to get caught up in Western materialism. The Lao have exhibited the greatest resistance to Christianity. This resistance is often not apparent to Americans because of the politeness of Southeast Asians. The members of Laurel Bible Chapel learned about their resistance from other agents.

The History of Laurel Bible Chapel

Laurel Bible Chapel was caught up in world events in 1975 when they responded to the verse of the day on a Sunday morning. One of the Sunday school classes was studying "hindrances to prayer" in contemplating the meaning of Proverbs 21:13, which states "whoever stops his ears at the cry of the poor, he shall cry himself, but shall not be heard." They wondered if God might stop listening to their prayers if they refused to listen to the cry of those in need. This led them to their first visit to Camp Pendleton, north of San Diego, where they made contact with a Vietnamese family who were professing Christians and helped them to get settled.

In 1979, other Vietnamese started coming to Laurel Bible Chapel. They preferred to come to Laurel Bible Chapel rather than go to a Vietnamese-speaking church because the people there were attempting to help them by providing counseling. The church then started helping sponsor some of the relatives who were attending church.

That same year a young Christian came to San Diego for the summer with a burden to help Cambodians. He was a Bible institute student from Illinois and had a few months to give himself to ministry before going back to school. Through the love and interest of this man a small class of Cambodians grew to about 40 over the summer.

While picking up children and adults for Sunday school, the church discovered a house with sixty refugees. They had been placed there by a sponsor! The church began helping some of these locate housing. One member took 17 to his own home. This was the beginning of the work in the town of El Cajon with several hundred Chinese Cambodians.

The Bible class quickly grew to 150, about half of whom were Chinese living in El Cajon. When the number grew so large that Laurel Bible Chapel was not able to continue busing the Chinese the 15 miles to their church, work was started with the Chinese in El Cajon.

After the number meeting at the church had been

reduced to about 75 by the departure of the Chinese, it quickly grew back again to 150. Today on Sundays there are about 220 Cambodians meeting during the afternoon. Four churches are now involved. Leaders are developing for the group from among the Cambodians themselves.

But Laurel Bible Chapel's concern for refugees did not stop there. Although they felt they had all they could handle with the Cambodian/Vietnamese work, two of their members had a vision to reach out to the Cubans. They already had a small Spanish group with about 40 on Sunday mornings. However, one of their members sponsored over 100 Cubans. The first Sunday in March 1982, the Spanish congregation with the Cubans was able to obtain its own building. They now have a Spanish-speaking church.

Others were concerned about Laotians. There was a Hmong church in town and three Vietnamese churches besides Laurel Bible Chapel, but no ministry to the Lao. The church had sponsored a few Laotians, but they had not seen any fruit or interest in the gospel on the part of those they helped. One weekday, a member Christian from another church introduced a member from Laurel Bible Chapel to a Lao who had become nominally Christian while in Thailand. He subsequently came to know Christ as his Savior. After four weeks, he asked if he could attend their church. Subsequently, he brought first eight, then 21, then 35 other Laotians with him.

Since no one in the church spoke Lao, and at that time the Lao spoke limited English, the church had to work through two interpreters. While one member taught the group in English, another translated into French, and one of the Laotians translated from French into Lao. When the group grew to 150, Laurel Bible Chapel made arrangements for them to meet in another church two blocks away. Laurel Bible Chapel still has about 150 Laotians on Sunday mornings.

Lessons Learned

There would be little interest on the part of many of the refugees initially if it had not been for the church's going into their homes and showing them the love of Christ by meeting some basic needs. This often meant showing up with a 50-pound bag of rice, providing a bed, or taking a wife to the doctor. There were many who continued to have no interest in the gospel. However, Laurel Bible Chapel tried to communicate that it was not necessary for those they were helping to profess Christ in order to be helped. To show the love of Christ, Chapel friends would try to help them in any way they could.

The language most suitable for evangelism is obviously the native language of the refugee. The language of the refugee sometimes differs within a given country. For instance, there are some Vietnamese from Laos who do not understand the Lao language beyond the level of basic communication. The gospel needs to be communicated to them in Vietnamese. There are ethnic Chinese from Cambodia, Laos and Vietnam who do very well understand the language of their country, but they speak one or more dialects of Chinese fluently.

With some, the gospel can be communicated effectively in two or more languages. There are some from Cambodia who prefer to go to the Lao services. There are some Chinese who, given the option, choose the Cambodian meetings rather than going to a Chinese-speaking church made up of Chinese speakers from many countries. Some loyalties are obviously stronger than language similarity.

There are prevailing needs unmet. Often there is a need for employment. There is a need for love and friendship. There are far more refugees open for love and attention than there are Christians willing and able to give them. With 26,000 refugees in San Diego, the task is a large one. The greatest needs are found among the recently arrived refugees.

Often, refugees are devastated by our culture. They have survived the regimes of Pol Pot and Heng Samrin in Kampuchea, or Laotian or Vietnamese Communism, but they are faced with more subtle enemies in the United States. They learn that divorce is an easy way out of marriage. They sometimes become quite materialistic when they see it is possible to get ahead in our society. They are often corrupted by the humanistic education most of them receive in public elementary or adult schools. They do not relate the greatness of America to the Judeo-Christian value system.

They also bring over attitudes from their own cultures that need to change. In the country they left, the government was their enemy. There was no honesty in the government's dealings with them or their dealing with the government. Each got what they could out of the other. The result is that they are afraid of the police. They do not want to contact the police when a crime has been committed against them. If they go on welfare, they seldom report honestly. The government was their enemy, so they do not have to be honest. They often bring with them the kind of corruption that helped pave the way for Communism to take their land. Laurel Bible Chapel discovered the need to help them understand that some elements of the Indochinese cultures were wrong and destructive and to teach them values of honesty and uprightness taught in the Word of God.

The most effective way Laurel Bible Chapel found to reach the Indochinese was to disciple those who showed a desire and ability for Christian leadership. The refugees can more effectively reach their own people. As Americans, the members of Laurel Bible

Chapel cannot communicate with them as well as someone from their own culture. The best thing to do was to train leadership, continue to work with the leadership and then stay in the background. Laurel Bible Chapel believes that the reason for the growth of their Cambodian and Laotian ministries was primarily the development of leadership.

The Indochinese cannot be effectively reached just by teaching them the Bible or handing them literature. A church must get involved with their lives and be interested in them as whole persons. A bag of rice is generally a better introduction than a gospel tract. After a refugee has been in the United States for a period of time, and some basic needs have been met, some of the lingering needs often are instruction in English as a second language in the home, job training, employment and home Bible studies which can be combined with learning English. When the refugees see that you have a genuine interest in them, they generally take an interest in what you have to say and what motivates you to want to give help. It does not take long before the door is open to present the gospel.

One question the members of Laurel Bible Chapel had to answer was how to measure any change actually taking place as a result of their efforts. They discovered that the best way to keep abreast of change was through personal discipleship and involvement in the lives of the refugees. They describe it as being like keeping track of one's own children. An intimate relationship with the refugee believers helps in knowing how they are doing and progressing.

One of the best signs that the Word of God is working in their lives is when it is apparent that some of the dead elements of their cultural background are dropping off. When they begin dealing honestly with others, when they are willing to tell a prospective landlord the truth of how many will be living in a house, progress is being made. When the father teaches the children to respect the authority of the mother as well as the father, when in giving their age they do not think, "Is it better to be older, or is it better to be younger?" but rather, "It is better to be honest!" then change is taking place. The refugees tend not to give much financially beyond a few coins in the collection, even if they can afford it; when they start giving to support one of their own people in the spread of the gospel, it is obvious that the gospel is taking root.

Problems

The experience of sponsoring refugees has been quite rewarding. With it have come some problems. Whether we like to admit it or not, many of us have our "comfort zone," and working with people from another culture can be somewhat unsettling. We have our ways that we do things together; they often do things differently. To minister effectively, we had to learn to differentiate between what is biblical and what is cultural. It was necessary to overlook some cultural differences in order to show the love of Christ to people. In other areas, they had to adjust to our culture, for instance to the need for babies to wear diapers since we have rugs in our nursery!

Although the church members do not consider themselves to be segregationists, they honestly feel uncomfortable among other cultures. The people at Laurel Bible Chapel have had to learn to adjust to others who do things differently together than they do. They had to learn that their fellowship was not based on culture but on a common Savior. It is a continual test to integrate the refugees into the fellowship of the local church with believers from outside their own cultural background.

Some Advice for Churches Interested in Sponsorship

1. Select only one language group at first; the languages and cultures of the Southeast Asians differ

from one country to another and one people group to another.

2. Do not expect the refugees you sponsor to act like Americans immediately. They learn the needed American ways and customs in time, but we have to be patient. They enrich our culture and our lives meanwhile.

3. Share the gospel with the refugees, but do not press too quickly for a decision. Often they will cooperate to be polite, but their early profession might not be genuine.

4. Help to meet the basic needs of the refugees, but don't shower them with too much help. Help them to help themselves so they will not have to remain dependent on you.

5. Because you sponsor them does not mean they have an obligation to attend all the meetings of the church. Their attendance should be voluntary. Most of them will want to attend, at least for a while.

6. Sponsoring several families is better than sponsoring just one family. If you have a small community of refugees from the same country, they will more likely stay with you than if you have only one family.

7. Do not try to isolate the family from other refugees of their own ethnic group in their community. They desire and need social contact with others of their own cultural background.

8. Provide the opportunity for them to cook their own food. Do not insist that they always eat American food, or food you think is better for them than what they are used to.

9. Read. World Relief publications on refugee cultures are excellent. Books like David Hesselgrave's **Communicating Christ Cross-Culturally,** (Zondervan, 1978) are very helpful.

10. When the family arrives, finalize tentative plans you made for the settlement prior to their arrival.

11. Have some live-in orientation in an American home, if possible. The refugees can more quickly learn acceptable American household procedures and customs in the home if they stay for a period of time with an American family.

12. Don't be bothered about tight quarters in the home. It will seem spacious to refugees by their former living standards.

Conclusion

What began as a ministry to refugees has in reality turned into a church planting ministry. In explaining and exemplifying our faith to others, we have become a stronger congregation, with knowledge and experience in cross-cultural evangelism and holistic ministry. Now when a missionary tells us about experiences in bringing Christ to other cultures, we can relate. In seeking to serve others, we have become stronger members of the Body of Christ.

Gary Coombs is the World Relief Refugee Service representative in the San Diego area. Prior to coming to California in 1974, he directed a Christian Serviceman's Center in Newport, Rhode Island and also served as an Emmaus Correspondence Course School regional director in New England. Before becoming involved full time with the refugee ministry in San Diego, he was principal of a Christian school.

Discovering a Plan for Refugee Evangelization

Loc Le-Chau
Burt N. Singleton

All that is said here is based on the assumption that in the last analysis, the responsibility for refugee ministry rests with the local church. Passing this responsibility to government agencies, denominational mission boards and parachurch organizations may be necessary because of the geographic separation of the refugees from the local church. But to ignore the biblical mandate of direct refugee ministry by the local church is to ignore the greatest possible opportunity for holistic ministry.

Editor's Note:

*This chapter has two complementary sections. The first, by Burt N. Singleton, was prepared in conjunction with the refugee study group at the 1980 Lausanne-sponsored Consultation on World Evangelization. Based upon the strategy workbook, **That Everyone May Hear,** prepared for COWE, it provides an example of how to use the workbook method to develop strategies specifically for refugee groups, emphasizing preparing the local church for ministry. (See Resources.)*

The second section, by Loc Le-Chau, demonstrates the impact of this approach on his actual ministry in refugee resettlement as Regional Director for World Relief Refugee Resettlement on the East Coast of the United States.

Together, these articles demonstrate the best approach to evangelistic strategy. Starting from the **people group** *itself, questions are derived to dynamically aid the formulation of specific ministries. This stands in opposition to efforts which* **originate** *in experience with a given method and modify available tools by attempting to make them applicable to the specific circumstances.*

If the local church recognizes the mandate for refugee ministry, it is then faced with the question of how to begin. The following guidelines are a development of the basic approach described in **That Everyone May Hear,** by Edward R. Dayton, MARC, 1979 (see **Resources**). They are intended to assist the local church in preparing a plan for a refugee ministry. The five general steps which follow facilitate matching the needs of the refugees with the capabilities of the local church. It may be necessary, however, to move through the steps both at more general and more specific levels of planning, viewing this as a cyclical process rather than as the outline of a plan itself. Gathering this information may identify several specific ministry opportunities for which detailed plans may then be developed. If you review the questionnaire in Appendix A, you will have a good beginning.

1. **What refugee group does God want you to reach?** With the refugee population of the world as large as it is, no single organization is capable of meeting all the needs of all the refugees. Each organization or individual who would undertake refugee evangelization

must make a selection. This selection should aim to match capabilities with needs, and not necessarily to respond to the most popular and current refugee situation. The following questions may assist in the selection process:

A. Are there any refugees groups within your country? How many? Where? How long have they been there? How long do you think they will remain?

B. Are there refugee groups whose language you already know?

C. What special gifts do you have for reaching a particular refugee group?

D. What successful experience have you had in reaching a particular kind of refugee?

E. Do you see a particular group of unreached people who are likely to become refugees in the future?

As one progresses in defining the strategy, it is possible that the above questions will have to be answered for a part rather than the whole of a refugee group. Strategy definition is not necessarily a linear process. Rather it tends to be more a circular process, addressing the same question at different planning levels.

2. What is this refugee group really like? We need to understand the physical, emotional, mental and spiritual needs of refugee groups to which God has called us and temporarily put aside those to which we are not called. We need to understand where they are as people. To increase our effectiveness, we must also understand where they are in terms of being refugees. Answers to the following questions will assist this process:

A. What is their country of origin?

B. Is the group homogeneous, or does it consist of

several specific people groups?

C. Why are these people refugees? What experiences have they already faced?

D. How long do you think they will be refugees?

E. What religious groups are found among the refugees?

F. What is the percentage who are adherents to each religion?

G. What percentage actually practice each religion?

H. What is the attitude of this refugee group toward Christianity?

I. What language is most suitable for presentation of the gospel?

J. What is the status of Scripture translation in the language you consider most suitable for the presentation of the gospel?

K. What appears to be the attitude of the refugee group toward religious change of any kind?

L. Is there a Christian witness present within the refugee group?

M. Is there a local Christian church in the country of refuge near the refugee group?

N. What is the attitude of the local church toward the refugee group?

O. What needs of the refugees have been met? What needs still have to be met?

P. What is likely to be the final destination of the refugee group?

Q. Who else could you consult who would have more information about this refugee group or might have some additional good questions?

A factor of major importance is understanding the original culture of the group as well as their present condition. For example, in a refugee camp, if it is normal procedure to give announcements to men and women together, it should not be assumed that the gospel message should be delivered in the same manner. Many cultural preferences of the refugees have had to be put aside as a result of their situation as refugees. Therefore, questions related to the presentation of the gospel should attempt to consider the viewpoints and preferences of people **before** they became refugees as well as the subsequent changes in their lives.

3. Who should reach this refugee group? In considering this strategy step, it is important not to overlook other members of the Body of Christ who may be interested or already involved in reaching these refugees. Refugee needs are so great that cooperation and coordination with other organizations and individuals will probably be required. Response resources include existing Christians who themselves are members of the refugee group, the local church in the country of refuge, and other Christian organizations outside the area who might have a potential interest in this group. To understand what God is doing through the Body, the following questions may help:

A. What churches, agencies or other groups of Christians are already working with this particular refugee group?

B. Which groups or agencies appear to understand the basic needs of these refugees?

C. Are the established churches in the country of refuge culturally acceptable to the local church among the refugees?

D. Are there Christian leaders among the refugee group?

E. If refugees are more likely to be resettled in a

third country instead of returning to their native country, what organizations are currently working with similar groups in the country of resettlement?

F. What organizations or agencies working with this group would be opposed to the proclamation of the gospel among this group?

G. What religious, spiritual or other forces hinder individuals and families from committing themselves to Christ in an open and active way?

H. If Christians are present in this group, what important factors, if any, seem to keep them from active and effective witness?

By understanding both the forces that favor evangelization and those opposed to it, you may conclude that a different refugee group would more nearly fit your capabilities, or that the group is being served adequately. If so, then you need to return to the first question above and begin again. This is a further demonstration that strategy definition is not necessarily linear but rather may lead back to previous steps as one collects more information.

4. How should this refugee group be reached? In choosing methods for the evangelization of a particular refugee group, one must be guided both by the cultural features of the group and by their status as refugees. Some methods, although culturally acceptable, may not be effective due to people's refugee status. For example, a farmer working his land from dawn to dusk may be too exhausted to listen to a cassette player in the evening. But as a refugee with little to do, the same farmer may listen to the same cassette over and over. Literate refugees may spend many hours reading available literature as refugees, which they would not take time to do when earning a living. Therefore, in considering methods, one needs to answer cultural questions and refugee status questions. Some of the following may be helpful:

A. In light of the current needs of the refugees, their cultural background, their understanding of the gospel, and the resources available, what methods do you believe are most likely to meet their spiritual needs?

B. Will these methods move these refugees toward Christ? When and how will the methods be changed because the people have moved toward Christ? How will they be modified to meet a change of status of the refugees?

C. Do these methods conform to biblical principles?

D. Where can you learn more about possible means or methods?

E. What organizations or individuals will probably cooperate with you?

A major factor to be considered at this point of strategy definition is not only **how** but **when.** Most refugee situations begin with the necessity for meeting physical needs. The evangelist who does not arrive to preach the gospel until the refugees are well fed, housed, healthy and occupied in organized activity has lost a significant opportunity and will be viewed as "one who visits" rather than "one who helps." This is not to imply that one should arrive early to preach to exhausted, sick and starving refugees, but experience has demonstrated that refugees are more open to the message of God's love brought by someone they have previously observed meeting physical needs in their midst. Whether this means training evangelists to do relief work, or relief workers to do evangelism, is of less consequence than the fact that the tasks go well together.

5. What will be the result? No one can predict the future, but God is in control. He expects us to think about the future and the outcome or goals of the activities we are about to undertake. By this means you can evaluate the direction and the effectiveness of the methods selected for this group of refugees. Ask yourself these questions:

A. If the approach is successful, what do you expect God to do?

B. How will you describe where these people are in their movement toward Christ?

C. How will you seek to measure spiritual changes among them?

D. What problems will you encounter in your approach? How will you overcome them or reduce their negative impact?

E. If members of this group become Christians, what kind of biblical worshiping fellowship would be most likely to continue to attract other members of the same group?

F. How will the Christians of this group integrate into: (1) their native national church when or if they return home, (2) the local church if they remain in the country of refuge, (3) another church in the country of resettlement, or (4) a new church formed by them?

If you are not able to describe the expected results in measurable terms, perhaps the previous steps of strategy definition require further study and possible revision.

Since refugee situations usually do not permit months of strategic planning, asking some simple "what if?" questions may be useful. As a minimum, you could devise a plan for the following possible alternatives:

If the people I am concerned about became refugees in another country, and I were to join them there, what strategy would I use if I knew:

a. that they would return home in six months; or

b. that they would remain in the country of refuge as legal settlers; or

c. that they would remain in the country of refuge as illegal settlers; or

d. that they would be resettled in a third country?

Such an exercise may provide some element of preparedness in the event one of these conditions becomes a reality.

Finally, when the local church has selected one or more areas of refugee ministry and has moved forward to carry out that ministry, positive results will not always be immediately apparent. This should be the cause not for abandoning future ministries, but rather for prayerfully seeking God's guidance and moving ahead with faith that He will provide harvest in His time.

AN EXPERIENCE IN REFUGEE RESETTLEMENT

This paper attempts to share general aspects of refugee work based on personal recall and impressions of thousands of records and reports. It is a summary of experience in refugee resettlement in the United States. It involves refugees from Southeast Asia, Afghanistan, Ethiopia and South Africa, Latin America and Central Europe.

The World Relief Refugee Services (WRRS) Regional Office in Washington, D.C., covers a six-state area surrounding the nation's capital. As the regional director, my main task was to develop as many sponsors as possible to place an average of 50 refugee cases, or approximately 200 people, per month. The purpose is to give to the refugee not only a home and an opportunity to develop a normal life, to be "self-reliant," but also a new life in the fullest sense. The sponsor, as a partner of World Relief, should be in a position to provide for the material, emotional and spiritual needs of the refugee.

The best type of sponsor for this type of holistic ministry is the church. The Regional Office's main objective in sponsorship development is therefore to identify churches that have a strong desire to reach out to the refugees and to share with them the richness of Christian life.

The Washington Office contacted about 1500 churches, the majority of which were Presbyterian, Christian and Missionary Alliance, Baptist, Assembly of God and independent churches. The regional director had personal contact with over 300 churches through visits, presentations, workshops and seminars. Many contacts have developed into lasting relationships and fellowships that have formed the core of support.

After leaving the Consultation on World Evangelization in Pattaya, Thailand, I took the liberty of distributing a paper presented to the Mini-Consultation on Refugees entitled "Discovering a Plan for Refugee Evangelization" to help the evangelical churches in America in their sponsoring of the refugees. The paper was prepared by Burt N. Singleton. Although it was not published officially as an appendix of the refugee paper, I thought it preserved experience and insights as well as discussion of the Mini-Consultation on Refugees group. It was indeed helpful.

Since I was partly responsible to organize and bring up a national network of Regional Offices for World Relief Refugee Services with regional directors, and I also used it in the Region I directed on the East Coast, well before the printing of the refugee report I shared the paper in a limited way.

This paper-questionnaire has helped many churches

that were challenged for the first time for this new ministry. Although for the majority of them, the refugee challenge presented to them is simpler and does not require a long struggle or even an elaborate process to come up with a decision, many parts of the paper have shed light on a number of areas that would otherwise be a hindrance in the planning phase or a cause for misunderstandings in sponsor-refugee relations.

At the outset, it is appropriate to note that most of the American churches contacted respond favorably almost immediately when called upon to take a refugee family home. Many of them realize that there is no time to ask too many questions. They set out to pray and to act upon the command of the Holy Spirit in moving quickly to the decision of sponsorship.

Many churches report that the parable of the Good Samaritan is good enough basis for their spontaneous decision. They are informed of the need, they open their churches and their homes, and they trust God for the resources to carry out the difficult tasks afterward. Many report that God's providence never fails them, and the whole experience is invariably an opportunity for the congregation or parish to grow in faith and in unity.

My experience is that when a church begins to debate with many questions asked, the process of decision making takes a long time, sometimes a year; meanwhile, the refugees in need of love keep flowing in. Most of the churches in this category conceive this kind of endeavor as a "project" among the many that the congregation has each budget year to keep itself busy. Another experience is that the bigger the churches are, the longer the time taken for a decision, whereas in smaller congregations--some have less than fifty members--more rooms are provided for the refugees more readily.

The following are those sections and questions that were found most helpful in the planning phase and the execution phase of a refugee sponsorship.

What Refugee Group Does God Want You to Reach?

Are there refugee groups whose language you already know? This reminds the congregation planning group that one of the major problems in resettling refugees, especially middle-aged and older adults, is **communication.** All the churches worked hard to make sure there was someone in the church or in the community surrounding the church that could speak the language of the refugee and do an adequate interpretation.

The Regional Office, acknowledging the vital importance of communication, has a multilingual staff and consultants readily available to the sponsors and to the refugees throughout the cities and states within the region. Many of the consultants are former missionaries now retired in the States, or else previously forced to leave the countries and the people they love.

What Is This Refugee Group Really Like?

This paragraph is helpful in sensitizing the sponsoring church to the need of understanding the refugees' background and situation. Some of the church refugee committees have used the questionnaire to research the background themselves; the majority rely on the abundant materials put out by World Relief and other national voluntary organizations with long-standing, extensive ministry in refugee work. The United States and state government agencies responsible for refugee programs, with the help of colleges contracted to do research and evaluation, also publish a variety of excellent reports, and books are available on specific aspects of resettlement experience.

Who Should Reach This Refugee Group?

Again, this paragraph concerns more the Christian resettlement agency. It was of great help to my office in its research and publication of notes, pamphlets and papers for the benefit of the individual church congregations involved in refugee ministry.

Some large denominations, such as Roman Catholics, Lutherans and Baptists, through their refugee and migration arms, have done extensive studies in this and produced significant amounts of related materials. To the independent evangelical churches associated with the National Association of Evangelicals (NAE), World Relief Refugee Services has not only provided information regarding congregations, churches being formed by the refugee group, and Christian leaders and trained ministers among the refugee population, but also encouraged, supported and trained them, if necessary. This special task has a top priority in its support services.

How Should This Refugee Group Be Reached?

This paragraph directly concerns the sponsoring church. Since the policy of World Relief is to work in partnership with the church, it looks on the church to provide the leadership in refugee evangelism.

Most of the churches are sensitive to the precarious physical, emotional and spiritual makeup of the refugee in the first months, or even years, in the country of resettlement. Accordingly, they are attentive in taking gradual steps toward sharing the Good News with their refugees. They make plans to introduce the refugee non-believers to their churches, without giving the impression of forcing or "proselytizing." In fact, the experience gained shows that the best way to share Christ with the refugees is to live out one's faith in Christ. Most of the refugees would see the special effect of Christ's love in the sponsor's life and believe, or at least become curious and ask questions leading to sharing of the Word.

Usually, the process of change takes a long time. Unfortunately, a small number of the sponsoring churches do not take seriously the advice set forth in this paragraph with regard to the aspects of **method** and **timing**--the **how** and **when**--in the strategy of evangelization. They allow impatience to take hold, and in their zeal to "save souls" have put the emphasis at the beginning of the resettlement process on having the refugees accept Christ in the first place. The result has been most unfortunate. The refugees accept without meaning it, or else in order to retain their integrity they leave the sponsor precipitously. Breakdowns in relationships happened this way more often in cases where the refugee was placed with individual Christian families of a certain evangelical conviction. The wisdom of the whole Church is simply lacking here.

So it is extremely important, as the paper seeks to bring out, that the how and the when in evangelization planning processes should be understood and appropriately balanced. We all know the why and what in evangelism work. But the result may vary greatly depending on how and when we do it, especially in the context of the refugee's culture and situation. At least for the refugees I have had the privilege to serve, deeds and examples are more important and a lot more helpful in the learning, discovering and changing process.

Quite a number of the churches involved encourage and support the formation of refugee congregations when there are large refugee groups resettled around the church.

An uplifting example is the Chestnut Street Baptist Church in Philadelphia. The Pastor, Dr. Yii, a Chinese immigrant from the Philippines, has worked closely with this writer using the Singleton strategy paper and discovered the vocation of his church. From a stagnant body of about twenty older women congregating in a deteriorating downtown area of the city, the church has grown within less than two years to a congregation of over 300 cosmopolitan members, comprising Vietnamese, Laotians, Kampucheans, Ethiopians and others. Moreover, the Chestnut Street Baptist Church houses on its premises, besides the American congregation which had grown dynamically as a result of the involvement with the refugees, a Laotian congregation, a Vietnamese congregation and an Ethiopian congregation, each pastored by Lao, Viet and Ethiopian ministers, sponsored by the Regional Office or located, contacted and sent by it.

Other similar examples of this sort of ministry are the Alexandria First Baptist Church and the Arlington Memorial Church.

What Will Be the Result?

One church in West Virginia and another church in Maryland have taken seriously the detailed questions grouped under the major strategy questions in this paragraph. Questions B and C have stirred their attention with regard to attitude and value change in the refugees' lives.

They have listed a number of Christian values in relationships (e.g., between husband and wife, parents and children) and concepts (e.g., money and material wealth) and observed the changes to detect any movement toward Christ as they shared their lives with the refugees.

This has proven to be useful to this writer in his own learning about evangelism, evangelization as a process, and certain truths about different cultures, approaches and groups. The refugees represent, in a way, a microcosm of the large mission field to be gained for Christ.

In brief, in the partnership between the resettlement agency and the churches, a division of labor seems to be most effective in approaching the whole spectrum of the refugees' needs and in ministering to them holistically. The church is better equipped for evangelism, a better environment for nurturing and development, while the Christian agency plays the supporting and undergirding role. The support of the agency should match the efforts of the church. Both have to cooperate and carefully coordinate plans for refugee evangelization.

Loc Le-Chau, a Vietnamese refugee himself, took part in organizing the Regional Offices of the World Relief Refugee Service and was director of the Washington, D.C., Regional Office. He attended the Consultation on World Evangelization in Pattaya, Thailand, and was a member of the mini-consultation on refugees. He is now serving as Special Assistant for Evangelism and Leadership in the World Vision Asia Regional Office.

Burt N. Singleton, Jr. is director of the Research and Information Division of World Vision International. During the height of the Vietnamese "Boat People" crisis, he served as the Operational Officer on board Seasweep, a service and supply ship operated on the South China Sea by World Vision to aid the refugees in their flight to freedom. In 1980, Singleton participated in the mini-consultation on refugees at the Consultation on World Evangelization in Pattaya, Thailand. In addition to his work through World Vision, he is a board member of the Navajo Gospel Mission.

Lessons Learned

Samuel Wilson

Throughout history, dislocation of peoples as refugees has been disruptive. But it is essential for us to see that the Holy Spirit has unleashed immense creativity as a direct consequence of and in response to these tragedies. It may well be that our "resistance to the Holy Spirit," like that of our forebears, makes such tragedy the only way He can bring His Church to open her eyes to what needs to be done. We often seem to look for His working only through the institutional forms. God insists on reminding us that both the Church and the world are in continual process.

Have we heard that reminder in the facts documented in these pages? What are the lessons our brothers and sisters have learned?

Refugees Are People Groups

"Refugee" is a category. But there is no such thing as a "ministry to refugees." Ministry must become specific. Most of us immediately recognize that there are natural groupings brought about by language. But what we have seen is that there are other groupings that more closely define a people group who happen to be refugees. First, there are their formal circumstances--the countries from which they come, their economic status, their religion, the situation that caused them to be refugees, and so forth. But we have also seen that each refugee group changes in the sense that it goes through various stages in transition. Refugees in holding camps may constitute groups quite different than refugees attempting to adjust to the country of resettlement.

Everything that we have learned about describing people groups and attempting to reach them with the gospel applies directly to refugees. (See **Resources.**)

Christian Love and Fellowship Are Real

In the first place, there is dramatic, winsome proof of the resources of Christian love and fellowship in times of deep need.

Sufferers share with human need more deeply because they are Christian. In times of disorientation, panic, loss of all anchor, those who know Christ not only find personal consolation and console one another, they reach out to minister in powerful testimony to the reality of the gospel to them.

Ministry to Refugees Is First a Healing Ministry

We must not underestimate the horrendous effects of dislocation. We need to be patient. Sometimes silence is the only effective response. At other times, there needs to be loving service. Refugees carry the physical and psychological marks of suffering. The trauma is evident. Those who seek to minister must do so in a sensitive, loving spirit.

Recent research with Chilean refugees in Canada indicates that it is even possible to recognize victims of torture by developing a profile of physical and psychological symptoms. The profile is able to distinguish real victims from those who are merely seeking attention. Refugees continue to hurt as a result of previous suffering. The reality of this must be taken into account by those who develop a ministry in the name of Christ. Everything learned in the articles in this book corroborates this deep need.

Confidence Must Be Won Slowly

There are instances where churches working in resettlement have been too forward too early in verbal witness and have not been effective. Likewise, vital contact with Christian celebration must be made, preferably with other nationals of similar background, before so much time has elapsed that the opportunity is lost.

In a time when personhood has been lost, identity is placed in doubt. The reinstitution of holidays, celebrations or social observances builds confidence and restores identity. Refugees need to observe old dates and customs. Such social events can become a powerful entree into intimate friendship and can meet a desperate and immediate need.

The refugee's gradual return to a more balanced life brings opportunity for developing wholeness in a new identity as a Christian, provided that the Christians have been willing first to reach out to understand and participate in the refugee's past. Sharing national occasions is a unique and powerful tool for identifying with refugees, to open this door even as they reconstruct their own identities.

Those Who Would Minister Must Be Flexible

Upheaval is always a time for creativity. The Church has best ministered at times of deep need when she has been flexible enough to minister on new terms and in new forms. The histories we have read in the preparation of this book bring this home with considerable force. Churches that have innovated, dedicating time and resources outside of routine church life, have been rewarded with rich ministry. Those that were unwilling to modify commitment or evolve new forms have not been so fruitful.

The phases of refugee pilgrimage offer a variety of options for ministry congenial to the built-in predispositions and predilections of a sweeping range of institutions.

Obviously, disaster relief is possible at the earliest stage, when, nearly totally destitute, refugees arrive somewhere and are grouped, usually in camps.

Organizations and agencies gifted in language teaching and literature have a prime opportunity when camp boredom sets in.

All the previous evangelistic and ministering skills of expatriates, former missionaries and those with cross-cultural experience are called to minister at the stage of resettlement.

Opportunity Is Vast if Not Limitless

If a church is ready for it, the ministry to individuals can mushroom into a group ministry, and ministry to one group can proliferate to others. Many, many needs go unmet through insensitivity or through inadequate commitment for whatever reason.

Love Must Be Demonstrated Before Verbal Witness Is Possible

Stated conversely, it is almost the unanimous opinion of those who have been effective in developing churches that initial verbal witness is counterproductive until love is shown by deeds in daily life.

Not all will be converted. This should hardly need to be expressed, but for some reason Christians feel witness by deeds should be more effective than witness by word or proclamation.

170

Timing Is Crucial

The opportunity to respond may not wait for "normal" channels and procedures. For refugees in a country of resettlement a powerful lesson to local congregations is that smaller churches are often more effective than larger ones. Most larger churches, for whatever reasons, are slower at making the necessary decisions. Some opportunities pass relatively quickly and must be seized with little delay. This seems to be true of the opportunity to meet refugees' needs.

The delay needed to get a decision through the machinery of a large church seems to develop caution and reserve. Smaller churches or well-knit groups within large congregations can and do act with dispatch; large churches on the whole seldom can. Delayed decisions are more apt to be negative. There is almost a defensiveness about not modifying programs and allowing refugees to change the status quo.

Language and Cultural Sensitivity in Outreach Are of Highest Priority

As truly gifted cross-cultural workers have known for hundreds of years, there is nothing more winsome than the ability to invest effort in maintaining the integrity of the person's group. You will learn and relearn all the lessons associated with cross-cultural contacts, whether on attitudes and use of time, space, resources, or relationships. Ask yourself continually: What do we (they) take for granted? Be especially careful of the effects of your perspective on attitudes. Your construction of the pastoral, caring attitude is necessary to effective ministry.

Leadership Development Must Be Emphasized

Responsibility must be given over. The challenge of ministry to "others" is a hurdle to overcome. For example, middle-class Westerners will discover unsuspected areas of prejudice when "different" people groups invade their homes, their schedules and their way of thinking about life. This ought not to be decried as racism but rather dealt with in the breadth of Christ's love as a practical outworking of understanding the meaning of unity across nations.

Give Essential but Not Total Help

Maintain a delicate balance between giving helpful support and creating demeaning dependence. Be prepared for independent decisions that may seem to convey ingratitude. Do not interpret them that way.

Be Prepared to "Tap Into" Informal Communication

The refugees, through family and other links, will "get the word" on conventional wisdom, which is sometimes, but not always, helpful. Be prepared to take advantage as they pick up information you have not given them.

Expect Some Surprises

Refugees represent the full social spectrum. We must work to keep a positive attitude toward giving when refugees insist on treating furnishings as theirs to barter or sell. We must not feel we have been used and allow resentment to rise. Give freely, with no strings attached.

One final lesson remains which points to the future. Only the locations and faces will change. The Church must avoid a sated attitude or a desperate spirit of "When will it end?" Humans will continue to treat others inhumanly, and refugees will continue to challenge the Church to creative, kingdom service. There is no expiration date on giving the cup of cold water. Neither is there a limitation on the multiple rewards of ministry.

Samuel Wilson is the current director of MARC. He has served with Christian and Missionary Alliance on the mission field in Peru for over a decade. Following his doctoral work in sociology at Cornell University, he served for eight years as a professor at Nyack College and the Alliance School of Theology and Missions.

Part 3

Expanded Descriptions— Refugees

Refugees:
A World Overview

Refugee statistics are difficult to collect and even more difficult to substantiate. For political reasons, many countries choose not to report refugees in their midst. They want to avoid world focus and embarrassment to the governments of the countries from which the refugees come. Sometimes the refugees choose not to register for fear of real or imagined consequences. As a result, the statistics are more likely to be understated. The usual estimate quoted worldwide is **16 million refugees.** However, the statistics in this report total **10 million,** which does not include **4.5 million internally displaced** within their country of origin, and therefore not legally defined as refugees. Also excluded from the current listing are more than **3 million** refugees who have been accepted for resettlement. Although they are no longer refugees in the sense that they are in process of attaining new citizenship, they continue to represent potential ministry for the church in the country of resettlement. Regardless of the exact number, definitions, legal protocol, and shifting areas in the world where major refugee flows occur, the measure of human misery these statistics represent is a tremendous challenge to Christians.

But whether 10 or 16 million people, it is too large a

number to deal with directly in ministry. In the section that follows, we discuss a way of viewing the total which makes reaching them possible. Through the use of the questions in the article entitled "Discovering a Plan for Refugee Evangelization," specific refugee groups may be defined at the neighborhood, local or national level within a larger refugee group. Thus the size of the refugee group may be defined consistent with the ministry resources that can be brought to the task at hand.

The following overview covers a summary of the world refugee situation, then focuses upon five major refugee population groups which are still too diverse to be considered as aggregate people groups. The expanded descriptions which follow, however, focus more finely on groups with common distinctives to assist in defining them for ministry opportunities.

1982 WORLD REFUGEE STATISTICS

Region	Country of Asylum	Origin	Official Estimate
Africa			
	Algeria	Western Sahara	65,000
	Angola		73,000
		Zaire	
		Namibia	
		South Africa	
	Botswana		1,500
		Angola	

	Namibia South Africa	
Burundi	Rwanda	55,000
Cameroon	Chad	20,000
Central African Republic	Chad	5,000
Djibouti	Ethiopia	30,000
Egypt	various	5,500
Ethiopia	Sudan	11,000
Kenya	Ethiopia Rwanda Uganda various	3,900
Lesotho	S. Africa	11,000
Nigeria	Chad	40,000
Rwanda	Burundi Uganda	10,000
Senegal	various	4,000
Somalia	Ethiopia	700,000
Sudan	Ethiopia Uganda Chad Zaire	500,000

	Country of Asylum	Origin	Official Estimate
	Swaziland	S. Africa	5,700
	Tanzania		156,000
		Burundi	
		Zaire	
	Uganda		113,000
		Rwanda	
		Zaire	
	Zaire		370,000
		Angola	
		Uganda	
		Zambia	
	Zambia		42,000
		Angola	
		Namibia	
		various	
	Other		30,000

TOTAL FOR AFRICA   **2,251,600**

Region	Country of Asylum	Origin	Official Estimate
Asia			
	Australia	various	304,000
	Bhutan	Tibet	1,500
	China	S.E. Asia	265,000

Hong Kong	Vietnam	14,000
India		3,300
	Afghanistan various	
Indonesia	Vietnam	6,000
Japan	Vietnam	1,800
Laos	Cambodia	3,800
Macao	Vietnam	1,200
Malaysia		99,000
	Philippines Vietnam Cambodia	
Nepal	Tibet	11,000
New Zealand	various	10,000
Papua New Guinea		1,000
	Indonesia	
Philippines	Vietnam	6,600
Singapore	Vietnam	500
Thailand		193,000
	Vietnam Laos	

	Cambodia	
Vietnam	Cambodia	33,000

TOTAL FOR ASIA		954,700

Region	Country of Asylum	Origin	Official Estimate
Europe	Austria	Eastern Europe	43,000
	Belgium	various	33,000
	Denmark	various	1,800
	France	various	150,000
	Germany (FRG)	various	94,000
	Greece	various	3,800
	Italy	various	14,000
	Netherlands	various	12,000
	Norway	various	6,000
	Portugal	Africa Latin America	7,600

Romania	Chile	1,000
Spain	Latin America S.E. Asia	40,000
Sweden	various	20,000
Switzerland	various	37,000
United Kingdom	various	148,000
Yugoslavia	various	2,000

TOTAL FOR EUROPE   **613,200**

Region	Country of Asylum	Origin	Official Estimate
Latin America	Argentina	Europe Latin America S.E. Asia	26,000
	Belize	El Salvador	7,000
	Bolivia	Europe Latin America	500
	Brazil		24,000

	Europe	
	Latin America	
Chile	Europe	1,500
Colombia	Latin America	2,000
Costa Rica		13,000
	El Salvador	
	Latin America	
Cuba	Latin America	3,000
Dominican Republic	Haiti	3,800
Ecuador	various	700
Guatemala	El Salvador	50,000 100,000
Honduras		25,000
	El Salvador	
	Nicaragua	
	Guatemala	
Mexico	El Salvador	70,000 140,000
Nicaragua	El Salvador	20,000
Panama	El Salvador	1,000
Peru		1,500
	Europe	
	Latin America	

Uruguay		1,700
	Europe	
	Latin America	
Venezuela		18,000
	Europe	
	Latin America	

TOTAL FOR LATIN AMERICA   **268,700–388,700**

Region	Country of Asylum	Origin	Official Estimate
North America	Canada	various	338,000
	U.S.A.	various	849,000

TOTAL FOR NORTH AMERICA   **1,187,000**

Region	Country of Asylum	Origin	Official Estimate
Middle East	Iran		110,000
		Afghanistan	
		Kurds	
		Iraq	

Lebanon		3,200
Pakistan		2,600,000
	Afghanistan	
Palestinian Refugees		1,884,000
	Jordan	733,000
	West Bank	334,000
	Ganza Strip	370,000
	Lebanon	232,000
	Syria	215,000
Other countries		40,000

TOTAL FOR MIDDLE EAST   **4,637,200**

REFUGEE TOTALS

Africa	2,251,600
Asia	954,700
Europe	613,200
Latin America (high estimate)	388,700
Middle East	4,637,200
North America	1,187,000
TOTAL	**10,032,400**

The Indochinese Refugees

The term Indochinese refugee is used in publications to designate those peoples from the nations of Vietnam, Kampuchea and Laos who have sought asylum elsewhere. For the period April 1975 to December 1981, voluntary repatriation was possible for 310,000 Khmer who had fled to Thailand and Laos. Ten thousand Laotians returned to their own land from temporary asylum in Thailand. Settlement in the country of first asylum is not possible to document since these refugees are often unregistered and subject to a gradual process of assimilation. Third country resettlement has been the most highly publicized form of solution to the Indochinese refugee problem. Since April 1975 an estimated 1,149,000 Indochinese refugees have been resettled in various parts of the world. The United States has received 567,000 refugees and Canada 81,500. As many as 266,000 Indochinese of ethnic Chinese background have been settled in China. Australia and New Zealand have received 59,400 and 4,200 respectively. Among the European nations, France leads with 83,600 resettled.

The nations of Asia generally do not favor resettlement programs within their own borders because of overtaxed economies, unemployment and potential friction with the refugee population. Several Asian nations, however, have borne the brunt of large refugee populations temporarily settled in their countries. Thailand has had more than 570,000 refugees cross its borders since 1975. Approximately 190,000 refugees remain in Thailand, the majority of whom are Khmer who may be repatriated in the near future. Over 159,000 refugees who escaped from Vietnam by boat landed in Malaysia. All but 16,000 of these were resettled in third countries by mid-1981. The remainder are to be settled elsewhere in time. Malaysia has granted permament settlement to approximately 1800 Khmer Muslims. Hong Kong has allowed some Vietnamese boat refugees of Chinese ethnic origin to remain. Camps have been constructed and programs maintained for boat people in Hong Kong. Eighty-four thousand have been resettled in third countries. The refugee processing centers in Bataan, the Philippines; and Galang, Indonesia, have been developed for the temporary care of the refugees and their preparation for life in third countries. As of June 1982, Bataan contained 10,000 and Galang 6,900 refugees awaiting processing.

While most Vietnamese refugees have been success-fully placed in third countries, the plight of the Laotian and Khmer refugees in holding sites continues. Since it is believed that these people will be repatriated even-tually, third countries have been reluctant to claim them. Some have lived in the camps for nearly three years.

In resettlement, employment opportunities are, of course, limited. Even professionals find themselves performing low-paying jobs. Many refugee families live on incomes well below the poverty level. Quite early in the process, the refugees themselves relocated. Those in remote rural settlements began to drift toward the urban centers, particularly where their kinfolk resided. The predominant reason refugees choose to settle in one country over another, irrespective of conditions or labor opportunities, is the presence of relatives in the country. Some refugee communities have become highly organized, producing their own publications and conducting their own forums. In some cases they have attempted to produce programs to inform local citizens about their cultures and customs.

Later waves of refugees have generally been less well educated, more amenable to "starting at the bottom" and eligible for less public assistance. In light of these difficulties, depression often infects refugees as they struggle with a new culture and language, and attempt to exist on scarce resources. Self-worth and personal dignity are eroded by the inability to find adequate employment.

In this situation, primary attention must now be directed towards integration within a host society. The prevailing needs of the Indochinese center around employment opportunities and language learning. In order for them to find jobs, they need at least a working knowledge of the primary languages of the countries in which they find themselves. This is significantly easier for Vietnamese who learned French in Vietnam and are resettled in France or Canada. It is extremely difficult for the Hmong who resettle in the United States or the Laotians in Spain.

The employment opportunities open to Indochinese refugees vary from country to country, and Christians should respond in an appropriate manner depending on the needs. If language learning surfaces as a major hurdle, Christians can help by providing tutoring. If unemployment prevails, particularly among older men, Christians should get involved in offering meaningful activity. As boredom becomes a problem, Christians must be ready to offer friendship and hope.

Indochinese refugees have perhaps received more mass media attention than any other refugee group. The issues at hand have captured the attention of concerned citizens who watch the world become smaller. The Indochinese spark notes both of criticism and of compassion as have few other groups in history.

Afghan Refugees

Since late 1979 some two million Afghan citizens have fled to neighboring Pakistan to escape the Soviet invasion of their homeland. This is the largest refugee community in the world and has created serious problems for their Pakistani hosts.

Afghan refugees reside in both official and unofficial encampments as either registered or unregistered aliens. Some manage to live with relatives, and those with some resources have rented quarters in the towns and villages nearby. Since Afghanistan presents a diverse ethnic population, it is assumed that the various ethnic groups represented in the refugee communities have tended to band together in Pakistan.

It is difficult to know exactly how many refugees are living in the settlements since they tend to flow back and forth across the border and are sometimes reregistered, thus inflating the official figures. By all accounts the refugee communities in Pakistan are expected to remain for a considerable time since the Soviets give no indication of leaving Afghanistan.

The Pakistani population of the Northwest Frontier Province and Baluchistan, the areas of greatest Afghan concentration, initially afforded the refugees a warm welcome owing to their ethnic and linguistic affinity with them, but the presence of so many refugees has taxed the resources of the provinces to the limit and created some dissonance between the refugees and the native population. An estimated three million head of livestock have accompanied the refugees and have browsed off the fragile vegetation of the region while seriously depleting and fouling the water resources of Pakistan. Continuous foraging for firewood by the refugees has almost completely denuded the area for miles around, and the ecological balance of the environment may have been destroyed by the human and animal impact on the resources of the region.

Politically, the potential for trouble between Pakistan and the Soviet Union is high because many Afghan men make forays into their country from Pakistan to harass Soviet troops and disrupt the administration of Afghanistan. Perhaps only 10 to 40 percent of the population of the refugee camps are adult males. The men are either seeking income elsewhere or engaging in guerrilla operations. In support of this view, the Shinwari and Afridi tribes which command the access routes to Pakistan are continually being wooed by the Afghan government in an effort to eliminate guerrilla action in Afghanistan.

Another feature of refugee life, particularly in Baluchistan, is that the benefits accorded the refugees often outstrip those available to the poverty-stricken Pakastani host population. Fear exists that the slender resources available for meeting Pakistani needs will be diverted to the Afghan refugees. The most recent Afghan arrivals in Pakistan suffer from malnutrition and other ailments far more than did those who arrived earlier, a possible indication of the hardness of life in Afghanistan under Soviet leadership. The fear of epidemics sweeping the settlements or the herds is an ever-present reality. The refugees urgently need a comprehensive public health and sanitation plan and disease prevention program.

A conspicuous problem which has cropped up in the refugee program is the fact that no Pashto language training was provided for non-Pashto speaking workers. Misunderstandings have arisen, and developmental projects have been occasionally canceled for this reason. Since the refugees are likely to remain in the economically depressed provinces of Pakistan for some time, the loss of potential income-generating projects through faulty communication processes is critical. Self-sufficiency for the refugees must be coordinated carefully with similar programs for the Pakistani population. Integration of long-term economic development programs with refugee projects is important to avoid duplication of effort.

A policy of dispersion and resettlement of Afghan refugees to other provinces of Pakistan has been contemplated. This integrative approach is favored by those officials in leadership positions who are concerned about the effects of large numbers of Afghans settled in colonies along the border regions of Pakistan. The strain placed on the economically deprived provinces of Baluchistan and the Northwest Frontier Province could be relieved as well. Official Pakistani policies favor cessation of the military conflict causing the mass refugee movement, and immediate repatriation of all refugees to Afghanistan. Most of the Afghans agree with the desire for repatriation, but only when political conditions allow them to do so without danger of persecution or death.

General indications suggest that while these Muslim Afghans are refugees in Pakistan they are more open to the gospel than they were while residing in their own country. Christians should make every effort to respond to the opportunities presented by current conditions.

Central America

During the initial stages of political and economic upheaval in Central America relatively small numbers of educated individuals fled persecution and terrorism. Subsequent military maneuvers and police activities caused large-scale movements of entire groups and particularly landless, uneducated peasants. Media networks of the world have issued conflicting reports. The stories emanating from the refugee groups indicate that severe repression and violence have been widespread. Official government communiques have often raised more questions than they have answered, and media documentaries of incredible horror and terror have proliferated. Thus, communication regarding the status of refugees in Central America is muddled. Cautious analysis of sources must be included in any review of written materials concerning the volatile state of affairs. The opportunities for Christian witness among refugees are complicated by the prevailing circumstances and the traditional approach to nominal

Christianity on the part of many of the refugees. Perhaps the unsettling events will awaken a new spiritual vitality among the displaced and a new heart of active involvement among church leaders.

Unofficial estimates of the number of Salvadorans and Guatemalans in Mexico alone range from 200,000 to 250,000. Guatemala may be host to as many as 100,000 Salvadorans, and Honduras may have 34,000. The number of refugees assisted by international agencies is significantly less than the actual number of people seeking asylum. No one really knows the extent of the problem.

Officials at the UNHCR have estimated that there are 300,000 refugees scattered along the Central American isthmus, including Panama and Mexico. Most of the refugees are poverty-stricken peasants who are illiterate and have little recourse for survival. Voluntary organizations have been faced with over-whelming problems as they have attempted to provide food, clothing and shelter. A few resettlement projects have been closed entirely by military intervention and political pressure. The UNHCR has been caught in the middle of these power struggles but continues to pursue any opportunities to provide assistance. There are currently over 91 projects among refugee groups throughout the region.

The Palestinian Refugees

In May 1948, the first of several Arab-Israeli wars began. By the time it was over, more than three-quarters of a million Palestinians had become refugees living in camps in Gaza, Jordan, Lebanon and Syria. In an ironic twist of history, the establishment of the state of Israel signaled the end of the forced Jewish diaspora as thousands of Jews from around the world flocked to their new homeland, but it also began the suffering of millions of Palestinian people who became refugees from their original homeland.

193

Why did the Palestinians leave their homes and country? Israeli Jews claim they left because invading Arab armies told them to, both for propaganda and military purposes. Palestinians claim they were forced to flee for their lives, citing the Israeli massacre of the inhabitants of the village of Deir Yassin in April 1948. Whatever the cause (and both sides' claims are at least partly true), the result was panic. Whole cities, towns, and villages were emptied of their inhabitants. Most refugees felt they could return as soon as the fighting was over. Instead, when the Arab armies were defeated, the Palestinians became pawns of Middle East politics. Their lands were confiscated, and the new state of Israel would not recognize their claims to the land.

More Palestinians were displaced during and after the "Six-Day War" in 1967 when Israeli forces drove through the Gaza Strip and the West Bank of Jordan to defeat the attacking Egyptian and Jordanian armies.

In response to the desperate needs of the Palestinians, the United Nations formed the United Nations Relief and Works Agency (UNRWA). Refugee camps were organized and are still supported by this agency. In addition to giving material support, UNRWA established schools and provided medical aid to Palestinian refugees.

The refugee camps have come a long way since the early tent camps. But overcrowding is still a problem. Most camp residents live in small houses of two rooms or less, and 88% of the houses have living spaces of 250 square feet or less. UNRWA has instituted several self-help projects designed to improve sanitation facilities and water availability as well as street and sewer conditions. Thirty of the 61 camps were improved by such projects in 1981. The principle of self-help has been accepted only reluctantly by some refugees. They see it as tending to give the camps a more permanent character and compromising their right to return to their lands with appropriate compensation for their losses.

Palestinian refugees in Lebanon suffered further when Israel invaded Southern Lebanon in the spring of 1982 to clear out the Palestinian Liberation Organization (PLO) military forces. Palestinian refugee camps were shelled, thousands of civilians were killed or wounded, and the refugees were displaced once again.

Not all Palestinians are registered as refugees. There is a wide range of experience and background among the Palestinians including class, family, education and geography. Palestinians are represented in all walks of life, from laborers in Lebanon to wealthy industrialists in Amman, Jordan, from contract workers in the Persian Gulf to doctors and lawyers in the United States. Yet despite this diversity they are generally united on the issue of autonomy and self-determination for a Palestinian homeland.

Of the 3.5 million Palestinians in the world today, over 1,885,000 are registered with UNRWA as refugees. Of this number, over 664,000 are living in 61 UNRWA camps. (Several of the 13 camps in Lebanon have been totally destroyed.) Overall, about 54% of the Palestinians (including those registered as refugees) live in the Arab world. About 45% live in Israel and are citizens of that country. A little more than 1% live elsewhere, including Europe and the United States. Of the registered refugees, 38.9% live in Jordan, 35.4% live under Israeli occupation, 12.3% live in Lebanon, and 11.4% live in Syria.

Palestinian refugees value educational opportunities highly. In 1978, UNRWA reported that there were 307,000 refugee pupils in UNRWA/UNESCO schools. In addition, over 78,000 Palestinians attended government or private schools. There are approximately 70,000

Palestinian university graduates, employed as follows: 50% in education, 17% in engineering, 10% in medicine and 15% in management.

The conditions of residence, naturalization, and employment available to the Palestinians differ widely from country to country. Job and personal security have been contingent upon their nominal legal status and the cross-current of Middle Eastern politics. In Jordan, for example, the Palestinians can accept Jordanian citizenship and passports. Many have become bankers, doctors and engineers, and some even occupy government posts. Yet in September 1970, the Jordanian army attacked Palestinian refugee camps to expel the PLO headquarters and military arm from Jordan. This forced the PLO to shift its base to Lebanon. In Lebanon, Palestinians have no extraterritorial rights and are legally considered as aliens. The general political atmosphere created by the influx of thousands of guerrilla fighters and their families allowed for considerable freedom for Palestinians, in practice. However, these new arrivals also upset the sensitive political balance between Muslim and Christian factions in Lebanon. Civil war erupted in 1975, and Lebanon was divided according to spheres of influence among the various sides, including a Palestinian area in the south. The Israeli invasion in 1982 caused the expulsion of the PLO from Beirut and the destruction of the refugee camps in the south.

The Palestinians have suffered greatly in the last 35 years. The trauma of fleeing for their lives, the boredom and high unemployment rate of camp life, the fear experienced in Israeli retaliation raids and now the demoralization of the PLO defeat in Lebanon have seriously affected their psychological state. This is particularly true among refugee children (64% of the refugee population are less than 20 years of age). These children do not know what life is with a secure place called "home," and they have watched their parents struggle to attain this desire.

Nearly all Palestinians are Muslims. The level of commitment varies from nominal to radical. Less than 1% are considered practicing Christians. A major hindrance ·to their acceptance of the gospel is their belief that all Christians are supporters of Zionism and of Israel.

Refugees in Africa

Much has been printed about the suffering of millions of African refugees. There is, however, no such thing as an African refugee. There are Ugandans in Sudan, Chadians in Cameroon, Angolans in Zaire, and Butus from Burundi in Tanzania. Black South African students live in Lesotho, and Eritreans live in Sudan. But each group merits careful consideration as a unique entity. Some similarities exist when one looks at the millions of Muslim refugees from Ethiopia in Somalia, but when considering rural farmers who escape to neighboring countries, one ask more than what their occupations have been.

The intertribal warfare which has compelled thousands of individuals to escape to nearby enclaves of families and friends has been going on for decades. Refugees are designated as such only when national boundaries are involved, and many of these were drawn as arbitrary designations by colonial politicians where land was taken by various powers irrespective of existing ethnic, cultural or social designations. It is not difficult to understand why refugees flee to nearby countries where individuals of like mind, culture and tradition reside. These refugees can resettle quickly with few visible consequences. Statisticians often lose track of social groupings when they are attempting to follow the movements of masses into various countries. Such is the case when researchers simply describe the origins of refugees and the countries in which they resettle. It is easy to state that there are 400,000 refugees from Uganda, Ethiopia and Chad in Sudan, but much more difficult to describe the distinctives of each group which set them apart. Yet it is crucial to get down to these specifics.

Thousands of urban Chadians from the city of N'Djamena who settle in rural villages in Cameroon have extremely different needs and challenges than do rural agriculturalists from Equatorial Guinea who also settle in Cameroon. Thus, it is futile to describe only the country of origin and the country of resettlement. Concerned individuals must make every effort to discover the various needs, desires and difficulties of each group of African refugees. Broad generalities can be beneficial as a starting point for individuals who want to learn about refugees. Only when specific traditions and social patterns are described, however, can one really begin to develop strategies for reaching members of each unique group. One is compelled to move beyond the generalities and learn to hunt for the specific qualities and characteristics that distinguish a people group.

The African scenario provides unprecedented opportunities to discover new means by which to exhort the local church to confront the needs of refugees. Most African refugees will never leave Africa. If possible, they will live in and among villages where language can be understood and where subsistence level farming can proliferate. This is not the case for Indochinese refugees or Palestinian refugees.

The entire plan for assisting refugees in Africa must be quite different from programs designed for Afghans in Pakistan, Indochinese in diaspora or Palestinians in the Middle East. There are actually more refugees in Africa than anywhere else in the world. This must be diagnosed with separate analytic criteria and each situation reviewed to determine appropriate action. Once again one comes full circle to the need to distinguish a people group to elaborate a strategy of ministry.

The following expanded descriptions are a beginning. They represent an initial effort to describe a few of the many groups of refugees among us.

Introduction to Expanded Descriptions

The following section contains descriptions of 41 refugee people groups in alphabetical order. Each group has a data table printed above the written description, containing information based on questionnaires completed by persons in the same country or otherwise knowledgeable about the people group. (Please see Appendix A for a sample of this questionnaire.)

In the data table, the most common name of the people group is given first, followed by the name of the country in which the group is located. Stars in front of the name indicate receptivity to the gospel: ******* = very receptive, ****** = receptive, and ***** = indifferent.

The following is a summary of the remaining data categories:

Alternate Names: Any alternate names or spellings for the people group.

Size of Group: Latest population estimate of the group.

MARC ID: An identification number by which information on the group is filed.

Any correspondence sent to MARC dealing with a group, sending corrections, updates, additions or requests for further information, should refer to that number.

Distinctives: Distinctive features that unify this group. Many different things may make a group distinct or cause them to consider themselves a people. Often several factors give them some kind of affinity toward one another or make them different from other groups. Respondents to the unreached peoples questionnaire were asked to indicate the relative importance of various factors in making the group distinctive. Those factors were speaking the same language, common political loyalty, similar occupation, racial or ethnic similarity, shared religious customs, common kinship ties, strong sense of unity, similar education level, common residential area, similar social class or caste, similar economic status, shared hobby or special interest, discrimination from other groups, unique health situation, distinctive legal status, similar age, common significant problems, and "other(s)."

Social Change: This represents an estimate of the overall rate at which culture and social change is taking place in the group--very rapid, rapid, moderate, slow or very slow.

Languages: Primary languages. Multilingual

communities often use different languages in different situations. They may learn one language in school, another in the market, and yet another in religious ceremonies. Respondents were asked to indicate the major languages used by the group as well as the place or function of each language. These functions are indicated by the following codes:

V - vernacular or common language
T - trade language or lingua franca
S - language used for instruction in schools
W- language used for any current or past Christian witness
G - language most suitable for presentation of the gospel
P - language used in any non-Christian ceremonies

The percentages listed next to the headings **speak** and **read** indicate the percentage of the total group that speak and read the language listed.

Scripture: Indicates the availability of various forms of biblical literature in the main language of the group.

Recordings: Indicates the availability of recordings, records or cassettes in the main language of the group. Recordings can include Bible readings, Bible stories with gospel applications, culturally adapted gospel messages, or basic Christian teaching, as well as music.

(Detailed information on recordings in specific languages can be obtained from Gospel Recordings U.S.A., 122 Glendale Boulevard, Los Angeles, California 90026, U.S.A.)

Christian Literacy: This indicates the percentage of Christians among the people (if any) over 15 years of age who can and do read in any language.

Religion: This indicates the primary religion(s) found among members of the group. The percentage shown next to **adherents** estimates the percentage of the group who would say that they follow the religion listed. The percentage next to **practicing** indicates the number who actively practice the religion listed (in the opinion of the researcher or reporter). Determining the percentage of those adhering to a certain religion versus the percentage of those practicing their faith is admittedly a subjective judgment. This figure is important, however, when considering Christian populations, because the definition of **unreached** used here depends on a measure of the church's strength, which must be drawn basically from its size and growth rate.

Churches and Missions: This indicates the primary Christian churches or missions, national or foreign, that are active in the area where the people group is concentrated. The figure under **membership** is the approximate number of full members of this church or mission denomination from the people group. The figure under **community** is the approximate number of adherents (including children) to the denomination or mission from the people group. These are not **all** the churches and missions among this group, only the ones that have been reported.

Openness to Religious Change: This is an estimate of how open the group is to religious change of any kind. Categories are very open, somewhat open, indifferent, somewhat closed and very closed.

Receptivity to Christianity: This is an estimate of the openness of the group to Christianity in particular. Categories are very receptive, receptive, indifferent, reluctant and very reluctant.

Evangelism Profile: People tend to come to Christ in more or less well-defined steps. This scale (based on a scale developed by Dr. James Engel of the Wheaton Graduate School) indicates the approximate percentage of the group at various levels of awareness of the gospel. The scale ranges from people with no awareness of Christianity to those who are active propagators of the gospel. A further explanation of this useful tool may be found in Edward Dayton's article "To Reach the Unreached" in **Unreached Peoples '79.**

Not Reported (nr): Whenever this appears in any category, it indicates that the information has not yet been received by the MARC computers. In future volumes of this series, information will be added as it becomes available.

Validity Code: An estimate of the accuracy and completeness of the data on a scale from one to nine. The code is:

1. The only information available at this point is the group name, country, language, population and primary religion. The percentage listed under practicing Christians is at best a rough estimate.

2. There has been more data collected than the "baseline" information in 1, but it is scanty or of poor quality.

3. About half of the information on the unreached peoples questionnaire (Appendix A) has been collected, and information on the Christian community, if any, is missing or probably inaccurate.

4. Almost all the data on the unreached peoples questionnaire has been collected, **or** the source document has supplied most of the necessary information.

5. Information has been supplied by a completed unreached peoples questionnaire **and** at least one other document.

6. In addition to 5, there is enough detailed information about the people group to write an accurate, up-to-date description.

7. There exists an extensive description of the people group in secular or Christian literature.

8. There has been a major research study (thesis or dissertation quality) done on the group which includes detailed information on the Christian community.

9. In addition to 8, the study includes a thorough exploration of evangelism strategy for the particular group, based on first-hand experience.

Following the data table with the basic information about the people group are several paragraphs further detailing the characteristics of the group.

A complete listing of all unreached people groups currently identified in the MARC files can be found in **Part 4.** For many of these groups there is more information available. To obtain the data on a particular group, just send in the reply page located in the back of this book.

Index of People Groups
With Expanded Descriptions

EXPANDED DESCRIPTIONS

Ansar Sudanese Refugees (Ethiopia)

ALTERNATE NAMES: not reported

SIZE OF GROUP: 11,000   **MARC ID:** 9010

DISTINCTIVES: ethnicity; residence; religion

SOCIAL CHANGE: very rapid

LANGUAGES: Arabic (51% speak; V)

SCRIPTURE: New Testament; **RECORDINGS:** yes

CHRISTIAN LITERACY: 12%

RELIGION: Islam; Christianity (-1% practicing)

CHURCHES AND MISSIONS	BEGAN	MEMBERSHIP	COMMUNITY
World Council of Churches	nr	nr	nr

OPENNESS TO RELIGIOUS CHANGE: not reported

RECEPTIVITY TO CHRISTIANITY: not reported

GROWTH RATE OF CHRISTIAN COMMUNITY: not reported

EVANGELISM PROFILE: not reported   **VALIDITY:** 4

Political upheaval and attempted coups by reactionary groups in Southern Sudan caused refugees to leave their settlements in 1975, 1976 and 1978. The numbers were significantly lower than previous waves of refugees and seemed to be related ethnically. Many of the refugees, approximately 11,000, were from the Ansar tribal group. They settled in two specific regions of Ethiopia where repatriation could be easily accomplished.

The refugees who were permitted to settle in Ethiopia became involved in a large agricultural development project which has been cooperatively operated by the European Economic Community, the World Food Program, and the Ethiopian government. A six-month training course was established for both refugees and nationals so that they could qualify for employment within the project.

Few missionaries or Christian relief workers have been involved in the project, and little is known about the status of Christianity among the Ansars in Ethiopia. They are believed to be Muslims who reacted to the liberalization of self-government by non-Muslims in Southern Sudan. They found solace and companionship among neighbors in Ethiopia who share common principles from the Koran. As in so many parts of Northern Africa, the confrontation between Islam and Christianity is intensifying, and the cost of discipleship has become a viable part of reality. Many Ansars despise the Christians and inflict severe reprisals upon Muslims who become Christians.

EXPANDED DESCRIPTIONS

Bakongo Angolan Refugees (Zaire)

ALTERNATE NAMES: Cabindan Refugees

SIZE OF GROUP: 600,000   **MARC ID:** 9026

DISTINCTIVES: discrimination; ethnicity; social class; residence

SOCIAL CHANGE: not reported

LANGUAGES: Kikongo (V); Portuguese (T)

SCRIPTURE: Bible; **RECORDINGS:** yes   **CHRISTIAN LITERACY:** nr

RELIGION: Animism (50% adherents); Christo-Paganism (49% adherents)

CHURCHES AND MISSIONS	BEGAN	MEMBERSHIP	COMMUNITY
Church of Christ	nr	nr	nr
Christian & Msny Alliance	nr	nr	nr

OPENNESS TO RELIGIOUS CHANGE: not reported

RECEPTIVITY TO CHRISTIANITY: not reported

GROWTH RATE OF CHRISTIAN COMMUNITY: not reported

EVANGELISM PROFILE: not reported   **VALIDITY:** 4

Angolans from Cabinda have settled in Zaire and are primarily from the Kikongo-speaking tribes of the Bakongo group. They are descendants of members of the kingdom of the Kongo who settled in the northwestern territories of Zaire as well as in the contemporary cities of Kinshasa and Cabinda. Thus, similarities in cultural traditions and language patterns are evident throughout the region. It has been possible for hundreds of Cabindans to settle among family or distant relatives in Zaire and preserve many aspects of their contemporary life-styles. Refugee families from Cabinda have been given a piece of land where they can plant both food and cash crops. Thousands of fruit trees were planted so that the settlers could supplement their diet and sell the surplus. Some individuals began selling agricultural products a short time after the new program was initiated. Cooperatives were formed to facilitate the marketing of agricultural produce and purchase of contemporary equipment. Merchants set up shop for basic items of necessity.

All programs were slow in developing due to a severe drought which rendered the land virtually worthless for two years. The refugees depended on charitable contributions of food from voluntary organizations. Thus, despite initial rehabilitation programs, there were needs for emergency relief. Refugees are now being trained as agriculturalists, and new vocational training programs allow self-sufficiency to be realized through the education of blacksmiths, carpenters, and small animal husbandry managers. A total of 12 villages were set up by October 1981. Public institutions such as clinics and dispensaries are open to rural Zaireans, so development among the refugees serves a dual role. By the time the settlements are self-sufficient they will constitute an important element in the rural development of Bas-Zaire. Initial efforts to assist a large number of Cabindan refugees in Zaire were assumed by personnel of the Christian and Missionary Alliance.

Funds were sent to establish supplementary feeding centers, school programs, and a library. Financial resources were exhausted at the same time that the government decided to move the refugees to more permanent settlements in rural village areas. C&MA developed a new strategy for evangelistic outreach with tent ministries, libraries, schools, and seed programs. The UNHCR became the chief administrative and financial resource for the refugee settlements.

Burmese Muslim Refugees (Bangladesh)

ALTERNATE NAMES: Rohingya Refugees

SIZE OF GROUP: 200,000   **MARC ID:** 9001

DISTINCTIVES: religion; language; discrimination

SOCIAL CHANGE: very rapid

LANGUAGES: Bengali (V)

SCRIPTURE: portions; **RECORDINGS:** yes **CHRISTIAN LITERACY:** 22%

RELIGION: Islam

CHURCHES AND MISSIONS: not reported

OPENNESS TO RELIGIOUS CHANGE: not reported

RECEPTIVITY TO CHRISTIANITY: not reported

GROWTH RATE OF CHRISTIAN COMMUNITY: not reported

EVANGELISM PROFILE: not reported   **VALIDITY:** 3

The continuing antipathy between the Burmese Buddhist majority and the Muslim minority of the western Arakan Hills region bordering Bangladesh flared into the open early in 1978. An estimated 200,000 Burmese Muslims fled Burma and encamped in the Chittagong region of eastern Bangladesh. The ostensible reason for this rapid exodus of the **Rohingya** (native born) was persecution by Burmese officials during a census check of the region euphemistically called "Operation Dragon King." The Burmese government countercharged, with some validity, that the more prosperous Arakan region had been entered by citizens of poorer Bangladesh's eastern provinces over the years. The Rohingya actually owe allegiance to both sides of the border. For generations, if not centuries, some have lived in Burma as Muslims. But religiously, linguistically and ethnically, they are allied with their Muslim neighbors in Bangladesh.

The presence of so many refugees in economically destitute Bangladesh sparked an immediate international crisis. Several squalid camps were established along the border, while other ad hoc settlements simply appeared. Basic necessities were in short supply, and even water was severely rationed. Tempers flared in both Rangoon and Dacca, and appeal was made to the United Nations for resolution of the problem. Under the U.N. High Commissioner for Refugees, the governments began talks aimed at resolving the problem. After considerable international pressure on Burma, a plan for repatriation was concluded in July, and nearly 100,000 refugees were repatriated by year's end. It was unclear, however, what future awaited several thousand Rohingya who could not verify their registration as former residents of Burma. Still, all this did little for those who claimed that their homes and possessions were destroyed or confiscated and relatives lost during the Burmese initiative.

Subsequently, during 1980, Rangoon proposed a citizenship law establishing two classes of citizens: indigenous and naturalized Burmese. Under the proposed law, the indigenous were narrowly defined, stirring fears among the Rohingya and other Burmese minorities that the events of 1978 might recur. The law was expected to result in severe social, economic and political disadvantages for those classed as naturalized citizens, further perpetuating the ethnic and religious distinctions in Burmese society.

EXPANDED DESCRIPTIONS

Burundian Hutu Refugees (Tanzania)

ALTERNATE NAMES: not reported
SIZE OF GROUP: 40,000   MARC ID: 9006
DISTINCTIVES: hobby or interest; ethnicity
SOCIAL CHANGE: moderate
LANGUAGES: Kirundi (100% speak; V)
SCRIPTURE: Bible; RECORDINGS: yes   CHRISTIAN LITERACY: 10%
RELIGION: Animism; Christianity (-1% practicing)

CHURCHES AND MISSIONS	BEGAN	MEMBERSHIP	COMMUNITY
Christian Refugee Service	nr	nr	nr

OPENNESS TO RELIGIOUS CHANGE: not reported
RECEPTIVITY TO CHRISTIANITY: not reported
GROWTH RATE OF CHRISTIAN COMMUNITY: not reported
EVANGELISM PROFILE: not reported   VALIDITY: 4

In Burundi, the Tutsi represent 14 percent of the total population. They have maintained control over the political, economic and social structures in Burundi for decades. The Hutu have been regarded as lower-class citizens and treated as subordinates. Following independence in 1962, the active involvement of Hutu in positions of official responsibility steadily declined. Discrimination against Hutu increased when rumors of a coup circulated in 1969. Fabricated stories of treachery instilled fear within the people, and purges in the government significantly reduced the participation of Hutu. Militant Hutus reacted by forming rebel factions which murdered and mutilated thousands of Tutsi citizens and soldiers. Counterattacks by government forces led by well-organized Tutsi wrought unprecedented havoc on Hutu settlements.

Indiscriminate violence resulted in the destruction of 80,000 educated Hutu, including thousands of Protestant pastors, school directors and teachers, as well as numerous Catholic priests. Thousands of poor, uneducated and terrified Hutu farmers poured across the borders of Burundi into Tanzania, where they settled among fellow Hutu in rural areas where they could maintain traditional life-styles without major changes. One missionary described the course of events as double genocide since the slaughter of 80,000 Hutu was in retaliation for the murders of 1500 Tutsi. The intent of the Tutsi was clear: they wanted to purge the Hutu of their employed and educated persons and leave a leaderless serfdom. Most Hutu did not stay in Burundi, but rather fled to Hutu villages in neighboring countries where they settled among family and friends. The nearly 40,000 refugees were indignant about the atrocities, and numerous guerrilla factions have arisen which now function as vigilante groups, striking back against Tutsi military personnel and civilians. Bitterness, hatred and vengeance remain prevailing attitudes among many refugees. The political and sociological factors remain complex, and most nations have attempted to stay clear of the battles between warring tribal groups.

Few organizations or individuals have sought to work among the refugees. In Tanzania, the Christian Refugee Service administers the entire program, facing numerous challenges with skill and realistic action. The churches are caught in the middle since many members have found themselves victims of circumstances. The complicated task of the church remains evident within Burundi among the Tutsi, and also among the Hutu of Tanzania.

214

Chadian Refugees (Nigeria)

ALTERNATE NAMES: not reported

SIZE OF GROUP: 3,000   **MARC ID:** 9043

DISTINCTIVES: legal status; residence; economic status

SOCIAL CHANGE: very rapid

LANGUAGES: Sara (V); Arabic (V, T); French (T)

SCRIPTURE: portions; **RECORDINGS:** yes **CHRISTIAN LITERACY:** 15%

RELIGION: Islam; Animism; Christianity (-1% practicing)

CHURCHES AND MISSIONS	BEGAN	MEMBERSHIP	COMMUNITY
Mennonite Church	nr	nr	nr
Maiduguri Church	nr	nr	nr

OPENNESS TO RELIGIOUS CHANGE: not reported

RECEPTIVITY TO CHRISTIANITY: not reported

GROWTH RATE OF CHRISTIAN COMMUNITY: not reported

EVANGELISM PROFILE: not reported   **VALIDITY:** 4

Civil warfare since 1979 has forced thousands of Chadians to become refugees. At one time during the fighting, over three- quarters of the population of the capital city, N'Djamena, had fled. While most refugees found sanctuary in neighboring Cameroon, some found their way to Nigeria. A camp was set up for them at Maiduguri. The UNHCR and the Nigerian government set about to meet the refugees' immediate needs for food, shelter and medical help. There was a small group of Christians among the refugees (about 30). At first they were afraid to make themselves known but with encouragement from local Christian students, they came together and formed a church. The students themselves bought materials and built a small church for the Christian refugees. The students helped them in leading services, but eventually one of the refugees took over as leader.

In addition to this help from students, a local Maiduguri church and the Mennonite Central Committee sought to aid the refugees. Christians brought clothes, food and cash for them. This aid was distributed through the new church.

Ministries to the refugees also included assistance to those refugees wishing to return to Chad, and teaching the local languages so the refugees could obtain job training and eventual employment. Local Christians were encouraged to teach Chadian Christians their job skills. Most of this ministry directly benefited the Chadian Christians, but they were encouraged to share these benefits with their neighbors.

Chadian Refugees from N'Djamena (Cameroon)

ALTERNATE NAMES: Chadian Refugees

SIZE OF GROUP: 100,000   **MARC ID:** 9005

DISTINCTIVES: significant problems; residence

SOCIAL CHANGE: very rapid

LANGUAGES: French (T); Arabic (T); Tribal Languages (V)

SCRIPTURE: not reported   **CHRISTIAN LITERACY:** 15%

RELIGION: Islam (52% adherents); Animism (47% adherents); Christianity (-1% practicing)

CHURCHES AND MISSIONS	BEGAN	MEMBERSHIP	COMMUNITY
Roman Catholic Church	nr	nr	nr

OPENNESS TO RELIGIOUS CHANGE: not reported

RECEPTIVITY TO CHRISTIANITY: not reported

GROWTH RATE OF CHRISTIAN COMMUNITY: not reported

EVANGELISM PROFILE: not reported   **VALIDITY:** 4

One-third of the entire population of the city of N'Djamena, in Chad, resettled in the village of Kousseri, Cameroon. Until 1980 there were only 12,000 residents in Kousseri which is 200 kilometers across the river from the bustling city of N'Djamena. As a result of military action in Chad, 100,000 from all walks of life fled N'Djamena to Kousseri. The government of Cameroon responded quickly with emergency supplies, including medicine, water, and food. Chadians settled into what they thought would be a brief time. The UNHCR began providing assistance when resources of Cameroon dwindled. Poorer refugees, who had no family or connections, settled in a rough straw and canvas shelter in open camps. The refugees have essentially run the camps themselves since they are used to the climate and the environment, as well as the fact that they know many of the neighbors. A school for the 4000 primary students was established, as well as a hospital. Life is hard out in the open where mud oozes in the wet season and turns to swirling dust in the dry season.

By October of 1981, the limbo of exile was terminated for more than 50,000 refugees who chose to repatriate. Life in N'Djamena has been as bad as in the camps, since the city and the infrastructure are no more. The emotional strength gained by being "home" has been enough to empower many of them to start over. Cooperatives have been formed for reconstruction of homes, businesses, mosques, cathedrals, and schools.

Many refugees did not want to return to N'Djamena since everything they had built had been destroyed. Many of them had been discouraged by failures in previous repatriation efforts. They had returned to N'Djamena but had found that the circumstances had not changed. They had been forced to flee for their lives time after time. They did not trust the situation in Chad and thus opted for a new life elsewhere. More than 50,000 refugees have stayed on in Cameroon. Hundreds of refugees from Kousseri have chosen to resettle in a new area of Chad which was set aside specifically for them.

Cham Refugees from Kampuchea (Malaysia)

ALTERNATE NAMES: Muslims from Kampuchea

SIZE OF GROUP: 1800   **MARC ID:** 91

DISTINCTIVES: language; ethnicity; residence; religion

SOCIAL CHANGE: not reported

LANGUAGES: Cham (100% speak; V); Khmer (75% speak/35% read; T); Vietnamese (10% speak)

SCRIPTURE: not reported   **CHRISTIAN LITERACY:** nr

RELIGION: Islam

CHURCHES AND MISSIONS	BEGAN	MEMBERSHIP	COMMUNITY
Khmer Evangelical Church	1924	nr	nr
Roman Catholic Church	1800	nr	nr

OPENNESS TO RELIGIOUS CHANGE: somewhat closed

RECEPTIVITY TO CHRISTIANITY: indifferent

GROWTH RATE OF CHRISTIAN COMMUNITY: not reported

EVANGELISM PROFILE: not reported   **VALIDITY:** 4

Unreached people groups do not remain static. This is well illustrated by the significant decline in the population of the Cham in Kampuchea. Whereas the expanded description of the Cham in **Unreached Peoples '80** indicated that there were 90,000 Cham in Kampuchea, the number has now declined to perhaps several thousand. This indicates the urgency of reaching specific groups before it is too late. In the case of the Cham, they were assaulted and murdered by the forces of Pol Pot. Thousands escaped to the forest but they were pursued and killed. The Cham were singled out as a specific minority group subject to annihilation because they practiced Islam. They have been compared to the Jews of Germany because they had such different cultural patterns, a distinct language and a separate religion from the mainstream of society. The few Cham who successfully concealed their identities often died from disease or starvation. Comparatively few escaped from Kampuchea. Documentation is sparse but that which is available is of interest to Christians. The government of Malaysia was willing to accept 1800 for resettlement from Thai refugee camps because they were Muslims. These refugees may never again hear the message of the gospel. Again, that is, if indeed they were evangelized while staying at the camps in Thailand.

The Western Cham were traditionally Sunni Muslims of the Shafi school. Whereas the Cham of Vietnam gradually lost many of their traditions which were related to Islamic teachings, the larger group of the Western Cham in Kampuchea retained most links with Islam. There were a few major developments in Kampuchea since matrilineal clans were prevalent and ancestor worship was held in high regard. The status of women was significantly higher than in most other Muslim groups and an animistic network of concepts and beliefs was incorporated into popular Islamic traditions.

The opportunity for Christians to reach the Cham has been greatly diminished. These solemn events can serve to remind us of the temporal nature of ministries to refugees, and the urgency of identifying specific groups which need to be reached.

EXPANDED DESCRIPTIONS

Chilean Refugees in Toronto (Canada)

ALTERNATE NAMES: not reported

SIZE OF GROUP: 10,000   MARC ID: 9023

DISTINCTIVES: not reported

SOCIAL CHANGE: very rapid

LANGUAGES: Spanish (100% speak/90% read; V); English (T)

SCRIPTURE: Bible; RECORDINGS: yes   CHRISTIAN LITERACY: 90%

RELIGION: Roman Catholic

CHURCHES AND MISSIONS: not reported

OPENNESS TO RELIGIOUS CHANGE: not reported

RECEPTIVITY TO CHRISTIANITY: indifferent

GROWTH RATE OF CHRISTIAN COMMUNITY: not reported

EVANGELISM PROFILE: not reported   VALIDITY: 4

Since the military coup in Chile in 1973 approximately 1,000,000 Chileans have left their country. Emigration to Canada has been estimated at 10,000 with the majority opting to live in Canadian urban centers--Montreal, Vancouver and Toronto. Some of Canada's western cities have more recently received Chileans. Canadian immigration law was relaxed to allow Chileans to enter the country as refugees though not all Chileans entering technically fit that description.

In metropolitan Toronto, the Chilean community has manifested the highest degree of community organization. This is thought to be due to the fact that they are nearly all professionals with experience in community organization. The circumstances of their migration under duress also contributes to their strong sense of community and local organization.

There is a relatively high level of stress evident among Chileans in Canada resulting from the great personal loss they feel. Uncertainty concerning their future, anxiety about loved ones still in Chile, and longing for return to their homeland dominate their thinking. The Chilean community is divided between those who hope for a rapid change in the political climate back home which will allow them to return and others who have responded fatalistically to their situation and have sought Canadian citizenship early in an attempt to moderate their lives as quickly as posssible.

Canada is welcoming Chileans with the expectation that they will contribute significantly to the development of the country. The multicultural society which is Canada may prove to be an ideal location for Chilean refugees to reconstruct their lives.

Dukwe Refugee Camp Residents (Botswana)

ALTERNATE NAMES: not reported

SIZE OF GROUP: 800   **MARC ID:** 9022

DISTINCTIVES: significant problems; residence; economic status; legal status

SOCIAL CHANGE: not reported

LANGUAGES: Tribal Languages (V); English (T)

SCRIPTURE: not reported   **CHRISTIAN LITERACY:** nr

RELIGION: Animism (80% adherents); Christianity (20% adherents)

CHURCHES AND MISSIONS	BEGAN	MEMBERSHIP	COMMUNITY
Lutheran World Federation	nr	nr	nr

OPENNESS TO RELIGIOUS CHANGE: not reported

RECEPTIVITY TO CHRISTIANITY: not reported

GROWTH RATE OF CHRISTIAN COMMUNITY: not reported

EVANGELISM PROFILE: not reported   **VALIDITY:** 4

The nature of the group of individuals residing at the Dukwe refugee camp in Botswana is significantly different than that of other refugee groups in Africa. Though these individuals show little common ethnic background, they became a group as refugees when they arrived in Dukwe camp. Though they are a temporary group, this is part of their social reality and causes them to form common bonds in response to shared desperation. Namibians, Zimbabweans and South Africans who have left their countries of origin for a number of reasons have little to bind them together as a group other than their present socioeconomic status. They are all unemployed, have few opportunities to be employed in the future and are not actively involved in educational or vocational training programs.

These 800 refugees have found it extremely difficult to fit in the mainstream of society, and prospects for the future are grim. The Dukwe camp offers the refugees an opportunity to face their dilemma objectively and adjust to the prevailing circumstances. For the first time in their lives they are offered a chance to begin basic vocational training and develop marketable skills.

Accommodations at Dukwe camp have improved considerably in recent months as stick huts with plastic coverings have been replaced by concrete cinder block flats. Development projects have proven beneficial as indicated by the availability of water which is now drawn from wells driven by windmill pumps. Several voluntary organizations, including the Botswana Council for refugees and Lutheran World Federation, have provided most of the basic services and necessities required by the refugees. Free education is available to all children under the Botswana refugee care program, and thus at least the young people will have opportunities to pursue a career and choose the life-styles they would like to live.

EXPANDED DESCRIPTIONS

Eritrean Refugees (Djibouti)

ALTERNATE NAMES: not reported

SIZE OF GROUP: 25,000   **MARC ID:** 9018

DISTINCTIVES: legal status; economic status; residence

SOCIAL CHANGE: slow

LANGUAGES: Somali (V); English (T)

SCRIPTURE: Bible; **RECORDINGS:** yes   **CHRISTIAN LITERACY:** 7%

RELIGION: Islam; Christianity (-1% practicing)

CHURCHES AND MISSIONS: not reported

OPENNESS TO RELIGIOUS CHANGE: somewhat open

RECEPTIVITY TO CHRISTIANITY: receptive

GROWTH RATE OF CHRISTIAN COMMUNITY: not reported

EVANGELISM PROFILE: not reported   **VALIDITY:** 4

Crowning the northeastern tip of the Horn of Africa lies Djibouti--a country in the midst of sharp contrasts, yet sharing the Islamic faith and the nomadic life-style of the camel herders with its neighbors Somalia and Ethiopia. It is the home of approximately 25,000 Eritreans from Northern Ethiopia.

As pastoral goat and camel herders, the Eritreans escaped to Djibouti with few possessions. They packed their portable houses, which are made of sticks and thatch, onto their livestock, gathered a few cooking utensils, bundled their clothing and fled. The fortunate ones arrived with their belongings. Others arrived with nothing: they had either been robbed along the way or had worn out their possessions and used up their supplies. Most refugees fell into the second category--the destitute. Some also lost family members before finally arriving across the border. For those who chose to register at the camps, adjustment to the sedentary life-style was not easy. Having been used to a great deal of solitude and open living space, they were suddenly surrounded by many neighbors and many new decisions. Even the food was strange. The herders normally subsisted on the resources derived from their livestock. In the camps they received protein-fortified grains and other unfamiliar dishes. A great deal of independence has been stifled since camp residents have been confined to a few parched acres.

A few individuals were given small plots of land to produce extra vegetables. What was not consumed was sold. Many of the children of the nomads experienced formal schooling for the first time as classes were offered at the primary level. As for medical care, those refugees suffering from tuberculosis and other respiratory diseases were cared for in more permanent housing facilities.

Water is in short supply and the desert sun is fierce. Daily activity is geared solely towards survival. The monotony is infrequently broken by visits from government officials and outside relief agencies. A few of the residents who are not herders but skilled craftsmen have fared somewhat better since they are able to manufacture and distribute their wares throughout the camps and local markets.

Camp residents are vulnerable in every way. Their needs are obvious and urgent. In some respects the opportunities for Christian witness may never be more readily available to the nomads who are localized and have a lot of empty time to fill. The drastic changes they have experienced make them more susceptible to new ways of thinking. The claims of Christ, when sensitively shared, will provide hope and comfort.

Eritrean Refugees (Sudan)

ALTERNATE NAMES: not reported

SIZE OF GROUP: 150,000   **MARC ID:** 9007

DISTINCTIVES: ethnicity; social class; education

SOCIAL CHANGE: slow

LANGUAGES: Ge'ez (V); Tigrinya (V); Galla (V); English (T)

SCRIPTURE: Portions **RECORDINGS:** yes **CHRISTIAN LITERACY:** nr

RELIGION: Islam; Orthodox; Animism

CHURCHES AND MISSIONS	BEGAN	MEMBERSHIP	COMMUNITY
Faith Evangelical Mission	nr	nr	nr
Eritrean Church in Sudan	nr	nr	nr

OPENNESS TO RELIGIOUS CHANGE: not reported

RECEPTIVITY TO CHRISTIANITY: not reported

GROWTH RATE OF CHRISTIAN COMMUNITY: not reported

EVANGELISM PROFILE: not reported   **VALIDITY:** 4

The struggles of Eritreans who fled urban areas of Ethiopia and now reside in Sudan are particularly distinct. Most young, well-educated Eritreans, who had regular contact with American and European servicemen, find refugee life depressing. Young women, who had received quality educations and actively participated in the political and economic infrastructure of Eritrean society, have undergone culture shock. They are poorly regarded by conservative villagers who believe that the role of women is within the confines of domestic life, which means they do the cooking, cleaning and child rearing. Cash-earning jobs for women are virtually nonexistent. They must either accept the status quo, or wander about towns without direction or purpose.

The voice of the Eritreans is not silent, particularly where educated individuals have the opportunity to promote development within Sudanese villages. It is often difficult for the villagers to appreciate the motives and manners of the foreigners who bring so many new ideas. Changes are not rapid, but after a number of years they do become evident. As conservative traditions are modified, and as education prevails, the attitudes of the refugees and the villagers have become mutually compatible.

Despite the tendency for many refugee groups to become downtrodden, Eritrean food, clothing styles, and behavioral patterns have been widely adopted by indigenous populations who have shared songs, casual attire, and survival skills with the refugees. Thus, there is a great deal of blending of cultures and traditions. The church has many new opportunities to promote biblical options among both the Eritrean refugees and the Sudanese. Changes have become more and more common in a shorter amount of time than ever before, and the church can assure a new role in providing direction to many who are seeking answers. The rights of refugees to pursue freedom and economic self-sufficiency must be preserved. Each group is reevaluating their customs and culture with new appreciation for what they maintain as well as the contributions of others.

EXPANDED DESCRIPTIONS

Haitian Refugees (United States of America)

ALTERNATE NAMES: not reported

SIZE OF GROUP: 40,000   **MARC ID:** 9044

DISTINCTIVES: age; discrimination; legal status; residence; ethnicity

SOCIAL CHANGE: very rapid

LANGUAGES: Creole (V)

SCRIPTURE: Bible; **RECORDINGS:** yes   **CHRISTIAN LITERACY:** nr

RELIGION: Folk Religion (90% adherents); Roman Catholic (8% adherents);
       Protestant (2% adherents)

CHURCHES AND MISSIONS: not reported

OPENNESS TO RELIGIOUS CHANGE: somewhat closed

RECEPTIVITY TO CHRISTIANITY: reluctant

GROWTH RATE OF CHRISTIAN COMMUNITY: not reported

EVANGELISM PROFILE: not reported   **VALIDITY:** 4

Although not legally recognized as refugees, more than 50,000 Haitians have sought asylum in the United States since 1970. They left the poorest country in the Western hemisphere and sought respite from the political and economic suppression of the current social system. Endless debate continues on their status within the United States. Numerous voluntary organizations have sought to minister among them.

Haitians fear not only the politicians but the spirits of this world. Vodun is their primary system of belief, and the rampant forces of Satan significantly hinder their well-being. Christians in the United States have not been exempt from prejudice and discrimination against Haitians. The racial question is a volatile one. Haitian refugees are black, they speak French Creole, many are uneducated, unskilled, and tend to portray behavior patterns different from most macro-and sub-cultural groups within the United States.

Detention centers have been established to house the Haitians, whom no one knew what to do with. The individuals detained were primarily males between 18 and 29 years of age who had few marketable skills in an era of high unemployment. Depression is common since boredom prevails, and uncertainty of the future stirs anxiety and anger. The Haitians in detention camps have not been particulary enthusiastic about learning English, a language they may never need to use, nor are they aware of the efforts to free them from captivity. It seems ironic that politicians in the United States will be the ones who determine the fate of the Haitians who escaped the politics and subsequent poverty so prevalent in Haiti.

Hmong Refugees (United States of America)

ALTERNATE NAMES: Meo Refugees; Miao Refugees

SIZE OF GROUP: 35,000   **MARC ID:** 9055

DISTINCTIVES: ethnicity; language; residence; religion

SOCIAL CHANGE: very rapid

LANGUAGES: Miao (V); English (T)

SCRIPTURE: Bible; **RECORDINGS:** yes   **CHRISTIAN LITERACY:** 1%

RELIGION: Buddhist-Animist; Christianity (-1% practicing)

CHURCHES AND MISSIONS	BEGAN	MEMBERSHIP	COMMUNITY
Lutheran Immig. & Refugee Svc.	nr	nr	nr

OPENNESS TO RELIGIOUS CHANGE: very open

RECEPTIVITY TO CHRISTIANITY: very receptive

GROWTH RATE OF CHRISTIAN COMMUNITY: not reported

EVANGELISM PROFILE: not reported   **VALIDITY:** 4

While the plight of all refugees is the sad story of dislocation and loss, that of the Hmong people of the highlands of Laos is particularly morose. These unfortunate people, through the outcome of a war not of their own making, have suffered greatly since the formal cessation of hostilities in Southeast Asia and have been forced to flee their ancestral homelands high in the mountains of Laos. Recruited by the CIA to perform guerilla operations against the Pathet Lao during the 1950s, they later became involved in similar operations against the army of North Vietnam. They continued their guerilla warfare following the collapse of the pro-U.S. governments in Laos and South Vietnam in 1975. In retaliation, the communist governments of Southeast Asia have systematically hunted and attacked the entire Hmong population. The Hmong, or Miao as they are also known, are closely related to the Chinese. They have long enjoyed the freedom of their mountain fortress and have a highly developed sense of their own culture and uniqueness. They are a proud, hard-working, resilient people who struggle with innovation and culture change.

The Hmong who have found refuge in the United States have had difficulty adjusting to their new environment. Strong group identification in large communities in the cities of Minneapolis/St.Paul; Missoula, Montana; Santa Ana, California; Providence, Rhode Island; and Denver have kept them from total despair. New arrivals in these communities from other locations in the United States testify to the benefit of experiencing the shock of American culture in community rather than in isolation.

The Hmong have shown a willingness to learn and adapt to their new environment and show every sign of being able to make the transition to American life. Education and facility in English, as for most refugee groups in the United States, are seen as critical skills necessary for survival and integration into the American labor force. While the younger Hmong are able to acquire these skills, much concern is voiced for the older people who suffer most from lack of a sense of purpose and meaning in the United States.

Usually the second year in the United States is the time when depression and frustration emerge. Ministry to the Hmong should ideally include elements to help them adjust and learn English as a basis for their future lives here. In this way the opportunity to present the gospel of Christ may be earned. Commitment to assisting the Hmong adjust to their new setting is an indispensable ingredient in spiritual ministry to these people.

Hmong Refugee Women in Ban Vinai (Thailand)

ALTERNATE NAMES: not reported

SIZE OF GROUP: 12,000   **MARC ID:** 9003

DISTINCTIVES: discrimination; legal status

SOCIAL CHANGE: very rapid

LANGUAGES: Miao (V)

SCRIPTURE: Bible; **RECORDINGS:** yes   **CHRISTIAN LITERACY:** 1%

RELIGION: Buddhist-Animist

CHURCHES AND MISSIONS	BEGAN	MEMBERSHIP	COMMUNITY
Christian & Msny Alliance	nr	nr	nr
World Vision International	1976	nr	nr

OPENNESS TO RELIGIOUS CHANGE: very open

RECEPTIVITY TO CHRISTIANITY: very receptive

GROWTH RATE OF CHRISTIAN COMMUNITY: not reported

EVANGELISM PROFILE: not reported   **VALIDITY:** 4

The Ban Vinai refugee camp in Thailand is populated by about 36,000 Hmong hill people from Laos. Women, the largest single group of camp residents, are particularly vulnerable to the constant threats of material, psychological, and physical insecurity. Cultural limitations on female assertiveness keep most Hmong women from complaining or asking for help. Men dominate the camp staff; thus, women do not feel they can disrupt the authority structure by becoming assertive about their basic human rights. General lack of access to resources further complicates life and makes it difficult for mothers providing primary care for infants and young children. High incidences of anemia, scarcity of food, limited safe water supplies and lack of space for homemaking all contribute to the Hmong women's difficulties. Intestinal illnesses and gynecological infections are hardly ever treated since Hmong women are unable within their cultural constraints to submit to examinations by male physicians.

At Ban Vinai, an estimated 2000 households are headed by women whose husbands are either dead or missing. Occasionally, a woman will become the second or even third wife of a man in order to provide for her family. This seriously jeopardizes her chances of resettlement in a third country since a man can only register one wife for resettlement.

In addition young, single women fear that their potential role of wife and mother will go unfulfilled, leaving them outcast and lacking in esteem. Other women are sexually abused or beaten by men. All these pressures conspire to cause a high incidence of attempted suicide among women in the camps. It is agreed that the women are not actually trying to take their lives by overdosing on antimalarial medicine, but simply seeking to draw attention to their plight, to be noticed or heard. In a society where the woman's place is not to verbalize her feelings, most women simply sit silently crying or take the route of getting the attention they need through bringing the specter of shame to the household.

All this points out that that ministry among Hmong women must be geared to effective counseling within their cultural context. New skills, which will raise their sense of self-esteem and enable them to become income earners, must be provided in any program to reach Hmong women. Training future leadership and teaching public health and craft skills help the spread of hope among the Hmong. Special orientation is needed for Hmong women who will eventually be resettled in third countries.

224

Iranian Bahai Refugees (Pakistan)

ALTERNATE NAMES: not reported

SIZE OF GROUP: 5,000   MARC ID: 9024

DISTINCTIVES: religion; language

SOCIAL CHANGE: very rapid

LANGUAGES: Farsi (V)

SCRIPTURE: Bible; RECORDINGS: yes   CHRISTIAN LITERACY: 35%

RELIGION: Bahaism; Christianity (-1% practicing)

CHURCHES AND MISSIONS: not reported

OPENNESS TO RELIGIOUS CHANGE: somewhat open

RECEPTIVITY TO CHRISTIANITY: receptive

GROWTH RATE OF CHRISTIAN COMMUNITY: not reported

EVANGELISM PROFILE: not reported   VALIDITY: 4

The Iranian Bahai refugees in Pakistan have been largely hidden by the Afghan refugee community which is reported to be the largest refugee community in the world today. While the Afghans have created serious problems for Pakistan in terms of providing for the refugees, at least international help has been forthcoming to deal with the problem. The absence of serious diplomatic ruptures over the Afghans present in Pakistan has allowed the issue to be publicized in international circles. This is not so with the several thousand refugees from Iran now in Pakistan who have fled the mullahs' regime.

Pakistan has sought to improve relations with Iran both diplomatically and economically and thus views the presence of Iranian refugees as a potential impediment to this. Pakistani officials, for instance, do not use the term "refugee" to refer to Iranians in Pakistan. Initially, Pakistan arrested some of the Iranians since technically they are illegal entrants subject to deportation, but more recently the Iranians have simply been ignored. The United Nations High Commissioner for Refugees' office has issued identity papers to the Iranians along with a subsistence allowance of two dollars per day. The attempt to find third countries willing to receive the refugees has met with complete failure. No third country has contributed money to their need, and the U.S. in particular is not willing to become involved.

The majority of these refugees are members of the Bahai sect. They are not regarded as a religious order by the Iranian leadership and thus have been persecuted and rendered virtually stateless. Pakistani Bahais have provided some help to the Iranian Bahais. The majority of the refugees settle in Karachi. Many Iranian Bahais are educated, and some have money. Concern is expressed for these people by the U.N. since they are totally disenfranchised, lacking status, protection, asylum, and employment. Persecution and threat of death await them in their homeland, so they cannot return.

EXPANDED DESCRIPTIONS

Iraqi Kurd Refugees (Iran)

ALTERNATE NAMES: not reported

SIZE OF GROUP: 300,000   **MARC ID:** 9028

DISTINCTIVES: ethnicity; language; discrimination

SOCIAL CHANGE: very rapid

LANGUAGES: Kurmanji (V); Turkish (T); Arabic (P); Persian (S)

SCRIPTURE: New Testament; **RECORDINGS:** yes   **CHRISTIAN LITERACY:** 26%

RELIGION: Islam; Christianity (-1% practicing)

CHURCHES AND MISSIONS: not reported

OPENNESS TO RELIGIOUS CHANGE: not reported

RECEPTIVITY TO CHRISTIANITY: not reported

GROWTH RATE OF CHRISTIAN COMMUNITY: not reported

EVANGELISM PROFILE: not reported   **VALIDITY:** 4

The Kurds are a mountain people whose homeland spans territory in five countries: Iran, Iraq, Turkey, Syria and the Soviet Union. Kurds are Muslims of the Sunni variety. They speak their own language while utilizing Turkish, Persian and Arabic for religious and educational purposes.

Originally herders with a strongly independent nature, the Kurds have experienced trouble throughout their history as they have moved back and forth across national boundaries pursuing their livelihood. The Kurds of Iraq, for instance, are known to have existed since the days of Alexander the Great. The total Kurdish population is estimated at around 12,000,000 while in Iraq they number approximately 2,000,000.

In Iraq, the Kurds have traditionally enjoyed considerable freedom since the Iraqi government has not, until recently, been sufficiently powerful to subdue them. The resulting policy afforded the Kurds a limited autonomy in their region which comprised roughly one-third of Iraq's total territory. The weakness of Iraq's military capacity encouraged the Kurds to continue to press for independence, however. By 1975 the Iraqi government was able to develop a stronger, more unified military capability with which they systematically forced the Kurds back into the Iranian border region. The struggle came to a close when Iran refused to come to the aid of the Kurds and sealed their border with Iraq in order to end the emigration from that country. An estimated 300,000 Kurds had moved to Iran by this time, three-quarters of whom returned to Iraq subsequently. Initially Iraqi Kurds in Iran settled in and around Teheran, not among their kin in Kurdish Iran. Several thousand more Kurds, including women and children, filtered into Iran subsequently to be localized in camps provided by the Iranian government. From this Iranian sanctuary Kurds conducted armed forays into Iraq in small-scale guerilla units. This only worsened the situation, and Iraq proceeded to bulldoze Kurdish villages and harass the Kurds left in Iraq. Their properties confiscated, the remaining Kurds have been resettled in villages removed from the border; thus a no-man's-land has been created at the border to control movement between Iraq and Iran, and to more closely monitor Kurdish activities.

While initially rather well provided for in Iran under the Shah's rule, the Kurds have fared less well under the rule of the Ayatollah Khomeini. They are likely to continue to be harassed in Iran, since the Kurds have not given up their dream of a national homeland, and the Iranian leadership is not disposed to grant their wish.

Jewish Refugees from U.S.S.R. (Israel)

ALTERNATE NAMES: not reported

SIZE OF GROUP: 170,000   **MARC ID:** 9013

DISTINCTIVES: discrimination; religion; education; significant problems

SOCIAL CHANGE: very rapid

LANGUAGES: Russian (85% speak; V); Yiddish (15% speak; V);
          English (T); Hebrew (T)

SCRIPTURE: Bible; **RECORDINGS:** yes   **CHRISTIAN LITERACY:** 99%

RELIGION: Secularism; Judaism; Christianity (-1% practicing)

CHURCHES AND MISSIONS: not reported

OPENNESS TO RELIGIOUS CHANGE: somewhat closed

RECEPTIVITY TO CHRISTIANITY: very reluctant

GROWTH RATE OF CHRISTIAN COMMUNITY: not reported

EVANGELISM PROFILE: not reported   **VALIDITY:** 4

The 2,100,000 or more Jews in the USSR are largely an urban population. A large number are well-educated and have held responsible positions, many of them involved in the arts (music and literature). While almost all speak Russian, they identify themselves culturally as Jews, but only a minority actively practice their religion.

Anti-Semitism has plagued Jewish people in Russia since the time of the Czars. Jews were barred from certain areas and were eventually prohibited from owning arable land. Prior to the Bolshevik Revolution in 1917, they endured attacks (pogroms) against their lives and property. The Communists eventually granted equality to the Jews superficially, while legally forbidding religious instruction. The major turning point in Soviet policy toward Jews occurred after Israel's Six-Day War in 1967. Official government stance against Israel made them suspect Soviet Jews of having divided loyalties.

Since 1971, over 250,000 Jews have left the Soviet Union because of this overt government policy of anti-Zionism, with its general anti-Semitic consequences. Jews saw opportunities previously open to them as closed off, and feared an even more limited future. The number of emigres increased after 1974 to a high of 51,000 in 1979. But it dropped severely just one year later to only 21,500. In order to emigrate, a Jew must present a letter of invitation from a party abroad. Once the invitation is submitted and application is made, the applicant is often subject to harrassment, such as the loss of a job or a demotion. Thus what began as an emigration process frequently becomes, through duress, a refugee movement. Extensive paperwork and arbitrary delays are also common. Up to 70% of applications for emigration are refused.

At first, most Jews continued on to Israel, but since 1978 almost 80% of the refugees try to come to America. Some 80,000 Soviet Jews have now come to America, where nearly 43% have chosen to settle in New York City. Generally, Soviet Jews who emigrate to Israel do so out of religious or Zionist convictions, while those who go to America are usually non-religious.

Soviet Jews arriving in other countries need help in finding jobs, understanding their new country's culture and learning a new language. While living in the Soviet Union, Jews maintain extensive kinship networks with each other. Losing this support is a major strain. Finding new friends and family who can replace that support is an important part of adjustment.

227

Khmer Refugees in Ontario (Canada)

ALTERNATE NAMES: Cambodian Refugees

SIZE OF GROUP: 600   **MARC ID:** 9046

DISTINCTIVES: language; age; religion; significant problems; residence

SOCIAL CHANGE: very rapid

LANGUAGES: Khmer (V); French (T)

SCRIPTURE: Bible; **RECORDINGS:** yes   **CHRISTIAN LITERACY:** nr

RELIGION: Buddhist-Animist

CHURCHES AND MISSIONS: not reported

OPENNESS TO RELIGIOUS CHANGE: somewhat open

RECEPTIVITY TO CHRISTIANITY: receptive

GROWTH RATE OF CHRISTIAN COMMUNITY: not reported

EVANGELISM PROFILE: not reported   **VALIDITY:** 4

Since 1979, approximately 2000 Khmers (Kampucheans) have entered Canada through a sponsorship program. While the majority have been settled in Quebec ostensibly to capitalize on their acquaintance with the French language, roughly 600 have settled in Ontario. Most have sponsors in urban Ottawa and Toronto although a few are found in smaller towns.

Those arriving in Ontario bring little professional skill to the labor market. Inability to function in English is another major drawback. Khmer generally require more help in English classes than other Southeast Asians.

While most refugees in Ontario are young and hardy, they had little opportunity to advance their education in their homeland. Malnutrition, bouts with disease, and eluding their Khmer Rouge enemies meant that they survived a desperate situation in Kampuchea.

The Khmer community in Ontario is organizing primarily to deal with problems of adjustment and to keep alive Khmer culture. There is evidence, however, that there are questions about retaining their traditional Buddhist religion, particularly among the young. To date, there has been no attempt made to reestablish religious services.

Khmer in Ontario are homesick and suffer from agonizing memories of atrocities endured while still in Kampuchea. Concern for family members, small incomes, and guilt since they were fortunate enough to escape while many of their compatriots perished are all coupled with the severe culture shock they have encountered in Ontario. This has created a surreal existence which is not easily overcome. This is further intensified by the expectation most have of returning to their homeland and thus they consider their time in Canada temporary. Since they did not leave their country willingly but only under severe duress, they have not been able to make the transition in thinking that is required of those who emigrate.

Women are especially disadvantaged in that their traditional roles of treasurer, household manager, shopper, and example to the children are often denied them. Forced to stay at home to tend children, immobilized by inability to drive, and totally dependent upon husbands and children for their windows to the world through inability to use English, the Khmer women find themselves isolated and without significance in modern Canadian life.

It appears that Khmer in Ontario are a people group much in need of Christian compassion first to understand their arduous journey to their new land and then to respond with acts of love, kindness and helpfulness in a sensitive way. Help in learning English and adjusting to their strange new environment would undoubtedly be paths to significant spiritual ministry.

Khmer Refugees (Belgium)

ALTERNATE NAMES: Cambodian Refugees

SIZE OF GROUP: 2,500   **MARC ID:** 9062

DISTINCTIVES: ethnicity; language; religion

SOCIAL CHANGE: moderate

LANGUAGES: Khmer (V); French (T)

SCRIPTURE: Bible; **RECORDINGS:** yes   **CHRISTIAN LITERACY:** nr

RELIGION: Buddhism

CHURCHES AND MISSIONS: not reported

OPENNESS TO RELIGIOUS CHANGE: indifferent

RECEPTIVITY TO CHRISTIANITY: not reported

GROWTH RATE OF CHRISTIAN COMMUNITY: not reported

EVANGELISM PROFILE: not reported   **VALIDITY:** 3

The flight of Khmer refugees during the Pol Pot regime in the late 1970s has resulted in the relocation of a few thousand to Belgium. Some Khmer have chosen to settle in Belgium because of the presence of relatives already in that country. For others, Belgium was simply a third choice for country of resettlement. For the most part, discrimination against the Khmer in Belgium has been minimal. Although securing employment is difficult during the present economic slowdown, most Khmer have managed to find domestic work or jobs in the cleaning industry. Some have opened successful restaurants featuring the exotic foods of mainland Southeast Asia. The Khmer have chosen to settle in the urban centers of Belgium, and relationships between Khmer and their hosts have been established smoothly.

Some are familiar with French while others are devoting time to French language lessons or, in some cases, to the study of Flemish. The Khmer in Belgium do not manifest the behavior of a tightly-knit community such as the Turks in Belgium but have rather dispersed themselves among the host population. The possibility that spies for the Khmer Rouge are active within the refugee community has intensified this and has kept the Khmer wary of one another.

The faction of the Khmer political spectrum loyal to Prince Sihanouk (Moulinaka) is the only well-organized one in Belgium. It has perpetuated cultural events and an active association with the Belgian Cambodian Friendship Organization which has served to promote Khmer causes. Through this vehicle, aid has been given to arriving Khmer in locating housing and jobs.

Maintenance of the Buddhist religious tradition is carried on through the Theravada Buddhist Association in Brussels. Plans to contruct a Buddhist temple are under way. A Buddhist priest from France visits monthly, and various festivals and celebrations are conducted under the auspices of the Buddhist Association. During these events a sense of community has developed among the Khmer in Belgium.

While the Khmer may consider their stay in Belgium temporary, it is unlikely that many of them will soon be able to return to their native land. As they become more integrated, they will increasingly associate their future with that of their adopted country. The friendship and help of the Christian community in Belgium could go a long way toward assisting these people in this process and in providing insights into Christianity for them to consider as they make their spiritual pilgrimage.

EXPANDED DESCRIPTIONS
Khmer Refugees (Laos)

ALTERNATE NAMES: Cambodian Refugees

SIZE OF GROUP: 10,400   **MARC ID:** 9049

DISTINCTIVES: not reported

SOCIAL CHANGE: very rapid

LANGUAGES: Khmer (V)

SCRIPTURE: Bible **RECORDINGS:** yes   **CHRISTIAN LITERACY:** nr

RELIGION: Buddhist-Animist

CHURCHES AND MISSIONS: not reported

OPENNESS TO RELIGIOUS CHANGE: not reported

RECEPTIVITY TO CHRISTIANITY: not reported

GROWTH RATE OF CHRISTIAN COMMUNITY: not reported

EVANGELISM PROFILE: not reported   **VALIDITY:** 4

The Khmer holocaust which took the lives of hundreds of thousands of Kampucheans during the period 1975-1979 resulted in the flight of thousands of the survivors across borders into neighboring countries. Most attention has been focused on those who fled through the jungle to Thailand where many still wait in refugee camps for a solution to their problem. By contrast, those who fled northeast into Laos have received little attention. It is estimated that some 3800 Kampuchean refugees are located in the three districts which form the border of Kampuchea: Saysetha, Samakisay and Sanamsay.

It is not hard to imagine the problems this situation presents both for the refugees and for the indigenous people of the region who must vie for the limited food, clothing and medical resources available from government sources. Local weather conditions have been unfavorable, and this has further restricted the government's efforts to assimilate the Kampuchean refugees.

It appears that efforts to reach refugees in Laos, while severely restricted at present in view of geopolitical realities, might be most successful if tied to the notion of progress especially through the vehicle of education.

Khmer Refugees, Unaccompanied Minors (Thailand)

ALTERNATE NAMES: Unaccompanied Cambodian Refugees

SIZE OF GROUP: 3,000   **MARC ID:** 9050

DISTINCTIVES: economic status; age; significant problems

SOCIAL CHANGE: not reported

LANGUAGES: Khmer (V)

SCRIPTURE: Bible; **RECORDINGS:** yes   **CHRISTIAN LITERACY:** nr

RELIGION: Buddhist-Animist

CHURCHES AND MISSIONS: not reported

OPENNESS TO RELIGIOUS CHANGE: not reported

RECEPTIVITY TO CHRISTIANITY: not reported

GROWTH RATE OF CHRISTIAN COMMUNITY: not reported

EVANGELISM PROFILE: not reported   **VALIDITY:** 3

At issue in the attempt to meet the needs of the Khmer in Thailand is the continuing influx of unaccompanied minors across the border. One source estimates there are 3000 of these children under 17 years old. Reunification with parents is the ultimate goal of those responsible for the welfare of the refugees but many are orphans with no hope of such reunion. Young people are resettled in a third country usually in a foster care arrangement so that family reunification may occur at a later date.

The insecurity, violence and psychological shock these young people have experienced is considered to be indelible. Their reactions to these experiences vary. For some, there is recurring talk of suicide. Others distrust and hate the adult world, as a result of the years of horror they have witnessed. Cases of parents finding children in the camps only to be repudiated by them have been reported.

If there is a sign of encouragement in this desperate picture, it may lie in the unquenchable thirst of Khmer children and youth for knowledge. Denied the opportunity to learn for years, Kampuchean children flock to makeshift schools at the prospect of learning. Educators feel this may be the key to the restoration of a healthy future in spirit, mind and body. UNICEF has respnded enthusiastically to this need by giving equal attention to meeting educational needs and nutritional needs. Not all these children react negatively to their former enemies. As in other areas where prolonged civil war has taken place, the resiliency of these youngest victims can be amazing. It is speculated that their optimistic reactions to hardship and disaster are defense mechanisms without which they might not have survived.

The legal status of these children has also been uncertain. As of March, 1981 the U.N. was hesitant to grant full refugee status to these children until the truth was known of their parents' whereabouts. This has delayed the resettlement of many orphaned children. Efforts are being made by U.S. Christian and other religious organizations to expedite this process.

EXPANDED DESCRIPTIONS

Kirgiz Afghan Refugees (Turkey)

ALTERNATE NAMES: Kirgiz Resettled Refugees

SIZE OF GROUP: 1,300   **MARC ID:** 9060

DISTINCTIVES: occupation; ethnicity; economic status; residence

SOCIAL CHANGE: not reported

LANGUAGES: Kirgiz (V); Turkish (T)

SCRIPTURE: portions; **RECORDINGS:** yes   **CHRISTIAN LITERACY:** nr

RELIGION: Islam (99% adherents); Christianity (-1% practicing)

CHURCHES AND MISSIONS: not reported

OPENNESS TO RELIGIOUS CHANGE: not reported

RECEPTIVITY TO CHRISTIANITY: not reported

GROWTH RATE OF CHRISTIAN COMMUNITY: not reported

EVANGELISM PROFILE: not reported   **VALIDITY:** 4

As the military conflict in Afghanistan dragged on it became evident that many refugees living in Pakistan would not be repatriated. Over 4000 refugees of Turkish origin who were residing in Pakistan were resettled in Eastern Turkey. Of this group, 1300 are members of the Kirgiz tribal group. They are Turkish-speakers and do share similar cultural patterns with the other groups resettled, and nearly all practice Islam.

Resettlement for the Kirgiz is difficult because the temperature is much higher than the mountain regions to which they are accustomed. The environment is therefore very different and the possibilities for livelihood limited. They are unable to raise the same herds of mountain sheep since the animals will not produce the same fur in the comparatively temperate climate. Nonetheless the Kirgiz hope to import yaks and goats so that they may build up their own herds once again. They also want to find swift horses on which to place their valuable saddles, one commodity they kept and carried to their new home. They are used to very active athletic events on horseback known as "Bazkashi" and are eager to return to herding livestock over endless mountain pastures interspersed with recreational activity. The confines of refugee camps are unacceptable and they anticipate that they can get on with their own way of life now that they are in Turkey.

The changes they have confronted due to displacement have brought them in contact with the Western world. They have responded by selling many of their fine artifacts to international exporters and will thus have contacts with individuals outside the traditional spheres. Despite the limitations of political and national regulations regarding proselytism there are now, perhaps for the first time ever, opportunities for establishing contact among Kirgiz.

Lao Refugees (Spain)

ALTERNATE NAMES: Laotian Refugees

SIZE OF GROUP: 1,000 **MARC ID:** 9056

DISTINCTIVES: ethnicity; language; residence; religion

SOCIAL CHANGE: very rapid

LANGUAGES: Lao (V); Spanish (T)

SCRIPTURE: Bible; **RECORDINGS:** yes **CHRISTIAN LITERACY:** 20%

RELIGION: Buddhist-Animist; Christianity (-1% practicing)

CHURCHES AND MISSIONS: not reported

OPENNESS TO RELIGIOUS CHANGE: indifferent

RECEPTIVITY TO CHRISTIANITY: indifferent

GROWTH RATE OF CHRISTIAN COMMUNITY: not reported

EVANGELISM PROFILE: not reported **VALIDITY:** 3

The refugees who are fortunate enough to leave the refugee camps in Thailand and make it to the borders of Spain are extremely respectful of their host country. After two months in a residence belonging to the Ministry of Works on the outskirts of Madrid where they are taught the rudiments of Castilian and learn to familiarize themselves with Spanish culture, they soon arrive in Avila. There they begin receiving the alloted 35,000 pesetas a month (about US$500), as well as medical assistance and language classes in Castilian, all provided by Spanish authorities.

They are received well by their Spanish hosts. They are considered respectful and hardworking. Most of the refugees want to work hard, save money and bring the rest of their families who remain in the Thai camps to be with them. The government provides them bicycles for transportation and assists them in finding jobs such as chauffeuring, masonry and mechanics. Many grow food on small plots of land provided them.

Very few Lao have adopted the Christian faith in their own country. Christianity among the ethnic Lao is normally regarded as the religion of the French colonists and of the Vietnamese that France brought to administer Laos when the Lao refused to cooperate with the French regime. Traditionally, the majority of the Lao are Buddhists. The highly individualistic emphasis of Buddhism and its mandates of lovingkindness toward all has led to a development of the Lao into a people tolerant of each other and of outsiders. Organizations and individuals of various persuasions may successfully minister to this group.

EXPANDED DESCRIPTIONS

Luvale Refugees from Angola (Zambia)

ALTERNATE NAMES: Angolan Refugees
SIZE OF GROUP: 11,000　　　　　　　MARC ID: 9061
DISTINCTIVES: residence; discrimination
SOCIAL CHANGE: not reported
LANGUAGES: Luvale (V)
SCRIPTURE: Bible; RECORDINGS: yes　　CHRISTIAN LITERACY: nr
RELIGION: Animism; Christianity

CHURCHES AND MISSIONS	BEGAN	MEMBERSHIP	COMMUNITY
Lutheran World Federation	nr	nr	nr
Zambia Churches Refugees Srvc	nr	nr	nr
Plymouth Brethren	nr	nr	nr

OPENNESS TO RELIGIOUS CHANGE: not reported
RECEPTIVITY TO CHRISTIANITY: not reported
GROWTH RATE OF CHRISTIAN COMMUNITY: not reported
EVANGELISM PROFILE: not reported　　　VALIDITY: 4

The northwest area of Zambia was the site of refuge for several Angolan people groups who fled conflicts between themselves and the Portuguese colonists. The Luvale, Luchazi, Chokwe and Mbunde settled in Zambia between 1910 and 1966. When Angolans began their war for independence against the Portuguese in 1966, many Angolan Luvale people fled into neighboring Zambia. As of June 1981, 28,000 Angolan refugees were in Zambia. Those immigrants who settled in Zambia in prior refugee movements provided both direction and welcoming relatives for many of the post-1966 refugees. Due to the repatriation of many Angolans in 1982, the Luvale refugee population is now estimated at 11,000.

New arrivals were given seed, agricultural tools and five-hectare plots of arable land for each family. Only about one-third of Meheba is under cultivation, so plenty of land is available if more refugees have to be settled there. The refugees raise these crops for their own use, and any surplus is sold for cash to the National Agriculture Marketing Board. A small cooperative exists through which its 250 members may buy basic necessities as well as make small loans. Schools and clinics were built, then turned over to the departments of education and health. A workshop was built and supplied necessary agricultural machinery and trucks which may be used by the refugees on a rental basis. There is also a piggery and a poultry unit.

Several Zambian villages have grown up around the perimeter of the refugee camps where they benefit not only from Meheba's economic momentum and agricultural surpluses, but from its schools and medical facilities. The UNHCR turned Meheba over to Zambian authority in 1982.

Luvale people believe that many diseases and accidents have spiritual origins. Since quarrels between neighbors give rise to the possibility of offending the spirits of their ancestors, the Luvale have shunned large rural settlements. Although this type of sorcery can be fought, the Luvale would usually move away from troublesome people or places where misfortune had occurred. The more established Luvale residents in Zambia consider the refugees from Angola to be more knowledgeable in traditional Luvale lore. Refugees have been approached to serve as diviners, sorcerers and doctors because they know more about "Luvale medicine."

Christian ministries have been effective, and no fewer than 36 churches of ten different denominations have been built by the refugees.

234

Marielitos in Florida (United States of America)

ALTERNATE NAMES: Mariel Boat People; Cuban Refugees; Cuban Boat People

SIZE OF GROUP: 125,000   **MARC ID:** 6565

DISTINCTIVES: discrimination; legal status; significant problems

SOCIAL CHANGE: rapid

LANGUAGES: Spanish (100% speak/90% read; V, T, S, G)

SCRIPTURE: Bible; **RECORDINGS:** yes   **CHRISTIAN LITERACY:** 90%

RELIGION: Secularism (50% adherents); Roman Catholic (45% adherents/10% practicing); Protestant (5% adherents/4% practicing)

CHURCHES AND MISSIONS: not reported

OPENNESS TO RELIGIOUS CHANGE: somewhat open

RECEPTIVITY TO CHRISTIANITY: receptive

GROWTH RATE OF CHRISTIAN COMMUNITY: slow growth

EVANGELISM PROFILE: not reported   **VALIDITY:** 4

In the spring of 1980, one percent of Cuba's population left their homes, jobs and even families in order to begin life anew in the United States. Over 125,000 Cubans were ferried from the island's Mariel Harbor in a flotilla of American fishing boats, yachts and sailboats, known as the "Freedom Flotilla." The refugees were soon called "Marielitos."

More than 90,000 Marielitos settled in Miami, Florida, where there was already a large Cuban community. Unlike previous Cuban refugees who were usually middle-class and upper-class professionals, Marielitos are mostly laborers, neither very skilled nor educated. They are predominantly males, ages 25 to 45, who either have no families or have left them behind. However, mixed with the majority of those Marielitos who were seeking new lives in America were an estimated 23,000 who were spending time in Cuban prisons or were mentally disturbed. About 1300 Cubans are still incarcerated in a federal prison in Atlanta, and an additional 530 are still detained because of severe mental problems. Furthermore, at least 25% of the inmates of the Dade County Jail (Miami) are Marielitos.

Therefore, it is not hard to understand the prejudices against all of the Marielitos living in Miami, both by the white community and by the established Cuban community. Compounding the Marielitos' problems further is a cutoff of U.S. Federal aid to Cuban refugees.

While most Marielitos have found jobs, as a whole they suffer from an unemployment rate of 20-25%. Low income housing, job training, and language training are some of their most pressing needs.

Although the Cuban population is officially 51% Christian, communist rule for two decades has discouraged Christian commitment. Only 2% of the people attend church regularly. Some 49% of Cuba's people claim no religious affiliation. Refugees from the early days of communist rule in Cuba tended to be more religious and had a high percentage of Protestants among them because they were fleeing the communist persecution. However, Marielito refugees tend to reflect the lack of Christian commitment of Cuban society today. Nevertheless, ministry opportunities abound for the Marielitos, including the sponsorship of refugees by Christian churches or families.

EXPANDED DESCRIPTIONS

Muslim Lebanese Refugees (Canada)

ALTERNATE NAMES: not reported

SIZE OF GROUP: 29,000   MARC ID: 9025

DISTINCTIVES: religion; legal status; ethnicity; residence

SOCIAL CHANGE: rapid

LANGUAGES: Arabic (V); French (T, V); English (T)

SCRIPTURE: Bible; RECORDINGS: yes   CHRISTIAN LITERACY: nr

RELIGION: Islam

CHURCHES AND MISSIONS: not reported

OPENNESS TO RELIGIOUS CHANGE: somewhat closed

RECEPTIVITY TO CHRISTIANITY: reluctant

GROWTH RATE OF CHRISTIAN COMMUNITY: not reported

EVANGELISM PROFILE: not reported   VALIDITY: 4

The Lebanese civil war in 1975 and the continued fighting since then have forced thousands of Lebanese, both Muslim and Christian, to flee. Approximately 58,000 Lebanese have found refuge in Canada; half of them are Muslim. Following the 1982 Israeli invasion of Lebanon, the Parliamentary Secretary to the Minister announced in Parliament the government's expectation of thousands more refugees.

Because of the French-speaking background of many of the Lebanese, most Lebanese settle in French-speaking Canada. Ottawa has a Lebanese population of 20,000; Montreal has between 15,000 and 20,000. Toronto has about 15,000, while Windsor, Ontario reports a community of some 3000. Lebanese refugees are found in various areas of the work force: in blue-collar jobs, professional fields, and commercial and retail trades.

Approximately 90% of these refugees speak Arabic. As part of a former French protectorate, many Lebanese speak French. English is also widely spoken.

Lebanese refugees can settle in Canada in one of three ways: 1) The approximately 1000 Lebanese visiting Canada may extend their visit up to one year with permission to work. At the end of the year their situation will be reviewed and a decision made as to their future status. 2) Lebanese visitors in Canada may apply for immigration status if they have relatives in Canada, and 3) Canadian citizens with relatives in Lebanon can sponsor them under relaxed criteria. Until the current situation in Lebanon is settled, no one under deportation order can be returned to Lebanon.

Nomadic Somali Refugees (Somalia)

ALTERNATE NAMES: Nomadic Refugees

SIZE OF GROUP: 700,000   **MARC ID:** 9027

DISTINCTIVES: economic status; legal status; ethnicity

SOCIAL CHANGE: moderate

LANGUAGES: Somali (V); Oromo (V)

SCRIPTURE: Bible; **RECORDINGS:** yes   **CHRISTIAN LITERACY:** 70%

RELIGION: Islam (90% adherents); Christianity (-1% practicing)

CHURCHES AND MISSIONS: not reported

OPENNESS TO RELIGIOUS CHANGE: somewhat open

RECEPTIVITY TO CHRISTIANITY: receptive

GROWTH RATE OF CHRISTIAN COMMUNITY: not reported

EVANGELISM PROFILE: not reported   **VALIDITY:** 4

Nomadic Somali refugees have fled civil war in Ethiopia by the hundreds of thousands. They are used to traveling throughout the parched deserts. For centuries they have meandered through the brush and sands of the scorching Ogaden in search of pasture for their livestock. They know how to survive and that is fortunate in view of the suppressive environmental factors they confront in Somalia. Most of the refugees are women and children who seek shelter from the fiery war in which their husbands and sons fight and die. There is little for the refugees to look forward to in Somalia. It is one of the poorest nations of the world and suffers from chronic food shortages and droughts. But the Somalis from Ethiopia want to survive, so they move on to regions where freedom prevails.

Approximately 75% of all Somali refugees have settled in camps. The rest are scattered throughout towns and villages of Somalia. Despite the economic problems which plague Somalia, there is no conceivable way to limit the settlement of refugees. They are regarded as brothers, and Islam provides specific teaching regarding the treatment of kindred peoples.

The most frustrating aspect of change for the refugees has been the loss of livestock. They can survive in the desert with limited resources; that they have done before. Without camels, goats and sheep, however, they are helpless. They have little sense of purpose or direction and see no hope for the future. They resist settling in agricultural villages. Instead, they yearn for the freedom to return to oasis and pasture with their own flocks.

Densely populated settlements are abnormal for the Somalis, and thus it is not unusual that abnormal diseases and problems proliferate. Water supplies are polluted, firewood scarce, and food virtually nonexistent. Non-profit relief agencies have been faced with overwhelming challenges in responding to the needs of the Somalis. Food has been shipped in to avert famine in the camps. Medical clinics have tended to the malnourished and sick. Development coordinators have installed sanitation facilities and have provided access to fresh water.

Long-term solutions are not yet evident, and the challenge of the church is particularly complicated since the Muslims forbid proselytizing the refugees. How God will work within the confines fo the Somali tragedy is not clear. Dedicated Christian doctors, nurses, development coordinators, and relief workers have much to contribute as they pour out their lives. The harvest is not yet evident, but the sowing continues with never-ending perseverance.

237

EXPANDED DESCRIPTIONS

Palestinian Refugees (Jordan)

ALTERNATE NAMES: not reported
SIZE OF GROUP: 1,160,800   MARC ID: 9020
DISTINCTIVES: political loyalty; ethnicity
SOCIAL CHANGE: not reported
LANGUAGES: Arabic (V)
SCRIPTURE: portions; RECORDINGS: yes CHRISTIAN LITERACY: 32%
RELIGION: Islam; Christianity (-1% practicing)
CHURCHES AND MISSIONS: not reported
OPENNESS TO RELIGIOUS CHANGE: not reported
RECEPTIVITY TO CHRISTIANITY: not reported
GROWTH RATE OF CHRISTIAN COMMUNITY: not reported
EVANGELISM PROFILE: not reported   VALIDITY: 4

The 1948 Arab-Israeli war caused thousands of Palestinians to flee their farms in the Galilee or their homes in Haifa, Jaffa, Acre and Jerusalem. More than half fled to nearby Jordan, while others found refuge in hastily built camps in the Gaza Strip, Syria and Lebanon. Most of them thought they could return to their homes when the fighting stopped. Instead, they became the helpless pawns of Middle Eastern politics. Another half-million Palestinians fled into Jordan after the 1967 Arab-Israeli war.

Today, nearly half of Jordan's population are Palestinian refugees. There are two sides to the Palestinian situation in Jordan. One is represented by the refugee camps still maintained by the U.N. Relief and Works Agency. Over 220,000 refugees live in the 10 camps in and around the capital city of Amman. They stay in the camps for several reasons (they are free to leave if they wish). Many cannot afford to live elsewhere because of the high cost of living in Jordan. Others stay because they wish to remain identified as refugees, without a homeland. The camps are no longer the squalid tent cities they were originally. The houses are small and neatly arranged. There are schools for all the children and medical facilities for all. Shops and small businesses provide some trade and jobs. However, the camps are overcrowded and people must cope with the frustration of waiting in lines for everything. Furthermore, the emotional stresses of being refugees for decades are particularly burdensome.

On the other hand, most Palestinians in Jordan have settled into Jordanian society as well as possible. King Hussein has given Jordanian citizenship to any refugee who desires it. Palestinians have become government officials, bankers, lawyers and doctors. Others work in the Persian Gulf states and send back to Jordan more than US$ 700 million annually. Much of the economic growth of Jordan can be attributed to the industriousness of the Palestinians.

The dream for most Palestinians in Jordan is to return "home" and establish their own independent state of Palestine. Many of the young men and women have joined one of the several Palestinian groups that seek the "liberation" of their homeland from Israel. Others would settle for an independent state located on the West Bank and the Gaza Strip. Christians ministering to Palestinians must recognize these deep feelings, since Palestinians often reject Christian witness outright because they see Christians as supporters of Israel and Zionism.

Rural Refugees from Eritrea (Sudan)

ALTERNATE NAMES: not reported

SIZE OF GROUP: 300,000   MARC ID: 9008

DISTINCTIVES: occupation; ethnicity

SOCIAL CHANGE: not reported

LANGUAGES: Tigre (V)

SCRIPTURE: New Testament; RECORDINGS: yes

CHRISTIAN LITERACY: not reported

RELIGION: Islam

CHURCHES AND MISSIONS: not reported

OPENNESS TO RELIGIOUS CHANGE: not reported

RECEPTIVITY TO CHRISTIANITY: not reported

GROWTH RATE OF CHRISTIAN COMMUNITY: not reported

EVANGELISM PROFILE: not reported   VALIDITY: 4

The opportunities for resettlement among Ethiopians with rural backgrounds are significantly different, meriting special attention. Fortunately for all, Sudan is willing to absorb refugees despite numerous socioeconomic problems which contribute to its status as one of the 25 least developed nations in the world.

Rural Ethiopians who flee to Sudan are moved to provincial settlements where they are assisted by government officials and non-profit organizations. Shelter is one of the more important necessities. Reed stalks, covered with mud or whitewashed lime, with available scraps of lumber or metal tied in as reinforcements, are fashioned into huts.

Work is another necessity. In settlements such as Um Gargur, each family is alloted 10 acres of nonirrigated land. They are able to raise sufficient vegetables and grains when it rains. Precipitation is seasonal, though, and the refugees work on their land during one season only. They must live on the fruits of their harvests for the remainder of the year. To supplement their diets they obtain work as migrant farmers in areas where there are irrigated fields.

A local infrastructure is developing as new cooperatives form to market goods produced on the irrigated farms. Merchants have opened stalls and booths with items of necessities. The UNHCR has assisted by providing tools, tractors, and seeds while the World Food Program provides basic items needed until the settlement becomes self-sufficient.

Whether or not churches have realized the opportunities for outreach in a new community which has no church remains unknown. There has been no indication on the part of church groups regarding the status of ministry among rural Ethiopians in Sudan.

EXPANDED DESCRIPTIONS

Rwandan Tutsi Refugees (Burundi)

ALTERNATE NAMES: not reported

SIZE OF GROUP: 49,000   MARC ID: 9041

DISTINCTIVES: residence; economic status

SOCIAL CHANGE: very slow

LANGUAGES: Kirundi (V)

SCRIPTURE: Bible; RECORDINGS: yes   CHRISTIAN LITERACY: nr

RELIGION: Animism (50% adherents); Roman Catholic (44% adherents); Protestant(6% adherents)

CHURCHES AND MISSIONS: not reported

OPENNESS TO RELIGIOUS CHANGE: very open

RECEPTIVITY TO CHRISTIANITY: very receptive

GROWTH RATE OF CHRISTIAN COMMUNITY: not reported

EVANGELISM PROFILE: not reported   VALIDITY: 4

National independence movements in Africa have often produced large refugee populations. Such was the case when Rwanda and Burundi became independent countries in 1962. They had formerly been a united territory under Belgian administration. The tensions of overpopulation, politics, and power struggles manifested themselves in ethnic rivalry. The Rwandan Hutus were tired of the suppressive reign of the Tutsi and revolted with violent aggression. A civil war broke out and 100,000 Tutsi were forced to flee from their lives. Nearly half of them joined families and friends in the concurrent upheaval in Burundi where Hutus left for Tanzania or Rwanda. The government of Burundi received the Tutsi from Rwanda with cordial generosity and provided the basic necessities of life despite overwhelming economic pressures.

Since the Rwandian Tutsi were settling among fellow Tutsi, there were few problems of adjustment and integration. The economic differences were significant at first since the local residents were established in official government positions and pursued elite careers. The refugees were settled in rural encampments and progressed only slightly in terms of personal advancement. In some respects the Tutsi refugees did not advance very quickly in society. Opportunities for educational training and employment were limited. They tilled the soil or sold basic wares and found it difficult to pursue individual interests despite similar language and culture patterns with the Burundian Tutsi.

Many refugees have not had the strong motivational or driving forces which push other refugee groups into the personal development mode. The church in Burundi must confront the special needs of the refugees from Rwanda and develop appropriate systems in order for the refugees to move beyond their present status. Too many similarities among groups can dim the differences and stifle creativity in the face of complacency.

South African Students (Lesotho)

ALTERNATE NAMES: not reported

SIZE OF GROUP: 11,500   **MARC ID:** 9014

DISTINCTIVES: legal status; occupation; ethnicity

SOCIAL CHANGE: very rapid

LANGUAGES: Afrikaans (V); English (V); Sotho (T); Tribal Languages (V)

SCRIPTURE: Bible; **RECORDINGS:** yes   **CHRISTIAN LITERACY:** 100%

RELIGION: Christianity (60% adherents); Animism

CHURCHES AND MISSIONS	BEGAN	MEMBERSHIP	COMMUNITY
Church of Lesotho	nr	nr	nr
Roman Catholic Church	nr	nr	nr

OPENNESS TO RELIGIOUS CHANGE: not reported

RECEPTIVITY TO CHRISTIANITY: not reported

GROWTH RATE OF CHRISTIAN COMMUNITY: not reported

EVANGELISM PROFILE: not reported   **VALIDITY:** 4

The government of Lesotho has two classifications of refugees: 1) those who are former students from South Africa, and 2) those who are political and/or rural refugees. Significant differences set them apart from each other. To begin with, former students have been exposed to many of the sociophilosophical ideologies of the world. They have lived in sprawling black townships of South Africa and are used to urban life-styles. When they arrive in Lesotho they are faced with a new environment in which they have had no experience, and lack the basic skills required for self-sufficiency. The challenge of moving from densely populated urban areas to sparsely populated farming regions are numerous. For individuals reared in the countryside, the openness and scenic mountain ranges are beautiful and familiar. But for the others, having left family behind, lacking experience and skills, the basic struggle to survive involves radical changes in lifestyle. Most students are not accustomed to hard physical labor, and the simplest chores in farming become major tasks.

Government officials in Lesotho have struggled with the issues involved in placing South African students in schools, since there is already a chronic shortage of teachers and facilities. They are aften more interested in placing a qualified student from Lesotho than a refugee from South Africa. They have, however, set aside 20% of the openings at the universities specifically for refugees. Programs to help refugees start cottage industries have been partially successful, but it has been difficult to integrate refugee students into traditional village settlements. The frustrations of students who cannot pursue their goals are often evident, and depression becomes a major hindrance.

Resources have been obtained from many different international agencies who are interested in the pursuit of education. Scholarships have been made available for refugee students who do not have sponsors and are unable to finance their education.

Most student refugees are young males between the ages of 16 and 22. They are confronted with many aspects of personal development and have few opportunities to express their deepest needs. The Church in Lesotho could develop a dynamic ministry to lonely, displaced students if individuals would befriend the refugee students, listen to them, and offer sound council. The task is not glamorous, nor is it easy. But the need to provide comfort and resources remains a challenge for Christians.

241

EXPANDED DESCRIPTIONS

Sudanese Repatriates (Sudan)

ALTERNATE NAMES: Former Sudanese Refugees

SIZE OF GROUP: 1,000,000   **MARC ID:** 9009

DISTINCTIVES: significant problems

SOCIAL CHANGE: not reported

LANGUAGES: Dinka (V); Nuer (V); Tribal Languages (V)

SCRIPTURE: portions; **RECORDINGS:** yes **CHRISTIAN LITERACY:** 12%

RELIGION: Animism (90% adherents); Christianity (-1% practicing)

CHURCHES AND MISSIONS	BEGAN	MEMBERSHIP	COMMUNITY
A.C.R.O.S.S.	nr	nr	nr
Africa Inland Church	nr	nr	nr
Catholic Relief Services	nr	nr	nr
Sudan Interior Church	nr	nr	nr

OPENNESS TO RELIGIOUS CHANGE: not reported

RECEPTIVITY TO CHRISTIANITY: not reported

GROWTH RATE OF CHRISTIAN COMMUNITY: not reported

EVANGELISM PROFILE: not reported   **VALIDITY:** 4

A synopsis of the repatriation of Southern Sudanese in 1972 and 1973 provides valuable insight into the nature and challenge of resettling refugees. Thousands of black Sudanese left their farms and villages during the undeclared civil conflict between northern Arab Muslims and southern blacks who were from animistic/Christian backgrounds. When the political officials of the capital recognized the right of self-government for the three southern regions of Sudan, the 17-year civil war ended. Months passed before the news of a peaceful resolution reached thousands of refugees camped in remote bush settlements. When they did return to their communities, they found few remains of schools, houses, or shops. There arose a concerted relief effort. Assistance was rendered by numerous secular and religious agencies, including a newly formed evangelical organization known as A.C.R.O.S.S. (the Africa Committee for Rehabilitation of Southern Sudan), which represented several cooperating agencies.

The initial demand for food taxed resources to the limit. Shipments of food from outside provided temporary relief from famine. Refugees were able to plant new crops after laborious weeding and plowing of fields which were long since overgrown. Former rebel guerrilla soldiers were given training and responsibilities in police operations. Farmers were given seeds and tools for subsistence crops, and professionals tended to the needs of individuals through their respective services.

Huge relief efforts averted major epidemics and mass starvation. The people, who were no longer refugees, rebuilt offices, schools, hospitals, and houses. The infusion of temporary monetary and technical assistance provided a suitable foundation for the reestablishment of a local economy; life slowly returned to normal.

The future of the country lies in the development schemes and political strategies, but for the time being repatriation occurrs in an admirable manner. The response of international agencies has been a key to the successful resettlement of refugees throughout Southern Sudan. The clear testimony of the effectiveness of cooperation foretells further interaction of organizations who seek to meet the needs of other refugees.

Tibetan Refugees (India)

ALTERNATE NAMES: not reported

SIZE OF GROUP: 100,000   **MARC ID:** 2033

DISTINCTIVES: language; political loyalty; ethnicity; religion; discrimination; legal status; residence

SOCIAL CHANGE: very rapid

LANGUAGES: Tibetan (100% speak/12% read; V); Hindustani

        (85% speak/45% read; T); English (10% speak/10% read; S)

SCRIPTURE: New Testament; **RECORDINGS:** yes   **CHRISTIAN**
LITERACY:100%

RELIGION: Buddhism (96% adherents); Protestant (1% adherents/1% practicing); Other (3% adherents)

CHURCHES AND MISSIONS	BEGAN	MEMBERSHIP	COMMUNITY
Moravian Church	nr	nr	nr

OPENNESS TO RELIGIOUS CHANGE: somewhat open

RECEPTIVITY TO CHRISTIANITY: indifferent

GROWTH RATE OF CHRISTIAN COMMUNITY: not reported

EVANGELISM PROFILE: not reported   **VALIDITY:** 4

The invasion of Tibet by the military forces of the People's Republic of China in 1959 resulted in the displacement of some 100,000 Tibetans. Most fled to the Daramsala region of northern India. Since that time the Tibetan refugee community has managed to develop an agricultural base in what was formerly a jungle region. Tibetans now supply one-fourth of India's corn, for instance. Small-scale craft industries and employment in road building in the Himalayas have been other pursuits of the Tibetan refugees.

The Dalai Lama, the Buddhist religious leader and political spokesman for Tibet, charged that China intended not only the political takeover of Tibet but also the destruction of Tibetan cultural and religious institutions and the elimination of Tibetan identity. The destruction of 1000 Buddhist monasteries by the Chinese invaders is poignant evidence of this charge. Also, at the time of the invasion there were about 110,000 monks in Tibet; there are scarcely a thousand left. There are some 5000 monks among the refugees in the Himalaya border regions and India.

In addition to the Tibetan refugees in India there are 4000 in Bhutan, 9000 in Nepal and over 1000 in Switzerland. Also, there are tiny communities of Tibetans residing in the U.S., Japan, Canada, and other Western European countries. In these instances they number only a few hundred in each place.

At first the Tibetan refugee situation received considerable media attention in the West. More recently, as the Dalai Lama's exile has continued, the Tibetan situation has receded into the background. The Chinese have made overtures to the Dalai Lama to return to Tibet in light of recent developments in Chinese policy toward those practicing various religions.

EXPANDED DESCRIPTIONS

Tibetan Refugees (Switzerland)

ALTERNATE NAMES: not reported

SIZE OF GROUP: 1,000   **MARC ID:** 9015

DISTINCTIVES: language; ethnicity; religion; political loyalty; residence

SOCIAL CHANGE: rapid

LANGUAGES: Tibetan (V); German (S, T)

SCRIPTURE: Bible; **RECORDINGS:** yes   **CHRISTIAN LITERACY:** nr

RELIGION: Buddhism

CHURCHES AND MISSIONS: not reported

OPENNESS TO RELIGIOUS CHANGE: very closed

RECEPTIVITY TO CHRISTIANITY: very reluctant

GROWTH RATE OF CHRISTIAN COMMUNITY: not reported

EVANGELISM PROFILE: not reported   **VALIDITY:** 4

Between 1912 and 1950, Tibet was governed as an autonomous kingdom. Following China's invasion and takeover in 1951, Tibetans were forced to change their centuries-old political, economic and religious structures. After years of enduring what the International Commission of Jurists concluded was genocide, the Tibetans revolted in 1959. The Chinese military stamped out the revolts forcing some 100,000 people, including the spiritual head, the Dalai Lama, to flee as refugees.

In 1963, the Federal Council of Switzerland authorized 1000 Tibetan refugees to be admitted to that country. Ten million Swiss francs have been allocated by the Association of Tibetan Homes in Switzerland and the Swiss Red Cross for the resettlement of the refugees in Switzerland. The Swiss government has announced that it is satisfied that these refugees are well established and need no further assistance.

The original Swiss plan called for resettling the Tibetans in high mountain valleys where they would be in a similar environment to their native land. However, most Tibetans found better job opportunities in the lower valleys. Hence, today there are groups of Tibetans scattered throughout German-speaking areas of Switzerland. There is now a Tibetan monastery near Rikon which serves as a religious and cultural center for Tibetans in Switzerland.

Most younger Tibetans have adapted readily to their new culture, adopting Swiss dress and speaking German. However, ties with their homeland are strongly encouraged and the monastery at Rikon tries to help this by having Tibetans come there for at least one or two weeks per year. There, they speak Tibetan, practice their religion and remember their cultural heritage.

Tibetan Buddhists have been very reluctant in accepting the gospel. Converts in Tibet were often persecuted and some were killed. After nearly 20 years in Switzerland, many cultural barriers against Christianity are breaking down, particularly among the young. This is apparent in that a few young Tibetans have married non-Tibetans in Switzerland. Nevertheless, many older Tibetans still desire to return to India, where they can be near their spiritual leader, the Dalai Lama.

Ugandan Asian Refugees (Canada)

ALTERNATE NAMES: Ismaili Refugees

SIZE OF GROUP: 6,000 MARC ID: 9011

DISTINCTIVES: religion; ethnicity; significant problems

SOCIAL CHANGE: not reported

LANGUAGES: Gujarati (V); English (T)

SCRIPTURE: RECORDINGS: yes CHRISTIAN LITERACY: nr

RELIGION: Islam

CHURCHES AND MISSIONS: not reported

OPENNESS TO RELIGIOUS CHANGE: not reported

RECEPTIVITY TO CHRISTIANITY: not reported

GROWTH RATE OF CHRISTIAN COMMUNITY: not reported

EVANGELISM PROFILE: not reported VALIDITY: 3

One segment of the many victims of Idi Amin's reign of terror were members of the East Africa Asian community. One particular group of Asians who belonged to the Ismaili sect of Islam in Uganda were resettled in Western Canada. The Ismaili split from the mainstream of Islam due to a disagreement over the method of choosing the head of the Islamic community as a whole. The Ismailis have come from predominantly urban backgrounds and have been part of a clearly defined sociological group.

They have lived in distinct residential areas which had specific parameters. Within Canada, the Ismailis have settled in urban areas with large concentrations of clustered family groupings. They move as quickly as possible from rented apartments to homes which they purchase just as they had done in Uganda and other cities of East Africa. Ismailis of Canada maintain close ties with other Ismaili communities throughout the world via a network of councils, which provide explicit instruction regarding appropriate behavioral patterns. The heads of the councils have discouraged smoking and drinking but encourage western styles of dress. The local mosque functions as an important center of community activity and perpetuates the cohesiveness of the group. Weekly prayer meetings are a regular part of religious tradition as is daily prayer at home and festive congregational celebrations in observance of special holy days.

Many Ismailis have stepped right into the free enterprise system of Canada with successful ingenuity. Young Ismailis are being trained to pursue careers in commercial businesses. There has been very active involvement of religous leaders in the lives of young businessmen so that both the religious and the business heritage of the Ismailis is preserved. The Ismailis appreciate the freedom and the opportunity to practice their traditional life-styles within Canada and seek to identify themselves as patriotic citizens. Challenges of economic opportunities within recessionary business climates are confronting young Ismailis who seek good jobs and positions of responsibility. The tensions of resettlement do not appear to threaten the identity or strength of the Ismaili community. Economic hardship poses major problems. The skills, ingenuity, and commitment are keeping the Ismaili community vibrant and growing together to face the future.

245

EXPANDED DESCRIPTIONS

Ugandan Refugees (Sudan)

ALTERNATE NAMES: not reported
SIZE OF GROUP: 100,000   **MARC ID:** 9048
DISTINCTIVES: legal status; economic status; residence
SOCIAL CHANGE: moderate
LANGUAGES: Acholi (V); Swahili (V, T); English (T)
SCRIPTURE: Bible; **RECORDINGS:** yes   **CHRISTIAN LITERACY:** nr
RELIGION: Animism; Christianity (-1% practicing)

CHURCHES AND MISSIONS	BEGAN	MEMBERSHIP	COMMUNITY
Norwegian Church Aid	nr	nr	nr
A.C.R.O.S.S.	nr	nr	nr

OPENNESS TO RELIGIOUS CHANGE: not reported
RECEPTIVITY TO CHRISTIANITY: not reported
GROWTH RATE OF CHRISTIAN COMMUNITY: not reported
EVANGELISM PROFILE: not reported   **VALIDITY:** 4

Over 100,000 Ugandans have settled in Southern Sudan despite the harshness of the environment. They left a much more pleasant land trying to end the threat to their lives. Thousands have left via dugout canoes in complete destitution. Approximately 50,000 were able to settle among friends and relatives, but 50,000 other individuals had no one to help them or to depend on. Fortunately, land is readily available and clusters of villages, comprised of 17 rural settlements, have been established for Ugandans. There is a busy road which links Uganda with Kenya and the refugees have been able to set up tea houses and rustic motels for the truck drivers who utilize the road.

Relief agencies have ready access to the village settlements and are able to provide medicine, food, tools and seeds to the refugees. Each family has been allotted approximately three and a half acres of land which is suitable for basic subsistence. The crops which grow are significantly different from those raised in Uganda, and the farmer must learn to cope with less rainfall, more insects, and dry winds. The Norwegian Church Aid, and A.C.R.O.S.S. (Africa Committee for the Relief of Southern Sudan) have been busy teaching Ugandans how to grow maize and sorghum. Waiting will continue as everyone observes whether ample rain promotes effective germination and then whether insects or animals destroy the crops. Drinking water remains a major problem, clear evidence of why the land was never previously utilized. Simple hand pumps are proving to be better than wells for providing adequate drinking supplies.

Ugandan Refugees (United Kingdom)

ALTERNATE NAMES: not reported

SIZE OF GROUP: 27,000   MARC ID: 9021

DISTINCTIVES: legal status; ethnicity; residence

SOCIAL CHANGE: very rapid

LANGUAGES: English (V)

SCRIPTURE: Bible; RECORDINGS: yes   CHRISTIAN LITERACY: nr

RELIGION: Hinduism; Islam; Sikhism

CHURCHES AND MISSIONS: not reported

OPENNESS TO RELIGIOUS CHANGE: not reported

RECEPTIVITY TO CHRISTIANITY: not reported

GROWTH RATE OF CHRISTIAN COMMUNITY: not reported

EVANGELISM PROFILE: not reported   VALIDITY: 4

Indians from South Asia went to East Africa as laborers for the British railways. Many stayed and became merchants, clerks, or middle managers. A three-tiered social structure developed in East Africa, with Europeans on top, Asians in the middle and blacks on the bottom. Independence for these nations did not change this situation very much. So, when Idi Amin seized power in Uganda in 1971, Asians became the scapegoats for economic and social troubles. In August 1972, Amin ordered the expulsion of all Asians at the end of three months. These Asians found themselves unwelcome in neighboring East African countries. Furthermore, India was reluctant to accept the bulk of the Asian refugees. But as a legacy of British colonialism, many Ugandan Asians still held British passports and/or citizenship. Hence, Great Britain was being pressured into accepting these people.

British immigration policies set strict limits for Asians immigrating to Britain. When all diplomatic means failed to dissuade Amin's plans, the British government set up the Uganda Resettlement Board, and the Conservative government launched a major campaign to persuade the public to welcome the refugees. Most of the refugees were forced to leave Uganda virtually penniless, their assets stolen or seized by the Ugandan government. More than 27,000 refugees came to Great Britain.

Upon their arrival in Britain, they were housed in camps until they could be permanently settled. They were advised on housing and job placement. It was suggested that they not settle in Birmingham, parts of London and other areas that had large Asian communities since they would not welcome more Asians (it is doubtful this advice was heeded). British welfare services took responsibility for their resettlement.

Asian refugees from Uganda were not a homogeneous lot. About 70% of Asian immigrants to East Africa were Gujarati-speaking Indians, while 26% were Punjabi-speaking, and about 4% were Konkani-speaking Christians from the Portuguese colony of Goa on the Indian subcontinent. The majority are Hindu, but there are sizable numbers of Muslims and Sikhs.

In Great Britain, Asians of all backgrounds see themselves as discriminated against. Furthermore, many young Asians, especially those born in Britain, feel that they belong there and not in the parent's homeland. Race riots, spawned by anti-Asian racial attacks, unemployment, bad housing, and a feeling of resentment against alleged discriminatory behavior by police, erupted in major British cities during the summer of 1981. Urban ministries of reconciliation, job training and placement, housing and legal services are needed in order to penetrate Asian people groups (including Asians from Uganda) with the gospel.

247

EXPANDED DESCRIPTIONS

Vietnamese Refugees (China)

ALTERNATE NAMES: not reported

SIZE OF GROUP: 2,000   **MARC ID:** 9000

DISTINCTIVES: discrimination; ethnicity; language

SOCIAL CHANGE: very rapid

LANGUAGES: Cantonese (V); Vietnamese(T)

SCRIPTURE: Bible; **RECORDINGS:** yes   **CHRISTIAN LITERACY:** nr

RELIGION: Traditional Chinese

CHURCHES AND MISSIONS: not reported

OPENNESS TO RELIGIOUS CHANGE: not reported

RECEPTIVITY TO CHRISTIANITY: not reported

GROWTH RATE OF CHRISTIAN COMMUNITY: not reported

EVANGELISM PROFILE: not reported   **VALIDITY:** 4

Since the breakdown of Sino-Vietnamese relations began in 1978, the People's Republic of China has received some 265,000 refugees from Vietnam. The Luliang State Farm in the border province of Yunnan is a designated refugee resettlement project which has received about 2000 ethnic Chinese refugees. These left Vietnam in 1978 as harassment of Chinese residents increased.

Since most of these refugees were urban dwellers in Vietnam, life in rural China holds little appeal. Unaccustomed to farm work, many of the refugees, who were formerly merchants, find the work difficult and rural society uninteresting. Most of the refugees speak only Vietnamese or dialects of Cantonese and are unable to communicate well with the host population.

Assimilation is difficult for the young. They despise agricultural work, and those studying Mandarin at the local schools resent being in classes with children ten years younger. Clad in jeans and T-shirts received from relatives abroad, the young identify more positively with life in the United States or Europe than with life in China. Most of the young want to emigrate to a third country. Poor food and low wages are general complaints. Some have left the farm for better-paying jobs in Macau, but many have returned when the rumors of such jobs turned out to be false. Others have taken to boats and headed for Hong Kong. Some petty crime attributed to the young has appeared in the camp according to officials.

The problems of Chinese refugee resettlement are admitted by Chinese authorities. The equivalent of almost three million U.S. dollars has been contributed toward the project by the government for farm equipment, housing and welfare. In addition, the International Red Cross has provided $100,000 for school buildings for the community. The Chinese government appealed for the first time to the United Nations High Commissioner for Refugees for assistance. The U.N. has responded by providing over 26 million dollars through 1981 to create jobs and provide farm equipment. Most of this aid has been designated for the poorest refugee camps on Hainan Island. To date, other nations have been reluctant to accept refugees from China. As a result those present in Chinese refugee camps have little hope of being accepted elsewhere. In spite of their difficulties, the Chinese authorities point out that the refugees now live in houses instead of tents as when they first arrived in the country.

Western Sahrawi Refugees (Algeria)

ALTERNATE NAMES: Sahrawi Refugees

SIZE OF GROUP: 70,000   **MARC ID:** 9012

DISTINCTIVES: political loyalty; religion; significant problems

SOCIAL CHANGE: very rapid

LANGUAGES: Arabic (V)

SCRIPTURE: Bible; **RECORDINGS:** yes   **CHRISTIAN LITERACY:** nr

RELIGION: Islam

CHURCHES AND MISSIONS: not reported

OPENNESS TO RELIGIOUS CHANGE: not reported

RECEPTIVITY TO CHRISTIANITY: not reported

GROWTH RATE OF CHRISTIAN COMMUNITY: not reported

EVANGELISM PROFILE: not reported   **VALIDITY:** 3

Spain relinquished the colonial territory of Western Sahara in 1975 and established the administration under the rule of Morocco and Mauritania. The residents of the region, who had formed an independent movement known as Polisario, resisted this pronouncement. Morocco and Mauritania forcibly occupied the territory and inflicted significant damage on the sociological, cultural and political infrastructures of the region. Approximately 70,000 Sahrawis fled and settled in temporary desert encampments where they were pursued by the Moroccan army, which claimed that it was fighting rebellious guerrillas. Unable to stand against the forces of the Moroccans and the harsh desert, the majority of Sahrawis escaped to Algeria.

By 1979 the 22 refugee camps were grouped into three provinces. The large units had been subdivided into cells of 11 adults with specific responsibilities of education, medical care and food distribution delegated to each adult. During the initial stages of the camps the refugees were grouped according to natural social tribal patterns. In an attempt to lessen the strength of tribalism these groups are now predetermined by national leaders. Much of the day is spent in educative programs including Arab culture, politics and military tactics. There is strong sentiment of Sahrawi nationalism. The scorching sun, irritating sandstorms, and cold nights cause life in the desert settlements to be very trying. The lack of adequate nutritional food, medicine and shelter compounds problems of the refugees, 80% of whom are women and children. In the initial stages of the camps only 10% of the tents were built by the Sahrawi from animal hair, and the canvas tents supplied by the foreign sources wore out very quickly. Blankets have also been in short supply. The health of the refugees has varied significantly depending on the availability of certain medicines for specific diseases which spread in epidemic proportion.

The refugees are waiting for resolution of the political and military conflicts which have stripped them of their rights to their own land. To return under foreign control would mean persecution and death. Thus they face the harsh reality of desert survival along with the psychological depression of being a landless people.

EXPANDED DESCRIPTIONS

Zimbabwean Refugees (Mozambique)

ALTERNATE NAMES: not reported
SIZE OF GROUP: 170,000   **MARC ID:** 9032
DISTINCTIVES: discrimination; residence
SOCIAL CHANGE: very rapid
LANGUAGES: Tribal Languages (V); English (T); Afrikaans (T)
SCRIPTURE: RECORDINGS: yes   **CHRISTIAN LITERACY:** 25%
RELIGION: Animism (75% adherents); Christianity (20% adherents)
CHURCHES AND MISSIONS: not reported
OPENNESS TO RELIGIOUS CHANGE: not reported
RECEPTIVITY TO CHRISTIANITY: not reported
GROWTH RATE OF CHRISTIAN COMMUNITY: not reported
EVANGELISM PROFILE: not reported   **VALIDITY:** 4

During the 1970s the phenomenon of black Zimbabwe's struggle for political equality escalated into a violent clash of wills which resulted in the disruption of life for many blacks in Zimbabwe.

Black guerrilla movements throughout the former country of Rhodesia created enormous pressure on the Ian Smith regime culminating in the demise of the white minority government in 1980. Prior to this, however, the crescendo of violence in Zimbabwe during the 70s led to the establishment of guerrilla sanctuaries in Mozambique and Zambia. In an attempt to root out the guerrillas, Rhodesian forces conducted forays into both nations in military actions designed to destroy guerrilla bases outside Rhodesia. Not only did these actions succeed in angering Rhodesia's neighbors since citizens of those countries were affected by these incursions, but countless Zimbabwean civilians seeking sanctuary in the two nations were killed. The attacks took the form of both air raids and infantry assaults. The Rhodesian explanation for these attacks on civilian refugee camps was that the camps sheltered and supported the guerrillas, thus making discrimination between the insurgents and general population impossible.

Although Zambia opened its borders to Zimbabweans fleeing from their country, three times as many fled to Mozambique by the late 1970s. There they were settled in five separate camps, and land was donated by the Mozambican government for crops. The refugees were affected by overcrowding, meager accomodations, disease and malnutrition. The goal of the camps was to eventually enable the refugees to provide a subsistence living for themselves by raising crops and some livestock. The continual attacks by Rhodesian forces resulting in the destruction of some of the camps and much of the farm equipment made it nearly impossible for the camps to achieve self-sufficiency.

The United Nations High Commissioner for Refugees protested the killing of refugees in the camps. The UNHCR and the International Committee of the Red Cross assisted in relief operations within Zimbabwe and among the refugees the latter organization appealed to the United States for monetary assistance for Zimbabwe.

The solution to the Mozambican refugee problem was expected to be eventual repatriation as soon as the political questions in Zimbabwe could be settled. While seen as a temporary problem, the continuing failure to resolve the Zimbabwean political situation created the need to develop longer-term maintenance plans for the refugees.

250

Zimbabwean Repatriates (Zimbabwe)

ALTERNATE NAMES: not reported
SIZE OF GROUP: 300,000   MARC ID: 9019
DISTINCTIVES: significant problems
SOCIAL CHANGE: very rapid
LANGUAGES: English (T); Afrikaans (60% speak; T); Tribal Languages (V)
SCRIPTURE: Bible; RECORDINGS: yes   CHRISTIAN LITERACY: 25%
RELIGION: Unknown; Christianity (-1% practicing)
CHURCHES AND MISSIONS: not reported
OPENNESS TO RELIGIOUS CHANGE: not reported
RECEPTIVITY TO CHRISTIANITY: not reported
GROWTH RATE OF CHRISTIAN COMMUNITY: not reported
EVANGELISM PROFILE: not reported   VALIDITY: 4

More Zimbabwean refugees were repatriated in a shorter amount of time than any other people group throughout history. By the time military conflict terminated, nearly 300,000 Zimbabweans had fled to Botswana, Zambia and Mozambique. When peace was restored they returned to their towns, villages and farms. The logistics involved were challenging as children sought parents whom they hadn't seen in years, and as the police attempted to register each refugee. Many refugees found ruined houses, fields and shops upon their return to former land holdings. The tasks at hand have required the help of relatives, friends and neighbors. Thatch-roofed homes have taken shape and fields have been replowed. Tools, seeds and fertilizer have been more difficult to come by, along with other basic agricultural supplies. Numerous secular and parochial organizations have pooled their resources and coordinated their efforts so that many of the basic elements of the local infrastructure could be restored. Water systems have been repaired, roads and bridges rebuilt, and some agricultural supplies distributed. It will undoubtedly take several seasons for the farmers to become self-sufficient once again.

Some elements of their lives will probably never return to normal.

The effects of mixing with peoples of other cultural traditions will undoubtedly alter certain aspects of lifestyles and ideologies. The value of material possessions has remained secondary to freedom and family welfare. The church can offer a sense of dynamic optimism as individuals seek to rebuild their lives within this growing redevelopment scenario. Christians can begin to look towards permanent church growth as many of the negative aspects of crisis situations are laid aside. The Zimbabweans have returned for good. They are home once again and the churches need to be a unifying force within each community.

Life is certainly not easy. It takes time to rebuild lives, but the key issue is the renewed freedom within each developing community. The farmers are back to work, the shop-keepers busy and the church alive once again.

Part 4

Registry of
the Unreached

Introduction
to the Registry

The information on the 3690 unreached peoples in the registry is presented in five different lists. Each list organizes the information differently. Only the first, which indexes the peoples alphabetically by group name, includes the estimated percentage of those that practice Christianity and a code that indicates the overall accuracy of the data. A more detailed explanation of the information contained in the following lists may be found at the beginning of each section.

Groups are also listed by receptivity to the gospel, principal professed religion, language and country. All five lists indicate those groups that are reported to be very receptive (***), receptive (**) or indifferent (*) to Christianity. There is also another code (79, 80, 81, 82 or 83) attached to the group name to indicate that a description has been written about this people group in **Unreached Peoples '79 (79)**, **Unreached Peoples '80 (80)**, **Unreached Peoples '81 (81)**, **Unreached Peoples '82 (82)** or **Unreached Peoples '83 (83)**.

A comparison with the indexes in previous volumes in this series will show that some early data has been changed. In a few cases, the group has been removed because of more accurate information. This reflects the ongoing nature of this data collection and research.

Index by Group Name

This is the basic listing of people groups in this registry. Peoples are listed by their primary **name,** and effort has been made to standardize names and use the most commonly accepted English spelling. This listing includes the **country** for which the information was provided, principal vernacular **language** used by the group, population estimate of the **group size** in the country listed and principal professed religion (**primary religion),** which in some cases is less than 40 percent of the total group membership.

In addition, this index includes the estimated percentage of the group that practices Christianity in any recognized tradition (**% Chr).** Included in this percentage are Protestant, Roman Catholic, Orthodox, African Independent and other Christian groups. Excluded from this percentage are Christo-pagans and Christian cultic groups. It is important to note that this figure is the estimated percentage of **practicing** Christians within the group. If the group was listed in **Unreached Peoples '80** or earlier, the figure recorded here will most likely be different, because those volumes recorded the percentage of **professing** Christians (or adherents), which most often will be a higher number. Thus, these figures should not be compared or used as a time series, since the changes indicate a different kind of data. Differences might also be due to a new and better data source or revised data, since we are continually updating our files.

This index also lists a validity code (**V**) which estimates the accuracy and completeness of the data on a scale from 1 to 9. See the introduction to the expanded descriptions for an explanation of this code.

The column labeled **Vol U.P.** indicates the year of the volume of **Unreached Peoples** in which a description of the group appears. The final column **(ID)** shows the identification number by which information on the group is filed in the unreached peoples database. Any correspondence sent to MARC dealing with the group should refer to that number.

Name	Country	Language	Group Size	Primary Religion	% Chr	V	UP	ID
Agariya in Bihar	India	Agariya	12,000	Hinduism	<1%			2602
Age	Cameroon	Age	5,000	Animism	0%		1	5206
Aghem	Cameroon	Aghem	7,000	Animism	0%		1	5207
Aghu	Indonesia	Aghu	3,000	Animism	<1%			2853
Agob	Papua New Guinea	Agob	1,000	Animism	0%		1	5906
Agoi	Nigeria	Agoi	4,000	Animism	<1%			2315
Aguacateco	Guatemala	Aguacateco	8,000	Animism	<1%			8002
Aguaruna	Peru	Aguaruna	22,000	Animism	<1%			3163
Agul	USSR	Agul	9,000	Islam	0%			5823
Agutaynon	Philippines	Agutaynon	7,000	Islam-Animist	<1%			3241
Agwagwune	Nigeria	Agwagwune	20,000	Animism	<1%			2316
Ahir in Maharashtra	India	Ahir	500,000	Islam	<1%			2603
**Ahl-i-Haqq in Iran	Iran	Kurdish dialects	133,000	Islam	0%	79	6	1237
Ahlo	Togo	Ahlo	3,000	Islam	0%			5621
Ahmadis in Lahore	Pakistan	Panjabi	60,000	Islam-Animist	0%	82	6	5016
Aibondeni	Indonesia	Aibondeni	200	Animism	<1%			2854
Aiku	Papua New Guinea	Aiku	800	Animism	0%		1	5907
Aikwakai	Indonesia	Aikwakai	400	Animism	<1%			2855
Aimol in Assam	India	Aimol	100	Hindu-Animism	<1%			2604
Aiome	Papua New Guinea	Aiome	900	Animism	<1%			5908
Aion	Papua New Guinea	Aion	800	Animism	<1%			5909
Airo-Sumaghaghe	Indonesia	Airo-Sumaghaghe	2,000	Animism	<1%			2856
Airoran	Indonesia	Airoran	400	Animism	<1%			5440
Aja	Sudan	Aja	1,000	Islam	0%			2605
Ajmeri in Rajasthan	India	Ajmeri	600	Hindu-Animist	<1%		3	1036
Aka	India	Aka	2,000	Animism	<1%			227
Akan, Brong	Ivory Coast	Akan, Brong	50,000	Islam-Animist	<1%		1	5115
Akawaio	Guyana	Akawaio	3,000	Christo-Paganism	<1%			2317
Ake	Nigeria	Ake	10,000	Animism	<1%	79	6	609
**Akha	Thailand	Akha	5,000	Ancestor Worship	0%		4	5824
Akhavakh	USSR	Akhavakh	nr	Unknown	0%			4064
***Akhdam	Yemen, Arab Republic	Arabic	15,000	Islam-Animist	<1%		1	2318
Akpa-Yache	Nigeria	Akpa-Yache	8,000	Islam-Animist	0%			5320
Akpafu	Ghana	Akpafu						
Akrukay	Papua New Guinea	Akrukay	200	Animism	<1%		4	5910
Alaba	Ethiopia	Alaban	50,000	Islam	3%		1	358
Aladian	Ivory Coast	Aladian	15,000	Islam-Animist	<1%		5	2228
Aiago	Nigeria	Aiago	35,000	Animism	2%		5	1058
Alak	Laos	Alak	8,000	Animism	<1%		1	112
Aiamblak	Papua New Guinea	Aiamblak	2,000	Animism	1%			5911
Alangan	Philippines	Alangan	6,000	Animism	<1%		4	3242
*Aiars	India	Allar	30,000	Christo-Paganism	0%		5	2017
Alas	Indonesia	Gayo	400	Folk Religion	0%			1133
Aiatil	Papua New Guinea	Aiatil	400	Animism	0%			5912
Aiauagat	Papua New Guinea	Aiauagat	300	Animism	0%	79	6	5913
*Alawites	Syria	Arabic	600,000	Islam	0%	80	6	1904
*Albanian Muslims	Albania	Albanian Tosk	1,700,000	Islam	0%		5	4000
*Albanians in Yugoslavia	Yugoslavia	Albanian (Gheg)	1,500,000	Islam	<1%			4036
Alege	Nigeria	Alege	1,000	Animism	<1%		1	2319

Name	Country	Language	Group Size	Primary Religion	% Chr	V	Vol UP	ID
Ansar Sudanese Refugees	Ethiopia	Arabic	11,000	Islam	<1%	4	83	9010
Ansus	Indonesia	Ansus	3,000	Animism	<1%	1		2864
Anuak	Ethiopia	Anuak	52,000	Animism	<1%	5		516
Anuak	Sudan	Anuak	30,000	Animism	4%	5		584
Anuki	Papua New Guinea	Anuki		Animism	<1%	1		5930
Anyanga	Togo	Anyanga	3,000	Islam-Animist	0%			5624
Apalai	Brazil	Apalai		Animism	1%	1		2145
**Apartment Residents-Seoul	Korea, Republic of	Korean	3,000	Animism	1%	4		301
**Apatani in Assam	India	Apartani	87,000	Folk Religion	1%	4		1026
*Apayao	Philippines	Isneg	11,000	Animism	9%	6		1201
Apinaye	Brazil	Apinaye	12,000	Christo-Paganism	<1%	1		2146
Apurina	Brazil	Apurina	200	Animism	<1%	1		2147
Ara	Indonesia	Ara	1,000	Animism	<1%	1		2865
Arab Immigrants in Bangui	Central African Republic	Arabic	75,000	Islam	0%	5	82	5045
Arab-Jabbari (Kamesh)	Iran	Arabic	5,000	Islam	0%	3		2044
Arab-Shaibani (Kamesh)	Iran	Arabic	16,000	Islam	0%	3		2045
Arabela	Peru	Arabela	200	Animism	<1%	5		3166
**Arabs in New Orleans	United States of America	Arabic	1,000	Islam	nr%	5	82	5008
Arabs of Khuzestan	Iran	Arabic	520,000	Islam	0%	4		2034
Aranadan in Tamil Nadu	India	Aranadan	600	Hindu-Animist	<1%	1		5931
Arandai	Indonesia	Arandai	2,300	Animism	<1%	1		2866
Arapaco	Brazil	Tucanoan	2,300	Animism	<1%	1		2148
Arapesh, Bumbita	Papua New Guinea	Arapesh, Bumbita	2,000	Animism	<1%	1		5932
Arapesh, Mountain	Papua New Guinea	Arapesh, Mountain	5,000	Animism	<1%	1		5933
Arapesh, Muhiang	Papua New Guinea	Arapesh, Muhiang	8,000	Animism	<1%	1		5934
Arawa	Nigeria	Hausa	200,000	Islam	<1%	4		644
Arawak	Guyana	Arawak	5,000	Christo-Paganism	<1%	1		5116
Arawe	Papua New Guinea	Arawe	3,000	Animism	<1%	1		5935
Arbore	Ethiopia	Arbore	2,000	Animism	<1%	1		3191
Archin	USSR	Archin	900	Unknown	0%			5827
Arecuna	Venezuela	Arecuna	14,000	Animism	<1%	1		5134
Argobba	Ethiopia	Argobba	3,000	Animism	<1%	1		3192
Arguni	Indonesia	Arguni	200	Animism	<1%	1		2867
*Arifama-Miniafia	Papua New Guinea	Arifama-Miniafia	2,000	Animism	1%			5936
Arigibi	Papua New Guinea	Arigibi	300	Animism	<1%	1		5937
Arinua	Papua New Guinea	Arinua	2,000	Animism	0%	1		5938
*Aranatas	India	Aranatan	2,000	Animism	<1%	4		2014
Arop	Papua New Guinea	Arop	2,000	Animism	<1%	1		5939
Arusha	Tanzania	Arusha	110,500	Animism	8%	5		5940
Arutani	Venezuela	Spanish	500	Animism	0%			5142
Arya in Andhra Pradesh	India	Arya	3,000	Hinduism	0%	1		5135
Asaro	Papua New Guinea	Asaro	12,700	Animism	<1%	1		2641
Asat	Papua New Guinea	Asat		Animism	<1%	1		5942
*Asian Students	Philippines	English	2,000	Animism	2%	4		5107
*Asienara	Indonesia	Asienara		Animism	7%	6	79	2868
*Asmat	Indonesia	Asmat	30,700	Animism	7%	6	79	205
Assumbo	Cameroon	Assumbo	10,000	Animism	<1%	1		5209

Name	Country	Language	Group Size	Primary Religion	% Chr	V	Vol UP	ID
Bafut	Cameroon	Bafut	25,000	Animism	0%	1		5211
Bagelkhandi in M.P.	India	Bagelkhandi	230,000	Hindu-Animist	<1%	1		2616
Baghati in H.P.	India	Baghati	4,000	Animist	<1%	1		2617
Bagirmi	Chad	Bagirmi	40,000	Islam-Animist	<1%	1		2209
***Bagobo	Philippines	Bagobo	35,000	Christo-Paganism	14%	5		4072
Bagri	Pakistan	Bagri	20,000	Hinduism	1%	4		268
Baguio Area Miners	Philippines	Ilocano	40,000	Nominal Christian	15%	5	81	5037
Bahais in Teheran	Iran	Farsi	45,000	Bahaism	0%	6	82	7004
Baham	Indonesia	Baham		Animism	<1%	3		2873
Baharlu (kamesh)	Iran	Turkish	8,500	Islam	0%	1		2046
Bahawalpuri in M.P.	India	Bahawalpuri	600	Animism	<1%	1		2618
Bahinemo	Papua New Guinea	Bahinemo	300	Animism	<1%	1		5952
Bai	Sudan	Bai	3,000	Islam	0%	1		5443
Baibai	Papua New Guinea	Baibai	1,300	Animism	<1%	1		5953
Baiga in Bihar	India	Baiga	11,000	Animism	0%	1		2619
Baining	Papua New Guinea	Baining	5,000	Animism	<1%	6	79	5954
Bajania	India	Gujarati Dialect	20,000	Hinduism	<1%	1		263
Bajau, Indonesian	Indonesia	Bajau, Indonesian	90,000	Islam-Animist	<1%	2		2874
Bajau, Land	Malaysia	Bajaus	1,000	Animism	<1%	1		4091
Baka	Cameroon	Baka	300	Animism	<1%	1		5212
Baka	Zaire	Baka		Animism				5689
Bakairi	Brazil	Bakairi		Animism	<1%	1		2150
Bakhtiaris	Iran	Bakhtiaris	590,000	Islam	0%	5	80	2031
Bakongo Angolan Refugees	Zaire	Kikongo	60,000	Animism	nr%	4	83	9026
**Bakuba	Zaire	Tshiluba	5,000	Islam-Animist	14%	1		1188
Bakwe	Ivory Coast	Bakwe	8,000	Animism	<1%	1		2281
***Bakwele	Congo	Bakwele	5,000	Christo-Paganism	0%	4		5291
***Balangao	Philippines	Balangao	5,000	Animism	3%	4		633
Balangaw	Philippines	Balangaw	50,000	Animism	<1%	1		3246
Balanta Refugees	Senegal	Balanta	60,000	Islam-Animist	0%	3		1142
Balantak	Indonesia	Balantak	125,000	Islam-Animist	<1%	1		9030
Balante	Guinea-Bissau	Balanta	100,000	Animism	7%	4		2875
Bali	Nigeria	Bali	1,000	Animism	<1%	1		594
Bali-Vitu	Papua New Guinea	Bali-Vitu	7,000	Animism	<1%	1		2328
Balinese	Indonesia	Balinese	2,000,000	Hinduism	0%	5		5955
Balkars	USSR	Balkar	60,000	Islam	1%	5		1094
Balmiki	Pakistan	Hindustani	20,000	Hinduism	1%	1		5813
Balong	Cameroon	Duala	5,000	Animism	<1%	5		254
Balti in Jammu	India	Balti	40,000	Islam	<1%	5		5213
Baluchi	Iran	Baluchi	1,100,000	Islam	0%	1		2620
Bam	Papua New Guinea	Bam	600	Animism	0%	6	80	2030
Bambara	Ivory Coast	Bambara	1,000,000	Islam	<1%	1		5956
Bambara	Mali	Bambara	1,000,000	not reported				2282
Bambuka	Nigeria	Bambuka	10,000	Animism	1%	5		604
Bamougoun-Bamenjou	Cameroon	Bamougoun-Bamenjou	31,000	Animism	0%	1		2329
Bamum	Cameroon	Bamum	75,000	Islam	nr%	1		5214
**Banai	Bangladesh	Bengali	2,000	Buddhist-Animist	1%	4		63
***Banaro	Papua New Guinea	Banaro	3,000	Animism	5%	4		195

Name	Country	Language	Group Size	Primary Religion	% Chr	V	UP	ID
Bandawa-Minda	Nigeria	Bandawa-Minda	10,000	Islam	<1%			2330
Bandi	Liberia	Bandi	32,000	Animism	6%	4		555
Bandjoun	Cameroon	Bandjoun	60,000	Animism	0%			5216
Banen	Cameroon	Banen	28,000	Animism	0%			5217
Banga	Nigeria	Banga	8,000	Islam	<1%			2331
Bangangte	Cameroon	Local Dialects	475,000	Islam	<1%			5218
Bangaru in Punjab	India	Bangri	4,000,000	Unknown	<1%			2621
Bangba	Zaire	Bangba	29,000	Hindu-Animism	0%			5692
Bangai	Indonesia	Bangai	200,000	Animism	<1%			2876
Baniwa	Brazil	Baniwa	3,000	Islam	<1%			2151
Banoni	Papua New Guinea	Banoni	1,000	Animism	<1%			5957
Bantuanon	Philippines	Bantuanon	50,000	Animism	<1%			3244
***Banyarwanda	Rwanda	Kinyarwanda	4,000,000	Christo-Paganism	6%	5		4027
Banyum	Senegal	Banyum	9,000	Animism	0%			5421
Banyum	Guinea-Bissau	Banyum	15,000	Islam-Animism	6%	4		593
***Baoule	Ivory Coast	Baule	4,000	Animism	9%	4		407
Barabaig	Tanzania	Tatoga	46,400	Animism	2%	5	79	5958
Barai	Papua New Guinea	Barai	400	Animism	0%			5444
Barambu	Sudan	Barambu	450	Islam	3%	5		2180
Barasano, Northern	Colombia	Barasano, Northern	400	Animism	2%	4		474
Barasano, Southern	Colombia	Janena	300	Animism	<1%			289
*barau	Indonesia	Barau	220,000	Animism	<1%	6	82	2877
*Berbers in Tokyo	Japan	Japanese	325,000	Buddhism	<1%			5009
Barie	Indonesia	Barie	230,000	Animism	<1%			2878
Bareli in Madhya Pradesh	India	Bareli	340,000	Hinduism	0%			2622
Barii	Sudan	Bari	400,000	Islam	<1%			5445
*Bariai	Papua New Guinea	Bariai	55,000	Animism	4%	6	80	5959
*Bariba	Benin	Bariba	300	Animism	<1%			246
Bariba	Nigeria	Bariba	600	Islam-Animism	<1%			7041
Barifi	Papua New Guinea	Barifi	1,000	Animism	<1%			5960
Barim	Papua New Guinea	Barim	1,000	Animism	<1%			5961
Barok	Papua New Guinea	Barok	4,000	Animism	<1%			5962
Baruga	Papua New Guinea	Baruga	170,000	Animism	<1%			5963
Baruya	Papua New Guinea	Baruya	60,000	Animism	<1%			7063
Basa	Cameroon	Bassa	4,000	Animism	0%			5219
Basakomo	Nigeria	not reported	8,000	Unknown	12%	4		550
Basari	Guinea	Basari	100,000	Animism	0%			5341
Basari	Senegal	Basari	20,000	Animism	0%			5422
Bashar	Nigeria	Basari	1,200,000	Animism	10%	5		2333
Bashgali	Afghanistan	Bashgali	9,000	Animism	<1%			2546
Bashir	USSR	Bashiri	70,000	Islam	0%	5	80	5001
Basila	Togo	Tatali	200,000	Animism	<1%			5025
Basketo	Ethiopia	Basketo	100,000	Islam-Animism	<1%			3192
***Basotho, Mountain	Lesotho	Southern Sesotho	30,000	Animism	8%	6	79	232
**Bassa	Liberia	Bassa		Animism	1%	5		3056
**Bassa	Nigeria	Bassa		Animism	8%	5		1056
Bata	Nigeria	Bata		Islam-Animism	<1%			2334

Name	Country	Language	Group Size	Primary Religion	% Chr	V	UP	ID
*Batak, Angkola	Indonesia	Batak, Angkola	400,000	Islam	6%	6	80	4002
Batak, Karo	Indonesia	Batak, Karo	400	Animism	<1%	1		2879
Batak, Palawan	Philippines	Batak, Palawan		Christo-Paganism	<1%	1		3245
Batak, Simalungun	Indonesia	Batak, Simalungun	800,000	Animism	<1%	1		2880
Batak, Toba	Indonesia	Batak, Toba	1,600,000	Animism	<1%	1		2881
Batanga-Ngolo	Cameroon	Batanga-Ngolo	9,000	Animism	206%	4		5220
**Batangeno	Philippines	Tagalog	nr	Nominal Christian	nr			4073
Bateg	Malaysia	Bateg	400	Animism	0%			4114
Bathudi in Bihar	India	Bathudi	74,000	Hinduism	0%			2623
Batsi	USSR	Batsi	3,000	Unknown	0%			5828
Batu	Nigeria	Batu	25,000	Islam	<1%			2335
Bau	Nigeria	Bau	2,000	Animism	<1%			5965
Baushi	Papua New Guinea	Baushi	3,000	Islam	<1%			2336
Bauwaki	Papua New Guinea	Bauwaki	400	Animism	<1%			5966
Bavenda	South Africa	Tschievenda	360,000	Animism	nr%			6564
Bawm	Bangladesh	Bawm	7,000	Islam	<1%			2561
Bawoyo	Zaire	Kiwoyo	10,000	Nominal Christian	20%			2067
Bayats	Iran	Bayat	nr	Islam-Animist	<1%			6571
Bayot	Gambia	Bayot	4,000	Islam-Animist	<1%			2266
	Guinea-Bissau	Bayot	3,000	Islam-Animist	0%			5348
	Senegal	Bayot	4,000	Islam-Animist	<1%			5423
Bazigar in Gujarat	India	Bazigar	100	Animism	0%			2626
Bebeli	Papua New Guinea	Bebeli	600	Animism	<1%			5967
Bediya in Bihar	India	Bediya	32,300	Animism	<1%			2627
Bedoanas	Indonesia	Bedoanas	39,000	Animism	<1%			2882
Beja	Ethiopia	Beja	91,000	Islam	<1%			3195
	Sudan	Beja	34,000	Islam	<1%			5446
Bekwarra	Nigeria	Bekwarra	50,000	Animism	0%			2337
Bembe	Zaire	Bembe	150,000	Animism	0%			5693
Bembi	Papua New Guinea	Bembi	400	Animism	0%			5968
Bena	Tanzania	Bena	14,000	Animism	<1%			5534
Benabena	Papua New Guinea	Benabena	5,000	Animism	<1%			5969
Bencho	Ethiopia	Bencho	9,000	Animism	0%			3196
Bende	Tanzania	Bende	60,000	Animism	0%			5535
Bene	Cameroon	Bene	nr	Animism	<1%			5221
Benga	Gabon	Benga		Animism	0%			5306
Bengali Refugees, Assam	India	Bengali	4,000,000	Islam	<1%			9054
Bengalis in London	United Kingdom	Bengali	15,000	Islam	0%		82	5038
Bengkulu	Indonesia	Bengkulu	25,000	Islam	0%			6563
Berba	Benin	Berba	44,000	Animism	<1%			5165
Berik	Indonesia	Berik	800	Animism	0%			2883
Berom	Nigeria	Berom	116,000	Animism	<1%			2338
Besisi	Malaysia	Besisi	7,000	Animism	0%			4109
Bete	India	Bete	3,000	Animism	1%			7049
*Bete	Ivory Coast	Bete	300,000	Animism	<1%			4128
Bethen	Cameroon	Bethen	10,000	Animism	0%			5222
Betsinga	Cameroon	Betsinga	10,000	Animism	0%			5223
Bette-Bende	Nigeria	Bette-Bende	40,000	Animism	<1%			2339
Bhakta	India	Bhakta	55,000	Hindu-Animist	<1%			2615

267

Name	Country	Language	Group Size	Primary Religion	% Chr	V	Vol UP	ID
Bitara	Papua New Guinea	Bitara	100	Animism	0%			5980
Bitare	Cameroon	Bitare	50,000	Animism	0%		79	5224
	Nigeria	Bitare	3,000	Islam-Animist	<1%			2342
Biti	Sudan	Biti	300	Islam	0%			5509
Biyom	Papua New Guinea	Biyom	400	Animism	0%			5981
**Black Caribs, Belize	Belize	Moreno	10,000	Christo-Paganism	1%	6		252
**Black Caribs, Guatemala	Guatemala	Moreno	2,000	Christo-Paganism	1%	5		251
**Black Caribs, Honduras	Honduras	Moreno	20,000	Christo-Paganism	1%	5		245
Boanaki	Papua New Guinea	Boanaki	2,000	Animism	nr%	4		5982
Boat People	Japan	Vietnamese	1,800	Ancestor Worship	0%			9036
Bobe	Cameroon	Bobe	600	Animism	<1%			5225
Bobo Fing	Mali	Bobo Fing	3,000	Animism	<1%			5373
Bobo Wule	Mali	Bobo Wule	366,000	Animism	<1%			5374
**Bodo Kachari	India	Bodo	610,000	Hindu-Animist	2%	4		2007
Bodo in Assam	India	Bodo	50,000	Animism	<1%			2641
Boghom	Nigeria	Boghom	1,000	Animism	<1%			2243
Bohutu	Papua New Guinea	Bohutu	31,000	Animism	<1%			5983
Boikin	Papua New Guinea	Boikin	40,000	Animism	2%			5984
**Boko	Benin	Boko (Busa)	87,000	Animism	<1%			444
Bokyi	Cameroon	Bokyi	87,000	Animism	<1%			5226
	Nigeria	Bokyi	5,000	Animism	<1%			2344
Bola	Papua New Guinea	Bola	5,000	Animism	<1%			5985
Bole	Nigeria	Bole	32,000	Islam	<1%			2345
***Bolinao	Philippines	Bolinao	26,000	Nominal Christian	19%	4	81	4058
Bolon	Upper Volta	Bolon	4,000	Islam-Animist	<1%			5661
Bolondo	Zaire	Bolondo	1,000	Animism	<1%			5596
Bom	Papua New Guinea	Bom	15,000	Animism	0%			5986
Boma	Cameroon	Bomboko	15,000	Animism	<1%			5697
Bomboko	Chad	Bomou	30,000	Islam-Animist	0%			5227
Bomou	Tanzania	Bomdei	2,000	Islam	<1%			2211
Bomdei	India	Bondo	100	Animism	<1%			5536
Bondo in Orissa	Indonesia	Bonerif	2,000	Hinduism	0%			2642
Bonerif	Indonesia	Bonggo	400	Animism	<1%			2888
Bonggo	Congo	Bongili	4,000	Animism	<1%			2889
Bongili	Sudan	Bongu	2,000	Animism	0%			5292
Bongu	Papua New Guinea	Bongu	2,000	Animism	0%			5451
	Cameroon	Bonkeng-Pendia	300	Animism	<1%			5987
Bonkeng-Pendia	Cameroon	Bonkiman	300	Animism	0%			5228
Bonkiman	Papua New Guinea	Bontoc, Central	1,000	Animism	<1%			5988
**Bontoc, Central	Philippines	Southern Bontoc	20,000	Animism	4%	5		632
**Bontoc, Southern	Philippines	Bor Gok	12,000	Christo-Paganism	0%	5		1060
Bor Gok	Sudan	Borai	6,000	Islam	0%			5463
Borai	Colombia	Boran	1,000	Animism	<1%			2081
Boran	Indonesia	Boran		Animism	<1%			2290
**Bororo	Ethiopia	Boran	132,000	Islam-Animist	3%	5		3198
*Bororo	Kenya	Bororo	37,000	Islam-Animist	1%	5		4077
Bosavi	Brazil	Bosavi	500	Animism	3%			441
Bosilewa	Papua New Guinea	Bosilewa	400	Animism	0%			5989
	Papua New Guinea	Bosilewa	400	Animism	<1%			5990

269

Name	Country	Language	Group Size	Primary Religion	% Chr	V	UP	Vol	ID
Buraka-Gbanziri	Congo	Buraka-Gbanziri	1,000	Animism	0%				5293
Buriat	China	Buriat	30,000	Traditional Chinese	<1%				2809
Buriat	USSR	Buriat	315,000	Buddhist-Animist	<1%				5831
Burig in Kashmir	China	Burig	148,000	Traditional Chinese	<1%				2810
Burig in Kashmir	India	Burig	132,000	Animism	<1%				2645
Burji	Ethiopia	Burji	20,000	Animism	<1%				3199
Burmese Muslim Refugees	Bangladesh	Bengali	200,000	Islam	0%	3		83	9001
Buru	Indonesia	Buru	6,000	Animism	<1%				2896
Burun	Papua New Guinea	Burun	3,000	Animism	<1%				6002
Burundian Hutu Refugees	Sudan	Kirundi	5,000	Islam	0%				5452
Burungi	Tanzania	Burungi	120,000	Animism	<1%	4		83	9006
**Bus Drivers, South Korea	Korea, Republic of	Korean	20,000	Unknown	7%	6		82	493
**Bus Girls in Seoul	Korea, Republic of	Korean	26,000	Secularism	8%	6		80	1195
Busa	Nigeria	Busa (Bokobarn Akiba)	50,000	Islam	8%				5023
Busah	Papua New Guinea	Busah	50,000	Islam	1%				1055
Busami	Indonesia	Busami	200	Animism	0%				6003
**Busanse	Ghana	Bisa (Busanga)	400	Animism	<1%				2897
*Bushmen (Heikum)	Namibia	Heikum	50,000	Animism	2%				1082
*Bushmen (Hiechware)	Zimbabwe	Kwe-Etshari	16,000	Animism	6%				563
*Bushmen (Kung)	Namibia	Xu	2,000	Animism	6%	6		79	588
Bushmen in Botswana	Botswana	Buka-khwe	10,000	Animism	6%				562
Bushoong	Zaire	Bushoong	30,000	Animism	7%				509
Bussa	Ethiopia	Bussa	100,000	Animism	<1%				5702
Butawa	Nigeria	Buta	1,000	Islam	0%				3200
Butung	Indonesia	Butung	20,000	Islam-Animist	<1%				548
**Buwid	Philippines	Buwid	200,000	Islam	8%	5		81	2898
Bviri	Sudan	Bviri	6,000	Animism	0%				4161
Bwa	Upper Volta	Buamu (Bobo Wule)	16,000	Islam	9%	6		80	5453
Bwaidoga	Zaire	Bwaidoga	35,000	Animism	<1%				468
Bwisi	Papua New Guinea	Bwisi	6,000	Animism	<1%				5703
Byangsi	Nepal	Byangsi	2,000	Animism	<1%				6004
Cacua	Colombia	Cacua	200	Buddhist-Animist	0%				5704
Caiwa	Brazil	Caiwa	7,000	Animism	<1%				6503
Cakchiquel, Central	Guatemala	Cakchiquel, Central	300,000	Animism	<1%				2182
Caluyanhon	Philippines	Caluyanhon	30,000	Christo-Paganism	<1%				2152
*Cambodians	Thailand	Northern Kamer	1,000,000	Buddhist-Animist	1%	5			8003
Campa	Peru	Campa	5,000	Animism	<1%				3250
Camsa	Colombia	Camsa	2,000	Animism	<1%				606
Candoshi	Brazil	Candoshi	1,000	Animism	<1%				2224
Canahua	Peru	Caneia	500	Animism	<1%				2183
Capanahua	Peru	Capanahua	150	Animism	<1%				3167
Cape Malays in Cape Town	South Africa	Afrikaans	150	Islam	7%	6		82	2153
Carapana	Colombia	Carapana	200	Animism	<1%				2205
Cashibo	Peru	Cashibo	2,000	Animism	<1%				5006
*Casiguranin	Philippines	Casiguranin	10,000	Nominal Christian	17%				2184
*Casual Laborers-Atlanta	United States of America	English	10,000	Secularism	nr%	5		82	3148
									4055
									5048
Cayapa	Ecuador	Cayapa	3,000	Animism	<1%				3158

Name	Country	Language	Group Size	Primary Religion	% Chr	V	Vol UP	ID
***Cebu, Middle-Class	Philippines	Cebuano	500,000	Christo-Paganism	12%	4		1079
***Central Thailand Farmers	Thailand	Thai	5,000,000	Buddhist-Animist	1%	5	81	645
Cewa	Zambia	Cewa	200,000	Animism	0%	4		5803
Ch'iang	China	Ch'iang	77,000	Traditional Chinese	<1%	4		2811
***Ch'ol Sabanilla	Mexico	Ch'ol	20,000	Christo-Paganism	5%	4		114
Ch'ol Tila	Mexico	Tila Chol	38,300	Animism	1%	5		1216
Chacobo	Bolivia	Chacobo		Animism	<1%	5		2132
Chad's Refugees from N'Djamena	Cameroon	Tribal Languages	100,000	Islam	<1%	4	83	9005
Chadian Refugees	Nigeria	Arabic	3,000	Islam	<1%	4	83	9043
Chagga	Tanzania	Chagga	800,000	Animism	0%	1		5537
Chaghatai	Afghanistan	Chaghatai	300,000	Islam	<1%	1		2547
Chakfem-Mushere	Nigeria	Chakfem-Mushere	5,000	Animism	<1%	1		2348
*Chakmas of Mizoram	India	Chakma	20,000	Buddhist-Animist	<1%	5	81	2011
Chakossi in Ghana	Ghana	Chakossi	31,000	Animism	1%	5		524
Chakossi in Togo	Togo	Chakossi	20,000	Animism	3%	4		598
Chala	Ghana	Chala	1,000	Islam-Animist	<1%	5		5324
Cham	Viet Nam	Cham	45,000	Hindu-Animist	1%	5		272
*Cham Refugees from Kampuchea	Kampuchea, Democratic	Cham	20,000	Islam	0%	6	83	91
Chamacoco, Bahia Negra	Paraguay	Chamacoco, Bahia Negra	1,000	Animism	<1%	1		5121
Chamalin	USSR	Chamalin	6,000	Unknown	0%	1		5832
Chamari in Madhya Pradesh	India	Chamari	5,000	Hindu-Animist	<1%	1		2647
Chamba Daka	Nigeria	Chamba Daka	66,000	Islam-Animist	<1%	1		2349
Chamba Leko	Nigeria	Chamba Leko	30,000	Islam-Animist	<1%	1		2350
Chambri	Papua New Guinea	Chambri	900	Animism	<1%	1		6005
Chameali in H.P.	India	Chameali	53,000	Hindu-Animist	<1%	1		2648
Chami	Colombia	Chami	3,000	Animism	<1%	1		2186
Chamicuro	Peru	Chamicuro	200	Animism	10%	4		3169
Chamorro	Turks and Caicos Islands	Chamorro	15,000	Christo-Paganism	7%	6	79	1001
Chamula	Mexico	Tzotzil (Chamula)	50,000	Christo-Paganism	0%	5	81	162
*Chang-Pa of Kashmir	India	Tibetan Dialect	7,000	Buddhist-Animist	<1%	1		701
Chara	Ethiopia	Chara	1,000	Animism	<1%	1		3201
Chatino, Nopala	Mexico	Chatino, Nopala	8,000	Christo-Paganism	0%	1		8017
Chatino, Panixtlahuaca	Mexico	Chatino, Panixtlahuaca	5,000	Christo-Paganism	<1%	1		8019
Chatino, Tataltepec	Mexico	Chatino, Tataltepec	2,000	Christo-Paganism	<1%	1		8018
Chatino, Yaitepec	Mexico	Spanish	2,000	Christo-Paganism	0%	1		8020
Chatino, Zacatepec	Mexico	Chatino, Zacatepec	500	Christo-Paganism	0%	1		8021
Chatino, Zenzontepec	Mexico	Chatino, Zenzontepec	4,000	Christo-Paganism	0%	1		8022
Chaudangsi	Nepal	Chaudangsi	2,000	Buddhist-Animist	<1%	1		6504
Chaungtha	Burma	Chaungtha	40,000	Buddhist-Animist	0%	1		2568
Chawai	Nigeria	Chawai		Animism	<1%	4		547
**Chayahuita Trotzil	Peru	Chayawita	6,000	Christo-Paganism	19%	3		84
Chenalhoa Trotzil	Mexico	Tzotzil, Chenalhoa		Animism	0%	1		5103
Chenapian	Papua New Guinea	Chenapian	200	Animism	<1%	1		6006
Chenchu in Andhra Pradesh	India	Chenchu	18,000	Hindu-Animist	<1%	1		2649
Chepang	Nepal	Chepang	10,000	Buddhist-Animist	0%	1		6505
Cherkess	USSR	Cherkess	40,000	Islam	0%	1		5810
Chero in Bihar	India	Chero	28,000	Animism	<1%	1		2810
**Chicanos in Denver	United States of America	Spanish	128,000	Nominal Christian	nr%	5	82	5029
Chiga	Uganda	Chiga	272,000	Animism	0%	1		5641

Name	Country	Language	Group Size	Primary Religion	% Chr	V	UP	ID
Chik-Barik in Bihar	India	Chik-Barik	30,000	Animism	<1%			2651
Chilean Refugees in	Argentina	Spanish	1,850	Nominal Christian	nr%	4	83	9031
*Chilean Refugees in Toronto	Canada	Spanish	10,000	Nominal Christian	nr%	4	83	9023
Chin	China	Chin	100,000	Traditional Chinese	<1%	1		2812
Chin, Asho	Burma	Chin, Asho	11,000	Buddhist-Animist	<1%	1		2569
Chin, Falam	Burma	Chin, Falam	92,000	Buddhist-Animist	<1%	1		2570
Chin, Haka	Burma	Chin, Haka	85,000	Buddhist-Animist	<1%	1		2571
Chin, Khumi	Burma	Chin, Khumi	30,000	Buddhist-Animist	<1%	1		2572
Chin, Ngawn	Burma	Chin, Ngawn	3,000	Buddhist-Animist	<1%	1		2573
Chin, Tiddim	Burma	Chin, Tiddim	38,000	Buddhist-Animist	<1%	1		2574
Chinanteco, Tepinapa	Mexico	Chinanteco, Tepinapa	3,000	Christo-Paganism	0%	1		8033
Chinanteco, Ayotzintepec	Mexico	Chinanteco, Ayotzintepec	2,000	Christo-Paganism	0%	1		8023
Chinanteco, Chiltepec	Mexico	Chinanteco, Chiltepec	3,000	Christo-Paganism	0%	1		8024
Chinanteco, Comaltepec	Mexico	Chinanteco, Comaltepec	2,000	Christo-Paganism	<1%	1		8025
Chinanteco, Lalana	Mexico	Chinanteco, Lalana	10,000	Christo-Paganism	<1%	1		8026
Chinanteco, Lealao	Mexico	Chinanteco, Lealao	5,000	Christo-Paganism	<1%	1		8027
Chinanteco, Ojitlan	Mexico	Chinanteco, Ojitlan	10,000	Christo-Paganism	<1%	1		8028
Chinanteco, Palantla	Mexico	Chinanteco, Palantla	11,000	Christo-Paganism	<1%	1		8029
Chinanteco, Quiotepec	Mexico	Chinanteco, Quiotepec	7,000	Christo-Paganism	<1%	1		8030
Chinanteco, Sochiapan	Mexico	Chinanteco, Sochiapan	2,000	Christo-Paganism	<1%	1		8031
Chinanteco, Tepetotutla	Mexico	Chinanteco, Tepetotutla	2,000	Christo-Paganism	<1%	1		8032
Chinanteco, Usila	Mexico	Chinanteco, Usila	5,000	Christo-Paganism	<1%	1		8034
Chinbok	Burma	Chinbok	21,000	Buddhist-Animist	<1%	1		2575
Chinese Businessmen	Hong Kong	Cantonese	10,000	Traditional Chinese	8%	5	81	2111
Chinese Factory Workers	Hong Kong	Cantonese	50,000	Traditional Chinese	2%	3		744
Chinese Fishermen	Malaysia	Hokkien	4,000	Traditional Chinese	0%	3		4142
**Chinese Hakka of Taiwan	Taiwan	Hakka	1,750,000	Traditional Chinese	1%	6	79	746
*Chinese Mainlanders	Taiwan	Mandarin	2,000,000	Traditional Chinese	8%	4		85
Chinese Muslims	Taiwan	Mandarin	45,000	Islam	<1%	5	81	7019
*Chinese Refugees in Macau	Macau	Cantonese	100,000	Traditional Chinese	1%	5	81	129
**Chinese Refugees in France	France	Mandarin	100,000	Traditional Chinese	2%	4	79	1226
*Chinese Restaurant Wrkrs.	France	Won Chow	50,000	Traditional Chinese	2%			1227
*Chinese Stud., Australia	Australia	Chinese Dialects	6,000	Secularism	5%	4		2119
**Chinese Students Glasgow	United Kingdom	Mandarin	1,000	Secularism	15%	4		2078
Chinese Villagers	Hong Kong	Cantonese	500,000	Traditional Chinese	1%	4		742
**Chinese in Amsterdam	Netherlands	Cantonese	15,000	Traditional Chinese	1%	3		735
**Chinese in Australia	Australia	Cantonese	30,000	Unknown	8%	4		747
**Chinese in Austria	Austria	Mandarin	1,000	Traditional Chinese	5%	4		753
**Chinese in Boston	United States of America	Hakka	20,000	Secularism	4%	6	82	5019
**Chinese in Brazil	Brazil	Cantonese	45,000	Traditional Chinese	8%	4		755
Chinese in Burma	Burma	Mandarin	600,000	Traditional Chinese	2%	4		751
Chinese in Costa Rica	Costa Rica	Mandarin and dialects	5,000	Unknown	1%	3		736
Chinese in Costa Rica	Costa Rica	Cantonese	4,000	Secularism	1%	3		4141
*Chinese in Holland	Netherlands	Mandarin	35,000	Unknown	1%	3		734
**Chinese in Indonesia	Indonesia	Indonesian	3,600,000	Traditional Chinese	6%	4		733
*Chinese in Japan	Japan	Mandarin	50,000	Traditional Chinese	1%	4		738
*Chinese in Korea	Korea, Republic of	Mandarin	20,000	Secularism	5%	4		298
*Chinese in Laos	Laos	Mandarin	25,000	Traditional Chinese	1%	4		101
*Chinese in Malaysia	Malaysia	Chinese dialects	4,000,000	Traditional Chinese	8%	5		408

Name	Country	Language	Group Size	Primary Religion	% Chr	Vol V	UP	ID
*Chinese in New Zealand	New Zealand	Cantonese	13,000	Traditional Chinese	4%		4	752
**Chinese in Panama	Panama	Spanish	25,000	Traditional Chinese	1%		3	4140
**Chinese in Puerto Rico	Puerto Rico	Hakka		Traditional Chinese	0%		2	748
**Chinese in Sabah	Malaysia	Hakka	180,000	Traditional Chinese	10%		4	740
**Chinese in Sarawak	Malaysia	Hakka	330,000	Traditional Chinese	7%		4	737
Chinese in Saudi Arabia	Saudi Arabia	Arabic	20,000	Islam	0%		3	4135
Chinese in South Africa	South Africa	Cantonese	9,000	Traditional Chinese	9%		4	756
Chinese in Thailand	Thailand	Hakka	3,600,000	Traditional Chinese	2%		4	749
**Chinese in United Kingdom	United Kingdom	Mandarin	110,000	Traditional Chinese	3%		4	1225
**Chinese in United States	United States of America	Mandarin	550,000	Traditional Chinese	9%		4	750
**Chinese in Vancouver B.C.	Canada	Cantonese	80,000	Traditional Chinese	6%		4	758
*Chinese in West Germany	German Federal Rep.	Mandarin	8,000	Traditional Chinese	2%		4	1228
*Chinese of W. Malaysia	Malaysia	Cantonese	3,500,000	Secularism	4%		1	757
Chinga	Cameroon	Chinga	13,000	Animism	0%		1	7050
Chingp'o	China	Chingp'o	100,000	Traditional Chinese	<1%		1	2813
Chip	Nigeria	Chip	6,000	Animism	<1%		1	2351
Chipaya	Bolivia	Chipaya		Animism	<1%		1	2133
Chiquitano	Bolivia	Chiquitano	20,000	Animism	<1%		1	2134
**Chiriguano	Argentina	Guarani (Bolivian)	20,000	Animism	8%		5	14
Chitralis	Pakistan	Khuwar	120,000	Islam	0%	79	6	1234
Chocho	Mexico	Spanish		Christo-Paganism	0%		7	8035
Chodhari in Gujarat	India	Chodhari	139,400	Hindu-Animist	<1%		1	2654
Chokobo	Nigeria	Chokobo		Animism	<1%		1	2352
Chokwe	Zambia	Chokwe	25,000	Animism	0%		1	5782
Chokwe (Lunda)	Angola	Chokwe	400,000	Animism	9%		5	149
Chola Naickans	India	Canarese	100	Animism	0%		3	124
Chopi	Mozambique	Chopi	400,000	Animism	<1%		1	5390
Chorote	Argentina	Chorote	500	Animism	<1%		1	2128
Chorote	Paraguay	Chorote		Animism	<1%		1	5122
Chorti	Guatemala	Chorti		Animism	nr		1	8004
**Chrau	Viet Nam	Jro	25,000	Animism	14%		4	394
Chuabo	Mozambique	Chwabo	15,000	Animism	9%		5	566
Chuang	China	Chuang	250,000	Animism	0%		1	7014
Chuave	Papua New Guinea	Chuave	20,000	Animism	<1%		1	6007
Chuj	Guatemala	Chuj	12,000	Animism	12%	81	5	8005
Chuj, San Mateo Ixtatan	Mexico	Chuj, San Mateo Ixtatan		Christo-Paganism	0%			8026
Chukot	USSR	Chukot	14,000	Unknown	0%		1	5823
Chulupe	Paraguay	Chulupe		Christo-Paganism	<1%		1	5833
Chungchia	China	Chungchia	1,508,000	Traditional Chinese	<1%		1	2814
Churahi in H.P.	India	Churahi	35,000	Hindu-Animist	<1%		1	2655
Chwang	China	Chwang	7,800,000	Traditional Chinese	<1%		1	2815
Cinta Larga	Brazil	Cinta Larga	500	Animism	<1%		1	2154
Circassian	Turkey	Circassian	113,000	Islam	<1%		1	2541
Circassians in Amman	Jordan	Arabic	17,000	Islam	0%	82	5	5018
Cirebon	Indonesia	Javanese, Tjirebon	2,500,000	Islam-Animist	<1%		5	1135
***Citak	Indonesia	Citak (Asmat)	7,000	Animism	<1%		5	1166
Cocama	Peru	Cocama	18,900	Animism	<1%		1	3170
Cocopa	Mexico	Cocopa	900	Christo-Paganism	0%		1	8037

273

Name	Language	Country	Group Size	Primary Religion	% Chr	V	UP	ID
Cofan	Cofan	Colombia	300	Animism	<1%			2188
Cogui	Cogui	Colombia		Animism	<1%	1		2189
***Coloureds in Eersterust	Afrikaans	South Africa	4,000	Animism	<1%			5040
***Copacabana Apt. Dwellers	Portuguese	Brazil	20,000	Secularism	15%	6	82	4116
Cora	Cora	Mexico	400,000	Nominal Christian	<1%	4		8038
**Coreguaje	Coreguaje	Colombia	8,500	Christo-Paganism	<1%			397
Cubeo	Cubeo	Colombia		Animism	<1%	4		2191
Cuiba	Cuiba	Colombia	2,000	Animism	<1%			2192
Cuicateco, Tepeuxila	Cuicateco, Tepeuxila	Mexico	10,000	Christo-Paganism	<1%			8039
Cuicateco, Teutila	Cuicateco, Teutila	Mexico	6,000	Christo-Paganism	<1%			8040
Cujareno	Cujareno	Peru	100	Animism	<1%			3171
Culina	Culina	Brazil	800	Animism	<1%			2155
*Cuna	Cuna	Colombia	600	Animism	7%	5	79	9
Curipaco	Curipaco	Colombia	3,000	Animism	<1%			2194
Cuyonon	Cuyonon	Philippines	49,000	Christo-Paganism	<1%			3251
Daba	Daba	Cameroon	31,000	Animism	<1%			7051
Dabra	Dabra	Indonesia	100	Animism	<1%			2900
Dadibi	Dadibi	Papua New Guinea	6,000	Animism	<1%			6008
Dadiya	Dadiya	Nigeria	2,000	Islam	<1%			2353
Daga	Daga	Papua New Guinea	6,000	Animism	<1%			6009
Dagada	Dagada	Indonesia	30,000	Animism	<1%			2901
Dagari	Dagari	Ghana	200,000	Animism	<1%	4		523
*Dagomba	Dagbanli	Upper Volta	150,000	Islam-Animist	1%	4		5663
Dagur	Dagur	China	350,000	Islam-Animist	<1%			525
Dahating	Dahating	Papua New Guinea	23,900	Traditional Chinese	<1%			2816
Dai	Dai	Burma		Buddhist-Animist	<1%			6010
Dair	Dair	Sudan	10,200	Islam	<1%			2576
Daju of Dar Dadju	Daju of Dar Dadju	Chad		Islam-Animist	0%			5454
Daju of Dar Fur	Daju	Sudan	27,000	Islam-Animist	<1%			2213
Daju of Dar Sila	Daju of Dar Sila	Chad	12,000	Islam-Animist	0%			5455
Daju of West Kordofan	Daju	Sudan	33,000	Islam-Animist	<1%			2214
*Daka	Daka	Nigeria		Islam	0%			5456
Dami	Dami	Papua New Guinea	10,000	Animism	3%	4		546
**Dan	Dan	Liberia	1,000	Animism	<1%	5		6011
*Danchi Dwellers in Tokyo	Japanese	Japan	270,000	Animism	2%	5		4126
*Dangaleat	Dangaleat	Chad	94,000	Islam-Animist	<1%	5	82	5359
*Dani, Baliem	Dani, Grand Valley	Indonesia	2,500,000	Secularism	2%			5005
Danu	Burmese	Burma	20,000	Animism	<1%			1219
Daonda	Daonda	Papua New Guinea	50,000	Animism	3%	6	79	2215
Darai	Darai	Nepal	70,000	Buddhism	0%	2		4148
Dargin	Dargin	USSR	100	Animism	0%			6012
Darmiya	Darmiya	Nepal	23,000	Buddhist-Animist	0%			6506
Dass	Dass	Nigeria	231,000	Islam	<1%			5834
Dathanik	Dathanik	Ethiopia	2,000	Buddhist-Animist	0%			6507
Davaweno	Davaweno	Philippines	9,000	Islam-Animist	<1%			2354
Davaweno	Davaweno	Philippines	18,000	Islam-Animist	<1%			3202
Dawawa	Dawawa	Papua New Guinea	13,000	Christo-Paganism	<1%			3252
Dawawa	Dawawa	Papua New Guinea		Animism	0%			6013
Dawoodi Muslims	Gujarati	India	225,000	Islam	0%	4		2004

Name	Country	Language	Group Size	Primary Religion	% Chr	V	UP	ID
Doghosie	Upper Volta	Doghosie	8,000	Islam-Animist	0%			5665
*Dogon	Mali	Dogon	312,100	Animism	10%	6	79	150
Dogoro	Papua New Guinea	Dogoro	100	Animism	0%			6021
Doigans	USSR	Dogan	5,000	Unknown	0%			5816
Dom	Papua New Guinea	Dom	5,000	Animism	<1%			6022
Dompago	Benin	Dompago	19,000	Animism	7%	4		515
Domu	Papua New Guinea	Domu	500	Animism	<1%			6023
Domung	Papua New Guinea	Domung	900	Animism	<1%			6024
Dongioi	Sudan	Dongioi	9,000	Islam	0%			5465
Dongo	Sudan	Dongo	100	Islam	0%			5490
Dongo	Zaire	Dongo	5,000	Animism	0%			5706
**Doohwaayo	Cameroon	Doohyaayo	15,000	Animism	12%	5		2661
**Dorlin in Andhra Pradesh	India	Dorli	24,000	Hindu-Animist	<1%			151
Dorobo	Kenya	Nandi	22,000	Animism	1%	4		490
Doromu	Tanzania	Hadza	3,000	Animism	1%			6025
Dorze	Ethiopia	Dorze	3,000	Animism	<1%			3204
Doura	Papua New Guinea	Doura	3,000	Animism	<1%			6026
*Drug Addicts in Sao Paulo	Brazil	Portuguese	200,000	Nominal Christian	nr%	5	82	5022
Druzes	Israel	Arabic	33,000	Folk Religion	0%	6	79	1230
Duau	Papua New Guinea	Duau	7,000	Animism	<1%			6027
**Dubla	India	Gujarati	200,100	Hindu-Animist	4%	4		122
Dubu	Indonesia	Dubu	12,000	Animism	<1%			2904
Duguir	Nigeria	Duguri	2,000	Islam	<1%			2360
Duguza	Nigeria	Duguza	10,000	Islam	<1%			2361
**Duka	Nigeria	Dukanci	800	Animism	1%	5		1054
Dukwe Refugee Camp Residents	Botswana	Tribal Languages	1,000	Animism	nr%	4	83	9022
Duma	Gabon	Duma	1,000	Animism	0%			5307
*Dumagat, Casiguran	Philippines	Dumagat	1,000	Animism	3%	6	81	2
Duna	Papua New Guinea	Duan	39,000	Animism	<1%			6028
Dungan	USSR	Dungan	20,000	Islam	0%			5836
Duru	Cameroon	Duru	160,500	Animism	6%	4		7040
Dusun	Malaysia	Kadazan	8,000	Animism	nr%	6	81	7023
Duvele	Indonesia	Duvele	500	Animism	<1%			2905
Dyan	Upper Volta	Dyan	8,000	Islam-Animist	0%	6	80	5666
Dyerma	Niger	Dyerma	50,000	Islam-Animist	<1%			4014
Dyerma	Nigeria	Dyerma	1,000,000	Islam-Animist	<1%			2362
Dyola	Gambia	Dyola	216,000	Islam-Animist	<1%			2267
Ebira	Nigeria	Ebira	325,000	Animism	<1%			2363
Ebrie	Ivory Coast	Ebrie	55,000	Animism	0%			2287
Edawapi	Papua New Guinea	Edawapi	4,000	Animism	<1%			6029
Edo	Nigeria	Edo	430,000	Animism	<1%			2364
Efik	Nigeria	Efik	10,000	Animism	12%	5		2365
Efutop	Nigeria	Efutop	80,000	Animism	<1%			2366
Eggon	Nigeria	Eggon	1,000	Animism	<1%			146
Eivo	Papua New Guinea	Eivo	100,000	Animism	12%	5		6030
Ejagham	Nigeria	Ejagham	15,000	Animism	<1%			2368
Ekagi	Indonesia	Ekagi	100,000	Animism	<1%			2906
Ekajuk	Nigeria	Ekajuk	15,000	Animism	<1%			2369

Name	Country	Language	Group Size	Primary Religion	% Chr	Vol V	Vol UP	ID
Eket	Nigeria	Eket	22,000	Animism	<1%			2370
Ekpeye	Nigeria	Ekpeye	30,000	Animism	<1%			2371
El Molo	Kenya	Samburu	1,000	Animism	3%	4		533
Eleme	Nigeria	Eleme	16,000	Animism	<1%			2372
Elkei	Papua New Guinea	Elkei	48,000	Animism	<1%	1		6031
Emai-Iuleha-Ora	Nigeria	Emai-Iuleha-Ora	2,000	Animism	<1%			2373
Embera, Northern	Colombia	Embera	2,000	Animism	0%			2196
Emerum	Papua New Guinea	Emerum	500	Animism	0%	1		6032
Emira	Papua New Guinea	Emira	4,000	Animism	<1%	1		6033
Emumu	Indonesia	Emumu	1,000	Animism	0%			2907
Endangen	Papua New Guinea	Endangen	500	Animism	<1%	1		6034
Enga	Papua New Guinea	Enga	110,000	Animism	0%	1		6035
Engenni	Nigeria	Engenni	10,000	Animism	<1%			5707
Enya	Zaire	Enya	4,000	Animism	<1%			2288
Eotile	Ivory Coast	Eotile	1,000	Islam-Animist	<1%			2375
Epie	Nigeria	Epie	12,000	Animism	nr%	4	83	9033
**Eritrean Refugees	Gabon	Tribal Languages	60,000	Nominal Christian	<1%	4	83	9018
**Eritrean Refugees	Djibouti	Somali	25,000	Islam	nr%	4	83	9007
**Eritrean Refugees	Sudan	Gaala	150,300	Islam	<1%			2910
Erokwanas	Indonesia	Erokwanas	200,300	Animism	<1%			2376
Esan	Nigeria	Otomo	700,000	Islam	<1%	4	83	9027
**Ethiopian Refugees	Somalia	Tigre	112,480	nst reported	nr%	3		9040
**Ethiopian Refugees, Yemen	Yemen, Arab Republic	Tigre	5,000	Islam	0%			7053
Eton	Cameroon	Eton	3,000	Animism	<1%			2377
Etulo	Nigeria	Etulo	5,000	Animism	<1%			2378
Evant	Nigeria	Evant	10,000	Animism	<1%			2817
Evenki	USSR	Evenki	25,000	Traditional Chinese	<1%			5837
Evenks	China	Evenk	10,000	Buddhist-Animist	0%			7020
Ewage-Notu	Papua New Guinea	Ewage-Notu	10,000	Animism	<1%	1		6036
Ewenkis	China	Altaic	20,000	Animism	nr%	5	81	5007
**Ex-Mental Patients in NYC	United States of America	Spanish	nr	Secularism	<1%	5	82	5024
**Expatriates in Riyadh	Saudi Arabia	English		Secularism	0%	5	82	5304
Fa D'Ambu	Equatorial Guinea	Fa D'Ambu	2,000	Animism	5%	6		1010
*Factory Workers	Hong Kong	Cantonese	40,000	Unknown	<1%	1		6037
Fagululu	Papua New Guinea	Fagululu	400	Animism	<1%	1		6038
Faiwol	Papua New Guinea	Faiwol	3,000	Animism	1%	5	79	1053
**Fakai	Nigeria	Faka	15,000	Animism	7%	1		159
**Flasha	Ethiopia	Agau	30,000	Judaism	2%	5		7054
Fali	Cameroon	Fali	25,000	Islam	<1%			1052
**Fali	Nigeria	Fali	2,000	Animism	<1%	5	82	6039
Fas	Papua New Guinea	Fas	900	Animism	<1%	1		6040
Fasu	Papua New Guinea	Fasu		Christo-Paganism	<1%			5043
*Favelados-Rio de Janeiro	Brazil	Portuguese	600,000	Christo-Paganism	0%			5471
Feroge	Sudan	Feroge	3,000	Islam	0%			6041
Finungwan	Papua New Guinea	Finungwan	400	Animism	0%			5541
Fipa	Tanzania	Fipa	78,000	Animism	2%	4		2107
Fishing Village People	Taiwan	Amoy	150,000	Traditional Chinese	2%			2911
Foau	Indonesia	Foau	200	Animism	<1%			6042
Foi	Papua New Guinea	Foi	3,000	Animism	<1%	1		

Name	Country	Language	Group Size	Primary Religion	% Chr	V	Vol UP	ID
Foran	Papua New Guinea	Foran	800	Animism	<1%			6043
Fordat	Indonesia	Fordat	10,000	Animism	<1%		1	2912
Fore	Papua New Guinea	Fore	16,000	Animism	<1%		1	6044
Fra-Fra	Ghana	Fra-Fra	230,000	Animism	<1%		4	656
Fula	Guinea	Fula	1,500,000	Islam	1%		5	406
	Sierra Leone	Fula	250,000	Islam	0%		5	4035
Fula, Cunda	Upper Volta	Fula	250,000	Islam-Animist	<1%		1	5667
Fula, Macina	Gambia	Fula, Macina	50,000	Islam-Animist	<1%		1	2268
Fula, Peuhala	Mali	Fula, Peuhala	450,000	Animism	0%		1	5376
*Fulah	Upper Volta	Fulah	300,000	Islam	1%		1	5377
*Fulani	Benin	Fulani	70,000	Islam-Animist	1%		5	140
Fulani	Cameroon	Fulani	250,000	Islam-Animist	1%	79	4	446
*Fulbe	Ghana	Fulani	6,000	Islam-Animist	0%		5	37
Fuliro	Zaire	Fuliro	56,000	Animism	<1%		5	1081
Fulnio	Brazil	Fulnio	2,000	Animism	0%		1	5708
Fungom, Northern	Cameroon	Fungom, Northern	15,000	Islam	0%		1	2157
Fungor	Sudan	Fungor	5,000	Animism	0%		1	7055
Furu	Zaire	Furu	5,000	Animism	0%		1	5472
Fuyuge	Papua New Guinea	Fuyuge	13,000	Animism	<1%		1	5709
Fyam	Nigeria	Fyam	14,000	Animism	<1%		1	6045
Fyer	Nigeria	Fyer	3,000	Animism	<1%		1	2379
Ga-Dang	Philippines	Ga-Dang	6,000	Animism	1%		5	2380
Gaanda	Nigeria	not reported	nr	Nominal Christian	1%		4	631
*Gabbra	Ethiopia	Gabrinja	12,000	Folk Religion	1%		4	2381
Gabbra	Kenya	Galla	20,000	Folk Religion	1%			234
Gabri	Chad	Gabri	20,000	Islam-Animist	<1%			715
Gadaban in Andhra Pradesh	India	Gadaba	70,000	Hindu-Animist	<1%			2216
Gaddi in Himachal Pradesh	India	Gaddi	70,000	Hindu-Animist	<1%			2662
Gade	Nigeria	Gade	25,000	Animism	<1%			2663
Gadsup	Papua New Guinea	Gadsup	7,000	Animism	1%		4	6046
Gagauzes	USSR	Gagauz	157,000	Christo-Paganism	<1%			5838
**Gagre	Pakistan	Punjabi	40,000	Animism	1%		4	264
Gagou	Ivory Coast	Gagou	25,000	Animism	1%			480
Gahuku	Papua New Guinea	Gahuku	8,000	Animism	1%			6047
Gaikundi	Papua New Guinea	Gaikundi	700	Animism	1%			6048
Gaina	Papua New Guinea	Gaina	1,000	Animism	1%			6049
Gal	Nigeria	Gal	1,200	Animism	<1%			6050
Galambi	Nigeria	Galambi	1,000	Islam	1%			2382
Galeshi	Iran	Galeshi	2,000	Islam	0%		3	2057
*Galla (Bale)	Ethiopia	Galla	750,000	Islam-Animist	7%		5	277
Galla of Bucho	Ethiopia	Gallinya (Oromo)	2,000	Christo-Paganism	<1%		3	404
Galla, Harar	Ethiopia	Gallinya	1,310,000	Islam	1%		5	367
Galler	Laos	Galler	50,000	Animism	1%			111
Gaiong in Assam	India	Galong	37,000	Hindu-Animist	<1%			2664
Gambai	Chad	Gambai	200,100	Islam-Animist	<1%			2217
Gamei	Papua New Guinea	Gamei	900	Animism	<1%			6051
Gami in Gujarat	India	Gami	140,000	Hindu-Animist	<1%			2665
Gan	Upper Volta	Gan	4,000	Islam-Animist	<1%		1	5668

Name	Country	Language	Group Size	Primary Religion	% Chr	Vol V	UP	ID
Gane	Indonesia	Gane	2,000	Animism	<1%			2913
Gangam	Togo	Gangam	16,200	Islam-Animist	0%	1		5628
Ganglau	Papua New Guinea	Ganglau		Animism	<1%	1		6052
Gangte in Assam	India	Gangte	6,000	Hindu-Animist	<1%	1		2666
Garuh	Papua New Guinea	Garuh	2,000	Animism	<1%	1		6053
Garus	Papua New Guinea	Garus		Animism	<1%	1		6054
Garuwahi	Papua New Guinea	Garuwahi		Animism	<1%	1		6055
Gawar-Bati	Afghanistan	Gawar-Bati	8,000	Islam	<1%	1		2548
Gawari in Andhra Pradesh	India	Gawari	21,000	Hindu-Animist	<1%	1		2668
Gawwada	Ethiopia	Gawwada	4,000	Animism	<1%	1		3205
Gayo in San Francisco	United States of America	English	200,000	Islam-Animist	0%	4	80	1132
Gbande	Guinea	Bandi	150,000	Secularism	0%	4	82	5010
Gbari	Nigeria	Gbari	500,000	Animism	3%	6	80	477
Gbaya	Nigeria	Gbaya	350,000	Animism	2%	6		158
Gbaya-Ndogo	Sudan	Gbaya-Ndogo		Islam	<1%	1		2384
Gbazantche	Benin	Gbazantche	9,000	Islam	0%			5491
Gberi	Sudan	Gberi		Islam	0%	3		447
Gedaged	Papua New Guinea	Gedaged		Animism	<1%	1		5473
Gedeo	Ethiopia	Gedeo	30,000	Animism	<1%	1		6056
Geishas in Osaka	Japan	Japanese	250,000	Secularism	<1%	5	82	3206
Geji	Nigeria	Geji		nr	Islam	<1%		5025
Genagane	Papua New Guinea	Genagane	3,000	Animism	<1%	1		2385
Gende	Papua New Guinea	Gende	8,000	Animism	0%			6057
Gera	Nigeria	Gera	13,000	Islam	<1%	1		6058
Geruma	Nigeria	Geruma	5,000	Islam	<1%	1		2386
Gesa	Indonesia	Gesa	5,200	Animism	<1%	1		2387
Ghale Gurung	Nepal	Ghale Gurung	10,000	Buddhist-Animist	0%	1		2914
Gheko	Burma	Gheko	4,000	Buddhist-Animist	<1%	1		6509
**Ghimeera	Ethiopia	Gimira	50,000	Animism	4%	5		2577
Ghol	Sudan	Ghol		Animism	0%			364
Ghotuo	Nigeria	Ghotuo	9,000	Animism	<1%	1		5460
Ghulfan	Sudan	Ghulfan	3,000	Islam	0%	1		2388
Gidar	Cameroon	Gidar	50,000	Islam	<1%	1		5474
	Chad	Gidar	50,000	Islam-Animist	<1%	1		7056
Gidicho	Ethiopia	Gidicho	500	Animism	<1%	1		2218
Gidra	Papua New Guinea	Gidra	2,000	Animism	0%	1		3207
Gilakis	Iran	Gilaki	1,950,000	Islam	1%	4		6059
Gilyak	USSR	Gilyak	4,000	Unknown	0%	1		2027
Gimi	Papua New Guinea	Gimi	18,000	Animism	<1%	1		5839
Ginuman	Papua New Guinea	Ginuman	800	Animism	<1%	1		6060
Gio	Liberia	Dan (Yacouba)	92,000	Animism	5%	5		190
Gira	Papua New Guinea	Gira	400	Animism	<1%	1		6061
Girawa	Papua New Guinea	Girawa		Animism	<1%	1		6062
Giri	Papua New Guinea	Giri	4,000	Animism	<1%	1		6063
Giryama	Kenya	Giryama	340,000	Animism	9%	4		6064
Gisei	Cameroon	Masa	10,000	Animism	<1%	4		534
Gisiga	Cameroon	Gisiga	30,500	Animism	11%	4		504
Gitua	Papua New Guinea	Gitua		Animism	<1%	1		6065

279

Name	Country	Language	Group Size	Primary Religion	% Chr	Vol V UP	ID
Gizra	Papua New Guinea	Gizra	600	Animism	0%	1	6066
**Glavda	Nigeria	Glavda	19,000	Animism	4%	5	1174
Gobasi	Papua New Guinea	Gobasi	1,000	Animism	0%	1	6067
Gobato	Ethiopia	Gobato		Animism	<1%	1	3208
Gobeze	Ethiopia	Gobeze	22,000	Animism	<1%	1	3209
***Godie	Ivory Coast	Godie	20,000	Animism	12%	4	2308
Goemai	Nigeria	Goemai		Animism	1%	1	2389
Gogo	Tanzania	Gogo	280,000	Animism	0%	1	5542
Gogodala	Papua New Guinea	Gogodala		Animism	0%	1	6008
Gokana	Nigeria	Gokana	54,000	Animism	<1%	1	2390
Gola	Liberia	Golana	47,000	Islam-Animist	0%	1	5360
	Sierra Leone	Mende		Islam-Animist	0%	1	5430
Golo	Chad	Golo	3,000	Islam-Animist	<1%	1	2219
*Gonds	India	Gondi	4,000,000	Animism	1%	5	641
Gonja	Ghana	Gonja	110,000	Islam-Animist	2%	5	1102
*Gorkha	India	Napali	180,000	Hinduism	0%	4	2009
Goroa	Tanzania	Goroa	180,000	Animism	0%	1	5543
Gorontalo	Indonesia	Gorontalo	500,000	Islam	<1%	1	2915
Gosha	Kenya	Gosha	3,000	Islam-Animist	0%	3	4134
Goudari	Iran	Goudari	3,000	Islam	0%	3	2059
Gouin-Turka	Upper Volta	Gouin-Turka	25,000	Islam-Animist	<1%	1	5669
Goulai	Chad	Goulai	30,000	Islam-Animist	<1%	1	2220
Gourency	Upper Volta	Gourendi	300,000	Animism	5%	4	94
**Gouro	Ivory Coast	Gouro	200,000	Animism	4%	4	194
Gouwar	Cameroon	Gouwar	5,000	Animism	0%	1	7057
Government officials	Thailand	Thai	100,000	Buddhism	0%	3	59
Grasia in Gujarat	India	Grasia	27,000	Hindu-Animist	<1%	1	2669
**Grebo	Liberia	Grebo Dialects	65,000	Animism	8%	4	689
Grunshi	Ghana	not reported	200,000	Animism	<1%	1	526
Gu	Benin	Gu	173,000	Animism	0%	1	5167
Guaiaqui	Paraguay	Guaiaqui	400	Animism	<1%	1	5124
Guajajara	Brazil	Guajajara	5,000	Animism	<1%	1	2158
Guajibo	Colombia	Guajibo	15,000	Animism	12%	5	2197
*Guajiro	Colombia	Guajiro	60,000	Animism	<1%	1	277
Guambiano	Colombia	Guambiano	9,000	Animism	0%	1	2199
Guana	Paraguay	Guana	3,000	Animism	0%	1	5125
***Guanano	Colombia	Guanano	3,800	Christo-Paganism	10%	6 79	442
***Guarani	Bolivia	Guarani	15,000	Christo-Paganism	1%	6 79	206
Guarayu	Bolivia	Guarayu	5,000	Christo-Paganism	<1%	1	605
Guarojio	Mexico	Guarojio	5,000	Christo-Paganism	n r%	1	8041
Guatemalan Refugees	Mexico	Spanish	70,000	Christo-Paganism	<1%	1	9057
Guayabero	Colombia	Guayabero	600	Animism	8%	5	1169
Gude	Cameroon	Gude	100,000	Animism	1%	4	502
	Nigeria	Gude	40,000	Animism	<1%	1	7042
Gudu	Nigeria	Gudu	1,000	Animism	<1%	1	2392
Guduf	Nigeria	Guduf	21,000	Animism	<1%	1	2393
Guere	Ivory Coast	Guere	120,000	Islam-Animist	1%	4	2289
Gugu-Yalanji	Australia	Gugu-Yalanji	1,500	Animism	<1%	1	430
Guhu-Samane	Papua New Guinea	Guhu-Samane	4,000	Animism	<1%	1	6069

Name	Country	Language	Group Size	Primary Religion	% Chr	V	UP	ID
Hehe	Tanzania	Hehe	192,000	Animism	0%	1		5548
Heiban	Sudan	Heiban	25,000	Islam	<1%	1		5476
Helong	Indonesia	Helong	5,000	Animism	<1%	1		2917
Herero	Botswana	Herero	10,000	Animism	0%	1		5175
	Namibia	Dhimba	40,000	Animism	<1%	1		5400
Heso	Zaire	Heso	6,000	Animism	0%	1		5767
**Hewa	Papua New Guinea	Hewa	2,000	Animism	5%	6	79	1238
Hezareh	Iran	Hezara'i	nr	Islam	<1%	3		2068
**High School Students	Hong Kong	Cantonese	453,000	Traditional Chinese	7%	4		2113
***Higi	Nigeria	Higi	150,000	Animism	7%	5		1118
Hixkaryana	Brazil	Hixkaryana	200	Animism	<1%	1		2160
Hkun	Burma	Shan	20,000	Buddhism	0%	2		4144
***Hmong Refugee Women, Ban Vinai	Thailand	Miao	12,000	Buddhist-Animist	0%	4	83	9003
***Hmong Refugees	United States of America	Miao	35,000	Buddhist-Animist	<1%	4	83	9055
Hmong, Twin Cities	United States of America	Miao	11,000	Nominal Christian	nr%	1		9034
Ho in Bihar	India	Ho	750,000	Hindu-Animist	<1%	1		2674
Hohodene	Brazil	Hohodene	1,000	Animism	<1%	1		2161
Holiya in Madhya Pradesh	India	Holiya	3,000	Hindu-Animist	0%	1		2675
Holoholo	Tanzania	Holoholo	5,000	Animism	0%	1		5549
Holu	Angola	Holu	12,000	Animism	0%	1		5149
Hopi	United States of America	Hopi	6,000	Animism	4%	5		382
*Hote	Papua New Guinea	Hote	3,000	Animism	<1%	1		6078
**Hotel Workers in Manila	Philippines	Pilipino	11,000	Nominal Christian	13%	5	81	7036
Hrangkhol	Burma	Hrangkhol	9,000	Buddhist-Animist	<1%	1		2579
Huachipaire	Peru	Huachipaire	200	Animism	<1%	1		3172
Huambisa	Peru	Huambisa	5,000	Animism	<1%	1		3173
Huasteco	Mexico	Huasteco	80,000	Animism	<1%	1		8042
**Huave	Mexico	Huave	18,000	Christo-Paganism	5%	5		113
Hui	China	Hui-hui-yu	5,200,000	Islam	0%	6	80	4006
**Huichol	Mexico	Huichol	8,000	Christo-Paganism	1%	4		8043
**Huistan Tzotzil	Angola	Tzotzil, Huistan	200,000	Christo-Paganism	<1%	2		682
Huitoto, Meneca	Mexico	Huitoto, Meneca	600	Animism	<1%	1		5104
Huitoto, Murui	Colombia	Huitoto, Murui	800	Animism	<1%	1		3142
Hukwe	Peru	Hukwe	9,000	Animism	<1%	4		3174
Hula	Angola	Hula	3,000	Animism	3%	1		511
Huli	Papua New Guinea	Huli	54,000	Animism	<1%	1		6079
Humene	Papua New Guinea	Humene	400	Animism	<1%	1		6080
Hunde	Papua New Guinea	Hunde	34,000	Animism	<1%	1		6081
Hunjara	Zaire	Hunjara	10,000	Animism	0%	1		5711
**Hunzakut	Papua New Guinea	Burushaski	200	Islam	<1%	6	79	6082
Hupda Maku	Pakistan	Hupda Maku	20,200	Animism	<1%	1		2236
Hwana	Colombia	Hwana	50,000	Islam-Animist	<1%	1		2202
Hwela-Numu	Nigeria	Hwela-Numu	60,000	Islam	<1%	1		2003
Hyam	Ivory Coast	Hyam	8,000	Animism	<1%	1		2398
Iatmul	Nigeria	Iatmul	20,000	Animism	<1%	4		6083
Ibaji	Papua New Guinea	Ibaji	30,000	Animism	nr%	1		544
**Ibani	Nigeria	Ibani	300	Animism	<1%	6	81	7024
Ibanag	Malaysia	Ibanag		Animism	<1%	1		3254

282

Name	Country	Language	Group Size	Primary Religion	% Chr	V	UP	ID
Ipiko	Papua New Guinea	Ipiko	200	Animism	<1%			6089
Ipili	Papua New Guinea	Ipili	6,000	Animism	<1%	1		6090
Iquito	Peru	Spanish	4,000	Animism	<1%	1		3175
Irahutu	Indonesia	Irahutu	4,000	Animism	<1%	4		2921
**Iranian Bahai Refugees	Pakistan	Farsi	5,000	Bahaism	<1%	4	83	9024
**Iraqi Kurd Refugees	Iran	Kurmanji	300,000	Islam	<1%	4	83	9028
Iraqw	Tanzania	Iraqw	218,000	Animism	1%	4		492
Iravas in Kerala	India	Malayalam	3,700,000	Hinduism	1%	4		4068
Iraya	Philippines	Iraya	6,000	Christo-Paganism	<1%	1		3259
Iresim	Indonesia	Iresim	100	Animism	<1%	1		2922
Iria	Indonesia	Iria	900	Animism	<1%	1		2923
***Irigwe	Nigeria	Irigwe	15,000	Animism	<1%			7046
Irulas in Kerala	India	Irula	10,000	Hinduism	0%	4		2012
Irumu	Papua New Guinea	Irumu	2,000	Animism	<1%	1		6091
Isanzu	Tanzania	Isanzu	12,000	Animism	<1%	1		5552
Isebe	Papua New Guinea	Isebe	800	Animism	<1%	1		6092
**Isekiri	Nigeria	Isekiri	33,000	Animism	<1%			2412
**Ishans	Nigeria	Esan	25,000	Nominal Christian	16%	5		4033
Isneg, Dibagat-Kabugao	Philippines	Isneg, Dibagat-Kabugao	10,000	Animism	<1%	1		3260
Isneg, Karagawan	Philippines	Isneg, Karagawan	8,000	Animism	<1%	1		3261
Isoko	Nigeria	Isoko	2,000	Animism	<1%	1		2413
Itawit	Philippines	Itawit	15,000	Christo-Paganism	<1%	1		3262
Itelmen	USSR	Itelmen		Unknown	0%	1		5841
Itik	Indonesia	Itik	100	Animism	<1%	1		2924
Itneg, Adasen	Philippines	Itneg, Adasen	4,000	Christo-Paganism	<1%	1		3263
Itneg, Binongan	Philippines	Itneg, Binongan	7,000	Christo-Paganism	<1%	1		3264
Itneg, Masadiit	Philippines	Itneg, Masadiit	100	Christo-Paganism	<1%	1		3265
Itonama	Bolivia	Itonama	100	Animism	<1%			2136
Ivbie North-Okpela-Atte	Nigeria	Ivbie North-Okpela-Atte	20,000	Animism	400%			2414
Iwa	Zambia	Iwa	15,000	Animism	0%			5800
*Iwaidja	Austria	Iwaidja	150	Animism	0%	4		390
Iwal	Papua New Guinea	Iwal	2,000	Animism	<1%	1		6093
Iwam	Papua New Guinea	Iwam	2,000	Animism	<1%	1		6094
Iwam, Sepik	Papua New Guinea	Iwam, Sepik	4,000	Animism	<1%	1		6095
Iwur	Indonesia	Iwur	1,000	Animism	0%	1		2925
Ixil	Guatemala	Cuyoibal	45,000	Christo-Paganism	<1%	4		646
Iyon	Cameroon	Iyon	4,000	Animism	0%	1		7059
Izarek	Nigeria	Izarek	2,000	Animism	<1%	1		2415
Izhor	USSR	Izhor	30,000	Animism	0%	1		2416
**Izi	Nigeria	Izi	1,000	Unknown	0%	4		5842
Jaba	Nigeria	Jaba	200,000	Animism	11%			89
Jabem	Papua New Guinea	Jabem	60,000	Animism	<1%	1		542
Jacalteco	Guatemala	Jacalteco	3,000	Animism	<1%	4		6096
Jagannathi in A.P.	India	Jagannathi	12,000	Hindu-Animist	<1%	1		8006
Jains	India	Hindi	2,000,000	Jain	<1%	4		2677
*Jama Mapun	Philippines	Cagayan	805,000	Islam-Animist	<1%	5	80	2005
**Jamaican Elite	Jamaica	Jamaican Patois	800,000	Secularism	0%			4117
Janamadi	Brazil	Janamadi	1,000	Animism	<1%	1		2162

Name	Country	Language	Group Size	Primary Religion	% Chr	V	Vol UP	ID
Juhai	Malaysia	Juhai	400	Animism	0%	2		4112
Jukun	Nigeria	not reported	20,000	Animism	<1%	4		539
Jyarung	China	Jyarung	70,000	Traditional Chinese	<1%	1		2819
**Kanjobal of San Miguel	Guatemala	K'anjobal	18,000	Ancestor Worship	10%	5		1207
Kaagan	Philippines	Kaagan	20,000	Christo-Paganism	<1%	1		3266
Kaalong	Cameroon	Kaalong	50,000	Animism	<1%	1		7060
Kaba	Central African Republic	Kaba	11,000	Animism	0%	1		5181
Kaba Dunjo	Central African Republic	Kaba Dunjo	17,000	Animism	0%	1		5182
Kabadi	Papua New Guinea	Kabadi	2,000	Animism	<1%	1		6098
Kabixi	Brazil	Kabixi		Animism	<1%	1		2163
Kabre	Benin	Kabre	35,000	Animism	0%	5		5168
Kabyle	Algeria	Kabyle	273,000	Islam	9%	6	79	192
Kachama	Ethiopia	Kachama	1,000,500	Animism	<1%	6		145
Kachchi in Andhra Pradesh	India	Kachchi	80,000	Hinduism	<1%	1		3214
Kachin in Shan State	Burma	Burmese	471,000	Buddhism	<1%	1		2682
Kadaklan-Barlig Bontoc	Philippines	Kadaklan-Barlig Bontoc	4,000	Animism	0%	2		4154
Kadar in Andhra Pradesh	India	Kadar		Hindu-Animist	<1%	1		3248
Kadara	Nigeria	Kadara	40,000	Animism	<1%	1		2683
Kadazans	Malaysia	Kadazans	110,000	Animism	9%	5		538
Kadiweu	Brazil	Kadiweu	600	Animism	<1%	2		4095
Kadugli	Sudan	Kadugli	19,000	Islam	0%	1		2164
Kae Sung Natives in Seoul	Korea, Republic of	Korean	20,000	Buddhism	<1%	5		5477
Kaeti	Indonesia	Kaeti	4,000	Animism	<1%	2		5015
*Kaffa	Ethiopia	Kaffenya (Kefa)	320,000	Animism	1%		82	2927
**Kafirs	Pakistan	Kafiristani (Bashgali)	3,000	Animism	<1%	6		363
Kagoma	Nigeria	Kagoma	6,000	Animism	2%	6	80	1233
Kagoro	Nigeria	Kagoro	30,000	Animism	<1%	6	79	2421
Kagoro	Mali	Logoro (Bambara)	59,000	Animism	<1%	2		552
Kagulu	Tanzania	Kagulu	66,000	Animism	<1%	4		5556
Kahluri in Andamans	India	Kahluri	200	Hindu-Animist	0%	1		2684
Kaian	Papua New Guinea	Kaian	700	Animism	<1%	1		6099
Kaibu	Nigeria	Kaibu	300	Animism	0%	1		2422
Kaiep	Papua New Guinea	Kaiep	12,000	Animism	<1%	1		6100
Kaikadi in Maharashtra	India	Kaikadi	300,000	Hindu-Animist	<1%	1		2685
Kaili	Indonesia	Kaili	7,000	Islam	<1%	1		2928
Kaingang	Brazil	Kaingang	700	Christo-Paganism	0%	1		2165
Kairi	Papua New Guinea	Kairi	3,000	Animism	<1%	1		6101
Kairiru	Papua New Guinea	Kairiru	600	Animism	<1%	1		6102
Kaiwai	Indonesia	Kaiwai	50,000	Animism	0%	1		2929
Kajang	Indonesia	Kajang	2,000	Animism	<1%	1		2930
Kaka	Cameroon	Kaka	37,000	Animism	0%	1		5241
Kaka	Central African Republic	Kaka	2,000	Animism	<1%	1		5183
Kakoa	Nigeria	Kaka	2,000	Islam	0%	1		2423
kakuna-Mamusi	Papua New Guinea	Kakoa	3,000	Animism	<1%	1		6103
**Kalagan	Papua New Guinea	Kakuna-Mamusi	3,000	Animism	<1%	1		6104
*Kalanga	Philippines	Kalagan	7,000	Islam	0%	1		630
Kalanga	Botswana	Chikalanga	3,000	Animism	1%	5		1163
Kalanga	Zimbabwe	Kalanga	150,000	Animism	2%	5		5410
Kalinga, Kalagua	Philippines	Kalinga, Kalagua	87,000	Animism	<1%	1		3268

Name	Country	Language	Group Size	Primary Religion	% Chr	V	UP	ID
Kapori	Indonesia	Kapori	100	Animism	<1%		1	2937
Kapriman	Papua New Guinea	Kapriman	1,000	Animism	<1%		1	6116
Kapuchin	USSR	Kapuchin	3,000	Unknown	0%		1	5845
Kara	Papua New Guinea	Kara	2,000	Animism	<1%		1	6117
*Karaboro	Upper Volta	Karaboro	32,000	Animism	0%		4	5558
Karachay	USSR	Karachay-Balkan	173,000	Islam-Animist	1%		1	4139
Karagas	USSR	Karagas	600	Unknown	0%			4042
Karaim	USSR	Karaim	1,000	Unknown	0%			5846
Karakalpak	USSR	Karakalpak	277,000	Islam	0%	6	80	5847
Karam	Papua New Guinea	Karam	11,000	Animism	<1%		1	4011
Karanga	Chad	Karanga	57,000	Islam-Animist	1%		1	6118
Karangi	Papua New Guinea	Karangi	200	Animism	<1%		1	2225
Karas	Indonesia	Karas	200	Animism	1%		1	6119
Karatin	USSR	Karatin	6,000	Animism	0%		1	2938
**Karbis	India	Mikir	300,000	Hindu-Animist	5%		5	5849
Kare	Papua New Guinea	Kare	39,000	Animism	1%		1	2120
Karekare	Nigeria	Karekare	80,000	Islam	1%		1	6120
Karen	Thailand	Sgaw Karen	40,000	Animism	1%	6	79	2427
Karen, Pwo	Thailand	Pwo Karen	4,000	Animism	1%		5	613
Kari	Central African Republic	Kari	40,000	Islam-Animist	0%		1	30
	Chad	Kari	1,000	Animism	0%		1	5185
Karipuna Creole	Brazil	Karipuna Creole	500	Animism	<1%		1	2226
Karipuna Do Guapore	Brazil	Karipuna Do Guapore	200	Animism	0%		1	5716
Kariya	Nigeria	Kariya	2,000	Islam	<1%		1	2168
Karkar	Papua New Guinea	Karkar	2,000	Animism	<1%		1	2169
Karko	Sudan	Karko	70,000	Islam	<1%		1	2428
Karmali in Dihar	India	Karmali	3,000	Hindu-Animist	<1%		1	6121
Karon Dori	Indonesia	Karon Dori	40,000	Animism	<1%		1	5480
Karon Pantai	Indonesia	Karon Pantai	900	Animism	<1%		1	2690
Karre	Central African Republic	Karre	400	Animism	0%		1	2939
Karua	Papua New Guinea	Karua	20,000	Animism	0%		1	2940
Kasanga	Guinea-Bissau	Kasanga	28,000	Islam-Animist	0%		1	5184
Kasele	Togo	Kasele		Islam-Animist	0%		1	6122
Kasem	Upper Volta	Kasem		Animism	0%		1	5351
**Kasena	Ghana	Kasem		Islam-Animist	0%		1	5629
**Kashmiri Muslims	India	Kashmiri	3,100,000	Islam	11%		4	1231
Kasseng	Laos	Kasseng	15,000	Animism	0%		1	657
Kasua	Papua New Guinea	Kasua	1,000	Animism	0%	6	79	109
Kasuweri	Indonesia	Kasuweri		Animism	<1%		5	6123
Katab	Nigeria	Katab	30,000	Islam	0%		1	2941
Katakari in Gujarat	India	Katakari	35,000	Animism	0%		1	2429
Katcha	Sudan	Katcha		Hindu-Animist	<1%		1	2691
Kate	Papua New Guinea	Kate	6,000	Animism	<1%		1	5481
Kati, Northern	Indonesia	Kati, Northern	8,000	Animism	<1%		1	6124
Kati, Southern	Indonesia	Kati, Southern	4,000	Animism	<1%		1	2942
Katiati	Papua New Guinea	Katiati	2,000	Animism	<1%		1	6125
Katla	Sudan	Katla	9,000	Islam	0%		1	5482

Name	Country	Language	Group Size	Primary Religion	% Chr	V	UP	ID
Katukina, Panoan	Brazil	Katukina, Panoan	200	Animism	<1%	1		2170
Kaugat	Indonesia	Kaugat	1,000	Animism	<1%	1		2944
Kaugel	Papua New Guinea	Kaugel	35,000	Animism	0%	3		6126
**Kaur	Indonesia	Kaur	50,000	Islam-Animist	<1%	1		4084
Kaure	Indonesia	Kaure	800	Animism	<1%	1		2945
Kavwol	Indonesia	Kavwol	500	Animism	<1%	1		2946
Kavwol	Papua New Guinea	Kavwol	500	Animism	0%	1		6127
Kaw	Burma	Kaw	30,000	Animism	0%	2		4152
Kawar in Madhya Pradesh	India	Kawar	34,000	Hindu-Animist	<1%	1		2692
Kawe	Indonesia	Kawe	300	Animism	<1%	1		2947
Kayabi	Brazil	Kayabi	300	Animism	<1%	1		2171
Kayagar	Indonesia	Kayagar	9,000	Animism	8%	4		233
Kayan	Burma	Padaung	18,000	Animism	0%	2		4156
Kayan	Malaysia	Kayan	12,000	Animism	0%	3		4102
Kayapo	Brazil	Kayapo	600	Animism	0%	4		1158
Kaygir	Indonesia	Kaygir		Animism	<1%	1		2948
Kayupulau	Indonesia	Kayupulau	4,000	Animism	<1%	1		2949
Kazakhs	Iran	Kazakhi	700,000	Islam-Animism	0%	6	81	7013
Kebu	Togo	Kebu	20,000	Islam-Animist	0%	1		2035
Kebumtamp	Bhutan	Kebumtamp	400,000	Buddhist-Animist	<1%	5	80	2536
Kedayanas	Malaysia	Kedayanas	25,000	Animism	0%	2		4094
Keer in Madhya Pradesh	India	Keer	30,000	Hindu-Animist	<1%	1		2693
Kei	Indonesia	Kei		Animism	<1%	1		2950
Keiga	Sudan	Keiga	6,000	Islam	<1%	1		5483
Keiga Jirru	Sudan	Keiga Jirru	1,000	Islam	0%	1		5484
**Kekchi	Guatemala	Kekchi	270,000	Christo-Paganism	3%	4		4034
Kela	Papua New Guinea	Kela	1,000	Animism	<1%	1		6128
Kelabit	Malaysia	Kelabit	17,000	Animism	n?%	3		7025
Kelao	Zaire	Kelao	100,000	Animism	0%	6	81	5717
Kele	China	Kele	23,000	Traditional Chinese	<1%	1		5308
Kele	Gabon	Kele	5,000	Animism	<1%	1		2822
Kemak	Indonesia	Kemak	50,000	Animism	<1%	1		2951
Kembata	Ethiopia	Kembata	250,000	Animism	<1%	1		3216
Kemok	Malaysia	Kemok	400	Animism	0%	2		4115
Kenati	Papua New Guinea	Kenati	600	Animism	<1%	1		6129
Kendari	Indonesia	Kendari	500,000	Islam-Animist	<1%	1		2952
Kenga	Chad	Kenga	25,000	Islam-Animist	<1%	1		2227
Kenyah	Indonesia	Kenyah	40,000	Animism	<1%	1		2953
Keopara	Papua New Guinea	Keopara	20,000	Animism	<1%	1		6130
*Kepas	Papua New Guinea	Kewa	15,000	Animism	<1%	3		130
Kera	Cameroon	Kera	35,000	Islam-Animist	<1%	4		5243
Kera	Chad	Kera	35,000	Animism	1%	4		2228
Kerewe	Tanzania	Kikerewe	2,000	Animism	<1%	1		243
Kerewo	Papua New Guinea	Kerewo	1,000	Animism	<1%	1		6131
Keriaka	Papua New Guinea	Keriaka	1,000	Animism	<1%	1		6132
Kerinchi	Indonesia	Kerinchi	170,000	Islam-Animist	<1%	1		2954
Ket	USSR	Ket	1,000	Unknown	0%	1		5850
Kewa, East	Papua New Guinea	Kewa, East	20,000	Animism	<1%	1		6133

Name	Country	Language	Group Size	Primary Religion	% Chr	V	UP	ID
Kewa, South	Papua New Guinea	Kewa, South	5,000	Animism	<1%	1		6134
Kewa, West	Papua New Guinea	Kewa, West	20,000	Animism	<1%	1		6135
Khakas	USSR	Khakas	67,000	Unknown	<1%	1		5851
Khalaj	Iran	Khalaj	20,000	Islam	<1%	1		2535
Khalka	China	Khalka	68,000	Traditional Chinese	<1%	1		2823
Kham	China	Kham	11,000	Traditional Chinese	<1%	1		2824
*Khamu	Nepal	Khamti	40,300	Buddhist-Animist	<1%	1		6512
Khamti in Assam	India	Khamu	6,000	Hindu-Buddhist	4%	1		2694
Khana	Thailand	Khana	90,000	Animism	5%	1		2087
Khandesi	Nigeria	Khandesi	20,000	Unknown	1%	1		1122
Khanti	India	Khanti	21,000	Hindu-Animist	0%	1		2695
Kharia in Bihar	USSR	Kharia	90,000	Unknown	1%	1		5852
Khasi in Assam	India	Khasi	384,000	Hindu-Animist	0%	1		2696
Khasonke	India	Khasonke	71,000	Hinduism	1%	1		2697
Khinalug	Mali	Khinalug	2,000	Islam	1%	1		5378
Khirwar in Madhya Pradesh	USSR	Khirwar	34,000	Unknown	0%	1		5853
**Khmer Refugees	India	Khmer	30,000	Hindu-Animist	1%	4	83	2698
**Khmer Refugees, Unaccd.	Thailand	Cambodia	34,000	Buddhist-Animist	1%	4		2094
Minors	Thailand	Khmer	30,000	Buddhist-Animist	0%	3		9050
Khojas, Agha Khani	India	Gujarati	175,000	Islam	0%	4		2006
Khowar	India	Khowar	7,000	Hindu-Animist	1%	1		2699
Khvarshin	USSR	Khvarshin	1,000	Unknown	0%	1		5854
Kiari	Papua New Guinea	Kiari	22,000	Animism	1%	1		6136
Kibet	Chad	Kibet	1,000	Islam-Animist	1%	1		2229
Kibiri	Papua New Guinea	Kibiri	16,000	Animism	0%	1		6137
Kichepo	Sudan	Kikepo	5,000	Animism	3%	1		704
Kikapoo	Mexico	Kikapoo	80,000	Christo-Paganism	0%	1		8044
Kilba	Nigeria	Kilba	2,000	Islam	1%	1		2430
Kilmera	Papua New Guinea	Kilmera	5,000	Animism	0%	1		6138
Kim	Central African Republic	Kim	3,000	Islam-Animist	1%	1		5186
Kimaghama	Indonesia	Kimaghama	15,000	Animism	1%	1		2230
Kimbu	Tanzania	Kimbu	7,000	Animism	0%	1		2955
*Kimyal	Indonesia	Kimyal		Animism	1%	1		5559
Kinalakna	Papua New Guinea	Kinalakna		Animism	0%	2		228
Kinaray-A	Philippines	Kinaray-A	288,000	Christo-Paganism	1%	1		6139
Kinga	Tanzania	Kinga	57,000	Animism	0%	4		3270
	Turkey	Kirghiz	1,300	Islam	1%	1		5560
Kirghiz Afghan Refugees	Afghanistan	Kirgiz	45,000	Islam	0%	5	80	9060
Kirgiz	China	Kirgiz	1,700,000	Islam-Animist	0%	6		2551
	USSR	Kirgiz	14,000	Islam	0%	1		4039
		Krifi	14,200	Islam	1%	1		4016
Kirifi	Nigeria	Kiriwina	74,000	Animism	0%	1		2431
Kiriwina	Papua New Guinea	Kis	4,000	Animism	1%	1		6140
Kis	Papua New Guinea	Kisan	57,000	Animism	0%	1		6141
Kisan in Bihar	India	Kisankasa	12,000	Hindu-Animist	1%	1		2700
Kisankasa	Tanzania	Kishanganjia	4,000	Animism	0%	1		5561
Kishanganjia in Bihar	India	Kishtwari		Hindu-Animist	1%	1		2701
Kishtwari in Jammu	India	Kisi		Hindu-Animist	0%	1		2702
Kisi	Tanzania	Kisi		Animism	0%	1		5562

Name	Country	Language	Group Size	Primary Religion	% Chr	V	Vol UP	ID
Konda-Dora (Andra Pradesh)	India	Konda-Dora	16,000	Hindu-Animist	<1%		1	2706
Koneraw	Indonesia	Koneraw	300	Animism	<1%		1	2957
Kongo	Angola	Kongo	756,000	Unknown	0%		1	5150
Konkani in Gujarat	India	Konkani	1,523,000	Hindu-Animist	<1%		1	2707
Konkomba	Ghana	Konkomba	175,000	Animism	9%	5		528
*Konkomba	Togo	Kom Komba	25,000	Animism	1%	4		253
Kono	Nigeria	Kono	2,000	Islam	<1%			2436
**Kono	Sierra Leone	Kono	133,600	Animism	5%	5		203
Konomala	Papua New Guinea	Konomala	20,000	Animism	<1%		1	6155
Konongo	Tanzania	Konongo	20,000	Animism	0%			5563
Konso	Ethiopia	Konso	30,000	Animism	<1%	5		517
Konyagi	Guinea	Konyagi	85,000	Islam-Animist	0%		1	5342
Koraga in Kerala	India	Koraga	2,200	Hindu-Animist	0%		1	2709
Korak	Papua New Guinea	Korak	2,000	Animism	<1%		1	6156
**Koranko	Sierra Leone	Kuranko (Maninka)	100,000	Islam-Animist	<1%	5		201
Korape	Papua New Guinea	Korape	4,000	Animism	<1%		1	6157
Korapun	Indonesia	Korapun	4,000	Animism	<1%		1	2958
***Koreans in Germany	German Federal Rep.	Korean	10,000	Unknown	4%	4		686
Koreans in Manchuria	China	Korean	3,000,000	Secularism	nr%	5		7007
*Koreans of Japan	Japan	Korean	600,000	Folk Religion	6%	5	81	57
*Korku in Madhya Pradesh	India	Korku	250,000	Animism	1%			198
Koro	Nigeria	Koro	35,000	Animism	<1%	5		572
Koroma	Sudan	Koroma	30,000	Animism	0%	5		706
Korop	Cameroon	Korop	10,000	Animism	0%	3		5247
	Nigeria	Korop	10,000	Animism	<1%		1	2437
Korwa in Bihar	India	Korwa	8,000	Hindu-Animist	<1%		1	2710
Koryak	USSR	Koryak	1,000	Unknown	0%			5857
Kosorong	Papua New Guinea	Kosorong	nr	Animism	<1%		1	6158
Kota	Gabon	Kota	900	Animism	<1%			5309
Kota in Tamil Nadu	India	Kota	15,000	Hindu-Animist	<1%		1	2711
Kotia in Andhra Pradesh	India	Kotia	31,000	Hindu-Animist	<1%		1	2768
Kotogut	Indonesia	Kotogut	31,000	Animism	0%		1	2959
Kotoko	Cameroon	Kotoko	75,000	Animism	0%			5248
	Chad	Kotoko		Islam-Animist	0%			2232
Kotokoli	Benin	Kotokoli	150,000	Islam	0%		3	448
	Togo	Kotokoli		Islam-Animist	0%	4		5631
Kotopo	Cameroon	Kotopo	10,000	Animism	0%	5		501
Kotta	India	Kota	1,000	Animism	0%		1	1098
Kouya	Ivory Coast	Kouya	6,000	Islam-Animist	0%			2292
Koval	Papua New Guinea	Koval	3,000	Animism	<1%		1	6159
Kove	Papua New Guinea	Kove	3,000	Animism	0%			6160
**Kowaao	Liberia	Kowaao	212,000	Hindu-Animist	3%	4		692
Koya in Andhra Pradesh	India	Koya	5,000	Animism	<1%			2712
Koyra	Ethiopia	Koyra	17,000	Animism	<1%		1	3217
Kpa	Cameroon	Kpa	250,000	Animism	<1%		1	5249
Kpelle	Guinea	Kpelle	250,000	Islam-Animist	6%	5		5343
	Liberia	Kpelle		Animism	0%			556
Kposo	Togo	Kposo	45,000	Islam-Animist	<1%		1	5632
Krachi	Ghana	Krachi	22,000	Islam-Animist	0%			5325

Name	Country	Language	Group Size	Primary Religion	% Chr	V	Vol UP	ID
*Krahn	Ivory Coast	Guere	250,000	Animism	3%	4		687
***Krahn	Liberia	Krahn	55,100	Animism	7%	4		83
Kreen-Akakore	Brazil	Kreen-Akakore		Animism	<1%	1		2173
Krim	Sierra Leone	Mende	3,000	Islam-Animist	0%	1		5432
Krio	Gambia	Krio	3,000	Islam-Animist	<1%	1		2269
Krisa	Papua New Guinea	Krisa	500	Animism	0%	1		6161
Krobou	Ivory Coast	Krobou	3,000	Islam-Animist	1%	4		2293
Krongo	Sudan	Krongo	121,000	Animism	1%	4		579
Krumen	Ivory Coast	Krumen	17,000	Animism	2%	4		4137
Kryz	USSR	Kryz	6,100	Unknown	0%	5		5858
Kuatinema	Brazil	Asurini		Animism	<1%	5		1159
Kube	Papua New Guinea	Kube	4,000	Animism	<1%			6162
Kubu	Indonesia	Kubu	25,000	Islam-Animist	nr%	6	81	7026
Kuda-Chamo	Indonesia	Local dialects	6,000	Animism	1%	6	80	1093
	Nigeria	Kuda-Chamo		Islam	<1%			2438
*Kudisai Vagh Makkal	India	Tamil	1,000,000	Hinduism	2%	3		695
Kudiya	India	Kudiya	100	Hindu-Animist	0%			2713
Kugbo	Nigeria	Kugbo	2,000	Animism	<1%			2439
*Kui	Thailand	Kui	160,000	Buddhist-Animist	1%	5		607
Kuikuro	Brazil	Kuikuro	100	Animism	<1%			2174
Kuka	Chad	Kuka	38,000	Islam-Animist	<1%			2233
Kukele	Cameroon	Kukele	33,000	Animism	<1%			5250
	Nigeria	Kukele	32,000	Animism	<1%			2440
*Kuknas	India	Kukni	125,000	Hindu-Animist	1%	4		701
Kukuwy	Papua New Guinea	Kukuya	11,000	Animism	<1%			6163
Kukwa	Congo	Kukwa	60,000	Animism	3%	4		5295
Kulango	Ivory Coast	Kulango	15,000	Islam-Animist	0%			481
Kulele	Ivory Coast	Kulele	8,000	Animism	<1%			2294
Kulere	Nigeria	Kulere	82,000	Islam-Animist	<1%			2441
**Kuluis in Himachal Pradesh	India	Kului	200,000	Hinduism	1%	5	81	3218
Kullo	Ethiopia	Kullo		Animism	<1%			2015
Kulung	Nigeria	Kulung	15,000	Islam-Animist	<1%			2442
Kumai	Papua New Guinea	Kumai	4,000	Animism	0%			6164
Kumam	Uganda	Kumam	100,000	Animism	<1%			5644
	Papua New Guinea	Kuman	66,000	Animism	<1%			6165
Kumauni in Assam	India	Kumauni	1,240,400	Hindu-Animist	<1%			2716
Kumdauron	Papua New Guinea	Kumdauron	60,300	Animism	<1%			5768
Kumu	Zaire	Kumu	70,000	Animism	<1%			5167
Kumukio	Papua New Guinea	Kumukio	60,000	Animism	<1%			3219
Kunama	Ethiopia	Kunama	21,000	Islam-Animist	0%			5353
Kunante	Guinea-Bissau	Kunante	8,000	Animism	<1%			5391
Kunda	Mozambique	LaLa-Bisa	40,000	Animism	0%			5790
	Zambia	Nyanja		Animism	0%			5411
Kuni	Zimbabwe	Kunda		Animism	0%			6168
**Kunimaipa	Papua New Guinea	Kunimaipa	9,000	Animism	0%			1202
Kunua	Papua New Guinea	Kunua		Christo-Paganism	6%	5		6169
Kuot	Papua New Guinea	Kuot	1,900	Animism	<1%			6170

293

Name	Country	Language	Group Size	Primary Religion	% Chr	Vol V	UP	ID
Kupia in Andhra Pradesh	India	Kupia	4,000	Hindu-Animist	<1%	1		2715
Kupsabiny	Uganda	Kupsabiny	60,900	Animism	0%	1		5645
Kurada	Papua New Guinea	Kurada		Animism	1%	6	80	6171
Kurds in Iran	Iran	Kurdish Dialects	2,000,000	Islam	1%	3		2036
Kurds in Kuwait	Kuwait	Kurdish	1,145,000	Islam	0%	6	79	4136
*Kurds of Turkey	Turkey	Kurdish (Kirmancho)	1,900,000	Islam	<1%	6		180
Kurfei	Niger	Hausa	50,000	Animism	1%	4		561
Kuria	Tanzania	Kuria	75,000	Animism	0%	1		5564
Kurichiya in Kerala	India	Kurichiya	12,000	Nominal Christian	<1%	5	81	2716
Kuruba in Tamil Nadu	India	Kuruba	8,000	Hindu-Animist	<1%	1		2717
Kurudu	Indonesia	Kurudu	1,000	Animism	<1%	1		2960
Kurumba	Upper Volta	Kurumba	86,000	Islam-Animist	<1%	1		5673
Kurux in Bihar	India	Kurux	1,240,000	Hindu-Animist	<1%	1		2718
**Kusaasi	Ghana	Kusaal	150,000	Animism	3%	5		1183
Kushi	Nigeria	Kushi	4,000	Islam	<1%	1		2443
Kusu	Zaire	Kusu	26,000	Animism	0%	1		5719
Kuteb	Nigeria	Kuteb	26,000	Animism	<1%	1		2444
Kutin	Cameroon	Kutin	400	Animism	0%	1		5251
Kutu	Tanzania	Kutu	17,000	Animism	0%	1		5565
Kuturmi	Nigeria	Kuturmi	3,000	Islam	<1%	1		2445
Kuvi in Orissa	India	Kuvi	190,000	Hindu-Animist	1%	6		2719
Kuwaa	Liberia	Kuwaa	6,000	Islam-Animist	0%	1		5362
Kuzamani	Nigeria	Kuzamani	1,000	Islam	0%	1		2446
Kvanadin	USSR	Kvanadin	6,000	Unknown	<1%	1		5859
Kwa	Nigeria	Kwa		Islam	<1%	1		2447
Kwadi	Angola	Kwadi	15,000	Animism	0%	1		5151
Kwakum	Cameroon	Kwakum	3,000	Animism	0%	1		5252
Kwale	Papua New Guinea	Kwale	700	Animism	<1%	1		6172
Kwambi	Namibia	Kwambi	30,000	Animism	<1%	1		5401
Kwanga	Papua New Guinea	Kwanga	25,000	Animism	<1%	1		6173
Kwangali	Angola	Kwangali		Animism	<1%	1		5152
Kwansu	Indonesia	Kwansu	400	Animism	0%	1		2961
Kwanyama	Angola	Kwanyama	100,000	Animism	<1%	1		5402
Kwanyama	Namibia	Kwanyama	150,000	Animism	0%	1		5153
Kwaya	Tanzania	Kwaya	35,000	Animism	0%	1		5566
Kwe-etshori	Botswana	Kwe-etshori	3,000	Animism	<1%	1		5176
Kwe-etshori	Zimbabwe	Kwe-etshori	1,000	Animism	0%	1		5412
Kwerba	Indonesia	Kwerba	2,000	Animism	10%	5		2962
Kwere	Tanzania	Kwere	63,000	Animism	<1%	1		491
Kwese	Zaire	Kwese	60,000	Animism	10%	5		5720
Kwesten	Indonesia	Kwesten	3,000	Animism	0%	1		2963
Kwoma	Papua New Guinea	Kwoma	2,000	Animism	<1%	1		6174
Kwomtari	Papua New Guinea	Kwomtari	800	Animism	0%	1		6175
Kyibaku	Nigeria	Kyibaku	20,000	Islam	<1%	1		2448
Laamang	Nigeria	Laamang	40,000	Islam	<1%	1		2449
Labans	India	Labaani	nr	Hindu-Buddhist	<1%	3		1041
Labbani in Andhra Pradesh	India	Tamil	nr	Islam	<1%	5		4045
Labhani of Jhoparpatti	India	Labhani	1,200,000	Hindu-Buddhist	<1%	1		2122
*Labourers of Jhoparpatti	India	Marathi	2,000	Hinduism	10%	4		2001

Name	Country	Language	Group Size	Primary Religion	% Chr	Vol V	UP	ID
Labu	Papua New Guinea	Labu	800	Animism	<1%	1		6176
Lacandon	Mexico	Lacandon	200	Christo-Paganism	<1%	1		8045
Ladakhi in Jammu	India	Ladakhi	60,000	Hindu-Buddhist	<1%	1		2720
Ladinos	Lebanon	Ladinos	7,000	Judaism	<1%	1		2538
Laewomba	Papua New Guinea	Laewomba	2,000	Animism	<1%	1		6177
Latofa	Sudan	Latofa	2,000	Islam	0%	1		5494
**Lahaulis in Punjab	India	Lahouli	18,000	Buddhism	<1%	4		2016
Lahu	Burma	Lahu	40,000	Animism	0%	2		4151
*Lahu	Thailand	Lahu	23,000	Animism	7%	5	81	2088
Lahul	China	Lahul	2,000	Traditional Chinese	<1%	1		2826
Laka	Cameroon	Laka	10,000	Animism	0%	4		500
Laka	Central African Republic	Laka	40,000	Animism	<1%	1		5187
	Chad	Lakal	40,000	Islam-Animist	<1%	1		2234
	USSR	Laka	6,000	Traditional Chinese	<1%	1		2827
Lakians	Nigeria	Lakian	86,000	Islam	0%	1		5812
Lakka	Zambia	Lakka	500	Islam	<1%	1		2450
Lala	India	Lala	125,000	Animism	0%	1		5785
Lalia	Zaire	Lalia	30,000	Animism	0%	1		5721
Laiung in Assam	India	Laiung	11,000	Hindu-Buddhist	<1%	1		2581
Lama	Burma	Lama	3,000	Buddhist-Animist	<1%	5		2589
Lamba	Benin	Lamba	29,000	Animism	3%	4		425
	Zaire	Lamba	29,000	Animism	<1%	1		5169
	Togo	Lamba	89,000	Animism	0%	1		5722
**Lambadi in Andhra Pradesh	India	Lambadi	1,300,000	Animism	nr%	5	81	5791
Lambi	Cameroon	Lambi	2,000	Animism	<1%	1		2018
Lambya	Malawi	Lambya	27,000	Animism	0%	1		5253
	Tanzania	Lambya	2,000	Animism	<1%	1		5366
Lame	Nigeria	Lame	2,000	Islam	<1%	1		5567
Lamogai	Papua New Guinea	Lamogai	2,000	Animism	0%	5	80	2451
Lampung	Indonesia	Komering	1,500,000	Islam-Animist	0%	1		6178
Landoma	Guinea	Landoma	4,000	Islam-Animist	0%	1		1134
	Guinea-Bissau	Landoma	5,000	Islam-Animist	0%	3		5344
Langi	Tanzania	Langi	95,000	Animism	0%	1		5354
*Lango	Ethiopia	Lango	560,400	Animism	0%	3		5568
Lango	Uganda	Lango	8,000	Animism	0%	1		680
Lanoh	Malaysia	Lanoh	1,910,500	Buddhism	<1%	1	79	5646
*Lao Refugees	Laos	Lao	1,000	Ancestor Worship	<1%	3	83	411
*Lao Refugees	Argentina	Lao	20,000	Buddhist-Animist	<1%	3	83	121
	Spain	Lao	12,000	Buddhist-Animist	<1%	4		9037
Lara	Thailand	Lara	1,900	Animism	<1%	1		9056
Laro	Indonesia	Lara	900	Islam	0%	1		2090
Laru	Nigeria	Laru	125,000	Animism	<1%	1		2964
Latdwalam	Sudan	Latdwalam	500	Islam	<1%	1		5495
Laudje	Indonesia	Lati	500	Animism	<1%	1		2452
	China	Laudje	125,000	Traditional Chinese	<1%	1		2829
Lavatbura-Lamusong	Indonesia	Lavatbura-Lamusong	1,000	Animism	<1%	1		2966
Lavongai	Papua New Guinea	Lavongai	10,000	Animism	<1%	1		6179
	Papua New Guinea							6180

295

Name	Country	Language	Group Size	Primary Religion	% Chr	V	Vol UP	ID
Lawa, Eastern	Thailand	Tibeto-Burman Dialect	3,000	Buddhist-Animist	<1%	5	81	7039
Lawa, Mountain	Thailand	Lawa	10,000	Buddhist-Animist	4%	5		612
Lebgo	Nigeria	Lebgo	30,000	Animism	<1%	5		2453
Lebong	Indonesia	Redjang-Lebong	nr	Islam	<1%	1		1090
Leco	Bolivia	Leco	200	Animism	<1%	1		2137
Lega	Zaire	Lega	150,000	Animism	<1%	1		5723
Lelemi	Ghana	Lelemi	15,000	Islam-Animist	<1%	1		5326
Lengua, Northern	Paraguay	Lengua, Northern	95,000	Animism	<1%	1		5126
Lenje	Zambia	Lenje	79,000	Animism	0%	1		5793
**Lepcha	India	Lepcha	18,000	Hindu-Buddhist	10%	4		2127
**Lepers of Cen. Thailand	Thailand	Thai	20,000	Buddhist-Animist	1%	6	81	236
**Lepers of N.E. Thailand	Thailand	Northeast Thai	200,500	Buddhism	1%	4		6181
Leron	Papua New Guinea	Leron	6,000	Animism	1%	1		2967
Letti	Indonesia	Letti	6,000	Buddhist-Animist	<1%	1		6513
Lhomi	Nepal	Lhomi	20,000	Islam	<1%	1		2830
Li	China	Li	1,000,000	Traditional Chinese	0%	5		1071
Ligbi	Ghana	Ligbi	2,000	Islam	<1%	4		482
	Ivory Coast	Ligbi	5,000	Islam-Animist	0%	1		5496
Liguri	Sudan	Liguri	26,000	Animism	<1%	1		6182
Lihir	Papua New Guinea	Lihir	12,000	Animism	0%	1		5727
Liko	Zaire	Liko	233,000	Animism	0%	4		5792
Lima	Zambia	Lima	470,000	Animism	0%	4		587
Limba	Sierra Leone	Limba	13,000	Animism	4%	4		2968
Lionese	Indonesia	Lio	2,000	Christo-Paganism	<1%	1		7009
*Lisu	China	Tibeto-Burman	2,000	Animism	0%	5	81	2089
	Thailand	Lisu	40,000	Unknown	6%	4		5860
Liv	USSR	Liv	44,000	Animism	0%	1		2454
Lo	Nigeria	Lo	3,000	Animism	<1%	4		483
Lobi	Ivory Coast	Lobi	900	Animism	1%	1		2723
Lodhi in Bihar	India	Lodhi	10,000	Hindu-Animist	<1%	4		5327
Logba	Ghana	Logba	100,000	Islam-Animist	0%	1		6183
Lohiki	Papua New Guinea	Lohiki	16,000	Animism	0%	3		137
**Loho Loho	Indonesia	Kolaka	80,000	Animism	nr%	5	81	2969
Loinang	Indonesia	Loinang	22,000	Islam-Animist	0%	1		5345
Loko	Guinea	Loko		Animism	1%	4		586
*Lokoro	Sierra Leone	Lokoro		Christo-Paganism	5%	4		1128
Lolo	Sudan	Yi	4,800,000	Animism	0%	4		7006
Loma	China	Loma	180,000	Animism	3%	4		479
	Guinea	Loma	60,000	Animism	12%	4		601
Lombi	Liberia	Lombi	8,000	Animism	0%	4		5729
Lombo	Zaire	Lombo		Animism	0%	4		5730
Lomwe	Zaire	not reported	1,000,000	Animism	9%	4		565
Longuda	Mozambique	Longuda	32,000	Islam	<1%	4		2455
Lore	Nigeria	Lore	140,000	Animism	<1%	1		2970
Lori	Indonesia	Lori		Islam	0%	1		5447
Lors	Sudan	Luri	600,000	Islam	<1%	5	80	2028
Lotsu-Piri	Iran	Lotsu-Piri	1,000	Islam	1%	5		2456
**Lotuka	Nigeria	Latuka	150,000	Other	6%	5		200
	Sudan							

Name	Country	Language	Group Size	Primary Religion	% Chr	Vol V	UP	ID
Lou-Baluan-Pam	Papua New Guinea	Lou-Baluan-Pam	1,000	Animism	<1%			6184
Loven	Laos	Loven	215,000	Buddhist-Animist	0%	5	81	107
Lozi	Zambia	Lozi	8,000	Animism	0%	1		5794
Lozi	Zimbabwe	Lozi	400,000	Buddhist-Animist	<1%	1		5413
Lu	China	Lu	4,700	Islam	0%	1		2831
Luac	Sudan	Luac	700	Animism	0%			5466
Luano	Zambia	Luano	18,000	Animism	0%	5	81	5787
Lubang Islanders	Philippines	Pilipino	1,000,000	Christo-Paganism	0%	5	81	7016
Lubu	Indonesia	Lubu	60,000	Islam	<1%			2971
Luchazi	Angola	Luchazi	34,000	Animism	<1%			5154
Luchazi	Zambia	Luchazi	4,000	Animism	<1%			5795
Lue	Cameroon	Lue	20,500	Animism	<1%			5255
Lugitama	Papua New Guinea	Lugitama	20,600	Animism	0%			6185
Luimbi	Angola	Luimbi	12,000	Animism	<1%			5155
Lukep	Papua New Guinea	Lukep	600	Animism	<1%			6186
Lumbu	Gabon	Lumbu	12,000	Animism	<1%			5310
Luna	Zaire	Luna	50,000	Animism	<1%			5132
Lunda	Angola	Lunda	50,000	not reported	nr%			5756
Lunda, Ndembu	Zambia	Lunda, Ndembu	100,000	Animism	0%			5294
Lundu	Cameroon	Lundu	24,000	Animism	<1%	4		571
Lungu	Nigeria	Lungu	10,000	Animism	<1%			5569
Luo	Tanzania	Luo	1,522,000	Animism	<1%			2524
Lushai in Assam from Angola	India	Lushai	270,000	Hindu-Animist	nr%	4		2579
Luvale Refugees from Angola	Zambia	Luvale	11,000	Animism	nr%	4	83	9061
Luwu	Indonesia	Luwu	500,000	Islam	<1%			2972
Luxemburgois	Luxembourg	letzburgesch	276,000	Nominal Christian	nr%	2		6561
Luyana	Angola	Luyana	4,000	Animism	0%			5157
Luyana	Zambia	Luyana	50,000	Animism	0%	1		5797
Lwalu	Zaire	Lwalu	20,000	Animism	<1%			5733
Lwena	Angola	Lwena	90,000	Animism	<1%			5158
Lwo	Sudan	Lwo	15,000	Islam	<1%			5497
Ma	Zaire	Ma	105,000	Animism	0%			5734
Maanyan	Indonesia	Maanyan	56,000	Animism	5%	6	79	2973
**Maasai	Kenya	Masai	9,000	Animism	5%			489
Maba	Chad	Maba	20,000	Islam	0%			2236
Maba	Sudan	Maba	10,600	Islam	<1%			5498
Maban-Jumjum	Sudan	Maban-Jumjum	10,000	Islam	<1%			5499
Maca	Paraguay	Maca	1,300	Animism	<1%			5127
Machiguenga	Peru	Machiguenga	6,000	Animism	<1%	3		3178
Macu	Colombia	Macu	3,000	Animism	<1%			242
Macuna	Colombia	Macuna	600	Animism	<1%			3144
**Macuxi	Brazil	Macuxi	6,000	Animism	5%	3		719
Madak	Papua New Guinea	Madak	3,000	Animism	<1%			6187
Madda	Nigeria	Madda	6,000	Animism	0%			2457
Madi	Sudan	Madi	30,000	Islam	0%			5500
Madi	Uganda	Madi	114,000	Animism	0%			5647
Madik	Indonesia	Madik	1,000	Animism	<1%			2974
**Magar	Nepal	Magar	300,000	Hindu-Animist	<1%	1		395
Maghi	Burma	Maghi	310,000	Buddhist-Animist	<1%			2582

Name	Country	Language	Group Size	Primary Religion	% Chr	Vol V	UP	ID
Magori	Papua New Guinea	Magori	200	Animism	<1%			6188
Maguindano	Philippines	Maguindano	700,000	Islam	1%	6	80	629
**Maguzawa	Nigeria	Hausa	100,000	Animism	1%	6	79	202
Mahali in Assam	India	Mahali	14,000	Hindu-Animist	<1%			2725
*Mahrah	Yemen, Democratic	Local dialects	50,000	Islam	0%	3		4066
Mahri	Oman	Mahri	50,000	Animism	400%			2539
Mai	Papua New Guinea	Mai		Animism	0%			6189
Mailu	Papua New Guinea	Mailu	5,000	Animism	<1%			6190
Maiongong	Brazil	Maiongong		Animism	<1%	3		718
Mairasi	Indonesia	Mairasi	1,000	Animism	<1%			2975
Maisan	Papua New Guinea	Maisan	2,000	Animism	<1%			6191
Maithili	Nepal	Maithili	1,000,000	Hindu-Animist	0%	4		398
Mawa	Papua New Guinea	Mawa	1,000	Animism	<1%			6192
Majhi	Nepal	Majhi	6,000	Buddhist-Animist	0%			6514
Majhwar in Madhya Pradesh	India	Majhwar	28,000	Hindu-Animist	0%			2726
Maji	Ethiopia	Maji	15,000	Animism	<1%			518
Majingai-Ngama	Chad	Majingai-Ngama	47,000	Islam-Animist	<1%	4		2237
Majingai-ngama	Central African Republic	Majingai-ngama	51,000	Animism	<1%			5188
Maka	Cameroon	Maka	2,000	Animism	0%			5256
Makarim	Papua New Guinea	Makarim	70,000	Animism	<1%			6193
Makasai	Indonesia	Makasai	18,000	Animism	0%			2976
Makere	Uganda	Makere	12,000	Animism	<1%			5648
Makian, West	Indonesia	Makian, West	100	Animism	<1%			2977
Maklew	Indonesia	Maklew		Animism	0%			2978
Makonde	Tanzania	not reported	550,100	Islam	6%	5		144
Makua	Mozambique	Makua	1,200,000	Animism	10%	4	81	564
Malaakkaras of Kerala	India	Malaamutha		Hindu-Animist	0%			2019
Malaiamai	Papua New Guinea	Malaiamai	300	Animism	<1%			6194
Malankuravan in Kerala	India	Malankuravan	5,000	Hindu-Animist	<1%			2727
Malapandaram in Kerala	India	Malapandaram	500	Hindu-Animist	<1%			2728
Malappanackers	India	Malappanackan	1,000	Animism	0%			2021
Malaryan in Kerala	India	Malaryan	5,000	Hindu-Animist	<1%			2729
Malas	Papua New Guinea	Malas	200	Animism	<1%			6195
Malasanga	Papua New Guinea	Malasanga	400	Animism	<1%			6196
Malavedan in Kerala	India	Malavedan	2,000	Hinduism	<1%			2730
*Malayalars	India	Malayalam	nr	Animism	6%	4		2020
Malayo	Colombia	Malayo		Hinduism	6%	4		696
Malays of Singapore	Singapore	Malay	300,000	Islam	<1%			120
Male	Ethiopia	Male	12,000	Animism	<1%			3221
Malek	Papua New Guinea	Malek	1,000	Animism	<1%			6197
Maleu	Papua New Guinea	Maleu	4,000	Animism	0%	6	79	6198
Mali in Andhra Pradesh	India	Mali	175,000	Hindu-Animist	0%			2731
Malila in Bihar	Tanzania	Malila	89,000	Hindu-Animist	0%			5570
Malki in Bihar	India	Malki		Animism	0%			6199
Malon	Papua New Guinea	Malon		Animism	0%			
Malpaharia in Assam	India	Malpaharia	3,000	Hindu-Animist	0%			2732
**Maltese	Malta	Maltese	330,000	Nominal Christian	nr%	2		6560
**Malvi in Madhya Pradesh	India	Malvi	644,000	Hindu-Animist	<1%	1		2734
**Mam Indian	Guatemala	Mam	470,000	Christo-Paganism	7%	5		1124

299

Name	Country	Language	Group Size	Primary Religion	% Chr	Vol V	UP	ID
**Manobo, Salug	Philippines	Manobo, Tigwa	4,000	Animism	4%	5		639
Manobo, Sarangani	Philippines	Manobo, Sarangani	15,000	Animism	<1%	1		3277
Manobo, Tagabawa	Philippines	Manobo, Tagabawa	10,000	Animism	<1%			3278
**Manobo, Tigwa	Philippines	Manobo, Tigwa	4,000	Animism	3%	5		640
**Manobo, Western Bukidnon	Philippines	Manobo, Binokid	12,000	Animism	6%	5		618
**Mansaka	Philippines	Manobo, Pulangi	5,000	Animism	1%	4		1171
Mansaka	Philippines	Mansaka	25,000	Christo-Paganism	10%	5		1035
Mansi	USSR	Mansi	8,000	Unknown	0%			5861
Mantera	Malaysia	Mantera	4,000	Animism	0%	2		4097
Mantion	Indonesia	Mantion	12,000	Animism	<1%	1		2984
Manu Park Panoan	Peru	Manu Park Panoan	200	Animism	<1%	1		3179
Manyika	Zimbabwe	Manyika	350,000	Animism	<1%	1		5414
Mao, Northern	Ethiopia	Mao, Northern	13,000	Islam-Animist	<1%	1		3222
Maou	Ivory Coast	Maou	80,000	Animism	<1%	1		2295
Mape	Papua New Guinea	Mape	5,300	Animism	<1%			6204
Mapena	Papua New Guinea	Mapena	300	Animism	<1%			6205
Mapoyo	Venezuela	Mapoyo	200	Animism	0%			5136
Mappillas	India	Malayalan	4,500,000	Islam	<1%	5		4026
Mapuche	Chile	Mapuche	300,000	Christo-Paganism	1%	5		48
Maquiritari	Venezuela	Maquiritari	5,000	Animism	<1%			5137
Mara in Assam	India	Mara	12,000	Hindu-Animist	<1%			2737
Maralango	Papua New Guinea	Maralango	2,000	Animism	<1%			6206
Maralinan	Papua New Guinea	Maralinan	2,000	Animism	<1%			6207
Maranao	Philippines	Maranao	500,000	Islam	2%	6	79	638
Maranao, Lanad	Chad	Maranao, Lanad	500,000	Islam-Animist	<1%			3279
Mararit	Chad	Mararit	42,000	Islam-Animist	<1%			2239
Marau	Indonesia	Marau	1,000	Animism	<1%			2985
Marba	Nigeria	Marba	30,000	Islam-Animist	<1%			2240
Marghi Central	Papua New Guinea	Marghi Central	135,000	Islam	<1%			2460
Mari	USSR	Mari	599,000	Animism	<1%			6208
Maria in Andhra Pradesh	India	Maria	2,000	Christo-Paganism	<1%			5862
**Marielito Refugees in Florida	United States of America	Spanish	125,000	Secularism	14%	4	83	6565
Marind	Indonesia	Marind	7,000	Animism	<1%			2986
Marind, Bian	Indonesia	Marind, Bian	900	Animism	<1%			2987
Maring	Papua New Guinea	Maring	8,000	Animism	<1%			6210
Marka	Upper Volta	Marka	39,000	Islam	0%			5675
Marubo	Brazil	Marubo	400	Animism	<1%			2175
Marwari in Gujarat	India	Marwari	6,810,000	Hindu-Animist	<1%			2739
Masa	Chad	Masa	80,000	Animism	6%	4		514
Masaba	Uganda	Masaba	110,000	Animism	0%			5650
Masakin	Sudan	Masakin	16,000	Islam	<1%			5501
Masalit	Sudan	Masalit	74,000	Islam-Animist	<1%			2241
	Sudan	Arabic	2,000	Islam	0%			5502
Masegi	Papua New Guinea	Masegi	2,000	Animism	<1%			6211
*Masengo	Ethiopia	Majangir	7,000	Animism	<1%	5		428
Masenrempulu	Indonesia	Masenrempulu	250,000	Islam	<1%	1		2988
Mashi	Zambia	Mashi	21,000	Animism	0%	1		5799

Name	Country	Language	Group Size	Primary Religion	% Chr	V	UP	ID
Me'en	Ethiopia	Me'en	38,000	Animism	<1%	1		3223
Meax	Indonesia	Meax	10,000	Animism	<1%	1		2991
Meban	Sudan	Maban-Jumjum	130,000	Animism	1%	4		578
Medipa	Papua New Guinea	Medipa	60,000	Animism	<1%	6		6214
**Meghwar	Pakistan	Marwari	100,000	Hinduism	1%	6	79	262
Mehek	Papua New Guinea	Mehek	4,000	Animism	<1%	6		6215
**Meitei	India	Manipuri	700,000	Hinduism	1%	6	79	293
**Mejah	India	Mejah	6,000	Animism	0%	4		1033
Meje	Uganda	Meje	13,000	Animism	0%	1		5649
Mekeo	Papua New Guinea	Mekeo	7,000	Animism	<1%	6		6216
Mekwei	Indonesia	Mekwei	1,000	Animism	<1%	1		2992
**Melanau of Sarawak	Malaysia	Melanau	61,000	Islam-Animist	1%	6	80	2122
Mende	Liberia	Mende	5,000	Animism	1%	5		5585
Mende	Sierra Leone	Mende	600,000	Animism	13%	5		5363
Menemo-Mogamo	Cameroon	Menemo-Mogamo	35,000	Animism	1%	5		5261
Mengen	Papua New Guinea	Mengen	6,000	Animism	<1%	6		6217
Menka	Cameroon	Menka	10,000	Animism	1%	5		5262
Menri	Malaysia	Menri	400	Animism	0%	2		4113
Menye	Papua New Guinea	Menye	13,000	Animism	0%	6		6218
**Meos of Rajasthan	India	Meo	30,000	Animism	9%	5		610
Mera Mera	Thailand	Rajasthani	500,000	Islam	0%	5	80	4017
Mesengo	Papua New Guinea	Mera Mera	1,000	Islam-Animist	<1%	1		6219
Mesme	Ethiopia	Mesengo	28,000	Islam-Animist	<1%	1		3224
Mesmedje	Chad	Mesme	28,000	Islam-Animist	<1%	1		2245
***Mestizos in La Paz	Chad	Mesmedje	400,000	Islam-Animist	4%	1	82	2246
Mianmin	Bolivia	Spanish	1,000	Christo-Paganism	<1%	5		5001
Miao	Papua New Guinea	Mianmin	2,800,000	Animism	<1%	6		6220
**Miching	China	Miao	300,000	Animism	<1%	5	81	2000
**Middle Class-Mexico City	India	Miching	2,000	Hindu-Animist	nr%	5	82	2002
Midob	Mexico	Saching	900	Nominal Christian	0%	5		5014
Midsivindi	Sudan	Midob	740,000	Islam	<1%	5		5003
Mien	Papua New Guinea	Midsivindi	10,000	Animism	<1%	7	81	7021
Migabac	China	Mien	6,000	Animism	<1%	6		5022
Migili	Papua New Guinea	Migabac	80,000	Animism	<1%	5		2467
Mikarew	Nigeria	Migili	15,000	Animism	1%	6		6223
**Military Personnel	Papua New Guinea	Mikarew	765,000	Animism	15%	4		4123
Mimi	Ecuador	Spanish	5,000,000	Nominal Christian	3%	3		2247
**Mimika	Chad	Mimi	300	Islam-Animist	1%	5	80	2741
Mina in Madhya Pradesh	Indonesia	Mimika	2,000	Christo-Paganism	<1%	6		2142
Minangkabau	India	Mina	4,000	Hindu-Animist	<1%	1		212
Minanibai	Indonesia	Minangkabau	300,000	Islam	0%	6		6224
Mindik	Papua New Guinea	Minanibai	6,000	Animism	<1%	6		6225
Minduumo	Papua New Guinea	Mindik	2,000	Animism	0%	5		5313
Mingat	Gabon	Minduumo	4,000	Animism	<1%	5		5863
Minianka	USSR	Mingat	300,000	Unknown	<1%	1		554
Mirdha in Orissa	Mali	Suppire	6,000	Animism	4%	4		2742
Miri	India	Mirdha	8,000	Hindu-Animist	<1%	1		5504
Miriam	Sudan	Miri	700	Islam	0%	1		6226
	Papua New Guinea	Miriam		Animism	<1%	1		

Name	Language	Country	Group Size	Primary Religion	% Chr	V	UP	ID
Mirung	Mirung	Bangladesh	12,000	Animism	1%		4	650
Mishmi in Assam	Mishmi	India	5,000	Hindu-Animism	<1%		1	2743
Miskito	Miskito	Nicaragua	20,000	Christo-Paganism	<1%		1	5110
Mitang	Mitang	Papua New Guinea		Animism	<1%		1	6227
Mitmit	Mitmit	Papua New Guinea	500	Animism	<1%		1	6228
**Mixes	Mixe	Mexico	60,000	Christo-Paganism	2%		5	1005
Mixteco, Amoltepec	Mixteco, Amoltepec	Mexico	6,000	Christo-Paganism	0%		1	8048
Mixteco, Apoala	Mixteco, Apoala	Mexico	6,000	Christo-Paganism	0%		1	8049
Mixteco, Central Puebla	Spanish	Mexico	3,000	Christo-Paganism	0%		1	8040
Mixteco, Eastern	Mixteco, Eastern	Mexico	15,000	Christo-Paganism	0%		1	5051
Mixteco, Eastern Putla	Mixteco, Eastern Putla	Mexico	7,000	Christo-Paganism	0%		1	5052
Mixteco, Huajuapan	Mixteco, Huajuapan	Mexico	3,000	Christo-Paganism	<1%		1	5053
Mixteco, Silacayoapan	Mixteco, Silacayoapan	Mexico	12,000	Christo-Paganism	0%		1	5054
Mixteco, Southern Puebla	Mixteco, Southern Puebla	Mexico	12,000	Christo-Paganism	<1%		1	5055
Mixteco, Southern Putla	Mixteco, Southern Putla	Mexico	3,000	Christo-Paganism	0%		1	5056
Mixteco, Tututepec	Mixteco, Tututepec	Mexico	2,000	Christo-Paganism	0%		1	5057
Mixteco, Yosondua	Mixteco, Yosondua	Mexico	15,000	Christo-Paganism	<1%		1	5058
*Mixteco,San Juan Mixtepic	Mixteco, Yosondua	Mexico	5,000	Animism	1%		4	409
Miya	Miya	Nigeria	13,000	Animism	1%		5	1175
Mo	Mo (Degha)	Ghana		Animism	<1%		5	1100
Moba	Mo	Ivory Coast	80,800	Islam-Animist	<1%		5	2296
	Bimoba	Ghana	70,000	Animism	8%		4	530
	Bimoba	Togo	45,000	Animism	<1%		4	597
Mober	Mober	Nigeria	170,000	Islam	4%		4	2468
***Mocha	Mocha	Ethiopia	2,000	Islam	0%		1	429
Modo	Modo	Sudan	2,000	Animism	<1%		1	5448
Moewehafen	Moewehafen	Papua New Guinea	33,000	Animism	0%		1	6229
Mofu	Mofu	Cameroon		Islam	0%		1	5263
Mogholi	Mogholi	Afghanistan	2,000	Islam-Animist	<1%		1	2552
Mogum	Mogum	Chad	6,000	Animism	<1%		1	2248
Moi	Moi	Indonesia	4,000	Animism	<1%		1	2994
Mokareng	Mokareng	Papua New Guinea	1,000	Animism	1%	6	79	6230
Moken	Moken	Burma		Animism	1%		1	157
Moken of Thailand	Local dialects	Thailand	5,000	Animism	1%		7	2092
*Mokole	Mokole	Benin	5,000	Islam-Animist	0%		3	449
*Molbog	Molbog	Philippines	7,000	Animism	0%		1	1039
Molof	Molof	Indonesia	200	Animism	<1%		1	2995
Momare	Momare	Papua New Guinea		Animism	<1%		1	6231
Mombum	Mombum	Indonesia	300	Animism	<1%		1	2996
Momoguns	Momoguns	Malaysia		Animism	<1%		2	4096
Momolili	Momolili	Papua New Guinea	110,000	Animism	<1%		1	6232
Mon	Mon	Burma	350,000	Buddhist-Animist	5%	5	81	2583
Mona	Mona	Ivory Coast	400,000	Animism	<1%		5	2297
Mongondow	Mongondow	Indonesia	50,000	Islam-Animist	<1%	5	81	2997
Mongour	Mongour	China	20,000	Traditional Chinese	<1%		1	2833
Moni	Moni	Indonesia	11,000	Animism	0%		1	2998
Monjombo	Monjombo	Central African Republic	30,000	Animism	0%		1	5191
Mono	Mono	Zaire	22,000	Animism	0%		1	5690
Monpa	Monpa	India		Buddhist-Animist	0%		3	1037

303

Name	Country	Language	Group Size	Primary Religion	% Chr	V	UP	ID
Montol	Nigeria	Montol	20,000	Islam	<1%	1		2469
Moor & Malays	Sri Lanka	Tamil	900,000	Islam	<1%	6	79	309
Moors in Mauritania	Mauritania	Arabic (Hassani)	1,000,000	Islam	0%	5		4043
**Mopan Maya	Belize	Mopan Maya	4,000	Christo-Paganism	15%	5		1206
	Guatemala	Mopan Maya	2,000	Christo-Paganism	15%	5		1205
Moqaddam	Iran	Moqaddam	1,000	Islam	0%	3		2069
Mor	Indonesia	Mor	1,000	Animism	<1%	1		2999
Morawa	Papua New Guinea	Morawa	800	Animism	0%	1		6233
Moreb	Sudan	Moreb	600	Islam	0%	1		5520
Moresada	Papua New Guinea	Moresada	200	Animism	0%	1		6234
Mori	Indonesia	Mori	200,000	Islam	0%	5	81	3000
Morigi	Papua New Guinea	Morigi	700	Animism	0%	1		6235
Morima	Papua New Guinea	Morima	3,000	Animism	<1%	4		6236
*Mororata	Bolivia	Aymara	500	Animism	<1%	1		6568
Moru	Ivory Coast	Moru	10,000	Islam-Animist	0%	1		2298
	Sudan	Moru	23,000	Islam	<1%	1		5511
Morunahua	Peru	Morunahua	300	Animism	<1%	1		3181
Morwap	Indonesia	Morwap	200	Animism	<1%	1		3576
Mosi	Tanzania	Mosi	240,000	Animism	<1%	1		4009
	Upper Volta	Moie	3,300,000	Animism	7%	6	80	3145
Motilon	Colombia	Motilon	3,000	Animism	<1%	1		5138
	Venezuela	Motilon	1,700	Animism	<1%	1		2137
Movima	Bolivia	Movima	22,000	Animism	0%	1		6237
Moxodi	Papua New Guinea	Moxodi	30,000	Animism	<1%	1		5367
Mpoto	Malawi	Mpoto	50,000	Animism	<1%	1		5577
	Tanzania	Mpoto	36,000	Animism	5%	5		3
Mru	Bangladesh	Murung	2,200	Islam-Animist	<1%	4		647
Mualthuam	India	Mualthuam	1,000	Animism	<1%	1		2249
Mubi	Chad	Mubi	3,000	Islam-Animist	0%	1		6238
Mugil	Papua New Guinea	Mugil	16,000	Animism	<1%	1		3136
Mujnane	Colombia	Muinane	10,000	Animism	<1%	1		6239
Mukawa	Papua New Guinea	Mukawa	2,000	Unknown	0%	1		5764
Mulimba	Cameroon	Mulimba	1,000	Hindu-Animist	<1%	1		5234
Multani in Punjab	India	Multani	3,000	Islam	<1%	5		2470
Mumbake	Nigeria	Mumbake	16,000	Animism	<1%	1		570
Mumuye	Nigeria	Mumuye	10,000	Animism	<1%	1		2584
Mun	Burma	Muna	200,000	Buddhist-Animist	<1%	5		3002
Muna	Indonesia	Muna	200,000	Islam-Animist	<1%	1		2250
Mundang in Assam	Chad	Mundang	77,000	Islam-Animist	0%	1		2745
Mundari in Bihar	India	Mundari	25,000	Hindu-Animist	<1%	1		2010
**Mundas in Bihar	India	Munda	5,000	Animism	<1%	1		5743
Mundu	Zaire	Mundu	2,000	Animism	<1%	1		3107
Munduruku	Brazil	Munduruku	14,700	Animism	0%	4		5265
Mungaka	Cameroon	Mungaka	100	Islam	<1%	1		3003
Munggui	Indonesia	Munggui	100	Animism	<1%	1		2553
Munji-Yidgha	Afghanistan	Munji-Yidgha	100	Islam	<1%	1		6240
Munkip	Papua New Guinea	Munkip		Animism	<1%	1		6241
Mup	Papua New Guinea	Mup		Animism	<1%	1		3108
Mura-Piraha	Brazil	Mura-Piraha		Animism	<1%	1		

304

Name	Country	Language	Group Size	Primary Religion	% Chr	V	UP	ID
Naka	Sudan	Naka	4,000	Islam	0%		1	5492
Nakama	Papua New Guinea	Nakama	900	Animism	<1%		1	6254
Nakanai	Papua New Guinea	Nakanai	8,000	Animism	<1%		1	6255
Nalik	Papua New Guinea	Nalik	3,000	Animism	<1%		1	6256
Naltya	Indonesia	Naltya	7,000	Animism	<1%		1	3006
Nalu	Guinea	Nalu	10,000	Islam-Animist	0%		1	5346
Nama	Namibia	Nama	15,000	Animism	<1%		1	5403
Nama	South Africa	Nama		Animism	0%		1	5437
Nambikuara	Brazil	Nambikuara	1,400	Animism	3%	5		379
Nambis	Papua New Guinea	Nambis	1,000	Animism	<1%		1	6257
Nambu	Papua New Guinea	Nambu	700	Animism	0%		1	6258
**Nambya	Zimbabwe	Nambya	40,000	Animism	8%	5		1161
Namuni	Papua New Guinea	Namuni	100	Animism	0%		1	6259
Nanai	China	Nanai		Traditional Chinese	<1%		1	2835
Nanai	USSR	Nanai	1,000	Unknown	0%		1	5864
Nancere	Chad	Nancere	12,000	Islam-Animist	<1%		1	2253
Nandi	Zaire	Nandi	35,000	Animism	<1%		1	5744
Nandu-Tari	Nigeria	Nandu-Tari	310,000	Islam	<1%		1	2471
Nankina	Papua New Guinea	Nankina	4,000	Animism	<1%		1	6260
Nao	Ethiopia	Nao	2,000	Animism	<1%		1	3226
Naoudem	Togo	Naoudem	90,000	Islam-Animist	<1%		1	5633
Nara	Papua New Guinea	Nara	25,000	Islam-Animist	<1%		1	3227
Nara	Ethiopia	Nara	700	Animism	<1%		1	6261
Naraguta	Nigeria	Naraguta	3,000	Animism	<1%		1	2472
Narak	Papua New Guinea	Narak	4,000	Animism	<1%		1	6262
Nasioi	Papua New Guinea	Nasioi	13,000	Animism	<1%		1	6263
Nata	Tanzania	Nata	17,000	Islam-Animist	0%		1	5580
Natemba	Togo	Natemba	1,000	Islam-Animist	<1%		1	5634
Natioro	Upper Volta	Natioro		Islam-Animist	<1%		1	5676
Nauna	Papua New Guinea	Nauna	100	Animism	0%		1	6264
Nawuri	Ghana	Nawuri	10,000	Animism	1%	5		1068
Nchimburu	Ghana	Nchumburu	1,000	Animism	7%	5		1069
Nchumbulu	Ghana	Nchumbulu	8,000	Islam-Animist	0%		1	5329
Nchumunu	Ghana	Nchumunu	57,000	Islam-Animist	0%		1	5330
Ndaaka	Zaire	Ndaaka	700	Animism	0%		1	5745
Ndali	Tanzania	Ndali	19,000	Animism	0%		1	5581
Ndam	Central African Republic	Ndam	2,000	Animism	0%		1	5192
Ndamba	Tanzania	Ndamba	178,000	Animism	0%		1	5582
Ndaonese	Indonesia	Ndao	10,000	Animism	0%		1	3007
Ndau	Zimbabwe	Ndau	1,000,000	Animism	<1%		1	5415
Nde-Nsele-Nta	Nigeria	Nde-Nsele-Nta	53,000	Animism	<1%		1	2473
**Ndebele	Zimbabwe	Sindebele	25,000	Animism	7%	6	79	1235
Ndengereko	Tanzania	Ndengereko	13,000	Animism	0%		1	5583
Ndjem	Cameroon	Ndjem	3,000	Animism	<1%		1	5266
Ndo	Zaire	Ndo		Animism	<1%		1	5746
Ndoe	Nigeria	Ndoe	4,000	Animism	<1%		1	2474
Ndogo	Central African Republic	Ndogo	4,000	Animism	0%		1	5193
Ndogo	Sudan	Ndogo		Unknown	0%		1	5512
Ndom	Indonesia	Ndom	500	Animism	<1%		1	3008

Name	Country	Language	Group Size	Primary Religion	% Chr	V	Vol UP	ID
Ngumba	Tanzania	Ngulu	13,000	Animism	0%			5588
Ngumbi	Cameroon	Ngumbi	10,000	Animism	<1%			5272
Ngunduna	Equatorial Guinea	Ngunduna	4,000	Animism	0%			5305
Ngurimi	Sudan	Ngurimi	9,000	Islam	0%			5487
Ngurimi	Tanzania	Ngurimi	8,000	Islam	0%			5488
Nguu	Tanzania	Nguu	46,000	Animism	0%			5599
Ngwoi	Cameroon	Ngwoi	4,000	Animism	0%			5590
Nharon	Botswana	Nharon	1,000	Animism	<1%			5593
Nhengatu	Brazil	Nhengatu	3,000	Animism	<1%			2476
Nias	Indonesia	Nias	230,000	Animism	<1%			5177
Nicaraguan Refugees	Costa Rica	Spanish	55,000	Nominal Christian	<1%			3110
Nielim	Chad	Nielim	1,000	Islam-Animist	nr%			3014
Nihali in Madhya Pradesh	India	Nihali	9,000	Hindu-Animist	<1%			9053
Nii	Papua New Guinea	Nii			<1%			2254
Nilamba	Tanzania	Nilamba	210,000	Animism	0%			2762
Nimadi in Madhya Pradesh	India	Nimadi	794,000	Hindu-Buddhist	<1%			6271
Nimboran	Indonesia	Nimboran	4,000	Animism	<1%			5591
Nimowa	Papua New Guinea	Nimowa	1,000	Animism	<1%			2763
Ninam	Brazil	Ninam			<1%			3015
*Ningerum	Papua New Guinea	Ningerum	500	Animism	<1%			6272
Ningrum	Indonesia	Ningrum	3,000	Animism	0%			3111
Niningo	Papua New Guinea	Niningo	4,000	Animism	<1%			41
Ninzam	Nigeria	Ninzam	500	Animism	<1%			3016
Nisa	Indonesia	Nisa	35,000	Islam	0%			6273
Nissan	Papua New Guinea	Nissan	2,000	Animism	<1%			2477
Nivkhi	USSR	Nivkhi	4,000	Animism	<1%			3017
Njadu	Indonesia	Njadu	9,000	Animism	0%			6274
Njalgulgule	Sudan	Njalgulgule	900	Unknown	<1%			5817
Nkem-Nkum	Nigeria	Nkem-Nkum	16,700	Animism	<1%			3018
Nkom	Cameroon	Nkom	30,000	Islam	0%			5513
Nkonya	Ghana	Nkonya	17,000	Animism	<1%			2478
*Nkoya	Zambia	Shinkoya	nr	Islam-Animist	0%			5274
Nkutu	Zaire	Nkutu	40,000	Animism	<1%			5331
***Nocte	India	Nocte	20,000	Animism	<1%			413
Nohu	Cameroon	Nohu	7,000	Animism	<1%			5755
Nomane	Papua New Guinea	Nomane	3,000	Animism	0%			1030
Nomu	Papua New Guinea	Nomu	800	Animism	<1%			5275
Nondiri	Papua New Guinea	Nondiri	2,000	Animism	<1%			6275
Norra	Burma	Norra	10,000	Buddhist-Animist	<1%			2585
North Africans in Belgium	Belgium	Arabic	90,000	Islam	<1%	6	80	4019
Northern Cagayan Negrito	Philippines	Northern Cagayan Negrito	556,000	Christo-Paganism	<1%			3292
Nosu	China	Nosu	1,000	Traditional Chinese	<1%			2837
*Nouni	Upper Volta	Nouni	50,000	Animism	3%			6278
Nsenga	Zambia	Nsenga	191,000	Animism	<1%			4129
Nsenga	Zimbabwe	Nsenga	16,000	Animism	0%			5802
Nso	Cameroon	Nso	100,000	Animism	<1%			5276

Name	Country	Language	Group Size	Primary Religion	% Chr	Vol V	UP	ID
Nsongo	Angola	Nsongo	15,000	Animism	<1%			5161
Ntomba	Zaire	Ntomba	50,000	Animism	0%	1		5756
Ntrubo	Ghana	Ntrubo	5,000	Animism	1%	5		1065
Ntrubo	Togo	Ntrubo	3,000	Islam-Animist	0%	1		5635
*Nuer	Ethiopia	Nuer	70,000	Animism	<1%	4		519
*Nuer	Sudan	Nuer	844,000	Animism	1%	6	79	576
Nuk	Papua New Guinea	Nuk	2,000	Animism	<1%	1		6279
Numana-Nunku-Gwantu	Nigeria	Numana-Nunku-Gwantu	15,000	Islam	<1%	1		2479
Numanggang	Papua New Guinea	Numanggang	2,000	Animism	<1%	1		6280
Nung	China	Nung	100,000	Traditional Chinese	<1%	1		2838
Nungu	Nigeria	Nungu	25,000	Animism	<1%	1		2480
Nunuma	Upper Volta	Nunuma	43,000	Islam-Animist	<1%	1		5677
**Nupe	Nigeria	Nupe	600,000	Islam	2%	5	80	4015
Nuristani	Afghanistan	Local dialects	67,000	Islam	0%	5	82	5031
Nurses in St. Louis	United States of America	English	30,000	Secularism	3%	4		4125
**Nyabwa	Ivory Coast	Nyabwa	15,000	Animism	2%	1		5369
Nyaheun	Laos	Nyaheun	34,000	Animism	<1%	1		5592
Nyakyusa	Malawi	Nyakyusa	193,000	Animism	0%	1		5757
Nyakyusa	Tanzania	Nyakyusa	12,000	Animism	0%	1		5593
Nyali	Zaire	Nyali	4,000	Animism	0%	6	80	5510
Nyambo	Tanzania	Nyambo	590,000	Islam	9%	1		487
Nyamusa	Sudan	Nyamusa	40,000	Animism	0%	1		5162
Nyamwezi	Tanzania	Nyamwezi	25,000	Animism	<1%	1		5277
Nyaneka	Angola	Nyaneka	3,000	Animism	0%	1		5758
Nyang	Cameroon	Nyang	252,000	Animism	0%	1		5333
Nyanga-Li	Zaire	Nyanga-Li	810,000	Islam-Animist	0%	1		5417
Nyangbo	Ghana	Nyangbo	4,000	Animism	<1%	3		5551
Nyanja	Zimbabwe	Nyanja	2,000	Animism	0%	1		450
Nyankole	Uganda	Nyankole	100,000	Animism	0%	1		5461
*Nyantruku	Benin	Aledjo	5,000	Islam	<1%	3		5163
Nyarueng	Sudan	Nyarueng	64,000	Animism	0%	1		5164
Nyemba	Angola	Nyemba	59,000	Animism	0%	1		5594
Nyengo	Angola	Nyengo	620,000	Animism	0%	1		5806
Nyiha	Tanzania	Nyiha	140,000	Animism	<1%	1		5652
Nyiha	Zambia	Nyiha	700,000	Animism	<1%	1		5653
Nyoro	Uganda	Nyoli	80,000	Animism	0%	1		
Nyuli	Uganda	Nyoli	3,000	Animism	<1%	1		
Nyungwe	Mozambique	Nyungwe	14,000	Animism	0%	1		5393
Nyzatom	Sudan	Topoza, Donyiro	40,000	Islam	0%	3		705
Nzakara	Central African Republic	Nzakara	275,000	Animism	<1%	1		5196
Nzanyi	Nigeria	Nzanyi	24,000	Islam-Animist	<1%	1		2481
Nzebi	Congo	Nzebi	5,000	Islam-Animist	0%	1		5296
Nzema	Ghana	Nzema	20,000	Animism	<1%	1		5334
Nzema	Ivory Coast	Nzema	70,300	Animism	<1%	1		2300
O'ung	Angola	O'ung	5,000	Animism	0%	1		5148
Obanliku	Nigeria	Obanliku	20,000	Islam-Animist	<1%	1		2482
Obolo	Nigeria	Obolo	70,300	Islam-Animist	<1%	1		2483
Ocaina	Peru	Ocaina	40,000	Animism	<1%	1		3182
Od	Pakistan	Odki	40,300	Hinduism	1%	4		265

Name	Country	Language	Group Size	Primary Religion	% Chr	V	Vol UP	ID
Odual	Nigeria	Odual	9,000	Animism	<1%	√	1	2484
Odut	Nigeria	Odut	700	Animism	<1%	√	1	2485
Ogan	Indonesia	Indonesian	200,000	Islam-Animist	0%	√	3	4085
Ogbia	Nigeria	Ogbia	22,000	Animism	<1%	√	1	2486
Oi	Laos	Oi	10,000	Animism	<1%	√	5	104
Oirat	China	Oirat	60,000	Traditional Chinese	<1%	√	1	2839
Oihi in Madhya Pradesh	India	Ojhi	11,000	Hindu-Animist	<1%	√	1	2764
Okobo	Nigeria	Okobo	11,000	Animism	<1%	√	1	2487
Okpamheri	Nigeria	Okpamheri	30,000	Animism	<1%	√	1	2488
Oksapmin	Papua New Guinea	Oksapmin	5,000	Animism	<1%	√	1	2681
Oliari in Orissa	India	Oliari	800	Hindu-Animist	<1%	√	1	2765
Olo	Papua New Guinea	Olari	9,000	Animism	<1%	√	1	6262
Olulumo-Ikom	Nigeria	Olulumo-Ikom	10,800	Animism	<1%	√	1	6282
Omati	Papua New Guinea	Omati	1,000	Animism	<1%	√	1	2489
Omie	Papua New Guinea	Omie	1,000	Animism	<1%	√	1	6283
Onank	Papua New Guinea	Onank	200	Animism	<1%	√	1	6284
Ong in Andamans	India	Ong	600	Hindu-Animist	<1%	√	1	6285
Onin	Indonesia	Onin	100	Animism	<1%	√	1	2766
Onjab	Papua New Guinea	Onjab	5,000	Animism	<1%	√	1	3019
Ono	Papua New Guinea	Ono		Animism	<1%	√	1	6286
Orang Kanak	Malaysia	Orang Kanak	4,000	Animism	0%	√	1	6287
Orang Laut	Malaysia	Orang Laut	4,000	Animism	0%	√	2	4100
Orang Ulu	Malaysia	Orang Ulu	4,000	Animism	0%	√	2	4101
Orejon	Peru	Orejon	25,000	Animism	<1%	√	1	4099
Oring	Nigeria	Oring	800	Animism	<1%	√	1	3183
Ormu	Indonesia	Ormu	1,400	Animism	<1%	√	1	2490
Oroch	USSR	Oroch	25,000	Unknown	0%	√	1	3020
Orok	USSR	Orok	13,000	Animism	<1%	√	1	5866
Orokaiva	Papua New Guinea	Orokaiva	50,000	Unknown	0%	√	1	5867
Orokolo	Papua New Guinea	Orokolo	25,000	Animism	<1%	√	1	6288
Oron	Nigeria	Oron	30,000	Animism	<1%	√	1	6289
Oronchon	China	Oronchon	600	Traditional Chinese	0%	√	1	2491
Oso	Cameroon	Oso	30,000	Animism	<1%	√	1	2840
Osum	Papua New Guinea	Osum	3,000	Animism	<1%	√	1	5778
Ot Danum	Indonesia	Ot Danum		Animism	<1%	√	1	6290
Otank	Nigeria	Otank		Animism	<1%	√	1	3021
Otomi, Eastern	Mexico	Otomi, Eastern	20,000	Christo-Paganism	<1%	√	1	2492
Otomi, Mezquital	Mexico	Otomi, Mezquital	100,000	Christo-Paganism	0%	√	1	5059
Otomi, Northwestern	Mexico	Otomi, Northwestern	40,000	Christo-Paganism	<1%	√	1	5060
Otomi, Southeastern	Mexico	Otomi, Southeastern	2,000	Christo-Paganism	<1%	√	1	5061
Otomi, State of Mexico	Mexico	Otomi	70,000	Christo-Paganism	0%	√	1	5062
Otomi, Tenango	Mexico	Otomi, Tenango	10,000	Christo-Paganism	<1%	√	1	5063
Otomi, Texcatepec	Mexico	Otomi, Texcatepec	8,000	Christo-Paganism	<1%	√	1	5064
Otoro	Sudan	Otoro	28,000	Christo-Paganism	<1%	√	1	5065
Ouaddai	Chad	Maba	320,000	Islam	1%	√	4	5514
Oubi	Ivory Coast	Oubi		Islam-Animist	<1%	√	1	310
Oyampipuku	Brazil	Oyampipuku	1,100	Animism	<1%	√	1	2301
Oyda	Ethiopia	Oyda	3,000	Animism	<1%	√	1	3112
Pacu	Brazil	Tucano	100	Animism	<1%	√	1	3228

Name	Country	Language	Group Size	Primary Religion	% Chr	V	Vol UP	ID
	Tanzania	Pare	99,000	Animism	0%	1		5596
Parengi in Orissa	India	Parengi	3,000	Hindu-Animist	<1%	1		2776
Paresi	Brazil	Paresi	400	Animism	<1%	1		3118
Parintintin	Brazil	Parintintin	200	Animism	<1%	1		3119
*Parsees	India	Gujarati	120,000	Secularism	<1%	5	81	2121
*Parsis in Bombay	India	Parsi	80,000	Zoroastrianism	0%	6	82	5039
Pashayi	Afghanistan	Pashayi	96,000	Islam-Animist	<1%	1		2554
Pashtuns	Iran	Pashtu	3,000	Islam	0%	6	80	2054
Pasismanua	Papua New Guinea	Pasismanua	6,000	Animism	<1%	1		6296
Patamona	Guyana	Patamona	3,000	Christo-Paganism	<1%	1		5117
Patelia in Gujarat	India	Patelia	23,000	Hindu-Animist	<1%	1		2778
Patep	Papua New Guinea	Patep	7,100	Animism	<1%	1		6297
Pato Tapuia	Brazil	Pato Tapuia		Animism	<1%	1		3120
Patpatar	Papua New Guinea	Patpatar	5,300	Animism	<1%	1		6298
Paumari	Brazil	Paumari	300	Animism	<1%	1		3121
Pawaia	Papua New Guinea	Pawaia	2,000	Animism	<1%	1		6299
Pay	Papua New Guinea	Pay	600	Animism	<1%	1		6300
Paya	Honduras	Spanish	300	Animism	<1%	1		8013
Paynamar	Papua New Guinea	Paynamar	200	Animism	0%	1		6301
Penan, Western	Malaysia	Penan		Animism	nr%	1		7027
Pende	Zaire	Pende	200,000	Hindu-Animist	0%	6	81	5759
Pengo in Orissa	India	Pengo	1,000	Secularism	<1%	1		2779
Pension Students-Madrid	Spain	Italian	2,000	Animism	nr%	5	82	5032
Peremka	Papua New Guinea	Peremka	200	Animism	0%	1		6302
Peri	Zaire	Peri	40,000	Islam	<1%	1		5760
Pero	Nigeria	Pero	20,000	Buddhist-Animist	<1%	1		2494
Persians of Iran	Iran	Persian	2,100,000	Animism	1%	6	80	4010
Phu Thai	Laos	Phu Thai	3,000	Animism	1%	5		102
Piapoco	Colombia	Piapoco	12,000	Animism	<1%	1		3148
Piaroa	Venezuela	Piaroa	50,000	Animism	<1%	1		5141
**Pila	Benin	Pila-Pila	600	Christo-Paganism	1%	4		237
Pila	Papua New Guinea	Pila	4,000	Animism	<1%	1		6303
Pilaga	Argentina	Pilaga	13,000	Animism	0%	1		2130
Pima Bajo	Mexico	Pima Bajo	800	Animism	<1%	1		5070
Pimbwe	Tanzania	Pimbwe	3,000	Animism	0%	1		5597
Piratapuyo	Brazil	Tucano	4,000	Islam	<1%	1		3122
Piro	Peru	Maniteneri	1,000	Islam	<1%	1		3184
Pisa	Indonesia	Pisa	175,000	Animism	0%	3		3025
Pishaghi	Iran	Pishaghi	100	Animism	<1%	1		2064
Pitu Uluna Salu	Indonesia	Pitu Uluna Salu	3,000	Islam	<1%	1		2495
Piu	Nigeria	Piu	5,000	Christo-Paganism	<1%	1		3026
Piya	Papua New Guinea	Piya	15,000	Hindu-Animist	6%	5		6304
**Plantation Workers	India	Local dialects	20,000	Christo-Paganism	<1%	1		2496
Pnar in Assam	Guatemala	Pnar	25,000	Christo-Paganism	<1%	1		4031
Pocomam, Central	Guatemala	Pocomam, Central	25,000	Christo-Paganism	<1%	1		2780
Pocomchi, Eastern	Guatemala	Pocomchi, Eastern		Animism	<1%	4		8007
Pocomchi, Western	Cameroon	Pocomchi, Western						8008
Podokwo		Podokwo						8009
								496

Name	Country	Language	Group Size	Primary Religion	% Chr	V	UP	ID
Podopa	Papua New Guinea	Podopa	3,000	Animism	<1%			6305
Podzo	Mozambique	Podzo	45,000	Animism	0%	1		5394
Pogolo	Tanzania	Pogolo	65,000	Animism	0%	1		5598
Poke	Zaire	Poke	46,000	Animism	0%	1		5761
Pokot	Uganda	Pokot	170,000	Animism	<1%			5654
Pol	Congo	Pol	2,000	Animism	0%	1		5298
Polci	Nigeria	Polci	6,000	Islam	<1%			2497
Pom	Indonesia	Pom	2,000	Animism	<1%			3027
Ponam-Andra-Hus	Papua New Guinea	Ponam-Andra-Hus	1,000	Animism	<1%			6306
Pondoma	Papua New Guinea	Pondoma	300	Animism	<1%			6307
Pongu	Nigeria	Pongu	4,800	Islam	<1%			2498
Poouch in Kashmir	India	Poochi	500,000	Islam	0%	4		4499
Popoloca, Ahuatempan	Mexico	Spanish	6,500	Christo-Paganism	0%	1		5071
Popoloca, Coyotepec	Mexico	Spanish	2,000	Christo-Paganism	0%	1		5072
Popoloca, Eastern	Mexico	Popoloca, Eastern	2,000	Christo-Paganism	<1%	1		5073
Popoloca, Northern	Mexico	Popoloca, Northern	1,000	Christo-Paganism	<1%	1		5074
Popoloca, Southern	Mexico	Spanish	8,000	Christo-Paganism	<1%	1		5075
Popoloca, Western	Mexico	Popoloca, Western	200	Christo-Paganism	<1%	1		5076
Popoluca, Oluta	Mexico	Spanish	6,000	Christo-Paganism	<1%	1		5077
Popoluca, Sayula	Mexico	Popoluca, Sayula	18,000	Christo-Paganism	0%	1		5078
Popoluca, Sierra	Mexico	Popoluca, Sierra	2,000	Christo-Paganism	0%	1		5079
Popoluca, Texistepec	Mexico	Spanish	2,000	Christo-Paganism	<1%	1		5080
Porapora	Papua New Guinea	Porapora	2,400	Animism	0%			6308
Porohanon	Philippines	Porohanon	23,000	Animism	<1%			3283
**Portuguese in France	France	Portuguese	150,000	Secularism	10%	4		1186
Prang	Ghana	Prang	5,000	Islam-Animist	0%			5335
***Prasuni	Afghanistan	Prasuni	2,000	Islam	<1%	4		2555
**Prisoners in Antananarivo	Korea, Republic of	Korean	45,000	Secularism	10%	4		5012
**Pro Hockey Players	United States of America	English	10,000	Secularism	2%	5	82	5010
Pu-I	China	Pu-I	1,311,000	Traditional Chinese	5%	6	82	2842
Puguli	Upper Volta	Puguli	600	Islam-Animist	<1%			5678
Puku-Geeri-Keri-Wipsi	Nigeria	Puku-Geeri-Keri-Wipsi	15,000	Islam	<1%			2499
Pular	Senegal	Fouta Toro	300,000	Animism	0%	3		1136
Pulie	Papua New Guinea	Pulie	200	Animism	<1%			6309
Punu	China	Punu	220,000	Traditional Chinese	<1%			2843
Puragi	Indonesia	Puragi	46,900	Animism	0%			5299
Purari	Papua New Guinea	Purari	6,000	Animism	<1%			3028
Purig-Pa of Kashmir	India	Purig-Skad	nr	Islam	400%	1		6310
Purum	Burma	Purum	300	Buddhist-Animist	<1%	5	81	7010
**Puyuma	Taiwan	Puyuma	6,000	Christo-Paganism	<1%	5	81	2587
Pye	Ivory Coast	Pye	300	Islam-Animist	nr%	5		7033
Pygmy (Binga)	Central African Republic	Local dialects	7,000	Animism	6%	5		2303
*Pygmy (Mbuti)	Zaire	Local dialects	30,000	Animism	0%	4		508
Pyu	Indonesia	local languages	40,000	Animism	1%		79	512
Qajars	Iran	Qajar	3,100	Islam	0%	3		2056
Qara'i	Iran	Qara'i	2,000	Islam	0%	3		2058

Name	Country	Language	Group Size	Primary Religion	% Chr	V	Vol UP	ID
Qaragozlu	Iran	Qaragozlu	2,000	Islam	0%	3		2060
Qashqa'i	Iran	Qashqa'i	350,000	Islam	0%	5	80	2038
Quaiquer	Colombia	Quaiquer	5,000	Animism	<1%	1		3149
Quarequena	Brazil	Tucano	300	Animism	<1%	4		2159
**Quechua	Bolivia	Quechua	1,000,000	Christo-Paganism	4%	4		033
	Peru	Quechua	3,000,000	Christo-Paganism	2%	5		10
**Quechua, Huancayo	Peru	Quechua, Huancayo	1,275,000	Animism	6%	5	79	1080
**Quiche	Guatemala	Quiche	500,000	Christo-Paganism	5%	6		152
**Quichua	Ecuador	Quichua	2,000,000	Christo-Paganism	6%	5	79	4070
Rabha in Assam	India	Rabha	10,000	Hindu-Animist	3%	4		676
Rabinal-Achi	Guatemala	Rabinal Achi	21,000	Christo-Paganism	4%	5		400
**Racetrack Residents	United States of America	Spanish	50,000	Secularism	10%	5	79	476
*Rai	Nepal	Rai	232,000	Hindu-Buddhist	0%	3		663
*Rai, Danuwar	Nepal	Danuwar Rai	12,000	Hindu-Animist	0%	3		661
Rai, Khaling	Nepal	Rai, Khaling	10,000	Buddhist-Animist	0%	1		6516
Rai, Kulunge	Nepal	Rai, Kulunge	10,000	Buddhist-Animist	0%	1		6524
Rai, Thulunge	Nepal	Rai, Thulunge	25,000	Buddhist-Animist	0%	1		6517
Rajasthani Muslims-Jaipur	India	Jaipuri	4,000	Islam	0%	6	82	5033
Rajbansi	Nepal	Rajbansi	15,000	Hindu-Animist	<1%	1		659
Ralte	Burma	Ralte	17,000	Buddhist-Animist	<1%	1		2888
*Rambutyo	Papua New Guinea	Rambutyo	200	Buddhism	<1%	4		6311
*Ramkamhaeng Un. Students	Thailand	Thai	600	Buddhism	0%	1		4053
Rangkas	Nepal	Rangkas	600	Buddhist-Animist	0%	1		6518
Rao	Papua New Guinea	Rao	3,000	Animism	0%	1		6312
Ratahan	Indonesia	Ratahan	150,000	Animism	<1%	1		3030
Rataning	Chad	Rataning	10,000	Islam-Animist	<1%	1		2255
Rauto	Papua New Guinea	Rauto	200	Animism	<1%	1		6313
*Rava in Assam	India	Rava	45,000	Hinduism	<1%	1		295
Rawang	Papua New Guinea	Rawa	6,000	Animism	<1%	5		6314
Rawa	China	Rawang	60,000	Animism	<1%	1		2844
Redjang	Indonesia	Rejang	300,000	Traditional Chinese	<1%	6	80	694
Refugee Doctors	Hong Kong	Cantonese	2,000	Traditional Chinese	<1%	3		9039
Rempi	Papua New Guinea	Rempile	20,000	Animism	<1%	3		6315
Rendille	Kenya	Rendille	30,000	Islam-Animist	<1%	1		4131
Reshe	Ethiopia	Reshe	10,000	Animism	<1%	1		2520
Reshiat	Bolivia	not reported	75,000	Animism	<1%	3		2740
Reyesano	India	Reyesano	21,000	Animism	<1%	1		2782
Riang in Assam	Burma	Riang	1,000	Hindu-Buddhist	<1%	1		2590
Riang-Lang	Indonesia	Riang-Lang	200	Buddhist-Animist	<1%	1		3031
Riantana	Brazil	Riantana	30,300	Animism	<1%	1		3123
Rikbaktsa	Nigeria	Rikbaktsa	20,000	Animism	<1%	1		2501
Roba	Papua New Guinea	Roba	200	Islam	<1%	1		6316
Roinji	Turkey	Roinji	400	Animism	<1%	1		2542
Romany	Papua New Guinea	Romany	20,000	Folk Religion	<1%	1		6317
Romkun	Papua New Guinea	Romkun	400	Animism	<1%	1		7064
Ronga	Mozambique	Ronga	400,000	Animism	0%	1		5395
Ronga	South Africa	Ronga	600,000	Animism	0%	1		5438
Roro	Papua New Guinea	Roro	8,000	Animism	<1%	1		6318

314

315

Name	Country	Language	Group Size	Primary Religion	% Chr	V	Vol UP	ID
Samburu	Kenya	Masai, Samburu	61.000	Animism	3%	4		535
Samo, Northern	Mali	Samo, Northern	50.000	Animism	0%	1		5380
	Upper Volta	Samo, Northern	70.000	Islam-Animist	<1%	1		5679
Samo, Southern	Upper Volta	Samo, Southern	8.000	Islam-Animist	0%	1		5680
*Samo-Kubo	Papua New Guinea	Samo	2.000	Animism	1%	4		386
Samogho	Mali	Samogho	10.000	Animism	0%	1		5381
San	Namibia	San	6.000	Animism	0%	1		5404
Sanapana	Paraguay	Sanapana	4.000	Animism	0%	1		5128
Sandawe	Tanzania	Sandawe	38.000	Animism	0%	1		5604
Sanga	Nigeria	Sanga	35.000	Islam	<1%	1		2505
	Zaire	Sanga	35.000	Animism	0%	1		5765
Sangil	Philippines	Sangil	8.000	Islam	1%	5		637
Sangir	Indonesia	Sangir	145.000	Animism	<1%	1		3036
Sangke	Indonesia	Sangke	300	Animism	<1%	1		3037
Sangu	Gabon	Sangu	18.300	Animism	<1%	1		5314
	Tanzania	Sangu	30.000	Animism	0%	1		5605
Sanio	Papua New Guinea	Sanio	600	Animism	<1%	1		6324
Santa	China	Santa	200.000	Traditional Chinese	<1%			2846
**Santhali	Nepal	Santhali	nr	Animism	20%	4		669
Santrokofi	Ghana	Sele	5.000	Islam-Animist	0%	1		5337
*Sanuma	Venezuela	Sanuma	300	Animism	1%	3		720
Sanuma	Brazil	Sanuma	4.000	Animism	<1%	1		5142
Sanza	Zaire	Sanza	15.000	Animism	0%	1		5766
Sapo	Liberia	not reported	30.000	Animism	12%	4		603
Saposa	Papua New Guinea	Saposa	1.000	Animism	<1%	6	80	6325
Sarakole	Senegal	Soninke	68.000	Islam	0%	1		1139
Saramaccan	Surinam	Saramaccan	20.000	Christo-Paganism	<1%	1		5131
Sarwa	Chad	Sarwa	400	Islam-Animist	<1%	1		2257
Sasak	Indonesia	Sasak	1.600.000	Islam-Animist	<1%	6	80	1095
Tasanis	Iran	Sasani	4.000	Islam	0%	3		2072
Sasaru-Enwan Igwe	Nigeria	Sasaru-Enwan Igwe	200	Islam	<1%	1		2506
Saseng	Papua New Guinea	Saseng	3.000	Animism	<1%	1		6326
Satere	Brazil	Satere	30.000	Animism	<1%	1		3124
Satnami (Madhya Pradesh)	India	Chhattisgarhi	1.000	Animism	2%	4		4076
Sau	Afghanistan	Sau	3.000	Islam	<1%	1		2556
Sauk	Papua New Guinea	Sauk	300	Animism	0%	1		6327
Sause	Papua New Guinea	Sause	500	Animism	<1%	1		3038
**Save	Benin	Save (Yoruba)	15.000	Animism	1%	4		451
**Sawi	Indonesia	Sawi	3.000	Animism	16%	5		1180
Sawos	Papua New Guinea	Sawos	50.000	Animism	0%	1		6329
Saya	Nigeria	Saya	400	Islam	<1%	1		2507
Sayyids	Yemen, Arab Republic	Arabic	500	Islam	<1%	4		4067
Secoya	Ecuador	Secoya		Animism	<1%	1		3161
Sekar	Indonesia	Sekar		Animism	<1%	1		3039
Sekayu	Indonesia	Indonesian	200.000	Islam-Animist	<1%	3		4090
Seko	Indonesia	Seko	275.000	Animism	0%	1		3040
Sekpele	Ghana	Sekpele		Islam-Animist	0%	1		5338
**Selakau of Sarawak	Malaysia	Selakau	5.000	Animism	7%	4		2124

Name	Country	Language	Group Size	Primary Religion	% Chr	V	UP	ID
Selepet	Papua New Guinea	Selepet	6,000	Animism	<1%			6330
Selkup	USSR	Selkup	4,000	Unknown	0%			5869
Semelai	Malaysia	Semelai	3,000	Animism	<1%			4110
Sempan	Indonesia	Sempan	2,000	Animism	0%			3041
Sena	Melanesia	Sena	115,000	Animism	0%			5370
Sena	Mozambique	Sena	85,000	Animism	0%			5396
Senggi	Indonesia	Senggi	340,100	Animism	<1%			3042
Senoi	Malaysia	Native Senoi		Animism	2%	5	81	1009
**Sentani	Indonesia	Sentani		Animism	<1%			3043
Senthang	Burma	Senthang		Buddhist-Animist	1%			2591
Senufo	Ivory Coast	Senari		Animism	2%			181
Sepen	Papua New Guinea	Sepen		Animism	<1%			6331
**Serawai	Indonesia	Serawai (Pasemah)		Islam-Animist	0%			1091
Sere	Sudan	Sere		Islam	9%	6	79	5515
Serere	Senegal	Serere	700,000	Animism	0%			215
Serere-Non	Senegal	Serere-Non	70,000	Islam-Animist	<1%			5426
Serere-Sine	Senegal	Serere-Sine	315,400	Islam-Animist	<1%			5427
Seri	Mexico	Seri		Christo-Paganism	<1%			5081
Serki	Papua New Guinea	Serki	200	Animism	<1%			6332
Serui-Laut	Indonesia	Serui-Laut	1,000	Animism	0%			3044
Setaui Keriwa	Papua New Guinea	Setaui Keriwa	400	Animism	<1%			6333
Setiali	Papua New Guinea	Setiali	200	Animism	<1%			6334
Seuci	Brazil	Tucano	400	Animism	<1%			3125
Seychellois	Seychelles	Creole	51,500	Secularism	10%	4		1199
Sha	Nigeria	Sha	180,500	Animism	<1%			2508
Shahsavans	Iran	Azerbaijani (Shahsavani)	152,000	Islam	0%			2043
Shambala	Tanzania	Shambala	800,000	Animism	0%			5606
Shan	Burma	Shan	300,000	Buddhist-Animist	0%			4143
Shan Chinese	Thailand	Shan	20,000	Buddhist-Animist	<1%			2086
Shanga	Nigeria	Shanga	5,000	Animism	1%	6	80	4157
***Shankilla (Kazza)	Ethiopia	Shankilla (Kazza)	20,000	Christo-Paganism	0%			568
Sharanahua	Peru	Sharanahua	2,000	Animism	<1%			3185
Sharchagpakha	Bhutan	Sharchagpakha	400,000	Buddhist-Animist	0%			2567
Shatt	Sudan	Shatt	9,000	Islam	<1%			5516
Shawiya	Algeria	Shawiya	150,000	Animism	<1%			2207
Sheko	Ethiopia	Sheko	23,000	Animism	0%			3229
*Sherpa	Nepal	Sherpa	20,000	Buddhism	<1%			671
**Shihu	United Arab Emirates	Shihu	10,000	Islam-Animist	0%			2543
Shilha	Morocco	Shilha	3,000,000	Islam-Animist	<1%			5388
Shilluk	Sudan	Shilluk	110,000	Islam-Animist	<1%			5517
Shina	Afghanistan	Shina	50,000	Islam-Animist	<1%			2557
Shinasha	Ethiopia	Shinasha	4,000	Animism	<1%			3230
Shipibo	Peru	Shipibo	15,000	Animism	<1%			3186
**Shirishana	Brazil	Shirishana	200	Animism	5%	5		721
**Shluh Berbers	Morocco	Tashilhait	2,000,000	Islam-Animist	<1%			4028
Shor	USSR	Shor	16,000	Unknown	<1%			5870
*Shourastra in Tamil Nadu	India	Shourastra	200,000	Hinduism	<1%			2023
Shua	Botswana	Shua	400	Animism	<1%			5178

Name	Country	Language	Group Size	Primary Religion	% Chr	V	Vol UP	ID
Shughni	Afghanistan	Shughni	3,000	Islam	<1%			2558
Shuwa Arabic	Nigeria	Shuwa Arabic	100,000	Islam	<1%			2519
Shwai	Sudan	Shwai	3,000	Islam	0%			5518
Siagha-Yenimu	Indonesia	Siagha-Yenimu		Animism	<1%			3045
Sialum	Papua New Guinea	Sialum	600	Animism	<1%			6335
Siane	Papua New Guinea	Siane	16,000	Animism	<1%			6336
Siar	Papua New Guinea	Siar	2,000	Animism	<1%			6337
Sibo	China	Sibo		Traditional Chinese	<1%			2847
Sidamo	Ethiopia	Sidamo	857,000	Islam-Animist	<1%			3231
Sikanese	Indonesia	Sikka	100,000	Animism	<1%			3047
Sikhule	Indonesia	Sikhule	20,000	Animism	<1%			3046
Sikkimese	India	Sikkimese	37,000	Hindu-Buddhist	<1%			2786
Simaa	Zambia	Simaa	40,000	Animism	0%			5808
Simba	Bolivia	Guarani	400	Animism	0%	4		6569
Simog	Papua New Guinea	Simog	100	Animism	<1%			6338
Sinagen	Papua New Guinea	Sinagen	200	Animism	<1%			6339
Sinagoro	Papua New Guinea	Sinagoro	12,000	Animism	<1%			6340
Sinaki	Papua New Guinea	Sinaki	200	Animism	<1%			6341
Sinasina	Papua New Guinea	Sinasina	20,000	Animism	<1%			6342
Sindamon	Papua New Guinea	Sindamon	200	Animism	<1%			6343
*Sindhi Muslims in Karachi	Pakistan	Sindhi	350,000	Islam-Animist	0%	6	82	5036
*Sindhis of India	India	Sindhi	3,000,000	Hinduism	1%	6		13
Sinhalese	Sri Lanka	Sinhala	9,200,000	Buddhism	6%	5		286
Sinsauru	Papua New Guinea	Sinsauru	400	Animism	<1%			6344
Sio	Papua New Guinea	Sio	2,000	Animism	<1%			6345
Siona	Colombia	Siona	300	Animism	<1%			3152
Sipoma	Papua New Guinea	Sipoma	300	Animism	<1%			6346
Sira	Gabon	Sira	17,000	Animism	0%			5315
Sirak	Papua New Guinea	Sirak	200	Animism	<1%			6347
Sirasira	Papua New Guinea	Sirasira	300	Animism	<1%			6350
Siri	Nigeria	Siri	2,000	Islam	<1%			2510
Siriano	Colombia	Siriano	600	Animism	<1%			3153
Siriono	Bolivia	Siriono	500	Animism	<1%			2141
Siroi	Papua New Guinea	Siroi	700	Animism	1%			6348
*Sisaala	Upper Volta	Isaalin	60,000	Animism	1%	4		658
Sisala	Ghana	Sisala	4,000	Islam-Animist	0%			5681
Siwai	Papua New Guinea	Siwai	6,000	Islam-Animist	1%			5339
Siwu	Ghana	Siwu	45,000	Animism	<1%	4		6349
*Slum Dwellers of Bangkok	Thailand	Thai	1,000	Buddhism	0%			4052
So	Cameroon	So		Animism	0%			5280
Sobei	Indonesia	Sobei		nr	1%	3		3048
Sochi	Pakistan	Sindhi		Hinduism	1%			255
Soga	Uganda	Soga	780,000	Animism	0%			5657
*Soh	Laos	Soh	15,000	Animism	1%	5	81	98
Soka Gakkai Believers	Japan	Japanese	6,500,000	Buddhism	0%	5		2091
Sokorok	Papua New Guinea	Sokorok	300	Animism	0%	3		6351
Solli	Zambia	Solli	32,000	Animism	0%			5809
Solorese Muslims	Indonesia	Solor	131,000	Islam	0%	5	81	3049

319

Name	Country	Language	Group Size	Primary Religion	% Chr	V	UP	ID
Suk	Kenya	not reported	133,000	Animism	8%	5		600
Suki	Papua New Guinea	Suki	1,000	Animism	<1%			6361
Suku	Zaire	Suku	74,000	Animism	0%			5771
Sukur	Nigeria	Sukur	10,400	Islam	<1%			2511
Sukurum	Papua New Guinea	Sukurum		Animism	<1%			6362
Sulka	Papua New Guinea	Sulka	1,000	Animism	<1%			6363
Sulung	India	Sulung	nr	Hindu-Buddhist	<1%			2789
Sumau	Papua New Guinea	Sumau	800	Animism	<1%			6364
Sumba	Indonesia	Sumba	400,000	Animism	<1%			1097
Sumbawa	Indonesia	Sumbawa	114,000	Islam	0%	5		3052
Sumbawa	Tanzania	Sumbawa	64,000	Animism	0%			5609
Sumu	Nicaragua	Sumu	2,000	Christo-Paganism	0%			5111
**Sundanese	Indonesia	Sundanese	20,000,000	Islam-Animist	<1%	6	80	273
Sungor	Chad	Sungor	39,000	Islam-Animist	<1%			2259
Sunwar	Nepal	Sunwar	20,000	Buddhist-Animist	0%			6519
Suppire	Mali	Suppire	300,000	Animism	0%			5384
Sura	Nigeria	Sura	40,000	Islam	<1%			2512
**Suri	Ethiopia	Suri	30,000	Animism	1%	4		521
**Suriguenos	Philippines	Surigueno	23,000	Secularism	7%	4		1191
Sursurunga	Papua New Guinea	Sursurunga	2,000	Animism	<1%			6365
Surubu	Nigeria	Surubu	2,000	Islam	<1%			2513
Surui	Brazil	Surui	300	Animism	<1%			3126
Susu	Guinea	Susu	815,000	Animism	nr			6562
Susu	Guinea-Bissau	Susu	2,000	Islam-Animist	<1%			5358
Susu	Sierra Leone	Susu	90,000	Islam-Animist	<1%			5435
Svan	USSR	Svan	35,000	Unknown	0%			5871
Swaga	Zaire	Swaga	121,000	Animism	0%			5772
Swaka	Zambia	Swaka	33,000	Animism	0%			5788
**Swatis	Pakistan	siSwati	600,000	Islam	9%	6	79	1232
Sylhetti	United Kingdom	Sylhetti	150,000	Islam	0%	5		4037
Syuwa	Nepal	Syuwa	4,000	Buddhist-Animist	0%	4		6566
**T'boli	Thailand	Tboli	150,000	Islam	3%	5	81	6520
Ta-Oi	Laos	Ta-Oi	25,000	Animism	<1%			624
Tabar	Papua New Guinea	Tabar	15,000	Animism	<1%			99
Tabasaran	USSR	Tabasaran	55,000	Animism	0%			6366
Tabi	Sudan	Tabi	10,000	Islam	0%			5872
Tabriak	Papua New Guinea	Tabriak	1,000	Animism	<1%			6367
Tacana	Bolivia	Tacana	100,000	Animism	<1%			5579
Tadjio	Indonesia	Tadjio	1,000	Animism	<1%			3043
Tadyawan	Philippines	Tadyawan	1,000	Animism	0%			3288
Tafi	Togo	Tafi	19,000	Islam-Animist	0%			5636
Tagal	Malaysia	Tagal	10,000	Animism	0%			7028
**Tagbanwa, Aborlan	Philippines	Tagbanwa	1,000	Animism	nr	5	81	1153
Tagbanwa, Kalamian	Philippines	Tagbanwa, Kalamian	19,000	Christo-Paganism	1%			636
***Tagin	India	Tagin	10,000	Animism	1%	6	81	1045
Tagula	Papua New Guinea	Tagula	25,000	Animism	<1%			6368
Tagwana	Ivory Coast	Tagwana	43,000	Islam-Animist	<1%			2304

Name	Country	Language	Group Size	Primary Religion	% Chr	V	Vol UP	ID
Tahit	Indonesia	Tehit	6,000	Animism	<1%	1		3063
Taikat	Indonesia	Taikat	8,600	Animism	<1%	1		3054
Tairora	Papua New Guinea	Tairora		Animism	<1%	6		6369
Taiwan-Chinese Un. Stud.	Taiwan	Mandarin	310,000	Secularism	nr%	5		7038
Tajik	Afghanistan	Damiri	3,600,000	Islam	0%	5		4040
Tajik	USSR	Persian (Tajiki)	2,500,000	Islam	0%	5	80	2053
Takalubi	Papua New Guinea	Takalubi	400	Animism	<1%	1		4041
Takankar	India	Takankar	11,000	Hindu-Animist	<1%	1		6370
Takemba	Benin	Takemba	10,000	Animism	0%	1		2775
Takestani	Iran	Takestani	220,000	Islam	<1%	1		5170
Takia	Papua New Guinea	Takia	11,000	Animism	<1%	1		2536
Talish	Nigeria	Tali	10,000	Islam	<1%	1		6371
*Talish	Iran	Talish	20,000	Islam	0%	3		2514
Talodi	Indonesia	Talo	90,000	Islam	<1%	3		2050
Tama	Sudan	Talodi	60,000	Islam-Animist	<1%	1		4089
Tamagario	Chad	Tama	4,000	Islam-Animist	<1%	1		5522
Taman	Indonesia	Tamagario	10,000	Islam-Animist	<1%	1		2260
Taman	Indonesia	Taman	600	Animism	<1%	1		3055
	Burma	Taman		Buddhist-Animist	<1%	3		2592
*Tamang in Bihar	Papua New Guinea	Tamang		Animism	<1%	1		6372
Tamaria in Bihar	Nepal	Tamaria	1,800,000	Hindu-Buddhist	nr	3		666
Tamazight	India	Tamazight	3,000	Hindu-Buddhist	0%	1		2790
Tambas	Morocco	Tambas	7,000	Islam-Animist	<1%	1		5389
Tambo	Nigeria	Tambo	400	Animism	0%	1		2515
Tamil	Zambia	Tami		Animism	<1%	1		5801
Tamil (Ceylonese)	Papua New Guinea	Tamil	1,420,000	Animism	5%	5		6373
**Tamil Laborers in Bombay	Sri Lanka	Tamil	3,000	Hinduism	<1%	5		287
Tamil Muslims in Madras	India	Tamil	50,000	Hinduism	<1%	6	82	5017
***Tamil Plantation Workers	India	Tamil	140,000	Islam	0%	6	82	5028
*Tamil in Yellagiri Hills	Malaysia	Tamil	4,000	Hinduism	1%	4		1109
*Tamils (Indian)	India	Tamil	600,000	Hinduism	2%	5		4025
**Tamils (Indian)	Malaysia	Tamil	1,200,000	Hinduism	7%	4	79	4
Tampulma	Sri Lanka	Tamil	8,000	Hinduism	5%	5		313
Tana	Ghana	Tampulensi	35,000	Animism	2%	5		1077
Tana	Central African Republic	Tana	35,000	Animism	<1%	1		5201
Tanahmerah	Chad	Tana	3,000	Islam-Animist	0%	3		2261
Tandanke	Indonesia	Tanahmerah	1,000	Animism	<1%	1		3056
Tandia	Senegal	Tandanke		Islam-Animist	0%	3		1145
Tangale	Indonesia	Tandia	100,000	Animism	<1%	1		3057
Tangchangya	Nigeria	Tangale	5,000	Islam	0%	1		2516
Tangsa	Bangladesh	Tangchangya	11,000	Animism	<1%	3		2564
**Tangsa	Papua New Guinea	Tangga	2,600	Animism	<1%	1		6374
Tangu	India	Tangsa	2,000	Animism	0%	1		1031
Tanguat	Papua New Guinea	Tangu	300	Animism	<1%	1		6375
Tani	Papua New Guinea	Tanguat	200	Animism	0%	1		6376
Tanimuca-Retuama	Papua New Guinea	Tani	700	Animism	<1%	1		6378
Tao't Bato	Colombia	Tanimuca-Retuama		Animism	<1%	4		3154
Tao-Suame	Philippines	not reported		Animism	0%	1		2106
	Papua New Guinea	Tao-Suame		Animism	0%			6377

Name	Country	Language	Group Size	Primary Religion	% Chr	V	UP	ID
Taori-Kei	Indonesia	Taori-Kei	100	Animism	<1%			3058
Tara	Indonesia	Tara	125,000	Animism	<1%			3059
Tarahumara, Northern	Mexico	Tarahumara, Northern	500	Christo-Paganism	0%			5082
Tarahumara, Rocoroibo	Mexico	Tarahumara, Rocoroibo	12,000	Christo-Paganism	<1%			5083
Tarahumara, Samachique	Mexico	Tarahumara, Samachique	40,000	Christo-Paganism	<1%			5084
Taram	Cameroon	Taram	3,000	Animism	0%			5283
Tarasco	Mexico	Tarasco	60,000	Christo-Paganism	<1%			5085
Targum	Israel	Targum	5	Judaism	<1%			2537
Tarof	Indonesia	Tarof	600	Animism	<1%			3060
Tarok	Nigeria	Tarok	60,000	Animism	<1%			2517
Tarpia	Indonesia	Tarpia	600	Animism	<1%			3061
Tat	USSR	Tat	17,000	Islam	0%			5873
Tatars	USSR	Tatar dialects	6,000,000	Islam	1%	6	80	4008
Tate	Tanzania	Tate	300	Animism	<1%			6379
Tatoga	Tanzania	Tatoga	22,000	Animism	<1%			5610
**Tatuyo	Colombia	Tatuyo	300	Animism	<1%			621
Tauade	Papua New Guinea	Tauade	11,000	Animism	<1%			6380
Taucouleur	Senegal	Tancouleur	500,000	Islam	0%	5	80	1137
Taungyo	Burma	Taungyo	200,000	Buddhist-Animist	0%			2593
Taungyoe	Burma	Burmese	18,000	Buddhism	0%	2		4147
Taupota	Papua New Guinea	Taupota	3,000	Animism	<1%			6381
Taurap	Indonesia	Taurap	200	Animism	<1%			3062
Tausug	Philippines	Tausug	500,000	Islam	1%	6	80	635
Tavara	Papua New Guinea	Tavara	9,000	Animism	0%			6382
Tawi-Pau	Papua New Guinea	Tawi-Pau	300	Animism	<1%			6383
Tawr	Burma	Tawr	700	Buddhist-Animist	0%			2594
Tayaku	Benin	Tayaku	10,000	Animism	0%	6		5171
Tchang	Cameroon	Tchang	100,000	Animism	0%			5284
Teda	Chad	Teda	10,000	Islam	0%			4012
Teda	Libya	Teda	120,000	Islam	0%			5364
*Teenbu	Niger	Lorhon	5,000	Islam-Animist	0%			5409
Tegali	Ivory Coast	Tegali	16,000	Animism	0%			311
Teimuri	Sudan	Teimuri	16,000	Islam	<1%	4		5523
Teimurtash	Iran	Teimurtash	77,000	Islam	0%	3		2051
Teke, Eastern	Iran	Teke, Eastern	71,000	Islam	0%	3		2052
Teke, Northern	Zaire	Teke, Northern	24,000	Animism	0%			5773
Teke, Southwestern	Congo	Teke, Southwestern	32,000	Animism	0%			5300
Telefol	Congo	Telefol	4,000	Animism	<1%			5301
Tem	Papua New Guinea	Kotokoli	100,000	Islam	5%	4		6384
Tembe	Togo	Tembe	300	Animism	0%			596
Tembo	Brazil	Tembo	30,000	Animism	0%			3127
Temein	Zaire	Temein	2,000	Islam	0%	2		5774
Temira	Sudan	Temira	7,000	Animism	<1%			5524
**Temne	Malaysia	Temne	1,000,000	Animism	6%	6	80	4108
*Tengger	Sierra Leone	Tenggerese	400,000	Hindu-Animist	<1%	5		123
*Tense	Indonesia	Teen	5,000	Animism	<1%			296
Teop	Ivory Coast	Teop	5,000	Animism	<1%			4122
Tepehua, Huehuetla	Papua New Guinea	Tepehua, Huehuetla	2,000	Christo-Paganism	<1%			6385
	Mexico							5086

Name	Country	Language	Group Size	Primary Religion	% Chr	V	UP	ID
Tiruray	Philippines	Tiruray	30,000	Animism	<1%		1	3290
Tlapaneco, Malinaltepec	Mexico	Tlapaneco, Malinaltepec	40,000	Christo-Paganism	<1%		1	5092
Toala	Indonesia	Toala	23,100	Animism	<1%		1	3068
Toaripi	Papua New Guinea	Toaripi	15,000	Animism	<1%		1	6394
Toba	Argentina	Toba	3,000	Animism	<1%		1	2131
Tobo	Papua New Guinea	Tobo		Animism	<1%		1	6395
Toda in Tamil Nadu	India	Toda	800	Hindu-Animist	<1%		1	2794
*Tofi	Benin	Tofi	33,000	Animism	3%	4		422
Togbo	Zaire	Togbo	6,000	Animism	0%		1	5691
Tojolabal	Mexico	Tojolabal	14,000	Christo-Paganism	<1%		1	5093
Tokkaru in Tamil Nadu	India	Tokkaru	1,300,200	Hindu-Animist	<1%		1	2660
Tol	Honduras	Tol		Animism	<1%		1	8014
Tombulu	Indonesia	Tombulu	40,000	Animism	<1%		1	3069
Tomini	Indonesia	Tomini	50,000	Animism	<1%		1	3070
Tonda	Papua New Guinea	Tonda	600	Animism	0%		1	6396
Tondanou	Indonesia	Tondanou	35,000	Animism	<1%		1	3071
Tonga	Botswana	Tonga	6,000	Animism	0%		1	5179
Tonga	Malawi	Tonga	62,000	Animism	<1%		1	5371
Tonga	Mozambique	Tonga	10,000	Animism	<1%		1	5397
*Tonga, Gwembe Valley	Zambia	Chitonga	90,000	Animism	2%	5	79	1160
Tonga	Zimbabwe	Chitonga	86,000	Animism	2%	7		188
Tongwe	Tanzania	Tongwe	8,000	Animism	0%		1	5611
Tonsea	Indonesia	Tonsea	90,000	Animism	<1%		1	3072
Tontemboa	Indonesia	Tontemboa	140,000	Animism	<1%		1	3073
*Topotha	Sudan	Toposa	60,000	Animism	2%	4	81	575
Toraja, Southern	Indonesia	Tae'	250,000	Animism	nr%	5		3074
Torau	Papua New Guinea	Torau	600	Animism	<1%		1	6397
Torricelli	Papua New Guinea	Torricelli	700	Animism	<1%		1	6398
Totis	India	Gondi	nr	Hinduism	<1%		3	1044
Totonaco, Northern	Mexico	Totonaco, Northern	15,000	Christo-Paganism	<1%		1	5094
Totonaco, Oxumatlan	Mexico	Totonaco, Oxumatlan	1,000	Christo-Paganism	0%		1	5095
Totonaco, Papantla	Mexico	Totonaco, Papantla	50,000	Christo-Paganism	<1%		1	5096
Totonaco, Sierra	Mexico	Totonaco, Sierra	100,000	Christo-Paganism	<1%		1	5097
Totonaco, Yecuatla	Mexico	Spanish	20,000	Christo-Paganism	0%		1	5098
*Toussian	Upper Volta	Toussian	3,100	Islam	8%	4		4123
Towei	Indonesia	Towei	100	Animism	<1%		1	3075
Trepo	Ivory Coast	Trepo	800	Islam-Animist	<1%		1	2306
Trio	Surinam	Trio	800	Animism	<1%		1	5132
Trique, San Juan Copala	Mexico	Trique, San Juan Copala	3,800	Christo-Paganism	<1%		1	5099
Tsaangi	Congo	Tsaangi	8,000	Christo-Paganism	0%		1	1197
**Tsachila	Ecuador	Colorado	10,000	Unknown	8%	5		5875
Tsakhur	USSR	Tsakhur	11,000	Islam	0%		1	3232
Tsamai	Ethiopia	Tsamai	7,000	Animism	<1%		1	2143
Tsimane	Bolivia	Tsimane	6,000	Animism	0%		1	5316
Tsogo	Gabon	Tsogo	15,000	Animism	<1%		1	5398
Tsonga	Mozambique	Tsonga	1,500,000	Animism	0%		1	5035
Tsou	Taiwan	Tsou	200,000	Animism	<1%	5	81	5399
Tswa	Zimbabwe	Tswa	300,000	Animism	0%		1	5418

Name	Country	Language	Group Size	Primary Religion	% Chr	V	UP	ID
Ukaan	Nigeria	Ukaan	18,000	Animism	<1%	4		2544
Ukpe-Bayobiri	Nigeria	Ukpe-Bayobiri	12,000	Animism	<1%	1		2522
Ukwuani-Aboh	Nigeria	Ukwuani-Aboh	150,000	Animism	<1%	1		2523
Ulchi	USSR	Ulchi		Unknown	0%	4		5818
Ulithi-Mall	Turks and Caicos Islands	Ulithi	2,000	Christo-Paganism	<1%	1		1004
Uilatan in Kerala	India	Uilatan	2,000	Hindu-Animist	<1%	4		2796
Umm Dorein	Sudan	Umm Dorein	500	Islam	0%	1		5507
Umm Gabralla	Sudan	Umm Gabralla	9,000	Islam	0%	1		5508
**Univ. Students of Japan	Japan	Japanese	2,000,000	Traditional Japanese	1%	4	82	2125
*Universitarios - Rosario	Argentina	Spanish	10,000	Nominal Christian	2%	6	79	5003
*University Students	France	French	800,000	Secularism	2%	4		702
**University Students, Chin	China	Mandarin	600,000	Secularism	<1%	4		6567
Urali in Kerala	India	Urali	1,000	Hindu-Animist	<1%	1		2797
Urarina	Peru	Urarina	4,000	Animism	<1%	1		3187
Urban Elite Vietnamese	United States of America	Vietnamese	90,000	Ancestor Worship	nr%	4		9035
**Urban Mestizos	Ecuador	Spanish	600,000	Nominal Christian	11%	5		4032
Urban Refugees in Lusaka	Zambia	Bantu Dialects		Nominal Christian	nr%	4	83	9038
Urhobo	Nigeria	Urhobo	340,800	Animism	<1%	1		2524
Uria	Indonesia	Uria	300	Animism	<1%	1		3080
Uruangnirin	Indonesia	Uruangnirin	300	Animism	<1%	1		3081
Urubu	Brazil	Urubu	500	Animism	<1%	1		3132
Urupa	Brazil	Urupa	300	Animism	<1%	1		3133
Uspanteco	Guatemala	Uspanteco	2,000	Animism	<1%	1		8011
Utugwang	Nigeria	Utugwang	12,000	Animism	<1%	1		2525
Uvbie	Nigeria	Uvbie	6,000	Animism	<1%	1		2526
**Uzbeks	Afghanistan	Uzbeki, Turkic	1,000,000	Islam-Animist	0%	6	79	1229
Uzekwe	Nigeria	Uzekwe	5,000	Animism	<1%	1		2527
Vagala	Ghana	Vagala	4,000	Animism	<1%	4		531
Vagari	Pakistan	Gujarati Dialect	30,000	Hinduism	<1%	5		267
Vagla	Ghana	Vagla	36,000	Islam-Animist	<1%	6	80	5340
*Vai	Liberia	Vai	30,000	Islam	<1%	1		688
Vaikino	Indonesia	Vaikino	3,000	Islam-Animist	0%	1		5436
Vaiphei in Assam	India	Vaiphei	14,000	Animism	<1%	4		3082
Vale	Central African Republic	Vale	12,000	Hindu-Buddhist	<1%	4		2798
Venda	Zimbabwe	Venda	1,000	Animism	0%	4		5203
Veps	USSR	Veps	38,000	Animism	0%	4		5420
Vere	Cameroon	Vere	16,000	Unknown	0%	4		5880
***Vere	Nigeria	Vere	20,000	Animism	9%	5		5287
Vidunda	Tanzania	Vidunda	11,000	Animism	1%	4		5177
**Vietnamese Refugees	Laos	Vietnamese	20,000	Buddhism	7%	4		5612
**Vietnamese Refugees	Australia	Vietnamese	8,000	Folk Religion	2%	4	83	2100
	China	Cantonese	2,500	Traditional Chinese	nr%	4		9026
**Vietnamese Refugees	Korea, Republic of	Vietnamese	140,000	Buddhism	nr%	4		9045
	Thailand	Vietnamese	2,700,000	Buddhism	7%	4		2083
	United States of America	Vietnamese		Buddhism	4%	4		1222
Vige	Upper Volta	Vige	4,000	Islam-Animist	<1%	1		5684
Vinza	Tanzania	Vinza	4,000	Asian-Animist	0%	1		5613
Vishavan in Kerala	India	Vishavan	200	Hindu-Animist	<1%	1		2799

Name	Country	Language	Group Size	Primary Religion	% Chr	Vol V	UP	ID
Wodani	Indonesia	Wodani	3,000	Animism	<1%		1	3094
Woi	Indonesia	Woi	1,000	Animism	<1%		1	3095
Woleat	Pacific Trust Islands	Woleat	1,000	Christo-Paganism	<1%	4		1003
Wolio	Indonesia	Wolio	25,000	Islam-Animist	<1%		1	3096
Wolof	Senegal	Wolof	1,500,000	Islam-Animist	<1%	6	80	96
Wolof, Gambian	Gambia	Wolof, Gambian	70,000	Islam-Animist	<1%		1	2272
Wom	Nigeria	Wom	10,000	Islam-Animist	<1%		1	2530
*Women Laborers	Taiwan	Amoy	1,200,000	Traditional Chinese	2%	4		2115
Wongo	Zaire	Wongo	8,000	Animism	0%		1	5776
Woro	Sudan	Woro	400	Islam	0%		1	5493
Wumbvu	Gabon	Wumbvu	100	Animism	0%		1	5318
Wungu	Tanzania	Wungu	8,000	Animism	0%		1	5617
Xavante	Brazil	Xavante	2,000	Animism	<1%		1	3138
Xerente	Brazil	Xerente	500	Animism	<1%		1	3139
Xokleng	Brazil	Xokleng	300	Animism	<1%		1	3140
Xu	Namibia	Xu	8,000	Animism	<1%		1	5406
Yafi	Indonesia	Yafi	200	Animism	<1%		1	3097
Yaghan	Chile	Yaghan	50	Christo-Paganism	0%		1	5114
Yagnobi	USSR	Yagnobi	2,000	Unknown	0%		1	5881
Yagua	Peru	Yagua	4,000	Animism	<1%		1	3188
Yahadian	Indonesia	Yahadian	700	Animism	<1%		1	3098
Yaka	Zaire	Yaka	200,000	Animism	<1%		1	5777
Yakan	Philippines	Yakan	97,000	Islam-Animist	1%	6	80	25
Yakha	Nepal	Yakha	5,000	Buddhist-Animist	0%		1	6523
Yakoma	Central African Republic	Yakoma	60,000	Animism	0%		1	5204
**Yala	Nigeria	Yala	25,000	Islam-Animist	5%	4		1011
*Yalunka	Sierra Leone	Yalunka	12,000	Animism	<1%	6	80	455
Yaly	Indonesia	Yaly	26,000	Animism	<1%		1	3099
Yambasa	Cameroon	Yambasa	1,000	Animism	<1%		1	5289
Yaminahua	Peru	Yaminahua	1,000	Animism	<1%		1	3189
Yanadi in Andhra Pradesh	India	Yanadi	210,000	Hindu-Animist	<1%		1	2802
Yandang	Nigeria	Yandang	10,000	Islam-Animist	<1%		1	2531
Yanga	Togo	Yanga	nr	Islam-Animist	<1%		1	5637
Yangbye	Burma	Yangbye	330,000	Buddhist-Animist	1%		1	2596
*Yanomamo	Brazil	Yanomam (Waica)	nr	Animism	1%	6	79	1059
Yanomamo	Venezuela	Yanomamo	nr	Animism	<1%	5		2024
Yans	Zaire	Yans	165,000	Animism	0%		1	5778
*Yanyula	Australia	Yanyula (Yanjula)	nr	Other	15%	4		230
**Yao	Malawi	Chiyao	600,150	Islam-Animist	2%	5		1006
Yao	Mozambique	Yao	220,000	Islam	12%	6	79	143
**Yao	Thailand	Yao (Mien Wa)	20,000	Animism	2%		1	611
*Yao Refugees from Laos	Thailand	Yao	7,000	Animism	4%	4		2097
Yaoure	Ivory Coast	Yaoure	14,000	Christo-Paganism	<1%		1	4120
Yaquis	Mexico	Yaqui	nr	Animism	4%	5		317
Yaruro	Venezuela	Yaruro	5,000	Animism	<1%		1	5145
Yasing	Cameroon	Yasing	25,000	Animism	0%		1	5290
Yaur	Indonesia	Yaur	400	Animism	<1%		1	3100
Yava	Indonesia	Yava	5,000	Animism	<1%		1	3101
Yazgulyam	USSR	Yazgulyam	2,000	Unknown	0%		1	5882

Name	Country	Language	Group Size	Primary Religion	% Chr	V	UP	ID
**Yei	Botswana	Yei	10,000	Animism	1%	5		1162
Yei	Indonesia	Yei	1,000	Animism	<1%	1		3102
Yela	Zaire	Yela	33,000	Animism	0%	1		5779
Yellow Uiguir	China	Yellow Uiguir	4,000	Traditional Chinese	<1%	1		2850
Yelmek	Indonesia	Yelmek		Animism	<1%	1		3103
Yemenis	Yemen, Arab Republic	Arabic (Eastern)	5,600,000	Islam	<1%	5	79	1061
Yerava in Karnataka	India	Yerava	11,300	Hindu-Animist	<1%	1		2803
Yeretuar	Indonesia	Yeretuar		Animism	<1%	1		3804
Yerukala in A.P.	India	Yerukala	70,000	Hindu-Animist	<1%	1		2804
Yeskwa	Nigeria	Yeskwa	13,000	Islam	<1%	1		2532
Yidinit	Ethiopia	Yidinit	600	Animism	<1%	1		3236
Yin-Kyar	Burma	Shan Dialects	2,000	Animism	0%	2		4146
Yin-Nett	Burma	Shan Dialects	2,000	Animism	0%	2		4145
Yinchia	Burma	Yinchia	4,000	Buddhist-Animist	0%	2		2597
Yinga	Cameroon	Yinga	300	Animism	1%	4		1157
Yoabu	Benin	Yoabu	8,000	Animism	0%	1		5172
Yogad	Philippines	Yogad	7,000	Animism	<1%	1		3291
Yonggom	Indonesia	Yonggom		Animism	<1%	1		3105
Yoruk	Turkey	Turkish (Danubian)	600,000	Islam	0%	5		4048
Yos	Burma	Yos	3,000	Buddhist-Animist	<1%	1		2598
Yotafa	Indonesia	Yotafa		Animism	<1%	1		3106
Yuana	Venezuela	Yuana	3,000	Animism	<1%	1		5146
Yucateco	Guatemala	Yucateco		Animism	<1%	1		8012
*Yucuna	Colombia	Yucuna	500	Christo-Paganism	<1%	5		5105
Yukagirs	USSR	Yukagir	500	Christo-Paganism	<1%	1		1185
Yukpa	Colombia	Yukpa		Unknown	0%	1		5820
Yukpa	Venezuela	Yukpa	3,000	Animism	<1%	1		3156
Yuku	China	Yuku	3,000	Traditional Chinese	<1%	1		5147
Yulu	Sudan	Yulu	4,000	Islam	<1%	1		2851
Yungur	Nigeria	Yungur	44,000	Islam	<1%	1		5531
Yuracare	Bolivia	Yuracare	3,000	Animism	<1%	1		2533
Yurak	USSR	Yurak	29,000	Animism	0%	1		2144
Yuruti	Colombia	Yuruti		Unknown	<1%	1		5883
Zaghawa	Chad	Zaghawa	61,200	Animism	<1%	1		3157
Zaghawa	Libya	Zaghawa		Islam-Animist	0%	1		2265
Zaghawa	Sudan	Zaghawa		Islam	<1%	1		5365
Zanaki	Tanzania	Zanaki	23,000	Islam	<1%	1		5532
Zangskari in Kashmir	India	Zangskari	3,000	Hindu-Animist	<1%	1		5618
Zapoteco, C.Sola De Vega	Mexico	Zapoteco, C.Sola De Vega	10,000	Christo-Paganism	<1%	1		2805
Zapoteco, Choapan	Mexico	Zapoteco, Choapan	9,000	Christo-Paganism	<1%	1		6528
Zapoteco, E Miahuatlan	Mexico	Zapoteco, E Miahuatlan	7,000	Christo-Paganism	<1%	1		6529
Zapoteco, E Ocotlan	Mexico	Zapoteco, E Ocotlan	5,000	Christo-Paganism	<1%	1		6530
Zapoteco, E Ziacolula	Mexico	Zapoteco, E Ziacolula		Christo-Paganism	0%	1		6531
Zapoteco, E Zimatlan	Mexico	Zapoteco, E Zimatlan	90,000	Christo-Paganism	<1%	1		6532
Zapoteco, Isthmus	Mexico	Zapoteco, Isthmus		Christo-Paganism	<1%	1		6533
Zapoteco, Mazaltepec	Mexico	Zapoteco, Mazaltepec	10,000	Christo-Paganism	<1%	1		6534
Zapoteco, Miahuatlan	Mexico	Zapoteco, Miahuatlan	15,000	Christo-Paganism	0%	1		6535
Zapoteco, Mitla	Mexico	Zapoteco, Mitla		Christo-Paganism	<1%	1		6526

Name	Country	Language	Group Size	Primary Religion	% Chr	V	Vol UP	ID
Zapoteco, N Isthmus	Mexico	Zapoteco, N Isthmus	7,000	Christo-Paganism	<1%			6538
Zapoteco, N Ocotlan	Mexico	Zapoteco, N Ocotlan	6,000	Christo-Paganism	0%			6539
Zapoteco, N Villa Alta	Mexico	Zapoteco, N Villa Alta	15,000	Christo-Paganism	<1%			6540
Zapoteco, NE Miahuatlan	Mexico	Zapoteco, NE Miahuatlan	2,000	Christo-Paganism	0%			6536
Zapoteco, NE Yautepec	Mexico	Zapoteco, NE Yautepec	3,000	Christo-Paganism	0%			6537
Zapoteco, NW Tehuantepec	Mexico	Zapoteco, NW Tehuantepec	5,000	Christo-Paganism	0%			6541
Zapoteco, Pochutla	Mexico	Zapoteco, Pochutla	2,000	Christo-Paganism	0%			6542
Zapoteco, S Ejutla	Mexico	Zapoteco, S Ejutla	2,000	Christo-Paganism	0%			6548
Zapoteco, S Villa Alta	Mexico	Zapoteco, S Villa Alta	8,000	Christo-Paganism	<1%			6546
Zapoteco, SC Zimatlan	Mexico	Zapoteco, SC Zimatlan		Christo-Paganism	nr			6549
Zapoteco, SE Miahuatlan	Mexico	Zapoteco, SE Miahuatlan	4,000	Christo-Paganism	0%			6547
Zapoteco, SW Ixtlan	Mexico	Zapoteco, SW Ixtlan	10,000	Christo-Paganism	0%			6550
Zapoteco, Srra De Juarez	Mexico	Zapoteco, Srra De Juarez	8,000	Christo-Paganism	<1%			6545
Zapoteco, Stgo Xanica	Mexico	Zapoteco, Stgo Xanica	4,000	Christo-Paganism	0%			6543
Zapoteco, Sto Dom Albarr	Mexico	Zapoteco, Sto Dom Albarr	2,000	Christo-Paganism	0%			6544
Zapoteco, Tabaa	Mexico	Zapoteco, Tabaa	5,000	Christo-Paganism	<1%			6527
Zapoteco, Villa Alta	Mexico	Zapoteco, Villa Alta	3,000	Christo-Paganism	<1%			6551
Zapoteco, W Miahuatlan	Mexico	Zapoteco, W Miahuatlan	3,000	Christo-Paganism	0%			6552
Zapoteco, W Ocotlan	Mexico	Zapoteco, W Ocotlan	20,000	Christo-Paganism	<1%			6553
Zapoteco, W Sola de Vega	Mexico	Zapoteco, W Sola de Vega	3,000	Christo-Paganism	0%			6554
Zapoteco, W Tlacolula	Mexico	Zapoteco, W Tlacolula	32,000	Christo-Paganism	<1%			6555
Zapoteco, W Yautepec	Mexico	Zapoteco, W Yautepec	2,000	Christo-Paganism	0%			6556
Zapoteco, W Zimatlan	Mexico	Zapoteco, W Zimatlan	6,000	Christo-Paganism	0%			6557
Zapoteco, Yalalag	Mexico	Zapoteco, Yalalag	2,000	Christo-Paganism	0%			6558
Zaramo	Tanzania	Zaramo	300,000	Islam-Animist	2%	5		147
**Zaranda Hill Peoples	Nigeria	local languages		Animism	2%	4		1178
Zari	Nigeria	Zari	4,000	Islam	<1%			2534
Zayse	Ethiopia	Zayse	21,000	Animism	<1%			3237
Zemi Naga of Assam	India	Jeme	16,000	Animism	nr%	6	81	7002
Zenaga	Mauritania	Zenaga	16,000	Islam	0%			5387
Zigwa	Tanzania	Zigwa	112,000	Animism	0%			5619
Ziimamu	Ethiopia	Ziimamu		Animism	<1%			3228
Zimba	Zaire	Zimba	50,000	Animism	0%			5781
Zimbabwean Refugees	Mozambique	Tribal Languages	170,000	Animism	nr%	4	83	9032
Zimbabwean Repatriates	Zambia	Tribal Languages	45,000	Christo-Paganism	nr%	4	83	9029
Zimbabwean Repatriates	Zimbabwe	Tribal Languages	300,000	Christo-Paganism	<1%	4	79	9019
Zinacantecos	Mexico	Tzotzil,Chenalho	10,000	Christo-Paganism	3%			95
Zoliang	India	Naga,Zoliang	50,000	Animism	<1%			1085
Zome	Burma	Zome	30,000	Buddhist-Animist	<1%			2599
Zome in Manipur	India	Zome	30,000	Hindu-Buddhist	<1%			2806
Zoque, Chimalapa	Mexico	Zoque,Chimalapa	6,000	Christo-Paganism	<1%			5106
Zoque, Copainala	Mexico	Zoque,Copainala	10,000	Christo-Paganism	<1%			5107
Zoque, Francisco Leon	Mexico	Zoque,Francisco Leon	12,000	Christo-Paganism	<1%			5108
Zoque, Tabasco	Mexico	Zoque,Tabasco	400	Christo-Paganism	<1%			5109
Zowla	Ghana	Ewe	800,000	Animism	2%	5		1101
Zulu	Malawi	Zulu	40,000	Animism	<1%	4		5372
Zuni	United States of America	English	6,000	Animism	1%	4		410

Index by Receptivity

This index lists groups by their reported attitude toward the gospel. The judgment of receptivity or resistance to the gospel is a subjective and difficult question. Oftentimes what appears to be resistance to the gospel turns out to be a rejection of the Western or foreign cultural trappings with which the gospel is offered. Or perhaps it is a resistance to the agents who bear witness because they come from a country or people not respected by those who are being asked to hear the gospel. Nonetheless, this index gives the considered judgment of those who have reported these unreached peoples. Within each category (very receptive, receptive, indifferent, reluctant, very reluctant and unknown) peoples are listed alphabetically by group name. Their country or location is also listed.

REGISTRY OF THE UNREACHED

Very Receptive

Adi, India
Akhdam, Yemen, Arab Republic
Azteca, Mexico (79)
Bagobo, Philippines
Banaro, Papua New Guinea
Banyarwanda, Rwanda
Baoule, Ivory Coast
Basotho, Mountain, Lesotho (79)
Bipim, Indonesia
Bolinao, Philippines
Cebu, Middle-Class, Philippines
Ch'ol Sabanilla, Mexico
Citak, Indonesia
Copacabana Apt. Dwellers, Brazil
Dan, Ivory Coast
Godie, Ivory Coast
Guarani, Bolivia (79)
Halam in Tripura, India
Higi, Nigeria
Hmong Refugees, United States of
    America (83)
Hmong Women at Ban Vinai, Thailand
    (83)
Irulas in Kerala, India
Kond, India
Koreans in Germany, German Federal
    Rep.
Krahn, Liberia
Maguzawa, Nigeria (79)
Matharis, India
Mestizos in La Paz, Bolivia (82)
Mocha, Ethiopia
Nocte, India
Paez, Colombia
Pakabeti of Equator, Zaire
Prasuni, Afghanistan
Rwandan Tutsi, Burundi, Burundi
    (83)
Shankilla (Kazza), Ethiopia
Tagin, India
Tamil Plantation Workers, Malaysia
Vere, Nigeria

Receptive

Adja, Benin
Afghan Refugees (NWFP), Pakistan
    (83)
Afo, Nigeria (80)
African Students in Cairo, Egypt
Ahl-i-Haqq in Iran, Iran (79)

Akha, Thailand (79)
Ampeeli, Papua New Guinea
Apartment Residents-Seoul, Korea,
    Republic of
Apatani in Assam, India
Apayao, Philippines
Arabs in New Orleans, U.S.A. (82)
Aymara, Bolivia
Azerbaijani, Afghanistan
Babur Thali, Nigeria (80)
Bachelors in Lagos, Nigeria (82)
Bakuba, Zaire
Balangao, Philippines
Banai, Bangladesh
Bassa, Nigeria
Batangeno, Philippines
Bhil, Pakistan
Bhils, India (79)
Bidayuh of Sarawak, Malaysia (81)
Bijogo, Guinea-Bissau
Bilan, Philippines
Black Caribs, Belize, Belize (79)
Black Caribs, Guatemala, Guatemala
Black Caribs, Honduras, Honduras
Bodo Kachari, India
Boko, Benin
Bontoc, Central, Philippines (81)
Bontoc, Southern, Philippines
Boran, Kenya
Bukidnon, Philippines
Bus Drivers, South Korea, Korea,
    Republic of
Bus Girls in Seoul, Korea, Republic
    of (82)
Busanse, Ghana
Buwid, Philippines (81)
Chayahuita, Peru
Chicanos in Denver, United States
    of America (82)
Chinese Hakka of Taiwan, Taiwan
    (79)
Chinese in Australia, Australia
Chinese in Boston, United States of
    America (82)
Chinese in Brazil, Brazil
Chinese in Indonesia, Indonesia
Chinese in Panama, Panama
Chinese in Sabah, Malaysia
Chinese in Sarawak, Malaysia
Chinese in United Kingdom, United
    Kingdom
Chinese in United States, United
    States of America
Chinese in Vancouver B.C., Canada
Chinese Refugees, France, France
    (79)
Chinese Stud., Australia, Australia
Chinese Students Glasgow, United
    Kingdom

Chiriguano, Argentina
Chrau, Viet Nam
Coreguaje, Colombia
Dagomba, Ghana
Dhodias, India
Dida, Ivory Coast
Djandeau, Zaire
Doohwaayo, Cameroon
Dubla, India
Duka, Nigeria
Eritrean Refugees, Djibouti (83)
Ex-Mental Patients in NYC, United
  States of America (82)
Fakai, Nigeria
Falasha, Ethiopia (79)
Fali, Nigeria
Gagre, Pakistan
Ghimeera, Ethiopia
Glavda, Nigeria
Gouro, Ivory Coast
Grebo, Liberia
Hadrami, Yemen, Democratic
Hajong, Bangladesh
Hazara in Kabul, Afghanistan (82)
Hewa, Papua New Guinea (79)
High School Students, Hong Kong
Hotel Workers in Manila,
  Philippines (81)
Huave, Mexico
Huila, Angola
Hunzakut, Pakistan (79)
Iban, Malaysia (81)
Ifugao (Kalangoya), Philippines
Ikalahan, Philippines
Indian Tamils - Colombo, Sri Lanka
  (82)
Indians, East, Trinidad and Tobago
  (79)
Iranian Bahai Refugees, Pakistan
  (83)
Ishans, Nigeria
Izi, Nigeria
Jamaican Elite, Jamaica
Japanese Students In USA, United
  States of America
Jarawa, Nigeria
Javanese of Pejompongan, Indonesia
Jimini, Ivory Coast
Jivaro (Achuara), Venezuela
K'anjobal of San Miguel, Guatemala
Kafirs, Pakistan (79)
Kalagan, Philippines
Kalinga, Tanudan, Philippines
Kalinga,Northern, Philippines (81)
Kankanay, Central, Philippines
Karbis, India
Kasena, Ghana
Kashmiri Muslims, India (79)
Kaur, Indonesia

Kekchi, Guatemala
Khmer Refugees, Thailand
Khmer Rfgs, Canada (83)
Koch, Bangladesh
Kohli, Kutchi, Pakistan
Kohli, Parkari, Pakistan
Kohli, Tharadari, Pakistan
Kohli, Wadiara, Pakistan
Kolam, India
Kono, Sierra Leone
Koranko, Sierra Leone
Kowaao, Liberia
Kuluis in Himachal Prades, India
  (81)
Kunimaipa, Papua New Guinea
Kusaasi, Ghana
Lahaulis in Punjab, India
Lambadi in Andhra Pradesh, India
  (81)
Lepcha, Sikkim
Lepers of Cen. Thailand, Thailand
  (81)
Lepers of N.E. Thailand, Thailand
Loho Loho, Indonesia
Lotuka, Sudan
Maasai, Kenya (79)
Macuxi, Brazil
Magar, Nepal
Mam Indian, Guatemala
Mamanua, Philippines (81)
Mangyan, Philippines
Manikion, Indonesia
Manjaco, Guinea-Bissau
Manobo, Cotabato, Philippines
Manobo, Salug, Philippines
Manobo, Tigwa, Philippines
Manobo, Western Bukidnon,
  Philippines
Mansaka, Philippines
Marielitos in Florida, United
  States of America (83)
Mawchis, India
Mazahua, Mexico
Meghwar, Pakistan (79)
Mejah, India
Melanau of Sarawak, Malaysia (80)
Meo, Thailand
Miching, India
Middle Class-Mexico City, Mexico
  (82)
Military Personnel, Ecuador
Mixes, Mexico
Mopan Maya, Guatemala
Mopan Maya, Belize
Mundas in Bihar, India
Muslim Immigrants in U.K., United
  Kingdom
Nafaara, Ghana (79)
Nambya, Zimbabwe

Ndebele, Zimbabwe (79)
Ndoro, Nigeria
Nepalese in India, India
Ngamo, Nigeria
Ngombe, Zaire
Nomadic Somali Refugees, Somalia (83)
Nupe, Nigeria
Nyabwa, Ivory Coast
Paniyan of Kerala, India (81)
Pila, Benin
Plantation Workers, Papua New Guinea
Portuguese in France, France
Prisoners, Korea, Republic of
Pro Hockey Players, United States of America (82)
Puyuma, Taiwan (81)
Quechua, Peru
Quechua, Bolivia
Quechua, Huanco, Peru
Quiche, Guatemala (79)
Quichua, Ecuador
Racetrack Residents, U.S.A. (79)
Saguye, Kenya
Saiva Vellala, India
Santhali, Nepal
Save, Benin
Sawi, Indonesia
Selakau of Sarawak, Malaysia
Senoi, Malaysia (81)
Serawai, Indonesia (81)
Shihu, United Arab Emirates
Shirishana, Brazil
Shluh Berbers, Morocco
Sisaala, Ghana
Somba, Benin
Subanen (Tuboy), Philippines
Subanen, Sindangan, Philippines (80)
Suena, Papua New Guinea
Sugut, Malaysia
Sundanese, Indonesia (80)
Suri, Ethiopia
Suriguenos, Philippines
Swazi, South Africa
T'boli, Philippines (81)
Tagbanwa, Aborlan, Philippines
Tamil Laborers in Bombay, India (82)
Tamils (Indian), Sri Lanka (79)
Tangsa, India
Tatuyo, Colombia
Temne, Sierra Leone (80)
Teribe, Panama
Teso, Kenya
Tsachila, Ecuador
Turkana Fishing Community, Kenya (79)

Univ. Students of Japan, Japan
University Students, Chin, China
Urban Mestizos, Ecuador
Uzbeks, Afghanistan (79)
Vietnamese Refugees, United States of America
Vietnamese Refugees, Thailand
Vietnamese Refugees, Australia
Vohras of Yavatmal, India
Wajita, Tanzania
Wanchoo, India
Wimbum, Cameroon
Yala, Nigeria
Yao, Thailand (79)
Yao, Malawi
Yei, Botswana
Zaranda Hill Peoples, Nigeria

Indifferent

Afawa, Nigeria (80)
Alars, India
Alawites, Syria (79)
Albanian Muslims, Albania (80)
Albanians in Yugoslavia, Yugoslavia
Americans in Geneva, Switzerland
Ami, Taiwan (81)
Anatolian Turks-Istanbul, Turkey (82)
Arnatas, India
Asian Students, Philippines
Asmat, Indonesia (79)
Ata of Davao, Philippines
Atta, Philippines
Atye, Ivory Coast
Barbers in Tokyo, Japan (82)
Bariba, Benin (80)
Bassa, Liberia
Batak, Angkola, Indonesia (80)
Bete, Ivory Coast
Bhojpuri, Nepal
Bororo, Brazil
Bosnian, Yugoslavia (80)
Bushmen (Hiechware), Zimbabwe
Bushmen (Kung), Namibia (79)
Cambodians, Thailand
Casiguranin, Philippines
Casual Laborers-Atlanta, United States of America (82)
Central Thailand Farmers, Thailand (81)
Chakmas of Mizoram, India (81)
Cham Refugees from Kampuc, Malaysia (83)
Chang-Pa of Kashmir, India (81)

335

REGISTRY OF THE UNREACHED

Nkoya, Zambia
Nouni, Upper Volta
Nuer, Ethiopia
Nuer, Sudan (79)
Nyantruku, Benin
Pala'wan, Philippines (81)
Parsees, India (81)
Parsis in Bombay, India (82)
Prisoners in Antananarivo,
  Madagascar (82)
Pygmy (Mbuti), Zaire (79)
Rai, Danuwar, Nepal
Ramkamhaeng Un. Students, Thailand
Rava in Assam, India
Ryukyuan, Japan
Samo-Kubo, Papua New Guinea
Sanuma, Brazil
Sherpa, Nepal
Shourastra in Tamil Nadu, India
Sindhis of India, India
Slum Dwellers of Bangkok, Thailand
Soh, Thailand (81)
Somahai, Indonesia
Students, German Federal Rep. (79)
Talo, Indonesia
Tamang, Nepal
Tamil in Yellagiri Hills, India
Tamils (Indian), Malaysia
Teenbu, Ivory Coast
Tense, Ivory Coast
Tertiary Level Youth, Iran
Thai Islam (Thai), Thailand
Thai University Students, Thailand
  (81)
Tibetan Refugees, India (83)
Tofi, Benin
Tonga, Zimbabwe
Topotha, Sudan
Toussian, Upper Volta
Universitarios - Rosario, Argentina
  (82)
University Students, France (79)
Vai, Liberia (80)
Warjawa, Nigeria
Wazinza, Tanzania
White Moors, Mauritania
Women Laborers, Taiwan
Yalunka, Sierra Leone (80)
Yanomamo, Brazil (79)
Yanyula, Australia
Yao Refugees from Laos, Thailand
Yucuna, Colombia

Reluctant

Aborigines in Brisbane, Australia
  (82)

Afar, Ethiopia (79)
Ahmadis in Lahore, Pakistan (82)
Alaba, Ethiopia
Alago, Nigeria
Arabs of Khuzestan, Iran
Barasano, Southern, Colombia
Bawoyo, Zaire
Bengalis in London, United Kingdom
  (82)
Bengkulu, Indonesia
Busa, Nigeria (80)
Butawa, Nigeria
Bwa, Upper Volta (80)
Cape Malays in Cape Town, South
  Africa (82)
Chinese Fishermen, Malaysia
Chitralis, Pakistan (79)
Chola Naickans, India
Chuj, San Mateo Ixtatan, Guatemala
Circassians in Amman, Jordan (82)
Dead-End Kids - Amsterdam,
  Netherlands (82)
Deccani Muslims-Hyderabad, India
  (82)
Digo, Kenya
Druzes, Israel (79)
Fishing Village People, Taiwan
Fra-Fra, Ghana
Fulani, Cameroon (79)
Ga-Dang, Philippines
Galla, Harar, Ethiopia
Gilakis, Iran
Gourency, Upper Volta
Government officials, Thailand
Guarayu, Bolivia
Gujarati, United Kingdom
Gujars of Kashmir, India (81)
Gypsies in Jerusalem, Israel (82)
Haitian Refugees, United States of
  America (83)
Hopi, United States of America
Ica, Colombia
Ifugao in Cababuyan, Philippines
Igbira, Nigeria (80)
Indians in Fiji, Fiji (79)
Indust.Workers Yongdungpo, Korea,
  Republic of
Iravas in Kerala, India
Ixil, Guatemala
Jama Mapun, Philippines (80)
Japanese in Brazil, Brazil (79)
Jewish Refugees from USSR, Israel
  (83)
Jews of Iran, Iran
Jews, Non-Sephardic of Mo, Canada
Jews, Sephardic of Montre, Canada
Kankanay, Northern, Philippines

336

Karen, Pwo, Thailand
Kayagar, Indonesia
Kerewe, Tanzania
Komering, Indonesia
Kotokoli, Benin
Krumen, Ivory Coast
Lamba, Togo
Lawa, Eastern, Thailand (81)
Lawa, Mountain, Thailand
Lubang Islanders, Philippines (81)
Maithili, Nepal
Malappanackers, India
Malays of Singapore, Singapore (79)
Mappillas, India
Mapuche, Chile
Mazandaranis, Iran
Miya, Nigeria
Moken, Burma (79)
Moken of Thailand, Thailand
Monpa, India
Mru, Bangladesh
Mualthuam, India
Musi, Indonesia
Muslim Gypsies in Skoplje,
  Yugoslavia (82)
Muslim Lebanese Refugees, Canada
  (83)
Nambikuara, Brazil
Nurses in St. Louis, United States
  of America (82)
Ogan, Indonesia
Palaung, Burma (79)
Pension Students-Madrid, Spain (82)
Poouch in Kashmir, India
Purig-Pa of Kashmir, India (81)
Rabinal-Achi, Guatemala
Rajasthani Muslims-Jaipur, India
  (82)
Rajbansi, Nepal
Sabbra, Kenya
Sama Bangingi, Philippines (80)
Sama Pangutaran, Philippines (80)
Sama-Badjaw, Philippines (79)
Sangil, Philippines
Satnamis (Madhya Pradesh), India
Sayyids, Yemen, Arab Republic
Senufo, Ivory Coast (80)
Simba, Bolivia
Sindhi Muslims in Karachi, Pakistan
  (82)
Sinhalese, Sri Lanka
Solorese Muslims, Indonesia (81)
Somali, Ajuran, Kenya (79)
Somali, Degodia, Kenya
Somali, Gurreh, Kenya
Somali, Ogadenya, Kenya
Street Vendors in Saigon, Viet Nam
  (82)
Swatis, Pakistan (79)

Sylhetti, United Kingdom
T'in, Thailand (81)
Tagbanwa, Kalamian, Philippines
Tamil (Ceylonese), Sri Lanka
Tengger, Indonesia
Tibetans in Bhutan, Bhutan (81)
Tonga, Gwembe Valley, Zambia (79)
Turkana, Kenya
Turkish Immigrant Workers, German
  Federal Rep. (79)
Vietnamese Refugees, Korea,
  Republic of
Watchi, Togo
Winji-Winji, Benin
Woleat, Pacific Trust Islands
Yakan, Philippines (80)
Yanomamo, Venezuela
Zowla, Ghana
Zuni, United States of America

Very Reluctant

Achehnese, Indonesia (80)
Arab Immigrants in Bangui, Central
  African Republic (82)
Arawa, Nigeria
Azerbaijani Turks, Iran (80)
Balinese, Indonesia
Baluchi, Iran (80)
Bhutias, Bhutan
Bugis, Indonesia (80)
Chamula, Mexico (79)
Dawoodi Muslims, India
Dendi, Benin
Divehi, Maldives (80)
Fula, Guinea
Fula, Sierra Leone
Fulah, Upper Volta
Gays in San Francisco, United
  States of America (82)
Guaiaqui, Paraguay
Gugu-Yalanji, Australia
Gwandara, Nigeria
Jains, India
Jemez Pueblo, United States of
  America
Kabyle, Algeria (79)
Kae Sung Natives in Seoul, Korea,
  Republic of (82)
Khojas, Agha Khani, India
Kotta, India
Kreen-Akakore, Brazil
Kurds in Iran, Iran (80)
Macu, Colombia
Maguindano, Philippines (80)

Malakkaras of Kerala, India (81)
Malayo, Colombia
Mandingo, Liberia (79)
Maranao, Philippines (79)
Maures, Senegal
Minangkabau, Indonesia (80)
Mirung, Bangladesh
Moor Malays, Sri Lanka (79)
Mumuye, Nigeria
Muslim Malays, Malaysia (80)
Muslims, United Arab Emirates (79)
Muslims (West Nile Dist.), Uganda
Muslims of Jordan, Jordan
North Africans in Belgium, Belgium
  (80)
Ouaddai, Chad
Paiute, Northern, United States of
  America
Redjang, Indonesia (80)
Shan, Thailand
Soka Gakkai Believers, Japan
Somali, Ethiopia
Tausug, Philippines (80)
Tem, Togo
Tepehuan, Southwestern, Mexico
Thai Islam (Malay), Thailand (80)
Tuareg, Niger (79)
Turkomans, Iran (80)
Turks in Basel, Switzerland (82)
Turks, Anatolian, Turkey
Ulithi-Mall, Turks and Caicos
  Islands
Wolof, Senegal (80)
Yaoure, Ivory Coast
Yaquis, Mexico
Yemenis, Yemen, Arab Republic (79)
Zemi Naga of Assam, India (81)

Not Reported

Abaknon, Philippines
Abanyom, Nigeria
Abau, Indonesia
Abau, Papua New Guinea
Abazin, Soviet Union
Abe, Ivory Coast
Abialang, Sudan
Abidji, Ivory Coast
Abie, Papua New Guinea
Abkhaz, Turkey
Abkhaz, Soviet Union
Abong, Nigeria
Abou Charib, Chad
Abu Leila, Sudan
Abua, Nigeria

Abujmaria (Madhya Pradesh, India
Abulas, Papua New Guinea
Abure, Ivory Coast
Ach'ang, China
Achagua, Colombia
Acheron, Sudan
Achi, Cubulco, Guatemala
Achi, Rabinal, Guatemala
Achipa, Nigeria
Achode, Ghana
Acholi, Uganda
Achual, Peru
Adamawa, Cameroon
Adele, Togo
Adhola, Uganda
Adiyan in Kerala, India
Adjora, Papua New Guinea
Adygei, Soviet Union
Adyukru, Ivory Coast
Aeka, Papua New Guinea
Aeta, Philippines
Afitti, Sudan
Afshars, Iran
Agajanis, Iran
Agarabi, Papua New Guinea
Agariya in Bihar, India
Age, Cameroon
Aghem, Cameroon
Aghu, Indonesia
Agob, Papua New Guinea
Agoi, Nigeria
Aguacateco, Guatemala
Aguaruna, Peru
Agul, Soviet Union
Agutaynon, Philippines
Agwagwune, Nigeria
Ahir in Maharashtra, India
Ahlo, Togo
Aibondeni, Indonesia
Aiku, Papua New Guinea
Aikwakai, Indonesia
Aimol in Assam, India
Aiome, Papua New Guinea
Aion, Papua New Guinea
Airo-Sumaghaghe, Indonesia
Airoran, Indonesia
Aja, Sudan
Ajmeri in Rajasthan, India
Aka, India
Akan, Brong, Ivory Coast
Akawaio, Guyana
Ake, Nigeria
Akhavakh, Soviet Union
Akpa-Yache, Nigeria
Akpafu, Ghana
Akrukay, Papua New Guinea
Aladian, Ivory Coast
Alak, Laos
Alamblak, Papua New Guinea

Alangan, Philippines
Alas, Indonesia
Alatil, Papua New Guinea
Alauagat, Papua New Guinea
Alege, Nigeria
Algerian Arabs in France, France
Alor, Kolana, Indonesia (81)
Alutor, Soviet Union
Ama, Papua New Guinea
Amahuaca, Peru
Amaimon, Papua New Guinea
Amanab, Indonesia
Amanab, Papua New Guinea
Amar, Ethiopia
Amarakaeri, Peru
Amasi, Cameroon
Ambai, Indonesia
Ambasi, Papua New Guinea
Amber, Indonesia
Amberbaken, Indonesia
Ambo, Zambia
Ambonese, Netherlands
Ambonese, Indonesia
Amo, Nigeria
Amsterdam Boat Dwellers,
  Netherlands
Amto, Papua New Guinea
Amuesha, Peru
Amuzgo, Guerrero, Mexico
Amuzgo, Oaxaca, Mexico
Ana, Togo
Anaang, Nigeria
Anal in Manipur, India
Andarum, Papua New Guinea
Andha in Andhra Pradesh, India
Andi, Soviet Union
Andoque, Colombia
Anem, Papua New Guinea
Anga in Bihar, India
Angaataha, Papua New Guinea
Angal Heneng, South, Papua New
  Guinea
Angal Heneng, West, Papua New
  Guinea
Angal, East, Papua New Guinea
Angas, Nigeria
Angaua, Papua New Guinea
Anggor, Papua New Guinea
Angoram, Papua New Guinea
Animere, Togo
Ankave, Papua New Guinea
Ankwe, Nigeria
Anor, Papua New Guinea
Ansar Sudanese Refugees, Ethiopia
  (83)
Ansus, Indonesia
Anuak, Ethiopia
Anuak, Sudan
Anuki, Papua New Guinea

Anyanga, Togo
Apalai, Brazil
Apinaye, Brazil
Apurina, Brazil
Ara, Indonesia
Arab-Jabbari (Kamesh), Iran
Arab-Shaibani (Kamesh), Iran
Arabela, Peru
Arafundi, Papua New Guinea
Aranadan in Tamil Nadu, India
Arandai, Indonesia
Arapaco, Brazil
Arapesh, Bumbita, Papua New Guinea
Arapesh, Mountain, Papua New Guinea
Arapesh, Muhiang, Papua New Guinea
Arawak, Guyana
Arawe, Papua New Guinea
Arbore, Ethiopia
Archin, Soviet Union
Arecuna, Venezuela
Argobba, Ethiopia
Arguni, Indonesia
Arifama-Miniafia, Papua New Guinea
Arigibi, Papua New Guinea
Arinua, Papua New Guinea
Arop, Papua New Guinea
Aruop, Papua New Guinea
Arusha, Tanzania
Arutani, Venezuela
Arya in Andhra Pradesh, India
Asaro, Papua New Guinea
Asat, Papua New Guinea
Asienara, Indonesia
Assumbo, Cameroon
Asu, Tanzania
Asuri in Bihar, India
Ata, Papua New Guinea
Aten, Nigeria
Ati, Philippines
Atoc, Sudan
Atruahi, Brazil
Attie, Ivory Coast
Atuot, Sudan
Au, Papua New Guinea
Au ei, Botswana
Aunalei, Papua New Guinea
Auyana, Papua New Guinea
Avatime, Ghana
Avikam, Ivory Coast
Avukaya, Sudan
Awa, Papua New Guinea
Awadhi, Nepal
Awar, Papua New Guinea
Awara, Papua New Guinea
Awin, Papua New Guinea
Awngi, Ethiopia
Awutu, Ghana
Awyi, Indonesia
Awyu, Indonesia

339

Ayana, Kenya
Aymara, Carangas, Chile
Ayoreo, Paraguay
Ayu, Nigeria
Azera, Papua New Guinea
Baali, Zaire
Babajou, Cameroon
Babri, India
Baburiwa, Indonesia
Bachama, Nigeria
Bada, Nigeria
Badagu in Nilgiri, India
Bade, Nigeria
Badyara, Guinea-Bissau
Bafut, Cameroon
Bagelkhandi in M.P., India
Baghati in H.P., India
Bagirmi, Chad
Bagri, Pakistan
Baguio Area Miners, Philippines
 (81)
Bahais in Teheran, Iran (82)
Baham, Indonesia
Baharlu (Kamesh), Iran
Bahawalpuri in M.P., India
Bahinemo, Papua New Guinea
Bai, Sudan
Baibai, Papua New Guinea
Baiga in Bihar, India
Baining, Papua New Guinea
Bajania, Pakistan (79)
Bajau, Indonesian, Indonesia
Bajau, Land, Malaysia
Baka, Cameroon
Baka, Zaire
Bakairi, Brazil
Bakhtiaris, Iran (80)
Bakongo Angolan Refugees, Zaire
 (83)
Bakwe, Ivory Coast
Bakwele, Congo
Balangaw, Philippines
Balanta, Senegal
Balanta Refugees, Senegal
Balantak, Indonesia
Balante, Guinea-Bissau
Bali, Nigeria
Bali-Vitu, Papua New Guinea
Balkars, Soviet Union
Balmiki, Pakistan
Balong, Cameroon
Balti in Jammu, India
Bam, Papua New Guinea
Bambara, Mali
Bambara, Ivory Coast
Bambuka, Nigeria
Bamougoun-Bamenjou, Cameroon
Bamum, Cameroon
Bandawa-Minda, Nigeria

Bandi, Liberia
Bandjoun, Cameroon
Banen, Cameroon
Banga, Nigeria
Bangangte, Cameroon
Bangaru in Punjab, India
Bangba, Zaire
Banggai, Indonesia
Baniwa, Brazil
Banoni, Papua New Guinea
Bantuanon, Philippines
Banyum, Senegal
Banyun, Guinea-Bissau
Barabaig, Tanzania (79)
Barai, Papua New Guinea
Barambu, Sudan
Barasano, Colombia
Barasano, Northern, Colombia
Barau, Indonesia
Bare'e, Indonesia
Bareli in Madhya Pradesh, India
Bari, Sudan
Bariai, Papua New Guinea
Bariba, Nigeria
Bariji, Papua New Guinea
Barim, Papua New Guinea
Barok, Papua New Guinea
Baruga, Papua New Guinea
Baruya, Papua New Guinea
Basaa, Cameroon
Basakomo, Nigeria
Basari, Togo
Basari, Guinea
Basari, Senegal
Bashar, Nigeria
Bashgali, Afghanistan
Bashkir, Soviet Union (80)
Basila, Togo
Basketo, Ethiopia
Bata, Nigeria
Batak, Karo, Indonesia
Batak, Palawan, Philippines
Batak, Simalungun, Indonesia
Batak, Toba, Indonesia
Batanga-Ngolo, Cameroon
Bateg, Malaysia
Bathudi in Bihar, India
Batsi, Soviet Union
Batu, Nigeria
Bau, Papua New Guinea
Baushi, Nigeria
Bauwaki, Papua New Guinea
Bavenda, South Africa
Bawm, Bangladesh
Bayats, Iran
Bayot, Gambia
Bayot, Guinea-Bissau
Bayot, Senegal
Bazigar in Gujarat, India

REGISTRY OF THE UNREACHED

Bua, Chad
Bual, Indonesia
Buang, Central, Papua New Guinea
Buang, Mangga, Papua New Guinea
Bube, Equatorial Guinea
Budibud, Papua New Guinea
Budug, Soviet Union
Budugum, Cameroon
Buduma, Nigeria
Buglere, Panama
Bugombe, Zaire
Buhid, Philippines
Builsa, Ghana
Buin, Papua New Guinea
Buja, Zaire
Buka-khwe, Botswana
Bukaua, Papua New Guinea
Buli, Indonesia
Buli, Upper Volta
Bulia, Zaire
Bullom, Northern, Sierra Leone
Bullom, Southern, Sierra Leone
Bulu, Papua New Guinea
Buna, Papua New Guinea
Bunabun, Papua New Guinea
Bunak, Indonesia
Bunama, Papua New Guinea
Bunann in Kashmir, India
Bungku, Indonesia
Bunu, Nigeria
Bura, Cameroon
Burak, Nigeria
Buraka-Gbanziri, Congo
Buriat, China
Buriat, Soviet Union
Burig, China
Burig in Kashmir, India
Burji, Ethiopia
Burmese Muslim Refugees, Bangladesh
   (83)
Buru, Indonesia
Burum, Papua New Guinea
Burun, Sudan
Burundian Hutu Refugees, Tanzania
   (83)
Burungi, Tanzania
Busah, Papua New Guinea
Busami, Indonesia
Bushmen (Heikum), Namibia
Bushmen in Botswana, Botswana
Bushoong, Zaire
Bussa, Ethiopia
Butung, Indonesia
Bviri, Sudan
Bwa, Zaire
Bwaidoga, Papua New Guinea
Bwisi, Zaire
Byangsi, Nepal
Cacua, Colombia

Caiwa, Brazil
Cakchiquel, Central, Guatemala
Caluyanhon, Philippines
Campa, Peru
Camsa, Colombia
Candoshi, Peru
Canela, Brazil
Capanahua, Peru
Carapana, Colombia
Cashibo, Peru
Cayapa, Ecuador
Cewa, Zambia
Ch'iang, China
Ch'ol Tila, Mexico
Chacobo, Bolivia
Chadian Refugees, Nigeria (83)
Chadian Rfgs, Cameroon (83)
Chagga, Tanzania
Chaghatai, Afghanistan
Chakfem-Mushere, Nigeria
Chakossi in Ghana, Ghana
Chakossi in Togo, Togo
Chala, Ghana
Cham, Viet Nam
Chamacoco, Bahia Negra, Paraguay
Chamalin, Soviet Union
Chamari in Madhya Pradesh, India
Chamba Daka, Nigeria
Chamba Leko, Nigeria
Chambri, Papua New Guinea
Chameali in H.P., India
Chami, Colombia
Chamicuro, Peru
Chamorro, Turks and Caicos Islands
Chara, Ethiopia
Chatino, Nopala, Mexico
Chatino, Panixtlahuaca, Mexico
Chatino, Tataltepec, Mexico
Chatino, Yaitepec, Mexico
Chatino, Zacatepec, Mexico
Chatino, Zenzontepec, Mexico
Chaudangsi, Nepal
Chaungtha, Burma
Chawai, Nigeria
Chenalhoa Tzotzil, Mexico
Chenapian, Papua New Guinea
Chenchu in Andhra Pradesh, India
Chepang, Nepal
Cherkess, Soviet Union
Chero in Bihar, India
Chiga, Uganda
Chik-Barik in Bihar, India
Chilean Refugees, Argentina
Chin, China
Chin, Asho, Burma
Chin, Falam, Burma
Chin, Haka, Burma
Chin, Khumi, Burma
Chin, Ngawn, Burma

Dimir, Papua New Guinea
Dinka, Sudan
Dinka, Agar, Sudan
Diodio, Papua New Guinea
Diola, Senegal
Diola, Guinea-Bissau (80)
Dirim, Nigeria
Dirya, Nigeria
Djuka, Surinam
Dobu, Papua New Guinea
Doe, Tanzania
Doga, Papua New Guinea
Doghosie, Upper Volta
Dogoro, Papua New Guinea
Dolgans, Soviet Union
Dom, Papua New Guinea
Dompago, Benin
Domu, Papua New Guinea
Domung, Papua New Guinea
Dongjoi, Sudan
Dongo, Sudan
Dongo, Zaire
Dorlin in Andhra Pradesh, India
Dorobo, Kenya
Dorobo, Tanzania
Doromu, Papua New Guinea
Dorze, Ethiopia
Doura, Papua New Guinea
Duau, Papua New Guinea
Dubu, Indonesia
Duguir, Nigeria
Duguza, Nigeria
Dukwe Camp Residents, Botswana (83)
Duma, Gabon
Duna, Papua New Guinea
Dungan, Soviet Union
Duru, Cameroon
Dusun, Malaysia (81)
Duvele, Indonesia
Dyan, Upper Volta
Dyerma, Niger (80)
Dyerma, Nigeria
Dyola, Gambia
Dyola, Guinea-Bissau
Dyola, Senegal
Ebira, Nigeria
Ebrie, Ivory Coast
Edawapi, Papua New Guinea
Edo, Nigeria
Efik, Nigeria
Efutop, Nigeria
Eggon, Nigeria
Eivo, Papua New Guinea
Ejagham, Nigeria
Ekagi, Indonesia
Ekajuk, Nigeria
Eket, Nigeria
Ekpeye, Nigeria
El Molo, Kenya

Eleme, Nigeria
Elkei, Papua New Guinea
Emai-Iuleha-Ora, Nigeria
Embera, Northern, Colombia
Emerum, Papua New Guinea
Emira, Papua New Guinea
Emumu, Indonesia
Endangen, Papua New Guinea
Enga, Papua New Guinea
Engenni, Nigeria
Enya, Zaire
Eotile, Ivory Coast
Epie, Nigeria
Equatorial Guin. Refugees, Gabon
Eritrean Refugees, Sudan (83)
Erokwanas, Indonesia
Esan, Nigeria
Ethiopian Refugees, Yemen, Yemen,
  Arab Republic
Eton, Cameroon
Etulo, Nigeria
Evant, Nigeria
Evenki, China
Evenks, Soviet Union
Ewage-Notu, Papua New Guinea
Ewenkis, China (81)
Fa D'Ambu, Equatorial Guinea
Fagululu, Papua New Guinea
Faiwol, Papua New Guinea
Fali, Cameroon
Fas, Papua New Guinea
Fasu, Papua New Guinea
Feroge, Sudan
Finungwan, Papua New Guinea
Fipa, Tanzania
Foau, Indonesia
Foi, Papua New Guinea
Foran, Papua New Guinea
Fordat, Indonesia
Fore, Papua New Guinea
Fula, Upper Volta
Fula, Cunda, Gambia
Fula, Macina, Mali
Fula, Peuhala, Mali
Fuliro, Zaire
Fulnio, Brazil
Fungom, Northern, Cameroon
Fungor, Sudan
Furu, Zaire
Fuyuge, Papua New Guinea
Fyam, Nigeria
Fyer, Nigeria
Gabbra, Kenya
Gabri, Chad
Gadaban in Andhra Pradesh, India
Gaddi in Himachal Pradesh, India
Gade, Nigeria
Gadsup, Papua New Guinea
Gagauzes, Soviet Union

Gagu, Ivory Coast
Gahuku, Papua New Guinea
Gaikundi, Papua New Guinea
Gaina, Papua New Guinea
Gal, Papua New Guinea
Galambi, Nigeria
Galeshis, Iran
Galla of Bucho, Ethiopia
Galler, Laos
Galong in Assam, India
Gambai, Chad
Gamei, Papua New Guinea
Gamti in Gujarat, India
Gan, Upper Volta
Gane, Indonesia
Gangam, Togo
Ganglau, Papua New Guinea
Gangte in Assam, India
Garuh, Papua New Guinea
Garus, Papua New Guinea
Garuwahi, Papua New Guinea
Gawar-Bati, Afghanistan
Gawari in Andhra Pradesh, India
Gawwada, Ethiopia
Gayo, Indonesia (80)
Gbande, Guinea
Gbari, Nigeria (80)
Gbaya, Nigeria
Gbaya-Ndogo, Sudan
Gbazantche, Benin
Gberi, Sudan
Gedaged, Papua New Guinea
Gedeo, Ethiopia
Geishas in Osaka, Japan (82)
Geji, Nigeria
Genagane, Papua New Guinea
Gende, Papua New Guinea
Gera, Nigeria
Geruma, Nigeria
Gesa, Indonesia
Ghale Gurung, Nepal
Gheko, Burma
Ghol, Sudan
Ghotuo, Nigeria
Ghulfan, Sudan
Gidar, Chad
Gidar, Cameroon
Gidicho, Ethiopia
Gidra, Papua New Guinea
Gilyak, Soviet Union
Gimi, Papua New Guinea
Ginuman, Papua New Guinea
Gio, Liberia
Gira, Papua New Guinea
Girawa, Papua New Guinea
Giri, Papua New Guinea
Giryama, Kenya
Gisei, Cameroon
Gisiga, Cameroon

Gitua, Papua New Guinea
Gizra, Papua New Guinea
Gobasi, Papua New Guinea
Gobato, Ethiopia
Gobeze, Ethiopia
Goemai, Nigeria
Gogo, Tanzania
Gogodala, Papua New Guinea
Gokana, Nigeria
Gola, Liberia
Gola, Sierra Leone
Golo, Chad
Gonja, Ghana
Goroa, Tanzania
Gorontalo, Indonesia
Gosha, Kenya
Goudari, Iran
Gouin-Turka, Upper Volta
Goulai, Chad
Gouwar, Cameroon
Grasia in Gujarat, India
Grunshi, Ghana
Gu, Benin
Guajajara, Brazil
Guajibo, Colombia
Guambiano, Colombia
Guana, Paraguay
Guarojio, Mexico
Guatemalan Refugees, Mexico
Guayabero, Colombia
Guayabevo, Colombia
Gude, Cameroon
Gude, Nigeria
Gudu, Nigeria
Guduf, Nigeria
Guere, Ivory Coast
Guhu-Samane, Papua New Guinea
Guinean Refugees, Gabon
Gujuri, Afghanistan
Gula, Chad
Gulfe, Cameroon
Gumasi, Papua New Guinea
Gumine, Papua New Guinea
Gumuz, Ethiopia
Gumuz, Sudan
Gurage, Ethiopia (80)
Gure-Kahugu, Nigeria
Gurensi, Ghana
Gurma, Upper Volta
Gurung, Nepal
Guruntum-Mbaaru, Nigeria
Gusap, Papua New Guinea
Guwot, Papua New Guinea
Gwa, Ivory Coast
Gwari Matai, Nigeria
Gwedena, Papua New Guinea
Gwere, Uganda
Gypsies, Soviet Union
Gypsies in Yugoslavia, Yugoslavia

Ha, Tanzania
Hadiyya, Ethiopia
Hahon, Papua New Guinea
Halbi in Madhya Pradesh, India
Halia, Papua New Guinea
Hallam, Burma
Hamtai, Papua New Guinea
Hangaza, Tanzania
Hani, China
Hanonoo, Philippines
Harari, Ethiopia
Harauti in Rajasthan, India
Hatsa, Tanzania
Havu, Zaire
Havunese, Indonesia
Haya, Tanzania
Hehe, Tanzania
Heiban, Sudan
Helong, Indonesia
Herero, Botswana
Herero, Namibia
Heso, Zaire
Hezareh, Iran
Hixkaryana, Brazil
Hkun, Burma
Hmong, Twin Cities, United States
  of America
Ho in Bihar, India
Hohodene, Brazil
Holiya in Madhya Pradesh, India
Holoholo, Tanzania
Holu, Angola
Hote, Papua New Guinea
Hrangkhol, Burma
Huachipaire, Peru
Huambisa, Peru
Huasteco, Mexico
Hui, China (80)
Huichol, Mexico
Huistan Tzotzil, Mexico
Huitoto, Meneca, Colombia
Huitoto, Murui, Peru
Hukwe, Angola
Hula, Papua New Guinea
Huli, Papua New Guinea
Humene, Papua New Guinea
Hunde, Zaire
Hunjara, Papua New Guinea
Hupda Maku, Colombia
Hwana, Nigeria
Hwela-Numu, Ivory Coast
Hyam, Nigeria
Iatmul, Papua New Guinea
Ibaji, Nigeria
Ibanag, Philippines
Ibibio, Nigeria
Icen, Nigeria
Idi, Papua New Guinea
Idoma, Nigeria

Idoma, North, Nigeria
Ifuago, Antipolo, Philippines
Ifugao, Ambanad, Philippines
Ifugao, Kiangan, Philippines
Ifumu, Congo
Igala, Nigeria
Igede, Nigeria
Ignaciano, Bolivia
Igora, Papua New Guinea
Igorot, Philippines
Iha, Indonesia
Ihceve, Nigeria
Ijo, Central-Western, Nigeria
Ijo, Northeast, Nigeria
Ijo, Northeast Central, Nigeria
Ikizu, Tanzania
Ikobi-Mena, Papua New Guinea
Ikulu, Nigeria
Ikundun, Papua New Guinea
Ikwere, Nigeria
Ila, Zambia
Ilongot, Philippines
Inallu, Iran
Inanwatan, Indonesia
Indians in Dubai, United Arab
  Emirates (82)
Indinogosima, Papua New Guinea
Inga, Colombia
Ingassana, Sudan
Ingushes, Soviet Union
Insinai, Philippines
Intha, Burma
Ipiko, Papua New Guinea
Ipili, Papua New Guinea
Iquito, Peru
Irahutu, Indonesia
Iraqi Kurd Refugees, Iran (83)
Iraqw, Tanzania
Iraya, Philippines
Iresim, Indonesia
Iria, Indonesia
Irigwe, Nigeria
Irumu, Papua New Guinea
Isanzu, Tanzania
Isebe, Papua New Guinea
Isekiri, Nigeria
Isneg, Dibagat-Kabugao, Philippines
Isneg, Karagawan, Philippines
Isoko, Nigeria
Itawit, Philippines
Itelmen, Soviet Union
Itik, Indonesia
Itneg, Adasen, Philippines
Itneg, Binongan, Philippines
Itneg, Masadiit, Philippines
Itonama, Bolivia
Ivbie North-Okpela-Atte, Nigeria
Iwa, Zambia
Iwal, Papua New Guinea

REGISTRY OF THE UNREACHED

Kaonde, Zaire
Kaonde, Zambia
Kapin, Papua New Guinea
Kapore, Papua New Guinea
Kapori, Indonesia
Kapriman, Papua New Guinea
Kapuchin, Soviet Union
Kara, Tanzania
Kara, Papua New Guinea
Karachay, Soviet Union
Karagas, Soviet Union
Karaim, Soviet Union
Karakalpak, Soviet Union (80)
Karam, Papua New Guinea
Karanga, Chad
Karangi, Papua New Guinea
Karas, Indonesia
Karatin, Soviet Union
Kare, Papua New Guinea
Karekare, Nigeria
Karen, Thailand (79)
Kari, Chad
Kari, Central African Republic
Kari, Zaire
Karipuna Creole, Brazil
Karipuna Do Guapore, Brazil
Kariya, Nigeria
Karkar, Papua New Guinea
Karko, Sudan
Karmali in Dihar, India
Karon Dori, Indonesia
Karon Pantai, Indonesia
Karre, Central African Republic
Karua, Papua New Guinea
Kasanga, Guinea-Bissau
Kasele, Togo
Kasem, Upper Volta
Kasseng, Laos
Kasua, Papua New Guinea
Kasuweri, Indonesia
Katab, Nigeria
Katakari in Gujarat, India
Katcha, Sudan
Kate, Papua New Guinea
Kati, Northern, Indonesia
Kati, Southern, Indonesia
Katiati, Papua New Guinea
Katla, Sudan
Katukina, Panoan, Brazil
Kaugat, Indonesia
Kaugel, Papua New Guinea
Kaure, Indonesia
Kavwol, Indonesia
Kavwol, Papua New Guinea
Kaw, Burma
Kawar in Madhya Pradesh, India
Kawe, Indonesia
Kayabi, Brazil
Kayan, Malaysia

Kayan, Burma
Kayapo, Brazil
Kaygir, Indonesia
Kayupulau, Indonesia
Kazakhs, Iran (80)
Kazakhs, China (81)
Kebu, Togo
Kebumtamp, Bhutan
Kedayanas, Malaysia
Keer in Madhya Pradesh, India
Kei, Indonesia
Keiga, Sudan
Keiga Jirru, Sudan
Kela, Papua New Guinea
Kelabit, Malaysia (81)
Kelah, Zaire
Kelao, China
Kele, Gabon
Kemak, Indonesia
Kembata, Ethiopia
Kemok, Malaysia
Kenati, Papua New Guinea
Kendari, Indonesia
Kenga, Chad
Kenyah, Indonesia
Keopara, Papua New Guinea
Kera, Chad
Kera, Cameroon
Kerewo, Papua New Guinea
Keriaka, Papua New Guinea
Kerinchi, Indonesia
Ket, Soviet Union
Kewa, East, Papua New Guinea
Kewa, South, Papua New Guinea
Kewa, West, Papua New Guinea
Khakas, Soviet Union
Khalaj, Iran
Khalka, China
Kham, China
Kham, Nepal
Khamti in Assam, India
Khana, Nigeria
Khandesi, India
Khanti, Soviet Union
Kharia in Bihar, India
Khasi in Assam, India
Khasonke, Mali
Khinalug, Soviet Union
Khirwar in Madhya Pradesh, India
Khmer Refugees, Laos (83)
Khmer Refugees, Belgium (83)
Khmer Unaced Minors, Thailand (83)
Khowar, India
Khvarshin, Soviet Union
Kiari, Papua New Guinea
Kibet, Chad
Kibiri, Papua New Guinea
Kichepo, Sudan
Kikapoo, Mexico

348

Kilba, Nigeria
Kilmera, Papua New Guinea
Kim, Chad
Kim, Central African Republic
Kimaghama, Indonesia
Kimbu, Tanzania
Kinalakna, Papua New Guinea
Kinaray-A, Philippines
Kinga, Tanzania
Kirgiz, Soviet Union (80)
Kirgiz, Afghanistan
Kirgiz, China
Kirgiz Afghans in Turkey, Turkey
  (83)
Kirgiz Refugees, Pakistan
Kirifi, Nigeria
Kiriwina, Papua New Guinea
Kis, Papua New Guinea
Kisan in Bihar, India
Kisankasa, Tanzania
Kishanganjia in Bihar, India
Kishtwari in Jammu, India
Kisi, Tanzania
Kissi, Guinea
Kita, Mali
Kiwai, Northeast, Papua New Guinea
Kiwai, Southern, Papua New Guinea
Kiwai, Wabuda, Papua New Guinea
Klaoh, Liberia
Koalib, Sudan (79)
Kobiana, Guinea
Kobon, Papua New Guinea
Koda in Bihar, India
Kodi, Indonesia
Koenoem, Nigeria
Kofyar, Nigeria
Kohoroxitari, Brazil
Kohumono, Nigeria
Koiari, Grass, Papua New Guinea
Koiari, Mountain, Papua New Guinea
Koita, Papua New Guinea
Kokant, Burma
Koke, Chad
Kol, Papua New Guinea
Kol in Assam, India
Kolbila, Cameroon
Kole, Cameroon
Koliku, Papua New Guinea
Kolom, Papua New Guinea
Kom in Manipur, India
Koma, Ghana
Koma, Nigeria
Koma, Cameroon
Koma, Central, Sudan
Komba, Papua New Guinea
Kombio, Papua New Guinea
Komi-Permyat, Soviet Union
Komi-Zyrian, Soviet Union
Komono, Upper Volta

Komutu, Papua New Guinea
Konabem, Cameroon
Konabem, Cameroon
Konda-Dora (Andra Pradesh, India
Koneraw, Indonesia
Kongo, Angola
Konkani in Gujarat, India
Konkomba, Ghana
Kono, Nigeria
Konomala, Papua New Guinea
Konongo, Tanzania
Konso, Ethiopia
Konyagi, Guinea
Koraga in Kerala, India
Korak, Papua New Guinea
Korape, Papua New Guinea
Korapun, Indonesia
Koreans in Manchuria, China (81)
Koro, Nigeria
Koroma, Sudan
Korop, Nigeria
Korop, Cameroon
Korwa in Bihar, India
Koryak, Soviet Union
Kosorong, Papua New Guinea
Kota, Gabon
Kota in Tamil Nadu, India
Kotia in Andhra Pradesh, India
Kotogut, Indonesia
Kotoko, Chad
Kotoko, Cameroon
Kotokoli, Togo
Kotopo, Cameroon
Kouya, Ivory Coast
Kovai, Papua New Guinea
Kove, Papua New Guinea
Koya in Andhra Pradesh, India
Koyra, Ethiopia
Kpa, Cameroon
Kpelle, Liberia
Kpelle, Guinea
Kposo, Togo
Krachi, Ghana
Krim, Sierra Leone
Krio, Gambia
Krisa, Papua New Guinea
Krobou, Ivory Coast
Krongo, Sudan
Kryz, Soviet Union
Kuatinema, Brazil
Kube, Papua New Guinea
Kubu, Indonesia (80)
Kubu, Indonesia (81)
Kuda-Chamo, Nigeria
Kudiya, India
Kugbo, Nigeria
Kuikuro, Brazil
Kuka, Chad
Kukele, Nigeria

Kukuwy, Papua New Guinea
Kukwa, Congo
Kulango, Ivory Coast
Kulele, Ivory Coast
Kulere, Nigeria
Kullo, Ethiopia
Kulung, Nigeria
Kumai, Papua New Guinea
Kumam, Uganda
Kuman, Papua New Guinea
Kumauni in Assam, India
Kumdauron, Papua New Guinea
Kumu, Zaire
Kumukio, Papua New Guinea
Kunama, Ethiopia
Kunante, Guinea-Bissau
Kunda, Mozambique
Kunda, Zimbabwe
Kunda, Zambia
Kunda, Zambia
Kuni, Papua New Guinea
Kunua, Papua New Guinea
Kuot, Papua New Guinea
Kupia in Andhra Pradesh, India
Kupsabiny, Uganda
Kurada, Papua New Guinea
Kurds in Kuwait, Kuwait
Kurfei, Niger
Kuria, Tanzania
Kurichiya in Kerala, India (81)
Kuruba in Tamil Nadu, India
Kurudu, Indonesia
Kurumba, Upper Volta
Kurux in Bihar, India
Kushi, Nigeria
Kusu, Zaire
Kuteb, Nigeria
Kutin, Cameroon
Kutu, Tanzania
Kuturmi, Nigeria
Kuvi in Orissa, India
Kuwaa, Liberia
Kuzamani, Nigeria
Kvanadin, Soviet Union
Kwa, Nigeria
Kwadi, Angola
Kwakum, Cameroon
Kwale, Papua New Guinea
Kwambi, Namibia
Kwanga, Papua New Guinea
Kwangali, Angola
Kwansu, Indonesia
Kwanyama, Angola
Kwanyama, Namibia
Kwaya, Tanzania
Kwe-etshori, Botswana
Kwe-etshori, Zimbabwe
Kwerba, Indonesia
Kwere, Tanzania

Kwese, Zaire
Kwesten, Indonesia
Kwoma, Papua New Guinea
Kwomtari, Papua New Guinea
Kyibaku, Nigeria
Laamang, Nigeria
Labans, India
Labbai, India
Labhani in Andhra Pradesh, India
Labu, Papua New Guinea
Lacandon, Mexico
Ladakhi in Jammu, India
Ladinos, Lebanon
Laewomba, Papua New Guinea
Lafofa, Sudan
Lahu, Burma
Lahul, China
Laka, Cameroon
Laka, Chad
Laka, China
Laka, Central African Republic
Lakians, Soviet Union
Lakka, Nigeria
Lala, Zambia
Lalia, Zaire
Lalung in Assam, India
Lama, Burma
Lamba, Benin
Lamba, Zaire
Lamba, Zambia
Lambi, Cameroon
Lambya, Malawi
Lambya, Tanzania
Lame, Nigeria
Lamogai, Papua New Guinea
Lampung, Indonesia (80)
Landoma, Guinea
Landoma, Guinea-Bissau
Langi, Tanzania
Lango, Uganda
Lanoh, Malaysia
Lao Refugees, Argentina
Lara, Indonesia
Laro, Sudan
Laru, Nigeria
Latdwalam, Indonesia
Lati, China
Laudje, Indonesia
Lavatbura-Lamusong, Papua New
  Guinea
Lavongai, Papua New Guinea
Lebgo, Nigeria
Lebong, Indonesia
Leco, Bolivia
Lega, Zaire
Lelemi, Ghana
Lengua, Northern, Paraguay
Lenje, Zambia
Leron, Papua New Guinea

Letti, Indonesia
Lhomi, Nepal
Li, China
Ligbi, Ivory Coast
Ligbi, Ghana
Liguri, Sudan
Lihir, Papua New Guinea
Liko, Zaire
Lima, Zambia
Limba, Sierra Leone
Lionese, Indonesia
Lisu, China (81)
Liv, Soviet Union
Lo, Nigeria
Lobi, Ivory Coast
Lodhi in Bihar, India
Logba, Ghana
Lohiki, Papua New Guinea
Loinang, Indonesia (81)
Loko, Sierra Leone
Loko, Guinea
Lolo, China (81)
Loma, Guinea
Loma, Liberia
Lombi, Zaire
Lombo, Zaire
Lomwe, Mozambique
Longuda, Nigeria
Lore, Indonesia
Lori, Sudan
Lors, Iran (80)
Lotsu-Piri, Nigeria
Lou-Baluan-Pam, Papua New Guinea
Loven, Laos (81)
Lozi, Zimbabwe
Lozi, Zambia
Lu, China
Luac, Sudan
Luano, Zambia
Lubu, Indonesia
Luchazi, Angola
Luchazi, Zambia
Lue, Cameroon
Lugitama, Papua New Guinea
Luimbi, Angola
Lukep, Papua New Guinea
Lumbu, Gabon
Luna, Zaire
Lunda, Angola
Lunda, Ndembu, Zambia
Lundu, Cameroon
Lungu, Nigeria
Luo, Tanzania
Lushai in Assam, India
Luvale Refugees from Angola,
  not reported (83)
Luwu, Indonesia
Luxemburgois, Luxembourg
Luyana, Angola

Luyana, Zambia
Lwalu, Zaire
Lwena, Angola
Lwo, Sudan
Ma, Zaire
Maanyan, Indonesia
Maba, Chad
Maba, Sudan
Maban-Jumjum, Sudan
Maca, Paraguay
Machiguenga, Peru
Macuna, Colombia
Madak, Papua New Guinea
Madda, Nigeria
Madi, Sudan
Madi, Uganda
Madik, Indonesia
Maghi, Burma
Magori, Papua New Guinea
Mahali in Assam, India
Mahri, Oman
Mai, Papua New Guinea
Mailu, Papua New Guinea
Maiongong, Brazil
Mairasi, Indonesia
Maisan, Papua New Guinea
Maiwa, Papua New Guinea
Majhi, Nepal
Majhwar in Madhya Pradesh, India
Maji, Ethiopia
Majingai-Ngama, Chad
Majingai-ngama, Central African
  Republic
Maka, Cameroon
Makarim, Papua New Guinea
Makasai, Indonesia
Makere, Uganda
Makian, West, Indonesia
Maklew, Indonesia
Makonde, Tanzania
Makua, Mozambique
Malalamai, Papua New Guinea
Malankuravan in Kerala, India
Malapandaram in Kerala, India
Malaryan in Kerala, India
Malas, Papua New Guinea
Malasanga, Papua New Guinea
Malavedan in Kerala, India
Male, Ethiopia
Malek, Papua New Guinea
Maleu, Papua New Guinea
Mali in Andhra Pradesh, India
Malila, Tanzania
Malki in Bihar, India
Malon, Papua New Guinea
Malpaharia in Assam, India
Malvi in Madhya Pradesh, India
Mama, Nigeria
Mamaa, Papua New Guinea

REGISTRY OF THE UNREACHED

Mamasani, Iran
Mambai, Indonesia
Mambila, Cameroon
Mambwe-Lungu, Tanzania
Mambwe-Lungu, Zambia
Mamprusi, Ghana
Mamprusi, Ghana
Mamvu-Efe, Zaire
Managalasi, Papua New Guinea
Manambu, Papua New Guinea
Mancang, Senegal
Manchu, China (81)
Manda, Tanzania
Mandar, Indonesia
Mandara, Nigeria
Mandaya, Philippines
Mandaya, Mansaka, Philippines
Mander, Indonesia
Manding, Senegal
Mandyak, Gambia
Manem, Indonesia
Mangap, Papua New Guinea
Mangbai, Chad
Mangbutu, Zaire
Manggarai Muslims, Indonesia (81)
Mangisa, Cameroon
Mangs in Maharashtra, India
Maninka, Guinea-Bissau
Maninka, Sierra Leone
Manjack, Senegal
Mankanya, Guinea-Bissau
Mankanya, Senegal
Manna-Dora in A.P., India
Mannan in Kerala, India
Mano, Liberia
Manobo, Agusan, Philippines
Manobo, Ata, Philippines
Manobo, Binokid, Philippines
Manobo, Dibabawon, Philippines
Manobo, Obo, Philippines
Manobo, Sarangani, Philippines
Manobo, Tagabawa, Philippines
Manobos, Pulangi, Philippines
Mansi, Soviet Union
Mantera, Malaysia
Mantion, Indonesia
Manu Park Panoan, Peru
Manyika, Zimbabwe
Mao, Northern, Ethiopia
Maou, Ivory Coast
Mape, Papua New Guinea
Mapena, Papua New Guinea
Mapoyo, Venezuela
Maquiritari, Venezuela
Mara in Assam, India
Maralango, Papua New Guinea
Maraliinan, Papua New Guinea
Maranao, Lanad, Philippines
Mararit, Chad

Marau, Indonesia
Marba, Chad
Marghi Central, Nigeria
Mari, Soviet Union
Mari, Papua New Guinea
Maria, Papua New Guinea
Maria in Andhra Pradesh, India
Marind, Indonesia
Marind, Bian, Indonesia
Maring, Papua New Guinea
Marka, Upper Volta
Marubo, Brazil
Marwari in Gujarat, India
Masa, Chad
Masaba, Uganda
Masakin, Sudan
Masalit, Chad
Masalit, Sudan
Masegi, Papua New Guinea
Masenrempulu, Indonesia
Mashi, Zambia
Massalat, Chad
Mataco, Argentina
Matakam, Cameroon
Matakam, Nigeria
Matawari, Surinam
Matbat, Indonesia
Matengo, Tanzania
Matipuhy-Nahukua, Brazil
Matlatzinca, Atzingo, Mexico
Matumbi, Tanzania
Maure, Mali
Mauri, Niger
Maviha, Mozambique
Mawak, Papua New Guinea
Mawan, Papua New Guinea
Mawes, Indonesia
Maxakali, Brazil
Mayo, Mexico
Mayoruna, Peru
Mba, Zaire
Mbaama, Gabon
Mbai, Chad
Mbai, Central African Republic
Mbala, Zaire
Mbangwe, Zaire
Mbanja, Zaire
Mbati, Central African Republic
Mbe, Nigeria
Mbede, Gabon
Mbembe, Cameroon
Mbembe (Tigong), Nigeria
Mbimu, Cameroon
Mbo, Cameroon
Mbo, Zaire
Mboi, Nigeria
Mbole, Zaire
Mbugwe, Tanzania
Mbukushu, Angola

Mbula-Bwazza, Nigeria
Mbum, Chad
Mbunda, Angola
Mbunga, Tanzania
Mbwela, Angola
Me'en, Ethiopia
Meax, Indonesia
Meban, Sudan
Medlpa, Papua New Guinea
Mehek, Papua New Guinea
Meje, Uganda
Mekeo, Papua New Guinea
Mekwei, Indonesia
Mende, Sierra Leone
Mende, Liberia
Menemo-Mogamo, Cameroon
Mengen, Papua New Guinea
Menka, Cameroon
Menri, Malaysia
Menye, Papua New Guinea
Meos of Rajasthan, India (80)
Mera Mera, Papua New Guinea
Mesengo, Ethiopia
Mesme, Chad
Mesmedje, Chad
Mianmin, Papua New Guinea
Miao, China (81)
Midob, Sudan
Midsivindi, Papua New Guinea
Mien, China (81)
Migabac, Papua New Guinea
Migili, Nigeria
Mikarew, Papua New Guinea
Mimi, Chad
Mina in Madhya Pradesh, India
Minanibai, Papua New Guinea
Mindik, Papua New Guinea
Minduumo, Gabon
Mingat, Soviet Union
Minianka, Mali
Mirdha in Orissa, India
Miri, Sudan
Miriam, Papua New Guinea
Mishmi in Assam, India
Miskito, Nicaragua
Mitang, Papua New Guinea
Mitmit, Papua New Guinea
Mixteco, Amoltepec, Mexico
Mixteco, Apoala, Mexico
Mixteco, Central Puebla, Mexico
Mixteco, Eastern, Mexico
Mixteco, Eastern Putla, Mexico
Mixteco, Huajuapan, Mexico
Mixteco, Silacayoapan, Mexico
Mixteco, Southern Puebla, Mexico
Mixteco, Southern Putla, Mexico
Mixteco, Tututepec, Mexico
Mixteco, Yosondua, Mexico
Mo, Ghana

Mo, Ivory Coast
Moba, Ghana
Moba, Togo
Mober, Nigeria
Modo, Sudan
Moewehafen, Papua New Guinea
Mofu, Cameroon
Mogholi, Afghanistan
Mogum, Chad
Moi, Indonesia
Mokareng, Papua New Guinea
Molof, Indonesia
Momare, Papua New Guinea
Mombum, Indonesia
Momoguns, Malaysia
Momolili, Papua New Guinea
Mon, Burma (81)
Mona, Ivory Coast
Mongondow, Indonesia (81)
Mongour, China
Moni, Indonesia
Monjombo, Central African Republic
Mono, Zaire
Montol, Nigeria
Moors in Mauritania, Mauritania
Moqaddam, Iran
Mor, Indonesia
Morawa, Papua New Guinea
Moreb, Sudan
Moresada, Papua New Guinea
Mori, Indonesia (81)
Morigi, Papua New Guinea
Morima, Papua New Guinea
Moru, Ivory Coast
Moru, Sudan
Morunahua, Peru
Morwap, Indonesia
Mosi, Tanzania
Mossi, Upper Volta (80)
Motilon, Colombia
Motilon, Venezuela
Movima, Bolivia
Moxodi, Papua New Guinea
Mpoto, Malawi
Mpoto, Tanzania
Mubi, Chad
Mugil, Papua New Guinea
Muinane, Colombia
Mukawa, Papua New Guinea
Mulimba, Cameroon
Multani in Punjab, India
Mumbake, Nigeria
Mun, Burma
Muna, Indonesia
Mundang, Chad
Mundari in Assam, India
Mundu, Zaire
Munduruku, Brazil
Mungaka, Cameroon

353

Munggui, Indonesia
Munji-Yidgha, Afghanistan
Munkip, Papua New Guinea
Mup, Papua New Guinea
Mura-Piraha, Brazil
Muria in Andhra Pradesh, India
Murik, Papua New Guinea
Murle, Sudan
Mursi, Ethiopia
Murut, Malaysia
Musak, Papua New Guinea
Musar, Papua New Guinea
Musei, Chad
Musgu, Chad
Muslim Community of Bawku, Ghana
Musom, Papua New Guinea
Muthuvan (Andra Pradesh), India
Mutu, Venezuela
Mutum, Papua New Guinea
Muwasi in Madhya Pradesh, India
Muyuw, Papua New Guinea
Mwanga, Tanzania
Mwatebu, Papua New Guinea
Mwera, Tanzania
Myaung-Ze, Burma
Nabak, Papua New Guinea
Nabi, Indonesia
Nadeb Maku, Brazil
Nafar, Iran
Nafri, Indonesia
Naga, Kalyokengnyu, India
Naga, Mao, India
Naga, Nruanghmei, India
Naga, Sangtam, India
Naga, Sema, India
Naga, Tangkhul, India
Naga, Wancho, India
Nagar in Madhya Pradesh, India
Nagarige, Papua New Guinea
Nagatman, Papua New Guinea
Nagovisi, Papua New Guinea
Nahsi, China
Nahu, Papua New Guinea
Naka, Sudan
Nakama, Papua New Guinea
Nakanai, Papua New Guinea
Nalik, Papua New Guinea
Naltya, Indonesia
Nalu, Guinea
Nama, Namibia
Nama, South Africa
Nambis, Papua New Guinea
Nambu, Papua New Guinea
Namuni, Papua New Guinea
Nanai, China
Nanai, Soviet Union
Nancere, Chad
Nandi, Zaire
Nandu-Tari, Nigeria

Nankina, Papua New Guinea
Nao, Ethiopia
Naoudem, Togo
Nara, Ethiopia
Nara, Papua New Guinea
Naraguta, Nigeria
Narak, Papua New Guinea
Nasioi, Papua New Guinea
Nata, Tanzania
Natemba, Togo
Natioro, Upper Volta
Nauna, Papua New Guinea
Nawuri, Ghana
Nchimburu, Ghana
Nchumbulu, Ghana
Nchumunu, Ghana
Ndaaka, Zaire
Ndali, Tanzania
Ndam, Central African Republic
Ndamba, Tanzania
Ndaonese, Indonesia
Ndau, Zimbabwe
Nde-Nsele-Nta, Nigeria
Ndengereko, Tanzania
Ndjem, Cameroon
Ndo, Zaire
Ndoe, Nigeria
Ndogo, Central African Republic
Ndogo, Sudan
Ndom, Indonesia
Ndomde, Tanzania
Ndoolo, Zaire
Ndop-Bamessing, Cameroon
Ndoro, Cameroon
Nduga, Indonesia
Ndunga, Zaire
Ndunpa Duupa, Cameroon
Negira, Papua New Guinea
Nek, Papua New Guinea
Nekgini, Papua New Guinea
Neko, Papua New Guinea
Nengaya, Papua New Guinea
Nentsy, Soviet Union
Newar in Kathmandu, Nepal (82)
Neyo, Ivory Coast
Ngada, Indonesia
Ngaing, Papua New Guinea
Ngalik, North, Indonesia
Ngalik, Southern, Indonesia
Ngalum, Indonesia
Nganasan, Soviet Union
Ngando, Central African Republic
Ngando, Zaire
Ngasa, Tanzania
Ngayaba, Cameroon
Ngbaka, Zaire
Ngbaka Ma'bo, Central African
  Republic
Ngbaka Ma'bo, Zaire

REGISTRY OF THE UNREACHED

Onjab, Papua New Guinea
Ono, Papua New Guinea
Orang Kanak, Malaysia
Orang Laut, Malaysia
Orang Ulu, Malaysia
Orejon, Peru
Oring, Nigeria
Ormu, Indonesia
Oroch, Soviet Union
Orok, Soviet Union
Orokaiva, Papua New Guinea
Orokolo, Papua New Guinea
Oron, Nigeria
Oronchon, China
Oso, Cameroon
Osum, Papua New Guinea
Ot Danum, Indonesia
Otank, Nigeria
Otomi, Eastern, Mexico
Otomi, Mezquital, Mexico
Otomi, Northwestern, Mexico
Otomi, Southeastern, Mexico
Otomi, State of Mexico, Mexico
Otomi, Tenango, Mexico
Otomi, Texcatepec, Mexico
Otoro, Sudan
Oubi, Ivory Coast
Oyampipuku, Brazil
Oyda, Ethiopia
Pacu, Brazil
Pahari Garhwali (Uttar Pr, India
Pai, Nigeria
Pai, China (81)
Paipai, Mexico
Paite in Assam, India
Paiwa, Papua New Guinea
Pak-Tong, Papua New Guinea
Pakaasnovos, Brazil
Palara, Ivory Coast
Palawano, Philippines
Palawano, Central, Philippines
Palembang, Indonesia
Palenquero, Colombia
Palestinian Refugees, Jordan (83)
Palestinian Refugees, Lebanon
Palikur, Brazil
Paloc, Sudan
Palpa, Nepal
Pambia, Central African Republic
Pame, Central Chichimeca, Mexico
Pame, Chichimeca-Jonaz, Mexico
Pame, Northern, Mexico
Pana, Central African Republic
Panare, Venezuela
Pande, Congo
Pangwa, Tanzania
Panika, India
Pankararu, Brazil
Pankhu, Bangladesh

Pantu, Indonesia
Pao, Burma
Pao in Madhya Pradesh, India
Paongan, China
Papapana, Papua New Guinea
Pape, Cameroon
Papel, Guinea-Bissau
Papuma, Indonesia
Parakanan, Brazil
Paranan, Philippines
Parawen, Papua New Guinea
Pardhan in Andhra Pradesh, India
Pare, Tanzania
Pare, Papua New Guinea
Parengi in Orissa, India
Paresi, Brazil
Parintintin, Brazil
Pashayi, Afghanistan
Pashtuns, Iran (80)
Pasismanua, Papua New Guinea
Patamona, Guyana
Patelia in Gujarat, India
Patep, Papua New Guinea
Pato Tapuia, Brazil
Patpatar, Papua New Guinea
Paumari, Brazil
Pawaia, Papua New Guinea
Pay, Papua New Guinea
Paya, Honduras
Paynamar, Papua New Guinea
Penan, Western, Malaysia (81)
Pende, Zaire
Pengo in Orissa, India
Peremka, Papua New Guinea
Peri, Zaire
Pero, Nigeria
Persians of Iran, Iran (80)
Phu Thai, Laos
Piapoco, Colombia
Piaroa, Venezuela
Pila, Papua New Guinea
Pilaga, Argentina
Pima Bajo, Mexico
Pimbwe, Tanzania
Piratapuyo, Brazil
Piro, Peru
Pisa, Indonesia
Pishagchi, Iran
Piti, Nigeria
Pitu Uluna Salu, Indonesia
Piu, Papua New Guinea
Piya, Nigeria
Pnar in Assam, India
Pocomchi, Eastern, Guatemala
Pocomchi, Western, Guatemala
Podokwo, Cameroon
Podopa, Papua New Guinea
Podzo, Mozambique
Pogolo, Tanzania

REGISTRY OF THE UNREACHED

Sanapana, Paraguay
Sandawe, Tanzania
Sanga, Nigeria
Sanga, Zaire
Sangir, Indonesia
Sangke, Indonesia
Sangu, Gabon
Sangu, Tanzania
Sanio, Papua New Guinea
Santa, China
Santrokofi, Ghana
Sanuma, Venezuela
Sanza, Zaire
Sapo, Liberia
Saposa, Papua New Guinea
Sarakole, Senegal (80)
Saramaccan, Surinam
Sarwa, Chad
Sasak, Indonesia (80)
Sasanis, Iran
Sasaru-Enwan Igwe, Nigeria
Saseng, Papua New Guinea
Satere, Brazil
Sau, Afghanistan
Sau, Papua New Guinea
Sauk, Papua New Guinea
Sause, Indonesia
Sawos, Papua New Guinea
Saya, Nigeria
Secoya, Ecuador
Sekar, Indonesia
Sekayu, Indonesia
Seko, Indonesia
Sekpele, Ghana
Selepet, Papua New Guinea
Selkup, Soviet Union
Semelai, Malaysia
Sempan, Indonesia
Sena, Malawi
Sena, Mozambique
Senggi, Indonesia
Sentani, Indonesia
Senthang, Burma
Sepen, Papua New Guinea
Sere, Sudan
Serere, Senegal (79)
Serere-Non, Senegal
Serere-Sine, Senegal
Seri, Mexico
Serki, Papua New Guinea
Serui-Laut, Indonesia
Setaui Keriwa, Papua New Guinea
Setiali, Papua New Guinea
Seuci, Brazil
Seychellois, Seychelles
Sha, Nigeria
Shahsavans, Iran (80)
Shambala, Tanzania
Shan, Burma

Shan Chinese, Burma
Shanga, Nigeria
Sharanahua, Peru
Sharchagpakha, Bhutan
Shatt, Sudan
Shawiya, Algeria
Sheko, Ethiopia
Shilha, Morocco
Shilluk, Sudan
Shina, Afghanistan
Shinasha, Ethiopia
Shipibo, Peru
Shor, Soviet Union
Shua, Botswana
Shughni, Afghanistan
Shuwa Arabic, Nigeria
Shwai, Sudan
Siagha-Yenimu, Indonesia
Sialum, Papua New Guinea
Siane, Papua New Guinea
Siar, Papua New Guinea
Sibo, China
Sidamo, Ethiopia
Sikanese, Indonesia
Sikhule, Indonesia
Sikkimese, India
Simaa, Zambia
Simog, Papua New Guinea
Sinagen, Papua New Guinea
Sinagoro, Papua New Guinea
Sinaki, Papua New Guinea
Sinasina, Papua New Guinea
Sindamon, Papua New Guinea
Sinsauru, Papua New Guinea
Sio, Papua New Guinea
Siona, Colombia
Sipoma, Papua New Guinea
Sira, Gabon
Sirak, Papua New Guinea
Sirasira, Papua New Guinea
Siri, Nigeria
Siriano, Colombia
Siriono, Bolivia
Siroi, Papua New Guinea
Sisala, Upper Volta
Siwai, Papua New Guinea
Siwu, Ghana
So, Cameroon
Sobei, Indonesia
Sochi, Pakistan
Soga, Uganda
Soh, Laos
Sokorok, Papua New Guinea
Soli, Zambia
Solos, Papua New Guinea
Som, Papua New Guinea
Somahai, Indonesia
Somrai, Chad
Somrai, Central African Republic

358

Sona, Papua New Guinea
Sondwari in M.P., India
Songe, Zaire
Songhai, Mali
Songhai, Niger
Songhai, Upper Volta
Songomeno, Zaire
Songoora, Zaire
Soninke, Gambia
Soninke, Mali
Soninke, Mauritania
Sonjo, Tanzania
Sopi, Sudan
Sora in Orissa, India
Sori-Harengan, Papua New Guinea
Soruba, Benin
South African Students, Lesotho (83)
Sowanda, Indonesia
Sowanda, Papua New Guinea
Students in Cuiaba, Brazil
Su, Cameroon
Sua, Papua New Guinea
Suain, Papua New Guinea
Suba, Tanzania
Subanun,Lapuyan, Philippines
Subi, Tanzania
Sudanese Repatriates, Sudan (83)
Suga, Cameroon
Suganga, Papua New Guinea
Sui, China
Sui, Papua New Guinea
Suk, Kenya
Suki, Papua New Guinea
Suku, Zaire
Sukur, Nigeria
Sukurum, Papua New Guinea
Sulka, Papua New Guinea
Sulung, India
Sumau, Papua New Guinea
Sumba, Indonesia
Sumbawa, Indonesia
Sumbwa, Tanzania
Sumu, Nicaragua
Sungor, Chad
Sunwar, Nepal
Suppire, Mali
Sura, Nigeria
Sursurunga, Papua New Guinea
Surubu, Nigeria
Surui, Brazil
Susu, Guinea-Bissau
Susu, Sierra Leone
Susu, Guinea
Svan, Soviet Union
Swaga, Zaire
Swaka, Zambia
Syuwa, Nepal
Ta-Oi, Laos

Tabar, Papua New Guinea
Tabasaran, Soviet Union
Tabi, Sudan
Tabriak, Papua New Guinea
Tacana, Bolivia
Tadjio, Indonesia
Tadyawan, Philippines
Tafi, Togo
Tagal, Malaysia (81)
Tagula, Papua New Guinea
Tagwana, Ivory Coast
Tahit, Indonesia
Taikat, Indonesia
Tairora, Papua New Guinea
Taiwan-Chinese Un. Stud., Taiwan
Tajik, Iran (80)
Tajik, Afghanistan
Tajik, Soviet Union
Takalubi, Papua New Guinea
Takankar, India
Takemba, Benin
Takestani, Iran
Takia, Papua New Guinea
Tal, Nigeria
Talish, Iran
Talodi, Sudan
Tama, Chad
Tamagario, Indonesia
Taman, Burma
Taman, Papua New Guinea
Tamaria in Bihar, India
Tamazight, Morocco
Tambas, Nigeria
Tambo, Zambia
Tami, Papua New Guinea
Tamil Muslims in Madras, India (82)
Tampulma, Ghana
Tana, Chad
Tana, Central African Republic
Tanahmerah, Indonesia
Tandanke, Senegal
Tandia, Indonesia
Tangale, Nigeria
Tangchangya, Bangladesh
Tangga, Papua New Guinea
Tangu, Papua New Guinea
Tanguat, Papua New Guinea
Tani, Papua New Guinea
Tanimuca-Retuama, Colombia
Tao't Bato, Philippines
Tao-Suame, Papua New Guinea
Taori-Kei, Indonesia
Tara, Indonesia
Tarahumara, Northern, Mexico
Tarahumara, Rocoroibo, Mexico
Tarahumara, Samachique, Mexico
Taram, Cameroon
Tarasco, Mexico
Targum, Israel

Tarof, Indonesia
Tarok, Nigeria
Tarpia, Indonesia
Tat, Soviet Union
Tatars, Soviet Union (80)
Tate, Papua New Guinea
Tatoga, Tanzania
Tauade, Papua New Guinea
Taucouleur, Senegal (80)
Taungyo, Burma
Taungyoe, Burma
Taupota, Papua New Guinea
Taurap, Indonesia
Tavara, Papua New Guinea
Tawi-Pau, Papua New Guinea
Tawr, Burma
Tayaku, Benin
Tchang, Cameroon
Teda, Chad (80)
Teda, Libya
Teda, Niger
Tegali, Sudan
Teimuri, Iran
Teimurtash, Iran
Teke, Eastern, Zaire
Teke, Northern, Congo
Teke, Southwestern, Congo
Telefol, Papua New Guinea
Tembe, Brazil
Tembo, Zaire
Temein, Sudan
Temira, Malaysia
Teop, Papua New Guinea
Tepehua, Huehuetla, Mexico
Tepehua, Pisa Flores, Mexico
Tepehua, Veracruz, Mexico
Tepehuan, Northern, Mexico
Tepehuan, Southeastern, Mexico
Tepeth, Uganda
Tepo, Ivory Coast
Tera, Nigeria
Terebu, Papua New Guinea
Terena, Brazil
Ternatans, Indonesia
Teso, Uganda
Thado in Assam, India
Thai-Ney, Burma
Thakali, Nepal
Thakur, India
Thami, Nepal
Thar in Bihar, India
Tharu, Nepal
Thoi, Sudan
Thuri, Sudan
Tiang, Papua New Guinea
Tibetan Refugees, Switzerland (83)
Ticuna, Brazil
Tidi, Papua New Guinea
Tidorese, Indonesia

Tiefo, Upper Volta
Tiene, Zaire
Tifai, Papua New Guinea
Tigak, Papua New Guinea
Tigon, Cameroon
Tikar, Cameroon
Timbe, Papua New Guinea
Timorese, Indonesia
Tindin, Soviet Union
Tinputz, Papua New Guinea
Tippera, Bangladesh
Tira, Sudan
Tirio, Papua New Guinea
Tirma, Sudan
Tiro, Indonesia
Tiruray, Philippines
Tlapaneco, Malinaltepec, Mexico
Toala, Indonesia
Toaripi, Papua New Guinea
Toba, Argentina
Tobo, Papua New Guinea
Toda in Tamil Nadu, India
Togbo, Zaire
Tojolabal, Mexico
Tokkaru in Tamil Nadu, India
Tol, Honduras
Tombulu, Indonesia
Tomini, Indonesia
Tonda, Papua New Guinea
Tondanou, Indonesia
Tonga, Botswana
Tonga, Malawi
Tonga, Mozambique
Tongwe, Tanzania
Tonsea, Indonesia
Tontemboa, Indonesia
Toraja, Southern, Indonesia (81)
Torau, Papua New Guinea
Torricelli, Papua New Guinea
Totis, India
Totonaco, Northern, Mexico
Totonaco, Oxumatlan, Mexico
Totonaco, Papantla, Mexico
Totonaco, Sierra, Mexico
Totonaco, Yecuatla, Mexico
Towei, Indonesia
Trepo, Ivory Coast
Trio, Surinam
Trique, San Juan Copala, Mexico
Tsaangi, Congo
Tsakhur, Soviet Union
Tsamai, Ethiopia
Tsimane, Bolivia
Tsogo, Gabon
Tsonga, Mozambique
Tsou, Taiwan (81)
Tswa, Mozambique
Tswa, Zimbabwe
Tswana, Namibia

360

361

Wobe, Ivory Coast
Wodani, Indonesia
Woi, Indonesia
Wolio, Indonesia
Wolof, Gambian, Gambia
Wom, Nigeria
Wongo, Zaire
Woro, Sudan
Wumbvu, Gabon
Wungu, Tanzania
Xavante, Brazil
Xerente, Brazil
Xokleng, Brazil
Xu, Namibia
Yafi, Indonesia
Yaghan, Chile
Yagnobi, Soviet Union
Yagua, Peru
Yahadian, Indonesia
Yaka, Zaire
Yakha, Nepal
Yakoma, Central African Republic
Yaly, Indonesia
Yambasa, Cameroon
Yaminahua, Peru
Yanadi in Andhra Pradesh, India
Yandang, Nigeria
Yanga, Togo
Yangbye, Burma
Yans, Zaire
Yao, Mozambique
Yaruro, Venezuela
Yasing, Cameroon
Yaur, Indonesia
Yava, Indonesia
Yazgulyam, Soviet Union
Yei, Indonesia
Yela, Zaire
Yellow Uighur, China
Yelmek, Indonesia
Yerava in Karnataka, India
Yeretuar, Indonesia
Yerukala in A.P., India
Yeskwa, Nigeria
Yidinit, Ethiopia
Yin-Kyar, Burma
Yin-Nett, Burma
Yinchia, Burma
Yinga, Cameroon
Yoabu, Benin
Yogad, Philippines
Yonggom, Indonesia
Yoruk, Turkey
Yos, Burma
Yotafa, Indonesia
Yuana, Venezuela
Yucateco, Guatemala
Yucateco, Mexico
Yukagirs, Soviet Union

Yukpa, Colombia
Yukpa, Venezuela
uku, China
Yulu, Sudan
Yungur, Nigeria
Yuracare, Bolivia
Yurak, Soviet Union
Yuruti, Colombia
Zaghawa, Chad
Zaghawa, Libya
Zaghawa, Sudan
Zanaki, Tanzania
Zangskari in Kashmir, India
Zapoteco, C Sola De Vega, Mexico
Zapoteco, Choapan, Mexico
Zapoteco, E Miahuatlan, Mexico
Zapoteco, E Ocotlan, Mexico
Zapoteco, E Tlacolula, Mexico
Zapoteco, E Zimatlan, Mexico
Zapoteco, Isthmus, Mexico
Zapoteco, Mazaltepec, Mexico
Zapoteco, Miamuatlan, Mexico
Zapoteco, Mitla, Mexico
Zapoteco, N Isthmus, Mexico
Zapoteco, N Ocotlan, Mexico
Zapoteco, N Villa Alta, Mexico
Zapoteco, NE Miahuatlan, Mexico
Zapoteco, NE Yautepec, Mexico
Zapoteco, NW Tehuantepec, Mexico
Zapoteco, Pochutla, Mexico
Zapoteco, S Ejutla, Mexico
Zapoteco, S Villa Alta, Mexico
Zapoteco, SC Zimatlan, Mexico
Zapoteco, SE Miahuatlan, Mexico
Zapoteco, Srra De Juarez, Mexico
Zapoteco, Stgo Xanica, Mexico
Zapoteco, Sto Dom Albarr, Mexico
Zapoteco, SW Ixtlan, Mexico
Zapoteco, Tabaa, Mexico
Zapoteco, Villa Alta, Mexico
Zapoteco, W Miahuatlan, Mexico
Zapoteco, W Ocotlan, Mexico
Zapoteco, W Sola de Vega, Mexico
Zapoteco, W Tlacolula, Mexico
Zapoteco, W Yautepec, Mexico
Zapoteco, W Zimatlan, Mexico
Zapoteco, Yalalag, Mexico
Zaramo, Tanzania
Zari, Nigeria
Zayse, Ethiopia
Zenaga, Mauritania
Zigwa, Tanzania
Zilmamu, Ethiopia
Zimba, Zaire
Zimbabwean Refugees, Zambia
Zimbabwean Refugees, Mozambique
 (83)
Zimbabwean Repatriates, Zimbabwe
 (83)

Index by Religion

This list indicates predominant professed religion, whether or not a majority of those who profess the religion are active practitioners. Many of the groups have more than one professed religion present, but only the one with the largest percentage of followers is indicated in this section.

African Independent

** Dida, Ivory Coast

Ancestor Worship

** Akha, Thailand (79)
   Boat People, Japan
** K'anjobal of San Miguel,
   Guatemala
   Lao Refugees, Argentina
   Urban Elite Vietnamese, United
   States of America

Animism

Abanyom, Nigeria
Abau, Indonesia
Abau, Papua New Guinea
Abie, Papua New Guinea
Abua, Nigeria
Abulas, Papua New Guinea
Achagua, Colombia
Achi, Cubulco, Guatemala
Achi, Rabinal, Guatemala
Acholi, Achual, Peru
Adamawa, Cameroon
Adhola, Uganda
*** Adi, India
** Adja, Benin
Adjora, Papua New Guinea
Aeka, Papua New Guinea
* Afawa, Nigeria (80)
** Afo, Nigeria (80)
Agarabi, Papua New Guinea
Age, Cameroon
Aghem, Cameroon
Aghu, Indonesia
Agob, Papua New Guinea
Agoi, Nigeria
Aguacateco, Guatemala
Aguaruna, Peru
Agwagwune, Nigeria
Aibondeni, Indonesia
Aiku, Papua New Guinea
Aikwakai, Indonesia
Aiome, Papua New Guinea
Aion, Papua New Guinea
Airo-Sumaghaghe, Indonesia

Airoran, Indonesia
Aka, India
Ake, Nigeria
Akpa-Yache, Nigeria
Akrukay, Papua New Guinea
Alago, Nigeria
Alak, Laos
Alamblak, Papua New Guinea
Alatil, Papua New Guinea
Alauagat, Papua New Guinea
Alege, Nigeria
Alor, Kolana, Indonesia (81)
Ama, Papua New Guinea
Amahuaca, Peru
Amaimon, Papua New Guinea
Amanab, Indonesia
Amanab, Papua New Guinea
Amar, Ethiopia
Amarakaeri, Peru
Amasi, Cameroon
Ambai, Indonesia
Ambasi, Papua New Guinea
Amber, Indonesia
Amberbaken, Indonesia
Ambo, Zambia
Ambonese, Netherlands
Ambonese, Indonesia
Amo, Nigeria
Amto, Papua New Guinea
Amuesha, Peru
Anaang, Nigeria
Anal in Manipur, India
Andarum, Papua New Guinea
Andha in Andhra Pradesh, India
Andoque, Colombia
Anem, Papua New Guinea
Angaataha, Papua New Guinea
Angal Heneng, South, Papua New
   Guinea
Angal Heneng, West, Papua New
   Guinea
Angal, East, Papua New Guinea
Angas, Nigeria
Angaua, Papua New Guinea
Anggor, Papua New Guinea
Angoram, Papua New Guinea
Ankave, Papua New Guinea
Ankwe, Nigeria
Anor, Papua New Guinea
Ansus, Indonesia
Anuak, Ethiopia
Anuak, Sudan
Anuki, Papua New Guinea
Apalai, Brazil
** Apatani in Assam, India
Apinaye, Brazil
Apurina, Brazil
Arabela, Peru
Arafundi, Papua New Guinea
Arandai, Indonesia

Arapaco, Brazil
Arapesh, Bumbita, Papua New Guinea
Arapesh, Mountain, Papua New Guinea
Arapesh, Muhiang, Papua New Guinea
Arawe, Papua New Guinea
Arbore, Ethiopia
Arecuna, Venezuela
Argobba, Ethiopia
Arguni, Indonesia
Arifama-Miniafia, Papua New Guinea
Arigibi, Papua New Guinea
Arinua, Papua New Guinea
* Arnatas, India
Arop, Papua New Guinea
Aruop, Papua New Guinea
Arusha, Tanzania
Arutani, Venezuela
Asaro, Papua New Guinea
Asat, Papua New Guinea
Asienara, Indonesia
* Asmat, Indonesia (79)
Assumbo, Cameroon
Asu, Tanzania
Asuri in Bihar, India
Ata, Papua New Guinea
* Ata of Davao, Philippines
Atruahi, Brazil
* Atta, Philippines
* Atye, Ivory Coast
Au, Papua New Guinea
Au ei, Botswana
Aunalei, Papua New Guinea
Auyana, Papua New Guinea
Awa, Papua New Guinea
Awar, Papua New Guinea
Awara, Papua New Guinea
Awin, Papua New Guinea
Awyi, Indonesia
Awyu, Indonesia
** Aymara, Bolivia
Ayoreo, Paraguay
Azera, Papua New Guinea
Baali, Zaire
Babajou, Cameroon
** Babur Thali, Nigeria (80)
Baburiwa, Indonesia
Bada, Nigeria
Badagu in Nilgiri, India
Bafut, Cameroon
Baghati in H.P., India
Baham, Indonesia
Bahawalpuri in M.P., India
Bahinemo, Papua New Guinea
Baibai, Papua New Guinea
Baiga in Bihar, India
Baining, Papua New Guinea

Baka, Cameroon
Baka, Zaire
Bakairi, Brazil
Bakongo Angolan Refugees, Zaire (83)
** Bakuba, Zaire
Bakwele, Congo
Balangaw, Philippines
Balanta, Senegal
Balanta Refugees, Senegal
Balante, Guinea-Bissau
Bali-Vitu, Papua New Guinea
Balong, Cameroon
Balti in Jammu, India
Bam, Papua New Guinea
Bamougoun-Bamenjou, Cameroon
*** Banaro, Papua New Guinea
Bandi, Liberia
Bandjoun, Cameroon
Banen, Cameroon
Bangba, Zaire
Baniwa, Brazil
Banoni, Papua New Guinea
*** Banyarwanda, Rwanda
Banyun, Guinea-Bissau
** Baoule, Ivory Coast
Barabaig, Tanzania (79)
Barai, Papua New Guinea
Barasano, Colombia
Barasano, Northern, Colombia
Barasano, Southern, Colombia
Barau, Indonesia
Bare'e, Indonesia
Bariai, Papua New Guinea
* Bariba, Benin (80)
Bariji, Papua New Guinea
Barim, Papua New Guinea
Barok, Papua New Guinea
Baruga, Papua New Guinea
Baruya, Papua New Guinea
Basakomo, Nigeria
Basari, Guinea
Basari, Senegal
Bashar, Nigeria
Basketo, Ethiopia
*** Basotho, Mountain, Lesotho (79)
* Bassa, Liberia
** Bassa, Nigeria
Batak, Karo, Indonesia
Batak, Simalungun, Indonesia
Batak, Toba, Indonesia
Batanga-Ngolo, Cameroon
Bateg, Malaysia
Bau, Papua New Guinea
Bauwaki, Papua New Guinea
Bavenda, South Africa
Bazigar in Gujarat, India
Bebeli, Papua New Guinea
Bediya in Bihar, India

367

Bedoanas, Indonesia
Bekwarra, Nigeria
Bembe, Zaire
Bembi, Papua New Guinea
Bena, Tanzania
Benabena, Papua New Guinea
Bencho, Ethiopia
Bende, Tanzania
Bene, Cameroon
Benga, Gabon
Berba, Benin
Berik, Indonesia
Berom, Nigeria
Besisi, Malaysia
Bete, India
* Bete, Ivory Coast
Bethen, Cameroon
Betsinga, Cameroon
Bette-Bende, Nigeria
Bharia in Madhya Pradesh, India
** Bhils, India (79)
Bhuiya in Bihar, India
Biafada, Guinea-Bissau
Biak, Indonesia
Biaka, Papua New Guinea
Biangai, Papua New Guinea
Bibling, Papua New Guinea
Biduanda, Malaysia
* Bijogo, Guinea-Bissau
** Bilan, Philippines
Biliau, Papua New Guinea
Bimin, Papua New Guinea
Binahari, Papua New Guinea
Binandere, Papua New Guinea
Binji, Zaire
Binumarien, Papua New Guinea
Birifor, Ghana
Bisa, Zambia
Bisaya, Malaysia (81)
Bisis, Papua New Guinea
Bitara, Papua New Guinea
Bitare, Cameroon
Biyom, Papua New Guinea
Boanaki, Papua New Guinea
Bobe, Cameroon
Bobo Fing, Mali
Bobo Wule, Mali
Bodo in Assam, India
Boghom, Nigeria
Bohutu, Papua New Guinea
Boikin, Papua New Guinea
** Boko, Benin
Bokyi, Nigeria
Bokyi, Cameroon
Bola, Papua New Guinea
Bolondo, Zaire
Bom, Papua New Guinea
Boma, Zaire

Bomboko, Cameroon
Bonerif, Indonesia
Bonggo, Indonesia
Bongili, Congo
Bongu, Papua New Guinea
Bonkeng-Pendia, Cameroon
Bonkiman, Papua New Guinea
** Bontoc, Central, Philippines
     (81)
Bora, Colombia
Borai, Indonesia
* Bororo, Brazil
Bosavi, Papua New Guinea
Bosilewa, Papua New Guinea
Bosngun, Papua New Guinea
Boya, Sudan
Bozo, Mali
Braj in Uttar Pradesh, India
Brao, Laos (79)
Brat, Indonesia
Breri, Papua New Guinea
Bruneis, Malaysia
Bua, Chad
Buang, Central, Papua New Guinea
Buang, Mangga, Papua New Guinea
Bube, Equatorial Guinea
Budibud, Papua New Guinea
Budugum, Cameroon
Bugombe, Zaire
Builsa, Ghana
Buin, Papua New Guinea
Buja, Zaire
Buka-khwe, Botswana
Bukaua, Papua New Guinea
** Bukidnon, Philippines
Bulia, Zaire
Bulu, Papua New Guinea
Buna, Papua New Guinea
Bunabun, Papua New Guinea
Bunak, Indonesia
Bunama, Papua New Guinea
Bunann in Kashmir, India
Bungku, Indonesia
Bunu, Nigeria
Bura, Cameroon
Buraka-Gbanziri, Congo
Burig in Kashmir, India
Burji, Ethiopia
Buru, Indonesia
Burum, Papua New Guinea
Burundian Hutu Refugees,
     Tanzania (83)
Burungi, Tanzania
Busah, Papua New Guinea
Busami, Indonesia
** Busanse, Ghana
Bushmen (Heikum), Namibia
* Bushmen (Hiechware), Zimbabwe
* Bushmen (Kung), Namibia (79)
Bushmen in Botswana, Botswana

Dorobo, Kenya
Dorobo, Tanzania
Doromu, Papua New Guinea
Dorze, Ethiopia
Doura, Papua New Guinea
Duau, Papua New Guinea
Dubu, Indonesia
** Duka, Nigeria
Dukwe Camp Residents, Botswana (83)
Duma, Gabon
* Dumagat, Casiguran, Philippines (81)
Duna, Papua New Guinea
Duru, Cameroon
Dusun, Malaysia (81)
Duvele, Indonesia
Edawapi, Papua New Guinea
Edo, Nigeria
Edo, Efutop, Nigeria
Eggon, Nigeria
Eivo, Papua New Guinea
Ejagham, Nigeria
Ekagi, Indonesia
Ekajuk, Nigeria
Eket, Nigeria
Ekpeye, Nigeria
El Molo, Kenya
Eleme, Nigeria
Elkei, Papua New Guinea
Emai-Iuleha-Ora, Nigeria
Embera, Northern, Colombia
Emerum, Papua New Guinea
Emira, Papua New Guinea
Emumu, Indonesia
Endangen, Papua New Guinea
Enga, Papua New Guinea
Engenni, Nigeria
Enya, Zaire
Epie, Nigeria
Erokwanas, Indonesia
Esan, Nigeria
Eton, Cameroon
Etulo, Nigeria
Evant, Nigeria
Ewage-Notu, Papua New Guinea
Ewenkis, China (81)
Fa D'Ambu, Equatorial Guinea
Fagululu, Papua New Guinea
Faiwol, Papua New Guinea
** Fakai, Nigeria
** Fali, Nigeria
Fas, Papua New Guinea
Fasu, Papua New Guinea
Finungwan, Papua New Guinea
Fipa, Tanzania
Foau, Indonesia
Foi, Papua New Guinea
Foran, Papua New Guinea

Fordat, Indonesia
Fore, Papua New Guinea
Fra-Fra, Ghana
Fula, Macina, Mali
Fula, Peuhala, Mali
Fuliro, Zaire
Fulnio, Brazil
Fungom, Northern, Cameroon
Furu, Zaire
Fuyuge, Papua New Guinea
Fyam, Nigeria
Fyer, Nigeria
Ga-Dang, Philippines
Gade, Nigeria
Gadsup, Papua New Guinea
** Gagre, Pakistan
Gagu, Ivory Coast
Gahuku, Papua New Guinea
Gaikundi, Papua New Guinea
Gaina, Papua New Guinea
Gal, Papua New Guinea
Galler, Laos
Gamei, Papua New Guinea
Gane, Indonesia
Ganglau, Papua New Guinea
Garuh, Papua New Guinea
Garus, Papua New Guinea
Garuwahi, Papua New Guinea
Gawwada, Ethiopia
Gbande, Guinea
Gbari, Nigeria (80)
Gedaged, Papua New Guinea
Gedeo, Ethiopia
Genagane, Papua New Guinea
Gende, Papua New Guinea
Gesa, Indonesia
** Ghimeera, Ethiopia
Ghotuo, Nigeria
Gidar, Cameroon
Gidicho, Ethiopia
Gidra, Papua New Guinea
Gimi, Papua New Guinea
Ginuman, Papua New Guinea
Gio, Liberia
Gira, Papua New Guinea
Girawa, Papua New Guinea
Giri, Papua New Guinea
Giryama, Kenya
Gisei, Cameroon
Gisiga, Cameroon
Gitua, Papua New Guinea
Gizra, Papua New Guinea
** Glavda, Nigeria
Gobasi, Papua New Guinea
Gobato, Ethiopia
Gobeze, Ethiopia
*** Godie, Ivory Coast
Goemai, Nigeria
Gogo, Tanzania
Gogodala, Papua New Guinea

Philippines
Isneg, Karagawan, Philippines
Isoko, Nigeria
Itik, Indonesia
Itonama, Bolivia
Ivbie North-Okpela-Atte, Nigeria
Iwa, Zambia
* Iwaidja, Austria
Iwal, Papua New Guinea
Iwam, Papua New Guinea
Iwam, Sepik, Papua New Guinea
Iwur, Indonesia
Iyon, Nigeria
Iyon, Cameroon
Izarek, Nigeria
** Izi, Nigeria
Jaba, Nigeria
Jabem, Papua New Guinea
Jacalteco, Guatemala
Jamamadi, Brazil
Jamden, Indonesia
Janjero, Ethiopia
Janjo, Nigeria
Jaqaru, Peru
** Jarawa, Nigeria
Jebero, Peru
Jeng, Laos
Jerawa, Nigeria
* Jibu, Nigeria
Jiji, Tanzania
Jimajima, Papua New Guinea
Jinja, Tanzania
Jinuos, China (81)
Jita, Tanzania
Jiye, Uganda
* Jiye, Sudan
Juhai, Malaysia
Jukun, Nigeria
Kaalong, Cameroon
Kaba, Central African Republic
Kaba Dunjo, Central African
  Republic
Kabadi, Papua New Guinea
Kabixi, Brazil
Kabre, Togo
Kabre, Benin
Kachama, Ethiopia
Kadaklan-Barlig Bontoc,
  Philippines
Kadara, Nigeria
Kadazans, Malaysia
Kadiweu, Brazil
Kaeti, Indonesia
** Kafirs, Pakistan (79)
Kagoro, Mali
Kagulu, Tanzania
Kaian, Papua New Guinea
Kaiep, Papua New Guinea
Kaili, Indonesia
Kairi, Papua New Guinea

Kairiru, Papua New Guinea
Kaiwai, Indonesia
Kajang, Indonesia
Kaka, Central African Republic
Kaka, Cameroon
Kakoa, Papua New Guinea
Kakuna-Mamusi, Papua New Guinea
** Kalagan, Philippines
* Kalanga, Botswana
Kalanga, Zimbabwe
Kalinga, Kalagua, Philippines
Kalinga, Limus-Linan,
  Philippines
Kalinga, Quinaang, Philippines
* Kalinga, Southern, Philippines
Kalokalo, Papua New Guinea
Kamano, Papua New Guinea
Kamantan, Nigeria
Kamayura, Brazil
* Kambari, Nigeria (80)
Kambera, Indonesia
Kamberataro, Indonesia
Kamberataro, Papua New Guinea
Kambot, Papua New Guinea
Kami, Tanzania
Kamkam, Cameroon
Kamnum, Papua New Guinea
Kamoro, Indonesia
Kampung Baru, Indonesia
Kamtuk-Gresi, Indonesia
* Kamuku, Nigeria (80)
Kana, Nigeria
Kandas, Papua New Guinea
Kaningra, Papua New Guinea
Kanite, Papua New Guinea
** Kankanay, Central, Philippines
Kankanay, Northern, Philippines
Kanu, Zaire
Kanum, Indonesia
Kanum, Papua New Guinea
Kao, Ethiopia
Kaonde, Zaire
Kaonde, Zambia
Kapin, Papua New Guinea
Kapore, Papua New Guinea
Kapori, Indonesia
Kapriman, Papua New Guinea
Kara, Tanzania
Kara, Papua New Guinea
* Karaboro, Upper Volta
Karam, Papua New Guinea
Karangi, Papua New Guinea
Karas, Indonesia
Kare, Papua New Guinea
Karen, Thailand (79)
Karen, Pwo, Thailand
Kari, Central African Republic
Kari, Zaire
Karipuna Creole, Brazil
Karipuna Do Guapore, Brazil

372

Koyra, Ethiopia
Kpa, Cameroon
Kpelle, Liberia
*** Krahn, Liberia
  * Krahn, Ivory Coast
Kreen-Akakore, Brazil
Krisa, Papua New Guinea
Krongo, Sudan
Krumen, Ivory Coast
Kuatinema, Brazil
Kube, Papua New Guinea
Kubu, Indonesia (80)
Kugbo, Nigeria
Kuikuro, Brazil
Kukele, Nigeria
Kukuwy, Papua New Guinea
Kukwa, Congo
Kulango, Ivory Coast
Kulere, Nigeria
Kumai, Papua New Guinea
Kumam, Uganda
Kuman, Papua New Guinea
Kumdauron, Papua New Guinea
Kumu, Zaire
Kumukio, Papua New Guinea
Kunda, Mozambique
Kunda, Zimbabwe
Kunda, Zambia
Kunda, Zambia
Kuni, Papua New Guinea
Kunua, Papua New Guinea
Kuot, Papua New Guinea
Kupsabiny, Uganda
Kurada, Papua New Guinea
Kurfei, Niger
Kuria, Tanzania
Kurudu, Indonesia
** Kusaasi, Ghana
Kusu, Zaire
Kutin, Cameroon
Kutu, Tanzania
Kwadi, Angola
Kwakum, Cameroon
Kwale, Papua New Guinea
Kwambi, Namibia
Kwanga, Papua New Guinea
Kwangali, Angola
Kwansu, Indonesia
Kwanyama, Angola
Kwanyama, Namibia
Kwaya, Tanzania
Kwe-etshori, Botswana
Kwe-etshori, Zimbabwe
Kwerba, Indonesia
Kwere, Tanzania
Kwese, Zaire
Kwesten, Indonesia
Kwoma, Papua New Guinea
Kwomtari, Papua New Guinea
Labu, Papua New Guinea

Laewomba, Papua New Guinea
  * Lahu, Thailand (81)
Lahu, Burma
Laka, Cameroon
Laka, Central African Republic
Lala, Zambia
Lalia, Zaire
Lamba, Togo
Lamba, Benin
Lamba, Zaire
Lamba, Zambia
** Lambadi in Andhra Pradesh, India
  (81)
Lambi, Cameroon
Lambya, Malawi
Lambya, Tanzania
Lamogai, Papua New Guinea
Langi, Tanzania
  * Lango, Ethiopia
Lango, Uganda
Lanoh, Malaysia
Lara, Indonesia
Latdwalam, Indonesia
Laudje, Indonesia
Lavatbura-Lamusong, Papua New
  Guinea
Lavongai, Papua New Guinea
Lebgo, Nigeria
Leco, Bolivia
Lega, Zaire
Lengua, Northern, Paraguay
Lenje, Zambia
Leron, Papua New Guinea
Letti, Indonesia
Lihir, Papua New Guinea
Liko, Zaire
Lima, Zambia
Limba, Sierra Leone
  * Lisu, Thailand
Lisu, China (81)
Lo, Nigeria
Lobi, Ivory Coast
Lohiki, Papua New Guinea
** Loho Loho, Indonesia
Loinang, Indonesia (81)
Loko, Sierra Leone
Lolo, China (81)
Loma, Guinea
Loma, Liberia
Lombi, Zaire
Lombo, Zaire
Lomwe, Mozambique
Lore, Indonesia
Lou-Baluan-Pam, Papua New Guinea
Lozi, Zimbabwe
Lozi, Zambia
Luano, Zambia
Luchazi, Angola
Luchazi, Zambia
Lue, Cameroon

Matbat, Indonesia
Matengo, Tanzania
Matipuhy-Nahukua, Brazil
Mauri, Niger
Maviha, Mozambique
Mawak, Papua New Guinea
Mawan, Papua New Guinea
Mawes, Indonesia
Maxakali, Brazil
Mayoruna, Peru
Mba, Zaire
Mbaama, Gabon
Mbai, Central African Republic
Mbala, Zaire
Mbangwe, Zaire
Mbanja, Zaire
Mbati, Central African Republic
Mbe, Nigeria
Mbede, Gabon
Mbembe, Cameroon
Mbembe (Tigong), Nigeria
Mbimu, Cameroon
Mbo, Cameroon
Mbo, Zaire
Mbole, Zaire
Mbugwe, Tanzania
Mbukushu, Angola
Mbunda, Angola
Mbunga, Tanzania
Mbwela, Angola
Me'en, Ethiopia
Meax, Indonesia
Meban, Sudan
Medlpa, Papua New Guinea
Mehek, Papua New Guinea
** Mejah, India
Meje, Uganda
Mekeo, Papua New Guinea
Mekwei, Indonesia
** Melanau of Sarawak, Malaysia
(80)
Mende, Sierra Leone
Menemo-Mogamo, Cameroon
Mengen, Papua New Guinea
Menka, Cameroon
Menri, Malaysia
Menye, Papua New Guinea
** Meo, Thailand
Mera Mera, Papua New Guinea
Mianmin, Papua New Guinea
Miao, China (81)
Midsivindi, Papua New Guinea
Mien, China (81)
Migabac, Papua New Guinea
Migili, Nigeria
Mikarew, Papua New Guinea
Minanibai, Papua New Guinea
Mindik, Papua New Guinea
Minduumo, Gabon
Minianka, Mali

Miriam, Papua New Guinea
Mirung, Bangladesh
Mitang, Papua New Guinea
Mitmit, Papua New Guinea
Miya, Nigeria
Mo, Ghana
Moba, Ghana
Moba, Togo
*** Mocha, Ethiopia
Moewehafen, Papua New Guinea
Mofu, Cameroon
Moi, Indonesia
Mokareng, Papua New Guinea
Moken, Burma (79)
Moken of Thailand, Thailand
* Mokole, Benin
Molof, Indonesia
Momare, Papua New Guinea
Mombum, Indonesia
Momoguns, Malaysia
Momolili, Papua New Guinea
Mongondow, Indonesia (81)
Moni, Indonesia
Monjombo, Central African
Republic
Mono, Zaire
Mor, Indonesia
Morawa, Papua New Guinea
Moresada, Papua New Guinea
Morigi, Papua New Guinea
Morima, Papua New Guinea
* Mororata, Bolivia
Morunahua, Peru
Morwap, Indonesia
Mosi, Tanzania
Mossi, Upper Volta (80)
Motilon, Colombia
Motilon, Venezuela
Movima, Bolivia
Moxodi, Papua New Guinea
Mpoto, Malawi
Mpoto, Tanzania
Mru, Bangladesh
Mualthuam, India
Mugil, Papua New Guinea
Muinane, Colombia
Mukawa, Papua New Guinea
Mumuye, Nigeria
** Mundas in Bihar, India
Mundu, Zaire
Munduruku, Brazil
Mungaka, Cameroon
Munggui, Indonesia
Munkip, Papua New Guinea
Mup, Papua New Guinea
Mura-Piraha, Brazil
Murik, Papua New Guinea
Murle, Sudan
* Murngin (Wulamba), Australia
Mursi, Ethiopia

376

Murut, Malaysia
Musak, Papua New Guinea
Musar, Papua New Guinea
Musom, Papua New Guinea
Mutum, Papua New Guinea
Muyuw, Papua New Guinea
Mwanga, Tanzania
Mwatebu, Papua New Guinea
Mwera, Tanzania
Myaung-Ze, Burma
Nabak, Papua New Guinea
Nabi, Indonesia
Nadeb Maku, Brazil
** Nafaara, Ghana (79)
Nafri, Indonesia
Nagarige, Papua New Guinea
Nagatman, Papua New Guinea
Nagovisi, Papua New Guinea
Nahu, Papua New Guinea
Nakama, Papua New Guinea
Nakanai, Papua New Guinea
Nalik, Papua New Guinea
Naltya, Indonesia
Nama, Namibia
Nama, South Africa
Nambikuara, Brazil
Nambis, Papua New Guinea
Nambu, Papua New Guinea
** Nambya, Zimbabwe
Namuni, Papua New Guinea
Nandi, Zaire
Nankina, Papua New Guinea
Nao, Ethiopia
Nara, Papua New Guinea
Naraguta, Nigeria
Narak, Papua New Guinea
Nasioi, Papua New Guinea
Nata, Tanzania
Nauna, Papua New Guinea
Nawuri, Ghana
Nchimburu, Ghana
Ndaaka, Zaire
Ndali, Tanzania
Ndam, Central African Republic
Ndamba, Tanzania
Ndaonese, Indonesia
Ndau, Zimbabwe
Nde-Nsele-Nta, Nigeria
** Ndebele, Zimbabwe (79)
Ndengereko, Tanzania
Ndjem, Cameroon
Ndo, Zaire
Ndoe, Nigeria
Ndogo, Central African Republic
Ndom, Indonesia
Ndomde, Tanzania
Ndoolo, Zaire
Ndop-Bamessing, Cameroon
** Ndoro, Nigeria
Ndoro, Cameroon

Nduga, Indonesia
Ndunga, Zaire
Negira, Papua New Guinea
Nek, Papua New Guinea
Nekgini, Papua New Guinea
Neko, Papua New Guinea
Nengaya, Papua New Guinea
Neyo, Ivory Coast
Ngaing, Papua New Guinea
Ngalik, North, Indonesia
Ngalik, Southern, Indonesia
Ngalum, Indonesia
** Ngamo, Nigeria
Ngando, Central African Republic
Ngando, Zaire
Ngasa, Tanzania
Ngayaba, Cameroon
Ngbaka, Zaire
Ngbaka Ma'bo, Central African
  Republic
Ngbaka Ma'bo, Zaire
Ngbandi, Zaire
Ngbee, Zaire
Ngemba, Cameroon
* Ngen, Ivory Coast
Ngeq, Laos
Ngere, Ivory Coast
Ngi, Cameroon
Ngindo, Tanzania
Ngiri, Zaire
** Ngombe, Zaire
Ngoni, Tanzania
Ngoni, Zambia
Ngulu, Malawi
Ngulu, Tanzania
Ngumba, Cameroon
Ngumbi, Equatorial Guinea
Ngurimi, Tanzania
Nguu, Tanzania
Ngwo, Cameroon
Nharon, Botswana
Nhengatu, Brazil
Nias, Indonesia
Nii, Papua New Guinea
Nilamba, Tanzania
Nimboran, Indonesia
Nimowa, Papua New Guinea
Ninam, Brazil
* Ningerum, Papua New Guinea
Ninggrum, Indonesia
Niningo, Papua New Guinea
Nisa, Indonesia
Nissan, Papua New Guinea
Njadu, Indonesia
Nkem-Nkum, Nigeria
Nkom, Cameroon
* Nkoya, Zambia
Nkutu, Zaire
*** Nocte, India
Nohu, Cameroon

377

Nomane, Papua New Guinea
Nomu, Papua New Guinea
Nondiri, Papua New Guinea
Notsi, Papua New Guinea
* Nouni, Upper Volta
Nsenga, Zimbabwe
Nsenga, Zambia
Nso, Cameroon
Nsongo, Angola
Ntomba, Zaire
Ntrubo, Ghana
* Nuer, Ethiopia
* Nuer, Sudan (79)
Nuk, Papua New Guinea
Numanggang, Papua New Guinea
Nungu, Nigeria
** Nyabwa, Ivory Coast
Nyaheun, Laos
Nyakyusa, Malawi
Nyakyusa, Tanzania
Nyambo, Tanzania
Nyamwezi, Tanzania (80)
Nyaneka, Angola
Nyang, Cameroon
Nyanga-Li, Zaire
Nyanja, Zimbabwe
Nyankole, Uganda
* Nyantruku, Benin
Nyemba, Angola
Nyiha, Tanzania
Nyiha, Zambia
Nyoro, Uganda
Nyuli, Uganda
Nyungwe, Mozambique
Nyzatom, Sudan
Nzakara, Central African
  Republic
Nzebi, Congo
O'ung, Angola
Obanliku, Nigeria
Obolo, Nigeria
Ocaina, Peru
Odual, Nigeria
Odut, Nigeria
Ogbia, Nigeria
Oi, Laos
Okobo, Nigeria
Okpamheri, Nigeria
Oksapmin, Papua New Guinea
Olo, Papua New Guinea
Olulumo-Ikom, Nigeria
Omati, Papua New Guinea
Omie, Papua New Guinea
Onank, Papua New Guinea
Onin, Indonesia
Onjab, Papua New Guinea
Ono, Papua New Guinea
Orang Kanak, Malaysia
Orang Laut, Malaysia
Orang Ulu, Malaysia

Orejon, Peru
Oring, Nigeria
Ormu, Indonesia
Orokaiva, Papua New Guinea
Orokolo, Papua New Guinea
Oron, Nigeria
Oso, Cameroon
Osum, Papua New Guinea
Ot Danum, Indonesia
Otank, Nigeria
Oyampipuku, Brazil
Oyda, Ethiopia
Pacu, Brazil
Pai, Nigeria
Paiwa, Papua New Guinea
Pak-Tong, Papua New Guinea
Pakaasnovos, Brazil
*** Pakabeti of Equator, Zaire
* Pala'wan, Philippines (81)
Palawano, Philippines
Palawano, Central, Philippines
Palenquero, Colombia
Palikur, Brazil
Pambia, Central African Republic
Pana, Central African Republic
Panare, Venezuela
Pande, Congo
Pangwa, Tanzania
** Paniyan of Kerala, India (81)
Pankararu, Brazil
Pantu, Indonesia
Papapana, Papua New Guinea
Pape, Cameroon
Papuma, Indonesia
Parakanan, Brazil
Parawen, Papua New Guinea
Pare, Tanzania
Pare, Papua New Guinea
Paresi, Brazil
Parintintin, Brazil
Pasismanua, Papua New Guinea
Patep, Papua New Guinea
Pato Tapuia, Brazil
Patpatar, Papua New Guinea
Paumari, Brazil
Pawaia, Papua New Guinea
Pay, Papua New Guinea
Paya, Honduras
Paynamar, Papua New Guinea
Penan, Western, Malaysia (81)
Pende, Zaire
Peremka, Papua New Guinea
Peri, Zaire
Piapoco, Colombia
Piaroa, Venezuela
** Pila, Benin
Pila, Papua New Guinea
Pilaga, Argentina
Pimbwe, Tanzania
Piratapuyo, Brazil

378

Setaui Keriwa, Papua New Guinea
Setiali, Papua New Guinea
Seuci, Brazil
Sha, Nigeria
Shambala, Tanzania
Shanga, Nigeria
Sharanahua, Peru
Sheko, Ethiopia
Shinasha, Ethiopia
Shipibo, Peru
** Shirishana, Brazil
Shua, Botswana
Siagha-Yenimu, Indonesia
Sialum, Papua New Guinea
Siane, Papua New Guinea
Siar, Papua New Guinea
Sikanese, Indonesia
Sikhule, Indonesia
Simaa, Zambia
Simba, Bolivia
Simog, Papua New Guinea
Sinagen, Papua New Guinea
Sinagoro, Papua New Guinea
Sinaki, Papua New Guinea
Sinasina, Papua New Guinea
Sindamon, Papua New Guinea
Sinsauru, Papua New Guinea
Sio, Papua New Guinea
Siona, Colombia
Sipoma, Papua New Guinea
Sira, Gabon
Sirak, Papua New Guinea
Sirasira, Papua New Guinea
Siriano, Colombia
Siriono, Bolivia
Siroi, Papua New Guinea
** Sisaala, Ghana
Siwai, Papua New Guinea
So, Cameroon
Sobei, Indonesia
Soga, Uganda
Soh, Laos
* Soh, Thailand (81)
Sokorok, Papua New Guinea
Soli, Zambia
Solos, Papua New Guinea
Som, Papua New Guinea
* Somahai, Indonesia
Somahai, Indonesia
** Somba, Benin
Somrai, Central African Republic
Sona, Papua New Guinea
Songe, Zaire
Songhai, Mali
Songomeno, Zaire
Songoora, Zaire
Sonjo, Tanzania
Sori-Harengan, Papua New Guinea
Soruba, Benin
Sowanda, Indonesia

Sowanda, Papua New Guinea
Su, Cameroon
Sua, Papua New Guinea
Suain, Papua New Guinea
Suba, Tanzania
** Subanen (Tuboy), Philippines
** Subanen, Sindangan, Philippines
(80)
Subi, Tanzania
Sudanese Repatriates, Sudan (83)
Suga, Cameroon
Suganga, Papua New Guinea
** Sugut, Malaysia
Sui, Papua New Guinea
Suk, Kenya
Suki, Papua New Guinea
Suku, Zaire
Sukurum, Papua New Guinea
Sulka, Papua New Guinea
Sumau, Papua New Guinea
Sumba, Indonesia
Sumbwa, Tanzania
Suppire, Mali
** Suri, Ethiopia
Sursurunga, Papua New Guinea
Surui, Brazil
Swaga, Zaire
Swaka, Zambia
** Swazi, South Africa
** T'boli, Philippines (81)
T'in, Thailand (81)
Ta-Oi, Laos
Tabar, Papua New Guinea
Tabi, Sudan
Tabriak, Papua New Guinea
Tacana, Bolivia
Tadjio, Indonesia
Tadyawan, Philippines
Tagal, Malaysia (81)
** Tagbanwa, Aborlan, Philippines
*** Tagin, India
Tagula, Papua New Guinea
Tahit, Indonesia
Taikat, Indonesia
Tairora, Papua New Guinea
Takalubi, Papua New Guinea
Takemba, Benin
Takia, Papua New Guinea
Tamagario, Indonesia
Taman, Papua New Guinea
Tambas, Nigeria
Tambo, Zambia
Tami, Papua New Guinea
Tampulma, Ghana
Tana, Central African Republic
Tanahmerah, Indonesia
Tandanke, Senegal
Tandia, Indonesia
Tangga, Papua New Guinea
** Tangsa, India

Vaikino, Indonesia
Vale, Central African Republic
Venda, Zimbabwe
*** Vere, Nigeria
Vere, Cameroon
Vidunda, Tanzania
Vinza, Tanzania
Vute, Nigeria
Wa, Burma
Wabo, Indonesia
Waimiri, Brazil
Waiwai, Brazil
** Wajita, Tanzania
Wala, Ghana
Walamo, Ethiopia
Wambon, Indonesia
** Wanchoo, India
Wanda, Tanzania
Wandamen, Indonesia
Wandji, Gabon
Wanggom, Indonesia
Wanji, Tanzania
Wano, Indonesia
Wapishana, Brazil
Wapishana, Venezuela
Warao, Venezuela
Ware, Mali
Warembori, Indonesia
Waris, Indonesia
* Warjawa, Nigeria
Warkay-Bipim, Indonesia
Waropen, Indonesia
Wasi, Tanzania
Watchi, Togo
Waura, Brazil
Wayana, Surinam
* Wazinza, Tanzania
Wetawit, Ethiopia
Wewewa, Indonesia
Widekum, Cameroon
** Wimbum, Cameroon
Wobe, Ivory Coast
Wodani, Indonesia
Woi, Indonesia
Wongo, Zaire
Wumbvu, Gabon
Wungu, Tanzania
Xavante, Brazil
Xerente, Brazil
Xokleng, Brazil
Xu, Namibia
Yafi, Indonesia
Yagua, Peru
Yahadian, Indonesia
Yaka, Zaire
Yakoma, Central African Republic
** Yala, Nigeria
Yaly, Indonesia
Yambasa, Cameroon
Yaminahua, Peru

* Yanomamo, Brazil (79)
Yanomamo, Venezuela
Yans, Zaire
** Yao, Thailand (79)
* Yao Refugees from Laos, Thailand
Yaoure, Ivory Coast
Yaruro, Venezuela
Yasing, Cameroon
Yaur, Indonesia
Yava, Indonesia
** Yei, Botswana
Yei, Indonesia
Yela, Zaire
Yelmek, Indonesia
Yeretuar, Indonesia
Yidinit, Ethiopia
Yin-Kyar, Burma
Yin-Nett, Burma
Yinga, Cameroon
Yoabu, Benin
Yogad, Philippines
Yonggom, Indonesia
Yotafa, Indonesia
Yuana, Venezuela
Yucateco, Guatemala
Yukpa, Colombia
Yukpa, Venezuela
Yuracare, Bolivia
Yuruti, Colombia
Zanaki, Tanzania
** Zaranda Hill Peoples, Nigeria
Zayse, Ethiopia
Zemi Naga of Assam, India (81)
Zigwa, Tanzania
Zilmamu, Ethiopia
Zimba, Zaire
Zimbabwean Refugees, Mozambique
(83)
Zoliang, India
Zowla, Ghana
Zulu, Malawi
Zuni, United States of America

Bahaism

Bahais in Teheran, Iran (82)
** Iranian Bahai Refugees, Pakistan
(83)

Buddhism

* Barbers in Tokyo, Japan (82)

Bhutias, Bhutan
Danu, Burma
Government officials, Thailand
Hkun, Burma
Japanese in Brazil, Brazil (79)
Kachin in Shan State, Burma
Kae Sung Natives in Seoul,
    Korea, Republic of (82)
Kalmytz, Soviet Union
Khmer Refugees, Belgium (83)
** Lahaulis in Punjab, India
* Lao, Laos (79)
** Lepers of N.E. Thailand,
    Thailand
Newar in Kathmandu, Nepal (82)
Palaung, Burma (79)
Pao, Burma
* Ramkamhaeng Un. Students,
    Thailand
Shan, Burma
* Sherpa, Nepal
Sinhalese, Sri Lanka
* Slum Dwellers of Bangkok,
    Thailand
Soka Gakkai Believers, Japan
Taungyoe, Burma
* Thai University Students,
    Thailand (81)
* Tibetan Refugees, India (83)
Tibetan Refugees, Switzerland
    (83)
Tibetans in Bhutan, Bhutan (81)
Vietnamese, Laos
** Vietnamese Refugees, United
    States of America
** Vietnamese Refugees, Thailand
Vietnamese Refugees, Korea,
    Republic of

Buddhist-Animist

* Ami, Taiwan (81)
** Banai, Bangladesh
Bote-Majhi, Nepal
Buriat, Soviet Union
Byangsi, Nepal
* Cambodians, Thailand
* Central Thailand Farmers,
    Thailand (81)
* Chakmas of Mizoram, India (81)
* Chang-Pa of Kashmir, India (81)
Chaudangsi, Nepal
Chaungtha, Burma
Chepang, Nepal
Chin, Asho, Burma
Chin, Falam, Burma

Chin, Haka, Burma
Chin, Khumi, Burma
Chin, Ngawn, Burma
Chin, Tiddim, Burma
Chinbok, Burma
Dai, Burma
Darai, Nepal
Darmiya, Nepal
Dhimal, Nepal
Evenks, Soviet Union
Ghale Gurung, Nepal
Gheko, Burma
Hallam, Burma
*** Hmong Refugees, United States of
    America (83)
*** Hmong Women at Ban Vinai,
    Thailand (83)
Hrangkhol, Burma
Intha, Burma
Janggali, Nepal
Jirel, Nepal
Kebumtamp, Bhutan
Kham, Nepal
** Khmer Refugees, Thailand
Khmer Refugees, Laos (83)
** Khmer Rfgs, Canada (83)
Khmer Unaccd Minors, Thailand
    (83)
Kokant, Burma
* Kui, Thailand
Lama, Burma
* Lao Refugees, Thailand
* Lao Refugees, Spain (83)
Lawa, Eastern, Thailand (81)
Lawa, Mountain, Thailand
** Lepers of Cen. Thailand,
    Thailand (81)
Lhomi, Nepal
Loven, Laos (81)
Lu, China
Maghi, Burma
Majhi, Nepal
Mon, Burma (81)
Monpa, India
Mun, Burma
Norra, Burma
Pai, China (81)
Palpa, Nepal
Phu Thai, Laos
Purum, Burma
Rai, Khaling, Nepal
Rai, Kulunge, Nepal
Rai, Thulunge, Nepal
Ralte, Burma
Rangkas, Nepal
Riang-Lang, Burma
Senthang, Burma
Shan, Thailand
Shan Chinese, Burma
Sharchagpakha, Bhutan

383

Street Vendors in Saigon, Vietnam (82)
Sunwar, Nepal
Syuwa, Nepal
Taman, Burma
Taungyo, Burma
Tawr, Burma
Thai-Ney, Burma
Thakali, Nepal
Thami, Nepal
Tuvinian, Soviet Union
Yakha, Nepal
Yangbye, Burma
Yinchia, Burma
Yos, Burma
Zome, Burma

Christo-Paganism

Abaknon, Philippines
Aeta, Philippines
Akawaio, Guyana
Alangan, Philippines
** Ampeeli, Papua New Guinea
Amuzgo, Guerrero, Mexico
Amuzgo, Oaxaca, Mexico
** Apayao, Philippines
Arawak, Guyana
Ati, Philippines
Aymara, Carangas, Chile
*** Azteca, Mexico (79)
*** Bagobo, Philippines
** Balangao, Philippines
Bantuanon, Philippines
Batak, Palawan, Philippines
** Bidayuh of Sarawak, Malaysia (81)
*** Bipim, Indonesia
** Black Caribs, Belize, Belize (79)
** Black Caribs, Guatemala, Guatemala
** Black Caribs, Honduras, Honduras
** Bontoc, Southern, Philippines
Buglere, Panama
Buhid, Philippines
Caluyanhon, Philippines
*** Cebu, Middle-Class, Philippines
*** Ch'ol Sabanilla, Mexico
Chamorro, Turks and Caicos Islands
Chamula, Mexico (79)
Chatino, Nopala, Mexico
Chatino, Panixtlahuaca, Mexico
Chatino, Tataltepec, Mexico
Chatino, Yaitepec, Mexico

Chatino, Zacatepec, Mexico
Chatino, Zenzontepec, Mexico
** Chayahuita, Peru
Chinanteco, Tepinapa, Mexico
Chinanteco, Ayotzintepec, Mexico
Chinanteco, Chiltepec, Mexico
Chinanteco, Comaltepec, Mexico
Chinanteco, Lalana, Mexico
Chinanteco, Lealao, Mexico
Chinanteco, Ojitlan, Mexico
Chinanteco, Palantla, Mexico
Chinanteco, Quiotepec, Mexico
Chinanteco, Sochiapan, Mexico
Chinanteco, Tepetotutla, Mexico
Chinanteco, Usila, Mexico
Chocho, Mexico
Chuj, San Mateo Ixtatan, Mexico
Chulupe, Paraguay
Cocopa, Mexico
Cora, Mexico
Cuicateco, Tepeuxila, Mexico
Cuicateco, Teutila, Mexico
Cuyonon, Philippines
Davaweno, Philippines
Djuka, Surinam
* Favelados-Rio de Janeiro, Brazil (82)
Gagauzes, Soviet Union
Galla of Bucho, Ethiopia
* Guanano, Colombia (79)
Guarayu, Bolivia
Guarojio, Mexico
Guatemalan Refugees, Mexico
Gypsies, Soviet Union
Hanonoo, Philippines
Huasteco, Mexico
** Huave, Mexico
Huichol, Mexico
Huistan Tzotzil, Mexico
* Ibataan, Philippines
Inga, Colombia
Iraya, Philippines
Itawit, Philippines
Itneg, Adasen, Philippines
Itneg, Binongan, Philippines
Itneg, Masadiit, Philippines
Ixil, Guatemala
Jemez Pueblo, United States of America
** Jivaro (Achuara), Venezuela
Kaagan, Philippines
* Kaffa, Ethiopia (80)
Kaingang, Brazil
** Kalinga,Northern, Philippines (81)
** Kekchi, Guatemala
Kikapoo, Mexico
Kinaray-A, Philippines
Komi-Permyat, Soviet Union
Komi-Zyrian, Soviet Union

385

Zapoteco, Mazaltepec, Mexico
Zapoteco, Miamuatlan, Mexico
Zapoteco, Mitla, Mexico
Zapoteco, N Isthmus, Mexico
Zapoteco, N Ocotlan, Mexico
Zapoteco, N Villa Alta, Mexico
Zapoteco, NE Miahuatlan, Mexico
Zapoteco, NE Yautepec, Mexico
Zapoteco, NW Tehuantepec, Mexico
Zapoteco, Pochutla, Mexico
Zapoteco, S Ejutla, Mexico
Zapoteco, S Villa Alta, Mexico
Zapoteco, SC Zimatlan, Mexico
Zapoteco, SE Miahuatlan, Mexico
Zapoteco, Srra De Juarez, Mexico
Zapoteco, Stgo Xanica, Mexico
Zapoteco, Sto Dom Albarr, Mexico
Zapoteco, SW Ixtlan, Mexico
Zapoteco, Tabaa, Mexico
Zapoteco, Villa Alta, Mexico
Zapoteco, W Miahuatlan, Mexico
Zapoteco, W Ocotlan, Mexico
Zapoteco, W Sola de Vega, Mexico
Zapoteco, W Tlacolula, Mexico
Zapoteco, W Yautepec, Mexico
Zapoteco, W Zimatlan, Mexico
Zapoteco, Yalalag, Mexico
Zimbabwean Refugees, Zambia
Zinacantecos, Mexico (79)
Zoque, Chimalapa, Mexico
Zoque, Copainala, Mexico
Zoque, Francisco Leon, Mexico
Zoque, Tabasco, Mexico

Folk Religion

* Alars, India
** Apartment Residents-Seoul,
   Korea, Republic of
* Deviant Youth in Taipei, Taiwan
   (82)
   Druzes, Israel (79)
* Gabbra, Ethiopia
   Gabbra, Kenya
* Gypsies in Spain, Spain (79)
   Haitian Refugees, United States
   of America (83)
   Indust.Workers Yongdungpo,
   Korea, Republic of
* Koreans of Japan, Japan
* Prisoners in Antananarivo,
   Madagascar (82)
   Romany, Turkey
** Vietnamese Refugees, Australia

Hindu-Animist

Abujmaria (Madhya Pradesh, India
Aimol in Assam, India
Ajmeri in Rajasthan, India
Aranadan in Tamil Nadu, India
Bagelkhandi in M.P., India
Balinese, Indonesia
Bangaru in Punjab, India
Bhakta, India
Bhattri, India
Bhilala, India
Bhoyari in Maharashtra, India
Bhumij in Assam, India
Bhunjia in Madhya Pradesh, India
Bijori in Bihar, India
Binjhwari in Bihar, India
Birhor in Bihar, India
** Bodo Kachari, India
Cham, Viet Nam
Chamari in Madhya Pradesh, India
Chameali in H.P., India
Chenchu in Andhra Pradesh, India
Chodhari in Gujarat, India
Churahi in H.P., India
** Dhodias, India
Dhurwa, India
Dorlin in Andhra Pradesh, India
** Dubla, India
Gadaban in Andhra Pradesh, India
Gaddi in Himachal Pradesh, India
Galong in Assam, India
Gamti in Gujarat, India
Gangte in Assam, India
Gawari in Andhra Pradesh, India
Grasia in Gujarat, India
** Hajong, Bangladesh
Halbi in Madhya Pradesh, India
Harauti in Rajasthan, India
Ho in Bihar, India
Holiya in Madhya Pradesh, India
** Indian Tamils - Colombo, Sri
   Lanka (82)
Jagannathi in A.P., India
Jatapu in Andhra Pradesh, India
Jaunsari in Uttar Pradesh, India
Kadar in Andhra Pradesh, India
Kahluri in Andamans, India
Kaikadi in Maharashtra, India
Kamar in Madhya Pradesh, India
Kanikkaran in Kerala, India
Kanjari in Andhra Pradesh, India
** Karbis, India
Karmali in Dihar, India
Katakari in Gujarat, India
Kawar in Madhya Pradesh, India
Keer in Madhya Pradesh, India
Khandesi, India

Kharia in Bihar, India
Khirwar in Madhya Pradesh, India
Khowar, India
Kisan in Bihar, India
Kishanganjia in Bihar, India
Kishtwari in Jammu, India
** Koch, Bangladesh
Koda in Bihar, India
** Kohli, Wadiara, Pakistan
Kol in Assam, India
** Kolam, India
Kom in Manipur, India
Konda-Dora (Andra Pradesh, India
Konkani in Gujarat, India
Koraga in Kerala, India
Korwa in Bihar, India
Kota in Tamil Nadu, India
Kotia in Andhra Pradesh, India
Koya in Andhra Pradesh, India
Kudiya, India
* Kuknas, India
Kumauni in Assam, India
Kupia in Andhra Pradesh, India
Kuruba in Tamil Nadu, India
Kurux in Bihar, India
Kuvi in Orissa, India
Lodhi in Bihar, India
Lushai in Assam, India
** Magar, Nepal
Mahali in Assam, India
Maithili, Nepal
Majhwar in Madhya Pradesh, India
Malakkaras of Kerala, India (81)
Malankuravan in Kerala, India
Malapandaram in Kerala, India
Malaryan in Kerala, India
Mali in Andhra Pradesh, India
Malki in Bihar, India
Malpaharia in Assam, India
Malvi in Madhya Pradesh, India
Manna-Dora in A.P., India
Mannan in Kerala, India
Mara in Assam, India
Maria in Andhra Pradesh, India
Marwari in Gujarat, India
** Mawchis, India
** Miching, India
Mina in Madhya Pradesh, India
Mirdha in Orissa, India
Mishmi in Assam, India
Multani in Punjab, India
Mundari in Assam, India
Muria in Andhra Pradesh, India
Muthuvan (Andra Pradesh), India
Muwasi in Madhya Pradesh, India
Naga, Kalyokengnyu, India
Nagar in Madhya Pradesh, India
Nihali in Madhya Pradesh, India
Ojhi in Madhya Pradesh, India
Ollari in Orissa, India

Ong in Andamans, India
Pahari Garhwali (Uttar Pr, India
Paite in Assam, India
Panika, India
Pardhan in Andhra Pradesh, India
Parengi in Orissa, India
Patelia in Gujarat, India
Pengo in Orissa, India
Pnar in Assam, India
Rabha in Assam, India
* Rai, Danuwar, Nepal
Rajbansi, Nepal
Sadan in Andamans, India
Sondwari in M.P., India
Takankar, India
Tengger, Indonesia
Thakur, India
Thar in Bihar, India
Toda in Tamil Nadu, India
Tokkaru in Tamil Nadu, India
Tugara, India
Ullatan in Kerala, India
Urali in Kerala, India
Vishavan in Kerala, India
Waddar in Andhra Pradesh, India
Wagdi in Rajasthan, India
Yanadi in Andhra Pradesh, India
Yerava in Karnataka, India
Yerukala in A.P., India
Zangskari in Kashmir, India

Hindu-Buddhist

Awadhi, Nepal
Kanauri in Uttar Pradesh, India
Khamti in Assam, India
Labans, India
Labhani in Andhra Pradesh, India
Ladakhi in Jammu, India
Lalung in Assam, India
** Lepcha, Sikkim
Naga, Mao, India
Naga, Nruanghmei, India
Naga, Sangtam, India
Naga, Tangkhul, India
Naga, Wancho, India
* Newari, Nepal
Nimadi in Madhya Pradesh, India
Pao in Madhya Pradesh, India
Rai, Nepal
Riang in Assam, India
Sikkimese, India
Sulung, India
* Tamang, Nepal
Tamaria in Bihar, India
Thado in Assam, India

Vaiphei in Assam, India
Zome in Manipur, India

Hinduism

Adiyan in Kerala, India
Agariya in Bihar, India
Anga in Bihar, India
Arya in Andhra Pradesh, India
Babri, India
Bagri, Pakistan
Bajania, Pakistan (79)
Balmiki, Pakistan
Bareli in Madhya Pradesh, India
Bathudi in Bihar, India
** Bhil, Pakistan
* Bhojpuri, Nepal
Bondo in Orissa, India
* Gorkha, India
Gujarati, United Kingdom
Gurung, Nepal
Indians in Dubai, United Arab
Emirates (82)
Indians in Fiji, Fiji (79)
* Indians In Rhodesia, Zimbabwe
** Indians, East, Trinidad and
Tobago (79)
Iravas in Kerala, India
*** Irulas in Kerala, India
Jharia in Orissa, India
Juang in Orissa, India
Kachchi in Andhra Pradesh, India
Khasi in Assam, India
** Kohli, Kutchi, Pakistan
** Kohli, Parkari, Pakistan
** Kohli, Tharadari, Pakistan
* Kudisai Vagh Makkal, India
** Kuluis in Himachal Prades, India
(81)
* Labourers of Jhoparpatti, India
Malavedan in Kerala, India
Mangs in Maharashtra, India
*** Matharis, India
** Meghwar, Pakistan (79)
* Meitei, India (79)
** Nepalese in India, India
Od, Pakistan
* Rava in Assam, India
** Saiva Vellala, India
* Shourastra in Tamil Nadu, India
* Sindhis of India, India
Sochi, Pakistan
Sora in Orissa, India
Tamil (Ceylonese), Sri Lanka
* Tamil in Yellagiri Hills, India
** Tamil Laborers in Bombay, India
(82)

*** Tamil Plantation Workers,
Malaysia
* Tamils (Indian), Malaysia
** Tamils (Indian), Sri Lanka (79)
Tharu, Nepal
Totis, India
Vagari, Pakistan

Islam

Abazin, Soviet Union
Abialang, Sudan
Abkhaz, Turkey
Abong, Nigeria
Abu Leila, Sudan
Achehnese, Indonesia (80)
Acheron, Sudan
Achipa, Nigeria
Adygei, Soviet Union
** Afghan Refugees (NWFP), Pakistan
(83)
Afitti, Sudan
** African Students in Cairo, Egypt
Afshars, Iran
Agajanis, Iran
Agul, Soviet Union
Ahir in Maharashtra, India
** Ahl-i-Haqq in Iran, Iran (79)
Ahmadis in Lahore, Pakistan (82)
Aja, Sudan
Alaba, Ethiopia
* Alawites, Syria (79)
* Albanian Muslims, Albania (80)
* Albanians in Yugoslavia,
Yugoslavia
Algerian Arabs in France, France
* Anatolian Turks-Istanbul, Turkey
(82)
Ansar Sudanese Refugees,
Ethiopia (83)
Ara, Indonesia
Arab Immigrants in Bangui,
Central African Republic (82)
Arab-Jabbari (Kamesh), Iran
Arab-Shaibani (Kamesh), Iran
** Arabs in New Orleans, United
States of America (82)
Arabs of Khuzestan, Iran
Arawa, Nigeria
* Asian Students, Philippines
Aten, Nigeria
Atoc, Sudan
Atuot, Sudan
Avukaya, Sudan
Awngi, Ethiopia
Ayu, Nigeria

** Azerbaijani, Afghanistan
Azerbaijani Turks, Iran (80)
Bachama, Nigeria
Bade, Nigeria
Badyara, Guinea-Bissau
Baharlu (Kamesh), Iran
Bai, Sudan
Bajau, Indonesian, Indonesia
Bakhtiaris, Iran (80)
Balkars, Soviet Union
Baluchi, Iran (80)
Bambara, Mali
Bambuka, Nigeria
Bandawa-Minda, Nigeria
Banga, Nigeria
Banggai, Indonesia
Barambu, Sudan
Bari, Sudan
Bashgali, Afghanistan
Bashkir, Soviet Union (80)
* Batak, Angkola, Indonesia (80)
Batu, Nigeria
Baushi, Nigeria
Bawm, Bangladesh
Bayats, Iran
Beja, Ethiopia
Beja, Sudan
Bengali Refugees, Assam, India
Bengalis in London, United
  Kingdom (82)
Bengkulu, Indonesia
Bhatneri, India
Bilen, Ethiopia
Bimanese, Indonesia
Binawa, Nigeria
Binga, Sudan
Bingkokak, Indonesia
Biti, Sudan
Bole, Nigeria
Bondei, Tanzania
Bongo, Sudan
Bor Gok, Sudan
* Bosnian, Yugoslavia (80)
Bovir-Ahmadi, Iran
Brahui, Pakistan
Bual, Indonesia
Buduma, Nigeria
Burak, Nigeria
Burmese Muslim Refugees,
  Bangladesh (83)
Burun, Sudan
Busa, Nigeria (80)
Butawa, Nigeria
Bviri, Sudan
Cape Malays in Cape Town, South
  Africa (82)
Chadian Refugees, Nigeria (83)
Chadian Rfgs, Cameroon (83)
Chaghatai, Afghanistan
* Cham Refugees from Kampuc,

Malaysia (83)
Cherkess, Soviet Union
Chinese in Saudi Arabia, Saudi
  Arabia
Chinese Muslims, Taiwan (81)
Chitralis, Pakistan (79)
Circassian, Turkey
Circassians in Amman, Jordan
  (82)
Dadiya, Nigeria
Dair, Sudan
Daju of West Kordofan, Sudan
Dargin, Soviet Union
Dawoodi Muslims, India
Daza, Chad
Deccani Muslims, India
Deccani Muslims-Hyderabad, India
  (82)
Dendi, Benin
Deno, Nigeria
Dera, Nigeria
* Dewein, Liberia
Digo, Kenya
Dinka, Agar, Sudan
Diola, Guinea-Bissau (80)
Dirya, Nigeria
Divehi, Maldives (80)
Dongjoi, Sudan
Dongo, Sudan
Duguir, Nigeria
Duguza, Nigeria
Dungan, Soviet Union
Dyerma, Nigeria
Eritrean Refugees, Sudan (83)
** Eritrean Refugees, Djibouti (83)
Fali, Cameroon
Feroge, Sudan
Fula, Guinea
Fula, Sierra Leone
Fulah, Upper Volta
Fungor, Sudan
Galambi, Nigeria
Galeshis, Iran
Galla, Harar, Ethiopia
Gawar-Bati, Afghanistan
Gbaya, Nigeria
Gbaya-Ndogo, Sudan
Gbazantche, Benin
Gberi, Sudan
Geji, Nigeria
Gera, Nigeria
Geruma, Nigeria
Ghol, Sudan
Ghulfan, Sudan
Gilakis, Iran
Gorontalo, Indonesia
Goudari, Iran
Guinean Refugees, Gabon
Gujuri, Afghanistan
Gumuz, Sudan

389

REGISTRY OF THE UNREACHED

Gure-Kahugu, Nigeria
Guruntum-Mbaaru, Nigeria
Gwari Matai, Nigeria
Gypsies in Jerusalem, Israel (82)
Gypsies in Yugoslavia, Yugoslavia
** Hadrami, Yemen, Democratic
Harari, Ethiopia
** Hazara in Kabul, Afghanistan (82)
Heiban, Sudan
Hezareh, Iran
Hui, China (80)
** Hunzakut, Pakistan (79)
Hwana, Nigeria
Hyam, Nigeria
Ikulu, Nigeria
Inallu, Iran
Ingushes, Soviet Union
Iraqi Kurd Refugees, Iran (83)
Jamshidis, Iran
Jara, Nigeria
Jati, Afghanistan
** Javanese of Pejompongan, Indonesia
Jera, Nigeria
Jimbin, Nigeria
** Jimini, Ivory Coast
Kabyle, Algeria (79)
Kadugli, Sudan
Kagoma, Nigeria
Kaibu, Nigeria
Kaka, Nigeria
Kamo, Nigeria
Kanga, Sudan
Kanuri, Nigeria (80)
Karakalpak, Soviet Union (80)
Karekare, Nigeria
Kariya, Nigeria
Karko, Sudan
** Kashmiri Muslims, India (79)
Katab, Nigeria
Katcha, Sudan
Katla, Sudan
Kazakhs, Iran (80)
Keiga, Sudan
Keiga Jirru, Sudan
Khalaj, Iran
Khasonke, Mali
Khojas, Agha Khani, India
Kilba, Nigeria
Kirgiz, Afghanistan
Kirgiz, China
Kirgiz Afghans in Turkey, Turkey (83)
Kirgiz Refugees, Pakistan
Kirifi, Nigeria
Kita, Mali
Koma, Central, Sudan
Kono, Nigeria
Kotokoli, Benin
Kuda-Chamo, Nigeria

Kunama, Ethiopia
Kurds in Iran, Iran (80)
Kurds in Kuwait, Kuwait
* Kurds of Turkey, Turkey (79)
Kushi, Nigeria
Kuteb, Nigeria
Kuturmi, Nigeria
Kuzamani, Nigeria
Kwa, Nigeria
Kyibaku, Nigeria
Laamang, Nigeria
Labbai, India
Lafofa, Sudan
Lakians, Soviet Union
Lakka, Nigeria
Lame, Nigeria
Laro, Sudan
Laru, Nigeria
Lebong, Indonesia
Ligbi, Ivory Coast
Ligbi, Ghana
Longuda, Nigeria
Lori, Sudan
Lors, Iran (80)
Lotsu-Piri, Nigeria
Luac, Sudan
Lubu, Indonesia
Luwu, Indonesia
Lwo, Sudan
Maba, Sudan
Maban-Jumjum, Sudan
Madi, Sudan
Maguindano, Philippines (80)
* Mahrah, Yemen, Democratic
Makonde, Tanzania
Malays of Singapore, Singapore (79)
Mamasani, Iran
Mandar, Indonesia
Mandara, Nigeria
Mandingo, Liberia (79)
Manggarai Muslims, Indonesia (81)
Mappillas, India
Maranao, Philippines (79)
Marghi Central, Nigeria
Marka, Upper Volta
Masakin, Sudan
Masalit, Sudan
Masenrempulu, Indonesia
Matakam, Nigeria
Matumbi, Tanzania
Maures, Senegal
Mazandaranis, Iran
Mboi, Nigeria
Mbula-Bwazza, Nigeria
Meos of Rajasthan, India (80)
Midob, Sudan
Minangkabau, Indonesia (80)
Miri, Sudan
Mober, Nigeria
Modo, Sudan

Mogholi, Afghanistan
Montol, Nigeria
Moor Malays, Sri Lanka (79)
Moors in Mauritania, Mauritania
Moqaddam, Iran
Moreb, Sudan
Mori, Indonesia (81)
Moru, Sudan
Mumbake, Nigeria
Munji-Yidgha, Afghanistan
Muslim Community of Bawku, Ghana
Muslim Gypsies in Skoplje,
  Yugoslavia (82)
** Muslim Immigrants in U.K.,
  United Kingdom
Muslim Lebanese Refugees, Canada
  (83)
Muslim Malays, Malaysia (80)
Muslims, United Arab Emirates
  (79)
Muslims (West Nile Dist.),
  Uganda
Muslims of Jordan, Jordan
Nafar, Iran
Naka, Sudan
Nandu-Tari, Nigeria
Nginyukwur, Sudan
Ngirere, Sudan
Ngizim, Nigeria
Ngok, Sudan
Ngunduna, Sudan
Nguqwurang, Sudan
Ngwoi, Nigeria
Ninzam, Nigeria
Njalgulgule, Sudan
** Nomadic Somali Refugees, Somalia
  (83)
North Africans in Belgium,
  Belgium (80)
Numana-Nunku-Gwantu, Nigeria
** Nupe, Nigeria
Nuristani, Afghanistan (80)
Nyamusa, Sudan
Nyarueng, Sudan
Nzanyi, Nigeria
Otoro, Sudan
Ouaddai, Chad
Palembang, Indonesia
Palestinian Refugees, Jordan
  (83)
Palestinian Refugees, Lebanon
Paloc, Sudan
Pankhu, Bangladesh
Pashtuns, Iran (80)
Pero, Nigeria
Persians of Iran, Iran (80)
Pishagchi, Iran
Piti, Nigeria
Piya, Nigeria
Polci, Nigeria

Pongu, Nigeria
Poouch in Kashmir, India
*** Prasuni, Afghanistan
Puku-Geeri-Keri-Wipsi, Nigeria
Purig-Pa of Kashmir, India (81)
Qajars, Iran
Qara'i, Iran
Qaragozlu, Iran
Qashqa'i, Iran (80)
Rajasthani Muslims-Jaipur, India
  (82)
Redjang, Indonesia (80)
Rukuba, Nigeria
Rumaya, Nigeria
Rural Eritreans, Sudan (83)
Ruruma, Nigeria
Rut, Sudan
Rutul, Soviet Union
** Saguye, Kenya
Sama Pangutaran, Philippines
  (80)
Sanga, Nigeria
Sangil, Philippines
Sarakole, Senegal (80)
Sasanis, Iran
Sau, Afghanistan
Saya, Nigeria
Sayyids, Yemen, Arab Republic
Sere, Sudan
Shahsavans, Iran (80)
Shatt, Sudan
Shawiya, Algeria
** Shihu, United Arab Emirates
Shilluk, Sudan
Shughni, Afghanistan
Shuwa Arabic, Nigeria
Shwai, Sudan
Siri, Nigeria
Solorese Muslims, Indonesia (81)
Somali, Ethiopia
Somali, Ajuran, Kenya (79)
Somali, Degodia, Kenya
Somali, Gurreh, Kenya
Somali, Ogadenya, Kenya
Soninke, Gambia
Soninke, Mali
Soninke, Mauritania
Sopi, Sudan
Sukur, Nigeria
Sumbawa, Indonesia
Sura, Nigeria
Surubu, Nigeria
Susu, Guinea
Swatis, Pakistan (79)
Sylhetti, United Kingdom
Tabasaran, Soviet Union
Tajik, Iran (80)
Tajik, Afghanistan
Tajik, Soviet Union
Takestani, Iran

Tal, Nigeria
Talish, Iran
Talodi, Sudan
Tamil Muslims in Madras, India
  (82)
Tangale, Nigeria
Tangchangya, Bangladesh
Tat, Soviet Union
Tatars, Soviet Union (80)
Taucouleur, Senegal (80)
Tausug, Philippines (80)
Teda, Chad (80)
Teda, Libya
Tegali, Sudan
Teimuri, Iran
Teimurtash, Iran
Tem, Togo
Temein, Sudan
Tera, Nigeria
Ternatans, Indonesia
* Tertiary Level Youth, Iran
Thoi, Sudan
Thuri, Sudan
Tippera, Bangladesh
Tira, Sudan
Tirma, Sudan
* Toussian, Upper Volta
Tsakhur, Soviet Union
Tuareg, Niger (79)
Tula, Nigeria
Tulishi, Sudan
Tumale, Sudan
Tumma, Sudan
Tumtum, Sudan
Turkish Immigrant Workers,
  German Federal Rep. (79)
Turkish Workers, Belgium (80)
Turkomans, Iran (80)
Turks in Basel, Switzerland (82)
Turks, Anatolian, Turkey
Turkwam, Nigeria
Twi, Sudan
Ugandan Asian Refugees, United
  Kingdom (83)
Ugandan Asian Refugees, Canada
  (83)
Uighur, Afghanistan
Uigur, China (80)
Umm Dorein, Sudan
Umm Gabralla, Sudan
* Vai, Liberia (80)
** Vohras of Yavatmal, India
Waja, Nigeria
Weda, Indonesia
Western Sahrawis Refugees,
  Algeria (83)
* White Moors, Mauritania
Winji-Winji, Benin
Woro, Sudan
Yao, Mozambique

Yemenis, Yemen, Arab Republic
  (79)
Yeskwa, Nigeria
Yoruk, Turkey
Yulu, Sudan
Yungur, Nigeria
Zaghawa, Libya
Zaghawa, Sudan
Zari, Nigeria
Zenaga, Mauritania

Islam-Animist

Abe, Ivory Coast
Abidji, Ivory Coast
Abou Charib, Chad
Abure, Ivory Coast
Achode, Ghana
Adele, Togo
Adyukru, Ivory Coast
Afar, Ethiopia (79)
Agutaynon, Philippines
Ahlo, Togo
Akan, Brong, Ivory Coast
*** Akhdam, Yemen, Arab Republic
Akpafu, Ghana
Aladian, Ivory Coast
Alas, Indonesia
Ana, Togo
Animere, Togo
Anyanga, Togo
Attie, Ivory Coast
Avatime, Ghana
Avikam, Ivory Coast
Awutu, Ghana
Ayana, Kenya
Bagirmi, Chad
Bajau, Land, Malaysia
Bakwe, Ivory Coast
Balantak, Indonesia
Bali, Nigeria
Bambara, Ivory Coast
Banyum, Senegal
Bariba, Nigeria
Basila, Togo
Bata, Nigeria
Bayot, Gambia
Bayot, Guinea-Bissau
Bayot, Senegal
Bidyogo, Guinea-Bissau
Bilala, Chad
Bile, Nigeria
Bimoba, Ghana
Bimoba, Togo
Bira, Indonesia
Birifor, Upper Volta
Bitare, Nigeria

392

393

Mandyak, Gambia
Mangbai, Chad
Maninka, Guinea-Bissau
Maninka, Sierra Leone
Manjack, Senegal
Mankanya, Guinea-Bissau
Mankanya, Senegal
Maou, Ivory Coast
Maranao, Lanad, Philippines
Mararit, Chad
Marba, Chad
Masalit, Chad
Massalat, Chad
Maure, Mali
Mbai, Chad
Mbum, Chad
Mende, Liberia
Mesengo, Ethiopia
Mesme, Chad
Mesmedje, Chad
Mimi, Chad
Mo, Ivory Coast
Mogum, Chad
* Molbog, Philippines
Mona, Ivory Coast
Moru, Ivory Coast
Mubi, Chad
Muna, Indonesia
Mundang, Chad
Musei, Chad
Musgu, Chad
Musi, Indonesia
Nalu, Guinea
Nancere, Chad
Naoudem, Togo
Nara, Ethiopia
Natemba, Togo
Natioro, Upper Volta
Nchumbulu, Ghana
Nchumunu, Ghana
Ndunpa Duupa, Cameroon
Nielim, Chad
Nkonya, Ghana
Ntrubo, Togo
Nunuma, Upper Volta
Nyangbo, Ghana
Nzema, Ivory Coast
Nzema, Ghana
Ogan, Indonesia
Oubi, Ivory Coast
Palara, Ivory Coast
Papel, Guinea-Bissau
Pashayi, Afghanistan
Prang, Ghana
Puguli, Upper Volta
Pye, Ivory Coast
Rataning, Chad
Rendille, Kenya
Runga, Chad
Safaliba, Ghana

Sakuye, Kenya
Sama Bangingi, Philippines (80)
Sama, Siasi, Philippines
Sama, Sibuku, Philippines
Sama-Badjaw, Philippines (79)
Samo, Northern, Upper Volta
Santrokofi, Ghana
Sarwa, Chad
Sasak, Indonesia (80)
Sekayu, Indonesia
Sekpele, Ghana
** Serawai, Indonesia (81)
Serere-Non, Senegal
Serere-Sine, Senegal
Shilha, Morocco
Shina, Afghanistan
** Shluh Berbers, Morocco
Sidamo, Ethiopia
Sindhi Muslims in Karachi,
   Pakistan (82)
Sisala, Upper Volta
Siwu, Ghana
Somrai, Chad
Songhai, Niger
Songhai, Upper Volta
Subanun,Lapuyan, Philippines
** Sundanese, Indonesia (80)
Sungor, Chad
Susu, Guinea-Bissau
Susu, Sierra Leone
Tafi, Togo
Tagwana, Ivory Coast
* Talo, Indonesia
Tama, Chad
Tamazight, Morocco
Tana, Chad
Teda, Niger
Tepo, Ivory Coast
Thai Islam (Malay), Thailand
   (80)
* Thai Islam (Thai), Thailand
Tidorese, Indonesia
Tiefo, Upper Volta
Trepo, Ivory Coast
Tunya, Chad
Tupuri, Chad
Tura, Ivory Coast
** Uzbeks, Afghanistan (79)
Vagla, Ghana
Vai, Sierra Leone
Vige, Upper Volta
Voko, Cameroon
Wara, Upper Volta
Win, Upper Volta
Wolio, Indonesia
Wolof, Senegal (80)
Wolof, Gambian, Gambia
Wom, Nigeria
Yakan, Philippines (80)
* Yalunka, Sierra Leone (80)

Yandang, Nígeria
Yanga, Togo
** Yao, Malawi
Zaghawa, Chad
Zaramo, Tanzania

Jain

Jains, India

Judaism

** Falasha, Ethiopia (79)
* Jewish Imgrnts.-American, Israel
* Jewish Imgrnts.-Argentine,
  Israel
* Jewish Imgrnts.-Australia,
  Israel
* Jewish Imgrnts.-Brazilian,
  Israel
* Jewish Imgrnts.-Mexican, Israel
* Jewish Imgrnts.-Uruguayan,
  Israel
* Jewish Immigrants, Other, Israel
  Jews in Venice, Italy (82)
  Jews of Iran, Iran
  Jews, Non-Sephardic of Mo,
  Canada
  Jews, Sephardic of Montre,
  Canada
  Ladinos, Lebanon
  Targum, Israel

Nominal Christian

  Baguio Area Miners, Philippines
  (81)
** Batangeno, Philippines
  Bawoyo, Zaire
*** Bolinao, Philippines
* Casiguranin, Philippines
** Chicanos in Denver, United
  States of America (82)
  Chilean Refugees, Argentina
* Chilean Refugees in Toron,
  Canada (83)
*** Copacabana Apt. Dwellers,
  Brazil

* Drug Addicts in Sao Paulo,
  Brazil (82)
  Equatorial Guin. Refugees,
  Gabon
  Hmong, Twin Cities, United
  States of America
** Hotel Workers in Manila,
  Philippines (81)
** Ishans, Nigeria
* Jeepney Drivers in Manila,
  Philippines (81)
** Kalinga, Tanudan, Philippines
  Kurichiya in Kerala, India (81)
  Luxemburgois, Luxembourg
* Maltese, Malta
** Middle Class-Mexico City, Mexico
  (82)
** Military Personnel, Ecuador
  Nicaraguan Refugees, Costa Rica
  Refugees from El Salvador,
  Belize
  Salvadoran Refugees, Honduras
  South African Students, Lesotho
  (83)
* Universitarios - Rosario,
  Argentina (82)
** Urban Mestizos, Ecuador

Peyote Religion

  Paiute, Northern, United States
  of America

Secularism

  Aborigines in Brisbane,
  Australia (82)
* Americans in Geneva, Switzerland
  Amsterdam Boat Dwellers,
  Netherlands
** Bachelors in Lagos, Nigeria (82)
** Bus Girls in Seoul, Korea,
  Republic of (82)
* Casual Laborers-Atlanta, United
  States of America (82)
** Chinese in Boston, United States
  of America (82)
* Chinese in Korea, Korea,
  Republic of
* Chinese in West Germany, German
  Federal Rep.
** Chinese Stud., Australia,
  Australia
* Coloureds in Eersterust, South
  Africa (82)

395

* Danchi Dwellers in Tokyo, Japan (82)
  Dead-End Kids - Amsterdam, Netherlands (82)
** Ex-Mental Patients in NYC, United States of America (82)
* Expatriates in Riyadh, Saudi Arabia (82)
  Gays in San Francisco, United States of America (82)
  Geishas in Osaka, Japan (82)
* Industrial Workers, Taiwan (81)
** Jamaican Elite, Jamaica
** Japanese Students In USA, United States of America
  Jewish Refugees from USSR, Israel (83)
  Koreans in Manchuria, China (81)
** Marielitos in Florida, United States of America (83)
  Nurses in St. Louis, United States of America (82)
* Parsees, India (81)
  Pension Students-Madrid, Spain (82)
** Portuguese in France, France
** Prisoners, Korea, Republic of
** Pro Hockey Players, United States of America (82)
** Racetrack Residents, United States of America (79)
  Seychellois, Seychelles
* Students, German Federal Rep. (79)
  Students in Cuiaba, Brazil
** Suriguenos, Philippines
  Taiwan-Chinese Un. Stud., Taiwan
* University Students, France (79)
** University Students, Chin, China

Traditional Chinese

  Ach'ang, China
  Buriat, China
  Burig, China
  Ch'iang, China
  Chin, China
  Chinese Businessmen, Hong Kong (81)
  Chinese Factory Workers, Hong Kong
  Chinese Fishermen, Malaysia
** Chinese Hakka of Taiwan, Taiwan (79)
** Chinese in Australia, Australia
* Chinese in Austria, Austria
** Chinese in Brazil, Brazil
  Chinese in Burma, Burma

** Chinese in Indonesia, Indonesia
* Chinese in Japan, Japan
* Chinese in Laos, Laos
* Chinese in Malaysia, Malaysia
* Chinese in New Zealand, New Zealand
** Chinese in Panama, Panama
  Chinese in Puerto Rico, Puerto Rico
** Chinese in Sabah, Malaysia
** Chinese in Sarawak, Malaysia
* Chinese in South Africa, South Africa
* Chinese in Thailand, Thailand
** Chinese in United Kingdom, United Kingdom
** Chinese in United States, United States of America
** Chinese in Vancouver B.C., Canada
* Chinese Mainlanders, Taiwan
* Chinese of W. Malaysia, Malaysia
* Chinese Refugees in Macau, Macau (81)
** Chinese Refugees, France, France (79)
* Chinese Restaurant Wrkrs., France
** Chinese Students Glasgow, United Kingdom
  Chinese Villagers, Hong Kong
  Chingp'o, China
  Chungchia, China
  Chwang, China
  Dagur, China
  Evenki, China
  Fishing Village People, Taiwan
  Hani, China
** High School Students, Hong Kong
  Jyarung, China
  Kalmytz, China
  Kam, China
  Kelao, China
  Khalka, China
  Kham, China
  Lahul, China
  Laka, China
  Lati, China
  Li, China
  Manchu, China (81)
  Mongour, China
  Nahsi, China
  Nanai, China
  Nosu, China
  Nung, China
  Oirat, China
  Oronchon, China
  Paongan, China
  Pu-I, China

Punu, China
Rawang, China
Refugee Doctors, Hong Kong
Salar, China
Santa, China
Sibo, China
Sui, China
Vietnamese Refugees, China (83)
Wa, China
* Women Laborers, Taiwan
Yellow Uighur, China
Yuku, China

Traditional Japanese

* Inland Sea Island Peoples, Japan
* Japanese in Korea, Korea, Republic of
* Ryukyuan, Japan
** Univ. Students of Japan, Japan

Zoroastrianism

* Parsis in Bombay, India (82)

Other

** Lotuka, Sudan
* Yanyula, Australia

Unknown

Abkhaz, Soviet Union
Akhavakh, Soviet Union
Alutor, Soviet Union
Andi, Soviet Union
Archin, Soviet Union
Bangangte, Cameroon
Basaa, Cameroon
Batsi, Soviet Union
Botlikh, Soviet Union
Budug, Soviet Union
** Bus Drivers, South Korea, Korea, Republic of

Chamalin, Soviet Union
* Chinese in Amsterdam, Netherlands
Chinese in Costa Rica, Costa Rica
* Chinese in Holland, Netherlands
Chukot, Soviet Union
Didoi, Soviet Union
Dolgans, Soviet Union
* Factory Workers, Hong Kong
Gilyak, Soviet Union
* Havasupai, United States of America
Itelmen, Soviet Union
Izhor, Soviet Union
Kapuchin, Soviet Union
Karagas, Soviet Union
Karaim, Soviet Union
Karatin, Soviet Union
Ket, Soviet Union
Khakas, Soviet Union
Khana, Nigeria
Khanti, Soviet Union
Khinalug, Soviet Union
Khvarshin, Soviet Union
Kongo, Angola
*** Koreans in Germany, German Federal Rep.
Koryak, Soviet Union
Kryz, Soviet Union
Kvanadin, Soviet Union
Liv, Soviet Union
Mansi, Soviet Union
Mingat, Soviet Union
Mulimba, Cameroon
Naga, Sema, India
Nanai, Soviet Union
Ndogo, Sudan
Nentsy, Soviet Union
Nganasan, Soviet Union
Nivkhi, Soviet Union
Oroch, Soviet Union
Orok, Soviet Union
Saams, Soviet Union
Selkup, Soviet Union
Shor, Soviet Union
Svan, Soviet Union
Tindin, Soviet Union
Tsaangi, Congo
Udegeis, Soviet Union
Udin, Soviet Union
Ulchi, Soviet Union
Veps, Soviet Union
Yagnobi, Soviet Union
Yazgulyam, Soviet Union
Yukagirs, Soviet Union
Yurak, Soviet Union
Zimbabwean Repatriates, Zimbabwe (83)

Not Reported

Bamum, Cameroon
Ethiopian Refugees, Yemen, Arab Republic
Lunda, Ndembu, Zambia

Index by Language

Groups are listed according to their primary vernacular language. In many cases, groups are bilingual or trilingual, speaking several languages including a more commonly known trade language.

Abaknon	Abaknon, Philippines
Abanyom	Abanyom, Nigeria
Abau	Abau, Indonesia
	Abau, Papua New Guinea
Abazin	Abazin, Soviet Russia
Abe	Abe, Ivory Coast
Abialang	Abialang, Sudan
Abie	Abie, Papua New Guinea
Abkhaz	Abkhaz, Turkey
	Abkhaz, Soviet Russia
Abong	Abong, Nigeria
Abou Charib	Abou Charib, Chad
Abu Leila	Abu Leila, Sudan
Abua	Abua, Nigeria
Abujmaria	Abujmaria (Madhya Pradesh, India
Abulas	Abulas, Papua New Guinea
Abure	Abure, Ivory Coast
Ach'ang	Ach'ang, China
Achagua	Achagua, Colombia
Achehnese	Achehnese, Indonesia (80)
Acheron	Acheron, Sudan
Achi, Cubulco	Achi, Cubulco, Guatemala
Achi, Rabinal	Achi, Rabinal, Guatemala
Achipa	Achipa, Nigeria
Achode	Achode, Ghana
Acholi	Acholi, Uganda
Achual	Achual, Peru
Adele	Adele, Togo
Adhola	Adhola, Uganda
Adi	* Adi, India
Adidji	Abidji, Ivory Coast
Adiyan	Adiyan in Kerala, India
Adjora	Adjora, Papua New Guinea
Adygei	Adygei, Soviet Russia
Adyukru	Adyukru, Ivory Coast
Aeka	Aeka, Papua New Guinea
Aeta	Aeta, Philippines
Afanci	* Afawa, Nigeria (80)
Afar	Afar, Ethiopia (79)
Afitti	Afitti, Sudan
Afrikaans	Cape Malays in Cape Town, South Africa (82)
	* Coloureds in Eersterust, South Africa (82)
Afshari	Afshars, Iran
	Inallu, Iran
Agajanis	Agajanis, Iran
Agarabi	Agarabi, Papua New Guinea
Agariya	Agariya in Bihar, India
Agau	** Falasha, Ethiopia (79)
Age	Age, Cameroon
Aghem	Aghem, Cameroon
Aghu	Aghu, Indonesia
Agob	Agob, Papua New Guinea
Agoi	Agoi, Nigeria
Aguacateco	Aguacateco, Guatemala
Aguaruna	Aguaruna, Peru
Agul	Agul, Soviet Russia
Agutaynon	Agutaynon, Philippines
Agwagwune	Agwagwune, Nigeria
Ahir	Ahir in Maharashtra, India
Ahlo	Ahlo, Togo

Aibondeni		Aibondeni, Indonesia
Aiku		Aiku, Papua New Guinea
Aikwakai		Aikwakai, Indonesia
Aimol		Aimol in Assam, India
Aiome		Aiome, Papua New Guinea
Aion		Aion, Papua New Guinea
Airo-Sumaghaghe		Airo-Sumaghaghe, Indonesia
Airoran		Airoran, Indonesia
Aja		Aja, Sudan
Ajmeri		Ajmeri in Rajasthan, India
Aka		Aka, India
Akan, Brong		Akan, Brong, Ivory Coast
Akawaio		Akawaio, Guyana
Ake		Ake, Nigeria
Akha	**	Akha, Thailand (79)
Akhavakh		Akhavakh, Soviet Russia
Akpa-Yache		Akpa-Yache, Nigeria
Akpafu		Akpafu, Ghana
Akrukay		Akrukay, Papua New Guinea
Alaban		Alaba, Ethiopia
Aladian		Aladian, Ivory Coast
Alago		Alago, Nigeria
Alak		Alak, Laos
Alamblak		Alamblak, Papua New Guinea
Alangan		Alangan, Philippines
Alatil		Alatil, Papua New Guinea
Alauagat		Alauagat, Papua New Guinea
Albanian (Gheg)	*	Albanians in Yugoslavia
Albanian Tosk	*	Albanian Muslims, Albania (80)
Aledjo	*	Nyantruku, Benin
Alege		Alege, Nigeria
Allar	*	Alars, India
Alor, Kolana		Alor, Kolana, Indonesia (81)
Altaic		Ewenkis, China (81)
Alutor		Alutor, Soviet Russia
Ama		Ama, Papua New Guinea
Amahuaca		Amahuaca, Peru
Amaimon		Amaimon, Papua New Guinea
Amanab		Amanab, Indonesia
		Amanab, Papua New Guinea
Amar		Amar, Ethiopia
Amarakaeri		Amarakaeri, Peru
Amasi		Amasi, Cameroon
Ambai		Ambai, Indonesia
Ambasi		Ambasi, Papua New Guinea
Amber		Amber, Indonesia
Amberbaken		Amberbaken, Indonesia
Ambo		Ambo, Zambia
Ambonese		Ambonese, Netherlands
		Ambonese, Indonesia
Ami	*	Ami, Taiwan (81)
Amo		Amo, Nigeria
Amoy		Fishing Village People, Taiwan
	*	Women Laborers, Taiwan
Ampale	**	Ampeeli, Papua New Guinea
Amto		Amto, Papua New Guinea
Amuesha		Amuesha, Peru
Amuzgo, Guerrero		Amuzgo, Guerrero, Mexico
Amuzgo, Oaxaca		Amuzgo, Oaxaca, Mexico
Ana		Ana, Togo

Anaang	Anaang, Nigeria
Anal	Anal in Manipur, India
Andarum	Andarum, Papua New Guinea
Andha	Andha in Andhra Pradesh, India
Andi	Andi, Soviet Russia
Andoque	Andoque, Colombia
Anem	Anem, Papua New Guinea
Anga	Anga in Bihar, India
Angaataha	Angaataha, Papua New Guinea
Angal Heneng, South	Angal Heneng, So. Papua New Guinea
Angal Heneng, West	Angal Heneng West Papua New Guinea
Angal, East	Angal, East, Papua New Guinea
Angas	Angas, Nigeria
Angaua	Angaua, Papua New Guinea
Anggor	Anggor, Papua New Guinea
Angoram	Angoram, Papua New Guinea
Animere	Animere, Togo
Ankave	Ankave, Papua New Guinea
Ankwai	Ankwe, Nigeria
Anor	Anor, Papua New Guinea
Ansus	Ansus, Indonesia
Anuak	Anuak, Ethiopia
	Anuak, Sudan
Anuki	Anuki, Papua New Guinea
Anyanga	Anyanga, Togo
Apalai	Apalai, Brazil
Apartani	** Apatani in Assam, India
Apinaye	Apinaye, Brazil
Apurina	Apurina, Brazil
Ara	Ara, Indonesia
Arabela	Arabela, Peru
Arabic	* Akhdam, Yemen, Arab Republic
	* Alawites, Syria (79)
	Algerian Arabs in France, France
	Ansar Sudanese Rfgs, Ethiopia (83)
	Arab Immigrants in Bangui, Central African Republic (82)
	Arab-Jabbari (Kamesh), Iran
	Arab-Shaibani (Kamesh), Iran
	** Arabs in New Orleans, U.S.A. (82)
	Arabs of Khuzestan, Iran
	Chadian Refugees, Nigeria (83)
	Chinese, Saudi Arabia
	Circassians in Amman, Jordan (82)
	Druzes, Israel (79)
	** Hadrami, Yemen, Democratic
	Masalit, Sudan
	Maures, Senegal
	Muslims, United Arab Emirates (79)
	Muslims of Jordan, Jordan
	North Africans, Belgium (80)
	Palestinian Refugees, Jordan (83)
	Palestinian Refugees, Lebanon
	Sayyids, Yemen, Arab Republic
	Western Sahrawi Rfgs, Algeria (83)
Arabic (Eastern)	Yemenis, Yemen, Arab Republic (79)
Arabic (Hassani)	Moors in Mauritania, Mauritania
Arafundi	Arafundi, Papua New Guinea
Aranadan	Aranadan in Tamil Nadu, India
Aranatan	* Arnatas, India
Arandai	Arandai, Indonesia

402

REGISTRY OF THE UNREACHED

Baali		Baali, Zaire
Babajou		Babajou, Cameroon
Babri		Babri, India
Baburiwa		Baburiwa, Indonesia
Bachama		Bachama, Nigeria
Bada		Bada, Nigeria
Badagu		Badagu in Nilgiri, India
Bade		Bade, Nigeria
Badyara		Badyara, Guinea-Bissau
Bafut		Bafut, Cameroon
Bagelkhandi		Bagelkhandi in M.P., India
Baghati		Baghati in H.P., India
Bagirmi		Bagirmi, Chad
Bagobo	***	Bagobo, Philippines
Bagri		Bagri, Pakistan
Baham		Baham, Indonesia
Bahasa Jawa	**	Javanese of Pejompongan, Indonesia
Bahasa Malaysia		Muslim Malays, Malaysia (80)
Bahawalpuri		Bahawalpuri in M.P., India
Bahinemo		Bahinemo, Papua New Guinea
Bai		Bai, Sudan
Baibai		Baibai, Papua New Guinea
Baiga		Baiga in Bihar, India
Baining		Baining, Papua New Guinea
Bajau, Indonesian		Bajau, Indonesian, Indonesia
Bajaus		Bajau, Land, Malaysia
Baka		Baka, Cameroon
		Baka, Zaire
Bakairi		Bakairi, Brazil
Bakhtiaris		Bakhtiaris, Iran (80)
Bakwe		Bakwe, Ivory Coast
Bakwele		Bakwele, Congo
Balangao	**	Balangao, Philippines
Balangaw		Balangaw, Philippines
Balanta		Balanta, Senegal
		Balanta Refugees, Senegal
		Balante, Guinea-Bissau
Balantak		Balantak, Indonesia
Bali		Bali, Nigeria
Bali-Vitu		Bali-Vitu, Papua New Guinea
Balinese		Balinese, Indonesia
Balkar		Balkars, Soviet Russia
Balti		Balti in Jammu, India
Baluchi		Baluchi, Iran (80)
Bam		Bam, Papua New Guinea
Bambara		Bambara, Mali
		Bambara, Ivory Coast
Bambuka		Bambuka, Nigeria
Bamougoun-Bamenjou		Bamougoun-Bamenjou, Cameroon
Bamum		Bamum, Cameroon
Banaro	***	Banaro, Papua New Guinea
Bandawa-Minda		Bandawa-Minda, Nigeria
Bandi		Bandi, Liberia
		Gbande, Guinea
Bandjoun		Bandjoun, Cameroon
Banen		Banen, Cameroon
Banga		Banga, Nigeria
Bangba		Bangba, Zaire
Banggai		Banggai, Indonesia
Bangri		Bangaru in Punjab, India

404

Baniwa	Baniwa, Brazil
Banoni	Banoni, Papua New Guinea
Bantu Dialects	Urban Refugees in Lusaka, Zambia
Bantuanon	Bantuanon, Philippines
Banyum	Banyum, Senegal
Banyun	Banyun, Guinea-Bissau
Barai	Barai, Papua New Guinea
Barambu	Barambu, Sudan
Barasano	Barasano, Colombia
Barasano, Northern	Barasano, Northern, Colombia
Barau	Barau, Indonesia
Bare'e	Bare'e, Indonesia
Bareli	Bareli in Madhya Pradesh, India
Bari	Bari, Sudan
Bariai	Bariai, Papua New Guinea
Bariba	* Bariba, Benin (80)
	Bariba, Nigeria
Bariji	Bariji, Papua New Guinea
Barim	Barim, Papua New Guinea
Barok	Barok, Papua New Guinea
Baruga	Baruga, Papua New Guinea
Baruya	Baruya, Papua New Guinea
Basaa	Basaa, Cameroon
Basari	Basari, Togo
	Basari, Guinea
	Basari, Senegal
Bashar	Bashar, Nigeria
Bashgali	Bashgali, Afghanistan
Basila	Basila, Togo
Basketo	Basketo, Ethiopia
Bassa	* Bassa, Liberia
	** Bassa, Nigeria
Bata	Bata, Nigeria
Batak, Angkola	* Batak, Angkola, Indonesia (80)
Batak, Karo	Batak, Karo, Indonesia
Batak, Palawan	Batak, Palawan, Philippines
Batak, Simalungun	Batak, Simalungun, Indonesia
Batak, Toba	Batak, Toba, Indonesia
Batanga-Ngolo	Batanga-Ngolo, Cameroon
Bateg	Bateg, Malaysia
Bathudi	Bathudi in Bihar, India
Batsi	Batsi, Soviet Russia
Batu	Batu, Nigeria
Bau	Bau, Papua New Guinea
Baule	*** Baoule, Ivory Coast
Baushi	Baushi, Nigeria
Bauwaki	Bauwaki, Papua New Guinea
Bawm	Bawm, Bangladesh
Bayat	Bayats, Iran
Bayot	Bayot, Gambia
	Bayot, Guinea-Bissau
	Bayot, Senegal
Bazigar	Bazigar in Gujarat, India
Bebeli	Bebeli, Papua New Guinea
Bediya	Bediya in Bihar, India
Bedoanas	Bedoanas, Indonesia
Beja	Beja, Ethiopia
	Beja, Sudan
Bekwarra	Bekwarra, Nigeria
Bembe	Bembe, Zaire

405

REGISTRY OF THE UNREACHED

Bembi	Bembi, Papua New Guinea
Bena	Bena, Tanzania
Benabena	Benabena, Papua New Guinea
Bencho	Bencho, Ethiopia
Bende	Bende, Tanzania
Bene	Bene, Cameroon
Benga	Benga, Gabon
Bengali	** Banai, Bangladesh
	Bengali Refugees, Assam, India
	Bengalis in London, U.Kingdom (82)
	Burmese Muslim Rfgs Bangladesh (83)
	** Hajong, Bangladesh
	** Koch, Bangladesh
Bengkulu	Bengkulu, Indonesia
Berba	Berba, Benin
Berik	Berik, Indonesia
Berom	Berom, Nigeria
Besisi	Besisi, Malaysia
Bete	Bete, India
	* Bete, Ivory Coast
Bethen	Bethen, Cameroon
Betsinga	Betsinga, Cameroon
Bette-Bende	Bette-Bende, Nigeria
Bhakta	Bhakta, India
Bharia	Bharia in Madhya Pradesh, India
Bhatneri	Bhatneri, India
Bhattri	Bhattri, India
Bhilala	Bhilala, India
Bhojpuri	* Bhojpuri, Nepal
	Tharu, Nepal
Bhoyari	Bhoyari in Maharashtra, India
Bhuiya	Bhuiya in Bihar, India
Bhumij	Bhumij in Assam, India
Bhunjia	Bhunjia in Madhya Pradesh, India
Biafada	Biafada, Guinea-Bissau
Biak	Biak, Indonesia
Biaka	Biaka, Papua New Guinea
Biangai	Biangai, Papua New Guinea
Biatah	** Bidayuh of Sarawak, Malaysia (81)
Bibling	Bibling, Papua New Guinea
Biduanda	Biduanda, Malaysia
Bidyogo	Bidyogo, Guinea-Bissau
	** Bijogo, Guinea-Bissau
Bijori	Bijori in Bihar, India
Biksi	Biksi, Indonesia
Bilaan	** Bilan, Philippines
Bilala	Bilala, Chad
Bile	Bile, Nigeria
Bilen	Bilen, Ethiopia
Biliau	Biliau, Papua New Guinea
Bima	Bimanese, Indonesia
Bimin	Bimin, Papua New Guinea
Bimoba	Bimoba, Ghana
	Bimoba, Togo
	Moba, Ghana
	Moba, Togo
Binahari	Binahari, Papua New Guinea
Binandere	Binandere, Papua New Guinea
Binawa	Binawa, Nigeria
Bine	Bine, Papua New Guinea

Binga		Binga, Sudan
Bingkokak		Bingkokak, Indonesia
Binjhwari		Binjhwari in Bihar, India
Binji		Binji, Zaire
Binumarien		Binumarien, Papua New Guinea
Bipim	***	Bipim, Indonesia
Bira		Bira, Indonesia
Birhor		Birhor in Bihar, India
Birifor		Birifor, Ghana
		Birifor, Upper Volta
Bisa		Bisa, Zambia
		Bousansi, Upper Volta
Bisa (Busanga)	**	Busanse, Ghana
Bisaya		Bisaya, Malaysia (81)
Bisis		Bisis, Papua New Guinea
Bitara		Bitara, Papua New Guinea
Bitare		Bitare, Nigeria
		Bitare, Cameroon
Biti		Biti, Sudan
Biyom		Biyom, Papua New Guinea
Boanaki		Boanaki, Papua New Guinea
Bobe		Bobe, Cameroon
Bobo Fing		Bobo Fing, Mali
Bobo Wule		Bobo Wule, Mali
Bodo		Bodo in Assam, India
	**	Bodo Kachari, India
Boghom		Boghom, Nigeria
Bohutu		Bohutu, Papua New Guinea
Boikin		Boikin, Papua New Guinea
Boko (Busa)	**	Boko, Benin
Bokyi		Bokyi, Nigeria
		Bokyi, Cameroon
Bola		Bola, Papua New Guinea
Bole		Bole, Nigeria
Bolinao	***	Bolinao, Philippines
Bolon		Bolon, Upper Volta
Bolondo		Bolondo, Zaire
Bom		Bom, Papua New Guinea
Boma		Boma, Zaire
Bomboko		Bomboko, Cameroon
Bondei		Bondei, Tanzania
Bondo		Bondo in Orissa, India
Bonerif		Bonerif, Indonesia
Bonggo		Bonggo, Indonesia
Bongili		Bongili, Congo
Bongo		Bongo, Sudan
Bongu		Bongu, Papua New Guinea
Bonkeng-Pendia		Bonkeng-Pendia, Cameroon
Bonkiman		Bonkiman, Papua New Guinea
Bontoc, Central	**	Bontoc, Central, Philippines (81)
Bor Gok		Bor Gok, Sudan
Bora		Bora, Colombia
Borai		Borai, Indonesia
Boran		Boran, Ethiopia
	**	Boran, Kenya
		Sabbra, Kenya
Bororo	*	Bororo, Brazil
Bosavi		Bosavi, Papua New Guinea
Bosilewa		Bosilewa, Papua New Guinea
Bosngun		Bosngun, Papua New Guinea

REGISTRY OF THE UNREACHED

Bote-Majhi	Bote-Majhi, Nepal
Botlikh	Botlikh, Soviet Russia
Bowili	Bowili, Togo
Boya	Boya, Sudan
Bozo	Bozo, Mali
Brahui	Brahui, Pakistan
Braj	Braj in Uttar Pradesh, India
Brao	Brao, Laos (79)
Brat	Brat, Indonesia
Breri	Breri, Papua New Guinea
Bruneis	Bruneis, Malaysia
Bua	Bua, Chad
Bual	Bual, Indonesia
Buamu (Bobo Wule)	Bwa, Upper Volta (80)
Buang, Central	Buang, Central, Papua New Guinea
Buang, Mangga	Buang, Mangga, Papua New Guinea
Bube	Bube, Equatorial Guinea
Budibud	Budibud, Papua New Guinea
Budug	Budug, Soviet Russia
Buduma	Buduma, Nigeria
Bugis	Bugis, Indonesia (80)
Buglere	Buglere, Panama
Bugombe	Bugombe, Zaire
Buhid	Buhid, Philippines
Buin	Buin, Papua New Guinea
Buja	Buja, Zaire
Buka-khwe	Bushmen in Botswana, Botswana
Bukaua	Bukaua, Papua New Guinea
Buli	Builsa, Ghana
	Buli, Indonesia
	Buli, Upper Volta
Bulia	Bulia, Zaire
Bullom, Northern	Bullom, Northern, Sierra Leone
Bullom, Southern	Bullom, Southern, Sierra Leone
Bulu	Bulu, Papua New Guinea
Buna	Buna, Papua New Guinea
Bunabun	Bunabun, Papua New Guinea
Bunak	Bunak, Indonesia
Bunama	Bunama, Papua New Guinea
Bunan	Bunann in Kashmir, India
Bungku	Bungku, Indonesia
Bunu	Bunu, Nigeria
Bura	Bura, Cameroon
Bura (Babur)	** Babur Thali, Nigeria (80)
Burak	Burak, Nigeria
Buraka-Gbanziri	Buraka-Gbanziri, Congo
Buriat	Buriat, China
	Buriat, Soviet Russia
Burig	Burig, China
	Burig in Kashmir, India
Burji	Burji, Ethiopia
Burmese	Danu, Burma
	Kachin in Shan State, Burma
	Taungyoe, Burma
Buru	Buru, Indonesia
Burum	Burum, Papua New Guinea
Burun	Burun, Sudan
Burungi	Burungi, Tanzania
Burushaski	** Hunzakut, Pakistan (79)
Busa (Bokobarn Akiba)	Busa, Nigeria (80)

Busah		Busah, Papua New Guinea
Busami		Busami, Indonesia
Bushoong		Bushoong, Zaire
Bussa		Bussa, Ethiopia
Buta		Butawa, Nigeria
Butung		Butung, Indonesia
Buwid	**	Buwid, Philippines (81)
Bviri		Bviri, Sudan
Bwa		Bwa, Zaire
Bwaidoga		Bwaidoga, Papua New Guinea
Bwisi		Bwisi, Zaire
Byangsi		Byangsi, Nepal
Cacua		Cacua, Colombia
Cagayan		Jama Mapun, Philippines (80)
Caiwa		Caiwa, Brazil
Cakchiquel, Central		Cakchiquel, Central, Guatemala
Caluyanhon		Caluyanhon, Philippines
Cambodia	**	Khmer Refugees, Thailand
Campa		Campa, Peru
Camsa		Camsa, Colombia
Canarese		Chola Naickans, India
Candoshi		Candoshi, Peru
Canela		Canela, Brazil
Cantonese		Chinese Businessmen, Hong Kong (81)
		Chinese Factory Workers, Hong Kong
	*	Chinese in Amsterdam, Netherlands
	**	Chinese in Australia
		Chinese in Costa Rica
	*	Chinese in New Zealand
	*	Chinese in South Africa
	**	Chinese in Vancouver B.C. Canada
	*	Chinese of W. Malaysia
	*	Chinese Refugees in Macau (81)
		Chinese Villagers, Hong Kong
	*	Factory Workers, Hong Kong
	**	High School Students, Hong Kong
		Refugee Doctors, Hong Kong
		Vietnamese Refugees, China (83)
Capanahua		Capanahua, Peru
Carapana		Carapana, Colombia
Cashibo		Cashibo, Peru
Casiguranin	*	Casiguranin, Philippines
Cayapa		Cayapa, Ecuador
Cebuano	***	Cebu, Middle-Class, Philippines
Cewa		Cewa, Zambia
Ch'iang		Ch'iang, China
Ch'ol	***	Ch'ol Sabanilla, Mexico
Chacobo		Chacobo, Bolivia
Chagga		Chagga, Tanzania
Chaghatai		Chaghatai, Afghanistan
Chakfem-Mushere		Chakfem-Mushere, Nigeria
Chakma	*	Chakmas of Mizoram, India (81)
Chakossi		Chakossi in Ghana, Ghana
		Chakossi in Togo, Togo
Chala		Chala, Ghana
Cham		Cham, Viet Nam
	*	Cham Rfgs, Malaysia (83)
Chamacoco, Bahia Negra		Chamacoco, Bahia Negra, Paraguay
Chamalin		Chamalin, Soviet Russia
Chamari		Chamari in Madhya Pradesh, India

Chamba Daka	Chamba Daka, Nigeria
Chamba Leko	Chamba Leko, Nigeria
Chambri	Chambri, Papua New Guinea
Chameali	Chameali in H.P., India
Chami	Chami, Colombia
Chamicuro	Chamicuro, Peru
Chamorro	Chamorro, Turks & Caicos Islands
Chara	Chara, Ethiopia
Chatino, Nopala	Chatino, Nopala, Mexico
Chatino, Panixtlahuaca	Chatino, Panixtlahuaca, Mexico
Chatino, Tataltepec	Chatino, Tataltepec, Mexico
Chatino, Zacatepec	Chatino, Zacatepec, Mexico
Chatino, Zenzontepec	Chatino, Zenzontepec, Mexico
Chaudangsi	Chaudangsi, Nepal
Chaungtha	Chaungtha, Burma
Chawai	Chawai, Nigeria
Chayawita	** Chayahuita, Peru
Chenapian	Chenapian, Papua New Guinea
Chenchu	Chenchu in Andhra Pradesh, India
Chepang	Chepang, Nepal
Cherkes	Cherkess, Soviet Russia
Chero	Chero in Bihar, India
Chhattisgarhi	Satnamis (Madhya Pradesh), India
Chiga	Chiga, Uganda
Chik-Barik	Chik-Barik in Bihar, India
Chikalanga	* Kalanga, Botswana
Chin	Chin, China
Chin, Asho	Chin, Asho, Burma
Chin, Falam	Chin, Falam, Burma
Chin, Haka	Chin, Haka, Burma
Chin, Khumi	Chin, Khumi, Burma
Chin, Ngawn	Chin, Ngawn, Burma
Chin, Tiddim	Chin, Tiddim, Burma
Chinanteco, Ayotzintepec	Chinanteco, Ayotzintepec, Mexico
Chinanteco, Chiltepec	Chinanteco, Chiltepec, Mexico
Chinanteco, Comaltepec	Chinanteco, Comaltepec, Mexico
Chinanteco, Lalana	Chinanteco, Lalana, Mexico
Chinanteco, Lealao	Chinanteco, Lealao, Mexico
Chinanteco, Ojitlan	Chinanteco, Ojitlan, Mexico
Chinanteco, Palantla	Chinanteco, Palantla, Mexico
Chinanteco, Quiotepec	Chinanteco, Quiotepec, Mexico
Chinanteco, Sochiapan	Chinanteco, Sochiapan, Mexico
Chinanteco, Tepetotutla	Chinanteco, Tepetotutla, Mexico
Chinanteco, Tepinapa	Chinanteco, Tepinapa, Mexico
Chinanteco, Usila	Chinanteco, Usila, Mexico
Chinbok	Chinbok, Burma
Chinese dialects	* Chinese in Malaysia, Malaysia
	** Chinese Stud., Australia
Chinese, Min-Nan	* Deviant Youth/Taipei, Taiwan (82)
Chinga	Chinga, Cameroon
Chingp'o	Chingp'o, China
Chip	Chip, Nigeria
Chipaya	Chipaya, Bolivia
Chiquitano	Chiquitano, Bolivia
ChiTonga	* Tonga, Zimbabwe
	Tonga, Gwembe Valley, Zambia (79)
Chiyao	** Yao, Malawi
Chodhari	Chodhari in Gujarat, India
Chokobo	Chokobo, Nigeria
Chokwe	Chokwe, Zambia

410

Dakhni (Urdu)		Deccani Muslims, India
Dami		Dami, Papua New Guinea
Dan		Dan, Liberia
	***	Dan, Ivory Coast
Dan (Yacouba)		Gio, Liberia
Dangaleat		Dangaleat, Chad
Dangi	**	Bhils, India (79)
Dani, Grand Valley	*	Dani, Baliem, Indonesia (79)
Danuwar Rai	*	Rai, Danuwar, Nepal
Daonda		Daonda, Papua New Guinea
Darai		Darai, Nepal
Dargin		Dargin, Soviet Russia
Dari	**	Afghan Refugees (NWFP), Pakistan (83)
		Tajik, Iran (80)
Darmiya		Darmiya, Nepal
Dass		Dass, Nigeria
Dathanik		Dathanik, Ethiopia
Davaweno		Davaweno, Philippines
Dawawa		Dawawa, Papua New Guinea
Day		Day, Central African Republic
Dazaga		Daza, Chad
De	*	Dewein, Liberia
Dedua		Dedua, Papua New Guinea
Degeme		Degema, Nigeria
Degenan		Degenan, Papua New Guinea
Dem		Dem, Indonesia
Demta		Demta, Indonesia
Dendi		Dendi, Benin
Dengese		Dengese, Zaire
Deno		Deno, Nigeria
Deori		Deori in Assam, India
Dera		Dera, Nigeria
Desano		Desano, Brazil
Dghwede		Dghwede, Cameroon
Dhaiso		Dhaiso, Tanzania
Dhanka		Dhanka in Gujarat, India
Dhanwar		Dhanwar in Madhya Pradesh, India
Dhimal		Dhimal, Nepal
Dhimba		Herero, Namibia
Dhodia Dialects	**	Dhodias, India
Dhuwal	*	Murngin (Wulamba), Australia
Dia		Dia, Papua New Guinea
Dida	**	Dida, Ivory Coast
Didinga		Didinga, Sudan
Didoi		Didoi, Soviet Russia
Digo		Digo, Tanzania
		Digo, Kenya
Dimasa		Dimasa in Cachar, India
Dime		Dime, Ethiopia
Dimir		Dimir, Papua New Guinea
Dinka		Dinka, Sudan
Dinka, Agar		Dinka, Agar, Sudan
Diodio		Diodio, Papua New Guinea
Diola		Diola, Senegal
		Diola, Guinea-Bissau (80)
Dirim		Dirim, Nigeria
Dirya		Dirya, Nigeria
Divehi		Divehi, Maldives (80)
Djuka		Djuka, Surinam
Dobu		Dobu, Papua New Guinea

Endangen		Endangen, Papua New Guinea
Enga		Enga, Papua New Guinea
Engenni		Engenni, Nigeria
English		Aborigines in Brisbane, Australia (82)
	*	Americans in Geneva, Switzerland
	*	Asian Students, Philippines
	*	Casual Laborers-Atlanta, U.S.A. (82)
	*	Expatriates in Riyadh, Saudi Arabia (82)
		Gays in San Francisco, U.S.A. (82)
	*	Havasupai, U.S.A.
	*	Jewish Imgrnts.-American, Israel
	*	Jewish Imgrnts.-Australia, Israel
		Jews, Non-Sephardic of Mo, Canada
		Nurses in St. Louis, U.S.A. (82)
	**	Pro Hockey Players, U.S.A. (82)
		Ugandan Asian Refugees, U.K. (83)
		Zuni, U.S.A.
English with Hindi	**	Indians, East, Trinidad & Tobago (79)
Enya		Enya, Zaire
Eotile		Eotile, Ivory Coast
Epie		Epie, Nigeria
Erokwanas		Erokwanas, Indonesia
Esan		Esan, Nigeria
	**	Ishans, Nigeria
Eton		Eton, Cameroon
Etulo		Etulo, Nigeria
Evant		Evant, Nigeria
Evenk		Evenks, Soviet Russia
Evenki		Evenki, China
Ewage-Notu		Ewage-Notu, Papua New Guinea
Ewe		Zowla, Ghana
Fa D'Ambu		Fa D'Ambu, Equatorial Guinea
Fagululu		Fagululu, Papua New Guinea
Faiwol		Faiwol, Papua New Guinea
Faka	**	Fakai, Nigeria
Fali	**	Fali, Nigeria
		Fali, Cameroon
Farsi		Bahais in Teheran, Iran (82)
	**	Iranian Bahai Refugees, Pakistan (83)
		Jews of Iran, Iran
Fas		Fas, Papua New Guinea
Fasu		Fasu, Papua New Guinea
Feroge		Feroge, Sudan
Finungwan		Finungwan, Papua New Guinea
Fipa		Fipa, Tanzania
Foau		Foau, Indonesia
Foi		Foi, Papua New Guinea
Foran		Foran, Papua New Guinea
Fordat		Fordat, Indonesia
Fore		Fore, Papua New Guinea
Fouta Toro		Pular, Senegal
Fra-Fra		Fra-Fra, Ghana
French		Jews, Sephardic of Montre, Canada
		Muslim Lebanese Refugees, Canada (83)
	*	University Students, France (79)
Fula		Fula, Guinea
		Fula, Upper Volta
		Fula, Sierra Leone
		Fula, Cunda, Gambia
Fula, Macina		Fula, Macina, Mali

414

Fula, Peuhala	Fula, Peuhala, Mali
Fulani	Adamawa, Cameroon
	Fulah, Upper Volta
	Fulani, Cameroon (79)
	* Fulani, Benin
	* Fulbe, Ghana
Fuliro	Fuliro, Zaire
Fulnio	Fulnio, Brazil
Fungom, Northern	Fungom, Northern, Cameroon
Fungor	Fungor, Sudan
Furu	Furu, Zaire
Fuyuge	Fuyuge, Papua New Guinea
Fyam	Fyam, Nigeria
Fyer	Fyer, Nigeria
Ga-Dang	Ga-Dang, Philippines
Gabri	Gabri, Chad
Gabrinja	* Gabbra, Ethiopia
Gadaba	Gadaban in Andhra Pradesh, India
Gaddi	Gaddi in Himachal Pradesh, India
Gade	Gade, Nigeria
Gadsup	Gadsup, Papua New Guinea
Gagou	Gagu, Ivory Coast
Gaguaz	Gagauzes, Soviet Russia
Gahuku	Gahuku, Papua New Guinea
Gaikundi	Gaikundi, Papua New Guinea
Gaina	Gaina, Papua New Guinea
Gal	Gal, Papua New Guinea
Galambi	Galambi, Nigeria
Galeshi	Galeshis, Iran
Galla	Eritrean Refugees, Sudan (83)
	Gabbra, Kenya
	* Galla (Bale), Ethiopia
	** Saguye, Kenya
Galler	Galler, Laos
Gallinya	Galla, Harar, Ethiopia
Gallinya (Oromo)	Galla of Bucho, Ethiopia
Galong	Galong in Assam, India
Gambai	Gambai, Chad
Gamei	Gamei, Papua New Guinea
Gamti	Gamti in Gujarat, India
Gan	Gan, Upper Volta
Gane	Gane, Indonesia
Gangam	Gangam, Togo
Ganglau	Ganglau, Papua New Guinea
Gangte	Gangte in Assam, India
Garuh	Garuh, Papua New Guinea
Garus	Garus, Papua New Guinea
Garuwahi	Garuwahi, Papua New Guinea
Gawar-Bati	Gawar-Bati, Afghanistan
Gawari	Gawari in Andhra Pradesh, India
Gawwada	Gawwada, Ethiopia
Gayo	Alas, Indonesia
	Gayo, Indonesia (80)
Gbari	Gbari, Nigeria (80)
Gbaya	Gbaya, Nigeria
Gbaya-Ndogo	Gbaya-Ndogo, Sudan
Gbazantche	Gbazantche, Benin
Gberi	Gberi, Sudan
Ge	** Adja, Benin
	Watchi, Togo

415

Gedaged		Gedaged, Papua New Guinea
Gedeo		Gedeo, Ethiopia
Geji		Geji, Nigeria
Genagane		Genagane, Papua New Guinea
Gende		Gende, Papua New Guinea
Gera		Gera, Nigeria
German	*	Students, German Federal Rep. (79)
Geruma		Geruma, Nigeria
Gesa		Gesa, Indonesia
Ghale Gurung		Ghale Gurung, Nepal
Gheko		Gheko, Burma
Ghol		Ghol, Sudan
Ghotuo		Ghotuo, Nigeria
Ghulfan		Ghulfan, Sudan
Gidar		Gidar, Chad
		Gidar, Cameroon
Gidicho		Gidicho, Ethiopia
Gidra		Gidra, Papua New Guinea
Gilaki		Gilakis, Iran
Gilyak		Gilyak, Soviet Russia
Gimi		Gimi, Papua New Guinea
Gimira	**	Ghimeera, Ethiopia
Ginuman		Ginuman, Papua New Guinea
Gira		Gira, Papua New Guinea
Girawa		Girawa, Papua New Guinea
Giri		Giri, Papua New Guinea
Giryama		Giryama, Kenya
Gisiga		Gisiga, Cameroon
Gitua		Gitua, Papua New Guinea
Gizra		Gizra, Papua New Guinea
Glavda	**	Glavda, Nigeria
Gobasi		Gobasi, Papua New Guinea
Gobato		Gobato, Ethiopia
Gobeze		Gobeze, Ethiopia
Godie	***	Godie, Ivory Coast
Goemai		Goemai, Nigeria
Gogo		Gogo, Tanzania
Gogodala		Gogodala, Papua New Guinea
Gokana		Gokana, Nigeria
Gola		Gola, Liberia
Golo		Golo, Chad
Gondi	*	Gonds, India
		Totis, India
Gonja		Gonja, Ghana
Goroa		Goroa, Tanzania
Gorontalo		Gorontalo, Indonesia
Gosha		Gosha, Kenya
Goudari		Goudari, Iran
Gouin-Turka		Gouin-Turka, Upper Volta
Goulai		Goulai, Chad
Gourendi		Gourency, Upper Volta
Gouro	**	Gouro, Ivory Coast
Gouwar		Gouwar, Cameroon
Grasia		Grasia in Gujarat, India
Grebo Dialects	**	Grebo, Liberia
Gu		Gu, Benin
Guaiaqui		Guaiaqui, Paraguay
Guajajara		Guajajara, Brazil
Guajibo		Guajibo, Colombia
Guajiro	*	Guajiro, Colombia

Guambiano	Guambiano, Colombia
Guana	Guana, Paraguay
Guanano	* Guanano, Colombia (79)
Guarani	*** Guarani, Bolivia (79)
	Simba, Bolivia
Guarani (Bolivian)	** Chiriguano, Argentina
Guarayu	Guarayu, Bolivia
Guarojio	Guarojio, Mexico
Guayabero	Guayabero, Colombia
	Guayabevo, Colombia
Gude	Gude, Cameroon
	Gude, Nigeria
Gudu	Gudu, Nigeria
Guduf	Guduf, Nigeria
Guere	Guere, Ivory Coast
	* Krahn, Ivory Coast
Gugu-Yalanji	Gugu-Yalanji, Australia
Guhu-Samane	Guhu-Samane, Papua New Guinea
Gujarati	Dawoodi Muslims, India
	** Dubla, India
	Gujarati, United Kingdom
	* Indians In Rhodesia, Zimbabwe
	Khojas, Agha Khani, India
	* Parsees, India (81)
	Ugandan Asian Refugees, Canada (83)
	** Vohras of Yavatmal, India
Gujarati Dialect	Bajania, Pakistan (79)
	Vagari, Pakistan
Gujarati, Koli	** Kohli, Kutchi, Pakistan
	** Kohli, Parkari, Pakistan
	** Kohli, Tharadari, Pakistan
	** Kohli, Wadiara, Pakistan
Gujari	Gujars of Kashmir, India (81)
Gujuri	Gujuri, Afghanistan
Gula	Gula, Chad
Gulfe	Gulfe, Cameroon
Gumasi	Gumasi, Papua New Guinea
Gumine	Gumine, Papua New Guinea
Gumuz	Gumuz, Ethiopia
	Gumuz, Sudan
Gurage Dialects	Gurage, Ethiopia (80)
Gure-Kahugu	Gure-Kahugu, Nigeria
Gurenne	Gurensi, Ghana
Gurma	Gurma, Upper Volta
Gurung	Gurung, Nepal
Guruntum-Mbaaru	Guruntum-Mbaaru, Nigeria
Gusap	Gusap, Papua New Guinea
Guwot	Guwot, Papua New Guinea
Gwa	Gwa, Ivory Coast
Gwandara	Gwandara, Nigeria
Gwari Matai	Gwari Matai, Nigeria
Gwedena	Gwedena, Papua New Guinea
Gwere	Gwere, Uganda
Ha	Ha, Tanzania
Hadiyya	Hadiyya, Ethiopia
Hadza	Dorobo, Tanzania
Hahon	Hahon, Papua New Guinea
Hakka	** Chinese Hakka of Taiwan, Taiwan (79)
	** Chinese in Brazil, Brazil
	Chinese in Puerto Rico, Puerto Rico

417

Hakka	** Chinese in Sabah, Malaysia
	* Chinese in Thailand, Thailand
Halbi	Halbi in Madhya Pradesh, India
Halia	Halia, Papua New Guinea
Hallam	Hallam, Burma
Hamtai	Hamtai, Papua New Guinea
Hangaza	Hangaza, Tanzania
Hani	Hani, China
Hanonoo	Hanonoo, Philippines
Harari	Harari, Ethiopia
Harauti	Harauti in Rajasthan, India
Hassaniya (Arabic)	* White Moors, Mauritania
Hatsa	Hatsa, Tanzania
Hausa	Arawa, Nigeria
	Kurfei, Niger
	*** Maguzawa, Nigeria (79)
	Mauri, Niger
Hausa, Ghana	Muslim Community of Bawku, Ghana
Havu	Havu, Zaire
Havunese	Havunese, Indonesia
Haya	Haya, Tanzania
Hazaragi	** Hazara in Kabul, Afghanistan (82)
Hebrew	* Jewish Imgrnts.-Argentine, Israel
	* Jewish Imgrnts.-Brazilian, Israel
	* Jewish Imgrnts.-Mexican, Israel
	* Jewish Imgrnts.-Uruguayan, Israel
	* Jewish Immigrants, Other, Israel
Hehe	Hehe, Tanzania
Heiban	Heiban, Sudan
Heikum	Bushmen (Heikum), Namibia
Helong	Helong, Indonesia
Herero	Herero, Botswana
Heso	Heso, Zaire
Hewa	** Hewa, Papua New Guinea (79)
Hezara'i	Hezareh, Iran
Higi	*** Higi, Nigeria
Hindi	Jains, India
Hindustani	Balmiki, Pakistan
	Indians in Fiji, Fiji (79)
Hixkaryana	Hixkaryana, Brazil
Ho	Ho in Bihar, India
Hohodene	Hohodene, Brazil
Hokkien	Chinese Fishermen, Malaysia
Holiya	Holiya in Madhya Pradesh, India
Holoholo	Holoholo, Tanzania
Holu	Holu, Angola
Hopi	Hopi, U.S.A.
Hote	Hote, Papua New Guinea
Hrangkhol	Hrangkhol, Burma
Huachipaire	Huachipaire, Peru
Huambisa	Huambisa, Peru
Huasteco	Huasteco, Mexico
Huave	** Huave, Mexico
Hui-hui-yu	Hui, China (80)
Huichol	Huichol, Mexico
Huila	** Huila, Angola
Huitoto, Meneca	Huitoto, Meneca, Colombia
Huitoto, Murui	Huitoto, Murui, Peru
Hukwe	Hukwe, Angola
Hula	Hula, Papua New Guinea

Iresim	Iresim, Indonesia
Iria	Iria, Indonesia
Irigwe	Irigwe, Nigeria
Irula	*** Irulas in Kerala, India
Irumu	Irumu, Papua New Guinea
Isaalin	** Sisaala, Ghana
Isanzu	Isanzu, Tanzania
Isebe	Isebe, Papua New Guinea
Isekiri	Isekiri, Nigeria
Isneg	** Apayao, Philippines
Isneg, Dibagat-Kabugao	Isneg, Dibagat-Kabugao, Philippines
Isneg, Karagawan	Isneg, Karagawan, Philippines
Isoko	Isoko, Nigeria
Italian	Jews in Venice, Italy (82)
	Pension Students-Madrid, Spain (82)
Itawit	Itawit, Philippines
Itelmen	Itelmen, Soviet Russia
Itik	Itik, Indonesia
Itneg, Adasen	Itneg, Adasen, Philippines
Itneg, Binongan	Itneg, Binongan, Philippines
Itneg, Masadiit	Itneg, Masadiit, Philippines
Itonama	Itonama, Bolivia
Ivbie North-Okpela-Atte	Ivbie North-Okpela-Atte, Nigeria
Iwa	Iwa, Zambia
Iwaidja	* Iwaidja, Austria
Iwal	Iwal, Papua New Guinea
Iwam	Iwam, Papua New Guinea
Iwam, Sepik	Iwam, Sepik, Papua New Guinea
Iwur	Iwur, Indonesia
Iyon	Iyon, Nigeria
	Iyon, Cameroon
Izarek	Izarek, Nigeria
Izhor	Izhor, Soviet Russia
Izi	** Izi, Nigeria
Jaba	Jaba, Nigeria
Jabem	Jabem, Papua New Guinea
Jacalteco	Jacalteco, Guatemala
Jagannathi	Jagannathi in A.P., India
Jaipuri	Rajasthani Muslims-Jaipur, India (82)
Jamaican Patois	** Jamaican Elite, Jamaica
Jamamadi	Jamamadi, Brazil
Jamden	Jamden, Indonesia
Jamshidi	Jamshidis, Iran
Janena	Barasano, Southern, Colombia
Janggali	Janggali, Nepal
Janjero	Janjero, Ethiopia
Janjo	Janjo, Nigeria
Japanese	* Barbers in Tokyo, Japan (82)
	* Danchi Dwellers in Tokyo, Japan (82)
	Geishas in Osaka, Japan (82)
	* Inland Sea Island Peoples, Japan
	Japanese in Brazil, Brazil (79)
	* Japanese in Korea, Korea, Republic of
	** Japanese Students In USA, U.S.A.
	Soka Gakkai Believers, Japan
	** Univ. Students of Japan, Japan
Jaqaru	Jaqaru, Peru
Jara	Jara, Nigeria
Jaranchi	** Jarawa, Nigeria
Jatapu	Jatapu in Andhra Pradesh, India

Kei	Kei, Indonesia
Keiga	Keiga, Sudan
Keiga Jirru	Keiga Jirru, Sudan
Kekchi	** Kekchi, Guatemala
Kela	Kela, Papua New Guinea
	Kelah, Zaire
Kelabit	Kelabit, Malaysia (81)
Kelao	Kelao, China
Kele	Kele, Gabon
Keley-i	Ifuago, Antipolo, Philippines
Kemak	Kemak, Indonesia
Kembata	Kembata, Ethiopia
Kemok	Kemok, Malaysia
Kenati	Kenati, Papua New Guinea
Kendari	Kendari, Indonesia
Kenga	Kenga, Chad
Kenyah	Kenyah, Indonesia
Keopara	Keopara, Papua New Guinea
Kera	Kera, Chad
	Kera, Cameroon
Kerewo	Kerewo, Papua New Guinea
Keriaka	Keriaka, Papua New Guinea
Kerinchi	Kerinchi, Indonesia
Ket	Ket, Soviet Russia
Kewa	* Kepas, Papua New Guinea
Kewa, East	Kewa, East, Papua New Guinea
Kewa, South	Kewa, South, Papua New Guinea
Kewa, West	Kewa, West, Papua New Guinea
Khakas	Khakas, Soviet Russia
Khalaj	Khalaj, Iran
Khalka	Khalka, China
Kham	Kham, China
	Kham, Nepal
Khamti	Khamti in Assam, India
Khamu	* Khamu, Thailand
Khana	Khana, Nigeria
Khandesi	Khandesi, India
Khanti	Khanti, Soviet Russia
Kharia	Kharia in Bihar, India
Khasi	Khasi in Assam, India
Khasonke	Khasonke, Mali
Khinalug	Khinalug, Soviet Russia
Khirwar	Khirwar in Madhya Pradesh, India
Khmer	Khmer Refugees, Laos (83)
	Khmer Refugees, Belgium (83)
	** Khmer Rfgs, Canada (83)
	Khmer Unaced Minors, Thailand (83)
Khowar	Khowar, India
Khuwar	Chitralis, Pakistan (79)
Khvarshin	Khvarshin, Soviet Russia
Kiari	Kiari, Papua New Guinea
Kibet	Kibet, Chad
Kibiri	Kibiri, Papua New Guinea
Kichepo	Kichepo, Sudan
Kijita	** Wajita, Tanzania
Kikapoo	Kikapoo, Mexico
Kikerewe	Kerewe, Tanzania
Kikongo	Bakongo Angolan Refugees, Zaire (83)
Kilba	Kilba, Nigeria

Kilmera	Kilmera, Papua New Guinea
Kim	Kim, Chad
	Kim, Central African Republic
Kimaghama	Kimaghama, Indonesia
Kimbu	Kimbu, Tanzania
Kimyal	* Kimyal, Indonesia
Kinalakna	Kinalakna, Papua New Guinea
Kinaray-A	Kinaray-A, Philippines
Kinga	Kinga, Tanzania
Kinyarwanda	*** Banyarwanda, Rwanda
Kirgiz	Kirgiz, Soviet Russia (80)
	Kirgiz, Afghanistan
	Kirgiz, China
	Kirgiz Afghans in Turkey, Turkey (83)
Kiriwina	Kiriwina, Papua New Guinea
Kirundi	Burundian Hutu Refugees, Tanzania (83)
	*** Rwandan Tutsi, Burundi, Burundi (83)
Kis	Kis, Papua New Guinea
Kisan	Kisan in Bihar, India
Kisankasa	Kisankasa, Tanzania
Kishanganjia	Kishanganjia in Bihar, India
Kishtwari	Kishtwari in Jammu, India
Kisi	Kisi, Tanzania
Kissi	Kissi, Guinea
	* Kissi, Liberia
Kissi, Southern	* Kissi, Sierra Leone
Kiwai, Northeast	Kiwai, Northeast, Papua New Guinea
Kiwai, Southern	Kiwai, Southern, Papua New Guinea
Kiwai, Wabuda	Kiwai, Wabuda, Papua New Guinea
Kiwoyo	Bawoyo, Zaire
Kizinza	* Wazinza, Tanzania
Klaoh	Klaoh, Liberia
Koalib (Nuba)	Koalib, Sudan (79)
Kobiana	Kobiana, Guinea
Kobon	Kobon, Guinea
Koda	Koda in Bihar, India
Kodi	Kodi, Indonesia
Koenoem	Koenoem, Nigeria
Kofyar	Kofyar, Nigeria
Kohoroxitari	Kohoroxitari, Brazil
Kohumono	Kohumono, Nigeria
Koiari, Grass	Koiari, Grass, Papua New Guinea
Koiari, Mountain	Koiari, Mountain, Papua New Guinea
Koita	Koita, Papua New Guinea
Kokant	Kokant, Burma
Koke	Koke, Chad
Kol	Kol, Papua New Guinea
	Kol in Assam, India
Kolaka	** Loho Loho, Indonesia
Kolami	** Kolam, India
Kolbila	Kolbila, Cameroon
Kole	Kole, Cameroon
Koliku	Koliku, Papua New Guinea
Kolom	Kolom, Papua New Guinea
Kom	Kom in Manipur, India
Kom Komba	* Konkomba, Togo
Koma	Koma, Ghana
	Koma, Nigeria
	Koma, Cameroon
Koma, Central	Koma, Central, Sudan

Komba	Komba, Papua New Guinea
Kombio	Kombio, Papua New Guinea
Komering	Komering, Indonesia
	Lampung, Indonesia (80)
Komi-Permyat	Komi-Permyat, Soviet Russia
Komi-Zyrian	Komi-Zyrian, Soviet Russia
Komo	* Komo, Ethiopia
Komono	Komono, Upper Volta
Komutu	Komutu, Papua New Guinea
Konabem	Konabem, Cameroon
	Konabem, Cameroon
Konda-Dora	Konda-Dora (Andra Pradesh, India
Koneraw	Koneraw, Indonesia
Kongo	Kongo, Angola
Konkani	Konkani in Gujarat, India
Konkomba	Konkomba, Ghana
Kono	** Kono, Sierra Leone
	Kono, Nigeria
Konomala	Konomala, Papua New Guinea
Konongo	Konongo, Tanzania
Konso	Konso, Ethiopia
Konyagi	Konyagi, Guinea
Koraga	Koraga in Kerala, India
Korak	Korak, Papua New Guinea
Korape	Korape, Papua New Guinea
Korapun	Korapun, Indonesia
Korean	** Apartment Residents-Seoul, Korea, Rep.
	** Bus Drivers, Korea, Republic of
	** Bus Girls in Seoul, Korea, Rep. (82)
	Indust.Workers Yongdungpo, Korea, Rep
	Kae Sung Natives in Seoul, Korea, (82)
	*** Koreans in Germany, German Federal Rep.
	Koreans in Manchuria, China (81)
	* Koreans of Japan, Japan
	** Prisoners, Korea, Republic of
Korku	* Korku in Madhya Pradesh, India
Koro	Koro, Nigeria
Koroma	Koroma, Sudan
Korop	Korop, Nigeria
	Korop, Cameroon
Korwa	Korwa in Bihar, India
Koryak	Koryak, Soviet Russia
Kosorong	Kosorong, Papua New Guinea
Kota	Kota, Gabon
	Kota in Tamil Nadu, India
	Kotta, India
Kotia	Kotia in Andhra Pradesh, India
Kotogut	Kotogut, Indonesia
Kotoko	Kotoko, Chad
	Kotoko, Cameroon
Kotokoli	Kotokoli, Benin
	Kotokoli, Togo
	Tem, Togo
Kotopo	Kotopo, Cameroon
Kouya	Kouya, Ivory Coast
Kovai	Kovai, Papua New Guinea
Kove	Kove, Papua New Guinea
Kowaao	** Kowaao, Liberia
Koya	Koya in Andhra Pradesh, India
Koyra	Koyra, Ethiopia

Kuria		Kuria, Tanzania
Kurichiya		Kurichiya in Kerala, India (81)
Kurmanji		Iraqi Kurd Refugees, Iran (83)
Kuruba		Kuruba in Tamil Nadu, India
Kurudu		Kurudu, Indonesia
Kurumba		Kurumba, Upper Volta
Kurux		Kurux in Bihar, India
Kusaal	**	Kusaasi, Ghana
Kushi		Kushi, Nigeria
Kusso		Mbukushu, Angola
Kusu		Kusu, Zaire
Kuteb		Kuteb, Nigeria
Kutin		Kutin, Cameroon
Kutu		Kutu, Tanzania
Kuturmi		Kuturmi, Nigeria
Kuvi		Kuvi in Orissa, India
Kuwaa		Kuwaa, Liberia
Kuzamani		Kuzamani, Nigeria
Kvanadin		Kvanadin, Soviet Russia
Kwa		Kwa, Nigeria
Kwadi		Kwadi, Angola
Kwakum		Kwakum, Cameroon
Kwale		Kwale, Papua New Guinea
Kwambi		Kwambi, Namibia
Kwanga		Kwanga, Papua New Guinea
Kwangali		Kwangali, Angola
Kwansu		Kwansu, Indonesia
Kwanyama		Kwanyama, Angola
		Kwanyama, Namibia
Kwaya		Kwaya, Tanzania
Kwe-Etshari	*	Bushmen (Hiechware), Zimbabwe
Kwe-etshori		Kwe-etshori, Botswana
		Kwe-etshori, Zimbabwe
Kwerba		Kwerba, Indonesia
Kwere		Kwere, Tanzania
Kwese		Kwese, Zaire
Kwesten		Kwesten, Indonesia
Kwoma		Kwoma, Papua New Guinea
Kwomtari		Kwomtari, Papua New Guinea
Kyibaku		Kyibaku, Nigeria
Laamang		Laamang, Nigeria
Labaani		Labans, India
Labhani		Labhani in Andhra Pradesh, India
Labu		Labu, Papua New Guinea
Lacandon		Lacandon, Mexico
Ladakhi		Ladakhi in Jammu, India
Ladinos		Ladinos, Lebanon
Laewomba		Laewomba, Papua New Guinea
Lafofa		Lafofa, Sudan
Lahouli	**	Lahaulis in Punjab, India
Lahu	*	Lahu, Thailand (81)
		Lahu, Burma
Lahul		Lahul, China
Laka		Laka, Cameroon
		Laka, China
		Laka, Central African Republic
Lakal		Laka, Chad
Lakian		Lakians, Soviet Russia
Lakka		Lakka, Nigeria
Lala		Lala, Zambia

426

427

	Buka-khwe, Botswana
	Kubu, Indonesia (80)
*	Mahrah, Yemen, Democratic
	Moken of Thailand, Thailand
	Nuristani, Afghanistan (80)
**	Plantation Workers, Papua New Guinea
	Pygmy (Binga), Burundi
	Pygmy (Binga), Central African Rep.

Local Languages	*	Pygmy (Mbuti), Zaire (79)
	**	Zaranda Hill Peoples, Nigeria
Lodhi		Lodhi in Bihar, India
Logba		Logba, Ghana
Logoro (Bambara)		Kagoro, Mali
Lohiki		Lohiki, Papua New Guinea
Loinang		Loinang, Indonesia (81)
Loko		Loko, Sierra Leone
		Loko, Guinea
Lokoro	*	Lokoro, Sudan
Loma		Loma, Guinea
		Loma, Liberia
Lombi		Lombi, Zaire
Lombo		Lombo, Zaire
Longuda		Longuda, Nigeria
Lore		Lore, Indonesia
Lorhon	*	Teenbu, Ivory Coast
Lori		Bovir-Ahmadi, Iran
		Lori, Sudan
Lotsu-Piri		Lotsu-Piri, Nigeria
Lou-Baluan-Pam		Lou-Baluan-Pam, Papua New Guinea
Loven		Loven, Laos (81)
Lozi		Lozi, Zimbabwe
		Lozi, Zambia
Lu		Lu, China
Luac		Luac, Sudan
Luano		Luano, Zambia
Lubu		Lubu, Indonesia
Luchazi		Luchazi, Angola
		Luchazi, Zambia
Lue		Lue, Cameroon
Lugbara		Muslims (West Nile Dist.), Uganda
Lugitama		Lugitama, Papua New Guinea
Luimbi		Luimbi, Angola
Lukep		Lukep, Papua New Guinea
Lumbu		Lumbu, Gabon
Luna		Luna, Zaire
Lunda		Lunda, Angola
Lunda, Ndembu		Lunda, Ndembu, Zambia
Lundu		Lundu, Cameroon
Lungu		Lungu, Nigeria
Luo		Luo, Tanzania
Luri		Lors, Iran (80)
		Mamasani, Iran
Lushai		Lushai in Assam, India
Luteso	**	Teso, Kenya
Luwu		Luwu, Indonesia
Luyana		Luyana, Angola
		Luyana, Zambia
Lwalu		Lwalu, Zaire
Lwena		Lwena, Angola
Lwo		Lwo, Sudan

428

Ma	Ma, Zaire
Maanyan	Maanyan, Indonesia
Maba	Maba, Chad
	Maba, Sudan
	Ouaddai, Chad
Maban-Jumjum	Maban-Jumjum, Sudan
	Meban, Sudan
Maca	Maca, Paraguay
Machiguenga	Machiguenga, Peru
Macu	Macu, Colombia
Macuna	Macuna, Colombia
Macuxi	** Macuxi, Brazil
Madak	Madak, Papua New Guinea
Madda	Madda, Nigeria
Madi	Madi, Sudan
	Madi, Uganda
Madik	Madik, Indonesia
Mafaara	** Nafaara, Ghana (79)
Magar	** Magar, Nepal
Maghi	Maghi, Burma
Magori	Magori, Papua New Guinea
Maguindano	Maguindano, Philippines (80)
Mahali	Mahali in Assam, India
Mahri	Mahri, Oman
Mai	Mai, Papua New Guinea
Mailu	Mailu, Papua New Guinea
Maiongong	Maiongong, Brazil
Mairasi	Mairasi, Indonesia
Maisan	Maisan, Papua New Guinea
Maithili	Maithili, Nepal
Maiwa	Maiwa, Papua New Guinea
Majangiir	* Masengo, Ethiopia
Majhi	Majhi, Nepal
Majhwar	Majhwar in Madhya Pradesh, India
Maji	Maji, Ethiopia
Majingai-Ngama	Majingai-Ngama, Chad
	Majingai-ngama, Central African Rep.
Maka	Maka, Cameroon
Makarim	Makarim, Papua New Guinea
Makasai	Makasai, Indonesia
Makere	Makere, Uganda
Makian, West	Makian, West, Indonesia
Maklew	Maklew, Indonesia
Makua	Makua, Mozambique
Mala, Pattani	Thai Islam (Malay), Thailand (80)
Malagasy	* Prisoners/Antananarivo, Madagascar (82)
Malalamai	Malalamai, Papua New Guinea
Malamutha	Malakkaras of Kerala, India (81)
Malankuravan	Malankuravan in Kerala, India
Malapandaram	Malapandaram in Kerala, India
Malappanackan	Malappanackers, India
Malaryan	Malaryan in Kerala, India
Malas	Malas, Papua New Guinea
Malasanga	Malasanga, Papua New Guinea
Malavedan	Malavedan in Kerala, India
Malay	Malays of Singapore, Singapore (79)
Malayalam	Indians in Dubai, United Arab Emirates (82)
	Iravas in Kerala, India
	* Malayalars, India
Malayalan	Mappillas, India

429

Malayo		Malayo, Colombia
Male		Male, Ethiopia
Malek		Malek, Papua New Guinea
Maleu		Maleu, Papua New Guinea
Mali		Mali in Andhra Pradesh, India
Malila		Malila, Tanzania
Malinke, Senegalese		Manding, Senegal
Malki		Malki in Bihar, India
Malon		Malon, Papua New Guinea
Malpaharia		Malpaharia in Assam, India
Maltese	*	Maltese, Malta
Malvi		Malvi in Madhya Pradesh, India
Mam	**	Mam Indian, Guatemala
Mama		Mama, Nigeria
Mamaa		Mamaa, Papua New Guinea
Mambai		Mambai, Indonesia
Mambila		Mambila, Cameroon
Mambwe-Lungu		Mambwe-Lungu, Tanzania
		Mambwe-Lungu, Zambia
Mampruli		Mamprusi, Ghana
		Mamprusi, Ghana
Mamvu-Efe		Mamvu-Efe, Zaire
Managalasi		Managalasi, Papua New Guinea
Manambu		Manambu, Papua New Guinea
Manchu		Manchu, China (81)
Manda		Manda, Tanzania
Mandar		Mandar, Indonesia
Mandara		Mandara, Nigeria
Mandarin	*	Chinese in Austria, Austria
	**	Chinese in Boston, U.S.A. (82)
	*	Chinese in Holland, Netherlands
	*	Chinese in Japan, Japan
	*	Chinese in Korea, Korea, Rep.
	*	Chinese in Laos, Laos
	**	Chinese in United Kingdom,
	**	Chinese in United States, U.S.A.
	*	Chinese in German Federal Rep.
	*	Chinese Mainlanders, Taiwan
		Chinese Muslims, Taiwan (81)
	**	Chinese Refugees, France (79)
	**	Chinese Students Glasgow, U. K.
		Taiwan-Chinese Un. Stud., Taiwan
	**	University Students, Chin, China
Mandarin and dialects		Chinese in Burma, Burma
	**	Chinese in Sarawak, Malaysia
Mandaya		Mandaya, Philippines
Mandaya, Mansaka		Mandaya, Mansaka, Philippines
Mander		Mander, Indonesia
Mandingo		Mandingo, Liberia (79)
Mandyak		Mandyak, Gambia
Mandyako	**	Manjaco, Guinea-Bissau
Mandyale		Manjack, Senegal
Manem		Manem, Indonesia
Mangap		Mangap, Papua New Guinea
Mangbai		Mangbai, Chad
Mangbutu		Mangbutu, Zaire
Manggarai		Manggarai Muslims, Indonesia (81)
Mangisa		Mangisa, Cameroon
Maninka		Maninka, Guinea-Bissau
		Maninka, Sierra Leone

Manipuri	*	Meitei, India (79)
Maniteneri		Piro, Peru
Mankanya		Mancang, Senegal
		Mankanya, Guinea-Bissau
		Mankanya, Senegal
Manna-Dora		Manna-Dora in A.P., India
Mannan		Mannan in Kerala, India
Mano		Mano, Liberia
Manobo	*	Ata of Davao, Philippines
Manobo, Agusan		Manobo, Agusan, Philippines
Manobo, Ata		Manobo, Ata, Philippines
Manobo, Binokid		Manobo, Binokid, Philippines
	**	Manobo, Wstrn Bukidnon, Philippines
Manobo, Binukid	**	Bukidnon, Philippines
Manobo, Dibabawon		Manobo, Dibabawon, Philippines
Manobo, Obo		Manobo, Obo, Philippines
Manobo, Pulangi		Manobos, Pulangi, Philippines
Manobo, Sarangani		Manobo, Sarangani, Philippines
Manobo, Tagabawa		Manobo, Tagabawa, Philippines
Manobo, Tigwa	**	Manobo, Salug, Philippines
	**	Manobo, Tigwa, Philippines
Mansaka	**	Mansaka, Philippines
Mansi		Mansi, Soviet Russia
Mantera		Mantera, Malaysia
Mantion		Mantion, Indonesia
Manu Park Panoan		Manu Park Panoan, Peru
Manyika		Manyika, Zimbabwe
Mao, Northern		Mao, Northern, Ethiopia
Maou		Maou, Ivory Coast
Mape		Mape, Papua New Guinea
Mapena		Mapena, Papua New Guinea
Mapoyo		Mapoyo, Venezuela
Mapuche		Mapuche, Chile
Maquiritari		Maquiritari, Venezuela
Mara		Mara in Assam, India
Maralango		Maralango, Papua New Guinea
Maraliinan		Maraliinan, Papua New Guinea
Maranao		Maranao, Philippines (79)
Maranao, Lanad		Maranao, Lanad, Philippines
Mararit		Mararit, Chad
Marathi	*	Labourers of Jhoparpatti, India
		Mangs in Maharashtra, India
Marau		Marau, Indonesia
Marba		Marba, Chad
Marghi Central		Marghi Central, Nigeria
Mari		Mari, Soviet Russia
		Mari, Papua New Guinea
Maria		Maria, Papua New Guinea
		Maria in Andhra Pradesh, India
Marind		Marind, Indonesia
Marind, Bian		Marind, Bian, Indonesia
Maring		Maring, Papua New Guinea
Marka		Marka, Upper Volta
Marubo		Marubo, Brazil
Marwari	**	Bhil, Pakistan
		Marwari in Gujarat, India
	**	Meghwar, Pakistan (79)
Masa		Budugum, Cameroon
		Gisei, Cameroon
		Masa, Chad

431

REGISTRY OF THE UNREACHED

Masaba		Masaba, Uganda
Masai	**	Maasai, Kenya (79)
Masai, Samburu		Samburu, Kenya
Masakin		Masakin, Sudan
Masalit		Masalit, Chad
Masegi		Masegi, Papua New Guinea
Masenrempulu		Masenrempulu, Indonesia
Mashi		Mashi, Zambia
Massalat		Massalat, Chad
Mataco		Mataco, Argentina
Matakam		Matakam, Cameroon
		Matakam, Nigeria
Matawari		Matawari, Surinam
Matbat		Matbat, Indonesia
Matengo		Matengo, Tanzania
Matipuhy-Nahukua		Matipuhy-Nahukua, Brazil
Matlatzinca, Atzingo		Matlatzinca, Atzingo, Mexico
Matumbi		Matumbi, Tanzania
Maure		Maure, Mali
Maviha		Maviha, Mozambique
Mawak		Mawak, Papua New Guinea
Mawan		Mawan, Papua New Guinea
Mawchi	**	Mawchis, India
Mawes		Mawes, Indonesia
Maxakali		Maxakali, Brazil
Mayo		Mayo, Mexico
Mayoruna		Mayoruna, Peru
Mazahua	**	Mazahua, Mexico
Mazandarani		Mazandaranis, Iran
Mba		Mba, Zaire
Mbaama		Mbaama, Gabon
Mbai		Mbai, Chad
		Mbai, Central African Republic
Mbala		Mbala, Zaire
Mbangwe		Mbangwe, Zaire
Mbanja		Mbanja, Zaire
Mbati		Mbati, Central African Republic
Mbe		Mbe, Nigeria
Mbede		Mbede, Gabon
Mbembe		Mbembe, Cameroon
		Mbembe (Tigong), Nigeria
Mbimu		Mbimu, Cameroon
Mbo		Mbo, Cameroon
		Mbo, Zaire
Mboi		Mboi, Nigeria
Mbole		Mbole, Zaire
Mbugwe		Mbugwe, Tanzania
Mbula-Bwazza		Mbula-Bwazza, Nigeria
Mbum		Mbum, Chad
Mbunda		Mbunda, Angola
Mbunga		Mbunga, Tanzania
Mbwela		Mbwela, Angola
Me'en		Me'en, Ethiopia
Meax		Meax, Indonesia
Medlpa		Medlpa, Papua New Guinea
Mehek		Mehek, Papua New Guinea
Mejah	**	Mejah, India
Meje		Meje, Uganda
Mekeo		Mekeo, Papua New Guinea
Mekwei		Mekwei, Indonesia

Melanau	**	Melanau of Sarawak, Malaysia (80)
Mende		Gola, Sierra Leone
		Krim, Sierra Leone
		Mende, Sierra Leone
		Mende, Liberia
Menemo-Mogamo		Menemo-Mogamo, Cameroon
Mengen		Mengen, Papua New Guinea
Menka		Menka, Cameroon
Menri		Menri, Malaysia
Menye		Menye, Papua New Guinea
Meo	**	Meo, Thailand
Mera Mera		Mera Mera, Papua New Guinea
Mesengo		Mesengo, Ethiopia
Mesme		Mesme, Chad
Mesmedje		Mesmedje, Chad
Mianmin		Mianmin, Papua New Guinea
Miao	***	Hmong Refugees, U.S.A. (83)
	***	Hmong Women/Ban Vinai,Thailand (83)
		Hmong, Twin Cities, U.S.A.
		Miao, China (81)
Miching	**	Miching, India
Midob		Midob, Sudan
Midsivindi		Midsivindi, Papua New Guinea
Mien		Mien, China (81)
Migabac		Migabac, Papua New Guinea
Migili		Migili, Nigeria
Mikarew		Mikarew, Papua New Guinea
Mikir	**	Karbis, India
Mimi		Mimi, Chad
Mimika	*	Mimika, Indonesia
Mina		Mina in Madhya Pradesh, India
Minamanwa	**	Mamanua, Philippines (81)
Minangkabau		Minangkabau, Indonesia (80)
Minanibai		Minanibai, Papua New Guinea
Mindik		Mindik, Papua New Guinea
Minduumo		Minduumo, Gabon
Mingat		Mingat, Soviet Russia
Mirdha		Mirdha in Orissa, India
Miri		Miri, Sudan
Miriam		Miriam, Papua New Guinea
Mirung		Mirung, Bangladesh
Mishmi		Mishmi in Assam, India
Miskito		Miskito, Nicaragua
Mitang		Mitang, Papua New Guinea
Mitmit		Mitmit, Papua New Guinea
Mixe	**	Mixes, Mexico
Mixteco	*	Mixteco,San Juan Mixtepic, Mexico
Mixteco, Amoltepec		Mixteco, Amoltepec, Mexico
Mixteco, Apoala		Mixteco, Apoala, Mexico
Mixteco, Eastern		Mixteco, Eastern, Mexico
Mixteco, Eastern Putla		Mixteco, Eastern Putla, Mexico
Mixteco, Huajuapan		Mixteco, Huajuapan, Mexico
Mixteco, Silacayoapan		Mixteco, Silacayoapan, Mexico
Mixteco, Southern Puebla		Mixteco, Southern Puebla, Mexico
Mixteco, Southern Putla		Mixteco, Southern Putla, Mexico
Mixteco, Tututepec		Mixteco, Tututepec, Mexico
Mixteco, Yosondua		Mixteco, Yosondua, Mexico
Miya		Miya, Nigeria
Mo		Mo, Ivory Coast
Mo (Degha)		Mo, Ghana

433

Mober	Mober, Nigeria
Mocha	*** Mocha, Ethiopia
Modo	Modo, Sudan
Moewehafen	Moewehafen, Papua New Guinea
Mofu	Mofu, Cameroon
Mogholi	Mogholi, Afghanistan
Mogum	Mogum, Chad
Moi	Moi, Indonesia
Mokareng	Mokareng, Papua New Guinea
Moken	Moken, Burma (79)
Mokole	* Mokole, Benin
Molbog	* Molbog, Philippines
Mole	Mossi, Upper Volta (80)
Molof	Molof, Indonesia
Momare	Momare, Papua New Guinea
Mombum	Mombum, Indonesia
Momoguns	Momoguns, Malaysia
Momolili	Momolili, Papua New Guinea
Mon	Mon, Burma (81)
Mona	Mona, Ivory Coast
Mongondow	Mongondow, Indonesia (81)
Mongour	Mongour, China
Moni	Moni, Indonesia
Monjombo	Monjombo, Central African Republic
Mono	Mono, Zaire
Monpa	Monpa, India
Montol	Montol, Nigeria
Mopan Maya	** Mopan Maya, Guatemala
	** Mopan Maya, Belize
Moqaddam	Moqaddam, Iran
Mor	Mor, Indonesia
Morawa	Morawa, Papua New Guinea
Moreb	Moreb, Sudan
Moreno	** Black Caribs, Belize, Belize (79)
	** Black Caribs, Guatemala, Guatemala
	** Black Caribs, Honduras, Honduras
Moresada	Moresada, Papua New Guinea
Mori	Mori, Indonesia (81)
Morigi	Morigi, Papua New Guinea
Morima	Morima, Papua New Guinea
Moru	Moru, Ivory Coast
	Moru, Sudan
Morunahua	Morunahua, Peru
Morwap	Morwap, Indonesia
Mosi	Mosi, Tanzania
Motilon	Motilon, Colombia
	Motilon, Venezuela
Movima	Movima, Bolivia
Moxodi	Moxodi, Papua New Guinea
Mpoto	Mpoto, Malawi
	Mpoto, Tanzania
Mualthuam	Mualthuam, India
Mubi	Mubi, Chad
Mugil	Mugil, Papua New Guinea
Muinane	Muinane, Colombia
Mukawa	Mukawa, Papua New Guinea
Mulimba	Mulimba, Cameroon
Multani	Multani in Punjab, India
Mumbake	Mumbake, Nigeria
Mumuye	Mumuye, Nigeria

434

Nambikuara		Nambikuara, Brazil
Nambis		Nambis, Papua New Guinea
Nambu		Nambu, Papua New Guinea
Nambya	**	Nambya, Zimbabwe
Namuni		Namuni, Papua New Guinea
Nanai		Nanai, China
		Nanai, Soviet Russia
Nancere		Nancere, Chad
Nandi		Dorobo, Kenya
		Nandi, Zaire
Nandu-Tari		Nandu-Tari, Nigeria
Nankina		Nankina. Papua New Guinea
Nao		Nao, Ethiopia
Naoudem		Naoudem, Togo
Napali	*	Gorkha, India
Nara		Nara, Ethiopia
		Nara, Papua New Guinea
Naraguta		Naraguta, Nigeria
Narak		Narak, Papua New Guinea
Nasioi		Nasioi, Papua New Guinea
Nata		Nata, Tanzania
Natemba		Natemba, Togo
Natioro		Natioro, Upper Volta
Native Senoi	**	Senoi, Malaysia (81)
Nauna		Nauna, Papua New Guinea
Nawuri		Nawuri, Ghana
Nchumbulu		Nchumbulu, Ghana
Nchumburu		Nchimburu, Ghana
Nchumunu		Nchumunu, Ghana
Ndaaka		Ndaaka, Zaire
Ndali		Ndali, Tanzania
Ndam		Ndam, Central African Republic
Ndamba		Ndamba, Tanzania
Ndao		Ndaonese, Indonesia
Ndau		Ndau, Zimbabwe
Nde-Nsele-Nta		Nde-Nsele-Nta, Nigeria
Ndengereko		Ndengereko, Tanzania
Ndjem		Ndjem, Cameroon
Ndo		Ndo, Zaire
Ndoe		Ndoe, Nigeria
Ndogo		Ndogo, Central African Republic
		Ndogo, Sudan
Ndom		Ndom, Indonesia
Ndomde		Ndomde, Tanzania
Ndoolo		Ndoolo, Zaire
Ndop-Bamessing		Ndop-Bamessing, Cameroon
Ndoro	**	Ndoro, Nigeria
		Ndoro, Cameroon
Nduga		Nduga, Indonesia
Ndunga		Ndunga, Zaire
Ndunpa Duupa		Ndunpa Duupa, Cameroon
Negira		Negira, Papua New Guinea
Nek		Nek, Papua New Guinea
Nekgini		Nekgini, Papua New Guinea
Neko		Neko, Papua New Guinea
Nengaya		Nengaya, Papua New Guinea
Nentsy		Nentsy, Soviet Russia
Nepali	**	Nepalese in India, India
Nevo		Neyo, Ivory Coast
Newari		Newar in Kathmandu, Nepal (82)

436

Newari	* Newari, Nepal
Ngada	Ngada, Indonesia
Ngaing	Ngaing, Papua New Guinea
Ngalik, North	Ngalik, North, Indonesia
Ngalik, Southern	Ngalik, Southern, Indonesia
Ngalum	Ngalum, Indonesia
Ngamo	** Ngamo, Nigeria
Nganasan	Nganasan, Soviet Russia
Ngando	Ngando, Central African Rep.
	Ngando, Zaire
Ngasa	Ngasa, Tanzania
Ngayaba	Ngayaba, Cameroon
Ngbaka	Ngbaka, Zaire
Ngbaka Ma'bo	Ngbaka Ma'bo, Central African Rep.
	Ngbaka Ma'bo, Zaire
Ngbandi	Ngbandi, Zaire
Ngbee	Ngbee, Zaire
Ngemba	Ngemba, Cameroon
Ngen	* Ngen, Ivory Coast
Ngeq	Ngeq, Laos
Ngi	Ngi, Cameroon
Ngindo	Ngindo, Tanzania
Nginyukwur	Nginyukwur, Sudan
Ngirere	Ngirere, Sudan
Ngiri	Ngiri, Zaire
Ngizim	Ngizim, Nigeria
Ngok	Ngok, Sudan
Ngombe	** Ngombe, Zaire
Ngoni	Ngoni, Tanzania
	Ngoni, Zambia
Ngulu	Ngulu, Malawi
	Ngulu, Tanzania
Ngumba	Ngumba, Cameroon
Ngumbi	Ngumbi, Equatorial Guinea
Ngunduna	Ngunduna, Sudan
Nguqwurang	Nguqwurang, Sudan
Ngurimi	Ngurimi, Tanzania
Nguu	Nguu, Tanzania
Ngwo	Ngwo, Cameroon
Ngwoi	Ngwoi, Nigeria
Nharon	Nharon, Botswana
Nhengatu	Nhengatu, Brazil
Nias	Nias, Indonesia
Nielim	Nielim, Chad
Nihali	Nihali in Madhya Pradesh, India
Nii	Nii, Papua New Guinea
Nilamba	Nilamba, Tanzania
Nimadi	Nimadi in Madhya Pradesh, India
Nimboran	Nimboran, Indonesia
Nimowa	Nimowa, Papua New Guinea
Ninam	Ninam, Brazil
Ningerum	* Ningerum, Papua New Guinea
Ninggrum	Ninggrum, Indonesia
Niningo	Niningo, Papua New Guinea
Ninzam	Ninzam, Nigeria
Nisa	Nisa, Indonesia
Nissan	Nissan, Papua New Guinea
Nivkhi	Nivkhi, Soviet Russia
Njadu	Njadu, Indonesia
Njalgulgule	Njalgulgule, Sudan

Nkem-Nkum	Nkem-Nkum, Nigeria
Nkom	Nkom, Cameroon
Nkonya	Nkonya, Ghana
Nkutu	Nkutu, Zaire
Nocte	*** Nocte, India
Nohu	Nohu, Cameroon
Nomane	Nomane, Papua New Guinea
Nomu	Nomu, Papua New Guinea
Nondiri	Nondiri, Papua New Guinea
Norra	Norra, Burma
Northeast Thai	** Lepers of N.E. Thailand, Thailand
Northern Cagayan Negrito	Northern Cagayan Negrito, Philippines
Northern Kamer	* Cambodians, Thailand
Northern Kankanay	Kankanay, Northern, Philippines
Nosu	Nosu, China
Notsi	Notsi, Papua New Guinea
Nouni	* Nouni, Upper Volta
Nsenga	Nsenga, Zimbabwe
	Nsenga, Zambia
Nso	Nso, Cameroon
Nsongo	Nsongo, Angola
Ntomba	Ntomba, Zaire
Ntrubo	Ntrubo, Ghana
	Ntrubo, Togo
Nuer	* Nuer, Ethiopia
	* Nuer, Sudan (79)
Nuk	Nuk, Papua New Guinea
Numana-Nunku-Gwantu	Numana-Nunku-Gwantu, Nigeria
Numanggang	Numanggang, Papua New Guinea
Nung	Nung, China
Nungu	Nungu, Nigeria
Nunuma	Nunuma, Upper Volta
Nupe	** Nupe, Nigeria
Nyabwa	** Nyabwa, Ivory Coast
Nyaheun	Nyaheun, Laos
Nyakyusa	Nyakyusa, Malawi
	Nyakyusa, Tanzania
Nyambo	Nyambo, Tanzania
Nyamusa	Nyamusa, Sudan
Nyamwezi	Nyamwezi, Tanzania (80)
Nyaneka	Nyaneka, Angola
Nyang	Nyang, Cameroon
Nyanga-Li	Nyanga-Li, Zaire
Nyangbo	Nyangbo, Ghana
Nyanja	Nyanja, Zimbabwe
Nyankole	Nyankole, Uganda
Nyarueng	Nyarueng, Sudan
Nyaturu	Turu, Tanzania
Nyemba	Nyemba, Angola
Nyiha	Nyiha, Tanzania
	Nyiha, Zambia
Nyoro	Nyoro, Uganda
Nyuli	Nyuli, Uganda
Nyungwe	Nyungwe, Mozambique
Nzakara	Nzakara, Central African Republic
Nzanyi	Nzanyi, Nigeria
Nzebi	Nzebi, Congo
Nzema	Nzema, Ivory Coast
	Nzema, Ghana
O'ung	O'ung, Angola

REGISTRY OF THE UNREACHED

Pakabeti	***	Pakabeti of Equator, Zaire
Pala'wan	*	Pala'wan, Philippines (81)
Palara		Palara, Ivory Coast
Palaung		Palaung, Burma (79)
Palawano		Palawano, Philippines
Palawano, Central		Palawano, Central, Philippines
Palembang		Palembang, Indonesia
Palikur		Palikur, Brazil
Paloc		Paloc, Sudan
Palpa		Palpa, Nepal
Pambia		Pambia, Central African Republic
Pame, Central Chichimeca		Pame, Central Chichimeca, Mexico
Pame, Northern		Pame, Northern, Mexico
Pamiri		Tajik, Afghanistan
Pana		Pana, Central African Republic
Panare		Panare, Venezuela
Pande		Pande, Congo
Pangwa		Pangwa, Tanzania
Panika		Panika, India
Paniyan	**	Paniyan of Kerala, India (81)
Panjabi		Ahmadis in Lahore, Pakistan (82)
Pankhu		Pankhu, Bangladesh
Pantu		Pantu, Indonesia
Pao		Pao, Burma
		Pao in Madhya Pradesh, India
Paongan		Paongan, China
Papapana		Papapana, Papua New Guinea
Pape		Pape, Cameroon
Papel		Papel, Guinea-Bissau
Papuma		Papuma, Indonesia
Parakanan		Parakanan, Brazil
Paranan		Paranan, Philippines
Parawen		Parawen, Papua New Guinea
Pardhan		Pardhan in Andhra Pradesh, India
Pare		Pare, Tanzania
		Pare, Papua New Guinea
Parengi		Parengi in Orissa, India
Paresi		Paresi, Brazil
Parintintin		Parintintin, Brazil
Parji		Dhurwa, India
Parsi	*	Parsis in Bombay, India (82)
Pashayi		Pashayi, Afghanistan
Pashtu		Pashtuns, Iran (80)
Pasismanua		Pasismanua, Papua New Guinea
Patamona		Patamona, Guyana
Patelia		Patelia in Gujarat, India
Patep		Patep, Papua New Guinea
Pato Tapuia		Pato Tapuia, Brazil
Patpatar		Patpatar, Papua New Guinea
Paumari		Paumari, Brazil
Pawaia		Pawaia, Papua New Guinea
Pay		Pay, Papua New Guinea
Paynamar		Paynamar, Papua New Guinea
Penan		Penan, Western, Malaysia (81)
Pende		Pende, Zaire
Pengo		Pengo in Orissa, India
Peremka		Peremka, Papua New Guinea
Peri		Peri, Zaire
Pero		Pero, Nigeria
Persian		Persians of Iran, Iran (80)

Purum		Purum, Burma
Puyuma	**	Puyuma, Taiwan (81)
Pwo Karen		Karen, Pwo, Thailand
Pye		Pye, Ivory Coast
Pyu		Pyu, Indonesia
Qajar		Qajars, Iran
Qara'i		Qara'i, Iran
Qaragozlu		Qaragozlu, Iran
Qashqa'i		Qashqa'i, Iran (80)
Quaiquer		Quaiquer, Colombia
Quechua	**	Quechua, Peru
	**	Quechua, Bolivia
Quechua, Huancayo	**	Quechua, Huanco, Peru
Quiche	**	Quiche, Guatemala (79)
Quichua	**	Quichua, Ecuador
Rabha		Rabha in Assam, India
Rabinal Achi		Rabinal-Achi, Guatemala
Rai		Rai, Nepal
Rai, Khaling		Rai, Khaling, Nepal
Rai, Kulunge		Rai, Kulunge, Nepal
Rai, Thulunge		Rai, Thulunge, Nepal
Rajasthani		Meos of Rajasthan, India (80)
Rajbansi		Rajbansi, Nepal
Ralte		Ralte, Burma
Rambutyo		Rambutyo, Papua New Guinea
Rangkas		Rangkas, Nepal
Rao		Rao, Papua New Guinea
Ratahan		Ratahan, Indonesia
Rataning		Rataning, Chad
Rauto		Rauto, Papua New Guinea
Rava	*	Rava in Assam, India
Rawa		Rawa, Papua New Guinea
Rawang		Rawang, China
Redjang-Lebong		Lebong, Indonesia
Rejang		Redjang, Indonesia (80)
Rempi		Rempi, Papua New Guinea
Rendille		Rendille, Kenya
Reshe		Reshe, Nigeria
Reyesano		Reyesano, Bolivia
Riang		Riang in Assam, India
Riang-Lang		Riang-Lang, Burma
Riantana		Riantana, Indonesia
Rikbaktsa		Rikbaktsa, Brazil
Roinji		Roinji, Papua New Guinea
Romany	*	Gypsies in Spain, Spain (79)
		Romany, Turkey
Romany (Serbian Kaldnash)		Gypsies in Yugoslavia, Yugoslavia
Romany Dialect		Gypsies in Jerusalem, Israel (82)
Romany Dialects		Muslim Gypsies in Skoplje, Yugo.(82)
Romkun		Romkun, Papua New Guinea
Ronga		Ronga, Mozambique
		Ronga, South Africa
Roro		Roro, Papua New Guinea
Rotokas		Rotokas, Papua New Guinea
Ruihi		Ruihi, Tanzania
Rukuba		Rukuba, Nigeria
Rumaya		Rumaya, Nigeria
Runga		Runga, Chad
		Runga, Central African Republic
Rungi		Rungi, Tanzania

REGISTRY OF THE UNREACHED

Sasaru-Enwan Igwe		Sasaru-Enwan Igwe, Nigeria
Saseng		Saseng, Papua New Guinea
Satere		Satere, Brazil
Sau		Sau, Afghanistan
		Sau, Papua New Guinea
Sauk		Sauk, Papua New Guinea
Sause		Sause, Indonesia
Save (Yoruba)	**	Save, Benin
Sawi	**	Sawi, Indonesia
Sawos		Sawos, Papua New Guinea
Saya		Saya, Nigeria
Secoya		Secoya, Ecuador
Sekar		Sekar, Indonesia
Seko		Seko, Indonesia
Sekpele		Sekpele, Ghana
Selakau	**	Selakau of Sarawak, Malaysia
Sele		Santrokofi, Ghana
Selepet		Selepet, Papua New Guinea
Selkup		Selkup, Soviet Russia
Semelai		Semelai, Malaysia
Sempan		Sempan, Indonesia
Sena		Sena, Malawi
		Sena, Mozambique
Senari		Senufo, Ivory Coast (80)
Senggi		Senggi, Indonesia
Sentani		Sentani, Indonesia
Senthang		Senthang, Burma
Sepen		Sepen, Papua New Guinea
Serawai (Pasemah)	**	Serawai, Indonesia (81)
Serbo-Croation	*	Bosnian, Yugoslavia (80)
Sere		Sere, Sudan
Serere		Serere, Senegal (79)
Serere-Non		Serere-Non, Senegal
Serere-Sine		Serere-Sine, Senegal
Seri		Seri, Mexico
Serki		Serki, Papua New Guinea
Serui-Laut		Serui-Laut, Indonesia
Setaui Keriwa		Setaui Keriwa, Papua New Guinea
Setiali		Setiali, Papua New Guinea
Sgaw Karen		Karen, Thailand (79)
Sha		Sha, Nigeria
Shamatali		Yanomamo, Venezuela
Shambala		Shambala, Tanzania
Shan		Hkun, Burma
		Shan, Thailand
		Shan, Burma
		Shan Chinese, Burma
		Thai-Ney, Burma
Shan Dialects		Yin-Kyar, Burma
		Yin-Nett, Burma
Shanga		Shanga, Nigeria
Shankilla (Kazza)	***	Shankilla (Kazza), Ethiopia
Sharanahua		Sharanahua, Peru
Sharchagpakha		Bhutias, Bhutan
		Sharchagpakha, Bhutan
Shatt		Shatt, Sudan
Shawiya		Shawiya, Algeria
Sheko		Sheko, Ethiopia
Sherpa	*	Sherpa, Nepal
Shihu	**	Shihu, United Arab Emirates

444

Solos	Solos, Papua New Guinea
Somagai	* Somahai, Indonesia
Somahai	Somahai, Indonesia
Somali	** Eritrean Refugees, Djibouti (83)
	Somali, Ethiopia
	Somali, Degodia, Kenya
	Somali, Gurreh, Kenya
	Somali, Ogadenya, Kenya
Somali (Ajuran)	Somali, Ajuran, Kenya (79)
Somba (Detammari)	** Somba, Benin
Somrai	Somrai, Chad
	Somrai, Central African Republic
Sona	Sona, Papua New Guinea
Sondwari	Sondwari in M.P., India
Songe	Songe, Zaire
Songhai	Songhai, Mali
	Songhai, Niger
	Songhai, Upper Volta
Songomeno	Songomeno, Zaire
Songoora	Songoora, Zaire
Soninke	Sarakole, Senegal (80)
	Soninke, Gambia
	Soninke, Mali
	Soninke, Mauritania
Sonjo	Sonjo, Tanzania
Sopi	Sopi, Sudan
Sora	Sora in Orissa, India
Sori-Harengan	Sori-Harengan, Papua New Guinea
Soruba	Soruba, Benin
Sough	** Manikion, Indonesia
Southern Bontoc	** Bontoc, Southern, Philippines
Southern Sesotho	*** Basotho, Mountain, Lesotho (79)
Sowanda	Sowanda, Indonesia
	Sowanda, Papua New Guinea
Spanish	Arutani, Venezuela
	Chatino, Yaitepec, Mexico
	** Chicanos in Denver, U.S.A. (82)
	Chilean Refugees, Argentina
	* Chilean Rfgs/Toronto, Canada (83)
	** Chinese in Panama, Panama
	Chocho, Mexico
	** Ex-Mental Patients/NYC, U.S.A.(82)
	Iquito, Peru
	Jebero, Peru
	** Marielitos in Florida, U.S.A. (83)
	*** Mestizos in La Paz, Bolivia (82)
	** Middle Class-Mexico City, Mex.(82)
	** Military Personnel, Ecuador
	Mixteco, Central Puebla, Mexico
	Mutu, Venezuela
	Nicaraguan Refugees, Costa Rica
	Paipai, Mexico
	Palenquero, Colombia
	Pame, Chichimeca-Jonaz, Mexico
	Paya, Honduras
	Popoloca, Ahuatempan, Mexico
	Popoloca, Coyotepec, Mexico
	Popoloca, Southern, Mexico
	Popoluca, Oluta, Mexico
	Popoluca, Texistepec, Mexico

447

Tadjio		Tadjio, Indonesia
Tadyawan		Tadyawan, Philippines
Tae'		Toraja, Southern, Indonesia (81)
Tafi		Tafi, Togo
Tagal		Tagal, Malaysia (81)
Tagalo	**	Batangeno, Philippines
Tagbanwa	**	Tagbanwa, Aborlan, Philippines
Tagbanwa, Kalamian		Tagbanwa, Kalamian, Philippines
Tagin	***	Tagin, India
Tagula		Tagula, Papua New Guinea
Tagwana		Tagwana, Ivory Coast
Taikat		Taikat, Indonesia
Tairora		Tairora, Papua New Guinea
Taiwanese (Hoklo)	*	Industrial Workers, Taiwan (81)
Takalubi		Takalubi, Papua New Guinea
Takankar		Takankar, India
Takemba		Takemba, Benin
Takestani		Takestani, Iran
Takia		Takia, Papua New Guinea
Tal		Tal, Nigeria
Talish		Talish, Iran
Talo	*	Talo, Indonesia
Talodi		Talodi, Sudan
Tama		Tama, Chad
Tamachek		Tuareg, Niger (79)
Tamagario		Tamagario, Indonesia
Taman		Taman, Burma
		Taman, Papua New Guinea
Tamang	*	Tamang, Nepal
Tamaria		Tamaria in Bihar, India
Tamazight		Tamazight, Morocco
Tambas		Tambas, Nigeria
Tambo		Tambo, Zambia
Tami		Tami, Papua New Guinea
Tamil	**	Indian Tamils – Colombo, Sri Lanka (82)
	*	Kudisai Vagh Makkal, India
		Labbai, India
		Moor Malays, Sri Lanka (79)
	**	Saiva Vellala, India
		Tamil (Ceylonese), Sri Lanka
	*	Tamil in Yellagiri Hills, India
	**	Tamil Laborers in Bombay, India (82)
		Tamil Muslims in Madras, India (82)
	***	Tamil Plantation Workers, Malaysia
	*	Tamils (Indian), Malaysia
	**	Tamils (Indian), Sri Lanka (79)
Tampulensi		Tampulma, Ghana
Tana		Tana, Chad
		Tana, Central African Republic
Tanahmerah		Tanahmerah, Indonesia
Tancouleur		Taucouleur, Senegal (80)
Tandanke		Tandanke, Senegal
Tandia		Tandia, Indonesia
Tangale		Tangale, Nigeria
Tangchangya		Tangchangya, Bangladesh
Tangga		Tangga, Papua New Guinea
Tangsa	**	Tangsa, India
Tangu		Tangu, Papua New Guinea
Tanguat		Tanguat, Papua New Guinea
Tani		Tani, Papua New Guinea

Tepo	Tepo, Ivory Coast
Tera	Tera, Nigeria
Terebu	Terebu, Papua New Guinea
Terena	Terena, Brazil
Teribe	** Teribe, Panama
Ternate	Ternatans, Indonesia
Teso	Teso, Uganda
Tewa (Jemez)	Jemez Pueblo, U.S.A.
Thado	Thado in Assam, India
Thai	* Central Thai Farmers, Thailand (81)
	Government officials, Thailand
	** Lepers of Cen. Thailand, (81)
	* Ramkamhaeng Un. Students, Thailand
	* Slum Dwellers of Bangkok, Thailand
	* University Students, Thailand (81)
Thai, Southern	* Thai Islam (Thai), Thailand
Thakali	Thakali, Nepal
Thakur	Thakur, India
Thami	Thami, Nepal
Thar	Thar in Bihar, India
Thoi	Thoi, Sudan
Thuri	Thuri, Sudan
Tiang	Tiang, Papua New Guinea
Tibetan	* Tibetan Refugees, India (83)
	Tibetan Refugees, Switzerland (83)
	Tibetans in Bhutan, Bhutan (81)
Tibetan Dialect	* Chang-Pa of Kashmir, India (81)
Tibeto-Burman	Jinuos, China (81)
	Lisu, China (81)
Tibeto-Burman Dialect	Lawa, Eastern, Thailand (81)
Ticuna	Ticuna, Brazil
Tidi	Tidi, Papua New Guinea
Tidore	Tidorese, Indonesia
Tiefo	Tiefo, Upper Volta
Tiene	Tiene, Zaire
Tifai	Tifai, Papua New Guinea
Tigak	Tigak, Papua New Guinea
Tigon	Tigon, Cameroon
Tigre	Ethiopian Refugees, Yemen, Arab Rep
	Rural Eritreans, Sudan (83)
Tikar	Tikar, Cameroon
Tila Chol	Ch'ol Tila, Mexico
Timbe	Timbe, Papua New Guinea
Timorese	Timorese, Indonesia
Tinputz	Tinputz, Papua New Guinea
Tippera	Tippera, Bangladesh
Tira	Tira, Sudan
Tirio	Tirio, Papua New Guinea
Tirma	Tirma, Sudan
Tiro	Tiro, Indonesia
Tiruray	Tiruray, Philippines
Tlapaneco, Malinaltepec	Tlapaneco, Malinaltepec, Mexico
Toala	Toala, Indonesia
Toaripi	Toaripi, Papua New Guinea
Toba	Toba, Argentina
Tobo	Tobo, Papua New Guinea
Toda	Toda in Tamil Nadu, India
Tofi	* Tofi, Benin
Togbo	Togbo, Zaire
Tojolabal	Tojolabal, Mexico

450

Tugara	Tugara, India
Tukude	Tukude, Indonesia
Tula	Tula, Nigeria
Tulishi	Tulishi, Sudan
Tumale	Tumale, Sudan
Tumawo	Tumawo, Indonesia
Tumma	Tumma, Sudan
Tumtum	Tumtum, Sudan
Tunebo, Cobaria	Tunebo, Cobaria, Colombia
Tung	Tung-Chia, China (81)
Tunya	Tunya, Chad
	Tunya, Central African Republic
Tupuri	Tupuri, Chad
	Tupuri, Cameroon
Tura	Tura, Ivory Coast
Turkana	Turkana, Kenya
**	Turkana Fishing Community, Kenya (79)
Turkic	Kirgiz Refugees, Pakistan
Turkish	* Anatolian Turks-Istanbul, Turkey (82)
	Baharlu (Kamesh), Iran
	Nafar, Iran
	Turkish Immgrnt Wrkers, Germany FDR (79)
Turkish (Danubian)	Yoruk, Turkey
Turkish, Osmanli	Turks, Anatolian, Turkey
Turkomani	Turkomans, Iran (80)
Turkwam	Turkwam, Nigeria
Turu	Turu, Indonesia
Tuvin	Tuvinian, Soviet Russia
Tuyuca	Tuyuca, Brazil
Twi	Twi, Sudan
Tzeltal, Bachajon	Tzeltal, Bachajon, Mexico
Tzeltal, Highland	Tzeltal, Highland, Mexico
Tzotzil (Chamula)	Chamula, Mexico (79)
Tzotzil, Chenalho	Zinacantecos, Mexico (79)
Tzotzil, Chenalhoa	Chenalhoa Tzotzil, Mexico
Tzotzil, Huistan	Huistan Tzotzil, Mexico
Tzutujil	Tzutujil, Guatemala
Udegeis	Udegeis, Soviet Russia
Udin	Udin, Soviet Russia
Udmurt	Udmurt, Soviet Russia
Uduk	Uduk, Sudan
Uhunduni	Uhunduni, Indonesia
Uighur	Uighur, Afghanistan
Uigur	Uigur, China (80)
Ukaan	Ukaan, Nigeria
Ukpe-Bayobiri	Ukpe-Bayobiri, Nigeria
Ukwuani-Aboh	Ukwuani-Aboh, Nigeria
Ulchi	Ulchi, Soviet Russia
Ulithi	Ulithi-Mall, Turks and Caicos Islands
Ullatan	Ullatan in Kerala, India
Umm Dorein	Umm Dorein, Sudan
Umm Gabralla	Umm Gabralla, Sudan
Urali	Urali in Kerala, India
Urarina	Urarina, Peru
Urhobo	Urhobo, Nigeria
Uria	Uria, Indonesia
Uruangnirin	Uruangnirin, Indonesia
Urubu	Urubu, Brazil
Urupa	Urupa, Brazil
Uspanteco	Uspanteco, Guatemala

452

Utugwang	Utugwang, Nigeria
Uvbie	Uvbie, Nigeria
Uzbeki, Turkic	** Uzbeks, Afghanistan (79)
Uzekwe	Uzekwe, Nigeria
Vagala	Vagala, Ghana
Vagla	Vagla, Ghana
Vai	* Vai, Liberia (80)
	Vai, Sierra Leone
Vaikino	Vaikino, Indonesia
Vaiphei	Vaiphei in Assam, India
Vale	Vale, Central African Republic
Various dialects	** African Students in Cairo, Egypt
	** Mangyan, Philippines
Venda	Venda, Zimbabwe
Veps	Veps, Soviet Russia
Vere	*** Vere, Nigeria
	Vere, Cameroon
Vidunda	Vidunda, Tanzania
Vietnamese	Boat People, Japan
	Street Vendors in Saigon, Viet Nam (82)
	Urban Elite Vietnamese, U.S.A.
	Vietnamese, Laos
	** Vietnamese Refugees, U.S.A.
	** Vietnamese Refugees, Thailand
	** Vietnamese Refugees, Australia
	Vietnamese Refugees, Korea, Republic of
Vige	Vige, Upper Volta
Vinza	Vinza, Tanzania
Vishavan	Vishavan in Kerala, India
Vute	Vute, Nigeria
Wa	Wa, China
	Wa, Burma
Wabo	Wabo, Indonesia
Waddar	Waddar in Andhra Pradesh, India
Wagdi	Wagdi in Rajasthan, India
Waimiri	Waimiri, Brazil
Waiwai	Waiwai, Brazil
	Waiwai, Guyana
Waja	Waja, Nigeria
Walamo	Walamo, Ethiopia
Wali	Wala, Ghana
Wambon	Wambon, Indonesia
Wanchoo	** Wanchoo, India
Wanda	Wanda, Tanzania
Wandamen	Wandamen, Indonesia
Wandji	Wandji, Gabon
Wanggom	Wanggom, Indonesia
Wanji	Wanji, Tanzania
Wano	Wano, Indonesia
Wapishana	Wapishana, Brazil
	Wapishana, Guyana
	Wapishana, Venezuela
Wara	Wara, Upper Volta
Warao	Warao, Venezuela
Ware	Ware, Mali
Warembori	Warembori, Indonesia
Waris	Waris, Indonesia
Warji	* Warjawa, Nigeria
Warkay-Bipim	Warkay-Bipim, Indonesia
Waropen	Waropen, Indonesia

453

Wasi	Wasi, Tanzania
Waura	Waura, Brazil
Wayana	Wayana, Surinam
Weda	Weda, Indonesia
Wetawit	Wetawit, Ethiopia
Wewewa	Wewewa, Indonesia
Widekum	Widekum, Cameroon
Win	Win, Upper Volta
Winji-Winji	Winji-Winji, Benin
Wobe	Wobe, Ivory Coast
Wodani	Wodani, Indonesia
Woi	Woi, Indonesia
Woko	Voko, Cameroon
Woleat	Woleat, Pacific Trust Islands
Wolio	Wolio, Indonesia
Wolof	Wolof, Senegal (80)
Wolof, Gambian	Wolof, Gambian, Gambia
Wom	Wom, Nigeria
Won Chow	* Chinese Restaurant Wrkrs., France
Wongo	Wongo, Zaire
Woro	Woro, Sudan
Wumbvu	Wumbvu, Gabon
Wungu	Wungu, Tanzania
Xavante	Xavante, Brazil
Xerente	Xerente, Brazil
Xokleng	Xokleng, Brazil
Xu	* Bushmen (Kung), Namibia (79)
	Xu, Namibia
Yafi	Yafi, Indonesia
Yaghan	Yaghan, Chile
Yagnobi	Yagnobi, Soviet Russia
Yagua	Yagua, Peru
Yahadian	Yahadian, Indonesia
Yaka	Yaka, Zaire
Yakan	Yakan, Philippines (80)
Yakha	Yakha, Nepal
Yakoma	Yakoma, Central African Republic
Yala	** Yala, Nigeria
Yalunka	* Yalunka, Sierra Leone (80)
Yaly	Yaly, Indonesia
Yambasa	Yambasa, Cameroon
Yaminahua	Yaminahua, Peru
Yanadi	Yanadi in Andhra Pradesh, India
Yandang	Yandang, Nigeria
Yanga	Yanga, Togo
Yangbye	Yangbye, Burma
Yanomam (Waica)	* Yanomamo, Brazil (79)
Yans	Yans, Zaire
Yanyula (Yanjula)	* Yanyula, Australia
Yao	Yao, Mozambique
	* Yao Refugees from Laos, Thailand
Yao (Mien Wa)	** Yao, Thailand (79)
Yaoure	Yaoure, Ivory Coast
Yaqui	Yaquis, Mexico
Yaruro	Yaruro, Venezuela
Yasing	Yasing, Cameroon
Yaur	Yaur, Indonesia
Yava	Yava, Indonesia
Yazgulyam	Yazgulyam, Soviet Russia
Yei	** Yei, Botswana

Zapoteco, Sto Dom Albarr	Zapoteco, Sto Dom Albarr, Mexico
Zapoteco, SW Ixtlan	Zapoteco, SW Ixtlan, Mexico
Zapoteco, Tabaa	Zapoteco, Tabaa, Mexico
Zapoteco, Villa Alta	Zapoteco, Villa Alta, Mexico
Zapoteco, W Miahuatlan	Zapoteco, W Miahuatlan, Mexico
Zapoteco, W Ocotlan	Zapoteco, W Ocotlan, Mexico
Zapoteco, W Sola de Vega	Zapoteco, W Sola de Vega, Mexico
Zapoteco, W Tlacolula	Zapoteco, W Tlacolula, Mexico
Zapoteco, W Yautepec	Zapoteco, W Yautepec, Mexico
Zapoteco, W Zimatlan	Zapoteco, W Zimatlan, Mexico
Zapoteco, Yalalag	Zapoteco, Yalalag, Mexico
Zaramo	Zaramo, Tanzania
Zari	Zari, Nigeria
Zayse	Zayse, Ethiopia
Zenaga	Zenaga, Mauritania
Zighvana(Dghwede)	* Dghwede, Nigeria
Zigwa	Zigwa, Tanzania
Zilmamu	Zilmamu, Ethiopia
Zimba	Zimba, Zaire
Zome	Zome, Burma
	Zome in Manipur, India
Zoque, Chimalapa	Zoque, Chimalapa, Mexico
Zoque, Copainala	Zoque, Copainala, Mexico
Zoque, Francisco Leon	Zoque, Francisco Leon, Mexico
Zoque, Tabasco	Zoque, Tabasco, Mexico
Zulu	Zulu, Malawi

Index by Country

Groups are listed by the countries for which information has been reported by questionnaires. In most cases, this means they are listed in the country where they are primarily located. Many peoples are found in several countries. This listing is limited to the country for which the MARC files have information. Groups are listed alphabetically under each country listed. Please note that not all countries will be found in this index. Peoples have not been reported from every country. Cambodia is listed under its new name, Kampuchea. The Republic of China is listed as Taiwan. Dahomey is listed under its current name, Benin. The French Territory of the Afars and the Issas is listed under its new name, Djibouti. The population estimate given is an indication of the size of that people in that one country. In some cases, this is only a part of a large people to be found in several other countries as well.

AFGHANISTAN

**	Azerbaijani	5,000
	Bashgali	10,000
	Chaghatai	300,000
	Gawar-Bati	8,000
	Gujuri	10,000
**	Hazara in Kabul (82)	300,000
	Jati	1,000
	Kirgiz	45,000
	Mogholi	2,000
	Munji-Yidgha	14,000
	Nuristani (80)	67,000
	Pashayi	96,000
***	Prasuni	2,000
	Sau	1,000
	Shina	50,000
	Shughni	3,000
	Tajik	3,600,000
	Uighur	3,000
**	Uzbeks (79)	1,000,000

ALBANIA

*	Albanian Muslims (80)	1,700,000

ALGERIA

	Kabyle (79)	1,000,000
	Shawiya	150,000
	Western Sahrawi Rfgs(83)	70,000

ANGOLA

	Chokwe (Lunda)	400,000
	Holu	12,000
**	Huila	200,000
	Hukwe	9,000
	Kongo	756,000
	Kwadi	15,000
	Kwangali	25,000
	Kwanyama	100,000
	Luchazi	60,000
	Luimbi	20,000
	Lunda	50,000
	Luyana	4,000
	Lwena	90,000
	Mbukushu	6,000
	Mbunda	59,000
	Mbwela	100,000
	Nsongo	15,000
	Nyaneka	40,000
	Nyemba	100,000
	O'ung	5,000

ARGENTINA

	Chilean Refugees	1,850
**	Chiriguano	15,000
	Chorote	500

	Lao Refugees	1,500
	Mataco	10,000
	Pilaga	4,000
	Toba	15,000
*	Universitarios-Rosario82)	10,000

AUSTRALIA

	Aborigines/Brisbane (82)	8,000
***	Chinese in Australia	30,000
**	Chinese Stud., Australia	6,000
	Gugu-Yalanji	5,000
*	Murngin (Wulamba)	4,000
**	Vietnamese Refugees	8,000
*	Yanyula	150

AUSTRIA

*	Chinese in Austria	1,000
*	Iwaidja	150

BANGLADESH

**	Banai	2,000
	Bawm	7,000
	Burmese Muslim Rfgs(83)	200,000
**	Hajong	17,000
**	Koch	35,000
	Mirung	12,000
	Mru	50,000
	Pankhu	600
	Tangchangya	8,000
	Tippera	38,000

BELGIUM

	Khmer Refugees (83)	2,500
	North Africans/Belgm(80)	90,000
	Turkish Workers (80)	60,000

BELIZE

**	Black Caribs, Belize (79)	10,000
**	Mopan Maya	4,000
	Rfgs from El Salvador	2,000

BENIN

**	Adja	250,000
*	Bariba (80)	400,000
	Berba	44,000
**	Boko	40,000
	Dendi	40,000
	Dompago	19,000
*	Fulani	70,000
	Gbazantche	9,000
	Gu	173,000
	Kabre	35,000
	Kotokoli	75,000
	Lamba	29,000

458

*	Mokole	7,000
*	Nyantruku	4,000
**	Pila	50,000
**	Save	15,000
**	Somba	60,000
	Soruba	5,000
	Takemba	10,000
	Tayaku	10,000
*	Tofi	33,000
	Winji-Winji	5,000
	Yoabu	8,000

BHUTAN

	Bhutias	780,000
	Kebumtamp	400,000
	Sharchagpakha	400,000
	Tibetans in Bhutan (81)	5,000

BOLIVIA

**	Aymara	850,000
	Chacobo	300
	Chipaya	100
	Chiquitano	20,000
***	Guarani (79)	15,000
	Guarayu	5,000
	Ignaciano	5,000
	Itonama	100
	Leco	200
***	Mestizos in La Paz (82)	400,000
*	Mororata	500
	Movima	1,000
**	Quechua	1,000,000
	Reyesano	1,000
	Simba	400
	Siriono	500
	Tacana	4,000
	Tsimane	6,000
	Yuracare	3,000

BOTSWANA

	Au ei	5,000
	Buka-khwe	9,000
	Bushmen in Botswana	30,000
	Dukwe Camp Resdnts (83)	800
	Herero	10,000
*	Kalanga	150,000
	Kwe-etshori	3,000
	Nharon	3,000
	Shua	400
	Tonga	6,000
**	Yei	10,000

BRAZIL

	Apalai	100
	Apinaye	200
	Apurina	1,000

	Arapaco	300
	Atruahi	500
	Bakairi	300
	Baniwa	3,000
*	Bororo	500
	Caiwa	7,000
	Canela	1,000
**	Chinese in Brazil	45,000
	Cinta Larga	500
***	Copacabana Apt.Dwellers	400,000
	Culina	800
	Desano	1,000
*	Drug AddictsSaoPaulo(82)	200,000
*	Favelados-RiodeJnero(82)	600,000
	Fulnio	2,000
	Guajajara	5,000
	Hixkaryana	200
	Hohodene	1,000
	Jamamadi	1,000
	Japanese in Brazil (79)	750,000
	Kabixi	100
	Kadiweu	600
	Kaingang	7,000
	Kamayura	100
	Karipuna Creole	500
	Karipuna Do Guapore	200
	Katukina, Panoan	200
	Kayabi	300
	Kayapo	600
	Kohoroxitari	600
	Kreen-Akakore	100
	Kuatinema	100
	Kuikuro	100
**	Macuxi	6,000
	Maiongong	100
	Marubo	400
	Matipuhy-Nahukua	100
	Maxakali	400
	Munduruku	2,000
	Mura-Piraha	100
	Nadeb Maku	200
	Nambikuara	400
	Nhengatu	3,000
	Ninam	500
	Oyampipuku	100
	Pacu	100
	Pakaasnovos	800
	Palikur	500
	Pankararu	2,000
	Parakanan	500
	Paresi	400
	Parintintin	200
	Pato Tapuia	100
	Paumari	300
	Piratapuyo	800
	Quarequena	300
	Rikbaktsa	200
*	Sanuma	300
	Satere	3,000
	Seuci	400

459

**	Shirishana	200
	Students in Cuiaba	20,000
	Surui	300
	Tembe	300
	Terena	5,000
	Ticuna	8,000
	Tucano	2,000
	Tuyuca	500
	Urubu	500
	Urupa	300
	Waimiri	1,000
	Waiwai	1,000
	Wapishana	2,000
	Waura	100
	Xavante	2,000
	Xerente	500
	Xokleng	300
*	Yanomamo (79)	3,000

BURMA

Chaungtha	40,000
Chin, Asho	11,000
Chin, Falam	92,000
Chin, Haka	85,000
Chin, Khumi	30,000
Chin, Ngawn	5,000
Chin, Tiddim	38,000
Chinbok	21,000
Chinese in Burma	600,000
Dai	10,000
Danu	70,000
Gheko	4,000
Hallam	11,000
Hkun	20,000
Hrangkhol	9,000
Intha	80,000
Kachin in Shan State	80,000
Kaw	30,000
Kayan	18,000
Kokant	50,000
Lahu	40,000
Lama	3,000
Maghi	310,000
Moken (79)	5,000
Mon (81)	350,000
Mun	10,000
Myaung-Ze	7,000
Norra	10,000
Palaung (79)	150,000
Pao	100,000
Purum	300
Ralte	17,000
Riang-Lang	20,000
Senthang	10,000
Shan	800,000
Shan Chinese	20,000
Taman	10,000
Taungyo	200,000
Taungyoe	18,000

Tawr	700
Thai-Ney	5,000
Wa	50,000
Yangbye	330,000
Yin-Kyar	2,000
Yin-Nett	2,000
Yinchia	4,000
Yos	5,000
Zome	30,000

BURUNDI

	Pygmy (Binga)	30,000
***	Rwandan Tutsi,Burndi83)	49,000

CAMEROON

Adamawa	380,000
Age	5,000
Aghem	7,000
Amasi	10,000
Assumbo	10,000
Babajou	500
Bafut	25,000
Baka	15,000
Balong	5,000
Bamougoun-Bamenjou	31,000
Bamum	75,000
Bandjoun	60,000
Banen	28,000
Bangangte	475,000
Basaa	170,000
Batanga-Ngolo	9,000
Bene	60,000
Bethen	10,000
Betsinga	10,000
Bitare	50,000
Bobe	600
Bokyi	87,000
Bomboko	3,000
Bonkeng-Pendia	2,000
Budugum	10,000
Bura	100,000
Chadian Rfgs (83)	100,000
Chinga	13,000
Daba	31,000
Dghwede	13,000

**	Doohwaayo	15,000
	Duru	20,000
	Eton	112,000
	Fali	50,000
	Fulani (79)	250,000
	Fungom, Northern	15,000
	Gidar	50,000
	Gisei	10,000
	Gisiga	30,000
	Gouwar	5,000
	Gude	100,000
	Gulfe	36,000
	Iyon	4,000

Kaalong	50,000		Yasing	25,000
Kaka	2,000		Yinga	300
Kamkam	800			
Kera	15,000		**CANADA**	
Kolbila	1,000			
Kole	300	*	Chilean Rfgs/Toronto(83)	10,000
Koma	15,000	**	Chinese in VancouverB.C.	80,000
Konabem	3,000		Jews, Non-Sephardic	120,000
Konabem	3,000		Jews, Sephardic/Montreal	26,000
Korop	10,000	**	Khmer Rfgs (83)	600
Kotoko	31,000		Muslim Lebanese Rfgs(83)	29,000
Kotopo	10,000		Ugandan Asian Rfgs(83)	6,000
Kpa	17,000			
Kutin	400		**CENTRAL AFRICAN REPUBLIC**	
Kwakum	3,000			
Laka	10,000		Arab Imgrnts/Bangui(82)	5,000
Lambi	1,000		Day	2,000
Lue	4,000		Kaba	11,000
Lundu	24,000		Kaba Dunjo	17,000
Maka	51,000		Kaka	37,000
Mambila	40,000		Kari	4,000
Mangisa	14,000		Karre	40,000
Matakam	140,000		Kim	5,000
Mbembe	25,000		Laka	40,000
Mbimu			Majingai-ngama	47,000
Mbo	23,000		Mbai	73,000
Menemo-Mogamo	35,000		Mbati	15,000
Menka	10,000		Monjombo	11,000
Mofu	33,000		Ndam	700
Mulimba	3,000		Ndogo	4,000
Mungaka	14,000		Ngando	2,000
Ndjem	25,000		Ngbaka Ma'bo	17,000
Ndop-Bamessing	17,000		Nzakara	3,000
Ndoro	10,000		Pambia	2,000
Ndunpa Duupa	1,000		Pana	20,000
Ngayaba	1,000		Pygmy (Binga)	2,000
Ngemba	34,000		Runga	13,000
Ngi	10,000		Somrai	50,000
Ngumba	10,000		Tana	35,000
Ngwo	10,000		Tunya	800
Nkom	30,000		Vale	1,000
Nohu	7,000		Yakoma	5,000
Nso	100,000			
Nyang	10,000		**CHAD**	
Oso	25,000			
Pape	1,000		Abou Charib	25,000
Podokwo	25,000		Bagirmi	40,000
So	6,000		Bilala	42,000
Su	500		Bomou	15,000
Suga	10,000		Bua	20,000
Taram	3,000		Daju of Dar Dadju	27,000
Tchang	100,000		Daju of Dar Sila	33,000
Tigon	25,000		Dangaleat	20,000
Tikar	13,000		Daza	159,000
Tupuri	70,000		Gabri	20,000
Vere	20,000		Gambai	200,000
Voko	1,000		Gidar	50,000
Widekum	10,000		Golo	3,000
** Wimbum	50,000		Goulai	30,000
Yambasa	26,000		Gula	3,000

461

Jongor	16,000	Chungchia	1,500,000
Kanembu	2,000	Chwang	7,800,000
Karanga	57,000	Dagur	23,000
Kari	40,000	Evenki	7,000
Kenga	25,000	Ewenkis (81)	10,000
Kera	5,000	Hani	138,000
Kibet	22,000	Hui (80)	5,200,000
Kim	5,000	Jinuos (81)	10,000
Koke	1,000	Jyarung	70,000
Kotoko	31,000	Kalmytz	70,000
Kuka	38,000	Kam	830,000
Laka	40,000	Kazakhs (81)	700,000
Maba	56,000	Kelao	23,000
Majingai-Ngama	47,000	Khalka	68,000
Mangbai	2,000	Kham	11,000
Mararit	42,000	Kirgiz	90,000
Marba	30,000	Koreans in Manchuria (81)	3,000,000
Masa	80,000	Lahul	2,000
Masalit	74,000	Laka	6,000
Massalat	23,000	Lati	500
Mbai	73,000	Li	1,000,000
Mbum	20,000	Lisu (81)	470,000
Mesme	28,000	Lolo (81)	4,800,000
Mesmedje	11,000	Lu	400,000
Mimi	15,000	Manchu (81)	200,000
Mogum	6,000	Miao (81)	2,800,000
Mubi	36,000	Mien (81)	740,000
Mundang	100,000	Mongour	50,000
Musei	60,000	Nahsi	160,000
Musgu	75,000	Nanai	1,000
Nancere	35,000	Nosu	556,000
Nielim	2,000	Nung	100,000
Ouaddai	320,000	Oirat	60,000
Rataning	10,000	Oronchon	2,000
Runga	13,000	Pai (81)	1,000,000
Sarwa	400	Paongan	8,000
Somrai	50,000	Pu-I	1,311,000
Sungor	39,000	Punu	220,000
Tama	60,000	Rawang	60,000
Tana	35,000	Salar	31,000
Teda (80)	10,000	Santa	200,000
Tunya	800	Sibo	21,000
Tupuri	60,000	Sui	160,000
Zaghawa	61,000	Tung-Chia (81)	1,100,000
		Uigur (80)	4,800,000
CHILE		** Univ. Students, China	600,000
		Vietnamese Refugees (83)	2,000
Aymara, Carangas	20,000	Wa	300,000
Mapuche	300,000	Yellow Uighur	4,000
Yaghan	50	Yuku	4,000
CHINA		**COLOMBIA**	
Ach'ang	10,000	Achagua	100
Buriat	30,000	Andoque	100
Burig	148,000	Barasano	400
Ch'iang	77,000	Barasano, Northern	450
Chin	100,000	Barasano, Southern	400
Chingp'o	100,000	Bora	400
Chuang (81)	12,000,000	Cacua	200

462

463

Gumuz	53,000	Kota	
Gurage (80)	750,000	Lumbu	12,000
Hadiyya	700,000	Mbaama	12,000
Harari	13,000	Mbede	45,000
Janjero	1,000	Minduumo	4,000
Kachama	500	Sangu	18,000
* Kaffa (80)	320,000	Sira	17,000
Kao	600	Tsogo	15,000
Kembata	250,000	Wandji	6,000
* Komo	20,000		
Konso	30,000	**GAMBIA**	
Koyra	5,000		
Kullo	82,000	Bayot	4,000
Kunama	70,000	Fula, Cunda	70,000
* Lango	8,000	Krio	3,000
Maji	15,000	Wolof, Gambian	70,000
Male	12,000		
Mao, Northern	13,000	**GERMAN FEDERAL REPUBLIC**	
* Masengo	7,000		
Me'en	38,000	* Chinese in West Germany	5,000
Mesengo	28,000	*** Koreans in Germany	10,000
*** Mocha	170,000	* Students (79)	850,000
Mursi	6,000	Turkish Wrkrs (79)	1,200,000
Nao	5,000		
Nara	25,000	**GHANA**	
* Nuer	70,000		
Oyda	3,000	Achode	5,000
Reshiat	10,000	Akpafu	8,000
*** Shankilla (Kazza)	20,000	Avatime	10,000
Sheko	23,000	Awutu	85,000
Shinasha	4,000	Bimoba	50,000
Sidamo	857,000	Birifor	40,000
Somali	1,000,000	Builsa	97,000
** Suri	30,000	** Busanse	50,000
Tsamai	7,000	Chakossi in Ghana	31,000
Walamo	910,000	Chala	1,000
Wetawit	28,000	Dagari	200,000
Yidinit	600	** Dagomba	350,000
Zayse	21,000	Fra-Fra	230,000
Zilmamu	3,000	* Fulbe	6,000
		Gonja	110,000
FIJI		Grunshi	200,000
		Gurensi	250,000
Indians in Fiji (79)	265,000	** Kasena	70,000
		Koma	1,000
FRANCE		Konkomba	175,000
		Krachi	22,000
Algerian Arabs in France	800,000	** Kusaasi	150,000
** Chinese Rfgs France (79)	100,000	Lelemi	15,000
* Chinese Restaurant Wrkrs	50,000	Ligbi	6,000
** Portuguese in France	150,000	Logba	3,000
* University Students (79)	800,000	Mamprusi	80,000
		Mamprusi	91,000
GABON		Mo	13,000
		Moba	80,000
Benga		Muslim Commty./Bawku	20,000
Duma	10,000	** Nafaara (79)	40,000
Equatorial Guin. Refugees	60,000	Nawuri	10,000
Guinean Refugees	1,200,000	Nchimburu	7,000
Kele	15,000	Nchumbulu	1,000

464

Nchumunu	8,000	
Nkonya	17,000	
Ntrubo	5,000	
Nyangbo	3,000	
Nzema	275,000	
Prang	5,000	
Safaliba	3,000	
Santrokofi	5,000	
Sekpele	11,000	
** Sisaala	60,000	
Siwu	5,000	
Tampulma	8,000	
Vagala	3,000	
Vagla	6,000	
Wala	60,000	
Zowla	800,000	

GUATEMALA

Achi, Cubulco	15,000
Achi, Rabinal	21,000
Aguacateco	8,000
** Black Caribs, Guatemala	2,000
Cakchiquel, Central	300,000
Chorti	25,000
Chuj	15,000
Chuj, San Mateo Ixtatan	19,000
Ixil	45,000
Jacalteco	12,000
** K'anjobal of San Miguel	18,000
** Kekchi	270,000
** Mam Indian	470,000
** Mopan Maya	2,000
Pocomchi, Eastern	20,000
Pocomchi, Western	25,000
** Quiche (79)	500,000
Rabinal-Achi	21,000
Tzutujil	5,000
Uspanteco	15,000
Yucateco	3,000

GUINEA

Basari	4,000
Fula	1,500,000
Gbande	66,000
Kissi	266,000
Kobiana	300
Konyagi	85,000
Kpelle	250,000
Landoma	4,000
Loko	16,000
Loma	180,000
Nalu	10,000
Susu	815,000

GUINEA-BISSAU

Badyara	10,000
Balante	100,000

Banyun	15,000	
Bayot	3,000	
Biafada	15,000	
Bidyogo	10,000	
** Bijogo	25,000	
Diola (80)	15,000	
Dyola		
Kasanga	400	
Kunante	6,000	
Landoma	5,000	
Maninka	65,000	
** Manjaco	80,000	
Mankanya	35,000	
Papel	36,000	
Susu	2,000	

GUYANA

Akawaio	3,000
Arawak	5,000
Patamona	1,000
Waiwai	1,000
Wapishana	4,000

HONDURAS

** Black Caribs, Honduras	20,000
Paya	300
Salvadoran Refugees	30,000
Tol	200

HONG KONG

Chinese Businessmen (81)	10,000
Chinese Factory Workers	500,000
Chinese Villagers	500,000
* Factory Workers	40,000
** High School Students	453,000
Refugee Doctors	2,000

INDIA

Abujmaria MadhyaPrdesh	11,000
*** Adi	80,000
Adiyan in Kerala	3,000
Agariya in Bihar	12,000
Ahir in Maharashtra	133,000
Aimol in Assam	100
Ajmeri in Rajasthan	600
Aka	2,000
* Alars	400
Anal in Manipur	7,000
Andha in Andhra Pradesh	65,000
Anga in Bihar	424,000
** Apatani in Assam	11,000
Aranadan in Tamil Nadu	600
* Arnatas	700
Arya in Andhra Pradesh	3,000
Asuri in Bihar	5,000
Babri	10,000

	Badagu in Nilgiri	110,000	
	Bagelkhandi in M.P.	230,000	
	Baghati in H.P.	4,000	
	Bahawalpuri in M.P.	600	
	Baiga in Bihar	11,000	
	Balti in Jammu	40,000	
	Bangaru in Punjab	4,000,000	
	Bareli in Madhya Pradesh	230,000	
	Bathudi in Bihar	74,000	
	Bazigar in Gujarat	100	
	Bediya in Bihar	32,000	
	Bengali Refugees, Assam	4,000,000	
	Bete	3,000	
	Bhakta	55,000	
	Bharia in Madhya Pradesh	5,000	
	Bhatneri	200	
	Bhattri	100,000	
	Bhilala	247,000	
**	Bhils (79)	800,000	
	Bhoyari in Maharashtra	5,000	
	Bhuiya in Bihar	5,000	
	Bhumij in Assam	50,000	
	Bhunjia/Madhya Pradesh	5,000	
	Bijori in Bihar	2,000	
	Binjhwari in Bihar	49,000	
	Birhor in Bihar	600	
	Bodo in Assam	510,000	
**	Bodo Kachari	610,000	
	Bondo in Orissa	2,000	
	Braj in Uttar Pradesh	6,000,000	
	Bunann in Kashmir	2,000	
	Burig in Kashmir	132,000	
*	Chakmas of Mizoram (81)	20,000	
	Chamari/Madhya Pradesh	5,000	
	Chameali in H.P.	53,000	
*	Chang-Pa of Kashmir (81)	7,000	
	Chenchu/Andhra Pradesh	18,000	
	Chero in Bihar	28,000	
	Chik-Barik in Bihar	30,000	
	Chodhari in Gujarat	139,000	
	Chola Naickans	100	
	Churahi in H.P.	35,000	
	Dawoodi Muslims	225,000	
	Deccani Muslims		
	Deccani Msls-Hydrbd(82)	500,000	
	Deori in Assam	15,000	
	Dhanka in Gujarat	10,000	
	Dhanwar/Madhya Pradesh	21,000	
**	Dhodias	300,000	
	Dhurwa	20,000	
	Dimasa in Cachar	38,000	
*	Dog-Pa of Ladakh (81)	2,000	
	Dorlin in Andhra Pradesh	24,000	
**	Dubla	200,000	
	Gadaban/Andhra Pradesh	20,000	
	Gaddi/Himachal Pradesh	70,000	
	Galong in Assam	37,000	
	Gamti in Gujarat	140,000	
	Gangte in Assam	6,000	
	Gawari in Andhra Pradesh	21,000	

*	Gonds	4,000,000	
*	Gorkha	180,000	
	Grasia in Gujarat	27,000	
	Gujars of Kashmir (81)	150,000	
***	Halam in Tripura	20,000	
	Halbi in Madhya Pradesh	350,000	
	Harauti in Rajasthan	334,000	
	Ho in Bihar	750,000	
	Holiya in Madhya Pradesh	3,000	
	Iravas in Kerala	3,700,000	
***	Irulas in Kerala	10,000	
	Jagannathi in A.P.	1,000	
	Jains	2,000,000	
	Jatapu in Andhra Pradesh	36,000	
	Jaunsari in Uttar Pradesh	60,000	
	Jharia in Orissa	2,000	
	Juang in Orissa	12,000	
	Kachchi/Andhra Pradesh	471,000	
	Kadar in Andhra Pradesh	800	
	Kahluri in Andamans	66,000	
	Kaikadi in Maharashtra	12,000	
	Kamar in Madhya Pradesh	10,000	
	Kanauri in Uttar Pradesh	30,000	
	Kanikkaran in Kerala	10,000	
	Kanjari in Andhra Pradesh	60,000	
**	Karbis	300,000	
	Karmali in Dihar	70,000	
**	Kashmiri Muslims (79)	3,100,000	
	Katakari in Gujarat	5,000	
	Kawar in Madhya Pradesh	34,000	
	Keer in Madhya Pradesh	3,000	
	Khamti in Assam	300	
	Khandesi	20,000	
	Kharia in Bihar	90,000	
	Khasi in Assam	384,000	
	Khirwar/Madhya Pradesh	34,000	
	Khojas, Agha Khani	175,000	
	Khowar	7,000	
	Kisan in Bihar	74,000	
	Kishanganjia in Bihar	57,000	
	Kishtwari in Jammu	12,000	
	Koda in Bihar	14,000	
	Kol in Assam	80,000	
**	Kolam	60,000	
	Kom in Manipur	7,000	
***	Kond	900,000	
	Konda-Dora AndraPradsh	16,000	
	Konkani in Gujarat	1,523,000	
	Koraga in Kerala	2,000	
*	Korku in Madhya Pradesh	250,000	
	Korwa in Bihar	10,000	
	Kota in Tamil Nadu	900	
	Kotia in Andhra Pradesh	15,000	
	Kotta	1,000	
	Koya in Andhra Pradesh	212,000	
*	Kudisai Vagh Makkal	1,000,000	
	Kudiya	100	
*	Kuknas	125,000	
**	Kuluis/H.P. (81)	200,000	
	Kumauni in Assam	1,240,000	

466

	Zangskari in Kashmir	5,000
	Zemi Naga of Assam (81)	16,000
	Zoliang	50,000
	Zome in Manipur	30,000

INDONESIA

	Abau	3,000
	Achehnese (80)	2,200,000
	Aghu	3,000
	Aibondeni	200
	Aikwakai	400
	Airo-Sumaghaghe	2,000
	Airoran	400
	Alas	30,000
	Alor, Kolana (81)	90,000
	Amanab	3,000
	Ambai	6,000
	Amber	300
	Amberbaken	5,000
	Ambonese	80,000
	Ansus	3,000
	Ara	75,000
	Arandai	2,000
	Arguni	200
	Asienara	700
*	Asmat (79)	30,000
	Awyi	400
	Awyu	18,000
	Baburiwa	200
	Baham	500
	Bajau, Indonesian	50,000
	Balantak	125,000
	Balinese	2,000,000
	Banggai	200,000
	Barau	300
	Bare'e	325,000
*	Batak, Angkola (80)	
	Batak, Karo	400,000
	Batak, Simalungun	800,000
	Batak, Toba	1,600,000
	Bedoanas	300
	Bengkulu	25,000
	Berik	800
	Biak	40,000
	Biksi	200
	Bimanese	300,000
	Bingkokak	150,000
***	Bipim	500
	Bira	75,000
	Bonerif	100
	Bonggo	400
	Borai	1,000
	Brat	20,000
	Bual	150,000
	Bugis (80)	3,500,000
	Buli	1,000
	Bunak	50,000
	Bungku	180,000
	Buru	6,000

	Busami	400
	Butung	200,000
**	Chinese in Indonesia	3,600,000
	Cirebon	2,500,000
***	Citak	7,000
	Dabra	100
	Dagada	30,000
*	Dani, Baliem (79)	50,000
	Dem	2,000
	Demta	800
	Dubu	100
	Duvele	500
	Ekagi	100,000
	Emumu	1,000
	Erokwanas	300
	Foau	200
	Fordat	10,000
	Gane	2,000
	Gayo (80)	200,000
	Gesa	200
	Gorontalo	500,000
	Havunese	40,000
	Helong	5,000
	Iha	6,000
	Inanwatan	1,000
	Irahutu	4,000
	Iresim	100
	Iria	900
	Itik	100
	Iwur	1,000
	Jambi	850,000
	Jamden	14,000
**	Javanese of Pejompongan	5,000
	Kaeti	4,000
	Kaili	300,000
	Kaiwai	600
	Kajang	50,000
	Kambera	200,000
	Kamberataro	1,000
	Kamoro	8,000
	Kampung Baru	400
	Kamtuk-Gresi	5,000
	Kanum	300
	Kapori	100
	Karas	200
	Karon Dori	5,000
	Karon Pantai	3,000
	Kasuweri	1,000
	Kati, Northern	8,000
	Kati, Southern	4,000
	Kaugat	1,000
**	Kaur	50,000
	Kaure	800
	Kavwol	500
	Kawe	300
	Kayagar	9,000
	Kaygir	4,000
	Kayupulau	600
	Kei	30,000
	Kemak	50,000

Tahit	6,000	**	Ahl-i-Haqq in Iran (79)	500,000
Taikat	600		Arab-Jabbari (Kamesh)	13,000
* Talo	90,000		Arab-Shaibani (Kamesh)	16,000
Tamagario	4,000		Arabs of Khuzestan	520,000
Tanahmerah	3,000		Azerbaijani Turks (80)	6,000,000
Tandia	400		Bahais in Teheran (82)	45,000
Taori-Kei	100		Baharlu (Kamesh)	8,000
Tara	125,000		Bakhtiaris (80)	590,000
Tarof	600		Baluchi (80)	1,100,000
Tarpia	600		Bayats	
Taurap	200		Bovir-Ahmadi	110,000
Tengger	400,000		Galeshis	2,000
Ternatans	42,000		Gilakis	1,950,000
Tidorese	26,000		Goudari	2,000
Timorese	300,000		Hezareh	
Tiro	75,000		Inallu	5,000
Toala	100		Iraqi Kurd Refugees (83)	300,000
Tombulu	40,000		Jamshidis	1,000
Tomini	50,000		Jews of Iran	93,000
Tondanou	35,000		Kazakhs (80)	3,000
Tonsea	90,000		Khalaj	20,000
Tontemboa	140,000		Kurds in Iran (80)	2,000,000
Toraja, Southern (81)	250,000		Lors (80)	600,000
Towei	100		Mamasani	110,000
Tukude	45,000		Mazandaranis	1,620,000
Tumawo	400		Moqaddam	1,000
Turu	800		Nafar	4,000
Uhunduni	14,000		Pashtuns (80)	3,000
Uria	300		Persians of Iran (80)	2,000,000
Uruangnirin	300		Pishagchi	1,000
Vaikino	14,000		Qajars	3,000
Wabo	900		Qara'i	2,000
Wambon	2,000		Qaragozlu	2,000
Wandamen	4,000		Qashqa'i (80)	350,000
Wanggom	1,000		Sasanis	1,000
Wano	2,000		Shahsavans (80)	180,000
Warembori	400		Tajik (80)	15,000
Waris	2,000		Takestani	220,000
Warkay-Bipim	300		Talish	20,000
Waropen	6,000		Teimuri	10,000
Weda	900		Teimurtash	7,000
Wewewa	55,000	*	Tertiary Level Youth	
Wodani	3,000		Turkomans (80)	550,000
Woi	1,000			
Wolio	25,000		**ISRAEL**	
Yafi	200			
Yahadian	700		Druzes (79)	33,000
Yaly	12,000		Gypsies in Jerusalem (82)	300
Yaur	400	*	Jewish Imgrnts.-American	30,000
Yava	5,000	*	Jewish Imgrnts.-Argntine	20,000
Yei	1,000	*	Jewish Imgrnts.-Australia	1,000
Yelmek	400	*	Jewish Imgrnts.-Brazilian	4,000
Yeretuar	300	*	Jewish Imgrnts.-Mexican	1,000
Yonggom	2,000	*	Jewish Imgrnts.-Uruguayn	3,000
Yotafa	3,000	*	Jewish Immigrants, Other	6,000
			Jewish Rfgs/USSR (83)	170,000
IRAN			Targum	5,000
Afshars	290,000			
Agajanis	1,000			

470

ITALY

Jews in Venice (82)	700

IVORY COAST

Abe	30,000
Abidji	23,000
Abure	25,000
Adyukru	51,000
Akan, Brong	50,000
Aladian	15,000
Attie	160,000
* Atye	210,000
Avikam	8,000
Bakwe	5,000
Bambara	1,000,000
*** Baoule	1,200,000
* Bete	300,000
*** Dan	270,000
** Dida	120,000
Ebrie	50,000
Eotile	4,000
Gagu	25,000
*** Godie	20,000
** Gouro	200,000
Guere	120,000
Gwa	8,000
Hwela-Numu	50,000
** Jimini	42,000
Kouya	6,000
* Krahn	250,000
Krobou	3,000
Krumen	17,000
Kulango	60,000
Kulele	15,000
Ligbi	20,000
Lobi	40,000
Maou	80,000
Mo	800
Mona	6,000
Moru	10,000
Neyo	5,000
* Ngen	20,000
Ngere	150,000
** Nyabwa	30,000
Nzema	24,000
Oubi	1,000
Palara	10,000
Pye	6,000
Senufo (80)	300,000
Tagwana	43,000
* Teenbu	5,000
* Tense	5,000
Tepo	20,000
Trepo	3,000
Tura	20,000
Wobe	40,000
Yaoure	14,000

JAMAICA

** Jamaican Elite	800,000

JAPAN

* Barbers in Tokyo (82)	220,000
Boat People	1,800
* Chinese in Japan	50,000
* Danchi Dwllers/Tokyo(82)	2,500,000
Geishas in Osaka (82)	
* Inland Sea Island Peoples	1,000,000
* Koreans of Japan	600,000
* Ryukyuan	1,000,000
Soka Gakkai Believers	6,500,000
** Univ. Students of Japan	2,000,000

JORDAN

Circassians/Amman (82)	17,000
Muslims of Jordan	2,430,000
Palestinian Refugees (83)	1,160,800

KENYA

Ayana	5,000
** Boran	37,000
Digo	168,000
Dorobo	22,000
El Molo	1,000
Gabbra	12,000
Giryama	340,000
Gosha	3,000
** Maasai (79)	100,000
Rendille	20,000
Sabbra	18,000
** Saguye	30,000
Sakuye	8,000
Samburu	61,000
Somali, Ajuran (79)	25,000
Somali, Degodia	70,000
Somali, Gurreh	54,000
Somali, Ogadenya	100,000
Suk	133,000
** Teso	110,000
Turkana	224,000
** Turkana Fishermen (79)	20,000

KOREA, REPUBLIC OF

** Apt Residents-Seoul	87,000
** Bus Drivers, South Korea	26,000
** Bus Girls in Seoul (82)	50,000
* Chinese in Korea	20,000
Indust.Wrkers Yongdungpo	140,000
* Japanese in Korea	5,000
Kae Sung Ntves/Seoul (82)	20,000
** Prisoners	45,000
Vietnamese Refugees	500

KUWAIT

Kurds in Kuwait	145,000

LAOS

	Alak	8,000
	Brao (79)	18,000
*	Chinese in Laos	25,000
	Galler	50,000
	Jeng	500
	Kasseng	15,000
	Khmer Refugees (83)	10,400
*	Lao (79)	1,910,000
	Loven (81)	25,000
	Ngeq	50,000
	Nyaheun	15,000
	Oi	10,000
	Phu Thai	100,000
	Soh	15,000
	Ta-Oi	15,000
	Vietnamese	20,000

LEBANON

Ladinos	7,000
Palestinian Refugees	240,000

LESOTHO

***	Basotho, Mountain (79)	70,000
	South African Stdents (83)	11,500

LIBERIA

	Bandi	32,000
*	Bassa	200,000
	Dan	94,000
*	Dewein	5,000
	Gio	92,000
	Gola	47,000
**	Grebo	65,000
*	Kissi	35,000
	Klaoh	81,000
**	Kowaao	7,000
	Kpelle	200,000
***	Krahn	55,000
	Kuwaa	6,000
	Loma	60,000
	Mandingo (79)	30,000
	Mano	65,000
	Mende	5,000
	Sapo	30,000
*	Vai (80)	30,000

LIBYA

Teda	16,000
Zaghawa	

LUXEMBOURG

Luxemburgois	276,000

MACAU

*	Chinese Rfgs/Macau (81)	100,000

MADAGASCAR

*	Prisoners/Ant'rivo (82)	10,000

MALAWI

Lambya	20,000
Mpoto	22,000
Ngulu	476,000
Nyakyusa	34,000
Sena	115,000
Tonga	62,000
** Yao	600,000
Zulu	40,000

MALAYSIA

	Bajau, Land	90,000
	Bateg	400
	Besisi	7,000
**	Bidayuh of Sarawak (81)	110,000
	Biduanda	4,000
	Bisaya (81)	3,000
	Bruneis	25,000
*	Cham Rfgs/Kmpuchea(83)	1,800
	Chinese Fishermen	4,000
*	Chinese in Malaysia	4,000,000
**	Chinese in Sabah	180,000
**	Chinese in Sarawak	330,000
*	Chinese of W. Malaysia	3,500,000
	Dusun (81)	160,000
**	Iban (81)	30,000
	Juhai	400
	Kadazans	110,000
	Kayan	12,000
	Kedayanas	25,000
	Kelabit (81)	17,000
	Kemok	400
	Lanoh	400
	Mantera	4,000
**	Melanau of Sarawak (80)	61,000
	Me i	400
	Momoguns	110,000
	Murut	38,000
	Muslim Malays (80)	5,500,000
	Orang Kanak	4,000
	Orang Laut	4,000
	Orang Ulu	4,000
	Penan, Western (81)	3,000
**	Selakau of Sarawak	5,000
	Semelai	3,000
**	Senoi (81)	340,000

**	Sugut	10,000
	Tagal (81)	19,000
***	Tamil Plantation Workers	140,000
*	Tamils (Indian)	600,000
	Temira	7,000

MALDIVES

| | Divehi (80) | 120,000 |

MALI

	Bambara	1,000,000
	Bobo Fing	3,000
	Bobo Wule	366,000
	Bozo	
*	Dogon (79)	312,000
	Fula, Macina	50,000
	Fula, Peuhala	450,000
	Kagoro	30,000
	Khasonke	71,000
	Kita	150,000
	Maure	58,000
	Minianka	300,000
	Samo, Northern	50,000
	Samogho	10,000
	Songhai	130,000
	Soninke	283,000
	Suppire	300,000
	Ware	2,000

MALTA

| * | Maltese | 330,000 |

MAURITANIA

	Moors in Mauritania	1,000,000
	Soninke	22,000
*	White Moors	
	Zenaga	16,000

MEXICO

	Amuzgo, Guerrero	20,000
	Amuzgo, Oaxaca	5,000
***	Azteca (79)	250,000
***	Ch'ol Sabanilla	20,000
	Ch'ol Tila	38,000
	Chamula (79)	50,000
	Chatino, Nopala	8,000
	Chatino, Panixtlahuaca	5,000
	Chatino, Tataltepec	2,000
	Chatino, Yaitepec	2,000
	Chatino, Zacatepec	500
	Chatino, Zenzontepec	4,000
	Chenalhoa Tzotzil	16,000
	Chinanteco, Tepinapa	3,000
	Chinanteco, Ayotzintepec	2,000
	Chinanteco, Chiltepec	3,000

	Chinanteco, Comaltepec	2,000
	Chinanteco, Lalana	10,000
	Chinanteco, Lealao	5,000
	Chinanteco, Ojitlan	10,000
	Chinanteco, Palantla	11,000
	Chinanteco, Quiotepec	7,000
	Chinanteco, Sochiapan	2,000
	Chinanteco, Tepetotutla	1,000
	Chinanteco, Usila	5,000
	Chocho	3,000
	Chuj, San Mateo Ixtatan	3,000
	Cocopa	900
	Cora	8,000
	Cuicateco, Tepeuxila	10,000
	Cuicateco, Teutila	6,000
	Guarojio	5,000
	Guatemalan Refugees	70,000
	Huasteco	80,000
**	Huave	18,000
	Huichol	8,000
	Huistan Tzotzil	11,000
	Kikapoo	5,000
	Lacandon	200
	Matlatzinca, Atzingo	2,000
	Mayo	30,000
**	Mazahua	150,000
**	Mddle Class-MexCity(82)	
**	Mixes	60,000
	Mixteco, Amoltepec	6,000
	Mixteco, Apoala	6,000
	Mixteco, Central Puebla	3,000
	Mixteco, Eastern	15,000
	Mixteco, Eastern Putla	7,000
	Mixteco, Huajuapan	3,000
	Mixteco, Silacayoapan	15,000
	Mixteco, Southern Puebla	12,000
	Mixteco, Southern Putla	3,000
	Mixteco, Tututepec	2,000
	Mixteco, Yosondua	15,000
*	Mixteco,SanJuan Mixtepic	15,000
*	Nahua, North Puebla	55,000
	Otomi, Eastern	20,000
	Otomi, Mezquital	100,000
	Otomi, Northwestern	40,000
	Otomi, Southeastern	2,000
	Otomi, State of Mexico	70,000
	Otomi, Tenango	10,000
	Otomi, Texcatepec	8,000
	Paipai	300
	Pame, Cntral Chichimeca	3,000
	Pame, Chichimeca-Jonaz	1,000
	Pame, Northern	2,000
	Pima Bajo	1,000
	Popoloca, Ahuatempan	6,000
	Popoloca, Coyotepec	500
	Popoloca, Eastern	2,000
	Popoloca, Northern	6,000
	Popoloca, Southern	1,000
	Popoloca, Western	8,000
	Popoluca, Oluta	200

Popoluca, Sayula	6,000
Popoluca, Sierra	18,000
Popoluca, Texistepec	2,000
Seri	400
Tarahumara, Northern	500
Tarahumara, Rocoroibo	12,000
Tarahumara, Samachique	40,000
Tarasco	60,000
Tepehua, Huehuetla	2,000
Tepehua, Pisa Flores	300
Tepehua, Veracruz	900
Tepehuan, Northern	5,000
Tepehuan, Southeastern	8,000
Tepehuan, Southwestern	6,000
Tlapaneco, Malinaltepec	40,000
Tojolabal	14,000
Totonaco, Northern	15,000
Totonaco, Oxumatlan	1,000
Totonaco, Papantla	50,000
Totonaco, Sierra	100,000
Totonaco, Yecuatla	500
Trique, San Juan Copala	8,000
Tubar	100
Tzeltal, Bachajon	20,000
Tzeltal, Highland	25,000
Yaquis	14,000
Yucateco	500,000
Zapoteco, C Sola De Vega	3,400
Zapoteco, Choapan	10,000
Zapoteco, E Miahuatlan	9,000
Zapoteco, E Ocotlan	7,000
Zapoteco, E Tlacolula	5,000
Zapoteco, E Zimatlan	5,000
Zapoteco, Isthmus	90,000
Zapoteco, Mazaltepec	
Zapoteco, Miamuatlan	10,000
Zapoteco, Mitla	15,000
Zapoteco, N Isthmus	7,000
Zapoteco, N Ocotlan	6,000
Zapoteco, N Villa Alta	15,000
Zapoteco, NE Miahuatlan	2,000
Zapoteco, NE Yautepec	2,000
Zapoteco, NW Tehuantpec	5,000
Zapoteco, Pochutla	2,000
Zapoteco, S Ejutla	2,000
Zapoteco, S Villa Alta	8,000
Zapoteco, SC Zimatlan	
Zapoteco, SE Miahuatlan	4,000
Zapoteco, Srra De Juarez	8,000
Zapoteco, Stgo Xanica	4,000
Zapoteco, Sto Dom Albarr	2,000
Zapoteco, SW Ixtlan	10,000
Zapoteco, Tabaa	5,000
Zapoteco, Villa Alta	3,000
Zapoteco, W Miahuatlan	3,000
Zapoteco, W Ocotlan	20,000
Zapoteco, W Sola de Vega	3,000
Zapoteco, W Tlacolula	32,000
Zapoteco, W Yautepec	2,000
Zapoteco, W Zimatlan	2,000

Zapoteco, Yalalag	6,000
Zinacantecos (79)	10,000
Zoque, Chimalapa	6,000
Zoque, Copainala	10,000
Zoque, Francisco Leon	12,000
Zoque, Tabasco	400

MOROCCO

	Shilha	3,000,000
**	Shluh Berbers	2,000,000
	Tamazight	1,800,000

MOZAMBIQUE

Chopi	400,000
Chuabo	250,000
Kunda	60,000
Lomwe	1,000,000
Makua	1,200,000
Maviha	70,000
Nyungwe	700,000
Podzo	45,000
Ronga	400,000
Sena	85,000
Tonga	10,000
Tsonga	1,500,000
Tswa	200,000
Yao	220,000
Zimbabwean Rfgs (83)	170,000

NAMIBIA

	Bushmen (Heikum)	16,000
*	Bushmen (Kung) (79)	10,000
	Herero	40,000
	Kwambi	30,000
	Kwanyama	150,000
	Nama	10,000
	San	6,000
	Tswana	11,000
	Xu	8,000

NEPAL

	Awadhi	317,000
*	Bhojpuri	810,000
	Bote-Majhi	6,000
	Byangsi	2,000
	Chaudangsi	2,000
	Chepang	10,000
	Darai	3,000
	Darmiya	2,000
	Dhimal	8,000
	Ghale Gurung	10,000
	Gurung	172,000
	Janggali	9,000
	Jirel	3,000
	Kham	40,000
	Lhomi	10,000

	Dyerma	50,000		Ivbie North-Okpela-Atte	20,000
	Ebira	325,000		Iyon	2,000
	Edo	430,000		Izarek	30,000
	Efik	30,000	**	Izi	200,000
	Efutop	10,000		Jaba	60,000
	Eggon	80,000		Janjo	6,000
	Ejagham	100,000		Jara	40,000
	Ekajuk	15,000	**	Jarawa	150,000
	Eket	22,000		Jera	23,000
	Ekpeye	30,000		Jerawa	70,000
	Eleme	16,000	*	Jibu	20,000
	Emai-Iuleha-Ora	48,000		Jimbin	2,000
	Engenni	10,000		Jukun	20,000
	Epie	12,000		Kadara	40,000
	Esan	200,000		Kagoma	6,000
	Etulo	3,000		Kaibu	700
	Evant	5,000		Kaka	2,000
**	Fakai	15,000		Kamantan	5,000
**	Fali	25,000	*	Kambari (80)	100,000
	Fyam	14,000		Kamo	3,000
	Fyer	3,000	*	Kamuku (80)	20,000
	Gade	25,000		Kana	90,000
	Galambi	1,000		Kanuri (80)	3,000,000
	Gbari (80)	500,000		Karekare	39,000
	Gbaya	350,000		Kariya	2,000
	Geji	3,000		Katab	30,000
	Gera	13,000		Khana	90,000
	Geruma	5,000		Kilba	80,000
	Ghotuo	9,000		Kirifi	14,000
**	Glavda	19,000		Koenoem	3,000
	Goemai	80,000		Kofyar	40,000
	Gokana	54,000		Kohumono	12,000
	Gude	40,000		Koma	15,000
	Gudu	1,000		Kono	2,000
	Guduf	21,000		Koro	35,000
	Gure-Kahugu	5,000		Korop	10,000
	Guruntum-Mbaaru	10,000		Kuda-Chamo	4,000
	Gwandara	25,000		Kugbo	2,000
	Gwari Matai	200,000		Kukele	32,000
***	Higi	150,000		Kulere	8,000
	Hwana	20,000		Kulung	15,000
	Hyam	60,000		Kushi	4,000
	Ibaji	20,000		Kuteb	26,000
	Ibibio	2,000,000		Kuturmi	3,000
	Icen	7,000		Kuzamani	1,000
	Idoma	300,000		Kwa	1,000
	Idoma, North	56,000		Kyibaku	20,000
	Igala	350,000		Laamang	40,000
	Igbira (80)	400,000		Lakka	500
	Igede	70,000		Lame	2,000
	Ihceve	5,000		Laru	1,000
	Ijo, Central-Western	340,000		Lebgo	30,000
	Ijo, Northeast	400,000		Lo	2,000
	Ijo, Northeast Central	8,000		Longuda	32,000
	Ikulu	6,000		Lotsu-Piri	2,000
	Ikwere	200,000		Lungu	10,000
	Irigwe	15,000		Madda	30,000
	Isekiri	33,000	***	Maguzawa (79)	100,000
**	Ishans	25,000		Mama	20,000
	Isoko	20,000		Mandara	20,000

476

Marghi Central	135,000	
Matakam	2,000	
Mbe	14,000	
Mbembe (Tigong)	3,000	
Mboi	3,000	
Mbula-Bwazza	8,000	
Migili	10,000	
Miya	5,000	
Mober	45,000	
Montol	20,000	
Mumbake	10,000	
Mumuye	200,000	
Nandu-Tari	4,000	
Naraguta	3,000	
Nde-Nsele-Nta	10,000	
Ndoe	3,000	
** Ndoro	10,000	
** Ngamo	18,000	
Ngizim	40,000	
Ngwoi	1,000	
Ninzam	35,000	
Nkem-Nkum	16,700	
Numana-Nunku-Gwantu	15,000	
Nungu	25,000	
** Nupe	600,000	
Nzanyi	14,000	
Obanliku	20,000	
Obolo	70,000	
Odual	9,000	
Odut	700	
Ogbia	22,000	
Okobo	11,000	
Okpamheri	30,000	
Olulumo-Ikom	10,000	
Oring	25,000	
Oron	50,000	
Otank	3,000	
Pai	2,000	
Pero	20,000	
Piti	2,000	
Piya	3,000	
Polci	6,000	
Pongu	4,000	
Puku-Geeri-Keri-Wipsi	15,000	
Reshe	30,000	
Rukuba	50,000	
Rumaya	2,000	
Ruruma	2,000	
Sanga	5,000	
Sasaru-Enwan Igwe	4,000	
Saya	50,000	
Sha	500	
Shanga	5,000	
Shuwa Arabic	100,000	
Siri	2,000	
Sukur	10,000	
Sura	40,000	
Surubu	2,000	
Tal	10,000	
Tambas	3,000	

Tangale		100,000
Tarok		60,000
Tera		46,000
Tula		19,000
Turkwam		6,000
Ukaan		18,000
Ukpe-Bayobiri		12,000
Ukwuani-Aboh		150,000
Urhobo		340,000
Utugwang		12,000
Uvbie		6,000
Uzekwe		5,000
*** Vere		20,000
Vute		1,000
Waja		30,000
* Warjawa		70,000
Wom		10,000
** Yala		60,000
Yandang		10,000
Yeskwa		13,000
Yungur		44,000
** Zaranda Hill Peoples		10,000
Zari		4,000

OMAN

Mahri	50,000

PACIFIC TRUST ISLANDS

Woleat	1,000

PAKISTAN

** Afghan Rfgs (NWFP) (83)		1,835,000
Ahmadis in Lahore (82)		60,000
Bagri		20,000
Bajania (79)		20,000
Balmiki		20,000
** Bhil		800,000
Brahui		745,000
Chitralis (79)		120,000
** Gagre		40,000
** Hunzakut (79)		10,000
** Iranian Bahai Rfgs (83)		5,000
** Kafirs (79)		3,000
Kirgiz Refugees		1,200
** Kohli, Kutchi		50,000
** Kohli, Parkari		100,000
** Kohli, Tharadari		40,000
** Kohli, Wadiara		40,000
** Meghwar (79)		100,000
Od		40,000
Sindhi Mslms/Karachi(82)		350,000
Sochi		
Swatis (79)		600,000
Vagari		30,000

PANAMA

	Buglere	2,000
**	Chinese in Panama	25,000
**	Teribe	1,000

PAPUA NEW GUINEA

	Abau	3,000
	Abie	600
	Abulas	33,000
	Adjora	2,000
	Aeka	3,000
	Agarabi	12,000
	Agob	1,000
	Aiku	800
	Aiome	900
	Aion	800
	Akrukay	200
	Alamblak	2,000
	Alatil	400
	Alauagat	300
	Ama	400
	Amaimon	400
	Amanab	3,000
	Ambasi	500
**	Ampeeli	1,000
	Amto	200
	Andarum	700
	Anem	1,000
	Angaataha	800
	Angal Heneng, South	15,000
	Angal Heneng, West	25,000
	Angal, East	10,000
	Angaua	2,000
	Anggor	1,000
	Angoram	4,000
	Ankave	2,000
	Anor	600
	Anuki	500
	Arafundi	1,000
	Arapesh, Bumbita	2,000
	Arapesh, Mountain	5,000
	Arapesh, Muhiang	8,000
	Arawe	2,000
	Arifama-Miniafia	2,000
	Arigibi	300
	Arinua	2,000
	Arop	2,000
	Aruop	500
	Asaro	12,000
	Asat	700
	Ata	1,000
	Au	4,000
	Aunalei	2,000
	Auyana	7,000
	Awa	2,000
	Awar	600
	Awara	900
	Awin	7,000
	Azera	400

	Bahinemo	300
	Baibai	300
	Baining	5,000
	Bali-Vitu	7,000
	Bam	600
***	Banaro	3,000
	Banoni	1,000
	Barai	2,000
	Bariai	3,000
	Bariji	300
	Barim	600
	Barok	1,000
	Baruga	1,000
	Baruya	4,000
	Bau	2,000
	Bauwaki	400
	Bebeli	600
	Bembi	400
	Benabena	14,000
	Biaka	400
	Biangai	1,000
	Bibling	2,000
	Biliau	600
	Bimin	400
	Binahari	800
	Binandere	3,000
	Bine	2,000
	Binumarien	200
	Bisis	400
	Bitara	100
	Biyom	400
	Boanaki	2,000
	Bohutu	1,000
	Boikin	31,000
	Bola	5,000
	Bom	1,000
	Bongu	400
	Bonkiman	300
	Bosavi	400
	Bosilewa	400
	Bosngun	700
	Breri	700
	Buang, Central	6,000
	Buang, Mangga	3,000
	Budibud	200
	Buin	9,000
	Bukaua	5,000
	Bulu	200
	Buna	900
	Bunabun	500
	Bunama	5,000
	Burum	3,000
	Busah	200
	Bwaidoga	5,000
	Chambri	900
	Chenapian	200
	Chuave	20,000
	Dadibi	6,000
	Daga	6,000
	Dahating	900
	Dami	1,000

Kerewo	2,000	Mailu	5,000
Keriaka	1,000	Maisan	2,000
Kewa, East	20,000	Maiwa	1,000
Kewa, South	5,000	Makarim	2,000
Kewa, West	20,000	Malalamai	300
Kiari	1,000	Malas	200
Kibiri	1,000	Malasanga	400
Kilmera	2,000	Malek	1,000
Kinalakna	200	Maleu	4,000
Kiriwina	14,000	Malon	3,000
Kis	200	Mamaa	200
Kiwai, Northeast	4,000	Managalasi	4,000
Kiwai, Southern	10,000	Manambu	2,000
Kiwai, Wabuda	2,000	Mangap	2,000
Kobon	7,000	Mape	5,000
Koiari, Grass	2,000	Mapena	300
Koiari, Mountain	2,000	Maralango	2,000
Koita	2,000	Maraliinan	2,000
Kol	2,000	Mari	300
Koliku	300	Maria	2,000
Kolom	100	Maring	8,000
Komba	10,000	Masegi	2,000
Kombio	2,000	Mawak	1,000
Komutu	500	Mawan	200
Konomala	600	Medlpa	60,000
Korak	200	Mehek	4,000
Korape	4,000	Mekeo	7,000
Kosorong	1,000	Mengen	6,000
Kovai	3,000	Menye	13,000
Kove	3,000	Mera Mera	1,000
Krisa	500	Mianmin	2,000
Kube	4,000	Midsivindi	900
Kukuwy	1,000	Migabac	1,000
Kumai	4,000	Mikarew	6,000
Kuman	66,000	Minanibai	300
Kumdauron	400	Mindik	2,000
Kumukio	300	Miriam	700
Kuni	2,000	Mitang	500
** Kunimaipa	9,000	Mitmit	100
Kunua	1,000	Moewehafen	2,000
Kuot	900	Mokareng	1,000
Kurada	900	Momare	400
Kwale	700	Momolili	2,000
Kwanga	5,000	Morawa	800
Kwoma	2,000	Moresada	200
Kwomtari	800	Morigi	700
Labu	800	Morima	3,000
Laewomba	2,000	Moxodi	700
Lamogai	1,000	Mugil	2,000
Lavatbura-Lamusong	1,000	Mukawa	1,000
Lavongai	10,000	Munkip	100
Leron	500	Mup	100
Lihir	5,000	Murik	2,000
Lohiki	900	Musak	200
Lou-Baluan-Pam	1,000	Musar	500
Lugitama	500	Musom	500
Lukep	600	Mutum	400
Madak	3,000	Muyuw	3,000
Magori	200	Mwatebu	200
Mai	200	Nabak	12,000

480

Nagarige	600	Porapora	400
Nagatman	500	Pulie	200
Nagovisi	5,000	Purari	6,000
Nahu	5,000	Rambutyo	1,000
Nakama	900	Rao	3,000
Nakanai	8,000	Rauto	200
Nalik	3,000	Rawa	6,000
Nambis	1,000	Rempi	500
Nambu	700	Roinji	300
Namuni	100	Romkun	400
Nankina	2,000	Roro	8,000
Nara	700	Rotokas	4,000
Narak	4,000	Saep	500
Nasioi	13,000	Sakam	400
Nauna	100	Saki	2,000
Negira	400	Salt	6,000
Nek	1,000	* Samo-Kubo	2,000
Nekgini	500	Sanio	600
Neko	200	Saposa	1,000
Nengaya	600	Saseng	200
Ngaing	900	Sau	3,000
Nii	9,000	Sauk	300
Nimowa	1,000	Sawos	2,000
* Ningerum	3,000	Selepet	6,000
Niningo	500	Sepen	900
Nissan	2,000	Serki	200
Nomane	3,000	Setaui Keriwa	400
Nomu	800	Setiali	200
Nondiri	2,000	Sialum	600
Notsi	1,000	Siane	16,000
Nuk	2,000	Siar	2,000
Numanggang	2,000	Simog	100
Oksapmin	5,000	Sinagen	200
Olo	9,000	Sinagoro	12,000
Omati	800	Sinaki	300
Omie	1,000	Sinasina	20,000
Onank	100	Sindamon	200
Onjab	100	Sinsauru	400
Ono	5,000	Sio	2,000
Orokaiva	25,000	Sipoma	300
Orokolo	13,000	Sirak	200
Osum	600	Sirasira	300
Paiwa	2,000	Siroi	700
Pak-Tong	1,000	Siwai	6,000
Papapana	200	Sokorok	300
Parawen	500	Solos	3,000
Pare	1,000	Som	100
Pasismanua	6,000	Sona	2,000
Patep	7,000	Sori-Harengan	600
Patpatar	5,000	Sowanda	900
Pawaia	2,000	Sua	4,000
Pay	600	Suain	900
Paynamar	200	** Suena	2,000
Peremka	200	Suganga	500
Pila	600	Sui	1,000
Piu	100	Suki	1,000
** Plantation Workers	5,000	Sukurum	400
Podopa	3,000	Sulka	1,000
Ponam-Andra-Hus	1,000	Sumau	800
Pondoma	300	Sursurunga	2,000

Tabar	2,000		Chamicuro	200
Tabriak	1,000	**	Chayahuita	6,000
Tagula	2,000		Cocama	18,000
Tairora	8,000		Cujareno	100
Takalubi	400		Huachipaire	200
Takia	11,000		Huambisa	5,000
Taman	600		Huitoto, Murui	800
Tami	400		Iquito	200
Tangga	5,000		Jaqaru	2,000
Tangu	2,000		Jebero	3,000
Tanguat	600		Machiguenga	10,000
Tani	2,000		Manu Park Panoan	200
Tao-Suame	700		Mayoruna	1,000
Tate	300		Morunahua	200
Tauade	11,000		Ocaina	300
Taupota	3,000		Orejon	300
Tavara	9,000		Piro	3,000
Tawi-Pau	300	**	Quechua	3,000,000
Telefol	4,000	**	Quechua, Huanco	275,000
Teop	5,000		Sharanahua	2,000
Terebu	4,000		Shipibo	15,000
Tiang	800		Urarina	4,000
Tidi	500		Yagua	4,000
Tifai	3,000		Yaminahua	1,000
Tigak	4,000			
Timbe	11,000		**PHILIPPINES**	
Tinputz	2,000			
Tirio	300		Abaknon	10,000
Toaripi	23,000		Aeta	500
Tobo	3,000		Agutaynon	7,000
Tonda	600		Alangan	6,000
Torau	600	**	Apayao	12,000
Torricelli	700	*	Asian Students	2,000
Tuam	600	*	Ata of Davao	10,000
Tubetube	1,000		Ati	2,000
		*	Atta	1,000
PARAGUAY		***	Bagobo	35,000
			Baguio Area Miners (81)	40,000
Ayoreo	700	**	Balangao	5,000
Chamacoco, Bahia Negra	1,000		Balangaw	5,000
Chorote			Bantuanon	50,000
Chulupe	8,000		Batak, Palawan	400
Guaiaqui	400	**	Batangeno	
Guana	3,000	**	Bilan	75,000
Lengua, Northern	95,000	***	Bolinao	26,000
Maca	600	**	Bontoc, Central (81)	20,000
Sanapana	4,000	**	Bontoc, Southern	12,000
			Buhid	6,000
PERU		**	Bukidnon	100,000
		**	Buwid (81)	6,000
Achual	5,000		Caluyanhon	30,000
Aguaruna	22,000	*	Casiguranin	10,000
Amahuaca	2,000	***	Cebu, Middle-Class	500,000
Amarakaeri	500		Cuyonon	49,000
Amuesha	5,000		Davaweno	13,000
Arabela	200	*	Dumagat, Casiguran (81)	1,000
Campa	5,000		Ga-Dang	6,000
Candoshi	3,000		Hanonoo	6,000
Capanahua	500	**	Hotel Workers,Manila(81)	11,000
Cashibo	2,000		Ibanag	300

482

REGISTRY OF THE UNREACHED

SEYCHELLES

Seychellois	51,000

SIERRA LEONE

Bullom, Northern	167,000
Bullom, Southern	40,000
Fula	250,000
Gola	1,000
* Kissi	48,000
** Kono	133,000
** Koranko	100,000
Krim	3,000
Limba	233,000
Loko	80,000
Maninka	64,000
Mende	600,000
Susu	90,000
** Temne (80)	1,000,000
Vai	3,000
* Yalunka (80)	25,000

SIKKIM

** Lepcha	18,000

SINGAPORE

Malays of Singapore (79)	300,000

SOMALIA

** Nomdic Smali Ref. (83)	700,000

SOUTH AFRICA

Bavenda	360,000
Cape Malys/Cape Twn(82)	150,000
* Chinese in South Africa	9,000
* Coloreds in Eersterust (2)	20,000
Nama	15,000
Ronga	600,000
** Swazi	500,000

SOVIET UNION

Abazin	25,000
Abkhaz	83,000
Adygei	100,000
Agul	9,000
Akhavakh	5,000
Alutor	2,000
Andi	9,000
Archin	900
Balkars	60,000
Bashkir (80)	1,200,000
Batsi	3,000
Botlikh	4,000
Budug	2,000
Buriat	315,000
Chamalin	6,000

Cherkess	40,000
Chukot	14,000
Dargin	231,000
Didoi	7,000
Dolgans	5,000
Dungan	39,000
Evenks	25,000
Gagauzes	157,000
Gilyak	4,000
Gypsies	175,000
Ingushes	158,000
Itelmen	1,000
Izhor	1,000
Kalmytz	137,000
Kapuchin	3,000
Karachay	173,000
Karagas	600
Karaim	1,000
Karakalpak (80)	277,000
Karatin	6,000
Ket	1,000
Khakas	67,000
Khanti	21,000
Khinalug	2,000
Khvarshin	2,000
Kirgiz (80)	1,700,000
Komi-Permyat	153,000
Komi-Zyrian	322,000
Koryak	8,000
Kryz	6,000
Kvanadin	6,000
Lakians	86,000
Liv	2,000
Mansi	8,000
Mari	599,000
Mingat	4,000
Nanai	12,000
Nentsy	29,000
Nganasan	1,000
Nivkhi	4,000
Oroch	1,000
Orok	400
Rutul	12,000
Saams	2,000
Selkup	4,000
Shor	16,000
Svan	35,000
Tabasaran	55,000
Tajik	2,500,000
Tat	17,000
Tatars (80)	6,000,000
Tindin	5,000
Tsakhur	11,000
Tuvinian	139,000
Udegeis	2,000
Udin	4,000
Udmurt	700,000
Ulchi	2,000
Veps	16,000
Yagnobi	2,000

Yazgulyam	2,000	Kanga		6,000
Yukagirs		Karko		2,000
Yurak	29,000	Katcha		6,000
		Katla		9,000
SPAIN		Keiga		6,000
		Keiga Jirru		1,000
* Gypsies in Spain (79)	200,000	Kichepo		16,000
* Lao Refugees (83)	1,000	Koalib (79)		320,000
Pension Stdnts-Madrid(82)	2,000	Koma, Central		3,000
		Koroma		30,000
SRI LANKA		Krongo		121,000
		Lafofa		2,000
** Indian TamilsColombo(82)		Laro		3,000
Moor Malays (79)	900,000	Liguri		2,000
Sinhalese	9,200,000	* Lokoro		22,000
Tamil (Ceylonese)	1,420,000	Lori		1,000
** Tamils (Indian) (79)	1,200,000	** Lotuka		150,000
		Luac		700
SUDAN		Lwo		20,000
		Maba		9,000
Abialang	7,000	Maban-Jumjum		20,000
Abu Leila	4,000	Madi		6,000
Acheron	1,000	Masakin		16,000
Afitti	3,000	Masalit		27,000
Aja	1,000	Meban		130,000
Anuak	30,000	Midob		2,000
Atoc	5,000	Miri		8,000
Atuot	8,000	Modo		2,000
Avukaya	5,000	Moreb		600
Bai	3,000	Moru		23,000
Barambu	46,000	Murle		40,000
Bari	340,000	Naka		4,000
Beja	91,000	Ndogo		4,000
Binga	1,000	Nginyukwur		4,000
Biti	300	Ngirere		4,000
Bongo	2,000	Ngok		21,000
Bor Gok	6,000	Ngunduna		9,000
Boya	15,000	Nguqwurang		8,000
Burun	5,000	Njalgulgule		900
Bviri	16,000	* Nuer (79)		844,000
Dair	200	Nyamusa		1,000
Daju of Dar Fur	12,000	Nyarueng		2,000
Daju of West Kordofan	6,000	Nyzatom		80,000
Didinga	30,000	Otoro		28,000
Dinka	1,940,000	Paloc		14,000
Dinka, Agar	16,000	Rural Eritreans (83)		300,000
Dongjoi	9,000	Rut		500
Dongo	100	Sere		4,000
Eritrean Refugees (83)	150,000	Shatt		9,000
Feroge	3,000	Shilluk		110,000
Fungor	5,000	Shwai		3,000
Gbaya-Ndogo	2,000	Sopi		2,000
Gberi	600	Sudanese Repatriates(83)		1,000,000
Ghol	2,000	Tabi		10,000
Ghulfan	3,000	Talodi		1,000
Gumuz	40,000	Tegali		16,000
Heiban	25,000	Temein		2,000
Ingassana	35,000	Thoi		400
* Jiye	7,000	Thuri		154,000
Kadugli	19,000	Tira		10,000

485

Tirma	9,000	
* Topotha	60,000	
Tulishi	9,000	
Tumale	1,000	
Tumma	5,000	
Tumtum	7,000	
Twi	9,000	
Uduk	7,000	
Ugandan Refugees (83)	100,000	
Umm Dorein	500	
Umm Gabralla	9,000	
Woro	400	
Yulu	2,000	
Zaghawa		

SURINAM

Djuka	20,000
Matawari	1,000
Saramaccan	20,000
Trio	800
Wayana	600

SWITZERLAND

* Americans in Geneva	45,000
Tibetan Refugees (83)	1,000
Turks in Basel (82)	3,000

SYRIA

* Alawites (79)	600,000

TAIWAN

* Ami (81)	99,000
** Chinese Hakka,Taiw.(79)	1,750,000
* Chinese Mainlanders	2,000,000
Chinese Muslims (81)	45,000
* Deviant Youth,Taipei(82)	80,000
Fishing Village People	150,000
* Industrial Workers (81)	500,000
** Puyuma (81)	7,000
Saisiat (81)	3,000
Taiwan-Chinese Un. Stud.	310,000
Tsou (81)	4,000
* Women Laborers	1,200,000

TANZANIA

Arusha	110,000
Asu	110,000
Barabaig (79)	49,000
Bena	150,000
Bende	9,000
Bondei	30,000
Burundian Hutu Rfgs (83)	40,000
Burungi	20,000
Chagga	800,000
Dhaiso	12,000

Digo	30,000
Doe	8,000
Dorobo	3,000
Fipa	78,000
Gogo	280,000
Goroa	180,000
Ha	286,000
Hangaza	54,000
Hatsa	2,000
Haya	276,000
Hehe	192,000
Holoholo	5,000
Ikizu	9,000
Iraqw	218,000
Isanzu	12,000
Jiji	3,000
Jinja	66,000
Jita	71,000
Kagulu	59,000
Kami	180,000
Kara	32,000
Kerewe	35,000
Kimbu	15,000
Kinga	57,000
Kisankasa	4,000
Kisi	4,000
Konongo	20,000
Kuria	75,000
Kutu	17,000
Kwaya	35,000
Kwere	63,000
Lambya	7,000
Langi	95,000
Luo	1,522,000
Makonde	550,000
Malila	175,000
Mambwe-Lungu	16,000
Manda	10,000
Matengo	58,000
Matumbi	72,000
Mbugwe	8,000
Mbunga	10,000
Mosi	240,000
Mpoto	36,000
Mwanga	27,000
Mwera	110,000
Nata	10,000
Ndali	57,000
Ndamba	19,000
Ndengereko	53,000
Ndomde	12,000
Ngasa	1,000
Ngindo	85,000
Ngoni	85,000
Ngulu	13,000
Ngurimi	12,000
Nguu	46,000
Nilamba	210,000
Nyakyusa	193,000
Nyambo	4,000

UGANDA

Acholi	
Adhola	200,000
Chiga	272,000
Gwere	162,000
Jiye	34,000
Kumam	100,000
Kupsabiny	60,000
Lango	560,000
Madi	114,000
Makere	18,000
Masaba	110,000
Meje	13,000
Muslims (West Nile Dist.)	45,000
Nyankole	810,000
Nyoro	620,000
Nyuli	140,000
Pokot	170,000
Rwamba	60,000
Saamia	124,000
Soga	780,000
Tepeth	4,000
Teso	830,000

UNITED ARAB EMIRATES

Indians in Dubai (82)	24,000
Muslims (79)	752,000
** Shihu	10,000

UNITED KINGDOM

Bengalis in London (82)	15,000
** Chinese, U.K.	110,000
** Chinese Students, Glasg	1,000
Gujarati	300,000
** Muslim Immigrants,U.K.	500,000
Sylhetti	150,000
Ugandan Asian Rfgs(83)	27,000

UNITED STATES OF AMERICA

** Arabs,New Orleans(82)	1,000
* Casual Lbrs,Atlnta(82)	3,000
** Chicanos in Denver (82)	121,000
** Chinese in Boston (82)	20,000
** Chinese in United States	550,000
** Ex-Mental Patients(82)	20,000
Gays,San Francisco (82)	150,000
Haitian Refugees (83)	40,000
* Havasupai	300
*** Hmong Refugees (83)	35,000
Hmong, Twin Cities	11,000
Hopi	6,000
** Japanese Students In USA	
Jemez Pueblo	2,000
** Marielitos in Florida (83)	125,000
Nurses in St. Louis (82)	3,000
Paiute, Northern	5,000

** Pro Hockey Players (82)	600
** Racetrack Residents (79)	50,000
Urban Elite Vietnamese	90,000
** Vietnamese Refugees	2,700,000
Zuni	6,000

UPPER VOLTA

Birifor	50,000
Bolon	4,000
Bousansi	140,000
Buli	60,000
Bwa (80)	140,000
Dagari	150,000
Doghosie	8,000
Dyan	8,000
Fula	250,000
Fulah	300,000
Gan	4,000
Gouin-Turka	25,000
Gourency	300,000
Gurma	250,000
* Karaboro	40,000
Kasem	28,000
Komono	6,000
Kurumba	86,000
Marka	39,000
Mossi (80)	3,300,000
Natioro	1,000
* Nouni	50,000
Nunuma	43,000
Puguli	5,000
Samo, Northern	70,000
Sisala	4,000
Songhai	35,000
Tiefo	7,000
* Toussian	20,000
Vige	4,000
Wara	2,000
Win	20,000

VENEZUELA

Arecuna	14,000
Arutani	100
** Jivaro (Achuara)	20,000
Mapoyo	200
Maquiritari	5,000
Motilon	3,000
Mutu	300
Panare	1,000
Piaroa	12,000
Sanuma	4,000
Wapishana	20,000
Warao	15,000
Yanomamo	
Yaruro	5,000
Yuana	300
Yukpa	3,000

VIETNAM

Cham	45,000
** Chrau	15,000
Street Vendors/Saigon(82)	

YEMEN, ARAB REPUBLIC

*** Akhdam	
Ethiopian Rfgs, Yemen	480
Sayyids	
Yemenis (79)	5,600,000

YEMEN, DEMOCRATIC

| ** Hadrami | 151,000 |
| * Mahrah | 50,000 |

YUGOSLAVIA

* Albanians in Yugoslavia	1,500,000
* Bosnian (80)	1,740,000
Gypsies in Yugoslavia	800,000
Mslm Gypsies/Skoplje(82)	23,000

ZAIRE

Baali	38,000
Baka	3,000
Bakongo Angolan Rfgs(83)	600,000
** Bakuba	75,000
Bangba	29,000
Bawoyo	10,000
Bembe	50,000
Binji	64,000
Bolondo	1,000
Boma	15,000
Bugombe	12,000
Buja	200,000
Bulia	45,000
Bushoong	100,000
Bwa	35,000
Bwisi	6,000
Dengese	4,000
** Djandeau	26,000
Dongo	5,000
Enya	7,000
Fuliro	56,000
Furu	5,000
Havu	262,000
Heso	6,000
Hunde	34,000
Kanu	4,000
Kaonde	20,000
Kari	1,000
Kelah	100,000
Kumu	60,000
Kusu	26,000
Kwese	60,000
Lalia	30,000

Lamba	80,000
Lega	150,000
Liko	26,000
Lombi	8,000
Lombo	10,000
Luna	50,000
Lwalu	21,000
Ma	5,000
Mamvu-Efe	40,000
Mangbutu	8,000
Mba	20,000
Mbala	200,000
Mbangwe	2,000
Mbanja	81,000
Mbo	2,000
Mbole	100,000
Mono	30,000
Mundu	5,000
Nandi	310,000
Ndaaka	5,000
Ndo	13,000
Ndoolo	5,000
Ndunga	3,000
Ngando	121,000
Ngbaka	700,000
Ngbaka Ma'bo	17,000
Ngbandi	137,000
Ngbee	30,000
Ngiri	6,000
** Ngombe	5,000
Nkutu	40,000
Ntomba	50,000
Nyanga-Li	25,000
*** Pakabeti of Equator	3,000
Pende	200,000
Peri	40,000
Poke	46,000
* Pygmy (Mbuti) (79)	40,000
Rwamba	48,000
Sakata	75,000
Salampasu	60,000
Sanga	35,000
Sanza	15,000
Songe	500,000
Songomeno	40,000
Songoora	1,000
Suku	74,000
Swaga	121,000
Teke, Eastern	71,000
Tembo	30,000
Tiene	25,000
Togbo	6,000
Wongo	8,000
Yaka	200,000
Yans	165,000
Yela	33,000
Zimba	50,000

ZAMBIA

Ambo	1,000
Bisa	83,000
Cewa	200,000
Chokwe	25,000
Ila	39,000
Iwa	15,000
Kaonde	116,000
Kunda	21,000
Kunda	8,000
Lala	125,000
Lamba	89,000
Lenje	79,000
Lima	12,000
Lozi	215,000
Luano	4,000
Luchazi	34,000
Lunda, Ndembu	100,000
Luyana	50,000
Mambwe-Lungu	121,000
Mashi	21,000
Ngoni	257,000
* Nkoya	
Nsenga	191,000
Nyiha	59,000
Sala	11,000
Simaa	40,000
Soli	32,000
Swaka	33,000
Tambo	7,000
Tonga, Gwembe Vally(79)	86,000
Urban Refugees in Lusaka	800
Zimbabwean Refugees	45,000

ZIMBABWE

* Bushmen (Hiechware)	2,000
* Indians In Rhodesia	10,000
Kalanga	87,000
Kunda	40,000
Kwe-etshori	2,000
Lozi	8,000
Manyika	350,000
** Nambya	40,000
Ndau	178,000
** Ndebele (79)	1,000,000
Nsenga	16,000
Nyanja	252,000
* Tonga	90,000
Tswa	300,000
Tswana	30,000
Venda	38,000
Zimbabwean Repatrts(83)	300,000

Appendices

Appendix A
Unreached Peoples
Questionnaire

REACHING THE UNREACHED

Part of a program being carried out jointly by the Strategy Working Group of the Lausanne Committee for World Evangelization and MARC, the Missions Advanced Research and Communication Center, which is a ministry of World Vision International.

919 West Huntington Drive, Monrovia, California, USA

There are over 3 billion people in the world who do not know Jesus Christ as Lord and Savior. Large numbers of these people are not being reached by the gospel because they are hidden among larger populations or because the gospel message has not been expressed in ways that they can understand and respond to.

They are unreached people.

It has been estimated that there are at least 15,000 major unreached people groups, the vast majority of which have not been identified as to where they are and how they can be reached. This is a task for Christ's Church throughout the world. This is your task.

In order to understand and locate these unreached people the Strategy Working Group of the Lausanne Committee for World Evangelization has been working with the Missions Advanced Research and Communication Center (MARC). The early results of this research were presented at the Lausanne Congress on World Evangelization in 1974. Since then this worldwide effort has continued.

The on-going results are published annually in a directory entitled *Unreached Peoples*. As new information comes in from around the world, basic data about each group is listed and some 80 to 100 groups are described in detail. Information on each group is available for your use from MARC.

By publishing whatever information is available, the *Unreached Peoples* directory acts as a bridge between those who are discovering new unreached people, and those whom God has chosen to seek them out with the good news. Your contribution is important!

This questionnaire has been designed to make that task as simple as possible. We ask that you supply whatever information you can, trusting that the Lord of the Harvest has others who will supply what is missing.

Thank you for being a part of this grand vision that every person in the world may have an opportunity to know Jesus Christ.

52479A

FINDING THE UNREACHED: YOU CAN HELP!

You can help locate unreached people groups

You are part of a worldwide network of concerned Christians. There are millions upon millions of people in the world who have had little or no contact with the gospel of Jesus Christ. Because of this, we are asking you to help the Church locate and identify these peoples so it can reach them.

Within each country there are distinct and unique groups of people who may be unreached. This questionnaire is designed to help you describe such groups so that Christians everywhere may pray and consider how these groups might be reached with the gospel. This information will be continuously compiled and made available to the Church and her mission agencies. It appears each year in an annual directory, *Unreached Peoples*, produced by David C. Cook.

There are many different groups of people in the world. How varied they are! Consequently, this questionnaire may not always ask the best questions for understanding a particular people. The questions have been asked in a way that will give comparative information to as large a number of Christians as possible. Where you feel another form of question would better suit your situation, please feel free to comment.

What is a "people group"?

A people group is a part of a society that has some basic characteristics in common that cause it to feel a sense of oneness, and set it apart from other groups. It may be unified by language, religion, economic status, occupation, ethnic origin, geographic location, or social position. For example, a distinct group based on ethnic, language and geographic characteristics might be the Quechua of Bolivia; a sociological group might be the urban university and college students of Colombia, or the urban industrial workers of France. It is important to see that groups may share a common way of life and sense of oneness because of social, occupational or economic characteristics, as well as because of language or ethnic origin. Therefore, whenever possible, *describe the smallest number of persons who make up a distinct group;* that is, don't say that all persons in a region or province are a group, rather describe the specific subgroups within that region or province.

Who are the "unreached and unevangelized people"?

Christians have different definitions of the terms "unreached" or "unevangelized." For the purposes of this worldwide effort, we describe an unreached or unevangelized people as a people who has not received or responded to the gospel. This unresponsiveness may be due to lack of opportunity, to lack of understanding, or because the people has not received enough information about the gospel message in its own language through the eyes of its own culture so that it can truly respond to Christ.

We consider a people "unreached" when less than 20 percent of the members of the group are *practicing* Christians, that is, are active members of the Christian community. By "Christian" we mean adherents (church members, families and followers) of the historic Christian communions; Protestant, Anglican, Roman Catholic, Orthodox and such independent groups as may claim the Bible as the basis of faith and Jesus Christ as Lord and Savior. A group less than 20 percent Christian may yet need Christians from outside the group to help with the evangelism task.

How you can provide information

The attached questionnaire has two parts. If you only have information for the first part, send that in now.

Please fill in one questionnaire for *each* people group with which you are familiar. Do not put several groups on one questionnaire. (If you need more questionnaires, ask for extra copies or photocopy this one, or typewrite the questions you are answering on a separate sheet of paper.) We realize that one person may not have all the answers to these questions. Just answer what you can. PLEASE DO NOT WAIT UNTIL YOU HAVE ALL THE INFORMATION REQUESTED ON THIS QUESTIONNAIRE. SEND WHAT YOU HAVE. Other people may provide information that you do not have. Thank you for your help!

When you have completed this questionnaire, please return it to:

Unreached Peoples Program Director
c/o MARC, 919 W. Huntington Drive, Monrovia, CA 91016 U.S.A.

SURVEY QUESTIONNAIRE FOR UNEVANGELIZED AND UNREACHED PEOPLES

Do you see a group of people who are unreached or unevangelized? Identify them! As the Lord spoke to Ezekiel of old, so He speaks to us today. "Son of man, What do you see"?

Answers to the questions on these two pages will provide the minimum information needed to list this people group in the *Unreached Peoples* annual.

After you have read the directions, type or print your answers so they can be easily read. It is unlikely that you will have all the information requested. Do the best you can. What information you are lacking others may supply. If your information is a best guess or estimate, merely place an "E" after it. Send in what you have as soon as possible. Please ignore the small numbers next to the answers. They help others prepare your answers for the *Unreached Peoples* annual.

"For this reason I bow my knees before the Father, from whom every family in heaven and on earth is named . . ."
Ephesians 3:14-15 (RSV)

1. Name of the group or people: _____

2. Alternate name(s) or spelling: _____

3. Country where located: _____

4. Approximate size of the group in this country: _____

5. Vernacular or common language: _____

6. Lingua franca or trade language: _____

7. Name of religious groups found among this people:

	% who are adherents of this religion	% who practice this religion
CHRISTIAN GROUPS:		
Protestant	_____ %	_____ %
Roman Catholic	_____ %	_____ %
Eastern Orthodox	_____ %	_____ %
Other Christian: _____ *(name)*	_____ %	_____ %
NON-CHRISTIAN GROUPS OR SECULARISM:		
_____	_____ %	_____ %
_____	_____ %	_____ %
_____	_____ %	_____ %
_____	_____ %	_____ %
TOTAL FOR ALL GROUPS:	100 %	

"Brethren, My heart's desire and prayer to God for them is that they may be saved."
Romans 10:1 (RSV)

8. In your opinion, what is the attitude of this people toward Christianity?

(01)☐ Strongly favorable   (02)☐ Somewhat favorable   (03)☐ Indifferent   (04)☐ Somewhat opposed   (05)☐ Strongly opposed

9. Questionnaire completed by:

Name: _____ Date: _____

Organization: _____

Address: _____

_____

10. Who else might be able to provide information about this people?

Name	Organization (if any)	Address

11. If you are aware of any publications describing this people, please give title and author.

_____

12. What other information do you have that could help others to understand this people better? What do you feel would help in evangelizing them?   *(Use additional sheet if necessary.)*

"And how are they to believe in him of whom they have never heard? And how are they to hear without a preacher?"
Romans 10:14 (RSV)

13. Are you also sending in pages 3 and 4? ☐ Yes   ☐ No

Please send whatever information you have immediately. Do not wait until you have every answer.

Mail to:

Unreached Peoples Program Director
c/o MARC, 919 W. Huntington Drive, Monrovia, CA 91016 USA

Name of people group described_____ Your name _____ Date ____

If you have any more information about this people group, please complete the following two pages as best you can. If not, please send in pages one and two now. If you can obtain more information later, send it in as soon as possible.

PEOPLE DISTINCTIVES—What makes them different? Why are they a people group?

14. A number of different things contribute to create a distinctive people or group, one that in some way shares a common way of life, sees itself as a particular group having an affinity toward one another, and differs to some extent from other groups or peoples. What would you say makes the people you are describing distinctive? Check the appropriate box of as many of the following descriptions as *are important* in making this people distinctive. Use the following scale: "High" importance, "Medium" importance, "Low" importance. For example, if you thought that the fact that they had a common political loyalty was of medium importance in unifying and making a group distinctive, you would place an "X" in the middle box under "Medium".

Importance   Importance

High / Medium / Low

(01)☐ ☐ ☐ Same language
(02)☐ ☐ ☐ Common political loyalty
(03)☐ ☐ ☐ Similar occupation
(04)☐ ☐ ☐ Racial or ethnic similarity
(05)☐ ☐ ☐ Shared religious customs
(06)☐ ☐ ☐ Common kinship ties
(07)☐ ☐ ☐ Strong sense of unity
(08)☐ ☐ ☐ Similar education level
(09)☐ ☐ ☐ Other(s) _____
        (please write in)

(10)☐ ☐ ☐ Common residential area
(11)☐ ☐ ☐ Similar social class or caste
(12)☐ ☐ ☐ Similar economic status
(13)☐ ☐ ☐ Shared hobby or special interest
(14)☐ ☐ ☐ Discrimination from other groups
(15)☐ ☐ ☐ Unique health situation
(16)☐ ☐ ☐ Distinctive legal status
(17)☐ ☐ ☐ Similar age
(18)☐ ☐ ☐ Common significant problems

15. How rapidly would you say the lifestyle of this people is changing? (check one)

(01)☐ Very Slow Change   (02)☐ Slow Change   (03)☐ Moderate Change   (04)☐ Rapid Change   (05)☐ Very Rapid Change

"And to him was given dominion and glory and kingdom, that all peoples, nations, and languages should serve him." Daniel 7:14 (RSV)

PEOPLE LANGUAGES—What do they speak?

Please list the various languages used by the members of this people:

LANGUAGE TYPE	Primary name(s) of their language(s)	Approximate % who *speak* this language	Approximate % of people over 15 years of age who *read* this language
16. Vernacular or common language:	_____	_____ %	_____ %
17. Lingua franca or trade language:	_____	_____ %	_____ %
18. Language used for instruction in schools:	_____	_____ %	_____ %
19. Language suitable for presentation of the gospel:	_____	_____ %	_____ %

20. If there is Christian witness at present, what language(s) is being used? _____

21. Place an "x" in the boxes that indicate the status of Scripture translation *in the language you consider most suitable for communicating the gospel* (question 19):

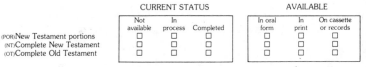

	CURRENT STATUS			AVAILABLE		
	Not available	In process	Completed	In oral form	In print	On cassette or records
(POR)New Testament portions	☐	☐	☐	☐	☐	☐
(NT)Complete New Testament	☐	☐	☐	☐	☐	☐
(OT)Complete Old Testament	☐	☐	☐	☐	☐	☐

22. Of the <u>Christians</u> present among this people, what percent *over 15 years of age can* and *do* read any language?

_____ %

CHRISTIAN WITNESS TO THIS PEOPLE—Who is trying to reach them?

23. If there are Christian churches or missions (national or foreign) now active *within the area or region where this people is concentrated,* please give the following information:

(If there are none, check here: ☐)

CHURCH OR MISSION Name of church, denomination	YEAR Year work began in this area	MEMBERS Approximate number of full members from this people	ADHERENTS Approximate number of adherents (community including children)	WORKERS Approximate numbers of trained pastors and evangelists from this people
_____	_____	_____	_____	_____
_____	_____	_____	_____	_____
_____	_____	_____	_____	_____

24. What is the growth rate of the total Christian community among this people group?

(01)☐ Rapid growth   (02)☐ Slow growth   (03)☐ Stable   (04)☐ Slow decline   (05)☐ Rapid decline

25. In your opinion, what is the attitude of this people to religious change of any kind?

(01)☐ Very open   (02)☐ Somewhat open   (03)☐ Indifferent   (04)☐ Somewhat closed   (05)☐ Very closed

26. In your opinion, what is the attitude of this people toward Christianity?

(01)☐ Strongly favorable   (02)☐ Somewhat favorable   (03)☐ Indifferent   (04)☐ Somewhat opposed   (05)☐ Strongly opposed

27. Most people move through a series of more or less well-defined stages in their attitude toward Christianity. Parts of a people group will be further along than other parts. Here are ten categories that attempt to show this progression. However, locating people in some of these categories can be difficult, so to make things simpler some categories are combined in the questions that follow.

In your estimation, what percentage of this people can be described as those who: (These percentages are exclusive. Do not include people more than once. Your total should add up to 100%.)

Have no awareness of Christianity . . . . _____ %

Have awareness of the existence of Christianity . . . . _____ %

Have some knowledge of the gospel . . . . _____ %

Understand the message of the gospel . . . . _____ %

See the personal implications of the gospel . . . . ⎫

Recognize a personal need that the gospel can meet . . . . ⎬ _____ %

Are being challenged to receive Christ . . . . ⎭

Have decided for Christ, but are not incorporated into a fellowship (may be evaluating their decision) . . . . _____ %

Are incorporated into a fellowship of Christians . . . . _____ %

Are active propagators of the gospel . . . . _____ %

                                                                    TOTAL   100 %

28. On the whole, how accurate is the information you have given us?

(V)☐ Very accurate   (F)☐ Fairly accurate   (E)☐ Good estimate   (G)☐ Mainly guesses

29. Are you willing to have your name publically associated with this information?

☐ No   ☐ Yes   ☐ Yes, with qualifications: _____

Appendix B
Definitions

People Group: a significantly large sociological grouping of individuals who perceive themselves to have a common affinity for one another. From the viewpoint of evangelization this is the largest possible group within which the gospel can spread without encountering barriers of understanding or acceptance.

Unreached People Group: a people group among which there is no indigenous community of believing Christians with adequate numbers and resources to evangelize this people group without outside (cross-cultural) assistance.

Hidden People Group: unreached people group.

Frontier People: unreached people group.

Frontier Mission: mission agency attempting to reach an unreached people group.

Reached People Group: a people group with adequate indigenous believers and resources to evangelize this group without outside (cross-cultural) assistance.

Reported People Group: a people group that someone has reported as possibly unreached.

Verified People Group: a people group that has been verified as a people group and as an unreached people group.

Evaluated People Group: an unreached people group about which adequate research has been completed to permit interested Christians outside the group to make a decision to attempt to reach it.

Selected People Group: an unreached people group that someone or some agency sufficient to the task has made a commitment to reach.

Supported People Group: an unreached people group for which adequate resources are provided (usually through church/mission partnership) for the agency to move ahead.

Engaged People Group: an unreached people group among which initial field work has begun with the intent of planting an evangelizing, culturally indigenous church.

Unreached Peoples Desk: a clearinghouse located at MARC for information and contacts related to selecting, supporting and engaging specific unreached people groups. It can be directly reached by calling (213) 574-9025 or by writing c/o MARC, 919 W. Huntington Drive, Monrovia, CA 91016, U.S.A.

Appendix C
Resources

1. Unreached Peoples

Beaver, R. Pierce, ed. **The Gospel and Frontier Peoples.** Pasadena: William Carey Library, 1973.

Dayton, Edward R. **That Everyone May Hear.** Monrovia: MARC, 1979.

_____ **Planning Strategies for Evangelism** (6th Edition). Monrovia: MARC, 1979.

Dayton, Edward R. and David A. Fraser, **Planning Strategies for World Evangelization.** Grand Rapids: William B. Eerdmans Publishing Company, 1980.

Daily Prayer Guides, Pasadena, CA: Frontier Fellowship, monthly.

Department of State. **Background Notes.** Washington, D.C.: U.S. Government Printing Office, updated regularly.

Douglas, J., ed. **Let the Earth Hear His Voice.** Minneapolis: World Wide Publications, 1975.

Europa Publications, Ltd. **Europa World Year Book.** London.

Grimes, Barbara, ed. **Ethnologue.** Huntington Beach:

Wycliffe Bible Translators, 1978.

Hedlund, Roger E., ed. **World Christianity: South Asia.** Monrovia: MARC, 1980.

Holland, Clifford, ed. **World Christianity: Central America.** Monrovia: MARC, 1981.

Johnstone, Patrick J. **Operation World.** Bromley, Kent, England: STL Publications, 1978 (available in the U.S. from the William Carey Library, P.O. Box 128C, Pasadena, CA 91104).

Kane, J. Herbert, **Global View of Christian Mission.** Grand Rapids: Baker Book Co., 1971.

Keyes, Lawrence, **The New Age of Missions: A Study of Third World Missionary Societies,** Pasadena: Fuller Theological Seminary, Doctoral Dissertation, 1981.

Lausanne Occasional Paper No. 1: The Pasadena Consultation--Homogeneous Unit, Wheaton, IL: Lausanne Committee for World Evangelization, 1978.

Consultation on Gospel and Culture. **Lausanne Occasional Paper No. 2: The Willowbank Report--Gospel and Culture,** Wheaton, IL: Lausanne Committee for World Evangelization, 1978.

Stott, John. **Lausanne Occasional Paper No. 3: The Lausanne Covenant--An Exposition,** Wheaton, IL: Lausanne Committee for World Evangelization, 1975.

North American Conference on Muslim Evangelization. **Lausanne Occasional Paper No. 4: The Glen Eyrie Report--Muslim Evangelization,** Wheaton, IL: Lausanne Committee for World Evangelization, 1978.

Consultation on World Evangelization, Mini-Consultation on Reaching Refugees. **Lausanne Occasional Paper No. 5: Thailand Report--Christian Witness to Refugees,** Wheaton, IL: Lausanne Committee for World Evangelization, 1980.

Consultation on World Evangelization, Mini-

Consultation on Reaching Chinese. **Lausanne Occasional Paper No. 6: Thailand Report--Christian Witness to the Chinese People,** Wheaton, IL: Lausanne Committee for World Evangelization, 1980.

Consultation on World Evangelization, Mini-Consultation on Reaching Jewish People. **Lausanne Occasional Paper No. 7: Thailand Report--Christian Witness to the Jewish People,** Wheaton, IL: Lausanne Committee for World Evangelization, 1980.

Consultation on World Evangelization, Mini-Consultation on Reaching Secularists. **Lausanne Occasional Paper No. 8: Thailand Report--Christian Witness to Secularized People,** Wheaton, IL: Lausanne Committee for World Evangelization, 1980.

Consultation on World Evangelization, Mini-Consultation on Reaching Large Cities. **Lausanne Occasional Paper No. 9: Thailand Report--Christian Witness to Large Cities,** Wheaton, IL: Lausanne Committee for World Evangelization, 1980.

Consultation on World Evangelization, Mini-Consultation on Reaching Nominal Christians among Roman Catholics. **Lausanne Occasional Paper No. 10: Thailand Report--Christian Witness to Nominal Christians among Roman Catholics,** Wheaton, IL: Lausanne Committee for World Evangelization, 1980.

Lebar, Frank M., ed. **Ethnic Groups of Insular Southeast Asia (Vol. 1).** New Haven: Human Relations Area Files Press, 1972.

_____ **Ethnic Groups of Insular Southeast Asia (Vol. 2).** New Haven: Human Relations Area Files Press, 1975.

Lebar, Frank M., G. C. Hickey, and J. K. Musgrave. **Ethnic Groups of Mainland Southeast Asia.** New Haven: Human Relations Area Files Press, 1964.

Luzbetak, Louis J. **The Church and Cultures.** Illinois:

Divine Word Publications, 1963.

Maloney, Clarence. **People of South Asia.** New York: Holt, Rinehart and Winston, 1974.

MARC. **You Can So Get There From Here (5th Edition).** Monrovia, CA: MARC, 1981.

MARC. **Unreached Peoples Prayer Cards** (Europe Only). Monrovia: MARC, 1981.

McCurry, Don M., ed. **The Gospel and Islam: A 1978 Compendium.** Monrovia, CA: MARC, 1979.

_____ **World Christianity: Middle East.** Monrovia, CA: MARC, 1979.

Murdock, George P. **Africa: Its Peoples and Their Culture History.** New York: McGraw-Hill, 1959.

Nida, Eugene A., ed. **The Book of a Thousand Tongues.** New York: United Bible Societies, 1972.

Pentecost, Edward C. **Reaching the Unreached.** South Pasadena, CA: William Carey Library, 1974.

Read, William R., and Frank A. Ineson. **Brazil 1980: The Protestant Handbook.** Monrovia: MARC, 1973.

Steward, Julian H. **Handbook of South American Indians.** New York: Cooper Square Pub., 1959.

Tindale, Norman B. **Aboriginal Tribes of Australia.** Berkeley: Univ. of Calif. Press, 1975.

Unreached Peoples Desk. A clearinghouse located at MARC for information and contacts related to selecting, supporting and engaging specific unreached people groups. MARC, 919 West Huntington Drive, Monrovia, CA 91016, U.S.A. (213) 574-9025.

Wagner, C. Peter. **Frontiers in Missionary Strategy.** Chicago: Moody Press, 1971.

Wagner, C. Peter, and Edward R. Dayton, eds. **Unreached Peoples '79: The Challenge of the Church's**

Unfinished Business. Illinois: David C. Cook Pub. Co., 1979.

_____ **Unreached Peoples '80: The Challenge of the Church's Unfinished Business.** Elgin, Illinois: David C. Cook Pub. Co., 1980.

_____ **Unreached Peoples '81: The Challenge of the Church's Unfinished Business with Special Section on the Peoples of Asia,** Elgin, Illinois: David C. Cook Pub. Co., 1981.

Wauchope, Robert, ed. **Handbook of Middle American Indians: Guide to Ethnohistorical Sources (Vols. 1-15).** Austin: Univ. of Texas Press, 1964.

Weekes, Richard V. **Muslim Peoples: A World Ethnographic Survey.** Connecticutt: Greenwood Press, 1978.

Wilson, Samuel, ed. **Mission Handbook: North American Protestant Ministries Overseas (12th Edition).** Monrovia: MARC, 1980.

Wilson, Samuel, and Edward R. Dayton, eds. **Unreached Peoples '82: The Challenge of the Church's Unfinished Business, Focus on Urban Peoples.** Elgin, Illinois: David C. Cook Pub. Co., 1982.

Wong, James, Peter Larson, and Edward Pentecost. **Missions from the Third World.** Singapore: Church Growth Study Center, 1973.

Audiovisual

Dayton, Edward R. **That Everyone May Hear.** Monrovia: MARC, 1979.

2. Refugees

Africa's Refugees and UNHCR. UNHCR, 1982.

Bernard, William S. "Immigrants and Refugees: Their Similarities, Difference and Needs." **International Migration,** 14(3) 1976, pp. 267-281.

Bibliography on Refugees, No. 4. Oct.-Nov. 1980. UNHCR.

Brown, Francis J., ed. Refugees: The Annals of the American Academy of Political and Social Science, No. 203. May 1979.

Chaney, Elsa M. Women in International Migration. Office of Women in Development, AID, 1980.

Congressional Research Service, Library of Congress. Review of U.S. Refugee Resettlement Programs and Policies. U.S. Government Printing Office, 1980.

D'Souza, Frances, ed. Refugees: A Special Issue Devoted to Viewpoints, Case Studies and Theoretical Considerations on the Care and Management of Refugees. Disasters: The International Journal of Disasters Studies and Practice, Vol. 3, No. 4, 1979. Oxford: Pergamon Press.

_____ Refugee Dilemma: International Recognition and Acceptance, Minority Rights Group, 1980.

David, Henry P. Involuntary International Migration: Adaptation of Refugees. International Migration, 7(3/4) 1969, pp. 67-105.

Early, Tracy. Refugees: "The Majority Are Women." Response. April 1982.

Edgren, James Andrews. Patterns for Ministry Among Refugee Peoples--The Vietnamese Experience. Unpublished Doctoral Thesis, Wesley Theological Seminary, 1981.

Encyclopedia Britannica, 1980 Book of the Year. Refugees. Chicago: Encyclopedia Britannica, Inc., pp. 593-596. 1980.

Eversole, Helena. Women Refugees. Trip Report, December 15-29, 1980. Unpublished Document, World

Vision/U.S.

Hanson, Christopher T. "Behind the Paper Curtain, Asylum Policy Versus Asylum Practice." **New York University Review of Law and Social Change,** Winter 1978.

ICM in Facts. Intergovernmental Committee for Migration, 1981.

ICVA News (Qrtly.) International Council of Voluntary Agencies (ICVA), 13 rue Gautier, 1201 Geneva, Switzerland.

International Catholic Migration Commission Annual Report. International Catholic Migration Commission, 1980.

Jacob, Sol. **Refugees: A Challenge to South African Churches.** South African Council of Churches, 1982.

Keller, Stephen L. **Uprooting and Social Change: The Role of Refugees in Development.** Delhi: Manohar Book Service, 1975.

Langlois, Joseph E. **Description and Directory of National Organizations and People Involved in the Processing and Resettlement of Indochinese Refugees in America.** Washington, D.C.: Indochina Refugee Action Center, 1979.

Logan, Muriel, and George Otis, Jr., eds. **Palestine and South Lebanon.** Situation Report No. 2. Issachar, 1982.

Newland, Kathleen. **Worldwatch Paper #43.** "Refugees: The New International Politics of Displacement." Worldwatch Institute: Washington, D.C., March 1981.

Norwood, Frederick A. **Strangers and Exiles: A History of Religious Refugees.** 2 Vols. Nashville: Abingdon Press, 1969.

Palestine Refugees Today, No. 98. Vienna, Austria: UNRWA Headquarters. January 1982.

People on the Move: Victims on the Altar of the Golden Calf. Pro Mundi Vita, 1981.

Refugee Reports, Vol. 3, No. 3. Jan. 15, 1982.

Refugees: Africa's Challenge. London: Christian Aid, 1978.

Report of the United Nations High Commissioner for Refugees. United Nations, 1979.

Schechtman, Joseph B. **The Refugee in the World: Displacement and Integration.** New York: A. S. Barnes, 1963.

Selected Bibliography: Refugees and Refugee Migration. Church World Service, Oct. 1980.

Sobel, Lester A., editor. **Refugees: A World Report.** New York: Facts on File, 1979.

Tabori, Paul. **The Anatomy of Exile: A Semantic and Historical Study.** London: Harrap, 1972.

UNHRC. **Refugee Women.** United Nations High Commissioner for Refugees, 1981.

UNHCR in Thailand. UNHCR, 1981.

UNRWA. **A Survey of United Nations Assistance to Palestine Refugees.** United Nations, 1980.

U.S. Senate, Committee on the Judiciary, Report by the Congressional Research Service, Library of Congress. **Review of U.S. Refugee Resettlement Programs and Policies.** Washington, D.C.: U.S. Government Printing Office, 1979.

————————————— **World Refugee Crises: The International Community's Response.** U.S. Government Printing Office, 1979.

Zachariah, K. C., and Julien Conde. **Migration in West Africa.** Oxford University Press, 1981.

3. Ministry to Refugees

The following materials relate to various aspects of refugees for those involved or wishing to be involved in ministry among refugee peoples. Included here are works that will increase cultural awareness, help in understanding the trauma of the refugee experience and aid in focusing on the appropriate evangelism strategies.

A Guide to Congregations Resettling Southeast Asian Refugees. Minneapolis, MN: Lutheran Social Service of Minnesota, n.d.

About Indo-Asian Refugees. Melbourne, Australia: Dept. of Migrants, Refugees and Ethnic Affairs, n.d.

Afghani. Center for Applied Linguistics, 1981.

An Introduction to the Various Ethnic Groups from Laos. Orientation Supplement/Hmong Series No. 8. New York: Lutheran Immigration and Refugee Service.

Anderson, Lorna. **You and Your Refugee Neighbors,** Pasadena, CA: William Carey Library, 1980.

Andrianoff, David I. and Jean. **Lao and Hmong Refugee Response: A Comparison.** Unpublished manuscript, 1982.

_____ **Church Growth Principles Relevant to Thailand's Indochinese Refugees,** unpublished manuscript, 1978.

_____ **An Accurate Picture of the Hmong Church in Exile: Prolegomena to Church Growth Study in a Refugee Situation.** Unpublished manuscript, 1978.

Armour, Monica, Paula Knudson, Jeffrey Meeks, V. Lynn Tyler, and Deborah L. Coon, editors. **The Indochinese: New Americans.** Brigham Young University, 1981.

509

Bentz, Thomas. **New Immigrants: Portraits in Passage.** New York: The Pilgrim Press, 1981.

Bjork, D. **An Update on "Reaching Newcomers to North America." Study and Recommendations.** IFMA/EFMA Convention, Kansas City, 1981.

Briefing Document on the Refugee Problem in Somalia. International Disaster Institute, 1980.

Cambodia: A Resource Guide for Teachers. Berkeley, CA: Berkeley United School District, 1976.

Church World Service. "Mental Health Problems of Indochinese Refugees in the United States." **Refugees and Human Rights Newsletter.** Vol. IV, No. 3, spring 1980.

Coles, Robert. **Uprooted Children: The Early Life of Migrant Farm Workers.** Pittsburgh: University of Pittsburgh Press, 1970.

Crist, Evamae Barton. **Take This House.** Scottsdale PA: Herald Press, 1977.

Diaz Briquets, Sergio, and Lisandro Perez. **Cuba: The Demography of Revolution.** Population Reference Bureau, 1981.

Erickson, Erik H. "Identity and Uprootedness in Our Time." **Uprooting and Resettlement.** London: World Federation for Mental Health, 1960.

Fieg, John Paul and George W. Renwick, eds. **Interact: Guidelines for Thais and North Americans.** Intercultural Press, 1980.

Glimpses of Hmong History and Culture, No. 16, Indochinese Refugee Education Guides, General Information Series. National Indochinese Clearing House, Arlington, VA: Center for Applied Linguistics, n.d.

Gordon, Arthur. **A Guide to Two Cultures: American . . . Indochinese.** Interagency Task Force for Indochina

Refugees, 1975.

Gregerson, M., and O. Thomas, eds. **Notes from Indochina on Ethnic Minority Cultures.** Summer Institute of Linguistics Museum of Anthopology, 1980.

Grodka, Sonia, and Gerhard Hennes. **Homeless No More: A Discussion of Integration Between Sponsor and Refugee.** New York: The National Council of Churches, 1960.

History and Culture of Vietnam: An Introduction. Orientation Supplement/Vietnamese Series No. 1. New York: Lutheran Immigration and Refugee Service, n.d.

Hoff, Hans. "Home and Identity," **Uprooting and Resettlement.** London: World Federation for Mental Health, 1960.

——————————— "The Young Refugee." **Growing Up in a Changing World.** London: World Federation for Mental Health, 1958.

Indochinese Cultural and Service Center. **Sponsoring Refugees: A Guide for Sponsors.** Portland, OR: The Neighborhood House, n.d.

Indochinese Materials Center. **Bibliography of Education and Resettlement Materials for Indochinese Refugees.** Kansas City, MO: U.S. Dept. of Education, n.d.

Indochinese Refugee Education Guides. Washington, D.C.: English Language Resource Center, Center for Applied Linguistics, n.d.

It's a Cosmopolitan World. Melbourne, Australia: Dept. for Migrants, Refugees and Ethnic Affairs, n.d.

Kampuchean Chronicles. National Federation of UNESCO Associations in Japan, 1980.

Kansier, Chris, Linda Williams, Debra Giel and Nancy DeMarre. **The Hmong in St. Paul: A Culture in Transition.** Community Planning Organization, Inc.,

1980.

Kehler, Larry. **Making Room for "Strangers."** Menno-nite Central Committee, Canada, 1980.

Kessner, Thomas, and Betty Boyd Caroli. **Today's Immigrants, Their Stories.** Oxford University Press, 1981.

Kino, F. F. "Refugee Psychoses in Great Britain: Aliens' Paranoid Reaction." **Journal of Medical Science.** No. 97, 1959.

Laos: The Land and Its People, Supplement No. 4. New York: Lutheran Immigration and Refugee Service, May 1978.

Lin, Keh-Ming, Laurie Tazuma and Minoru Masuda. "Adaptational Problems of Vietnamese Refugees: Health and Mental Health Status." **Archives General Psychiatry.** No. 16, August 1979.

Living With Other Faiths. Melbourne, Australia: Anglican Information Office, 1981.

Lutheran Immigration and Refugee Service. **Cambodia: The Land and Its People.** World Relief Refugee Services, 1976.

_____ **Face to Face: The Ministry of Refugee Resettlement.** Orientation Manual for Con-gregations. New York: Lutheran Council in the USA, n.d.

More, Faye, and Al Braun. **Results of a Questionnaire to Sponsors of Southeast Asian Refugees.** Ontario Ministry of Culture and Recreation, n.d.

Mutiso, Roberta M. **Counseling of Refugees in Africa.** Paper presented at Pan African Conference on Refu-gees, Arusha, Tanzania, May 1979.

Office of Family Assistance. **A Guide to Two Cultures--Indochinese.** Washington, D.C.: Interagency

Task Force for Indochinese Refugees, 1976.

Peoples and Cultures of Cambodia, Laos and Vietnam. Center for Applied Linguistics, 1981.

Pfister-Ammende, Maria. "Uprooting and Resettlement as a Sociological Problem," **Uprooting and Resettlement.** London: World Federation for Mental Health, 1960.

Planck, Jane. **An Organization and Welcome Guide for Groups Sponsoring Indochinese Refugees.** Available from Julia Vadala Taft, Director, Interagency Task Force, U.S. Government, n.d.

"Please Listen to What I'm Not Saying." Canberra, Australia: Dept. of Immigration and Ethnic Affairs, 1982.

Preparing for Sponsorship. World Vision of Canada, n.d.

Robinson, Court. **Special Report: Physical and Emotional Health Care Needs of Indochinese Refugees.** Indochinese Refugee Action Center, 1980.

Senate Standing Committee on Foreign Affairs and Defense, Australia. **Indochinese Refugee Resettlement--Australia's Involvement.** Australian Government Publishing Service, 1982.

Refugee Service of the Commission on Inter-Church Aid, Refugee and World Service. **Are the Haitians Claiming Asylum in the United States Really Refugees?** World Council of Churches, 1980.

——————————— **The Churches and the World Refugee Crisis.** World Council of Churches, 1981.

Refugees--The Cry of the Indochinese. Asian Relations Center, 1980.

Seelye, H. Ned. **Sequencing Training for Intercultural Communication During the First Six Months of Residence Abroad.** Address at the Language and Intercultural Research Center "Bridges of Understanding Symposium," Nov. 3-Dec. 2, 1978, Provo, Utah: Language and Intercultural Research Center, Brigham Young University, n.d.

Smalley, William A. "The Gospel and the Cultures of Laos," **Practical Anthropology,** Vol. 3, No. 3, 1956.

Stahr, James A. "Reaching Out in Six Languages," **Interest,** Vol. 46, No. 8, September 1981.

Stein, B. N. "Occupational Adjustment of Refugees: The Vietnamese in the United States," **International Migration Review,** No. 13, Spring 1979.

Stepick, A. **Haitian Refugees in the U.S.** Minority Rights Group Ltd., 1982.

The Hmong: Their History and Culture. Orientation Supplement/Hmong Series No. 8, New York: Lutheran Immigration and Refugee Service.

The Resettlement of Indochinese Refugees in the U.S.: A Selected Bibliography, Washington D.C.: Indochina Refugee Action Center, September 1980.

Their New Life in the United States. Center for Applied Linguistics, 1981.

Thuy, Vuong G., **Getting to Know the Vietnamese and Their Culture.** New York: Fredrick Ungar, 1976.

United HAIS Service. **A Guide to Working with Vietnamese Refugees.** Washington, D.C.: Emigration and Refugee Services, United States Catholic Conference, n.d.

UNHCR Special Report: Refugee Integration. UNHCR, n.d.

Vek, Hmong Taing. **Ordeal in Cambodia.** Here's Life Publishers, 1980.

Weinberg, Abraham A. **Migration and Belonging: A Study of Mental Health and Adjustment in Israel.** The

Hague: M. Nijhoff, 1961.

Who Is My Neighbor? Inter-Church Committee for Refugees, Canada, 1981.

Zwingmann, Charles, and Maria Pfister-Ammende. **Uprooting and After.** New York: Springer-Verlag, 1973.

4. Directory of Organizations Related to Refugees

Source: **World Refugee Survey, 1982,** U.S. Committee for Refugees.

A. INTERNATIONAL ORGANIZATIONS

International Commitee for Migration (ICM), P.O. Box 100, CH-1211 Geneva 19, Switzerland. Director: James Carlin. Representatives: New York--Richard Scott, 60 East 42nd St., Suite 2122, New York, NY 10165. (212) 599-0440; California--William Anderson, Building 500, Rm. 42, Hamilton AFB, CA 94934. (415) 883-0561; Washington, D.C.--Gretchen S. Brainerd, 1346 Connecticut Ave., NW, Suite 711, Washington, D.C. 20036. (202) 785-1909.

International Committee of the Red Cross (ICRC), 17 Avenue de la Paix, CH-1211 Geneva, Switzerland.

International Council of Voluntary Agencies (ICVA), 13 Rue Gautier, 1201 Geneva, Switzerland, 31 66 02 (Cable: VOLAG (Geneva), Telex: 22891 icva ch.). Executive Director: Anthony Kozlowski.

International Disaster Institute, 85 Marylebone High St., London W1M 3DE. Director: Dr. Frances D'Souza.

League of Red Cross Societies, 17 Chemin de Crets, P.O. Box 276, 1211 Geneva 19, Switzerland. 60 E 42nd St., Suite 1438, New York, NY

515

10017. New York office: (212) 661-5714. Secretary-General: Hans Hoegh.

Office of the United Nations High Commissioner for Refugees (UNHCR), Palais des Nations, 1211 Geneva 10, Switzerland. High Commissioner: Poul Hartling. Regional Office: UN Bldg., 3rd fl., New York, NY 10017. (212) 754-7600. Liaison Office: UNHCR, 1785 Massachusetts AVe. NW, Washington, D.C. 20036. (202) 387-8546.

United Nations Children's Fund (UNICEF), 866 UN Plaza, New York, NY 10017. (212) 754-1234. Executive Director: James Grant.

United Nations Relief and Works Agency for Palestine Refugees in the Near East (UNRWA), Vienna International Centre, Box 700, A1400 Vienna, Austria. Commissioner-General: Olof Rydbeck. New York Liaison Office: John Miles, UN Bldg., Rm. 937, New York, NY 10017. (212) 754-4214.

B. U.S. GOVERNMENT OFFICES

Department of State Bureau for Refugee Programs, Room 7532, 2201 C St. NW, Washington, D.C. 20520. (202) 632-5230. Director: Ambassador Richard D. Vine.

Department of Education, Office of Bilingual Education and Minority Languages Affairs, Refugee Children Assistance Staff, Reporters Building, 400 Maryland Ave. SW, Room 505, Washington, D.C. 20202. (202) 472-3520. Branch Chief: James Lockhart.

Department of Health and Human Services, Office of Refugee Resettlement, 330 C St. SW, Room 1229, Washington, D.C. 20201. (202) 245-0418. Director: Philip Hawkes.

Department of Justice, Immigration and

Naturalization Service, 425 Eye St. NW, Washington, D.C. 20530. (202) 633-2000. Commissioner: Alan C. Nelson.

House Judiciary Committee, 2137 Rayburn House Office Building, Washington, D.C. 20515. (202) 225-3951. Chairman: Peter W. Rodino, Jr. Subcommittee on Immigration, Refugees and International Law Chairman: Romano L. Mazzoli.

Office of the U.S. Coordinator for Refugee Affairs, Department of State, (S/R) Rm. 7526, 2201 C St. NW, Washington, D.C. 20520. (202) 632-3964. Coordinator: Ambassador H. Eugene Douglas.

Senate Judiciary Committee, 2226 Dirksen Senate Office Bldg., Washington, D.C. 20510. (202) 224-5225. Chairman: Strom Thurmond. Subcommittee on Immigration and Refugee Policy Chairman: Alan K. Simpson.

C. U.S. RESETTLEMENT AGENCIES

American Council for Nationalities Service, 20 W. 40th St., New York, NY 10018. (212) 398-9142. Executive Director: Wells C. Klien.

American Fund for Czechoslovak Refugees, 1790 Broadway, Room 710, New York, NY 10019. (212) 265-1919. President: Dr. Jan Papanek.

Buddhist Council for Refugee Rescue and Resettlement, City of 10,000 Buddhas, Box 217, Talmage, CA 95481. (707) 468-9155. Executive Director: Bhikshu Heng Ch'i.

Church World Service, 475 Riverside Dr., New York, NY 10115. (212) 870-2164. Executive Director: Paul F. McCleary.

Hebrew Immigrant Aid Society, Inc. (HIAS), 200

Park Ave. South, New York, NY 10003. (212) 674-6800. Executive Vice President: Leonard Seidenman.

International Rescue Committee, 386 Park Ave. South, New York, NY 10016. (212) 679-0010. Executive Director: Charles Sternberg.

Lutheran Immigration and Refugee Service/ Lutheran Council in the U.S.A., 360 Park Ave. South, New York, NY 10010. (212) 532-6350. Director: Ingrid Walter.

Migration and Refugee Services (MRS): United States Catholic Conference, 1312 Massachusetts Ave. NW, Washington, D.C. 20005. (202) 659-6618. Executive Director: John McCarthy.

Presiding Bishop's Fund for World Relief: Episcopal Church Center, 815 Second Ave., New York, NY 10017. (212) 687-9454 or 55. Executive Director: Reverend Samir J. Habiby.

Rav Tov, 125 Heyward St., Brooklyn, NY 11206. (212) 875-8300. Executive Director: Rabbi David Niederman.

Tolstoy Foundation, Inc., 250 W 57th St., Suite 1101, New York, NY 10107-0144. (212) 247-2922. Executive Director: Teymuraz Bagration.

World Relief Corporation/Refugee Services Division: National Association of Evangelicals, P.O. Box WRC, Nyack, NY 10960. (914) 268-4135. Associate Executive Director: Donald Bjork.

YMCA Refugee Resettlement Services, 101 N. Wacker Dr., Chicago, IL 60606. Director: Boris Kazimiroff. New York Office: 291 Broadway, New York, NY 10007. (212) 374-2285. Associate Director: Ray E. Day.

D. U.S. AID AND INFORMATION ORGANIZATIONS

Afghan Community in America, 139-15 95th Ave., Jamaica, NY 11435. (212) 658-3737. Chairman: Habib Mayar.

Afghanistan Relief Committee, Inc., 345 Park Ave., Suite 4100, New York, NY 10154. (212) 355-2931. President: Gordon A. Thomas.

Africare, Inc., 1601 Connecticut Ave. NW, Rm 600, Washington, D.C. 20009. (202) 462-3614. Executive Director: C. Payne Lucas.

Aid for Afghan Refugees (AFAR), 1052 Oak St., San Francisco, CA 94117. (415) 863-1450.

The American Council for Judaism Philathronpic Fund, 386 Park Ave. S., New York, NY 10016. (212) 684-1525. Executive Secretary: Mrs. Carolyn Kinsman.

American Council of Voluntary Agencies for Foreign Service, Inc., 200 Park Ave. S., New York, NY 10003. (212) 777-8210. Executive Director: Leon O. Marion.

American Friends Service Committee, 1501 Cherry St., Philadelphia, PA 19102. (215) 241-7000. Executive Secretary: Asia Bennett.

American Jewish Joint Distribution Committee, Inc., 60 E. 42nd St., New York, NY 10165. (212) 687-6200. President: Henry Taub.

American National Red Cross, 17th & D Sts. NW, Washington, D.C. 20006. (202) 737-8300.

American Near East Refugee Aid, 1522 K St. NW, Suite 202, Washington, D.C. 20005. (202) 347-2558. President: Dr. Peter Gubser.

American ORT (Organization for Rehabilitation Through Training) Federation, 817 Broadway,

New York, NY 10003. (212) 677-4400. Executive Vice President: Donald H. Klein.

American Refugee Committee, 2110 Nicollet Ave., Suite 210, Minneapolis, MN 55404. (612) 872-7060. National Director: Stanley B. Breen.

CARE, 660 First Ave., New York, NY 10016. (212) 686-3110. Executive Director: Dr. Philip Johnson.

Catholic Relief Services--USCC (CRS), 1011 First Ave., New York, NY 10022. (212) 838-4700. Executive Director: Most Rev. Edwin B. Broderick, D.D.

Citizens' Committee for Immigration Reform, 1828 L St. NW, Suite 1000, Washington D.C. 20036. (202) 331-1759. Executive Director: Nina K. Solarz.

Direct Relief Foundation, 2801 B De La Vina St., Santa Barbara, CA 93105. (805) 687-3694. Executive Director: Dennis Karche.

Eritrean Relief Committee, Inc., P.O. Box 1180, Grand Central Station, New York, NY 10163. (212) 866-4293. Executive Secretary: Tecle-H Menghsteab.

Freedom House, 20 W 40th St., New York, NY 10018. (212) 730-7744. Executive Director: Leonard R. Sussman.

Hadassah: The Women's Zionist Organization of America, Inc., 50 W 58th St., New York, NY 10019. (212) 355-7900. Executive Director: Aline Kaplan.

Holt International Children's Services, Inc., 1195 City View, Box 2880, Eugene, OR 97402. (503) 687-2202. Executive Director: David H. Kim.

Indochina Refugee Action Center (IRAC), 1424

16th St. NW, Suite 404, Washington, D.C. 20036. (202) 667-7810. Director: Jesse Bunch.

International Social Service, American Branch, 291 Broadway, 11th Fl., New York, NY 10007. (212) 964-7550. Executive Director: Mary Jane Fales.

Lawyers Committee for International Human Rights, 36 W 44th St., New York, NY 10036. (212) 921-2160. Executive Director: Michael Posner.

Lutheran World Relief, 360 Park Ave. S., New York, NY 10010. (212) 532-6350. Executive Director: Norman E. Barth.

MAP International, 327 W. Gunderson Dr., Wheaton, IL 60187. (312) 653-6010. President: Larry E. Dixon.

Mennonite Central Committee, 21 S. 12th St., Akron, PA 17501. (717) 859-1151. Executive Secretary: Reg Toews.

Minority Rights Group, 36 Craven St., London WC2N 5NG, U.K. (01) 930-6659. Director: Ben Whitaker. New York Branch: Sue Nichterlein, 35 Claremount Ave., Suite 4S, New York, NY 10027. (212) 864-7986.

National Council for International Health, 2121 Virginia Ave. NW, Suite 303, Washington, D.C. 20037. (202) 298-5901. Executive Director: Dr. Russell E. Morgan, Jr.

National Immigration, Refugee, and Citizenship Forum, 533 8th St. SE, Washington, D.C. 20003. (202) 544-0004. President: Rick Swartz.

Oxfam America, 115 Broadway, Boston, MA 02116. (617) 482-1211. Executive Director: Joe Short.

Refugee Resource Center of the Committee on Migration and Refugee Affairs, American Council of Voluntary Agencies for Foreign Service, Inc., 200 Park Avenue South, Room 1703, New York, NY 10003. (212) 674-6844.

The Salvation Army World Service Office (SAWSO), 1025 Vermont Ave. NW, Washington, D.C. 20005. (202) 833-5646. Director: John W. Wiggins.

Save the Children Federation, 54 Wilton Rd., Westport, CT 06880. (203) 226-7272. President: David L. Guyer.

Spanish Refugee Aid, Inc., 80 E. 11th. St., Rm. 412, New York, NY 10003. (212) 674-7451. Director: Nancy Macdonald.

U.S. Committee for Refugees, 20 W. 40th St., New York, NY 10018. (212) 398-9142. Executive Director: Wells C. Klein.

U.S. Committee for Somali Refugee Relief, Inc., 1900 L St. NW, Suite 708, Washington, D.C. 20036. (202) 833-9542. Director: Martin R. Ganzglass.

U.S. Committee for UNICEF, 331 E. 38th St., New York, NY 10016. (212) 686-5522. President: James R. Sheffield.

United Lithuanian Relief Fund of America, Inc., 2558 W. 69th St., Chicago, IL 60629. (312) 776-7582. President: Mary Rudis.

World Vision International, 919 W. Huntington Dr., Monrovia, CA 91016. (213) 357-7979. President: Dr. Ted W. Engstrom.

Appendix D
Follow-Up Information

It appears there is the following error/omission on page _____ of **Unreached Peoples '83:** _____

_____

_____

_____

_____

_____

_____

I would like to receive more information on the _____
_____ (name/ID of people
group).

Additional Comments: _____

_____

_____

_____

Name: _____

Date: _____

Address: _____

Please detach, insert in an envelope, and mail to:
Missions Advanced Research and Communication Center, 919 West Huntington Drive, Monrovia, CA 91016 U.S.A.